D1179451

GEORGE DALGARNO ON UNIVERSAL LANGUAGE

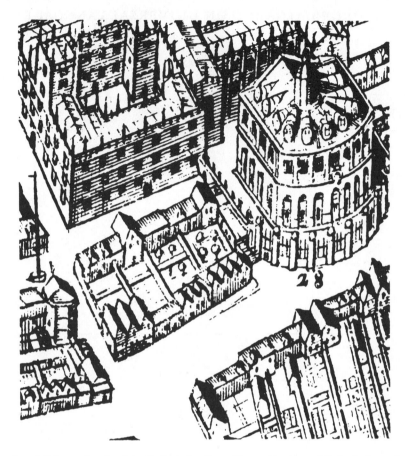

The site of Dalgarno's school in Oxford. Section of Loggan's map of Oxford, from *Oxonia Illustrata* (1675), enlarged to show the Little Printhouse that was constructed against the east side of the wall that ran round the Sheldonian Theatre. (Reproduced here from Harry Carter, *A History of the Oxford University Press* (1975), 67.)

George Dalgarno on Universal Language

The Art of Signs (1661), *The Deaf and Dumb Man's Tutor* (1680), and the Unpublished Papers

Edited with a Translation, Introduction, and Commentary by

DAVID CRAM AND JAAP MAAT

OXFORD

UNIVERSITY PRESS

OXFORD
UNIVERSITY PRESS

Great Clarendon Street, Oxford OX2 6DP

Oxford University Press is a department of the University of Oxford.
It furthers the University's objective of excellence in research, scholarship, and
education by publishing worldwide in

Oxford New York

Athens Auckland Bangkok Bogotá Buenos Aires Calcutta
Cape Town Chennai Dar es Salaam Delhi Florence Hong Kong Istanbul
Karachi Kuala Lumpur Madrid Melbourne Mexico City Mumbai
Nairobi Paris São Paulo Shanghai Singapore Taipei Tokyo Toronto Warsaw
with associated companies in Berlin Ibadan

Published in the United States
by Oxford University Press Inc., New York

British Library Cataloging in Publication Data
Data available

Library of Congress Cataloguing in Publication Data
Data applied for

ISBN 0-19-823732-4
1 3 5 7 9 10 8 6 4 2

Typeset in Swift
by Graphicraft Limited, Hong Kong
Printed in Great Britain
on acid-free paper by
Biddles Ltd., Guildford & King's Lynn

PREFACE

George Dalgarno was the author of two books, the first about the construction of a universal and philosophical language, the second on the teaching of language to the deaf. He lived in a time of profound change in the status of English and other vernaculars *vis-à-vis* Latin, and it is a measure of this sea change that, while his first book was written in Latin, his second was in English. Dalgarno was a fascinating and intellectually formidable character. Although himself only a humble schoolmaster, born and bred in Aberdeen, after his move to Oxford in the 1650s he associated closely with a number of scholars who later formed the nucleus of the Royal Society. This was a period when, for a complex variety of reasons, concern about linguistic questions occupied not just grammarians but scholars of all sorts, and Dalgarno debated issues concerning universal language with some of the leading scientists and mathematicians of the time.

A great deal has been written about seventeenth-century universal language schemes, including any number of book-length treatments (e.g., Funke 1929; Cornelius 1966; Salmon 1972; Knowlson 1975; Slaughter 1982; Strasser 1988; Hüllen 1989; Eco 1995; Stillman 1995). Much, indeed most, of this literature has been oriented towards the dominating figure of John Wilkins, focusing on his monumental *Essay towards a Real Character* of 1668, and on the place of universal language in the activities of the Royal Society. Dalgarno, whose *The Art of Signs* appeared in 1661 as a small octavo volume, is generally seen as a humble precursor to Wilkins. But in fact Wilkins, although a great synthesizer and popularizer, is arguably not a particularly great or original thinker on linguistic matters. Dalgarno, by contrast, represents a quite distinctive approach to the idea of universal language, and one that happened to be diametrically opposed to the position that Wilkins occupied. The present book invites a reading of Dalgarno on his own terms, and, as a result, offers a rather different panorama of the contemporary intellectual scene as viewed from Dalgarno's perspective. In fact it emerges that, while Dalgarno's position is original, it is not unique, since he was closer in spirit to other thinkers in the Royal Society circle such as Seth Ward and John Wallis than he was to Wilkins. He was also closer than Wilkins to continental thinkers who were concerned with this topic, and in particular makes useful counterpoint to Leibniz, who used Dalgarno's language scheme as one starting point for his own project.

The aim of this edition is to make Dalgarno's writings as accessible as possible to the modern reader. His texts in fact make difficult reading because they are densely and sometimes elliptically written, largely because his immediate audience was a highly informed and sophisticated one—as he himself put it, he writes 'ad solos doctos', for those who will know how to supply the necessary assumptions and inferences. And the fact that the central work is in Latin does not help. But in fact Dalgarno is a very *clear* and *consistent* thinker and writer, and he is easy to understand so long as one has the relevant contextual materials to hand. Our introduction is thus first and foremost an introduction to Dalgarno's texts, and only indirectly to the broader contemporary scene. The centrepiece of the book is an edition of the best-known work, *Ars Signorum*, which provides the original Latin text with a facing-page English translation, and notes. For convenience of reference this work will be referred to throughout by the English translation of the title: *The Art of Signs*. Other documents presented here that are essential to understanding the development of Dalgarno's thought—and that have been examined in some detail by a number of earlier scholars—include a number of broadsheets that he published in the later 1650s, and letters in which the early version of his scheme is explained.

Published here for the first time is a book-length 'Autobiographical Treatise', in which Dalgarno gives a blow-by-blow account of the various stages in the development of the scheme that saw light as *The Art of Signs*, and which serves as Dalgarno's own commentary on the published work. Dalgarno is known to have been intending this work for publication, since he said as much in print in the preface to his second book, but scholars had hitherto thought it to have been lost. Its happy discovery now provides a wealth of historical and intellectual detail with which the reader may reassess both contemporary and modern commentators on Dalgarno's work, and gives a vivid picture of both the development of Dalgarno's thought and his interaction with his peers. Furthermore, two shorter treatises are included, likewise previously unpublished, dealing with the nature of linguistic representation.

We also print Dalgarno's second book, published in 1680, which we shall refer to as *The Deaf and Dumb Man's Tutor*. Its full title reads *Didascalocophus or The Deaf and Dumb mans Tutor, to which is added A Discourse of the Nature and number of Double Consonants*. This volume in fact contains two quite separate tracts, both of which the author describes as spin-offs from his work on universal language. The first, from which the overall work takes its name, is a tract on teaching language to the deaf. The second is one of the earliest self-contained treatments of phonotactics, the study of constraints on the sequencing of sounds in language. This latter work complements Dalgarno's detailed analysis of speech sounds elsewhere, both in *The Art of Signs* and at various points in the unpublished papers.

The two editors of the present volume each devoted several years of individual study to seventeenth-century universal language schemes before joining forces for several further years of fruitful collaboration. Coming from rather different academic backgrounds—the one largely linguistic and the other mainly philosophical—they had each independently produced an English translation of *Ars Signorum*, being convinced that a close reading of the text was a sine qua non for historiography of whatever sort. Collaboration on a number of joint articles led in due course to the plan for a critical edition of *The Art of Signs*, complete with translation, and with an edition of the newly discovered unpublished materials. The ultimate advantage of joint work, of course, is the opportunity it gives us to declare that the faults that remain are the other chap's.

In acknowledging our indebtedness, we must first and foremost express our thanks to Christ Church College, Oxford, for permission to print an edition of the Dalgarno manuscript MS 162. But the work has been so long in gestation, and so many individuals have helped the editors at various stages in its preparation, that it would be hopeless to begin to thank all of them—though in a number of cases thanks have already been expressed in journal publications. We should like to extend a general thanks to colleagues in many places, and to library staff in Aberdeen, Paris, Guernsey, and Oxford in particular. Although we are not able to name them personally, they, like Dalgarno's ideal audience, will know who they are. Vivian Salmon and Werner Hüllen must, however, be mentioned as having given help and advice at various stages over the years. We also owe thanks to Emma Holloway for expert help in removing infelicities in our translation from the Latin, and to John Davey, Sarah Dobson, and Hilary Walford for helping to see a complicated text through the press.

David Cram and Jaap Maat

Oxford/Amsterdam
July 2000

Contents

Textual Note

In the transcription of Dalgarno's unpublished works, his erratic spelling, capitalization, and punctuation have largely been preserved. Where unambiguous sentence boundaries would not otherwise stand out, however, these have been normalized with full stop and capital letter. A number of additional paragraph breaks have been introduced for similar reasons. Abbreviations, which are not numerous, have been tacitly expanded—for example, y^t = that, w^t = with, & = and, Lang: = Language, and so on. Where parentheses occur, these are from the original manuscript. Square brackets indicate an editorial addition or expansion. Original material inserted from the margin or the facing page is enclosed within curly brackets, with the source indicated in square brackets—for example {[*from* fo. 43^v] . . . }. Foliation is indicated in angled brackets—for example, <fo. 33^r>. The folio number indicates that the text that follows is located on the folio with that number.

The foliation of the tracts transcribed from Christ Church MS 162 requires brief comment. For these, Dalgarno made used of a bound volume of paper, first using only the recto pages, and then inverting the book and writing on the verso. Additions and corrections were subsequently made both in the margins of the text, on the facing page, or on the verso, the place for insertion usually being flagged by letters or other marks. For this reason the foliation can sometimes run backwards, and can frequently appear confusing. It is.

Dalgarno's published tracts are in some places as poorly legible as his manuscripts. This applies in particular to the fonts used in the early broadsheets for the Greek expressions cited and for the Greek letters used in Dalgarno's own philosophical language. In deciphering such forms in *The Art of Signs* and *The Deaf and Dumb Man's Tutor* we have referred to the nineteenth-century Maitland Club edition of these works, but often arrived at a different reading of expressions from the philosophical language on the basis of logical reconstruction. In the interests of clarity, accents on the Greek examples cited have been standardized, following the pattern of the Maitland Club edition. In our translation of *The Art of Signs*, expressions from Dalgarno's own language have been highlighted in bold italic. To allow cross reference from other sources, the original pagination of the printed books has been indicated in the text in angled brackets—for example, <p. 7>. The page number indicates that the text that follows is located on the page with that number.

The following abbreviations have been used:

AS   *The Art of Signs*
D&D   *The Deaf and Dumb Man's Tutor*
CC   Christ Church MS 162

Introduction

At the beginning of 1657, when George Dalgarno was about 37 years of age, he moved from his native Aberdeen to Oxford. He thus became a resident of an important centre of intellectual activity. It was a period of great political turmoil, but this did not prevent scientific interests from being energetically and successfully pursued. Extensive contacts were sustained between learned men throughout Europe. In Oxford and London, a number of influential scholars organized experiments and meetings that were to result in the foundation of the Royal Society. Its members were concerned to advance and promote what was called the 'new philosophy'. Topics of scholarly debate were not confined to natural science, but included linguistic ones: an issue of primary interest was the construction of an artificial symbol system, designed to be a universal means of communication as well as an accurate representation of knowledge. The subject had been discussed since the early decades of the century in France as well as in England, but in the 1650s it was especially in England that the atmosphere of expectation reached its height. At the time he moved to Oxford, Dalgarno seems to have been largely unaware of this. When he describes himself in 'The Autobiographical Treatise' (see below, Part IV) as a 'great stranger at Oxford' (CC, fo. 27^r), he clearly refers to a lack of personal contacts, but it appears from his story that he was at first also a stranger in the intellectual sense. However, he soon compensated for this in both respects. He was to make a substantial contribution to the linguistic debate, and become the author of the first complete and fully-fledged philosophical language to be produced in the seventeenth century.

In what follows, a brief outline of the general context of Dalgarno's contribution will first be provided (Sect. 1). Next, the various stages of development of Dalgarno's scheme will be sketched (Sect. 2), followed by a description of the essentials of the philosophical language presented in *The Art of Signs* (Sect. 3). Further, some reactions to Dalgarno's language will be discussed (Sect. 4), and some background to his second book, *The Deaf and Dumb Man's Tutor*, will be provided (Sect. 5).

1. Seventeenth-Century Universal Language Schemes

1.1. *The intellectual background*

Seventeenth-century linguistics was characterized by two, partially antagonistic, tendencies. On the one hand, a highly critical attitude towards language prevailed, and an inclination to consider linguistic knowledge as inferior to knowledge of nature. Following Francis Bacon (1561–1626) in his depreciation of the Humanist ideal of literary education, many authors contrasted vain and useless knowledge of *words* with real and valuable knowledge of *things*. Rather than being considered as a source of wisdom, existing languages were seen as unduly irregular, and as being full of ambiguities and redundancies. The large portions of time needed to master them, it was felt, were largely wasted. Furthermore, it was believed that language might have a pernicious influence on thinking, both because of its intrinsic defects and through its abuse in practice. On the other hand, the period was characterized by an intense concern with semiotics, and a fascination with sign systems: cryptography, shorthand, and other notational systems were widely studied. Above all in mathematics, an increasingly prestigious discipline, the importance of developing new methods of notation was universally recognized. Combined with a general feeling that a renewal of learning was possible and that great scientific progress could be achieved by human power, these tendencies were the fertile soil on which a widespread concern with language planning could flourish.

Some writers on the European continent, notably Comenius, mixed religious concerns with the ones just outlined. In the opinion of several modern authors, a mystical approach to language was also instrumental in the seventeenth-century efforts to create a universal language. There is, however, little doubt that the interests of the English language planners, especially Dalgarno and Wilkins, were largely secular and quite explicitly anti-mystical.

The search for a new medium of communication was further stimulated by practical considerations and developments. In the course of the sixteenth and seventeenth centuries reports by missionaries brought about a more acute awareness of the great cultural and linguistic diversity among the nations of the world. Ever-expanding trade brought increasing problems in communication. In addition, the linguistic situation was drastically changed by the rise of the vernaculars and the gradual decline of Latin as the international language of the learned world.

Throughout the medieval period the study of language had been conducted within the framework of the 'trivium', consisting of the three liberal arts of grammar, logic, and rhetoric. Although the value of these traditions was increasingly questioned, their influence was still far-reaching. They each played an important part in shaping the various universal language schemes.

The grammatical tradition was relevant in that it provided the paradigm for the analysis of language structure. Dalgarno deviated from this tradition in proposing a thorough revision, or rather the abolishment, of the classical theory of word classes. For practical reasons, however, he refrained from carrying this proposal through in *The Art of Signs* (see Sect. 3.3.2 below). Grammatical theory was also important in that it contained a branch known as philosophical grammar, which posited that there is a universal structure underlying all languages, and that this is intimately connected with the basic categories of thought as well as those of reality. Dalgarno's philosophical language is clearly inspired by this tradition, although he himself claimed to have made a new departure in producing *The Art of Signs* (see the tract entitled 'On Interpretation' (CC, fo. 113ᵛ (see below, Part IV))).

The logical tradition exerted a profound influence on the work of the language planners in general and on Dalgarno in particular. He explicitly states that logic is to be the foundation of the art of signs, and he claims that learning his language is the best way to imbibe logical principles. Furthermore, he uses the so-called predicaments (that is, categories) as a starting point for the lexicon of his language. The predicaments were a standard subject of logical theory (see Sect. 3.2.1 below). In addition, Dalgarno not infrequently puts forward his arguments in explicitly syllogistic form, which suggests that logic was an integral part of his education in Aberdeen. At the same time however, he often expresses dissatisfaction with logical theory, and condemns various parts of it as useless and absurd (see e.g. *AS* 65).

Rhetoric, finally, was of primary importance in that it included the art of memory. Since the attractiveness of universal language schemes depended crucially on the ease with which they could be learned and remembered, mnemonics was of central concern to those engaged in the construction of such schemes. Mnemonic considerations were pivotal to the structure of Dalgarno's early scheme of 1657. In the philosophical language of *The Art of Signs* mnemonic principles are replaced by logical ones, but a separate chapter is added on 'mnemonic aids', as Dalgarno believed that the logical foundation of the radical words was undesirable from a mnemotechnical point of view (see *AS* 59; 'The Autobiographical Treatise', CC, fos. 48ᵛ–50ʳ).

Another important framework for linguistic theorizing was formed by two elements from the biblical tradition. In the first place, the story in Genesis concerning Adam giving names to the various kinds of creatures provided an unquestionable account of language origin. It was thus generally taken for granted that all people once spoke a single language that had been invented by Adam. It was further commonly believed that the Adamic language was more perfect than any of the languages currently in use, for Adam's prelapsarian state of perfect knowledge would have guaranteed that the names he gave to creatures were not arbitrary, but expressed the nature or essence of these creatures. The myth of the Adamic language engendered extensive speculation and debate as to which existing language was to be identified as its most direct descendant, and likewise inspired efforts to rediscover or to restore the original language of mankind by means of various occult or mystical practices. It has sometimes been suggested that the seventeenth-century schemes for a universal language were similarly motivated. Dalgarno's discussion of the subject shows, however, that he saw his own enterprise as quite unconnected with any kind of search for the primordial language. In his manuscripts he indeed addresses the issue of whether names are arbitrary or natural, but does so only to explain why sensible thinkers such as Plato could have seriously considered the matter at all. He invokes the Adamic language to illustrate his position, but this is precisely to maintain that even for God there is only one way of establishing a natural relationship between words and things. This is the very same way that is open to ordinary language users, and that Dalgarno primarily relies on for his own philosophical language—namely, the use of compound expressions. The meaning of the component parts of these expressions, Dalgarno points out, is necessarily arbitrary (see e.g. 'The Autobiographical Treatise', CC, fos. 47^v, 82^r, 114^v). He saw his own scheme not as an attempt to restore the Adamic language, but rather as resulting from the consistent application of general linguistic principles that are valid for all languages, including those of divine and Adamic origin.

The other element of the biblical tradition that was important for seventeenth-century views on language is the idea that the diversity of languages can be explained in terms of the story of the confusion of tongues at Babel. From this perspective, language diversity was seen to be a curse inflicted on human kind. The seventeenth-century mainstream was far enough secularized and certainly optimistic enough to believe that the invention of a remedy against the curse of Babel was both permissible and possible.

1.2. *Universal writing systems*

The first schemes for a new means of communication to appear in the seventeenth century were designed to be universal writing systems rather than complete languages. A major impetus for the development of such schemes came from the acquaintance with Chinese script, which was reported to enable speakers of mutually unintelligible languages to communicate in writing. It was again Francis Bacon who influentially pointed out—in *The Advancement of Learning* (1605)—that this feature of Chinese script was based upon a reversal of the relationship between spoken and written language. While alphabetical writing represented spoken sounds, Chinese characters—it was somewhat erroneously assumed—represented things directly, rather than representing them indirectly through spoken sounds. Spoken language, in this view, resulted from giving a particular pronunciation to the written symbols, instead of being primary signs of things that were represented in writing. Since such written symbols signified things rather than sounds, they were called 'real characters', as opposed to 'vocal characters', such as the letters of the alphabet. It is to be noted that the meaning of real characters, as Bacon emphasized, was just as much dependent on arbitrary convention as that of spoken words. He further stated that the use of real characters was unattractive from a practical point of view, because of the large number of symbols that was required.

Nevertheless, the concept of a 'real character' suggested to various scholars that it should be possible to devise a set of language-independent written symbols that could be used as a system of universal writing: speakers of diverse languages, it was believed, could simply 'read off' their own languages from the written text. Aside from Chinese characters, Arabic numerals as well as astronomical and chemical symbols were invoked as examples of such symbols that were already in use. All that was needed to obtain a convenient medium of international communication, these authors believed, was to invent real characters for all things and notions. Among the authors who made a proposal of this kind in print was John Wilkins (1614–72), who was to collaborate with Dalgarno in the 1650s and who eventually produced a rival universal language in 1668. In an early work called *Mercury, or the Secret and Swift Messenger* (1641) Wilkins proposed the construction of 'an Universal Character to express Things and Notions, as might be legible to all People and Countries, so that Men of several Nations might with the same ease both write and read it' (p. 56).

From the 1620s onwards, various attempts to implement the idea of a universal character were made, or at least announced. Most of these schemes were rudimentary sketches that never reached print, and some of them are now lost. The earliest printed scheme was published by Francis Lodwick (1619–94), in a tract called *A Common Writing, whereby two, although not understanding one the other's language, yet by the helpe thereof, may communicate their minds one to another* (1647). The work presents the outline of a system of non-phonetic symbols for designating verbs, to which diacritic signs are added that indicate a large variety of morphological and grammatical derivations and inflections. A second work was published in 1652: *The Groundwork, or foundation laid (or so intended) for the framing of a new perfect language: and an universal or common writing.* In this work Lodwick refines his analysis of derivational affixes, and he considers the addition of a spoken counterpart to his writing system. Lodwick was concerned with universal language schemes throughout his life. He was one of Dalgarno's financial supporters, and among his unpublished papers is a fairly detailed comment on Dalgarno's early scheme. In *The Art of Signs* (AS 79) Dalgarno praises Lodwick's scheme, although adding a rather dismissive comment.

In 1657 the Ipswich schoolmaster Cave Beck (1623–1706) published a book entitled *The Universal Character*, which contained a scheme that was based on simple principles. Beck provided an alphabetical list of English words, to each of which a number was assigned. Dictionaries of other languages were to be produced, it was announced, in which words were to be assigned the same number as the English semantic equivalents. Writing the numbers rather than the words would provide a universally understandable script. Beck added provisions for grammatical features, and he proposed a method for pronouncing numbers, thus enabling the system to serve as a spoken language. In *The Art of Signs* (AS 79), Dalgarno dismisses Beck's scheme as being nothing but a difficult way of writing or speaking English. In the 1660s, two schemes were published that followed closely similar principles: both Johann Joachim Becher's (1635–82) *Character, pro Notitia Linguarum Universali* (1661) and Athanasius Kircher's (1602–80) *Polygraphia Nova et Universalis* (1663) used numerals in the same way as Beck's scheme. Further, a Spanish Jesuit later identified as Pedro Bermudo devised a scheme called 'Arithmeticus Nomenclator', which circulated in manuscript form in Rome in 1653. The original scheme is no longer extant, but its essentials survive in a work by Caspar Schott (1664). Bermudo likewise proposed numbering words so as to use numerals as universal characters, although he arranged his word lists thematically rather than alphabetically.

1.3. *Philosophical language*

In various cases, schemes for a universal character formed the first stage in a development towards more ambitious projects, aimed at creating a language that would surpass existing ones in being better suited to the accurate representation of knowledge. This holds true for Lodwick, whose scheme for a 'common writing' developed into a sketch of the foundation for a 'new perfect language', which was to be at the same time a universal character. Likewise, Wilkins's project underwent fundamental changes with respect to the programmatic proposal in the *Mercury* of 1641, but he still described the provision of a 'Real universal character' as the principal goal of his mature scheme (1668: 13). Dalgarno's project also went through a stage in which he thought of it as a universal character, and the subtitle of *The Art of Signs* still refers to this aspect of the scheme. However, although Dalgarno at first endorsed the theoretical assumptions underlying the concept of a real and universal character, he became increasingly aware that they are untenable (see further Sect. 2.3).

In other cases, proposals for the construction of artificial languages were largely unrelated to the concept of a real and universal character as articulated by Wilkins and others. In 1629, the famous mathematician and philosopher René Descartes (1596–1650) wrote a letter to Marin Mersenne (1588–1648) in which he outlined the programme for an artificial philosophical language, in explicit contrast with a proposal for a universal character. Descartes criticized the latter project for being useless in practice and suggested instead the creation of a language based upon the ordering of simple ideas. Descartes added, however, that this would presuppose a perfect analysis of knowledge, and, further, that it would be illusory to expect such a language ever to be in actual use. Other writers who were more optimistic included Mersenne, who discussed the invention of 'the best of all possible languages' in his *Harmonie universelle* (1636). Although he did not elaborate an actual language scheme, Mersenne formulated criteria for a language to qualify as excellent, and he considered various methods of coining names for things. Tommaso Campanella (1568–1639) added an appendix to his work on philosophical grammar (1638), in which he presented some guidelines for the construction of a new language. The words of this language should be free from ambiguity and synonymy, and its grammar should follow philosophical principles.

Subsequent writers made a variety of proposals for constructing nomenclatures and languages on rational and scientific principles. Thus Cyprian Kinner

(d. 1649), one of Samuel Hartlib's many correspondents, is known to have worked on the construction of 'technical words' for plants, the syllables of which indicated properties of the plant designated by the word (DeMott 1958). Technical words were to be a prominent feature of both Dalgarno's and Wilkins's languages, although the value of this feature was a matter of dispute between them (see Sects. 2.4 and 3.2.1 below). A more fully elaborated scheme was produced by Comenius (Jan Amos Komensky, 1592–1670), the Bohemian educational reformer who devised an all-embracing programme for the attainment of universal peace. An important element of this programme was the creation of a universal language. As Comenius pointed out in *The Way of Light*, written in 1641 but not published until 1668, the universal language was to be in conformity with the structure of reality. In a later work, the *Panglottia*, he elaborated this idea in more detail. This work was written *c.*1665-6—that is, some years after Dalgarno's *Art of Signs* had been published, but was printed for the first time only in the twentieth century (1966). In the *Panglottia*, Comenius recommended the use of sound symbolism as far as possible ('a' signifying largeness, 'o' roundness, and so on), and he estimated that a collection of 300 monosyllabic radical words could serve as the foundation of the entire lexicon through a combination of radical words and the use of various affixes. Several exchanges between Comenius and Dalgarno concerning universal language are known to have taken place (see Sect. 2.1 below).

Another scheme for a universal language to be based on philosophical principles was described by Thomas Urquhart (1611–?1660) in *Ekskubalauron* (1652), and again in *Logopandecteision* (1653). Rather than a fully developed scheme, Urquhart provided a list of characteristics of his language, claiming that the bulk of his work had been lost in the Battle of Worcester in 1651. As many of Urquhart's claims are too extravagant to be credible, modern commentators have been in doubt as to whether his flamboyant writings should be taken seriously at all. However, it is clear that he was familiar, at a very early stage, with the issues that were also occupying other language planners. This appears from the importance of both mathematics and mnemonics in his work, and from the itemization of features of his language. Thus Urquhart claimed that there 'ought to be a proportion betwixt the signe and thing signified' (item 3), that the words of his language were divided according to the Aristotelian categories (item 6), and that words signifying similar things should be similar to each other in form (item 9). Furthermore, he criticized existing languages in much the same way as both Dalgarno and Wilkins subsequently did. Urquhart received his university education at Aberdeen just as Dalgarno did, and, although there is no record of personal contacts between the two, it is certain that Dalgarno was familiar with Urquhart's writings on universal language. A letter written by Dalgarno in 1659 shows that he was expecting Urquhart to produce a more complete version of his universal language scheme (to Hartlib, 3 November 1659 (see below, Part V)).

By the time Dalgarno published his *Art of Signs*, or shortly afterwards, the young Isaac Newton (1642–1727) made notes concerning the creation of a philosophical language (Elliott 1957). Aside from the construction of technical words, Newton envisaged the provision of an elaborate grammatical apparatus. These notes were never published during Newton's lifetime, and they were probably unknown to his contemporaries. However, their existence shows how widespread the occupation with language planning was.

A final person to be mentioned in the present context is Seth Ward (1617–89), a noted mathematician and theologian who played an important part in the development of both Dalgarno's and Wilkins's schemes. In 1654, Ward and Wilkins jointly published a treatise in defence of the university curriculum, *Vindiciae Academiarum* (Ward 1654). In this treatise, Ward sketched the programme for an artificial symbol system reflecting the logical structure of discourse. We know that Ward himself did preliminary work on the execution of this programme, for Dalgarno relates, both in his 'Autobiographical Treatise' (CC, fo. 26^r) and in *The Art of Signs* (AS 78), that Ward showed him tables that he had drawn up for the purpose of devising real characters. However, it seems that Ward never achieved definitive results in this regard. There is evidence that in the 1670s he no longer considered the construction of an artificial language to be a goal worth pursuing (see Cram 1994). Ward was closely associated with Wilkins, who acknowledged a debt to him in his *Essay*. It was Ward who introduced Dalgarno to Wilkins, and Dalgarno in his broadsheets appealed to the support of both Wilkins and Ward in order to establish his own credentials. It appears from Dalgarno's treatise that Ward was involved in the debate that arose between Dalgarno and Wilkins soon after they had started to collaborate, although Ward refrained from taking sides with either party (CC, fos. 30^r, 45^r, 50^r). In *The Art of Signs* (AS 78) Ward is mentioned very favourably, while Wilkins's name is conspicuously absent in that context.

In summary, when Dalgarno appeared on the scene at the beginning of 1657, the construction of artificial symbol systems and universal languages was already a widely discussed topic, but few actual results had been achieved. All that was published were either programmatic proposals or tentative and incomplete sketches. Almost immediately after his arrival in Oxford, Dalgarno became one of the most prominent players in the field, his efforts culminating in the publication of *The Art of Signs* in 1661. The following section presents an outline of the development leading to the production of this main work.

2. THE DEVELOPMENT OF DALGARNO'S SCHEME

Between Dalgarno's first involvement with language planning and the publication of *The Art of Signs* in 1661 lies a period of four years. After this period, Dalgarno continued to be interested in linguistic matters. He produced several treatises in this area, which will be discussed below (Sect. 5). The present section is concerned with the first four years, in which Dalgarno's universal language scheme went through various stages of development. Initially, he attempted to improve a system of shorthand, which soon led him into drawing up a scheme for a universal character. After this followed a stage in which he proposed both a character and a spoken language, and finally he created his rational or philosophical language.

The various stages of Dalgarno's project can be followed through a rich documentary trail, a variety of sources being available.

First, Dalgarno advertised his scheme through a number of printed broadsheets, in which he claimed many advantages for his invention. One of these (see below, Part I, Broadsheet 2) includes both extensive details of his early scheme and also a number of theoretical reflections on the nature of the invention. In all, five different advertisements of this kind were produced, the first being published in May or June 1657, the last in late 1660 or early 1661, shortly before publication of *The Art of Signs*. These broadsheets are all reproduced in the present volume. In addition to the printed advertisements, a manuscript survives in Paris that contains much the same material as does the second broadsheet, allowing the development of Dalgarno's early scheme to be traced in still greater detail (see Maat and Cram 1998).

Secondly, Dalgarno produced several retrospective accounts of the development of his scheme: aside from a succinct summary in the appendix to *The Deaf and Dumb Man's Tutor* published in 1680 (D&D 96, 100–1), he relates in *The Art of Signs* (AS 78–81) how his treatment of the particles underwent profound changes as his aims shifted from shorthand to logic. His most detailed account is to be found in 'The Autobiographical Treatise', which was written around 1684.

Thirdly, the various stages that Dalgarno's project went through are documented by correspondence: not only did Dalgarno exchange letters concerning his scheme with other scholars, but comments on his scheme are also contained in letters from and to persons other than himself. A pivotal role in this regard was played by Hartlib, who solicited and obtained comments on Dalgarno's early scheme from a number of correspondents. Samuel Hartlib (1600–62) was a German who settled in London in the late 1620s. In the following decades, he was involved as a promoter, publisher, and patron, with numerous projects directed towards educational reform and the advancement of learning. It was through Hartlib that Dalgarno came into contact with Comenius and a number of other scholars. In late 1657 or early 1658, Dalgarno used Hartlib's house as a correspondence address. Since Hartlib was at the centre of a network of European philosophers and scholars who were in regular correspondence with each other, it was quite understandable that Dalgarno should turn to him in 1659 when he was anxious to discover news concerning rival universal language schemes (see the letter of 3 November 1659 (see below, Part V)).

Finally, various aspects of the development of Dalgarno's scheme are touched upon in contemporary accounts by Robert Plot (1676: 282–6), John Wallis (1678: 16–17), and Anthony Wood (1691: 506).

2.1. *From shorthand to universal character*

The first known reference to Dalgarno's early scheme dates from 11 April 1657. On that day, a Pole called Faustus Morstyn[1] wrote a letter to Hartlib 'concerning the inventor and the invention of a universal character'. Morstyn knew that Hartlib, having heard about the scheme, was curious to learn the details. He evidently assumes that Hartlib knows little or nothing about Dalgarno, and provides him with a biographical background and the following account of Dalgarno's work.

I am acquainted with the said inventor and indeed I know him through and through; we were thrown together first by the shared wrongs of adverse fortune, and thereafter the simplicity and honesty of his manners endeared him to me. By nationality he is a Scot, by parentage not noble but not ignoble either, for he was (as he tells me) born of a good family. His name is Dalgerno [*sic*]; he is of a virile age, is in somewhat straitened circumstances, and has a lively intellect whose acuteness has been whetted by poverty, that sister of a good mind. As regards the invention, I can pride myself with having been its instigator, for I provided the first occasion for it and likewise inferred what could be made of it. But far be it from me to seek laurels in trifles; I mention these things only so as to recount everything to you just as it happened.

 Some days ago there was in this town a certain master of brachigraphy [i.e. shorthand]. Since I was not anxious to buy this art at the price it was being offered, and was not able to comprehend all the details of it due to my imperfect knowledge of the English language on which the shorthand system was based, I prevailed upon several friends that we should at communal expense engage this Scot to gain a thorough knowledge of it, so that we could then find out from him what he had learned. Soon after he had gained a grasp of it all, he, following our arrangement, explained to us among other rules and observations that there occurred certain marks made with a single stroke of the pen which served to abbreviate whole sentences. On seeing these I exclaimed that marks of this sort could be adapted not just for the English language but for any language whatsoever, and by similar means I abbreviated various other notions of the mind. Taking occasion from this, the Scot did not idle or pause until he had arranged in classes a quantity of marks contrived along similar lines, and had developed a simple method whereby most of the concepts of the mind could be expressed in that character without difficulty. It is, however, not yet completed and polished, although Dr. Wilkins and Dr. Ward (who say that nothing similar of this sort has so far been invented, either by themselves or by any other) have devoted no little effort to bring this praiseworthy undertaking to a conclusion.[2]

It appears that when Morstyn thus introduced Dalgarno to Hartlib, Dalgarno had already made considerable progress in devising his first scheme, although

---

[1] 'Faustus Morsteyn, a nobleman of the Greater Poland, was created M. of A. by virtue of a dispens[sation] from the delegates.—He was a student or sojourner in the university several years purposely to obtain learning from the publ. libr. [i.e. the university library]' (Wood, 1691: ii. 197).
[2] Morstyn to Hartlib, 11 Apr. 1657; the Latin original is preserved in Sheffield, Hartlib MS 49/22/1A–2B.

it was not yet complete. Dalgarno's autobiographical treatise contains a personal account of the very first steps, including many additional details. Dalgarno's version differs conspicuously from Morstyn's in that the role of the latter receives no mention whatsoever. A possible explanation for this is that Dalgarno's account was written almost thirty years afterwards, and that what he remembered as a chain of individual intellectual events in fact involved some active participation of others.

Be this as it may, 'The Autobiographical Treatise' agrees with Morstyn's letter in essential points. Thus Dalgarno confirms that it was his study of a system of shorthand that inspired him to devise his first scheme. It is not known who the 'master of brachigraphy' was, but he may possibly be identified as Jeremiah Rich, who published a shorthand system in 1659 entitled *The Penns Dexterity*.[3] Rich's scheme is strongly reminiscent of Dalgarno's early one, being printed on one side of a single broadsheet, and having a set of rules for contractions 'by which a Sentence is Writt as soone as a Word'. Furthermore, it announces itself as 'Allowed by Authority and past the two universitys with great aprobation and aplause'. Shorthand was a subject widely studied and practised in England at the time, while being largely neglected elsewhere (Salmon 1972: 61–2). Furthermore, both Morstyn and Dalgarno relate that the next step was the invention of symbols for the purpose not only of shorthand, but of a universal character. This step is described by both as the result of a chance discovery, the realization that symbols intended to represent an English expression in a contracted way could also be used to represent equivalent expressions of other languages. Whether this insight was brought to Dalgarno's attention by Morstyn, as the latter claims, or was Dalgarno's own discovery, as he himself says, cannot be determined. However, in other instances in which 'The Autobiographical Treatise' can be compared with external sources, Dalgarno's account proves to be completely reliable.

According to Dalgarno, then, the universal character emerged from his efforts to model a shorthand system on Hebrew sentence structure, of which the large number of affixes struck him as characteristic. The conception was to render major words such as verbs and substantives by special symbols of the shorthand system, while treating 'particles'—that is, minor words such as prepositions and adverbs—as affixes, representing them by diacritic signs added to the symbol for the major word. However, in existing shorthand systems such diacritic signs were used for quite a different purpose: points positioned around a larger symbol were used to represent vowels. The problem thus became how to avoid confusion between signs for vowels and signs for particles. This could be solved by the use of 'real characters' instead of 'vocal' ones—that is, symbols that designate language-independent concepts rather than words of some existing

---

[3] An octavo booklet describing Rich's system was published in 1669, after his death; the title page states that he himself did not put his scheme into print during his lifetime, 'because it would have hindred his Practice'.

language. The shorthand systems that Dalgarno knew used a small number of such real characters. He himself resolved to use such symbols throughout, so that signs for vowels were no longer needed.

This solution immediately engendered a new problem, which had been recognized by authors such as Bacon and Wilkins in their discussions of the use of real characters for the purpose of a universal writing system. Dalgarno was, however, unaware of these discussions at the time. The problem he now faced was that a very large number of symbols would have to be invented, since the items to be represented were not sounds but things and concepts. Dalgarno sought to resolve this along two lines. First, he selected a limited number of items to be designated by a separate symbol, yielding a core vocabulary designating only things talked about in everyday conversation. Dalgarno used a dictionary in making the selection, so that strictly speaking the selected items were words rather than the things designated by them, but clearly Dalgarno disregarded the distinction. Secondly, he decided upon a specific arrangement of the items to be represented by the symbols. He considered four methods of arrangement, two of which were soon rejected. The first of these proposed an alphabetical order; the second a thematic order, as used in certain dictionaries and in Comenius' method of language teaching. The other two methods were both of great significance for Dalgarno's scheme: one employed a so-called predicamental order, and the other a mnemonic arrangement. For his early scheme, Dalgarno opted for the mnemonic arrangement, but in *The Art of Signs* he used the predicamental order—that is to say, a structure containing genera and species arranged according to the Aristotelian categories (see Sects. 1.1 above and 3.2.1 below). The merits and disadvantages of a predicamental order were one of the topics of debate that engaged Dalgarno and Wilkins some time after their collaboration began.

According to Dalgarno's own account, he had already made a first version of his shorthand system based on mnemonic principles before he realized that the system could also be used as a universal character. This revelation, by his own account, excited and stimulated him intensely (CC, fo. 24^r). He started looking for ways to make himself and his invention known, and in this he was successful: through John Owen, then vice-chancellor of Oxford, Dalgarno was put in touch with Seth Ward, who in turn introduced him to Wilkins. At the time, Wilkins was warden of Wadham College. He invited Dalgarno to the college, showed himself eager to learn about the scheme, and introduced Dalgarno into university circles. In this way Dalgarno experienced a dramatic change in circumstances. From being an unknown schoolmaster with an uncertain future, he now saw that his universal character might bring him fame and fortune.

All this had occurred before Morstyn wrote his letter to Hartlib on 11 April 1657, so that Morstyn's statement that the brachigrapher came to Oxford 'some days ago' cannot be taken literally; this must have been a matter of months rather than days. This is confirmed by a letter written by Dalgarno nine days afterwards (to Hartlib, 20 April 1657 (see below, Part V)), in which he addressed Hartlib directly for the first time. He here claimed that his design was 'now perfected', that Wilkins and Ward had formally approved the scheme, and that it was to be discussed by the delegates of the university later that week.[4] He further mentioned that he had obtained a testimonial from some prominent scholars at the University of Cambridge. Dalgarno's letter apparently had two purposes: his main aim was to secure Hartlib's support in promoting the scheme, but he also used the occasion to comment on the recently published universal character of Cave Beck, a report that Hartlib had sought in his correspondence with Morstyn. Dalgarno was strongly critical of Beck's scheme, contrasting it with 'another Treatise' of 1647 (undoubtedly by Lodwick), of which his appraisal was much more positive. In *The Art of Signs* (*AS* 79) he reiterated these judgements, this time identifying Lodwick, not Beck, by name. In his letter to Hartlib, Dalgarno further mentioned that Wilkins had shown him Beck's scheme in manuscript form 'long ago', which suggests that Dalgarno had already known Wilkins personally for some time when he wrote this.

By the end of April 1657 Dalgarno had thus not only completed a first version of a scheme that at once served the two purposes of shorthand and universal character, but had also assured himself of support from scholars in both universities. His next concern was to raise funds for the publication of the scheme. A first result of the appeal to Hartlib for support was that the latter asked friends and acquaintances, among whom were scholars as well as merchants, for comment on Dalgarno's project. Initially, the only information Hartlib had about the scheme came from the letters he had received from Morstyn and Dalgarno, and this is what he at first communicated to his correspondents. Shortly afterwards, he also circulated a printed sheet containing both a Latin and an English advertisement for Dalgarno's scheme (see below, Part I, Broadsheet 1). The original was printed some time in May or June 1657, as John Pell, one of Hartlib's correspondents who was at Zurich at the time, noted receipt on 4 July (Salmon 1966a: 358). On this broadsheet, Dalgarno announces the invention of an 'art' that provides both a universally understandable script and a better shorthand system than all existing ones. He further claims that the art can be learned in the space of two weeks time—a statement he later successfully sought to prove by practical experiment (see below, Part I, Broadsheet 4). The English part of the text contains a claim that was to become of primary concern to Dalgarno at a later stage, but that was clearly an important motive from the start—namely, that the practice of his art would bring 'a great deale of clearnesse to the acts of the understanding'. To enhance his credibility, Dalgarno emphasizes the support and attestation that Wilkins and Ward had given to his scheme.

---

[4] Of which Wilkins, Ward, and Wallis were members. On the history of the Delegacy at this period, see Carter (1975: 137–41); for lists of delegates, see Buckler (1756).

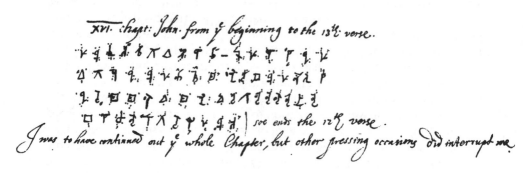

FIG. 1. Dalgarno's transcription of the first twelve verses of Chapter 16 of St John's Gospel into his real character, enclosed in a letter from Hartlib to Pell dated 3 July 1657 (BL Add. MS 4377, fo. 149ʳ). The accompanying note, in Dalgarno's hand, reads: 'I was to have continued out yᵉ whole Chapter, but other pressing occasions did interrupt me.'

Neither Dalgarno's letter nor the broadsheet advertisement contained any details revealing the actual workings of the scheme. However, there is evidence that some contemporaries at least had sight of models showing the scheme in operation. At the beginning of July, Hartlib had access to a sample: Dalgarno's transcription of the first twelve verses of Chapter 16 of St John's Gospel into his character (see Fig. 1).

On 3 July, Hartlib sent this specimen to Pell. In the accompanying letter, Hartlib shows himself convinced of its merits, praising the character for being 'so exact and compendious that the whole Bible will be printed in 9 or 10 sheets' (BL Add. MS 4377, fo. 149ʳ). Yet it is unlikely that without further explanation Pell could form a clear picture of how the character worked. A fuller explanation became available when Dalgarno's second and most detailed broadsheet (see below, Part I, Broadsheet 2) was printed, but this probably did not appear until several months afterwards. After that, Pell studied Dalgarno's scheme thoroughly, and his comments are extant (BL Add. MS 4377, fos. 153ʳ–154ʳ, 159ʳ–169ʳ; see Sect. 2.2.2 below). Besides Pell, Hartlib elicited comments from a series of other friends, apparently on the basis of the same information as that which was sent to Pell: Dalgarno's and Morstyn's letters, the first broadsheet, and the specimen transcribing the biblical fragment. A number of replies are preserved among Hartlib's papers.

Among the first recorded reactions is one by Robert Boyle (1627–91), who commented: 'Dalgerno's Vniversal Character will certainly bee far more stenographical then any short writing, but whether it will bee or how far a Real Character to all Nations that cannot bee yet determined' (noted in Hartlib's *Ephemerides*, Hartlib MS 29/6/9b). It appears that Boyle later considered Dalgarno's scheme valuable enough to be worth sponsoring, since his name occurs on the lists of patrons that were printed on later advertisements and in *The Art of Signs*. Another reply, by Robert Wood (1632–95), a fellow of Lincoln College, was initially sceptical. On 1 August 1657 he wrote: 'I have not faith yet to beleeve those effects he promises, will follow his designe' (Hartlib MS 33/1/23a). However, one week later, on 8 August, Wood wrote that, after talking more than once with Dalgarno, whom he says he finds 'a person exceeding ingenious', he now has a better opinion of the scheme: 'the invention I confesse is very acute & neatly contrived, & he has wrought in me a much better perswasion thereof, than I had. & yet I am not convinced that it will answer those ends proposed, at least not under a great many yeares . . . Yet this I conceive that it is already a much better way of shortwriting, then that commonly used' (Hartlib MS 33/1/25a).

Other correspondents showed themselves to be very interested in the scheme, without being able to assess it as yet. Thus in August 1657 Johann Morian (on whom see Turnbull 1947) requested more copies of the first broadsheet for distribution, adding that he awaited further explanation before he could understand the transcript of the biblical fragment (Hartlib MS 42/2/19a). In later letters to Hartlib (Nov. 1657, Hartlib MS 42/2/26b; Jan. 1658, Hartlib MS 31/18/2b, 56/2/1a) Morian said he was looking forward to using Dalgarno's universal character. Nicholas Mercator (Kauffmann, the clockmaker, d. 1687), who had seen a specimen of Dalgarno's universal character at Hartlib's, later wrote that other friends were curious to learn the details. In another letter, he asked for an explanation concerning what was apparently a specimen that Hartlib had sent in the meantime (Hartlib MS 56/1/114a, 56/1/115a).

An old friend of Hartlib's, Cheney Culpeper (1601–63),[5] in a first reaction likewise showed interest in Dalgarno's scheme, adding that people with whom he had discussed the news of the invention said that they thought it 'too good to be believed' (6 Sept. 1657, Hartlib MS 42/15/7a). Two weeks later Culpepper wrote that he had perused the papers concerning Dalgarno's scheme. He commented that the method of representing the particles, which, he emphasized, take up two-thirds of our language, was likely to give rise to confusion. He further raised the question whether or not Dalgarno's character was supposed to be based upon some analogy between thing and symbol. If not, he considered the symbols used to be rather inconvenient, as they seemed hard to write. He suggested positioning the symbols with respect to a line, so that a single symbol might have different meanings according to this position. Culpepper was enough impressed with Dalgarno to offer payment if he was willing to come to Kent in order to instruct Culpepper and his two daughters about the scheme (20 Sept. 1657, Hartlib MS 42/15/11b). Dalgarno almost certainly did not accept the offer, for Culpepper wrote on 6 October 1657 that he would be in London shortly, and expected on that occasion to 'understande more in an hower from Mr Dalgarnoe then I can at this distance in a weeke' (Hartlib MS 42/15/15a). Culpepper's name, like Boyle's, is on all three lists of sponsors printed in advertisements and in *The Art of Signs*.

---

[5] Eldest son of Sir Thomas Culpepper (1578–1662) of Hollingbourn, Kent. He matriculated at Hart Hall, 1618, and entered the Middle temple in 1621 (Foster 1891).

Hartlib asked two other acquaintances for an opinion on Dalgarno's scheme, both of whom were working on similar projects themselves. The first of these was John Beale (divine, natural philosopher, and writer, 1603–83), who emphasized both the importance and the difficulty of the kind of enterprise Dalgarno had embarked upon. Being as yet unable to judge the scheme, Beal expected that success was easier to attain in the field of shorthand than in that of a universal character. Yet he believed that progressive improvements of shorthand systems could in the end lead to a universal character (24 Aug. 1657, Hartlib MS 62/18/4a; 3 Nov. 1657, Hartlib MS 52/14a; 9 January 1658, Hartlib MS 31/1/61b).

The second acquaintance was Comenius, whose plan for a universal language as expounded in the manuscript 'Via Lucis' (1641) was known to Hartlib. On 11 January 1658, Comenius wrote: 'The inventions of Mr. Dalgarno can be held for miraculous, if they last. Eight days ago I sent (through Hartmann) the conditions which a new language ought to satisfy according to my plan, of which you are not unaware (through *Via Lucis*). I will await a reply' (Hartlib MS 7/128/1B). Samuel Hartmann, to whom Comenius refers, was in England at the time to collect funds for Bohemian exiles. Hartmann noted in his diary that he met Dalgarno in London on 8 December 1657, and that they talked at length about universal language. Dalgarno and Hartmann met again on 11 December, and once more on 2 February 1658 (Prümers 1899–1900: xiv. 152, 153; xv. 208). Hartmann also visited Hartlib, probably showing him the letter from Comenius concerning a new language. Hartlib was not impressed, for he wrote to Boyle: 'Mr Comenius hath sent lately to Mr Dalgarno his idea of it [i.e. of a 'philosophical character']; but it is so short and general that it is not worth the imparting' (Boyle 1772: vi. 99). Nothing is known about what exactly Dalgarno and Hartmann discussed, and it is uncertain whether Comenius ever received the reply he was awaiting. However, in his own published work on universal language, the *Panglottia*, Comenius makes a few positive references to Dalgarno's scheme.[6]

Thus, when the news about Dalgarno's scheme spread from April 1657 onwards, it met in general with a mixture of curiosity, expectation, and scepticism. A balanced assessment of the scheme was not possible until the second broadsheet appeared, which finally revealed many of the details of the scheme.

2.2. *The structure of the early scheme*

In 'The Autobiographical Treatise', Dalgarno relates that he first achieved a clear overall view of his invention after he had placed a large collection of particles above a collection of 'integral' words on one side of a sheet of paper (CC, fo. 23^r). The original broadsheet containing Dalgarno's second advertisement, entitled 'Tables of the Universal Character' (see below, Part I, Broadsheet 2), illustrates

---

[6] Comenius (1966: 300). A little earlier in the same chapter Comenius refers to Delgarno's [*sic*] treatment of points and accents as significant, and not just syllables (1966: 291).

this, although it represents a slightly later stage. One side of the broadsheet similarly contains a table of particles, arranged above a table of 'radical' words. The reverse side is filled by a dedicatory letter, and by four columns of densely printed text entitled 'Grammatical Observations', most of which concerns the explanation of the tables. The broadsheet thus contains a specific enough description of the early scheme, even though the printed sheet provides no clues concerning the shape of the symbols to be used, and lacks directions as to their use. For this reason, Dalgarno notes in the explanatory text that the tables are useful only if orally explained by himself. There is a surviving copy of the broadsheet (BL Add. MS 4377, fos. 145^r–146^v) on which these symbols are inserted in Dalgarno's own hand (partly reproduced in Fig. 2 below). The broadsheet was probably not printed until November 1657, but it is clear, on the basis of the Paris manuscripts, that the scheme was ready in virtually the same form by May of that year.

Two prominent features of the scheme are apparent at first glance. First, the title itself shows again that the scheme was designed to serve both as a universal character and as a system of shorthand. Secondly, the provision of the two distinct kinds of tables reflects Dalgarno's division of all words into radical words, on the one hand, to be represented by larger symbols, and particles, on the other hand, to be rendered by points and strokes around the larger symbols.

2.2.1. The Table of Particles.   The Table of Particles consists of a systematic enumeration of Latin words. The words are printed in four columns and nineteen rows. Each row contains twelve words (three in each column), so that the table contains 228 words in total. To represent the particles in his character, Dalgarno uses only nineteen different diacritic signs, one for each row. (Since various of these signs have the same shape as others, differing only in being rotated, Dalgarno claims in the explanatory text that he uses only seven distinct symbols. For example, the colon (:) is indicative of the second row, and horizontal twin dots (..) are indicative of the third row.) The twelve words in the same row are distinguished by means of the position of the sign. This position is indicated, first, by the column in which a word is printed, corresponding to positions before, after, above, and under the larger symbol, and, secondly, by whether the word is the first, second, or third word in a particular row and column. Thus the first row, first column, contains the words 'ego, tu, ille'. Each of these three is represented by a single dot '.' placed before a larger symbol representing some radical word. 'Ego' is represented by placing the dot at the top, 'tu' by placing it in the middle, and 'ille' by placing it at the bottom. In short, each of the nineteen diacritic signs has twelve distinct meanings according to twelve positions around a larger symbol.

A special place within the Table of Particles is occupied by the 'derivatives', which take up rows 18 and 19. Rather than by Latin words, these derivatives are represented in the table by names of grammatical categories. However, some of these names occur also in the other rows (e.g. first row, third and fourth columns). The Table of Derivatives is clearly modelled on Latin affixes.

In the explanatory text, Dalgarno claims that the Table of Particles is the key to his design, as anyone mastering this table 'is master of the whole art'. He further asserts that the table embodies 'a perfect scheme of a Logicall Grammer'. Dalgarno was clearly concerned with logical analysis of speech from an early stage onwards, and this was to remain a principal element of his linguistic work. Since he was convinced that logical structure resides primarily in the particles, he devoted much of his attention to the study of their meaning. In *The Art of Signs* he dwells at length on the subject, again stating that the particles are the key to the invention (*AS* 77–8). Furthermore, various passages in 'The Autobiographical Treatise' contain grammatical and logical observations on a number of particles, especially words expressing comparisons (CC, fos. 60^r–69^r). It will be seen below that, although the importance assigned to the particles was permanent, their treatment subsequently underwent drastic revision. Despite these later changes, several items on the list of specific observations concerning the Table of Particles of the early scheme are similar to considerations underlying the philosophical language of *The Art of Signs*. This is true, for instance, of the close affinity between personal and possessive pronouns (item 2; see Sect. 3.3.4 below); of the distinction between the copulative function of the verb 'to be' and its use in statements of existence (item 8; see *AS* 63 and Sect. 3.3.1 below); and of the emphasis given to the composite nature of many of the particles (items 3, 4, 6; see *AS* 83–4).

Dalgarno's early belief that the Table of Particles was the most accomplished and significant element of his scheme was supported by contemporaries (CC, fo. 28^r). He relates in *The Art of Signs* that, when 'some of the most learned men in the University of Oxford' saw the scheme of the whole art exhibited on one page, they admired it especially because of the treatment of the particles (*AS* 78). What these 'learned men' saw was either a copy of the broadsheet as printed below (Part I, Broadsheet 2), or a sheet very similar to it. Yet Dalgarno was subsequently to alter his treatment of the particles completely, after he had decided that he should no longer pursue a shorthand system but follow only logical principles. It appears from the comments on the broadsheet that he was aware at an early stage that shorthand and logic set different and at times antagonistic requirements, since he notes that many of the particles do not represent simple notions, but are included for the purpose of shorthand only.

2.2.2. The Table of Radicals.   The Table of Radicals is much larger than that of the particles. At first sight, the table looks like verse, consisting as it does of thirteen stanzas. These are all built on the same pattern, each stanza containing seven lines, while in every line six words are italicized. The italicized words are the radical words for the arrangement of which the table was designed. Since each stanza contains 42 (7×6) radical words, the thirteen stanzas together contain 546 radical words. Furthermore, as the radical words are accompanied by 'contraries', which are printed on the broadsheet in a column next to each stanza, the overall capacity of the Table of Radicals amounts to twice that number

(1,092). As some of the radical words on the table as printed lack a 'contrary', the total number of radical words is in fact 935.

There is purpose behind Dalgarno's choice of presentation. The 'Table of Radicals' is based on mnemonic principles, such that the stanzas might be learned by heart. Although, as Dalgarno emphasizes, the stanzas are nonsensical, they are not unintelligible. The idea is precisely to exploit the meaning of the radical words for their arrangement so as to make it easier to commit them to the memory. The non-italicized words in every line were added to make whole sentences, nonsensical stories supposedly being easier to memorize and recall than a list of unrelated words. Dalgarno even believed that the 'fictitious and foolish' quality of the stories meant that they would be more easily remembered than more sensible and serious ones. To enhance learnability, Dalgarno used two further mnemonic devices. As it is helpful to the memory that all stanzas have the same structure, he starts each line but the first in each stanza with the same word. For instance, the second line always begins with 'for', the third with 'but', and so on. In a letter to John Pell of 26 December 1657 (see below, Part V), Dalgarno explains that the resulting structure of the stanzas is mnemotechnically motivated. Thus the last two lines begin with 'nevertheless' and 'moreover' because 'varietie is operative on the memory'. A second device was offered for memorizing the order of the stanzas. The grammatical subject of the sentences in the first stanza is 'I', while the second stanza is written in the second person throughout, and so on, following the order of the particles as observed in the first column of the Table of Particles.

As to the 'contraries', Dalgarno apparently supposed that these could be easily remembered on account of their being antonyms. For example, if one knows where to find 'high' in the table, it will be easy to find 'low'. The tables of 'contraries' contain many open spaces. It is not certain whether Dalgarno intended to fill these places later on, or whether they were deliberately left open for lack of appropriate items, since for some words there is no obvious antonym. As Dalgarno notes, the 'contraries' are often coupled on the basis of some relation other than antonymy. In these cases, resemblance or some more general affinity between the things designated by the word appears to be the rationale. Thus 'honey' is coupled with 'wax', and 'bee' with 'wasp'.

Strictly speaking, the items arranged in the Table of Radicals are words, but Dalgarno clearly regarded these words as pointers to language-independent notions or things. Thus he says that synonymy is avoided in his scheme, because his intention is to 'express things and not the words of any Language' (see below, Part I, broadsheet 2, under the heading 'Of the Table of Radicall Characters', item 5). The Table of Radicals is, however, divided into two sections on the basis of linguistic criteria: the first contains 'radicall verbs and adjectives' (first to ninth stanzas), the second 'radicall substantives' (tenth to thirteenth stanzas). In fact, the division is not strictly observed in several cases, substantives occurring in the table of verbs and adjectives (e.g. 'heat') and verbs occurring in the table of substantives (e.g. 'barking'). As Dalgarno explains, in such cases the substantival or verbal form should be ignored, and the word is to be taken 'according as the nature of the notions is'—that is, although, for example, 'heat' may be expressed as a substantive, it should be conceived as a verb. It appears, then, that linguistic properties are part of what a notion is supposed to be. This lack of a sharp distinction between linguistic and mental (or logical) categories is not uncommon in other writers of the period, and it is also a feature of *The Art of Signs* (see Sect. 3.3.1). In the letter to Pell, Dalgarno explains that the division of the table into two sections is not of great importance, since verbs can be turned into nouns and vice versa, 'as the nature of the notion requires'.

The broadsheet offers no explanation as to how the radical words are to be represented in the character, probably because this would have caused complications in printing. Dalgarno's letter to Pell of December 1657 does offer such an explanation, however (see Fig. 2). The method is essentially as follows. Every stanza is represented by a symbol, to which short strokes are added. The symbols representing stanzas are the ones inserted by hand on the copy of the broadsheet. The place where these strokes are attached is indicative of the line where a radical word is to be found. Thus, if the stroke is attached to the top of the symbol, the first line is indicated. A stroke attached to the middle part of the symbol designates the second line, and a stroke attached to the bottom designates the third line. A different, hooked stroke attached in the same way to the symbol is indicative of the fourth, fifth, and sixth lines respectively. The seventh line is designated by a stroke that cuts through the symbol. The place of words within a line, finally, is identified by the direction in which the stroke points: if pointing upward to the left, the first word is designated, if pointing straight to the left, the second word, and so on (for the seventh line a slightly different method is used). The contraries are designated in the same fashion, using some kind of modification of the basic symbol, for which Dalgarno considered various methods. In the explanatory text, it is said that contraries are indicated by placing a single point in the middle. In the letter to Pell, Dalgarno says that contraries are to be indicated by reversing the position of the basic symbol, which is the method used with the symbols inserted by hand. In this way, Dalgarno managed to codify his 935 radical words by means of thirteen basic symbols (one for each stanza), and a series of systematic additions to the symbols that correspond to positions of words within the stanza. As for the shape of the symbols, Dalgarno explains in 'The Autobiographical Treatise' that he did not invent the symbols himself (CC, fo. 34ʳ), but does not identify the source he took them from. He may have referred to della Porta's well-known book on cryptography, *De Furtivis Literarum* (1602: 133), which, it is worth noting, contains a series of symbols similar to the ones used by Dalgarno.

FIG. 2. (opposite) Dalgarno's early scheme. *Above*: Parts of the broadsheet scheme (reduced), showing annotation in Dalgarno's hand added to the tables of particles and radicals (BL Add. MS 4377, fo. 145ᵛ). *Below*: Annotations by Pell showing the method of forming the radical characters following the broadsheet scheme (BL Add. MS fo. 154ʳ).

THE TABLE OF PARTICLES,

Before the character	after	above	under
1. Ego tu ille	me te illum	præt. præf. futurum	passivum & non
2. Nos vos illi	nos vos illos	plurale genitiv. dativ.	ideo quia quasi
3. Hoc illud aliud	hoc illud aliud	possum debeo oportet	nam nisi ne
4. Uterque reliqui solus	utrumque reliquos solum	imperat. utinam licet	quod si quamvis
5. Unusquisque alius neuter	unumquemque alium neutrum	hic illic alibi	sed tamen cum
6. Omnes aliquis nullus	omnes aliquem nullum	ubique alicubi nusquam	sic ut sicut
7. Omnia aliquid nihil	omnia aliquid nihil	sursum directe deorsum	primo deinde denique
8. Quis qualis talis	bene mediocriter male	antrorsum à latere retrorsum	partim dimidium potius
9. Ubi unde quo	fere præcipue perfecte	supra præter infra	omnino quodammodo præterea
10. Quid quare qua	certe possibile impossibile	extra intra undequaque	usque vix proxime
11. Quando quamdiu quousque	facile difficile frustra	simul juxta procul	tam quam secundum
12. Quantum quomodo quam	forte probabile falsum	contra inter circum	aut neque donec
13. Quot quotus quoties	contingens conveniens necesse	citra apud ultra	hucusque adhuc quoque
14. Tot toties tantum	nunc tunc tandem	per de pro	heri hodie cras
15. Solum satis nimis	iterum brevi diu	cum sine	raro sæpe semper
16. Cito opportune tarde	coram publice privatim	super ab ex	magnum parum multum
17. Statim aliquando nunquam	aliter particulariter Universaliter	ante penes post	valde magis maxime

Derivatives

18. Facere, actio, Infinitivus,	actor, substantiv. activ: sub. pass.	adjectiv. neutrum. adject. act. adj. pass.	abstractum, adverbium, potentia,
19. Officiū, Incipio, genus fæmininum,	Instrumentum, tempus, locus agendi	membrum, vestis, fructus	ars, vox animalis, morbus,

The TABLE of Radicall verbs and adjectives

1. Ego

6.¶. When I sit down upon a hie place, I'm sick with light and heat
12. For the many thick moistures, doe open wide my Empire pores
18. But when I sit upon a strong borrowed Horse, I ride and run most swiftly
24. Therefore if I can purchase this courtesie with civilitie, I care not the hirers babaritie
30. Because I'm perswaded they are wild villains, scornfully deceiving modest men
36. Neverthelesse I allowe their frequent wrongs, and will encourage them with obliging exhortations
42. Moreover I'l assist them to fight against robbers, when I have my long crooked sword.

2. Tu

6. Worthie friend be entreated, to extoll religion and holynes
12. F. true vertue being found giveth a rich blessing
18. B. your courage concealed in a prison, provokes flyers to pursue you
24. T. bold firme your victory against the heavie burdens of despaire
30. B. the great sufferings of miserie, kills wicked servants
36. N. you may constantly sell deare, and continue still your idle questions
42. M. you may remarke how chast virgins conceive, and afflict sleeping men with nakednes.

3. Ille

6. A wyse teacher knowes, what he affirmes and understands what he remembers
12. F. he chooseth rather to speake prophesies, then to please angry lovers
18. B. when he heares and sees clearly, they have promised to honour and thanke him
24. T. he therefore absolves them from false accusations, and praises their flourishing innocency
30. B. hard beginnings of good, begets a lively growth
36. N. he commanded presently to bind them, and lead them away and hang and burn them
42. M. he punished them so with hunger and thirst, that they cryed out eating is sweet.

4. Nos

6. We'l call this old mad man, and tickle him till he fart for laughter
12. F. the pleasant mirth of itching, will make him scratch his white snowie beard
18. B. sharp byting wounds, will bury his lustfull desires
24. T. we'll feed his lean barren corps, with fresh savoury dinners
30. B. filthie stinking roasts, move him fall a vomiting
36. N. we'l penetrate him with fearfull thunder, and kindle unhappy flames in him
42. M. we'l prove he divorced his wife for dancing, and inchanted her to refuse his kindnes.

CONTRARIES

1. Ego

Rise up, lowe, displace, whole, darke, cold,
F. few, thin, drie, shut, narrow, full,
B. stand, weake, lend, goe on foot, walke, slowe,
T. possesse, froward, rude, neglect, eloquent,
B. disswade, tame, serious, lascivious,
N. dissallow, rare, discourage, disobliedge, rebuke
M. resist, at peace, want, short, straight.

2. Tu

Unworthie enemie, threaten, abase, superstitious, prophane,
F. false, vitious, leeke, receive, poore, curse,
B. coward, tell, sett at liberty, pacifie, follow, defend,
T. let goe, inflable, yeeld, light, disburden, hope,
B. small, doe, prosperous, quicken, godlie, free,
N. unconstant, buy, cheap, leave of worke, answere
M. unchast, bring forth, comfort, wake, cloathe.

3. Ille

Foole, learne, doubt, denie, ignorant, forget,
F. reject, dumb, come to passe, offend, content, hate,
B. deafe, blind, obscure, performe, dishonour, unthankfull,
T. condemne, excuse, dispraise, wither, guilty,
B. soft, end, ill, corrupt, die, decrease,
N. obey, absent, loose, drawe, drowne, smoake,
M. spare, full, drinke, silent, fast, soure.

4. Nos

Appeare, young, sottish, pricke, belch, weep
F. unpleasant, sad, sore, rubbe, black, haile,
B. blunt, licke, cure, digge, covet,
T. poyson, fat, fertile, rotten, unsavory, suppe,
E. cleane, odoriferous, boyle, rest, stand, spit,
N. dare, lighten, quench, happy, sparkle,
M. improve, marry, play, conjure, graunt, unkind.

It appears from some final remarks on the broadsheet that Dalgarno was concerned to refute the objection that his scheme was incomplete. This was precisely the objection made by Wilkins soon after Dalgarno had finished his early scheme. The ensuing debate (see Sect. 2.4) can be perceived in the text of the broadsheet. Dalgarno answers the objection, initially by admission that the Table of Substantives is as yet incomplete, and that the addition of four or five stanzas is required. Apart from this minor defect, however, he claims his scheme to be quite sufficient to enable communication about ordinary matters. He continues with a claim that the extent of the tables is greater than it appears, as synonyms are avoided. In addition, he explains, only notions that enter into common discourse are to be catered for in the tables: words pertaining to institutions and practices that are peculiar to particular nations may be disregarded in a universal character, a point that Wilkins was himself to make in his *Essay* (1668: 295–6). Finally, as the character is intended only for ordinary discourse, it is, he contends, neither possible nor desirable to include the 'numberlesse multitude of the severall *species* of nature' in the tables. For specialized discourse, special tables including some of these species might be drawn up.

It must have been clear to Dalgarno, however, that, even if these points were granted, the collection of radical words contained in his tables was too limited to enable communication about everyday matters in a satisfactory way. In the letter to Pell, he makes clear that he was working on a method to overcome this limitation, presenting his solution as an additional advantage of his scheme. His method involved the use of radical words for forming compound expressions, so that, for instance, all names of diseases would consist of the radical word 'disease', combined with another radical word designating some salient feature of the disease in question. The advantage of this, Dalgarno explains, is that, whereas other languages involve learning separate words for 'calf' and 'lamb', for example, his own scheme treats such 'notions' as derivative, that is, as composed of 'cow + young', and 'sheep + young', respectively. He tells Pell in December 1657 that he has 'great companies brought together' of such expressions. It can thus be shown that Dalgarno was already exploiting at an early stage what was to be one of the main principles of *The Art of Signs*.

In conclusion, although Dalgarno's early scheme differed from the later language of *The Art of Signs* in various respects, several of the principles underlying his original design were to remain unaltered. Thus Dalgarno was concerned with learnability throughout, and never changed his belief that he should confine himself to the provision of a core vocabulary of radical words, on the basis of which all other expressions are to be formed through composition. Furthermore, from the start he criticized existing languages for being illogical and full of redundancies, claiming that both the early scheme and the language of *The Art of Signs* offered a more rational means of expression. Moreover, the importance assigned to the particles for the structure of speech was a constant feature of his approach. In addition, some specific points remained the same, such as the analysis of some of the particles, and the pairing of radical words on the basis of semantic opposition.

When John Pell received the broadsheet containing the tables, and Dalgarno's letter including a further explanation of the scheme, he was able to translate the sample of the character transcribing a fragment of St John's Gospel. Among his papers are notes in which he provides a Latin translation of the first seven characters with diacritics, which together render the first two verses of John 16 (BL Add. MS 4377, fo. 153ʳ). Pell further commented that he himself, unlike Dalgarno, would not strive to construct a universal writing and a shorthand system at the same time, the former purpose being quite enough. He found the figure of the basic characters of primary importance, and suggested the use of squares, to which strokes could be added in much the same way as in Dalgarno's scheme. For the convenience of the users, pre-printed sheets filled with blank squares could be produced (BL Add. MS 4377, fo. 159ʳ).

Another well-informed commentary on Dalgarno's early scheme was made by Francis Lodwick, who had done pioneering work in this area himself, and who never failed to be among those on the lists of Dalgarno's sponsors. Lodwick noted that the mnemonic arrangement of radical words into stories had the drawback that verbs had to be inflected for tense and that sometimes a substantive had to be used instead of 'the adjective primitive', so that the systematical division of the table was distorted, making it hard 'to find the primitive desired'. He further suggested arranging the particles into verses as well, and changing the stanzas so that they consisted of nine lines, each comprising nine radical words. Lodwick also proposed an alternative method of symbolizing the radical words, as well as a method for pronouncing the written symbols (BL Add. MS 932, fos. 13ʳ–15ʳ).

Lodwick in his notes thus addressed an aspect of Dalgarno's scheme that emerged soon after Dalgarno had finished a first version of his scheme. This was the construction of a spoken language in addition to a writing system. On the second broadsheet the language is only briefly mentioned, but it is clear from various independent sources that Dalgarno had been working on a spoken language for some time before this broadsheet was printed.

2.3. *A character and a language*

According to his own retrospective account, it was about three months after Dalgarno became acquainted with Wilkins that he started devising a spoken language (CC, fo. 35ᵛ). Since it is plausible that Dalgarno first met Wilkins in February or March 1657, this tallies well with the fact that Hartlib referred to Dalgarno's scheme as being both a character and a 'universal language' in his letter to Pell of 3 July 1657 (BL Add. MS 4377, fo. 149ʳ). Similarly, John Wood in his letter to Hartlib of 8 August refers to Dalgarno's 'Universal Character & Language' (Hartlib MS 33/1/25a). That Dalgarno started inventing a language in the spring or early summer of 1657 is further corroborated by manuscripts now preserved in Paris, which contain a faithful Latin translation of large portions of the material that is presented in the second broadsheet (Bibliothèque Mazarine MS 3788). These manuscripts also include an account of how the radical words of the tables are to be expressed in a language using ordinary alphabetical script. The unknown author notes that the scheme was explained to him in June and July 1657 at Oxford, by its inventor, 'a certain Scot, George Dalgerno', adding that the scheme had been invented in May of that year.

According to Dalgarno's own account, the creation of the language was brought about just as incidentally as that of the universal character (CC, fos. 34^r-36^r). He found in using his tables that his graphical symbols did not allow easy reference to radical words. For this reason, he started using letters to refer to stanzas and words. He did this at first 'by using letters according to the inartificial order they are placed in our Alphabet'. The Paris manuscripts show clearly how this was done: the first stanza was indicated by the syllable 'lo'. The first radical word, 'sit downe', was represented by 'loa', the second by 'lobe', the third by 'loce', and so on. Since this method did not represent lines but only stanzas and radical words, the letters of the alphabet were insufficient to represent all forty-two radical words in each stanza in this way. Dalgarno provided for this by adding another syllable, yielding words like 'loasi', 'lobesi', 'locesi', and so on. Dalgarno's statement that he abandoned this method after a short while is confirmation that he had just started working on his language when the Paris manuscripts were written. However, these papers show that Dalgarno had already by this time also devised a method for representing the particles by means of monosyllabic words, rendering, for example, 'ego, tu, ille' by 'ar, eir, ir', respectively. As far as the radical words are concerned, Dalgarno soon devised a more convenient and elegant method of representing these: he used monosyllabic words consisting of an initial consonant, a vowel in the middle position, and a final consonant, indicating the stanza, line, and radical word respectively. Thus artificial words emerged that codified the words in the tables in exactly the same way as did the graphical symbols, but which had the advantage of being easy to pronounce and read. For example, according to a copy of the broadsheet in the Bodleian Library (Wood 276 a 20) in which phonetic values are marked up in a hand that seems to be Dalgarno's, the artificial word 'BAD' indicated 'second stanza, first line, third word'—that is, 'entreat'. A parallel example, with differences of detail, can be found in 'The Autobiographical Treatise' (CC, fo. 35^r).

There is no reason to doubt the accuracy of Dalgarno's retrospective account, and the Paris manuscripts provide conclusive evidence that his version is correct on this particular point. In the light of this, the claim made by John Wallis that it was at his instigation that Dalgarno added a spoken language to his universal character does not seem to be accurate (Wallis 1678: 16). Given the circumstances in which the language developed, it is understandable why Dalgarno regarded the character and the language as two parallel and equivalent symbolisms:

they each represented the items enumerated in the tables in structurally the same way. Accordingly, he announces on the second broadsheet that alongside the written symbolism a language will be produced 'by the selfe same art' (see below, Part I, Broadsheet 2, 'Grammatical Observations').

Dalgarno reports that, when he first proposed the construction of a spoken language, he met with fairly strong opposition. Wilkins, for one, did not initially like the idea, but was convinced when Dalgarno showed how the system worked (CC, fo. 36^v). In the *Essay*, Wilkins was to provide two parallel symbolisms himself, a character and a language, both of which were based upon the very same method of codification as was used in Dalgarno's early scheme. The idea of providing a means of pronouncing the written symbols of which a universal character consisted was not new. Lodwick had proposed the addition of a spoken version to his universal script in the *Groundwork* of 1652. Ward, in the *Vindiciae Academiarum* of 1654, had suggested that the universal character he envisaged should be made effable, 'because it is a dul thing to discours by pointing and indication' (Ward 1654: 21). Beck's universal character of 1657 also contained a method for pronouncing the numerical characters he used. Why Dalgarno, unlike Lodwick, Ward, and Beck, encountered what was apparently rather forceful opposition may be explained by the fact that he, unlike the others, challenged the very framework from which the idea of a universal character derived its popularity in the first place (see Sect. 1.2 above). Whereas the others had thought of and presented their spoken versions of the universal writing expressly as an additional device solely for the convenience of face-to-face communication, Dalgarno looked upon his universal language as a valuable invention in its own right.

The objections to this idea clearly stimulated his critical skills, for he argues at length, both in *The Art of Signs* (AS 12–17) and in 'The Autobiographical Treatise' (CC, fos. 70^r–74^r), against the prejudices that he perceived to underlie his opponents' views. Their belief was that a system of real characters, signifying things directly rather than through spoken sounds, could provide an easy means for overcoming language barriers, whereas the creation of a new language would add to rather than remedy the curse of Babel. Dalgarno saw that this position was based on the erroneous assumption that written symbols signifying speech sounds are related to extra-linguistic reality in a quite different way from those that are not associated with specific speech sounds (the 'real characters'). Dalgarno argues that this distinction is quite illusory, since written words may just as well be considered real characters, if one disregards pronunciation. Conversely, a system of real characters can always be turned into an equivalent pronounceable system. He further draws attention to the naivety of the idea that a universal writing might be constructed simply by extending the use of symbols of the same kind as Arabic numerals. He is clearly referring to proposals such as those made by Wilkins in the *Mercury* (1641), and by Lodwick in *The Groundwork* (1652: 3) (see Sect. 1.2 above). Such systems, Dalgarno believed, could never 'reach all the ends and uses of Language' (CC, fo. 73^r).

At this point, it becomes clear how Dalgarno's concern with the construction of a universal language led to his involvement with the teaching of language to the deaf and dumb. The development of his scheme prompted him to articulate and refine his thoughts on the relationship between spoken and written language. In the course of this, the condition of a deaf and dumb person provided him with an illuminating perspective on this relationship, since it showed quite clearly that, contrary to what was assumed by his opponents, there is no order of priority between written and spoken language (see CC, fo. 71ʳ).

Although in Dalgarno's opinion neither written nor spoken language has a status superior to the other on a theoretical level, he emphasized that in practice each has advantages of its own, spoken language being most convenient for communication face to face, written language being capable of conveying messages over long distances (*AS* 13). Not long after he started creating his language, he realized that this was the 'better halfe' of the invention (CC, fo. 70ʳ), as the artificial words were equally capable of functioning as a universal character, while being pronounceable into the bargain. Furthermore, Dalgarno believed that the analysis of speech sounds reflected in alphabetical writing constituted the greatest achievement in linguistics ever made (*AS* 1–2; cf. CC, fo. 77ʳ), so that its use in an invention that was based upon rational principles must have seemed imperative. Intending at first to make no mention of the language for strategic reasons, he decided a little later, both for fear of being pre-empted by a competitor and for reasons of intellectual honesty, to put forward a language using alphabetical letters in addition to a 'mute' written character (CC, fo. 70ʳ). Accordingly, in a broadsheet that probably appeared in the beginning of 1658, Dalgarno refers to his scheme as 'an Universal Character and a new Rational Language' (see below, Part I, Broadsheet 3). A similar double characterization is used in *The Art of Signs*, the subtitle of which reads 'A Universal Character and Philosophical Language', thus indicating that two separate symbolisms are involved in one and the same scheme. In the text of *The Art of Signs* only the language is discussed, but the provision for a separate character is announced, having been omitted for the time being, it is said, for practical reasons (*AS* 17, 127). Looking back on this aspect of his project in the autobiographical manuscript, Dalgarno asserts that one further step in the development of his thoughts on the matter consisted in the insight that the provision of a language alone is quite sufficient, and that 'it is a manifest redundancy to provide for the same thing twice' (CC, fo. 73ʳ).

2.4. *The dispute with Wilkins*

Until recently, very little was known about the joint efforts of Dalgarno and Wilkins towards the construction of a universal language. The main source was a brief account by Wilkins in his *Essay*, where he says that his own work was occasioned by his assisting someone referred to as 'another person' in creating a 'real *Character*, from the Natural notion of things' (1668: Epistle to the Reader). Wilkins drew up tables classifying a large number of stones, animals, and plants for this other person, clearly Dalgarno, who refused, however, to make use of the tables. Unwilling to lose the fruit of so much work, Wilkins tells us, he went on to construct a scheme of his own. This short account could be supplemented by other contemporary writers, who identified Dalgarno by name, rectifying what was seen as a blatant omission on Wilkins's part. Thus Wallis wrote: 'This Enterprise of Mr. Dalgarno, gave occasion to Dr. Wilkins (the late Bishop of Chester) to pursue the same Design (as himself intimates in his Epistle)' (1678: 17). A perceptive short description of both Dalgarno's *Art of Signs* and Wilkins's *Essay* was provided by Robert Plot, who recapitulated the various stages of development that Dalgarno's project went through, and emphasized the contrast between the treatment of the 'species of natural bodies' in both works—Dalgarno relying on composition of radical words as much as possible, Wilkins preferring to reduce large numbers of these species to classificatory tables (Plot 1676: 282–5). A further comment was made by Wood, who says of *The Art of Signs*: 'This book, before it went to the press, the author communicated to Dr. Wilkins, who from there taking an hint of a greater matter, carried it on, and brought it up to what you see extant [i.e. in the *Essay*]' (1691: 506). Finally, an indication of why the tables that Wilkins drew up were rejected by Dalgarno is contained in a letter to Pell of December 1657, in which Dalgarno reports that Wilkins was drawing up tables using a 'philosophical' method— that is, arranging the items in the tables according to a 'predicamental' order (see Sects. 1.1, 2.1, 3.2.1). Dalgarno asserts that this method has two serious drawbacks: not only does it run counter to the principles of mnemonics, but it also depends on arbitrary distinctions that will give rise to unrestrained differences of opinion.

In short, what was known about the collaboration between Dalgarno and Wilkins amounted to the following: that, after Dalgarno had completed his early scheme, Wilkins urged him to rearrange the tables using the predicamental method; that Wilkins then proceeded to carry this out himself; and that Dalgarno refused to make use of the results. Since Dalgarno's 'Autobiographical Treatise' has come to light, it is known that the matter was debated at length by the two men, and the reasons for the disagreement have become clearer. Furthermore, the treatise clarifies various aspects of both Dalgarno's and Wilkins's work, giving further confirmation of the differences between their approaches.

When Wilkins first suggested that Dalgarno should change his tables, two reasons were given. First, he judged the tables to be defective, as they should include a far larger number of names of 'natural bodies' such as animals and plants. Secondly, he believed that a logical classification by genus, difference, and species (the predicamental order) was more appropriate for a design of this kind than Dalgarno's mnemonic arrangement. Neither of these arguments persuaded Dalgarno. As to the first, his intention had always been to confine himself in principle to the production of a core vocabulary of radical words, and to express all other concepts exclusively by means of composition, either with other radicals or with derivational affixes. His objections to the predicamental order, as noted, were that it makes the language hard to learn, and that it is impossible to establish an uncontroversial arrangement. The debate on these points was well advanced by the time Dalgarno's second broadsheet, containing the mnemonic tables, was printed, as can be inferred not only from his rejecting the inclusion of 'the numberlesse multitude of the severall species of nature' from the tables, but also from his emphasizing in the dedicatory letter that the choice of a mnemonic method was a deliberate one, which involved 'abstracting altogether from Philosophy' (see below, Part I, Broadsheet 2).

Both disputants adduced further arguments in support of their positions, but without succeeding in convincing the other. As interesting as the points of disagreement, perhaps, are the points on which they did agree. There was, for instance, no controversy concerning the impossibility of establishing definitions that specify the essential property of a thing. Aristotelian natural philosophy maintained the existence of so-called substantial forms, endowing things with a particular essence. An ideal definition specified the name of the genus to which a thing belongs together with the name of this essential property. Neither Wilkins nor Dalgarno believed that such definitions could be used as a basis for the radical words, because the essences, if they exist at all, are unknown to us. A relevant passage from Dalgarno's account (CC, fos. 48^{r}–47^{v}) shows the influence of the new science on the linguistic enterprise both men were engaged in, and provides important information on this aspect of their schemes.

A further point of agreement, consequent upon the previous one, was that the predicamental method entailed the more or less random listing of items within categories. Wilkins's tables accordingly distinguished the species of animals and plants belonging to the same category by assigning numbers to them. For example, in the *Essay* (where the tables are structurally similar to the ones originally drawn up for Dalgarno (see Wilkins 1668: Epistle to the Reader)), the category of 'whole-footed beasts' contains four species, in the order: 1. Horse, 2. Asse, 3. Camel, 4. Elephant (1668: 156). It was this numerical order that Dalgarno particularly objected to, as he was convinced that such an order is hard to memorize, especially if large numbers of items are involved. His own method was not to include names of species in the 'table of Radicals' at all, but to combine names of genera with a word designating some property that is specific enough to identify the species. Wilkins assessed both methods quite differently, maintaining that the predicamental order, though arbitrary to some extent, still enabled the radical words to contain descriptive content, while the compositional method would lead to lengthy periphrases.

It became clear in the course of the debate that both participants had radically different approaches towards the construction of a universal language. Dalgarno aimed to create a language that is rational both because it is efficiently

organized and because it agrees with the structure of thought; Wilkins aimed
to devise a language that is 'philosophical' in that its words provide a description of the things they refer to. In 'The Autobiographical Treatise', Dalgarno
elaborates on the principles underlying his own approach (CC, fos. 77^r–84^r). He
points out that the compositional method is necessarily used by all languages
because of the limited capacity of the memory and the vast number of things
for which expressions are to be formed. Further, the use of a few elements to
express many things is a mark of excellence, the compositional method being
employed even by God in naming Adam, and by Adam in naming the animals.
This leads him to formulate as a 'fundamental principle' that 'no notion is to be
expressed by a primitive Sign, which by its nature is capable of being exprest
by a derivation or composition' (CC, fo. 83^v). By the time he wrote the treatise,
he was also in a position to illustrate the superiority of his own approach to that
of Wilkins by means of examples taken from the *Essay*. In so doing, he points
out many instances of what he judged to be errors, omissions, and redundancies in the latter work. Wilkins's fundamental mistake, in Dalgarno's opinion,
was to attempt to force two incompatible designs into one—that is, to serve
the purposes of scientific classification and those of linguistic practice at the
same time.

The disagreement concerning the principles on which to build the artificial language was too deep for the collaboration to continue. After a declared
'breach of judgment', Dalgarno and Wilkins worked independently on their
own schemes. Dalgarno states that the difference of opinion did not lead to personal conflict, and this is confirmed by Wilkins's name on the list of sponsors
of *The Art of Signs*. However, in a letter to Hartlib written after the breach and
before publication of *The Art of Signs* (3 November 1659 (see below, Part V)),
Dalgarno voices suspicion about Wilkins's work, anticipating that he might
plagiarize his own scheme—and an obsolete version of it at that—without
due credit. Furthermore, in *The Art of Signs* he recalls that his early scheme was
assessed by scholars in the University of Oxford, mentioning Ward, but not
Wilkins. When exactly the breach took place is not certain, but Dalgarno's
report to Hartlib (3 November 1659) that he had held daily conversations with
Wilkins for almost a year suggests that the collaboration ended in the first
months of 1658.

2.5. *From mnemonics to philosophy*

A third advertisement for Dalgarno's scheme was published, in all probability,
early in 1658 ('News to the Whole World', see below, Part I, Broadsheet 3).
The invention is now described as 'an Universal Character, and a New Rational
Language', thus highlighting the spoken language more emphatically than
in the earlier broadsheet. At the same time, the use of the invention for the
purpose of shorthand has been given less prominence, although this is still

mentioned among the features and advantages of the scheme that are listed on the sheet (items 4 and 5). A novel development from the earlier broadsheets is the claim that the character will provide a means for communicating with the deaf and dumb (item 11). Dalgarno also now champions his scheme as extremely useful for language teaching (item 13). The broadsheet contains a list of persons who subscribe to the need for a design of this kind; it is perhaps significant that Wilkins's name is absent.

By the time this broadsheet appeared, Dalgarno had apparently moved to London, as he says he can be found at Hartlib's house. From Hartmann's diary, Dalgarno is known to have been in London in December 1657 and February 1658 (Prümers 1899–1900: xiv. 152, 153; xv. 208). A letter from him on 17 February 1658 to William Brierton was sent from London (printed below, Part V). In this, he asks for support in promoting his scheme, his thoughts on which have now fully matured. He encloses a testimony of the 'practical facility' of the scheme, based upon experiment. This might have been an earlier version of a pamphlet that was dated May 1658, and signed by Richard Love of the University of Cambridge. The sheet contains the testimony that two students mastered Dalgarno's character within a fortnight, having been trained during two hours a day (see below, Part I, Broadsheet number 4). In the same month, Dalgarno stayed at Cambridge, from whence he wrote to Hartlib with a copy of Love's testimony (see below, Part V).

After May 1658, the next reference to Dalgarno's project dates from November 1659, when he writes to Hartlib again, from Bishopston in Wiltshire (see below, Part V). He enquires if there is news about rival projects, showing himself, as noted, especially anxious about Wilkins's moves. He also tells Hartlib that he has continued working on his own scheme, and that a period of solitariness has contributed to its perfection. Dalgarno's absence from the scene for some period is borne out by 'The Autobiographical Treatise', which mentions a visit to Scotland for about a quarter of a year (CC, fo. 32^r). There is evidence that he returned from Scotland to Cambridge by the end of August 1658, and that he then went to Wiltshire to preach the gospel. Upon his return to Oxford, he found that what was left of the air of expectation concerning the creation of a universal character was now completely centred on Wilkins, and that he himself was no longer considered to be a proponent of any importance. Without identifying anybody by name, he relates that some people even thought he had plagiarized Wilkins's plan (CC, fo. 31^r). Typical of the atmosphere was a comment by Henry Oldenburg (c.1615–77), who wrote to Hartlib in July 1659 that, when it came to the design of a universal character, he had 'more confidence in Dr Wilkins . . . than in any other' (Hartlib MS 39/3/25a). Furthermore, John Owen, who had first put Dalgarno in touch with Wilkins two years previously, published a book in which he mentioned only Wilkins as a person engaged in the development of a universal language. In a conversation Owen fully acknowledged Dalgarno's pioneering role, and this encouraged the latter not to give up the project (CC, fo. 33^r).

Thus after an initial period of about a year, in which Dalgarno started his project, created his early scheme, and sought and found publicity as well as sponsors and collaborators, there followed a period in which he worked in isolation on the improvement of his scheme. It was during the latter period that he made a number of far-reaching changes.

In the first place, his growing perception that the requirements of shorthand conflict with those of a rationally instituted character and language prompted him to abandon the goal of a system for shorthand. The division into particles and radicals that was characteristic of the early scheme was both inspired by and primarily useful for the purpose of shorthand. On consideration, Dalgarno discovered that, from a logical point of view, the distinction between particles and radicals was unfounded. Since the particles are semantically derivative of radical words (see Sect. 3.3.4 for an explanation of this point), it would be redundant to have a separate class of particles. On the basis of 'Ockham's razor', forbidding the inclusion of redundant items, the particles were consequently discarded, and only radical words were retained. Furthermore, since the distinction between verbs and adjectives, on the one hand, and substantives, on the other hand, did not agree with the principles to be followed in the construction of a philosophical language, only one class of radical words was retained: the noun substantive, conceived as a category of words that 'signify the notion of a thing indefinitely' (see Sect. 3.3.1 below for discussion).

The second major change was that the mnemonic arrangement of radical words was after all replaced by a predicamental one. Dalgarno provides no explicit justification for this change; he simply states that this arrangement was his final choice. However, he does indicate that the choice was of relatively minor importance, saying that the mnemonic stanzas of the early scheme were an imitation of a predicamental order, stanzas corresponding to genera, lines to differences, and words to species. In addition, he clearly believed that the principle guiding the arrangement of the radical words is inessential as far as the forming of compounds is concerned. In the compounds that Dalgarno wanted to make use of as much as possible, one radical (for example, 'metal') performs the role of a genus, while another (for example, 'perfect') functions as a specific difference (the resulting compound meaning 'gold'). For the radical words to function in this way, it does not matter whether they are arranged mnemonically or predicamentally. Thus, provided that the compositional method is employed for the expression of most of the 'species of natural bodies', the use of the predicamental method in arranging the radical words is quite compatible with the approach that Dalgarno defended against Wilkins's suggestion to employ the predicamental method throughout. The debate concerned not so much the arrangement as the number of radical words.

Nevertheless, it does not seem implausible that the emphasis by Wilkins on the advantage of the predicamental arrangement—enabling the radical words to be partial descriptions rather than completely arbitrary names of the things they designate—persuaded Dalgarno to employ the device, albeit to a limited extent. In *The Art of Signs*, he draws attention to the non-arbitrariness of the radical words as an additional advantage of the design. This advantage was, however, bought at a high price, for the mnemonic facility of the early scheme was lost, and the objections that Dalgarno had levelled against the method favoured by Wilkins now seemed to apply to his own scheme. In 'The Auto-biographical Treatise', he addresses this point, explaining that his own scheme is much less liable to these objections than Wilkins's because of the much smaller number of radical words, and that, furthermore, he had established an additional mnemonic method to compensate for the loss of mnemonic advantages of the early scheme. In *The Art of Signs*, only an indication of how this worked is given, since there was no time to include a complete explanation (see *AS*, ch. VIII; CC, fo. 50^r).

Having reworked his scheme, Dalgarno decided that the resulting version was to be definitive, and he made efforts to have it printed as soon as possible, probably because he feared that one of his competitors would pre-empt his ideas (see the letter to Hartlib, 3 November 1659 (below, Part V)). Some time in 1660, but clearly after the Restoration, he published yet another broadsheet (see below, Part I, Broadsheet 5), consisting of three parts. The first is a short political essay written in a highly florid style, in which Dalgarno calls on all the nations of the world to participate in a project aimed at global linguistic unity, and summons all those who are in power to establish and procure peace through promoting the arts. The second part is a letter addressed to the newly restored king, Charles II, begging him more particularly to support Dalgarno's own art. The third part presents an outline of the contents of *The Art of Signs*. This pamphlet was intended to attract additional supporters for the scheme, and it may be safely assumed that it was also part of the petition that was addressed to the king. That the petition was successful seems to be demon-strated in the letter of recommendation issued from the palace and printed in *The Art of Signs* and in the occurrence of the name of the king's secretary in the list of sponsors. Thus Dalgarno was able to publish his book in 1661, pre-senting the first complete artificial and universal language in the seventeenth century.

3. The Philosophical Language of *The Art of Signs*

The present section introduces the essentials of the artificial language expounded in *The Art of Signs*. To support this, it provides background information on the logical and grammatical traditions with which Dalgarno assumed his readers would be familiar. The order of presentation is that followed by Dalgarno himself in his text, beginning with examination of the most simple elements (letters), followed by discussion of more complex items (words), and concluding with analysis of still more complex structures (sentences). This order, as well as reflecting Dalgarno's own methodological principles, follows the standard pattern underlying most classical and contemporary works on grammar.

Apart from the text of *The Art of Signs* proper, this introduction also makes reference to other elements of the work. These include the summary table of the alphabet contained in the prefatory matter (the 'Alphabetum'), the 'Lexicon Grammatico-Philosophicum' (reproduced as a fold-out table at the end of this volume), the 'Lexicon Latino-Philosophicum', and the 'Praxis', all of which are provided as appendices to the text. Of these, the 'Lexicon Grammatico-Philosophicum' is indispensable for a description of the philosophical language, since it is here that the essential details are to be found—namely, the lexicon of radical words, a list of particles, and the grammatical apparatus used to indicate word classes, degrees of comparison, and tenses and modes.

3.1. *The alphabet of the philosophical language*

As the title page indicates, and as the opening paragraphs of the first chapter show, Dalgarno claims that his language is based upon a general theory of symbolization: the art of signs. Thus the book starts out with a discussion of the simple elements of signs. The simple elements of the language are sounds, and Dalgarno accordingly presents a phonological theory that serves two closely related purposes. It both establishes an alphabet that, unlike existing ones, conforms to the 'rules of art', and, in addition, selects a number of sounds to be used in forming words of the philosophical language. The first purpose requires that the principal speech sounds are identified and unambiguously designated, each by a single letter. The second purpose implies that only those sounds that can be pronounced with ease by all people, whatever their native tongue may be, are eligible for use. The selection of simple sounds was also undertaken with a view to a more ambitious, philosophical goal—namely, to establish a connection between the simple elements of language, on the one hand, and the simple elements of either thought or reality, or both, on the other hand. As will be explained below (Sect. 3.2.2), this proved to be unachievable.

On the basis of both articulatory and acoustic criteria, Dalgarno establishes the following alphabet. He identifies seven open sounds or vowels, which divide into four 'gutturals': *a*, *η*, *e*, *i*, and three 'labials' *o*, *υ*, *u*. Further, there are three semi-closed sounds—that is, made by half closing the organs of speech: *s*, *r*, *l*. Finally, nine sounds made with the speech organs closed, or consonants, are distinguished on two grounds, first on the basis of where the closure is made, and, secondly on the basis of the sound being produced. The first criterion groups together sounds made by closing the lips: *m*, *b*, *p*; sounds produced by making a closure with the tongue: *n*, *d*, *t*; and sounds made by closing the throat: *ng*, *g*, *k*. The second criterion distinguishes the same group of nine letters into nasals: *m*, *n*, *ng*; suffocates: *b*, *d*, *g*; and mutes: *p*, *t*, *k*. In sum, if all principal sounds are enumerated in an order derived from phonological principles, the following alphabet emerges:

A H E I O Y U S R L M N NG B D G P T K.

In this alphabet, the most open sounds come first, and more open sounds generally precede more closed ones. Phonologically similar sounds follow immediately upon each other: guttural vowels, labial vowels, semi-closed sounds, nasal consonants, suffocate consonants, mute consonants. Dalgarno notes (*AS* 7) that simple sounds other than the ones just listed exist, but that these are not used in the language. This is not quite correct, in that some of these simple sounds are in fact used—namely, *f*, *v*, and *h*. As for *f* and *v*, these are derivative, phonologically speaking: in Dalgarno's opinion they arise by aspiration from *p* and *b* respectively. *F* is used, for reasons explained by Dalgarno (*AS* 6), instead of *ng*. To perform various auxiliary functions in the language, *V* was added to the alphabet. The replacement of *ng* by *f* and the addition of *v* are registered in the 'Alphabetum', which accordingly enumerates the following letters:

A H E I O Y U M N F B D G P T K S R L V.

It is to be noted that the character *H* is the capital eta (*H*) representing a vowel. *Y* is the capital upsilon (*Y*). Further, *s*, *r*, *l* appear after rather than before the consonants. This probably results from the fact that the 'Alphabetum' is designed not only to present a list of letters used in the language, but also to show which generic notions are designated by these letters when initial. Since, however, *r*, *l*, *v* do not function in this way, listing *s*, *r*, *l* in the phonologically appropriate place would have led to interrupting the list of generic notions.

The 'Alphabetum' omits *h*, which nonetheless is used in the language, as appears from both the 'Lexicon Grammatico-Philosophicum' and the 'Praxis'. It is used to perform exactly the same function as *r* does—namely, to indicate opposition. The only context in which *h* is used is immediately following *s*. In the text (*AS* 10–11), Dalgarno notes that the combination *sr* rarely occurs in existing languages, adding that the pressure of regularity forced him to use it in his own language and that it offers the advantage of being easy to pronounce. It appears that, after the text was completed, Dalgarno was not satisfied with his own justification and decided to sacrifice regularity to euphony. He changed his language on this point, replacing the combination *sr* wherever it occurred by *sh*. The two instances in which *sr* still occurs confirm this reconstruction of events: the list of particles in the 'Lexicon Grammatico-Philosophicum' contains the form *srʋd*, which is inconsistent with the Tables of Radical Words, which have *shʋd*. Moreover, the tables indicate that the form *sros* should be used where one would expect *shos*—namely, the opposite of *sos*. It is very likely that Dalgarno in revising his tables overlooked these forms.

The 'Alphabetum' further omits diphthongs. The text mentions six diphthongs as being easy to pronounce: *ai*, *ei*, *oi*, *au*, *eu*, *ou*. However, the latter three of these are not used in the philosophical language at all, whereas the first three are put to various uses: they occur in radical words, in words designating numbers, and in affixes.

The inconsistencies between the text of *The Art of Signs* and the various appendices are probably due to the fact that Dalgarno continued working on his project while hastily preparing his book for the press.

Dalgarno's concern to ensure that the words of his language would be easy to pronounce led him to devote special attention to the question of which sounds may be combined with which others. He mentions some of his results in *The Art of Signs* (AS 9–10), but he reserved most of these for separate treatment in *A Discourse of the Nature and Number of Double Consonants*, which was published in 1680 as an appendix to *The Deaf and Dumb Man's Tutor* (see below, Part III).

3.2. *The Lexicon*

3.2.1. The art of things versus the art of signs.

The words of Dalgarno's language fall into two types: radical words, and compound words formed out of radical words. The set of radical words is relatively small, consisting of 1,068 words. These radical words are derived from a comprehensive classification scheme, so that each radical word provides a partial description of the thing it designates. Compound words also provide such descriptive information, but in a different way—namely, by combining the meaning of two or more radical words into a more complex meaning. Both methods will be exemplified below. This double-layered structure of the lexicon is the result of a deliberate compromise between two distinct methods of constructing a lexicon, which it will be convenient to label 'encyclopaedic' and 'analytic' respectively. In Dalgarno's opinion, neither of these methods, if consistently applied throughout, would produce a practicable language. If all words needed for a language were to be constructed following the encyclopaedic method, deriving them from a classification scheme, the size of the lexicon would become unmanageably large. On the other hand, if the analytic method were applied in all cases, so that only logically primitive notions were to be assigned a radical word and all the others were to be made by means of composition, the complex words created would be far too long, and incomprehensible. For this reason, Dalgarno takes a middle course between the two extremes: the encyclopaedic method is applied in forming the lexicon of radical words, but the analytic method is used for all other words, being compounds in which the radical words function as primitive elements.

Dalgarno devotes two chapters of *The Art of Signs* (chs. III and IV) to a discussion of the theoretical starting points determining the structure of the lexicon. Since his argument on this matter is intricate and somewhat tortuous, it may be convenient to sum up its essential points here. First, Dalgarno maintains that 'the art of signs should follow the art of things' (AS 18). He goes on to explain that the latter art is concerned with establishing a 'regular series of things commonly called the Praedicamentum'. What Dalgarno is referring to here is the kind of classificatory table that was typically produced in manuals of logic to illustrate the theory of 'predicaments', which ultimately derives from Aristotle's treatise *The Categories*. The term 'predicament' was introduced by Latin writers as a translation of the term 'category'. The predicaments remained a standard subject treated by logic throughout the medieval and early modern period. In his treatise, Aristotle enumerated ten categories—that is, types of word meaning—claiming that the meaning of each uncombined word belongs to one of these. In the terminology of the later tradition, the ten categories were substance, quantity, quality, relation, place, time, position, state, action, passion (*Categories* IV, 1b25–8). In the third century AD, Porphyry wrote a commentary on the *Categories* entitled *Isagoge*, which was to be extremely influential in the subsequent centuries. Porphyry's commentary consists of an explanation of five concepts that later were called the 'predicables'—namely, genus, difference, species, property, and accident. Explaining the concepts of genus and species, Porphyry stated that each category contains a hierarchically ordered series of classes, of which the highest is a genus, and the lowest are species. The intermediate classes qualify as either genus or species depending on whether they are considered with respect to a lower or higher class respectively. Exemplifying such a hierarchy by means of the category of substance, Porphyry stated: 'Substance is itself a genus; under this is body; and under body animate body, under which is animal; under animal is rational animal, under which is man; under man are Socrates, Plato, and particular men' (1975: 35–6).

This hierarchical series of concepts became known as the Porphyrian tree, and it remained a stock component of learning for almost a millennium and a half. In scholastic logic, the predicaments and the predicables formed the core of the theory of terms. Logic handbooks usually provided Porphyrian trees for most of the predicaments, in which the basic concepts not only of substance, but also of quantity, quality, and so on, were enumerated and classified. These classificatory tables were thought of as furnishing a definition of the terms referring to the most fundamental components of both reality and knowledge. For instance, the place of the term 'man' in the classification shows that man is a rational animal. Thus logic provided the general framework of an all-embracing ontological theory, leaving it to the special sciences to treat the various subject areas of which the basic concepts were defined by the predicaments. It was common to group all nine predicaments other than substance together under the head of 'accident', which, although originally belonging to the predicables, in this manner acquired the status of a super-category. As a result, the primary division of all existing things was that into substance and accident.

In the course of the seventeenth century, the prestige of logic as a discipline declined, as the new science became an increasingly powerful rival to traditional learning. Although scholastic logic was often the object of scorn, it still formed a common ingredient of intellectual education, and many writers assumed general familiarity with the predicaments. Thomas Hobbes (1588–1679) included a survey of logical theory in his *De Corpore* (1655), which was the first part (systematically, though not chronologically) of a trilogy containing his philosophical system. In a chapter 'Of Names' he described the predicaments, exemplifying them by presenting four series of hierarchically arranged terms, belonging to the four chief predicaments: body, quantity, quality, and relation. He added, however: 'I have not yet seen any great use of the predicaments in philosophy' (*De Corpore* 1. 2. 16). It was conspicuous that Hobbes pruned the top from Porphyry's tree, putting 'body' rather than substance at the head of the first predicament, the first division being into 'Body' and 'Not-Body, or Accident'. This reflected Hobbes's materialism, according to which all existing things are corporeal.

Hobbes was suspected of atheism, and his views met fervent opposition by, among others, Ward and Wallis, who both produced treatises in which they refuted his philosophical and political doctrines as well as his geometrical results. One of the charges made by Ward against Hobbes in *Vindiciae Academiarum* was that 'Being is a superiour notion to Body, that Immateriall substance, or separated Substances, is no contradiction' (Ward 1654: 59, cf. *Leviathan*, ch. IV). Ward, as we have noted above, played a central part in the development of Dalgarno's scheme. Wallis, for his part, was prominent in the circle of scholars to which both Ward and Wilkins belonged. This context provides the background for a reading of Dalgarno's attack in *The Art of Signs* on 'the opinion of some writers of this century', that the predicamental doctrine is of no use (*AS* 18–19). Dalgarno is clearly referring here to Hobbes, as appears from the arguments that follow, which are directed against positing 'Body' and 'Not-Body' as highest genera, and against the atheism purportedly following from this. Even more explicitly, he had announced in the pamphlet 'Omnibus Omnino Hominibus' (below, Part I, Broadsheet 5), which previewed the contents of *The Art of Signs*, that Hobbes's approach to the concept of 'substance' would be overthrown, as well as his atheism. It is unclear why Dalgarno does not mention Hobbes by name in *The Art of Signs*, as he had done in the earlier pamphlet, particularly given his explicit reference to Descartes in the passage immediately following (*AS* 21). There may be significance in the fact that Hobbes was the former tutor of Charles II, with whom he re-established friendly relations after the Restoration of 1660. It is clear, however, that Dalgarno's arguments agree well with Ward's views, which were probably shared by most of his other patrons, several of whom belonged to the group of men who were to found the Royal Society. Hobbes was disfavoured by several leading figures in the Royal Society, and his later attempts to be elected as a fellow failed. Thus the text of *The Art of Signs* at this point is not dealing simply with a technicality of logical theory, but touches upon associated issues that were at the centre of the philosophical debate. This leads Dalgarno to insert a proof of the existence of God, and of the immortality of the soul, which in turn leads him to challenge the foundation of Descartes's epistemology.

The attack on Hobbes is embedded in what at first sight appears to be a straightforward defence of scholastic logic: metaphysics and logic are said to constitute one single art; it is maintained that it is the duty of the logician to provide a predicamental series of things, and that such a series is of great use for philosophy as it forms the basis of all proof. However, Dalgarno goes on to dissociate himself from Aristotelianism, pointing out that as yet a satisfactory predicamental series does not exist. Aristotle's ten categories are criticized for being arbitrary, and for failing to classify all notions unambiguously. Further, Dalgarno condemns Aristotle's distinction of a class of so-called transcendental notions as erroneous. Aristotle, possibly following Plato, observed that some terms cannot be subsumed under any of the categories, since they can be predicated of things falling under various or all categories. Instances of such terms are 'one', 'being', 'same', and 'other' (*Metaphysics* V. 1018[a]), as well as 'good' (*Ethica Nicomachea* I. 1096[a]; Kneale and Kneale 1962: 29–30). In the logical tradition, it was common to distinguish a class of so-called transcendental, or pervasive terms, including 'true', in addition to the ones discussed by Aristotle, which cannot be reduced to the predicaments (see e.g. Blundeville 1599: 13). Dalgarno rejects the distinction, and tries to show how 'one', 'true', and 'good' can in fact be reduced to the predicaments (*AS* 25–6). In doing so, he was possibly following up on a suggestion made by Arriaga, one of the 'schoolmen' with whose work Dalgarno says he was familiar (CC, fo. 39[r]), and who argued that 'transcendental predicates are really genera' (Arriaga 1653: 103). However, the argument Dalgarno offers was probably his own: he claims that the non-existence of transcendentals follows from the definition of the 'predicament' as a series of things contained under a single highest genus. This definition was indeed a very common one, but its scope was usually more limited than what Dalgarno takes it to be. The definition simply stated what an individual category is, whereas Dalgarno interprets it as pertaining to all categories taken together. He thus arrives at a position contrary to that of both Aristotle and Porphyry, who held that there cannot be a single genus of all existing things.

Having dismissed the Aristotelian categories as unsatisfactory, Dalgarno goes on to argue that it would be a 'noble undertaking' to try and establish a comprehensive predicamental series on a new basis. He immediately, however, gives his belief that a perfect series of this sort is unattainable, because of the weakness of the human mind, on the one hand, and the complexity of reality, on the other hand. Next he explains that there are two possible methods of constructing a predicamental series: one uses the most simple notions as a starting point, and shows how all other notions are composed out of these; the other subsumes both simple and complex notions under a classification scheme. The first method is termed the 'analytic' one by Dalgarno, and clearly provided the model for forming all words of his language other than radical ones. There are several clues, both in the text of *The Art of Signs* and in 'The Autobiographical Treatise', that Dalgarno considered this to be philosophically the most attractive method. Although the approach is not explained in any detail, what he had in mind was apparently a methodical arrangement of ideas similar to the one proposed by Descartes. It is not unlikely that Dalgarno was here pursuing ideas floated by Ward, who also envisaged a system of knowledge representation of this kind. That he describes the 'analytic' method as one of two possible 'predicamental' ones is curious, since the predicaments were traditionally and generally associated with the second, classificatory method. This second method was the one that Dalgarno followed in the tables containing his radical words, as he explicitly states (*AS* 29). He adds some directions as to how a predicamental series made according to the second, traditional method should be structured (*AS* 29–31). One of these directions is that divisions should be made by positive differences, in itself possibly another, implicit criticism of the treatment of the predicaments by Hobbes, who uses opposition by negation, such as 'Man–Not Man', throughout.

Our understanding of Dalgarno's position is further complicated by the discovery that he did not always live up to his own precepts: maintaining (*AS* 29) that dichotomy is the best of all divisions, he sometimes uses trichotomous divisions in his tables, stating (*AS* 37) that these may be just as perfect as dichotomous ones. Thus, having stated that the art of signs should be based upon the art of things, Dalgarno goes on to argue that the latter art is as yet defective, and that, although it would be useful to develop it further, it is impossible in principle to bring it to perfection. In chapter IV, he presents a series of arguments that defeat his initial programmatic statement still further, since they are aimed to show that, even if a perfect predicamental series could be established, this would not be a suitable foundation for the lexicon of the philosophical language. The arguments have been outlined above: neither the analytic nor the encyclopaedic—that is, what was generally known as the 'predicamental'—method could lead to a practicable language. Far from maintaining that the art of signs should follow the art of things (*AS* 18), Dalgarno concludes that 'this art of signs does not admit of strict philosophical rules' (*AS* 36). The purposes of philosophy and those of the art of signs prove to be incongruous after all.

The various twists in Dalgarno's explanation of the theoretical foundation of his language may be partly ascribed to his ambivalent attitude towards the application of the predicamental method. As noted, Dalgarno initially considered but soon rejected a predicamental arrangement of his radical words, opting instead for a mnemonic one. In the debate with Wilkins that subsequently ensued the drawbacks and merits of a predicamental arrangement played an important part, Dalgarno maintaining that the method was unattractive from a mnemonic point of view, and that any predicamental order would be arbitrary and likely to give rise to controversy. Although it seems that Dalgarno in the end yielded to Wilkins's pressure (see CC, fos. 30^v–31^r), at least as far as the formation of radical words was concerned, he clearly never shared the satisfaction of Wilkins with the predicamental method.

3.2.2. The lexicon of radical words.   In spite of Dalgarno's misgivings concerning the predicamental method, he discusses at some length the details of the classification scheme that he used as a basis for his radical words (chapter V). On many points the discussion is in fact quite summary, based on the supposition that few words will suffice for the learned, and he leaves the subject after reviewing about three-quarters of the tables, with a comment that there are other reasons for omitting further explanation (*AS* 49), clearly an oblique reference to the haste with which the book was written. The exact structure of the classification can be gathered only by combining the clues given in the text with the information in the tables containing the words of the 'Lexicon Grammatico-Philosophicum' (see the fold-out table at the end of this volume). The words are printed in columns, but they are supposed to be arranged in hierarchical order. The various levels in the hierarchy are indicated by typographical means, such as varying fonts and font sizes.

An outline of the main characteristics of the scheme at once demonstrates its novelty. To begin with, there is only one highest genus—namely, 'ens, res', or 'being, thing'. Further, Dalgarno replaces the traditional dichotomy into substance and accident by what he thinks is a more correct division: 'ens' is first subdivided into 'abstract' (or, equivalently, 'simple', or again 'incomplete') and 'concrete' (or, 'composite' or 'complete'). The first member of this pair is divided into 'substance' and 'accident', the second comprises all the things traditionally enumerated under 'substance'—that is, immaterial objects, plants, and animals. The result of Dalgarno's division is that the category of 'substance' yields place to the category of 'concretes'. Thus his scheme does, in effect, contain a broad division into things or substances, called 'concretes', on the one hand, and 'accidents', on the other hand.

The gist of Dalgarno's argument (see *AS* 37–8) against the traditional division seems to be that predicates belonging to substance, like 'stone', can in general be correctly applied to the very same objects as can predicates belonging to 'accident', like 'white'. Consequently, white stones seem somehow to belong to both 'substance' and 'accident'. However, if this interpretation is correct, it is hard to see how Dalgarno's alternative division solves the problem, for it can analogously be pointed out that white stones would seem to belong to both 'concrete' and 'accident', which would be equally unsatisfactory.

Schematically, the highest categories of Dalgarno's scheme are related as follows (indenting indicates subdivision):

Ens, res
    Abstract (simple, incomplete)
        Substance
        Accident
    Concrete (composite, complete)

Alternatively, Dalgarno indicates, the following trichotomy may be used, which is obtained by disregarding the genus 'abstract':

Ens, res
  Substance
  Accident
  Concrete

In the lexicon of radical words, it is this trichotomy that is used, and the genus 'abstract' does not occur as a radical word.

Of the three genera immediately following under 'Ens, res', only 'Accident' and 'Concrete' are further subdivided. The genus 'Concrete' contains the lower genera 'Imperfect' and 'Perfect', the latter consisting of the single species 'Man'. 'Imperfect' comprises corporeal things, and spiritual things. This is again reduced to a trichotomy by deleting the intermediate level of 'Imperfect' and 'Perfect', so that 'Concrete' is divided as follows:

Concrete
  Corporeal
  Spiritual
  Composite, i.e. Man

Of these, 'Man' is a category in its own right, without further subdivisions. The category of 'Spiritual Concretes' contains two species—namely, 'Soul' and 'Angel' (see AS 54)—which likewise are not further subdivided. The genus 'Corporeal', however, comprises a large number of lower genera and species, which is understandable as it functions as the overall category encompassing all objects in the world of nature, with the notable exception of man. The latter, as has been seen, was assigned a special place in the classification to avoid Hobbesian, materialist implications. In the text, Dalgarno uses the term 'material' sometimes as a synonym for 'corporeal'. The corporeal or material concretes, then, consist of mathematical, physical, and artificial concretes. In summary, the category of concretes is divided as follows:

Concrete
  Corporeal
    Mathematical
    Physical
    Artificial
  Spiritual
    Soul
    Angel
  Composite, i.e. Man

To subsume mathematical notions such as 'point', 'line', and so on under 'concretes' was a deliberate novelty, as they were commonly regarded as belonging to 'quantity', and hence to 'accident' (see AS 38–9). Also novel was Dalgarno's category of 'artificial concretes', comprising all kinds of man-made things, which were usually disregarded in the theory of predicaments. The issue was of some interest to philosophers: John Locke later argued that artificial things may just as well be classified as natural ones (*Essay*, III. vi. §41), against which Leibniz was to point out that scholastic philosophers had good reason to omit artificial things from their predicaments (*Nouveaux Essais*, III. vi). Dalgarno's position clearly connects with his rejection, explicitly stated (*AS* 44), of the doctrine of substantial forms, according to which each natural kind is characterized by an essence, or form, that is to be distinguished from the accidental properties any thing may have. In this regard, Dalgarno agreed with Wilkins, whom he reports in 'The Autobiographical Treatise' to have believed that 'the formes of things, if there were any such, are unknown to us' (CC, fo. 48ʳ; cf. Wilkins 1668: 289). It is, finally, under the physical concretes that one finds the kinds of things that were traditionally placed under substance: inanimate things like stones, and animate ones such as plants and animals. At this point, the classificatory structure of the tables is complicated, and at times obscure.

The other broad category immediately under the highest genus 'Ens, res'— that is, 'Accident'—is divided into eight subordinate genera. In contrast with the Tables of Concretes, the structure of the classification is completely perspicuous here: each of the eight genera immediately under 'Accident' contains a number of lower genera, which in turn contain a number of species. The lower genera range in number from three to nine; the species, from two to nine. The order in which the eight genera of accidents are listed is intended to match the order of the genera of concretes (see *AS* 45), starting with general accidents, through mathematical, general physical, and special physical accidents, the latter comprising sensible qualities and sensitive accidents, and concluding with accidents related to man (rational accident), and the man-made world: economical and political accidents. The following list summarizes the overall scheme of highest categories (the categories marked with an asterisk are further divided into lower genera and species).

Ens, res (being, thing)
   Substantia (substance)
   Ens completum, vel concretum (complete, or concrete being)
      Corpus (body)
         *Concretum Mathematicum (mathematical concrete)
         *Concretum Physicum (physical concrete)
         *Concretum Artefactum (artificial concrete)
      Spiritus (spirit)
         Anima (soul)
         Angelus (angel)
      Compositum, id est, Homo (composite, i.e. Man)
   Accidens (accident)
      *Accidens Commune (common accident)
      *Accidens Mathematicum (mathematical accident)
      *Physicum Generale (general physical (accident))

*Qualitas Sensibilis (sensible quality)
*Accidentia Sensitiva (sensitive accidents)
*Accidens Rationale (rational accident)
*Oeconomicum (economical/social (accident))
*Politicum (political (accident))

One can identify the elements of this scheme in the tables of the 'Lexicon Grammatico-Philosophicum'. The highest genera of the scheme—that is, Ens, Substantia, Accidens, Ens Completum, Corpus, Spiritus, Compositum—are enumerated at the top of the first column, in larger type. The three broad categories under 'Corpus', that is, the concretes, are listed first. The genus 'Concretum Mathematicum' follows immediately after the seven highest genera in the first column. The elaborate genus 'Concretum Physicum' occupies the rest of the first column and most of the second. At the bottom of the second column the genus 'Concretum Artefactum' starts, finishing towards the bottom of the third. After this follows a list of five words in large type, the status of one of which is not entirely clear: 'Homo seu Concretum Compositum' (Man or Composite Concrete) is clearly a repetition, and probably 'Concretum Spirituale' (Spiritual Concrete) repeats 'Spiritus' (Spirit), although it is represented by another word of the artificial language. This may be an inconsistency caused by insertions in the tables without appropriate adjustments elsewhere. The word for 'Deus' (God) is strictly speaking not a radical word, but a compound, consisting of words meaning 'first cause' (cf. *AS* 54, where 'sasva' rather than 'sava' is given as the correct form). The remainder of the tables, from the bottom of the third column up to and including most of the seventh column, is taken up by the eight categories of 'Accident' and their subdivisions.

The lexicon of radical words results from a combination of the philosophical alphabet with the classification scheme. Dalgarno's attempts to match the number of highest genera with that of the number of simple sounds failed (*AS* 50), since the various kinds of things outnumbered the simple sounds. This problem is solved by using combinations of simple sounds as characteristic of certain genera, an example of which will be seen immediately below. Throughout the tables, the order of the alphabet is retained. The seven highest genera of the scheme are designated by the seven vowels, to which the letter *v* is added: Av, *H*v, Ev, Iv, Ov, *Y*v, Uv (*AS* 50). The nine consonants plus the letter *s* are used to designate the eleven genera that are arranged under the seven highest ones and that contain lower genera. In this instance, there was a shortage of one simple sound, which is made up by using the combination *st* as though it were simple. The words signifying these eleven genera are completed by adding the ending *-eis* to the consonants, resulting in the following list:

Meis—Concretum Mathematicum (mathematical concrete)
Neis—Concretum Physicum (physical concrete)
Feis—Concretum Artefactum (artificial concrete)
Seis—Accidens Commune (common accident)

Beis—Accidens Mathematicum (mathematical accident)
Deis—Physicum Generale (general physical (accident))
Geis—Qualitas Sensibilis (sensible quality)
Peis—Accidentia Sensitiva (sensitive accidents)
Teis—Accidens Rationale (rational accident)
Steis—Oeconomicum (economical/social (accident))
Keis—Politicum (political (accident))

Up to this point, the mutual relationships between the various genera are not expressed by the radical words designating them. For instance, neither the fact that 'Iv—complete, or concrete being' falls under 'Av—being, thing', nor the fact that 'Feis' is subordinated to 'Iv', is encoded in the radical words. From this point onwards, however, the radical words are formed so as to be indicative of the classification scheme. How this is done can be explained most easily by looking at one of the genera of accidents, such as 'Teis—Accidens Rationale'. First, the lower genera falling under this genus are designated by words that are formed by adding a vowel to the initial consonant: TA, TH, TE, etc., which are made complete by the ending '-s'. Thus 'Teis' contains the lower genera called 'TAs', 'THs', 'TEs', 'TIs', 'TOs', 'TYs', 'TUs', each of which is a kind of 'rational accident'. These lower genera in turn contain a number of species, which are designated by words obtained by putting a final consonant after the vowel. For instance, the genus 'TIs—expression of the intellect' comprises the following list of species:

tim affirmare r. negare
tin loqui r. scribere
tif interpretari
tib docere r. discere
tid interrogare r. respondere
tig narrare
tip fama
tit definire r. distinguere
tik restringere r. ampliare

According to this scheme, for example, 'tim' means 'affirmare' (to affirm), while insertion of r yields 'trim', which means the opposite notion, 'negare' (to deny). In this way, two radical words may be associated with a single place on the table. In all, about a quarter of the places on the tables contains more than one radical word. In rare cases, three radical words are associated with a single place. This is when the middle between two opposite notions is designated, which is done by insertion of l. For instance, the notions 'past' and 'future' are to be rendered as 'daf' and 'draf' respectively, while 'present' is translated as 'dlaf'.

The radical words in the Tables of Concretes are formed in a similar, though different, way: rather than the vowels in second position, the final consonants indicate lower genera, while species are designated by the vowel. For instance, 'neit' means 'fish', and the species enumerated under this genus are all designated by a word of the form 'n__t'. Vowels inserted at the open place yield words signifying more specific kinds of fish: 'nat' means 'squamosus' (scaly), 'nit' means 'planus' (flat), etc. Further, Dalgarno uses various devices to account for additional levels in the classification. Thus between the genus 'Neis'—'physical concrete' and the species falling under it there are three intermediate genera rather than a single one. 'Physical concrete' is first divided into 'inanimatum', 'planta', and 'brutum' (beast); the latter is further divided into 'exanguious' and 'sanguineous', of which the latter comprises birds, fish, and terrestrial beasts. These three latter ones finally contain species—i.e. lowest categories of the classification. They are not species in the biological sense, which in Dalgarno's view should not be expressed by radical words, but by compounds. The intermediate genera are expressed by various combinations of the letters $p\,t\,k$, which together are characteristic of 'beast' (see AS 51–2), with the overall generic sign N. The method Dalgarno applied is not completely clear, and at times led to apparently unintended equivocation. For instance, 'neipteik' means both 'beast' and 'sanguineous beast'. A further complication in the Tables of Concretes is the occurrence of genera comprising 'parts' (see AS 52–3). Thus there are genera of 'parts of animals', an expression that occurs as a heading in the tables, without being expressed by a radical word. The various kinds of parts of animals are expressed by truncated words, which symbolizes their incomplete nature. This again led at times to ambiguities—for example, the word 'meis' means both 'head' and 'mathematical concrete'.

Dalgarno made a special provision for words designating numbers. The method is explained on the page containing the 'Alphabetum' (AS, sig. A8^r). The letter v, when initial, indicates that the word refers to a number. Two lists of letters are provided: a list of vowels supplemented by three diphthongs, and a list of consonants. The first digit of a numerical expression in Arabic notation is represented by an item from the first list, the second by an item from the second list. The third, fifth, etc., digits are again represented by items from the first list, and the fourth, sixth, etc., by items from the second list. In this way, Dalgarno ensured that words expressing numbers are always easy to pronounce. For example, '10,000' translates as 'valili', where 'a' represents '1', and both 'l' and 'i' represent '0'.

It has often been maintained that Dalgarno's scheme consists of seventeen highest genera. This statement is both false and misleading. It is false in that the number of seventeen is incorrect. This number is very probably based upon the enumeration in the 'Alphabetum', where seventeen genera are mentioned. However, the genus 'accidens oeconomicum' has been omitted from this list, apparently because this genus is characterized by the combination st, and it would have seemed inappropriate to include this in the alphabet. Moreover, the three genera (or two, if 'Spiritual Concrete' is intended to mean the same as 'Spirit') that are designated by diphthongs are omitted. For this reason, it would be more correct to say that there are eighteen, or twenty, or twenty-one highest genera. Alternatively, it would be equally justified to identify the seven genera designated by vowels as the highest genera of the scheme. But this would still be misleading in that the hierarchical relations between the genera are ignored, suggesting, contrary to fact, that all highest genera belong to the same level. In short, it is true that seventeen of the genera are designated by a single letter to which some ending is affixed; but this says very little about the structure of the classification.

In the caption above the tables of the 'Lexicon Grammatico-Philosophicum', Dalgarno claims that the radical words are established 'by art and design, observing an analogical conformity between things and signs'. This claim is clearly based upon the procedure followed in forming the radical words, which has just been outlined. According to this method, words for species indicate by their form to which genus, and to which higher genus, the species belongs. For instance, the word 'tim', beginning with 'ti', indicates that 'to affirm' belongs to the class of 'expressions of the intellect'. Further, the initial t shows that this class belongs to the 'rational accidents'. In this way, the words provide additional information besides the Latin equivalent which primarily defines their meaning. This is why Dalgarno is able to claim that the radical words are not established at random, but by art. Despite this, it should be noted that the additional information provided by the structure of the radical words is insufficient to define the thing designated by the word. This is because the final consonant (and in the Tables of Concretes the middle vowel) in the words for species merely serves to differentiate the species from others of the same kind, without specifying in which respect it differs. While 'tim', for example, refers to that expression of the intellect that is called 'to affirm', 'tin' signifies that expression of the intellect that is called 'to speak'. There is no indication of what distinguishes both kinds of expressions of the intellect. In the same vein, we can see within the class designated by 'tis' that items belonging to it are randomly listed. A similar observation can be made concerning the other levels of the classification: although the genus signified by 'tis' indicates by its form that it is a subclass of the higher genus 'teis', there is no clue, other than the meaning of the Latin expression defining its meaning, as to what makes this class differ from the other genera such as 'tas', 'tes', etc., which likewise demonstrate by their form their belonging to 'teis'. The descriptive information provided by the form of the radical words is thus necessarily incomplete as a consequence of the method followed in composing them. This point was fully appreciated by both Dalgarno and Wilkins, as is clear from the fact that the random, numerical order of the species was one of the issues in the debate on the predicamental method.

In this context it is interesting to note Dalgarno's mention (AS 42) of a possible alternative application of his table. Instead of the procedure proposed by himself—that is, to designate species such as 'elephant' by means of a compound expression—one might, he noted, use his tables to launch a different approach—namely, by listing the species in numerical order. He is clearly referring here to the method favoured by Wilkins and eventually implemented in his *Essay*, a reference that was, incidentally, recognized by Leibniz, who noted in his copy of 'The Art of Signs' on page 42: 'Ita fecit Wilkinsius' (Thus did Wilkins). Since Dalgarno undoubtedly regarded this method as inferior to his own, it is unclear why he mentioned it at all. Perhaps he intended to show that his design could be used in various ways. For his part, he envisaged a different method of endowing the words of his language with as much descriptive content as possible—namely, the use of compounds. This is the method he actually applied in creating all words other than radical ones.

3.2.3. The rest of the lexicon. While some 1,068 radical words formed the basis of Dalgarno's language, his proposed method of forming compound radical words allowed for a rich extension of the vocabulary. In the caption above the tables of the 'Lexicon Grammatico-Philosophicum' Dalgarno claims that 'the names thus formed contain descriptions of these things that correspond to their nature'. The text of *The Art of Signs* provides only brief hints as to how such names are to be formed. Dalgarno leaves it to the users of his language to form compounds in whatever way seems most appropriate to their circumstances. He indicates that every radical word may be combined with every other, provided, first, that a radical word retains its meaning when entering into a compound, and, secondly, that the combination is 'meaningful and to the point', and the 'reason for the composition is clear and plain to see' (*AS* 70, 71, 94). Further, he stipulates (*AS* 42–5) that names for species of animals and plants, as well as names for particular 'artificial concretes', are to be composed out of a word signifying a generic concept and a word signifying some salient feature of the species.

In his text Dalgarno demonstrates by example how such compounds can be formed. He also provides a concise dictionary, containing approximately 1,500 entries. This is the 'Lexicon Latino-Philosophicum', in which Dalgarno shows how Latin words that are not in his Tables of Radical Words are to be rendered in his language. This dictionary is obviously far from exhaustive. It is intended only to exemplify the method to be followed in forming compounds, which every user of the language is free to apply as the circumstances require, and also as the logical abilities of the speaker allow. This flexibility is in agreement with the principle repeatedly emphasized by Dalgarno, that freedom of composition is a mark of excellence in a language. He further announces the production of a larger dictionary for the benefit of the average man, a plan he never carried out.

The 'Lexicon Latino-Philosophicum', which is for the most part alphabetical (see *AS* 95–115), includes a section exemplifying the method of forming names for the species of inanimate things, plants, and animals (*AS* 115–17). It is this category of words that triggered the debate between Dalgarno and Wilkins on the radical words, Dalgarno maintaining that they should be expressed by compounds, while Wilkins insisted on including them in the tables of radicals.

This section of the 'Lexicon Latino-Philosophicum' is thematically arranged, and provides examples of the formation of words for species of 'mineral', 'ordinary stone', and 'precious stone' (*AS* 115); 'metal', 'herb', 'tree', 'exsanguinous beast' (*AS* 116); 'bird' and 'four-footed (animal)' (*AS* 117), all of which are generic terms listed in the tables of 'physical concretes'. For each of these genera, an example of a compound word designating a species belonging to it follows:

mineral (naf)
carbo—nafgrofn*η*m
coal—medium minerale nigrum ignis—mineral black fire

stone (n*η*f)
silex—n*η*fgab n*η*fn*η*m
flint—lapis durities, lapis ignis—stone hard, stone fire

gem (sn*η*f)
adamas—sn*η*fgab
diamond—lapis pretiosus durities—precious stone hard

metal (nef)
aurum—nefsis
gold—metallum perfectio—metal perfect

herb (neib)
gramen—nab
grass—herba bestiae vesca—herb edible for beasts

tree (sneid)
fraxinus—snags*υ*m bamrug
ash—arbor sterilis valde longum nucleus—very fruitless tree long kernel

exsanguinous beasts
apis—snapg*η*m
bee—brutum exangue aerium volatile detectipennis dulce—winged flying exsanguinous beast sweet

bird (neip)
aquila—naps*υ*f
eagle—avis carnivora maxime—carnivorous bird largest

quadruped (neik)
elephas—n*η*ks*υ*f
elephant—brutum solidipes maxime—whole-footed beast largest

These samples illustrate how species can be designated by combining the word for the general kind with a word expressing some salient feature of, or some property commonly associated with, the species. Thus the word 'sweet' joined to the word meaning 'flying insect' is supposed to distinguish 'bee' sufficiently from other flying insects. The same method is applied to artificial concretes such as 'cup' and 'spoon' (see *AS* 43–4). As the examples in the alphabetical section of the 'Lexicon Latino-Philosophicum' show, compound words for things other than 'concretes' are often modelled on the same pattern as well. Thus 'night' is rendered as 'dangrom'—that is, 'time darkness'—and 'day' is rendered as 'dangom'—that is, 'time light'. Not all compound words are formed in this way. In some cases, Dalgarno uses near-synonyms, as in the case of 'tos', which is a radical word meaning 'sign', but is also used as equivalent of both 'symbol' and 'omen'. In other cases, he uses more lengthy periphrases, such as 'dipu sηf domu sηf ef' for 'cicatrix' (scar)—that is, 'imprint of a cut of the flesh'.

Such examples show that Dalgarno, rather than prescribing exact definitions, relied to a large extent on the capacity of users of his language to convey meanings on the basis of well-chosen clues. Although it is certain that Dalgarno intended the radical words to function as unanalysed primitives within composite expressions, the translation of the latter into an existing language like English raises a problem. It is not entirely clear to what extent the classificatory surplus information carried by the radical words is to be spelled out in a translation of compounds. For instance, the Table of Radicals defines 'nηf' as 'solidipes'—that is, 'whole-footed'—but its place in the table further indicates that this is a species of 'physical concrete, beast, sanguineous, terrestrial'. If a translation of 'nηf' were to enumerate this entire list, this would suggest that all of this would be conveyed on each occasion of use, which is contrary to what Dalgarno envisaged (see e.g. *AS* 59). It seems most in line with Dalgarno's intentions, therefore, to make the decision depend on the availability in the target language of short expressions that are equivalent to radicals. Thus 'whole-footed beast' will do for 'nηf', just as 'neip' translates as 'bird', rather than as 'physical concrete, aerial sanguineous beast'. The equivalence of the latter long expression with 'avis' (bird) is explicitly stated in the tables of the 'Lexicon Grammatico-Philosophicum'.

A further important feature of Dalgarno's method of expressing things by means of compounds is evident in the samples: he offers two alternative translations for the word 'silex' (flint). This is an instance of the general rule that a single thing may often be designated by a variety of compound expressions. Thus, Dalgarno gives two alternative translations for 'elephant' in the text (*AS* 41) in addition to that quoted above from the 'Lexicon Latino-Philosophicum', and besides the translation for 'gold' already cited ('perfect metal') he gives 'nefsimap'—that is, 'the best metal' in the alphabetical section of the dictionary. He emphasizes it to be a consequence of the principles underlying his lexicon that the same meaning may be expressed by combinations of different simple notions, just as both 4 plus 4 and 3 plus 5 make 8 (*AS* 69).

Dalgarno's reliance on compounds was clearly inspired by the wish to make the words of his language capable of expressing a logical analysis of the concepts designated by them (see *AS* 68–9). Moreover, he was convinced that every language must necessarily make use of composition on the lexical level, since otherwise the number of different words required would become far too large to be practicable. His approach poses a question as to how the meaning of compounds is established. Dalgarno seems to have assumed that this is solely and

completely determined by the meaning of the radicals of which they are composed. This is, at least, suggested by his insistence that the same notion may
be expressed by various different compounds, and by his disapproval of the
parrot-like uttering of idiomatic phrases, the meaning of which cannot be
determined on the basis of their component parts (*AS* 69). It is evident, however,
that, without further regulation by the author of the philosophical language
or the conventionalized practice of a group of users, the meaning of the compound words will often be vague or underspecific. The vagueness of Dalgarno's
compounds was exposed in a stinging manner by Roger Daniel, who published
a caustic attack on *The Art of Signs* in 1662 (see Sect. 4 below). In 'The Autobiographical Treatise', Dalgarno makes clear that, despite objections of this kind,
he held to his opinion that the abundant use of compounds is both necessary
and commendable.

Despite his preferred approach, there are some special cases in which Dalgarno
does introduce conventions regulating the meaning of compounds. Thus he
indicates that 'spark' should be rendered as 'point fire' and that in general the
figure of corporeal things should be designated in a similar way (*AS* 39). Furthermore, he prescribes which compounds are to be used for designating stages of
life (*AS* 91), the measures of time (*AS* 92), and family relations (*AS* 92–3).

A final constraint on the use of compounds lies in the presence of a series
of grammatical inflections, which allow one to express a number of semantic
relations by means of affixes. There is a listing of these affixes in the 'Lexicon
Grammatico-Philosophicum' (see the fold-out table at the end of this volume).
The use of the affixes is discussed by Dalgarno in his chapter on grammar
(*AS*, ch. VIII).

3.3. *The grammar*

3.3.1. The logical foundation. The grammar of Dalgarno's language is
primarily based, as is the lexicon, on logical principles. Its key starting point
is that speech should reflect an analysis of thought, so that 'the external
logos is fully in accord with the internal one' (*AS* 68). The image of thought as
an internal, mental discourse had been prevalent for centuries; the notion
that linguistic expressions can be reduced to an underlying, logical form that
agrees with this internal process had often been connected with it. Dalgarno's
aim in designing the grammar was to provide the users of his language with
the means for a direct expression of the logical form of their thoughts,
unrestrained by the haphazard rules of ordinary languages. He claims that,
if his language is properly used, the distinction between semantic theory and
linguistic practice will disappear, equating the use of his language with the
true practice of logic (*AS* 69).

Chapter VIII of *The Art of Signs* is entitled 'On Grammatical Inflections';
the details about these inflections are to be found in the seventh and eighth

columns of the 'Lexicon Grammatico-Philosophicum' (see the fold-out table). In chapter VIII Dalgarno deals with two theoretical points: first, that strictly speaking there is only one part of speech, and, secondly, that the philosophical language contains a number of inflections indicating, among other things, various parts of speech. These inflections, he asserts, were included because it was necessary to compromise between logical rigour and linguistic practice.

Dalgarno points to the fact that the grammatical tradition usually distinguished eight different parts of speech. Both the seminal *Techne* attributed to Dionysius Thrax (*c*.100 BC) and Priscian's influential *Institutiones Grammaticae* (*c.* AD 500) list eight word classes, albeit that Priscian adds the interjection to the list, omitting the article that is absent from Latin (Robins 1990: 39, 66). The logical tradition, by contrast, commonly made a distinction between categorematic and syncategorematic terms, reckoning only the noun and the verb to be in the former group. Categorematic terms were thought of as significant in themselves: they designate some entity whether or not they occur in a proposition. Syncategorematic terms, such as 'every', derive their meaning from the function they perform when joined to other terms. Logicians considered all word classes other than noun and verb as belonging to the single class of syncategorematic terms. Dalgarno deviates from both traditions in maintaining that only the noun should count as a genuine part of speech. All the rest, including the verb, are 'inflections and cases of the noun' (*AS* 62).

Dalgarno offers a twofold argument to support the thesis that the noun is the only principal part of speech, assuming that, if it can be proved that the so-called substantive verb is derived from a noun, then all verbs are so derived. The term 'substantive verb' was introduced by Priscian as a translation of a Greek term meaning 'verb of existence'. In the grammatical tradition the distinction gained currency between, on the one hand, the verb substantive 'to be', which, according to some, both functions as a copula and signifies the existence of a thing, and, on the other hand, the verb adjective, which comprises all other verbs (Padley 1976: 46–7). What is more, both medieval and humanist grammarians as well as logicians commonly believed that the substantive verb formed part of the meaning of all verbs, so that the expression 'we love', for example, was held to be equivalent to 'we are loving'. Dalgarno explicitly cites this particular equivalence (*AS* 65). His assumption that if his proof is valid for the copula it will be valid for all verbs is clearly based on this analysis of the verb. Dalgarno's argument rests essentially on two elements: first, the statement that the copulative function of the verb 'to be' should be isolated from its use within a statement of existence, and secondly the claim that the copula refers to the mental act of judging—that is, to either affirmation (in positive statements) or negation (in negative ones). Since both affirmation and negation are complete notions that have their place in the predicamental series, they are 'essentially nominal' (*AS* 64)—that is, most properly expressed by a noun. It follows that the copula, and hence all verbs, ultimately derive from a noun.

Exactly why Dalgarno believed that 'every predicamental notion is a noun' (*AS* 62) is not explained; he simply posits this as uncontroversial. In chapter X he explains that the radical words of his language refer to notions 'in the abstract sense'—that is, regardless of the word class of the Latin word defining their meaning (*AS* 87). In 'The Autobiographical Treatise' he further states that in a philosophical language 'evry Radical word must be a noun Substantive, or rather signifying the notion of the thing indefinitely' (CC, fo. 37ʳ). It seems, then, that what Dalgarno had in mind was that the purely lexical meaning of a word is typically expressed by a noun substantive, and that all other word classes are characterized by additional meaning components, which are related to structural aspects. That Dalgarno asserts predicamental notions *to be* nouns may be simply a sloppy way of saying that such notions are most correctly, or typically, expressed by nouns. It is also possible that he would have agreed on this point, if pressed, that linguistic categories such as 'noun' are in fact applicable to mental entities. However the case may be, it will be seen below that Dalgarno's language in fact contains an affix that serves to turn radical words into substantives. If radical words occur without any affix, they function as particles.

He further explains that, since the copula is a sign of the act of judging, it would be logically more correct to designate the mental acts of affirming and negating each by a single unambiguous word, such as 'yes' and 'no' (*AS* 64). In the philosophical language, however, he uses the radical word 'tim', meaning 'affirmation', to designate the copula in positive statements, and its opposite 'trim', 'negation', for the copula in negative statements. In 'The Autobiographical Treatise', he records that he later became convinced that in fact, not two, but three different acts may be performed by the mind in judging, since the act of doubting should be added to the affirmative and negative acts (CC, fos. 60ʳ–63ʳ).

Although Dalgarno claims his language to be constructed in accord with logical principles, he dismisses a large part of logical theory as useless. Negation, according to Dalgarno, is 'an act of the mind, separating one thing from another' (*AS* 65). For this reason, negation operates at the level of the proposition, not at that of simple terms. Logical theory traditionally treated the subject of equipollence and conversion of propositions. Equipollence concerns the fact that propositions of different forms may have equal truth values. For instance, whenever 'Every A is B' is true, then also 'No A is not-B' is true. To bring out equivalences such as these, logicians coined terms such as 'not-stone'—a practice that Dalgarno strongly objects to. The subject of 'conversion' concerns the question if and when the subject and predicate term may change places within a proposition without changing its truth value. For instance, 'No A is B' may be harmlessly converted into 'No B is A', while 'All A are B' cannot in general be replaced by 'All B are A'. Seventeenth-century works on logic often claimed that equipollence was quite useless (e.g. Blundeville 1599: 64; Arnauld and Nicole 1662: ii, ch. 4), but conversion was generally regarded as important (Arnauld and Nicole 1662: ii, ch. 17). Dalgarno, however, condemns both subjects equally (*AS* 65).

3.3.2. Logical form versus inflectional system. Having established that in principle there is only one part of speech, Dalgarno goes on to explain that the grammar as well as the lexicon of his language results from a compromise between various antagonistic requirements. Logical rigour requires that each and every component of our concepts, as well as the mental acts performed on them, is expressed by a separate word. A strictly logical language, in Dalgarno's view, is free from grammatical inflections, since these are abbreviations of the truly logical expressions that explicitly mention every aspect of the thought expressed. Conciseness of speech, on the other hand, requires that abbreviations are used wherever possible. Again, Dalgarno takes a middle course between the two extremes, introducing a series of grammatical inflections so as to prevent over-elaborate expressions, while keeping the number of these inflections down. The result is shown in the 'Lexicon Grammatico-Philosophicum' (the fold-out table at the end of the volume). Towards the bottom of the seventh column there is a heading that reads 'Grammatical inflections: the single examples are to be regarded as rules admitting of no exceptions'. Under this heading, a list of forms is presented showing how radicals may be inflected for indicating various word classes, categories, and moods. The radical words 'sim' (good) and 'pon' (love) are used as paradigms, and most inflections are effected by suffixes. Below the relevant portion of the table is reproduced, with translation and commentary added where this seemed appropriate:

Sim bonus Radix, in oratione
> **particula**
slim indifferens medium
srim malus oppositum
simu bonitas
simmu bonitates

The first point indicated here is that a radical without any inflection is to be regarded as a particle. This will be discussed below (Sect. 3.3.4). There follows a list of four forms of the radical 'sim', exemplifying once more how the letters *l* and *r* may be inserted, yielding 'slim' (indifferent) and 'srim' (bad), to indicate a medium between opposites and opposition, respectively. Suffixing -*u* to the radical turns this into a noun substantive: 'simu' means 'goodness'. Doubling the final consonant before the ending -*u* indicates plural.

Adjectiva varia	**various adjectives**
pone amans activum	pone loving active
pono amatus passivum	pono loved passive
Sima bonus neutrum	Sim good neutre
ponemp amorosus et ax	ponemp amorous and over-amorous
ponomp amabilis	ponemp lovable
ponomb amandus	ponomp to be loved
ponemb amaturus	ponemb to be loving

Clearly, the radical 'sim' could not be used as a paradigm for most of these inflections. This illustrates Dalgarno's remark that 'not every notion is capable of taking all these inflections', and it shows why he states as a general rule that 'variability in the notion is the basis for variation in the word' (*AS* 67). This list also demonstrates that it may be problematic to rely on a single example in defining a general rule: the Latin suffix '-bilis' is in most cases equivalent in meaning to English '-able', which is the reason why 'amabilis' is rendered as 'lovable' above. In fact, 'lovely' translates 'amabilis' more correctly in most contexts.

Gradus Comparationis	Degrees of Comparison
simam valde bonus	simam very good
siman mediocriter bonus	siman moderately good
simaf parum bonus	simaf not good enough
simab melior	simab better
simad aeque bonus	simad equally good
simag minus bonus	simag less good
simap optimus	simap best
simat mediocriter bonus	simat moderately good
simak minime bonus	simak good in the least degree

This list seems to be superfluous in view of the radical words enumerated under the intermediate genus 'degrees of comparison' in the fourth column of the fold-out table. It is probably no coincidence that the inflections in the above list are characterized by the very same words as those occurring as radicals under that genus, in the same order (albeit that 'mediocriter', oddly, is used twice so that both 'siman' and 'simat' are defined as 'mediocriter bonus'). It seems likely that Dalgarno considered various possibilities for expressing comparative statements, either by radical words or by means of inflections, offering, possibly inadvertently, both possibilities. Dalgarno noticed this slip after his book was printed. In a copy containing 'errata' in his own hand, it is indicated that the comparates should be crossed out (Bodleian Library, 8° A 130 Linc). In the 'Praxis', in which Dalgarno supplies sample texts written in his language, he usually uses combinations of radical words rather than inflections, with the exception of the suffix *-ap* indicating superlative, which he sometimes uses (e.g. 'nηkbeisap' (*AS* 41) and in the particle 'shʋbapdan'). It is clear that Dalgarno thought the accurate expression of comparisons to be very important, as he believed that comparison is a crucial mental operation (*AS* 46). Both the text of *The Art of Signs* (*AS* 46–7, 84–5) and 'The Autobiographical Treatise' (CC, fos. 68[r]–69[r]) testify to his interest in the subject.

Flexiones temporis & modi	Inflections of tense and mood
ponre facio amare	ponre to make [a person] love
ponesa amavi	ponesa I [etc.] have loved
ponesη amaveram	ponesη I [etc.] had loved
ponese amabam	ponese I [etc.] loved

ponesi amo	ponesi I [etc.] love
poneso amato	poneso love [future]
ponoso amator imperative	ponoso be loved [future]
pones*v* amare	pones*v* to love
ponos*v* amari	ponos*v* to be loved
ponesai amanter	ponesai lovingly
ponompai amabiliter	ponompai lovably

Thus four tenses are expressed (perfect, pluperfect, imperfect, present). There is no future tense, an apparent omission, which is corrected in the handwritten annotations concerning the 'errata'. The form for the future tense that is supplied there shows that the suffix '-esu' should indicate future tense. This agrees with various occurrences of this suffix in the sample texts (and confirms the conjecture made by Shumaker (1982: 166)). In addition, there are four moods: future imperative (active and passive), and infinitive (active and passive). The adjective 'pone' and 'ponomp' become adverbs by means of a suffix -*(s)ai*.

Alia Derivativa Compendii Causa	**Other Derivatives for the sake of brevity**
ponel persona amans	ponel loving person
sunilli omnes personae	sunilli all persons
ponor amatum vel res amata	ponor loved thing
sunirri omnia vel res omnes	sunirri everything or all things
nηfim magnus lapis	nηfim big stone
nηfif lapillus	nηfif small stone
nηfind cumulus lapidum	nηfind heap of stones
oi Exoticum Angloi Galloi	oi Foreign English French

Suffixing the letter *l* to a radical word is significative of person. Likewise, if *r* is suffixed, this indicates that the radical refers to a thing. Between the suffixed *l* and *r* a vowel is inserted: *e* signifies the agent, *o* undergoing (see *AS* 87). Thus, besides 'ponel' (loving person), it is possible to form 'ponol' (person loved). If neither active nor passive person or thing is to be signified, *i* is inserted, following the general rule that *i* may be inserted everywhere for the sake of euphony without altering the meaning of the word (see *AS* 73). If *l* or *r* is duplicated and euphonic *i* is added, a plural form is indicated. Examples are provided of both a diminutive and an augmentative suffix, as well as a suffix signifying 'aggregate' or 'heap'. Finally, the suffix *oi* is demonstrated by words referring to inhabitants of some country, but serves also, as appears from the 'Praxis', to signify that the word to which it is affixed is a proper name. The result of Dalgarno's compromise between logic and practice thus appears to be that his language contains substantives, adjectives, verbs, and adverbs, rather than just the single part of speech identified by logical analysis. As will be seen, the language also includes six pronouns and a large number of 'particles'.

3.3.3. Syntax.   As most writers on grammar of his day, Dalgarno is brief on syntax. His main principle that speech should conform in structure to the

mental processes it expresses is emphasized once more in the context of syntax
(*AS* 72). The short chapter IX on syntax is for the most part devoted to the
description of nine particular rules. The first three of these are concerned with
word order (*AS* 73). A means of rendering a construction similar to the Latin
ablative absolute is also described (*AS* 73–4, rule 4), and it is explained that the
genitive (rule 5), dative, and ablative cases (rule 7) are to be expressed by means
of particles meaning 'of', 'to', and 'from' respectively (*AS* 74–6). Dalgarno
argues that genitive case and adjective, when logically analysed, are equivalent.
Wallis's grammar (1653: ch. V) contains similar observations. Rule 6 (*AS* 75) states
that the adjectival suffix may be combined with the suffixes indicating person
and thing, as explained above. Rule 8 concerns the expression of impersonal
verbs such as 'it is raining', which are rendered as 'the rain is raining' (*AS* 76).
This is in accord with the analysis of such verbs by humanist grammarians such
as Linacre and Sanctius (Padley 1976: 105). Under the same rule, Dalgarno also
discusses the expression of eternal, or necessary, propositions by means of the
radicals 'tim' (affirmation) and 'trim' (negation). If the verb 'to be' is inflected
for tense, the radical word 'dan' (time) is to be used as a verb, unless a particle
like 'yesterday' occurs in the sentence (*AS* 76–7). Finally, rule 9 states that the
substantive verb 'tim', which, as seen, is part of all other verbs logically speaking,
should be omitted if another verb occurs in the sentence (*AS* 77).

3.3.4. The particles.   It is not until the final chapter (X) that Dalgarno discusses what he claims to be the key to his invention and the most important
part of all languages—that is, the particles. By this term Dalgarno understands
all words that serve to modify and connect other words, by contrast with words
that have a meaning that is independent from their conjunction with other
words. The distinction closely resembles the logicians' one between categorematic and syncategorematic terms, although a similar distinction was implicit
in various more grammatically oriented theories as well (for example, the
Modistic grammarian Siger de Courtrai distinguished more principal and less
principal word classes (Bursill-Hall 1972: 45)). Dalgarno's inspiration came from
the logical rather than the grammatical tradition in this case as in many others:
in 'The Autobiographical Treatise' he explicitly identifies the particles with
the 'syncategoremata' (CC, fo. 38ʳ). Particles, in Dalgarno's definition, include
conjunctions, prepositions, and interjections (*AS* 87), as well as pronouns and
certain adverbs, as appears both from the examples he discusses in the text
and from a list he provides in the 'Lexicon Grammatico-Philosophicum' (see
fold-out table).
    Recapitulating the development of his scheme (*AS* 78–81), Dalgarno recalls
that he perceived the purposes of shorthand to be incompatible with those of a
philosophical language. The most considerable changes he subsequently made
to his scheme, he emphasizes, were those concerning the particles. Although
the particles are called 'the most primary part of speech' (*AS* 78), this does
not contradict the earlier argument that the noun is the only genuine part of

speech. The primacy of the particles is asserted with respect to their function. However, Dalgarno emphasizes that, just as all other kinds of words, the particles are derivative of predicamental notions, and these are to be identified with nouns. That the particles are derivative in this sense follows from a reasoning analogous to the one purportedly proving that the copula derives from a noun: since the function performed by any particle can be described using a noun designating this function, it follows that all particles are derived from nouns. Hence they are most appropriately expressed by using this noun. Thus, as the preposition 'with' is often used to indicate that the noun to which it is joined denotes a thing being used as an instrument, 'with' is more appropriately expressed as 'instrument'. Consequently, Dalgarno decided to do away with the particles as a separate word class, and to express everything—that is, both the categorematic and the syncategorematic (which he also calls the material and the formal) aspect of word meaning—by means of the radical words of his tables.

There remained obviously the need to distinguish between a word functioning as a substantive and the same word functioning as a particle: for instance, between 'instrument' denoting an instrument and 'instrument' meaning 'with'. The rule that is given (*AS* 83) describes how this it to be accomplished: a word from the Tables of Accidents without any suffix is a particle. Thus 'sab' means 'with'; adding the suffix -*u* yields 'sabu', which means 'instrument'. Just as with all words of Dalgarno's language, particles allow composition. Dalgarno observes that many particles are of a complex nature. In fact, some of them are so complex that it would be too laborious to express everything involved in the corresponding concept. In these cases, abbreviations are used, mentioning only the main components of the complex concept (see *AS* 84).

As an exception to the rule that everything is expressed by means of radical words, Dalgarno retained six words of his original collection of several hundreds that were designed to represent the particles. These six words are listed just above the grammatical inflections in the seventh column of the Lexicon Grammatico-Philosophicum. 'Lal, lηl, lel' represent the personal pronouns 'I, you, he' respectively. As appears from the 'Praxis', possessive pronouns are formed from these by adding the adjectival suffix '-a': 'lηla' meaning 'your'. Plural is formed just as with radical words, 'lalli' meaning 'we'. Further, the demonstrative, reflexive, and relative pronouns 'this, self, who' are represented by 'lol, lυl, lul' respectively. These pronouns are expressly introduced as pure abbreviations. Dalgarno shows for the personal pronouns, but not for the others (*AS* 81), that these can always be replaced by the nouns they stand for.

The method of forming particles using radical words is exemplified by the list of eighty-two words in the right-most column of the 'Lexicon Grammatico-Philosophicum'. The list is reproduced here, glossed as follows: the Latin equivalents of the radical words representing the Latin particles are put in parentheses on the same line as the reproduced items. An English translation of all Latin words is provided on the following line. In many cases, several English words are used to render a single Latin particle.

Etymologia praecipuarum particularum
Etymology of the most important particles

ab—sod, sam, bem (actio, causa efficiens, distantia)
by, away from—action, efficient cause, distance

ac—tηf (multiplicare [addere][7])
and—multiply [add]

ad—shod, brem (passio, contiguitas)
about, to, at—passion, contiguity

adhuc—slem, subdan (continuare, proportio-tempus)
hitherto, still—to continue, proportion-time

aliquis—sum, shun (unitas, pars)
someone, something—unity, part

an—tid (interrogare)
whether—to ask

ante—bef (ante)
before—before

apud—bem,[8] shυmbem (distantia, parum-distantia)
at, near—distance, little distance

at—slom, trηf, trimshaf (diversum, dividere, negare-impedimentum)
but, yet—diverse, divide, negate impediment

aut—trηb, slom (opposite of probare,[9] diversum)
or, or else—contradict/refute, diverse

circum—beg (circundans)
around—surrounding

citra—loliηb, shηg (hic-latus, carere)
on this side, without—this side, to lack

contra—shom (oppositum)
opposite—opposing

coram—bef, mηssi (ante, oculus + plural)
face to face, in presence of—before, eyes)

cum—slυb, dap, slam, sab (simul, praesentia, (causa) medium, instrumentum)
when, together with, since, with—simultaneously, presence, medium, instrument

cur—lulsas (qui-causa)
why—which cause

de—sηf, shop (pertinere, objectum)
of, about—pertain, object

---

[7] As appears from Dalgarno's manuscript annotations in a copy of *AS* in the Bodleian Library (8° A 130 Linc.), this should be 'tηn'—'to add'. The same error occurs in other instances, such as 'etiam', 'quoque', 'et', 'item', 'praeterea'.

[8] The opposite 'brem'—'contiguity' seems more appropriate.

[9] 'Trηb' is not in the Tables of Radicals, but signifies the opposite of 'tηb', which means 'probare' (to approve, to prove).

deinde—shʊbdan, shʊbsud (posterius-tempus, posterius-ordo)
thereafter, next—later time, later order

denique—shʊbapdan (posterius + superlative-tempus)
finally—latest time

deorsum—bηsbren (rectus-infra)
downwards—straight below

e, ex—san, bed (materia, extra)
out (of)—matter, outside

ergo—lelsas, trηm (ille-causa, inferre)
therefore—that[10]-cause, conclude

et—tηf (multiplicare [addere])
and—multiply [add][11]

etiam—tηf (multiplicare [addere])
also—multiply [add][12]

etsi—tηm (supponere)
even if—suppose

extra—bed (extra)
outside—outside

fere—sʊfshun, sʊmshʊf (maxime-pars, valde-minime)
almost—largest part, very little

forte—sak (fortuna)
maybe—fate

hic—loldad (hic-locus)
here—this place

jam—loldan (hic-tempus)
now, already—this time

ideo—lelsas (ille-causa)
therefore—that cause

illic—leldad (ille-locus)
there—that place

in—bred, dan (intra, tempus)
in—inside, time[13]

inter—bem, breg, gʊm (distantia, opposite of circundans, mixtio)
between, amid, among—distance, surrounded,[14] mixture

interdum—shundan (pars-tempus)
sometimes—part time

---

[10] Dalgarno sometimes uses the particle *lel* as an equivalent to 'he' (e.g. *AS* 73, 81). However, in this example, as in others below, he clearly intended it to mean 'that'—a usage that is more in agreement with the meaning of the Latin word *ille*.
[11] This should read 'tηn'. See n. 7.   [12] This should read 'tηn'. See n. 7.   [13] Cf. *AS* 86.
[14] 'Beg' is a radical meaning 'circundans' (surrounding); 'breg', though not occurring in the tables, signifies its opposite.

interim—luldan, loldan, dlaf (qui-tempus, hic-tempus, praesens)
meanwhile—which time, this time, present

intra—bred (intra)
inside—inside

invicem—sηt, sum, sum (vices, unitas, unitas)
in turn, mutually—alternation, unity, unity

ita—tim (affirmare)
yes—affirm

iterum—sen, vη (repetere,—)
again, a second time—repeat, two

item—tηf (multiplicare [addere])
also—multiply [add][15]

iuxta—brem, shumbem, slʋn, sos (contiguitas, multitudo-distantia, aeque, consentanea)
near, equally—contiguity, multitude [little][16] distance, equally, agreeing

magis—sʋn (magis)
more—more

nam—sas, sηf (causa, pertinere)
for—cause, pertain

ne—trim (negare)
that not, lest—negate

nimis—sʋd (excessus)
very much, too much—excess

nimis-parum—srʋd (defectus)
too little—defect

non—trim (negare)
not—negate

nunc—loldan (hic-tempus)
now—this time

ob—sham, sas, shom (finis, causa, oppositum)
because of—goal, cause, opposite[17]

omnis—sun (totum)
all, whole—whole

per—sod, sam, sab, sag, slam, brηn, blηn (actio, efficiens, instrumentum, exemplum, medium, transversum, secans)
through, by means of, with, by way of, by, along, over—action, efficient cause, instrument, example, means, transverse, intersecting

---

[15] This should read 'tηn'. See n. 7.
[16] Probably 'shumbem' is an error, 'shʋmbem' very probably being intended.
[17] This is probably because 'ob', when occurring in a compound verb, sometimes adds a notion of resistance or opposition to the sense of the verb.

post—shʊb, bref (posterius, post)
later, after—later, after

prae—sʊn, bef (magis, ante)
in comparison with, before—more, before

praeter—sʊn, brηn (magis, transversum)
except, more than, contrary to—more, transverse

praeterea—tηf, sʊn, shʊb (multiplicare [addere], magis, posterius)
besides, further, hereafter—multiply [add],[18] more, later

pro—sηt, sos, bef, sʊb (vices, consentanea, ante, prius)
in place of, like, for, before—alternation, agreeing, before, previously

prope—shʊmbem, sufshun, shʊmsuf (parum-distantia, reliquum-pars,
   parum-reliquum)
near, nearly—little distance, remaining part, little remaining

propter—sham, sas, shʊumbem (finis, causa, parum-distantia[19])
because of, near—goal, cause, little distance

quam—sʊs, tηg (gradus comparationis, mensurare)
how, as—degree of comparison, to measure

quasi—slʊn, ses (aeque, modus agendi)
just as, as if—aequally, manner of acting

qui, vel quis—lul
who, or somebody

quoque—tηf, slʊn (multiplicare [addere], aeque)
also—multiply [add],[20] aequally

satis—slʊd (satis)
enough—enough

sed—shom, trηf (oppositum, dividere)
but, however—opposite, divide

secundum—sos, shʊmbem (consentanea, parum-distantia)
following, next to—agreeing, little distance

sine—shηg, drap, sof (carere, absentia, privativum)
without—lack, absence, privative

simul—slʊb (simul)
at the same time—at the same time

sub—dηd, shʊb, bren (sustinere, posterius, infra)
underneath, immediately after, under—to sustain, later, below

super—drηd, bren (inniti, infra [supra][21])
over, above—to lean upon, below [above]

sursum—bηsben (positio-supra)
upwards, on high—position above

---

[18] This should read 'tηn'. See n. 7.
[19] Reading 'shʊmbem'.
[20] This should read 'tηn'. see n. 7.
[21] 'Bren' is obviously an error; 'ben' meaning 'supra'.

supra—ben (supra)
over, above—over, above

tam—slʊn, lolbes, lelbes (aeque, hic-situs, ille-situs)
so, so far—aequally, this place, that place

tamen—trimshaf, tηm (negare-impedimentum, supponere)
nevertheless, however—negate impediment, suppose

tandem—shʊbdanbam[22] (posterius-tempus-longum)
at last—later time long, i.e. after long time[23]

tenus—bηs, brem (positio, contiguitas)
up to, as far as—position, contiguity

trans—brηn, shomieb (transversum, oppositum-perimetrum)
across, on the other side—transverse, opposite perimeter

versus—bηs (positio)
towards—position

vel—trηb (opposite of probare[24])
or—contradict, refute

vix—shep (difficile)
hardly—difficult

ullus—av (ens, res)
any(one)—being, thing

ut—sham, slʊn (finis, aeque)
so that, as—goal, aequally

4. REACTIONS TO *THE ART OF SIGNS*

Dalgarno's work met with very little success. It is not certain whether he really expected his invention to evolve into a language used worldwide, as he says in *The Art of Signs*, but he must have been disappointed by the almost complete silence that followed its appearance. As noted above (Sect. 2.4), his work is mentioned in contemporary publications a few times, two of which are fairly brief references, primarily drawing attention to the fact that Dalgarno's work was a forerunner of that of Wilkins (Wallis 1678; Wood 1691). In addition, there is the account in Plot (1676), which gives a more elaborate though still sketchy account of the principles used in *The Art of Signs*.

The longest comment to appear in print was published shortly after *The Art of Signs*, in 1662. It consisted of a caustic attack on both the purposes and the

---

[22] The original has spaces: 'shʊb dan bam', which is anomalous. All other compounds in the list are written as a single word.

[23] The meaning of 'shʊb' according to the tables is 'posterius', but according to the list of particles it also translates 'post'—'after'. Further, a syntactic rule says that adjectives follow the noun (*AS* 73).

[24] Cf. 'aut' above.

method of *The Art of Signs*, and on its author personally (see Cram and Maat 1996). The attack formed a major part of the preface to an English translation of Comenius' *Janua Linguarum*. Comenius did not write the preface himself, and it is doubtful whether its contents ever came to his attention. The author of the attack was Roger Daniel, who produced an authorized English and Greek translation of the *Janua Linguarum*, which he published in England. Despite the vicious tone, Daniel's discussion of Dalgarno's work is quite sophisticated, showing that he was familiar with the details of and background to the artificial language.

As Daniel relates, he was first prompted to write the review of Dalgarno's language by what he felt to be a sign of intolerable arrogance—namely, the claim that an artificial language of one's own device could be more rational and convenient than languages that have been in existence for centuries, such as Latin, Greek, and Hebrew. Obviously, the underlying assumption that these languages are irrational, being full of irregularities, ambiguities, and redundancies, was flying in the face of Daniel's interests as a publisher and translator of a method of language teaching. He may also have been aware of Dalgarno's broadsheets, in which not only is the irrationality of existing languages emphasized, but the claim is made that the scheme is a useful 'Janua', thus being explicitly presented as a competitor to the book published by Daniel. He accordingly argues at length for the rationality of the classical languages, claiming that they contain wisdom that is ultimately derived from the Adamic language. He illustrates this by pointing out a series of etymological connections between various Latin, Greek, and Hebrew words, and contrasts Dalgarno's artificial words unfavourably with these. Daniel further argues that Dalgarno's language, far from being based upon rational principles, is a completely arbitrary institution without any proper philosophical foundation.

In Daniel's view, Dalgarno's hope that his language would at some time replace Latin as the international language of the learned was chimerical. Experience shows, he said, that, if an international auxiliary language is needed, some existing language can serve the purpose very well. His discussion of this point illustrates why Dalgarno had such difficulties arguing against those who believed that a universal *character* was a desirable invention, while opposing the construction of an artificial *language*. Daniel was clearly one of them: he strongly rejects the idea of an artificial language, but at the same time he emphasizes that a universal character would be both implementable and useful. Dalgarno's lengthy argument in chapter II of *The Art of Signs*, to the effect that such a position is inconsistent, thus seems to have been lost upon him.

Daniel makes two further points that concern the details of Dalgarno's language. First, he claims that its phonological starting points are flawed in that they disregard the diversity of speech sounds used by various nations, thus overlooking Dalgarno's explicit intention of employing only sounds that are universally used. Secondly, and more convincingly, he points out that in many cases Dalgarno's language uses long descriptive expressions where other languages use a single word. Yet these periphrases are often ambiguous, under-specifying the thing they supposedly designate. Thus the expression 'aquatic bird with large wings' may equally well designate a goose or a swan as a heron, which is the intended meaning.

Daniel's review is also personally insulting. Never mentioning Dalgarno by name, he says that the author of *The Art of Signs* should improve his own Latin rather than endeavour to instruct others in the way they should speak. The support he has got from several persons of great name, Daniel surmizes, must have been inspired by pity rather than admiration. He concludes his discussion of Dalgarno's work by using the artificial language the one and only time, calling anyone who wastes his time on rubbish of this sort 'nηkpim sυfa'—that is, 'the greatest ass'. Thus the single time that a person other than Dalgarno is known to have used his language in print was for the purposes of adding stylistic edge to a harsh critique of the language.

There is no direct evidence that Dalgarno was aware of Daniel's comments, but it is unlikely that he was not. In 'The Autobiographical Treatise', there are several remarks that seem to be indirect replies to Daniel. Thus Dalgarno admits his Latin to be poor (CC, fo. 40ʳ; see also *D&D*, Introduction). Further, he grants that his selection and arrangement of radical words is arbitrary, but emphasizes that this is necessarily so, and that his proposing some particular arrangement should not be taken as a sign of arrogance (CC, fo. 83ᵛ). Moreover, he defends his method of coining words for species against 'some considerable objections' (CC, fo. 79ʳ). Finally, he recognizes that, if people were to use his language, they would be wise in his own opinion, but 'great fools in the opinion of others' (CC, fo. 42ʳ).

In 1668, Wilkins's impressive folio volume containing the *Essay* was finally published, and in the eyes of most observers it was seen as overshadowing Dalgarno's modest booklet. Typical of this perspective is a comment by John Locke in a letter of 30 August 1681. Writing to his friend Toinard in Paris, who had requested that he send him two copies of *The Art of Signs*, one for himself and one for a friend who had plans in this area, Locke says he was able to find just one copy of *The Art of Signs* 'in all the bookshops in London or Oxford'. He adds that he has been unable to find out whether Dalgarno published another book on the subject, but he does send a copy of the *The Deaf and Dumb Man's Tutor*. As a final comment, Locke says (in French): 'If I knew the plan of your friend in this area, perhaps the book of Dr Wilkins the Rev. bishop of Chester who has written in folio in English *de Charactere universali* would be more appropriate if your friend understands English' (Locke 1976: ii. 436).

In the beginning of 1673, the young philosopher and mathematician Gottfried Wilhelm Leibniz (1646–1716) visited London, where he bought a copy of *The Art of Signs*. From a note pasted at the front of this copy, it appears that he discussed the topic of a universal language with Boyle and Oldenburg. Both men had been friends of Wilkins, who had died in November of the previous year. Leibniz noted that Dalgarno's invention was later perfected by Wilkins, a comment he might have borrowed from Wilkins's friends (Leibniz, A 6 3 170). Leibniz was himself concerned to construct a philosophical language throughout his life. He believed that his own plan was significantly different from what others had achieved, and he habitually referred to both Dalgarno and Wilkins in explaining this point to his correspondents.

Both from Leibniz's annotations in his copy of *The Art of Signs* and from a large number of manuscripts that were never published during his lifetime (often because they were not meant for publication), it appears that Leibniz studied Dalgarno's work very carefully. Apart from the marginal annotations, there are various papers containing excerpts of Dalgarno's lexicon (Leibniz, A 6 4 594–604; A 6 4 1009). In addition, Leibniz used Dalgarno's work (as well as that of Wilkins and others) for the implementation of his own project. At least five manuscripts, some of which are very long, are preserved among Leibniz's papers, which use Dalgarno's lexicon as a starting point for lists of definitions. One of these contains definitions, apparently made by Leibniz himself, of each of the more than 1,000 words of Dalgarno's 'Lexicon Grammatico-Philosophicum' (Leibniz 1903: 437–510). Other similar lists were compiled by Hodann, Leibniz's secretary from 1702 to 1704, who borrowed the definitions from various dictionaries. Dalgarno's alphabetical lexicon was also used as a basis for a list of definitions (Leibniz, A 6 4 53–7).

Thus, fifteen years after Dalgarno died, and more than twenty years after Locke found that *The Art of Signs* had become a rare book in England, there was a clerk at Hanover meticulously going through the tables of Dalgarno's lexicon, providing each of the items with a definition he had looked up in various dictionaries, or which had been produced by his employer, the famous philosopher Leibniz.

5. THE DEAF AND DUMB MAN'S TUTOR

Almost twenty years separate Dalgarno's best-known work, *The Art of Signs*, from his second publication, *Didascalocophus or The Deaf and Dumb Man's Tutor* (1680). In general outline, something is known of his life and occupation during these years. He had become, in the year of the publication of *The Art of Signs*, master of Queen Elizabeth College, Guernsey, with a wife who was a fellow Aberdonian, and by 1662 the first of at least seven children. By 1664 he was resident again in Oxford, as master of a school in the Parish of St Mary Magdalen. Here he remained until 1669, when he relinquished his interest in the school premises and returned once more to teach in Guernsey. Ill health in 1672 resulted in his return once more to Oxford, where he died in 1687. Residence in the university town presumably gave him the opportunity of association with some of the Oxford scholars who had interested themselves in his earlier work.

Although his publications on a universal language lay behind him, and it was reported to the Royal Society in 1685 that Dalgarno was ready to hand on his papers on the subject if another scholar could make use of them, he acknowledged in *The Deaf and Dumb Man's Tutor* that his new work had arisen from concerns first identified in his preparation for *The Art of Signs*. Lack of opportunity, until illness interrupted his regular employment, had prevented his further research and publication on these topics. His earlier work had indeed contained clear signals pointing to his later interests. As noted above (see Sect. 2.5), the link between universal character and the language of the deaf was explicitly established in the broadsheets advertising Dalgarno's early scheme. Following from this, many points in early chapters of *The Deaf and Dumb Man's Tutor* are closely tied with the arguments both of *The Art of Signs* and 'The Autobiographical Treatise'.

5.1. *The background: Bulwer, Holder, and Wallis*

Dalgarno's second book-length publication in fact consists of two independent and substantial works, *The Deaf and Dumb Man's Tutor* and *A Discourse of the Nature and Number of Double Consonants*. On the title page Dalgarno explains that both tracts are 'the first (for what the Author knows) that have been published on either of the Subjects'. This is, on the face of it, an extraordinary statement, for, as any informed reader in the 1680s would have known, Dalgarno was far from being the first in making a link between real character and the language of the deaf. It is difficult to explain why he made such a claim for novelty, although a brief summary of the history of scholarly interest in the teaching of the deaf since the 1640s provides some clues.[25]

One obvious predecessor, and the one making the most explicit connection between the language of the deaf and real character, was John Bulwer, whose *Chirologia* (1644) presents gesture both as a universal language and as a real character in the seventeenth-century sense (see Knowlson 1965 on the idea of gesture as a universal language in the seventeenth century). Thus, on the language of the hand, Bulwer (1644: 3) says: 'Nor doth the Hand in one speech or kinde of language serve to intimate and expresse our mind: It speakes all languages, and as an universall character of Reason, is generally understood and knowne by all Nations, among the formall differences of their tongue.' There had indeed been scholarly activity in this area closer to home and of more recent date. Reference to this can be found in Plot's *Natural History of Oxfordshire* (1676: 281-2), which, in a chapter on discoveries that have been made in the county, records the invention of a method to teach language to the deaf immediately before that of a universal character. Two names are linked by Plot with the real

[25] On the history of the teaching of the deaf in this period, see Kemp (1972: 11–14), Salmon (1972: 68–71), and Rée (1999: pt. two).

character—namely, those of Dalgarno and Wilkins—and two with surdo-mutism, namely, William Holder and John Wallis.

What Plot avoids mentioning, presumably with deliberation, and Dalgarno gives no hint of, is the acrimonious and public altercation on this subject between Holder and Wallis, who each claimed credit for original contributions to the subject. This was, incidentally, not the only acrimonious academic dispute in which Wallis became embroiled. The facts of the matter, as we know them, are as follows. Wallis claimed to have taught two deaf mutes to speak in the early 1660s; Daniel Whaley, then aged about 26, and Alexander Popham, aged about 12. In order to demonstrate Wallis's success, Whaley was paraded before the Royal Society on 21 May 1662, and subsequently before the King. In 1669, however, Holder published in his *Elements of Speech* an 'Appendix concerning Persons Deaf and Dumb', containing an assertion that he himself had been the first to teach this same Popham to speak. The claim was repeated in a pamphlet *A Supplement to the Philosophical Transactions of July, 1670, with some Reflexions on Dr John Wallis* (1678), in which Holder explicitly asserts that he had taught Popham in 1659 and that Wallis both knew of this and had personally witnessed the results. Wallis immediately replied with his *Defence of the Royal Society . . . In Answer to the Cavils of Dr. William Holder* (1678), in which he restated his own case and rebutted Holder's charges. The argument was a bitter one and contemporaries felt obliged to take sides; Aubrey and Wood, for example, both aligned themselves against Wallis.

This is not the place to adjudicate between the claims of Wallis and Holder (for a reasoned view, which tilts slightly in Holder's favour, see Kemp 1972: 12–13), but it is significant for our present purposes that the debate was at its fiercest and most public at precisely the time when Dalgarno was composing *The Deaf and Dumb Man's Tutor*, described, rather cheekily, as the first work on the subject 'for what the Author knows'. We can safely assume that Dalgarno was aware of the background and that in the debate he would have been sympathetic to the position of Wallis, whom he refers to in his work as 'The Learned and my worthy friend Dr *Wallis*' (p. 21). By 1680 their association had a long history. Wallis had been one of Dalgarno's advisers from the very inception of his scheme to devise a real character and in *A Defence of the Royal Society* (1678) Wallis presents himself publicly—whether accurately or not—as Dalgarno's primary patron and mentor, claiming credit for having given the advice that prompted Dalgarno to transform his scheme from a dumb character to spoken language.

There is evidence of Wallis's reaction on at least one occasion to Dalgarno's new work. In 1685 Dalgarno submitted two papers to the Oxford Philosophical Society, based on *The Art of Signs* and *The Deaf and Dumb Man's Tutor*. Wallis was then President of the Society and chaired the meeting on 24 March 1685, when the minutes described the subject of Dalgarno's papers (Gunther 1925: 133): 'one concerning the bringing a Philosophicall Language into practice, the other a compendium of a Book, not long since printed by him, entitled

Didascalocophus, which among other things undertakes to prove, that the Eye & Hand are more usefull Organs of knowledge, than the Tongue and Ear.' A lively discussion seems to have ensued, in which Wallis, not unsurprisingly, drags in a reference to the deaf mute Whaley:

This gave occasion to some Discourse concerning the Vigour and improvement of some one Sense, upon the Defect, or non-employment of one or more of the others; upon which Subject Mr. President was pleased to informe us, that Mr. Whaly (the deaf Gentleman, whom he taught to speak) could, when within doors, distinguish a Coach from a Cart in ye street by the motion, it made; when those, who were in company with him, could not discerne whether it were the one, or the other, by the noise, it made.

The reception of Dalgarno's work by the Society is significant. It was clearly characterized and discussed not primarily as a practical manual but rather as a theoretical disquisition on surdo-mutism. This reflects the members' appreciation of wherein lay the novelty in Dalgarno's work on the subject.

5.2. *The language of the deaf*

At the very outset of *The Deaf and Dumb Man's Tutor*, Dalgarno makes a direct link with *The Art of Signs*, which he says that he would now entitle 'On Sematology', if he were writing it in English. In the later work he develops a general taxonomy of the different types of sign, within which his earlier work can be located. He postulates that the interpretation of signs may be supernatural, natural, or artificial, which he refers to respectively by the terms 'chrematology' (relating to divinity), 'physiology' (relating to natural philosophy), and 'sematology' (relating to rational grammar). Sematology is distinguished from physiology in that it concerns artificial or instituted signs as distinct from the natural expression of passion in acts such as laughing, weeping, frowning.

Sematology—the interpretation of instituted signs—is now subdivided depending on the senses involved: so, pneumatology involves sounds and the ear, schematology, figures and the eye. The latter further subdivides into typology (grammatology), which is devoted to writing, and cheirology (dactylology), interpretation by movements of the fingers. This scheme can be represented in a tree diagram, as shown in Fig. 3. The analysis of the area of sematology developed here by Dalgarno links the present work not only to its predecessor *The Art of Signs*, but also to his treatise 'On Interpretation' (see below, Part IV), which was composed at approximately the same time.

Dalgarno explains that he has been led to coin a number of new words for the purposes of his typology. In fact, in these neologisms, as also in the content of this section, there is evidence that Dalgarno owes a specific debt to the two works on the language of the deaf by John Bulwer. Although this debt is not specifically acknowledged, Dalgarno's adoption of the terminology used by Bulwer and other aspects of his treatment suggest no effort to conceal an

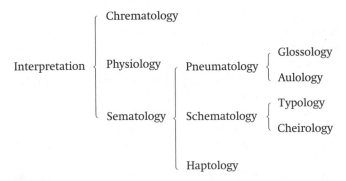

FIG. 3. A tree diagram of Dalgarno's scheme showing the position of sematology (the art of signs) and cheirology (the language of the deaf) within the general field of interpretation.

association with the earlier writer. The very form of the title immediately alerts a reader to Dalgarno's association with Bulwer: *Didascalocophus or The Deaf and Dumb Man's Tutor* carries a strong echo of Bulwer's publication *Philocophus: or the Deaf and Dumb Man's Friend* (1648). What is more, there is clear evidence that the original title Dalgarno gave to *The Deaf and Dumb Man's Tutor* was 'Cheirology', undoubtedly referring back to Bulwer's earlier work *Chirologia* (1644). This is clear from the fact that the second work in the volume, the treatise on double consonants, is announced on its own title page as *An Appendix to Cheirology*; and, moreover, the errata notes on the verso of the volume's main title page advise the reader to read *Didascalocophus* for *Cheirology* in various places where the latter had not been corrected.

In the first four chapters, Dalgarno's general treatment of the language of the deaf is, like that of Bulwer, intended to place the issue in the broader context of the theory of 'interpretation', a perspective that offers a contrast to the more functional and applied approach of Holder. Although Dalgarno shares some of Bulwer's speculative interests, their conclusions contain marked differences. Bulwer's *Chirologia* is concerned primarily with gesture as a natural language and universal character. In Dalgarno's typology, gesture in this sense qualifies as physiology. What absorbs Dalgarno, for his part, is the art of instituted or artificial signs, sematology; his concern with the language of the deaf is as a visual equivalent of spoken language. In these chapters he uses surdo-mutism as a vehicle for revisiting the philosophical issues that, as we have seen, he had first tackled when his work for *The Art of Signs* prompted him to develop his views on the relationship between speech and writing (see Sect. 2.3 above).

One of the few other references made by Dalgarno to the work of contemporary writers in this area concerns the well-known passage in Sir Kenelm Digby's *Of Bodies* (1644: 254–6), which introduced the ideas of Juan Pablo Bonet (1620) to the English speaking world. Digby gives a detailed report on Bonet's success in teaching a deaf Spanish lord to lip-read and to imitate sounds in languages unknown to him. Wherever else Dalgarno may have come across Digby's findings, with which he has serious disagreement, he would have found the celebrated passage quoted verbatim and in extenso in Bulwer's *Philocophus* (1648: 56–61). It is worth noting that Digby's account of Bonet's method was one of the major bones of contention between Holder and Wallis in the late 1670s. Wallis (1678: 20) maintained, in answer to an accusation from Holder, that when he taught Whaley and Popham to speak he had not known of Pablo Bonet's work, nor read the book by Sir Kenelm Digby, but had worked out his own method on the basis of the *Tractatus De Loquela*, prefixed to his *Grammar* (Wallis 1653). A note to this effect was added to the 1670 edition of the *Grammar* (Wallis 1972: 116–19).

For a modern reader of *The Deaf and Dumb Man's Tutor*, it remains difficult to gauge the effect on his contemporaries of Dalgarno's parsimonious references to the current literature on surdo-mutism, but this background shows some of the complexity of the scholarly debate on the subject, and the significance of the personal animosities involved, and goes some way to explain Dalgarno's apologetic but patronizing dismissal of Digby's report (see Wallis 1670: 20) and of course the lack of any reference whatsoever to Holder.

After the first four chapters, which include a lengthy attempt to show that, contrary to popular belief, deafness is no more serious an intellectual deficit than blindness, Dalgarno proceeds to consider the practicalities of teaching language to the deaf. Although they need not detain us, he has some interesting and humane pedagogical views—for instance, that a slow learner will do better with a slow master than the most learned doctor in the university, since what is primarily required is patience (*D&D* 48–9). Of more direct concern in connection with sematology are his remarks on the deaf man's dictionary (chapter VI) and on a grammar for deaf persons (chapter VII). The former chapter has some detailed remarks about the type of vocabulary items to be learned first—namely, things that are best known to the pupil: corporeal substances, whether natural or artificial, and relational terms (for example, father, brother, master) as well as absolutes. There is an echo of discussion elsewhere, both in *The Art of Signs* and in 'The Autobiographical Treatise', when Dalgarno proposes the ways in which the nomenclature or dictionary may be sorted: first, alphabetically, secondly, following the order of double consonants, and, thirdly, reduced to heads as in Junius' *Nomenclator*.

The discussion of the grammar for the deaf likewise touches on a range of morphological and syntactic issues that are treated at greater length in *The Art of Signs* and in the autobiographical tract, but which are reviewed here from a distinctive perspective. Under 'etymology' (the standard seventeenth-century label for what we now broadly term morphology), the comparative and superlative forms receive mention here again, as do participial forms in *-ing* and abstracts in *-ness*. The section on syntax starts with a general observation that, while this area is traditionally subdivided (that is, in Latin grammar) into agreement and government, this division does not work for a vernacular such as

English, which uses particles where Latin uses terminations (*D&D* 61–2). This gives a theoretical motivation for the structure of the remainder of the chapter, which proceeds to work through the various categories of 'particle': pronouns, the copula, conjunctions, prepositions, the metaphysical particles, and the comparates (see *AS*, ch. VIII, and Sect. 3.3.1. above).

The final chapter of *The Deaf and Dumb Man's Tutor* is concerned with finger spelling, or 'an alphabet upon the fingers', the antecedents of which are discussed by Siger (1968). An illustration in the text shows the proposed layout of the letters upon the various segments of the hand; vowels are to be indicated by a touch with the finger, consonants by a touch with the thumb. Dalgarno then goes on to show how consonant clusters may be indicated by the simultaneous touch of more than one digit. This latter technique means, of course, that the layout of the letters on the hand presupposes an analysis of the sequential patterning of the consonants and vowels in the language being used, in much the same way as the layout of modern typewriter keyboards is based on a prior analysis of the frequency and co-occurrence of letters. This is indeed the subject of the companion treatise in the volume, the analysis of double consonants, a treatise written several years earlier.

Dalgarno closes the work by proposing that there are uses for finger spelling other than teaching language to the deaf, just as elsewhere the multiple uses of the universal character were pointed up. His alphabet on the fingers, he says, may be used, first, for silence—for example, by those tending the sick; secondly, for secrecy—that is, as a manual equivalent of cryptography; and, thirdly, for pleasure—that is, 'it may be an ingenious and useful divertisement and pass-time for young people' (*D&D* 91–2).

5.3. *The treatise on double consonants*

Dalgarno's work on double consonants was likewise a spin-off from *The Art of Signs*. It was written seven years before *The Deaf and Dumb Man's Tutor* and is in many ways the more original piece, being in its own right a remarkable and distinctive example of Dalgarno's thinking. Although billed as an appendix, it is an independent work, and, at forty-one pages, a substantial one. It offers an early treatment of what is now called phonotactics, the study of the constraints on the serial ordering of sounds in human languages. Without wishing to draw too direct a parallel between seventeenth- and twentieth-century concerns in this area of phonology, there are interesting pre-echoes of structuralist thinking in Dalgarno's analysis, and it is felicitous, if fortuitous, that he lights on the term 'cardinal vowel' in a sense strikingly close to its modern technical usage.

For his purposes of teaching language to the deaf, Dalgarno has the aim of describing the phonological patterns of particular languages, be these of classical languages such as Greek or modern languages such as English and Polish.

But since the concern from which he first started is to establish the consonant clusters to be allowed in his philosophical language, he assumes a universalistic framework within which the language-specific facts are to be viewed.[26] His starting point is an examination of Hebrew, which he assumes to retain some vestiges of the original Adamic language. However, it is noteworthy that, in referring to the changes that Hebrew has undergone, he does not here invoke the biblical account of the diversification of languages at Babel, but refers to the 'common accidents which are known to change a language' of the sort that have transformed Latin into Italian and ancient Greek into modern Greek (D&D 98). Dalgarno then singles out a number of features of Hebrew that serve as surviving evidence of its Adamic origin. The first is directly relevant to phonotactics—namely, that in that language 'all their radical words consist generally of a single consonant, and a single vowel, succeeding one another alternatly' (D&D 99)—that is, canonical CVCV syllable structure, which he also sees as the most appropriate pattern for a philosophical language (D&D 96). Other features include the fact that Hebrew roots are typically 'triliteral radicals' (that is, of the form CVCVC); the fact that the writing system systematically distinguishes vowels from consonants (that is, the distinction between radical consonants and vocalic points), which Dalgarno compares to soul and body respectively; and the fact that in the Hebrew alphabet the letters are named by 'significant' words Aleph, Beth, and so on—that is, words that are a phonetic reflection of the sound they represent and are thus a real character.

After these introductory remarks Dalgarno gives a brief recapitulation of his analysis of simple sounds as previously set out in chapter I of *The Art of Signs*. In doing so he rehearses once again arguments concerning the velar nasal and the aspirates that concern him in the autobiographical tract.

The set of rules that Dalgarno develops for initial consonant clusters is based first of all on standard descriptions of Greek (D&D 115–20), with differences from English and other languages being indicated at various points. He first sets up three 'negative' rules, which preclude certain categories of sounds from co-occurring—for example, no liquid, by which he understands *l*, *m*, *n*, *r*, can come first in an initial cluster (with the exception in Greek of μνάομαι). These negative rules, he claims, hold also for Latin and for other 'modern languages'. His subsequent set of 'affirmative rules' are ones that apply specifically to Greek, and concern both double and triple consonants clusters.

When he moves on to consider final consonant clusters, his primary focus is on English, in which clusters abound, owing to the fact that roots are for the most part monosyllables. Having considered final pairs of consonants, he then sets up rules for final clusters of three (one of which must be *s*) and four consonants (two of which must be *s*, as in 'firsts' and 'thirsts').

---

[26] Bulwer, incidentally, draws a parallel distinction between chirologia, the natural and universal language of the hand, and chir-ethnica-logia, gestures specific to a given nation (Bulwer 1644: To the Reader).

Dalgarno finishes by asking what the maximum number of consonants is, both initial and final, that one may have in any one syllable. He draws examples here from English, Dutch, and French, as well as Greek, but he is clearly pleased that the prize is taken by a Polish monosyllable of nine letters, 'chrzaszcz'. This last example he had 'from the hand of a person of Honour of that Nation', an informant who may with certainty be identified as Faustus Morstyn (see Sect. 2.1 above). Dalgarno goes on to say 'this word I have often heard pronounced by Natives, and have myself been commended by them for the imitation: But to strangers it seems a barbarous sound, and reaches not the expressing of the power of all the letters with which it is written' (*D&D* 124). It is clear that Dalgarno's conception of the relationship between speech and writing, discussed elsewhere, enables him to maintain the distinction between the phonetics of a language and the (often imperfect) orthography with which it is associated.

6. BIBLIOGRAPHICAL NOTE

The fate of Dalgarno's manuscripts has not been a happy one. Papers of his that were recorded as having been read to the Oxford Philosophical Society were also recorded as having been preserved in the Society's Letterbook B (Letterbook A being for correspondence). Thus the minutes for the meeting of 24 March 1685 state that two papers by Dalgarno were presented, 'one concerning the bringing a Philosophicall Language into practice, the other a Compendium of a Book, not long since printed by him, entitled *Didascalocophus*', these being registered as 'Letterbook B, Paper 16th' (Gunther 1925: 133). The Letterbooks thus referred to (Letterbook A being for correspondence) later came to form a single volume known as 'Dr Plott's Letters' or as MS Ashmole 1813 (Gunther 1925: 223). This volume was later transferred to the Bodleian Library, but having lost some of its contents—including Dalgarno's paper No. 16—in the process. A note by Francis Madden inside the front cover of the manuscript says: 'This certainly contains 1813 and is closely connected with lot 363 in the Dawson Turner sale of 9 June 1859. FM.' The catalogue of the Dawson Turner sale here referred to indeed itemizes a selection of titles from the Oxford Philosophical Society papers, but does not mention the one by Dalgarno. The lot seems to have been split between Dublin and Cambridge (and perhaps elsewhere), but enquiries have found no trace of any paper by Dalgarno.

The missing papers just mentioned must clearly be related to the tracts preserved in the Christ Church MS 162, in particular 'The Autobiographical Treatise' (dealing with the philosophical language) and the tract 'On Interpretation' (dealing, among other things, with the language of the deaf). The dating of the manuscript is fully consistent with this link. It might further be mentioned that the Christ Church MS contains a set of untitled notes by Dalgarno on the topic of filtration, which can with some certainty be associated with the following item in the minutes of the meeting of the Oxford Philosophical Society of 24 February 1685: 'A Paper of Queries concerning Filtration, drawn up by Mr. Dalgarno, was read' (Gunther 1925: 124). Thus, although Dalgarno's papers themselves appear to have been lost, their substantial content was not.

The fate of the volume now known as Christ Church MS 162 is another odd story. This must have been left with Dalgarno's Aberdonian wife at his death in 1687. She had them in her own safe keeping until 1698, when she handed them on to another Aberdonian, David Gregory, who had recently been appointed to the chair of astronomy. A note to this effect has been made on the cover of the volume: 'Liber Manuscriptus Georgii Dalgarno Scoti ab ejus vidua D.G. tradit Maio 1698.' The volume thus came to be part of the Gregory collection at Christ Church, which was one of the first Oxford colleges to produce a printed catalogue of its manuscript holdings. For reasons that are not fully clear, however, the Dalgarno volume failed to be entered in the card catalogue that formed the central catalogue of manuscript holdings of Oxford colleges and that is to be found in the Bodleian Library. Thus, although a number of scholars over the years came to Oxford to do research on Dalgarno and his ideas, the existence of the set of unpublished tracts went unnoticed. They came to the notice of David Cram—in Aberdeen University Library as it happens—as he was doing a systematic trawl of printed catalogues of the Oxford colleges.

Prior to the present edition, Dalgarno's published works were reprinted twice. In 1834 the Maitland Club published *The Works of George Dalgarno of Aberdeen*, containing both *The Art of Signs* and *The Deaf and Dumb Man's Tutor*. A facsimile reprint of *The Art of Signs* was published by the Scolar Press in 1968, and a facsimile reprint of *The Deaf and Dumb Man's Tutor* appeared in 1971, with the same publisher. Part of *The Deaf and Dumb Man's Tutor* had earlier been reprinted in the journal *American Annals of the Deaf* (1837), ix. 14–64.

Dalgarno's 'Autobiographical Treatise' is published here for the first time, together with his other unpublished tracts, his two published books, and the complete set of his broadsheet publications. A translation of all Latin texts is provided, together with notes that are designed to be sufficient to clarify and not so many as to obfuscate. We hope that these texts, together with our introduction, will make Dalgarno's ideas accessible to a new generation of scholars.

CHRONOLOGY OF DALGARNO'S LIFE

c.1620

——   Birth of George Dalgarno at Old Aberdeen in Scotland.

1631

——   Matriculates at Marischal College, Aberdeen.

1657

——   Arrives in Oxford, where he starts a school.

11 Apr.   Letter from Faustus Morstyn to Hartlib introducing Dalgarno and mentioning the arrival of the brachigrapher in Oxford.

20 Apr.   Dalgarno's first letter to Hartlib, from Oxford, outlining the reception of his scheme at Oxford and Cambridge, mentioning its examination by Wilkins and Ward, and commenting on the schemes of Beck and Lodwick.

Apr.   Entry in Hartlib's diary refers to the role of Ward and Wallis in assisting 'a Scotchman' (Dalgarno), in his investigation of Real Characters.

Apr./May   Entry in Hartlib's diary records Robert Boyle's comments on the utility of Dalgarno's scheme.

2 May   Pell receives letter from Hartlib asking for an evaluation of Dalgarno's universal language scheme.

4 July   Pell receives from Hartlib copies of Dalgarno's broadsheet 'Character Vniversalis'.

18 July   Pell receives specimen from St John's Gospel in Dalgarno's character.

July   A visitor, who probably came from Paris, records notes on Dalgarno's early scheme, and makes a Latin translation of the mnemonic tables later contained in the broadsheet 'Tables of the Universal Character'.

1, 8 Aug.   Robert Wood writes letters to Hartlib, initially expressing scepticism, but later giving a moderately positive evaluation of Dalgarno's scheme.

24 Aug.   Johann Morian asks to be sent additional copies of Dalgarno's first broadsheet.

24 Aug.   John Beale sends a general comment on Dalgarno's scheme to Hartlib.

Sept.   Nicholas Mercator asks Hartlib for further details of Dalgarno's scheme.

The principal sources on which this epitome draws are Goodwin (1908), Salmon (1966a), Cram (1980, 1990), Cram and Maat (1996), and Maat and Cram (1998), to which reference should be made for further details. The main archival sources for Dalgarno's biography are: the Hartlib collection of manuscripts at the University of Sheffield, the Pell papers held in the British Library (Add. MS 4377), and records preserved in The Greffe, Guernsey.

6 Sept.	Sir Cheney Culpepper writes to Hartlib, expressing a desire to learn the details of Dalgarno's system.
8 Sept.	Letter from Hartlib to Boyle mentioning visit by Dalgarno, Morstyn, Culpepper, and another Polish gentleman.
20 Sept.	Sir Cheney Culpepper sends Hartlib his opinion of Dalgarno's transcription from St John's Gospel.
6 Oct.	Sir Cheney Culpepper gives additional comments on Dalgarno's scheme.
——	Publication of the broadsheet 'Tables of the Universal Character'.
30 Nov.	John Beale stresses the difficulty of the project Dalgarno is working on.
30 Nov.	Johann Morian sends Hartlib his positive evaluation of Dalgarno's scheme.
Dec.	Letter from Dalgarno to Pell giving a detailed account of his scheme.
8, 11 Dec.	Samuel Hartmann visits Dalgarno, talks at length about universal language, and communicates Comenius' plans in this area.

1658

——	John Pell makes notes commenting on the details of Dalgarno's scheme.
——	Francis Lodwick composes a report (for Hartlib) on Dalgarno's Universal Character.
1, 18 Jan.	Johann Morian reports receipt of copies of Dalgarno's broadsheets.
9 Jan.	John Beale in letter to Hartlib writes: 'I hope Mr Dalgarno has an eye upon Dr Wilkins attempts, that hee may not bee disrobed of the advantage of adding to Invention.'
11 Jan.	Comenius sends Hartlib a short comment on Dalgarno's scheme.
17 Feb.	Letter from Dalgarno in London to Brierton enclosing broadsheet advertisement and asking for support.
1 May	Publication of broadsheet 'The possibilitie and great usefulness of an Universall character', with recommendation from Richard Love, Corpus Christi College, Cambridge.
20 May	Letter from Dalgarno in Cambridge to Hartlib enclosing a copy of the Cambridge broadsheet.
31 Aug.	Dalgarno issued with pass at Dalkeith under General Monck's order, permitting him to travel to Cambridge, on his return from a visit of some months to Scotland.[1]

1659

| Sept. | Wilkins moves from Wadham College to Trinity College, Cambridge. |
| 3 Nov. | Letter to Hartlib from Dalgarno in Bishopston, Wiltshire, where he is preaching, reporting progress on his scheme, and expressing his fears that Wilkins might be pre-empting him. |

---

[1] We are grateful to Frances McDonald for drawing our attention to the entry in one of General Monck's order books (Worcester College, Oxford, Clarke MS 48, unfoliated) 'Passe for Mr George Dalgerno with his Horse, Sword & [man] to Cambridge'.

1660

——   Publication of the pamphlet 'Omnibus Omnino Hominibus', forming part of the petition to Charles II requesting support for Dalgarno's scheme.

1661

——   Publication of *The Art of Signs*.

——   Dalgarno master of Queen Elizabeth College, Guernsey.

12 Mar.   Letter requesting repairs to the schoolhouse roof at Queen Elizabeth College.

1662

——   In a preface to an English translation of Comenius's *Janua Linguarum*, the publisher, Roger Daniel, launches a caustic attack on *The Art of Signs*.

30 Apr.   Baptism of Martha, daughter of 'Sr. George Dalgarno, maistre du College' and 'Dorothee Jonston', Parish of St Peter Port, Guernsey.

1664

——   Dalgarno returns from Guernsey and is resident in Oxford.

17 Jan.   Baptism of daughter Mary, naming as his wife 'Margarett', registered in Parish of St Mary Magdalen, Oxford.

9 Feb.   Burial of daughter Mary, Parish of St Mary Magdalen, Oxford.

1665

4 May   Baptism of son George, Parish of St Mary Magdalen, Oxford.

30 June   Burial of son William, Parish of St Mary Magdalen, Oxford. (Birth date not traced.)

1667

——   Oxford Poll Tax return, Parish of St Mary Magdalen, lists Dalgarno's Guernsey pupils as lodgers in his household: 'Mr George Dol:Garno, gent; Margaret his wife; Susanna, Martha & George, children; Jane Box, wages £1; James Gill; Nich. Mesurier, John Martine, Nich. Martine, Will Haviland, Peter Monamy, William Merchant, John Sausmaries, Zachary Cary, Will. Crooke, Alexander Crooke, Lodgers'.

——   Subsidy of 1667, Parish of St Mary's, Oxford, lists a 'Mr Dollgardiner'.

28 Oct.   Baptism of daughter Mary, Parish of St Mary the Virgin, Oxford.

1668

——   Publication of Wilkins's *Essay towards a Real Character and a Philosophical Language*.

7 Feb.   Letter from de Havilland in Guernsey to Andros referring to payment of £20 to Dalgarno.

15 May   Letter from de Havilland to Andros mentioning admission of his son to an Oxford College.

1669

——   Dalgarno now resident in the Parish of St Mary the Virgin, Oxford.

14 Apr.   Lease from Mary Wood to Dalgarno, in which Dalgarno is styled MA of the University.

1 June   Baptism of daughter Margaret, Parish of St Mary the Virgin, Oxford.

4 Aug.   Relinquishes interest in the 'Little Print Shop', in which he had held his school.

1670

——   Second stint as schoolmaster in Guernsey.

8 Aug.   Dalgarno requests repairs to the schoolhouse.

7 Nov.   Letter of appointment as Master of Queen Elizabeth College.

1671

11 Sept.   Letter from de Havilland to Lord Hatton reporting that Dalgarno is dangerously ill.

1672

——   Dalgarno back in Oxford from Guernsey.

Jan.   Letter from Marsh to de Havilland concerning the latter's son.

9 June   Letter from Dalgarno to Lord Hatton.

20 June   Letter from de Havilland to Lord Hatton concerning Dalgarno's ill health.

22 July   Letter from Dalgarno to Lord Hatton concerning his ill health and his inclination not to return to Guernsey.

30 Sept.   Dalgarno in letter to Lord Hatton giving his resignation as Master of Queen Elizabeth College.

1674

8 Feb.   Baptism of son Charles, Parish of St Michael, Oxford.

1675

18 Apr.   Baptism of daughter Frances, Parish of St Michael, Oxford.

1680

——   Publication of *Didascalocophus, or the Deaf and Dumb Man's Tutor*.

1685

24 Feb.   Minutes of the Oxford Philosophical Society record the reading of 'A Paper of Queries concerning Filtration, drawn up by Mr. Dalgarno'.

28 Feb.   Minutes of the Oxford Philosophical Society record discussion of work by Dalgarno: 'A book was shown us written by Mr. Dalgarno and printed some years since but scarce yet published; the subject of it is *peri hermeneias* or the severall wayes of communicating thoughts.'

24 March   Minutes of the Oxford Philosophical Society record presentation of two papers by Dalgarno: 'one concerning the bringing a Philosophicall Language into practice, the other a Compendium of a Book . . . entitled *Didascalocophus*.' In a communication to the Secretary of the Royal Society, it is reported that Dalgarno prorposes 'bringing an Universall Character into practice' but is not currently working on the subject and promises to pass his papers on 'to any worthy undertaker'.

1687

25 Aug.   Dalgarno makes will.

28 Aug.   Death of Dalgarno.

30 Aug.   Burial 'in the north side of the church', Parish of St Mary Magdalen, Oxford.

1698

——   Dalgarno's papers handed by his widow to David Gregory (1661–1708), a fellow Aberdonian, who had been appointed Savilian professor of astronomy in Oxford in 1691.

PART I

DALGARNO'S FIRST SCHEME

Broadsheet 1

Character Universalis/A New Discovery of the Universal Character (1657)

CHARACTER VNIVERSALIS

Omnes Omnino homines, totius terrarum orbis Incolas, hic, vel alibi gentium, Doctos, Indoctos, linguarum plurium gnaros, ignaros, pariter Compello: Artem Novam (anxie, & laboriose, tamen frustra, ab altioris & primæ eruditionis viris, multis retro sæculis, quæsitam) *CHARACTEREM* scil: *UNIVERSALEM*, non luxurientis, & multipliciter variantis Orationis, sed simplicis, certæ, & Immutabilis *Rationis*, vobis discendam offero. *Scribam Celerem & Fidelem Interpretem*, appello; hoc, quod ejus adminiculo poterunt, omnium nationum homines, mutuo colloquio, inter se frui; illud, quod Scribens, quovis Idiomate loquentem, dupla celeritate vincere possit. Quandoquidem Myriades sententiarum dentur, quarum singula, unico, aut duobus characteribus, ijsq; ut plurimum, unico pennæ ductu delineatis, quibusdam distinctionum punctulis adjectis, perfecte conscribantur. Non Ægyptiorum hyeroglyphica ænigmatica, nec operosam & Infiniti prope laboris, (ut fama fert) Chynensium scripturam, sed artem perspicuam, facilem, brevem, celerem & expeditam trado: quicquid in ea memoria onerabit, unico chartæ folio, comprehendetur. Discenti, mediocris ingenij, & modicæ sedulitatis, unius septimanæ opus erit; altera deinde ad praxin accedente, perfectus artifex evadet: & quamvis in hac Inventione multum linguarum cognitioni (præcipue Hebraicæ & Arabicæ) debeam, artis tamen præcepta, tanta perspicuitate elaboravi, ut cujuslibet intellectu, supra linguam suam vernaculam, non sapientis, accomodentur. Nec reticendum est, plurima hujus Inventionis, Viris Celebratissimis & rei literariæ præsentis sæculi (salvo aliorum honore) vere ornamentis, Doctori scil: *Wilkins*, Collegij Whadamensis, in florentissima Academia Oxoniensi, præfecto dignissimo, & Doctori *Ward*, ejusdem Academiæ Professori Astronomico meritissimo (Cujus scripta, non ita pridem in lucem edita, hujus artis, non solum possibilitatem, probabilitatem, & utilitatem, sed & Inventionis methodum & rationem, non obscure testantur) deberi. *Artem Miram!* nullus non clamabit; at *Magis Veram!* mihi reclamare liceat.

Per GEO: DALGARNO

THE UNIVERSAL CHARACTER

I call upon each and every man, inhabitants of the whole world, of this and other nations, learned and unlearned, those who know many languages and those who do not: I bring to your attention a new art (sought after for many centuries with earnestness and industry, and yet in vain, by men of the highest and most eminent learning) namely a UNIVERSAL CHARACTER, based not on rank and ever varying linguistic usage, but on simple, certain, and immutable reason. This I call a *Swift Scribe* and *Faithful Interpreter*; the latter because with its help men of all nations may enjoy the benefit of conversing one with another; the former because what is spoken in any language can be written twice as fast. For there are numberless sentences that can each perfectly well be written by means of one or two characters, made for the most part by a single stroke of the pen, together with certain additional points of distinction. I propose nothing akin to the enigmatic Egyptian hieroglyphics, nor the laborious and (as is reported) near infinitely burdensome Chinese script, but an art that is perspicuous, easy, brief, swift, and convenient: all that will burden the memory will be contained on a single sheet of paper. A learner of average intelligence can with modest application learn it in one week, and after a second week devoted to the practice of it will emerge as fully proficient: and, although in this invention I owe much to a knowledge of various languages (notably Hebrew and Arabic), I have elaborated the precepts of this art, with so much perspicuity that they will be suitable to the capacity of anyone knowing no other language than their native one. Nor must I neglect to add that many things in this invention are due to those most illustrious men, truly distinguished among the learned of the present century (without disrespect to others), namely Dr *Wilkins*, eminent Warden of Wadham College in the highly reputed University of Oxford, and Dr *Ward*, distinguished Professor of Astronomy in the same university (whose writings not long since published on this art demonstrate clearly not just the possibility, probability, and usefulness of this invention, but also its methods and principles). '*What an art beyond belief!*' someone will cry; and my rejoinder to this may be: '*But a genuine one!*'.

By GEO: DALGARNO

A copy of this broadsheet is preserved in the British Library, Add. MS 4377, fo. 144^r.

A
NEW DISCOVERY

Of the UNIVERSAL CHARACTER, Containing also a more readie
and approved way of SHORT-HAND-WRITING,
then any heretofore practised in this Nation.

THis Art shall be of Common use, not to any one, or some few nations, but generally, to the whole world, and all the Inhabitants thereof, who are so farre civilized, that they can be any wayes capable of Instruction, and that in two maine respects: First, the people of all nations and languages, how different soever, by the præcepts and rules of this Art, shall be able to understand one another, as fully and clearely as if they should speake one unto another, in their owne proper Idioms, or, as if they had the gift of languages. Secondly, whereas there has been many laudable, and profitable Inventions in this nation, for a Compendious and contracted way of writing, yet take the best of those, or, them all together, they shall not be able to contract so much by an halfe as this, and that either for time or space, a current hand Indifferently practised in the rules, being able (if judgement and memorie could serve the hand) to write after two speakers at once. And albeit the best judgments shall be most profitted by it and soonest comprehend the difficulties of it, yet the method and præcepts of it shall be elaborate with such perspicuity, that by the help of a good Instructer it shall be made obvious to every ordinary capacity: And as the principall intended use of it shall be profitable to all, so shall the occasionale fruits of it be no lesse acceptable and usefull to the learned, the exercise of it bringing a great deale of clearnesse to the acts of the understanding, in Gramaticall, Logicall, and Metaphysicall Criticismes, and shall ripen the judgment to discover the superfluity of some languages and the sterility of others. The rules and full practise of the whole Art shall be attainable by any Person indifferently sedulous in a weeks time: The scrupulosities of those who quæstion the reality and truth of the thing undertaken, shall be satisfied by testimonies from the most eminent Doctors of both the Universities.

By GEO: DALGARNO

Broadsheet 2

Tables of the Universal Character (1657)

To The

Right Worshipfull, and eminently learned Doctors, D. *WILKINS*,
Warden of Wadham Colledge, and D. *WARD*, Professour
of Astronomy in the famous University of *Oxford*.

Srs:

Three reasons mainly have induced me to prefixe a line or two here,
inscribed to your names: first that I might give some publicke testimony
of my humble respects to your eminent worth among the learned of this
age, and of my thankfulnes for your singular favors and civilities conferred upon
me; next that I might vindicate my selfe from proving so farre injurious to your
honour, as to conceale from the world your labours and merit, in this present
literary affaire: for this I offer not so much as a dedication of what is mine, as
an ingenuous declaration that a great part of the worke is your owne: Lastly
that by the authority of your fame and names, I might guard my self from the
prejudices of ignorant and inconsiderate persons, who contenting themselves
with a stupid admiration of what their ancestors have already done, and not being
able to comprehend either the grounds or scope of art delivered by them, much
lesse the particulars wherein they faile, or the wayes of supplying their defects,
doe erect a *nil ultra*[1] within the narrow compasse of their owne capacities,
even anathematizing those who dare to say, there are Antipodes: But learned
worthies, you are of the number of those who have fortunately passed this pillar
of ignorance erected in the straights of knowledge, and have given an evident
demonstration, that there is yet a vast *America* of unmanured faculties in the
soule. That which I now propound is intended as an essay, towards the releife
of the confusion of languages, and how farre the principles I goe upon will
reach, ye know and have attested: my present designe is to give a proofe of
my undertakings, by presenting so much as may be sufficient to expresse the
common intercourse of mankinde: my method is simply memorative abstracting altogether from Philosophy: the periods of my table are composed more of
non sense then sense, so that he who carps at them upon this account, seems

A copy of this broadsheet is preserved in the British Library, Add. MS 4377, fos. 145ʳ–146ᵛ. This broadsheet is the one discussed by Dalgarno in the *The Art of Signs* (*AS* 78) and in 'The Autobiographical
Treatise' (CC, fo. 23ʳ). This shows his first attempt to set out the whole of his scheme on one side of
a single sheet, with the particles at the head and the radicals below. The radicals are arranged in
two tables, one of verbs and adjectives, and the other of substantives, each of these having its own
table of contraries displayed alongside.

  [1] 'There is nothing beyond'. The same tag is used in 'Omnibus Omnino Hominibus' (Broadsheet 5
below), fo. 141ʳ, and is obliquely referred to by the motto on the title page of *The Art of Signs*: 'hoc ultra',
which may be glossed as 'This is the way ahead'. The allusion here is to the words 'Ne plus ultra',
which, according to legend, were inscribed on the Pillars of Hercules. These were incorporated into
the motto of the Spanish royal coat of arms, the word 'ne' being struck out by Charles V when he
inherited the vast American possessions that went with the Crown of Aragon and Castile.

not to comprehend rightly the scope of the whole designe; neverthelesse such as they are I present them first unto your wor[ships], next unto all ingenuous and liberall spirits, whom to honour and serve shall bee the constant resolution of.

LEARNED WORTHIES

Your most oblidged servant

GEO. DALGARNO

GRAMMATICAL OBSERVATIONS

THe soules of men, though of a spirituall and heavenly substance; yet in respect of that neare and strict union betwixt them and their bodies while they are in this state of mortality, are not able to act & exert their intellectuall faculties, without the ministration of the corporeall organs of the Inferior faculties of the senses: the chief servants the body does afford the soule, are the eare and the eye, the one carrying in upon the understanding the species of things by the signes of variously and artificially modulated sounds; the other from the like artificiall variation of figures, which for the most part are not the immediate signes of things and the conceptions of the mind, but of sounds and words. Language as it consists both in sounds and figures, being that sole and great way of conveyance of the passions and affections of the mind mutually betwixt man & man; discovering even the most intimate motions and conceptions of the Soule, by which all humane societies are united, and the great affaires & transactions of the world are mannaged. It is scarce conceivable what advantages should redound to the generallity of mankind, if there should bee a rationall, artificiall, and compendious waye of communication invented and received, equally applicable to all Languages, by which the insuperable labour of attaineing of divers Languages might be remedied, in which all humane knowledge is so lockt up that none but those who devote themselves fully to that studie, are able to arrive at any perfection. What Irrationality is lying upon all Languages for want of Logicall rules, in Grammaticall flexions, and Sintax, rationall derivations, and art to help the memory in Lexicons; is not my purpose here to instance: yet I hope to the judicious and learned this shall in some measure *ipso facto* appeare in the serious weighing and considering the way and method of this attempt, which is undertaken for obviating that grand defect and imperfection Universally of all knowne Languages, to wit, by an artificiall variation of figures, answering to the like artificiall combination of the notions of things, and conceptions of the mind; and what is here done in figures, shall hereafter (by the assistance of God) bee performed by the selfe same art in sounds: and I am bold to affirme that any judicious man shall bee able to make a greater proficiency in this new language in a weekes tyme, then he can in a yeare in any other language, which ha's [*sic*] no affinity with his owne proper Idiome. But forbearing to insist in this place upon the nature of Language in a comtemplative way, my purpose is, only to set down briefly in so many words, the most necessary rules required for practicing this art, having designed these tables only for private use, & to bee communicated to none but those, who shall receive them from my owne hand, with an actuall explication of them *viva voce*, without which they can scarce be usefull to any. The parts of this designe are two, Radicall characters, and points of affixes: the first expressing the notions of nounes and verbs, the other their grammaticall flexions, circumstantiating particles, & rationall derivations.

Explication of the Table of Affixes.

THe Table of Affixes is divided into the Table of Particles and the Table of Derivatives, the art of both is to hold out the divers notions expressed in them, by contiguous affixed points about the Radicall character. The places of affixes about every Character are twelve, to wit, three above, three below, three before, and three after the Character. The points of affixe specifically distinct are only seven, whereof foure belonging to the Table of Particles have every one of them foure severall positions, which may be expressed thus, up, downe, right, and left hand, which holds uniformly in all the foure: so that the whole number of affixes, both of particles and derivatives extends to the number of nineteen, those nineteen keeping that same uniforme method and position upon all the foure quarters of the Character: so that every one of them according to the twelve places about the Character, where they are to be affixed, carries forth twelve severall distinct notions: as is evident from the table. It is to be observed for eviting of confusion, that those points which come to be affixed above and belowe be placed really without the body of the Character; and those before and after, are to be within the Character, keeping an equall distance between themselves; the first at the top, the second in the middle, the third at the bottome, which are places fully distinguishable and made use of in all brachygraphies. Above and below the places are thus distinguished, the first a little to the left hand, the second just over or under the very middle part of the Character, the third a little farther towards the left hand.

This Table is to be taken chiefe notice of, for in it consists the sintax of speech, the necessary flexions of nounes and verbs, and rationall derivations; yea in this Table is represented a perfect scheme of a Logicall Grammer which goes as farre beyond the Grammaticall way of all languages, in the rationality of its rules as it comes within them in facility, plainesse, & compendiousnesse; whosoever is able to mannage this Table aright is master of the whole art, for as herein lyes the chiefe rules of sintax; so those burden the memory more then all the Tables of nounes and verbs. This Table is set down in Latine because my purpose at the present is, chieffely to communicate it to schollers as also, because the distinct notions of particles are better rendred in the Latine then the English.

Of the Table of Particles.

THis Table containes a full enumeration of all the necessary and simple notions of particles requisite for binding and coupling together the radicall parts of speech, in any discourse: yea, the designe being intended to carry along a more compendious and contracted way of writing then any heretofore received; there are many notions of adverbs here made use of, which are not simple notions of particles, but might be derived from Radicall Characters, by the rule of derivatives. I shall subjoyne the particular rules in so many words referring the explication of them and examples to be done *viva voce*.

1. Persons and particles of Universallity and Particularity have places both before and after the radicall Character, for distinguishing them when they are agents, and when they are patients.

2. Affixes of persons are rendered personally with verbs, & as possessives with nouns.

3. The compound pronouns which (*ipse*) are expressed by twice writing the affixe of the simple, whether person or possessive.

4. Those particles which end in (ever) in English, and (*cunque*) in Latine, are also expressed by twice writing the simple affixe.

5. If two simple points of affixe come so to be written, that they express two severall particles they are to be set at a little more distance one from another, then they are set in the second place of affixes, where they expresse both but one simple notion.

6. Adverbs of motion, from, or to a place, are expressed by the adverb of rest, in place, and the particles (from) and (to).

7. In verbs expressing action or passion, there is no necessity of adding the affixe of the present tyme: but let it bee taken for rule, that those verbs written without any affixe of tyme are understood to bee of the present tyme.

8. Where nouns come to be coupled together without any other verb, but the substantive verb (sum)[2] for the more compendiousnesse, the verb (sum) may be expressed by the affixes of tyme, unless it be in propositions of (*est*) *secundi adjacentis*,[3] or some other few places, in which the radicall Character of the verb (sum) may be made use of.

9. Those particles which signify *adverbialiter* with verbs, being affixed with substantives they signify *adjectively*, such as *bene, male, præcipue, Universaliter*, &c.

[2] i.e. the copula 'to be'.   [3] i.e. the verb 'to be' as used to state existence.

10. The notions of (to goe) or (to come) are expressed, the first by a quadrangle, the other by a triangle, the reasons I can not enlarge here.

11. For reading any thing that is written in this Character, it is required first that the Table of Particles and Derivatives be perfectly understood, and had by heart; then let it be considered, whether the radicall Character be a noune or a verb, primitive or derivative, and if it be a verb, what tyme it's of, if it have persons before, or after it, what the notions of the other particles are affixed about it: which all being understood, the sense of the whole will immediately appeare: where it may be observed, that for the most part conjunctions are allwaies first read, adverbs or Logicall *modi* may be read either first or last, and yet the sense stand intire; the expression wherof is all here required: but a little practice will shew that there can scarce be error in reading, unlesse there be error first in writing.

12. If two or three particles come to be expressed with one ve[rb], which virtually & logically makes more the[n] one proposition then the sentence is either to be expressed logically by [again][4] writing the radicall Character, & every one of them it's proper affixes, otherwise if the Character before contractions cause, but once written, then the particle first to be read is set neerest the Character &c. e.g. I love you but not him, this is Logically resolved I love you, but I love not him &c.

Prepositions governing persons after verbs are to be set over the verb in their own place, and if there be two persons after the verb, to wit one governed by itself, and another by the preposition, that which is governed by the preposition is to be set at a little farther distance from the Character.

I am necessitated in respect of the narrow compasse of this sheet, whereunto I have confined my self to passe over the Table of Derivatives, without explication, as also many other usefull observations.

Of the Table of Radicall Characters.

THis Table is divided into the Table of Verbs and Adjectives, & the Table of Substantives: for understanding of the art and use of both, let it be observed.

Every particular table containes fourty two words, expressing so many severall distinct notions of things, (which this designe only considers without respect to synonymous words.)

---

[4] The printed broadsheet has 'man'. Although the printer has clearly made more than one error in setting this paragraph, perhaps because of the illegibility of the copy, the sense of the rule can be readily retrieved from the example given.

For helping of the memory to retaine these words, and render them readily by the Character, there is a story made up to couple them together, either by way of sense, or no sense, which somtimes is most helpfull to the memory: This story is divided in seven parts, to wit 1. a simple narration, 2. a continuance of the story by the particle (for) 3. (but,) 4. (therefore,) 5. (because;) & because variety is very operative upon the memory, the two last particles which are (neverthelesse) and (moreover,) give a quite contradiction, to what hath been spoken in the former part of the story, and this method is constantly observed thorowout the whole Tables. Again those seven parts of the story so distinguished, are contained in seven lines, whereof every one containes six words, and those again so composed among themselves, that three of them goe allwayes together by way of sense; Those words expressed in the Italicke Character, are but only expletive particles,[5] for binding the words belonging to the tables together, for helping the memory.

One of the great advantages of this art, is the expressing of all contraries by one uniforme rule, without any charge upon the memory: the rule is, *When the Character of the one contrary is had in the Tables, the other contrary is allwayes expressed by that same Character, with a single point put within it*: those contraries which are to be expressed with a single point added to the Character of it; contrary in the stories, are set *e diametro* opposite, to their owne contraries expressed in the story. Where it is to be observed, that I have not taken contraries allwayes from contrariety of nature, but from any ground of contradiction, which might help the memory, this being all I intend.

And it is to bee observed, that the order of the severall heads of the stories are carried on by the order of the particles of affixes, before the Character, that is the first story being made up in the first person: The second in the second person: The third in the third &c. The advantage of this is, the Character answering uniformly, by a numericall progression to this method, of the severall stories, he who hath any notion of the story, so that he can referre any word either to the story of *ego tu ille* &c. immediately he hath the Character to be written with. For it is again to be observed, That one Character carrieth out the fourty two words of every table, by fourty two severall distinct points of numeration which are affixed upon it, whereof all the characters I make use of, are equally capable: the way of doing whereof I referre to actuall explication, seeing the Character must be set down with my owne hand.

Briefly then for the attaining the perfect use of these tables: first the numerical way of the Character is to be learned, then the seven cardinall points of numeration upon the Character, answerable to the seven parts of every story: the seven distinguishing particles of the story are to be gotten by heart as they answer to the cardinall points of numeration upon the character; which by any of common capacity can upon a simple explication of the way be fully

---

[5] This is a slip; the expletive ones are those *not* in italics.

comprehended and taken. And this being once rightly understood carries out the whole designe; for the method of the tables amongst themselves, and the method of the distinguishing particles of the particular Tables (which is that same in all) being rightly understood and attained, there needs no more for doing all this designe is capable of, but to get exactly by heart those memorialls of the severall tables, which are composed by way of fictitious and foolish stories, which are apt to sticke more upon the memory then that which carries more sense and seriousnes with it. This being all then that is requisite for practising this art, to understand first the rules which are few, plaine, and easy, and then to get those few stories by heart; I am bold to affirme, that any man indifferently judicious and diligent, should be able both to write and read in this character in any subject so farre as the Tables will reach, in a week's tyme without the help of Tables set before him but simply, with the help of the memory. This I know will seem a thing impossible to many, but I hope experience shall confirme the truth of it.

It is to be observed, that all those words in the table of verbs and adjectives which are expressed in the stories either as substantives or adverbs, which is done only for the more conveniency of making up the stories, are to be taken radically for verbs, and adjectives, according as the nature of the notion is: so in the table of substantives all those words expressed in an Italick letter, are radically to be taken as substantives.

Then let it be observed that my main designe being to carry forth the common notions and conceptions of the minde, in the ordinary intercourse of mankind, if my Tables be not so full and comprehensive as many may judge they should bee; I give for a farther explication these following considerations, to be seriously weighed by the more judicious and learned. 1. The nature of this designe as it is intended for a common help & remedy of the imperfection & difficulty of the languages of all nations, (which is the chief and grand impediment that stops the familiar intercourse, commerce and mutuall communications between the people of severall nations:) requires only the expression of those notions and things, which are the same in all nations; so that the particular ceremonies, customes, and technick words of particular nations and languages fall not properly within the compasse of it, for if any notions of things proper to any particular nation should be expressed in other nations, they behooved to learn the nature of the thing, as well as the word or Character expressing it. 2. those common notions, necessary for making up discourse in all ordinary intercourse, consisting chieffely of particles which are *ligaturæ orationis*, coupling and binding together the radicall and principall parts of speech, and varying the formality of it, and verbs and adjectives by which are expressed the qualities of things, actions, and passions of the minde, motions, transactions of affaires &c. I hope there shall be scarce any simple notions of particles, and very few of verbs and adjectives found to be omitted. 3. I acknowledge the chief defect of my Tables will be in substantives: for I did strive only at the present to pitch upon those, which were most obvious and occurrent in ordinary discourse, as transcendent words, relations, members of the body &c. 4. I dare promise, that by adding foure or five more Tables composed in stories, (which God willing shall shortly be done) this designe shall be able to reach farther in communication and discourse then the most part of languages. 5. I desire it may be considered, that my intention being to expresse things and not the words of any Language; I take of that irrationality of all Languages of using many tymes multitudes of synonimous words for expressing that same thing. 6. It is worthie of observation by the learned, that beside that principall intended use of this designe, of facilitating the matter of language and communication, there are other choice advantages to be reaped by it: as chieffely, the practice of it teaches a man to abstract from the particular phrases of languages, which many tymes logically considered, are impertinencies and non sense, and to compose and expresse his thoughts in a plaine and rationall method, and (as I had it from an eminently learned person) it makes a man as it were dip his pen in his soul, before he deliver his thoughts: for it is the complaint of many learned men, that Rhetoricall flourishes of words doe often obscure best literature, and what strife hath been in the world meerly about words, is a thing too we'll known. 7. If the synonimous words of languages signifying that same simple notion, were collected and ranked together, (which for the use of weaker capacities is necessary and shall be done hereafter:) The extent of these Tables will appeare to reach a great length in communication. 8. This designe being chiefly intended for common intercourse as is said before, it is not to bee expected that it shall containe the numberlesse multitude of the severall *species* of nature and words of art & technick words of all trades, for this no language is able to doe, nor no one man able to understand, but those who would have those reduced to an artificiall way of expression, must make particular tables for every art and trade, which they must doe in all languages, notwithstanding there shall bee as many of the most common *species* of nature here expressed, as any language is able to doe without *Periphrases*.

TABLES OF THE VNIVERSAL CHARACTER

So contrived, that the practice of them exceed's all former wayes of short hand writing, and are applicable to all languages.

THE TABLE OF PARTICLES

Before the character	after
1. Ego tu ille	me te illum
2. Nos vos illi	nos vos illos
3. Hoc illud aliud	hoc illud aliud
4. Uterque reliqui solus	utrumque reliquos solum
5. Unusquisque alius neuter	unumquemque alium neutrum
6. Omnes aliquis nullus	omnes aliquem nullum
7. Omnia aliquid nihil	omnia aliquid nihil
8. Quis qualis talis	bene mediocriter male
9. Ubi unde quo	fere præcipue perfecte
10. Quid quare qua	certe possibile impossibile
11. Quando quamdiu quousque	facile difficile frustra
12. Quantum quomodo quam	forte probabile falsum
13. Quot quotus quoties	contingens conveniens necesse
14. Tot toties tantum	nunc tunc tandem
15. Solum satis nimis	iterum brevi diu
16. Cito opportune tarde	coram publice privatim
17. Statim aliquando nunquam	aliter particulariter universaliter

Derivatives

18. Facere, actio, infinitivus	actor, substantiv. activ., sub. pass.
19. Officium, incipio, genus fæmininum	instrumentum, tempus, locus agendi

The TABLE of Radicall verbs and adjectives

1. Ego

6. When I *sit down* upon a *hie place*, I'm *sick* with *light* and *heat*

12. For the *many thick moistures*, doe *open wide* my *Emptie* pores

18. But when sit *upon* a *strong borrowed* Horse, I *ride* and *run* most *swiftly*

24. Therefore if I can *purchase* this *courtesie* with *civilitie*, I *care* not the *hirers barbaritie*

30. Because I'm *perswaded* they are *wild villains*, *scornfully deceiving modest* men

36. Neverthelesse I *allowe* their *frequent wrongs* and will *encourage* them with *obliging exhortations*

42. Moreover I'l *assist* them to *fight* against *robbers*, when I *have* my *long crooked* sword.

above	*under*
præt., præs., futurum	passivum & non
plurale genitiv. dativ.	ideo quia quasi
possum debeo oportet	nam nisi ne
imperat. utinam licet	quod si quamvis
hic illic alibi	sed tamen cum
ubique alicubi nusquam	sic ut sicut
sursum directe deorsum	primo deinde denique
antrorsum à latere retrorsum	partim dimidium potius
supra præter infra	omnino quodammodo præterea
extra intra undequaque	usque vix proxime
simul juxta procul	tam quam secundum
contra inter circum	aut neque donec
citca apud ultra	hucusque adhuc quoque
per de pro	heri hodie cras
in cum sine	raro sæpe semper
super ab ex	magnum parum multum
ante penes post	valde magis maxime

adjectiv. neutrum, adj.act., adj. pass.	abstractum, adverbium, potentia
membrum, vestis, fructis	ars, vox animalis, morbus

Contraries

1. Ego

Rise up, lowe, displace, whole, darke, cold
F. few, thin, drie, shut, narrow, full
B. stand, weake, lend, goe on foot, walke, slowe
T. possesse, froward, rude, neglect, ____,[6] eloquent
B. disswade, tame, ____, serious, ____, lascivium
N. dissallow, rare, ____, discourage, disobliedge, rebuke
M. resist, at peace, ____, want, short, straight.

---

[6] The blanks in this table are place-holders indicating gaps where Dalgarno failed to find an appropriate 'opposite' word; in a few cases, where the original is ambiguous or obviously wrong, blanks have been tacitly inserted or moved according to what must have been intended.

2. Tu

6. *Worthie friend* be *entreated*, to *extoll religion* and *holynes*
12. F. *true vertue* being *found giveth* a *rich blessing*
18. B. your *courage concealed* in a *prison, provokes flyers* to *pursue* you
24. T. *hold firm* your *victory*, against the *heavie burdens* of *despaire*
30. B. the *great sufferings* of *misery, kills wicked servants*
36. N. you may *constantly sell deare*, and *continue* still your *idle questions*
42. M. you may *remarke* how *chast* virgins *conceive*, and *afflict sleeping* men with *nakednes*.

3. Ille

6. A *wyse teacher knowes*, what he *affirmes* and *understand's* what he *remembers*
12. F. he *chooseth* rather to *speake prophesies*, then to *please angry lovers*
18. B. when he *heares* and *sees clearly* they have *promised* to *honour* and *thanke* him
24. T. he therefore [*sic*] *absolves* them from *false accusations*, and *praises* their *flourishing innocency*
30. B. *hard beginnings* of *good, begett* a *lively growth*
36. N. he *commanded presently* to *bind* them, and *lead* them away and *hang* and *burn* them
42. M. he *punished* them so with *hunger* and *thirst*, that they *cryed* out *eating is sweet*.

4. Nos

6. We'l *call* this *old mad* man, and *tickle* him till he *fart* for *laughter*
12. F. the *pleasant mirth* of *itching*, will make him *scratch* his *white snowie* beard
18. B. *sharp byting wounds*, will *bury* his *lustfull desires*
24. T. we'll *feed* his *lean barren* corps, with *fresh savoury dinners*
30. B. *filthie stinking roasts, move* him *fall* a *vomitting*
36. N. we'l *penetrate* him with *fearfull thunder*, and *kindle unhappy flames* in him
42. M. we'l *prove* he *divorced* his wife for *dancing*, and *inchanted* her to *refuse* his *kindnes*.

5. Vos

6. You *vile breathlesse lyers, consider* your *wicked cutomes*
12. F. you *bowe down* with *deep groanings*, when you *use* your *flattering salutations*
18. B. you *contradict* the *comparisons* of *honest* men, and *vilipend* their *skilfull corrections*
24. T. your *seed* shall be *perfectly excluded*, and your *names blotted out* from *inheritance*
30. B. you *measure* the *creation* by *division*, and *hyde* the *world* with *coverings*
36. N. the very *despised shadowe* of your *comb*, shall be *accepted* with *sweating kisses*
42. M. your *wilfully ensnaring witnesses*, shall be *shot* through with a *rough plough*.

6. Illi

6. *Thriftie* men *paint* their *buildings*, only with *greasie blew* and *red*
12. F. by the *equality* of this *order*, they *take away* the *joynings* where the *raine poures in*
18. B. yet the *power* of the *frost* is so *nimble*, that it *impudently breakes* downe their *baking* houses
24. T. they *agree* to *spend cruelly*, before the *tempests tumble* done their place of *worship*
30. B. they would *vindicate* the *fitnesse* of *baptisme*, from *indiscreet* and *severe solitariness*
36. N. they *keep* themselves *unjustly armed*, to *hurt sincere undertakings*
42. M. they *force swimmers* to *admiration*, by *taking* their *beautifull sailes* from them.

2. Tu

Unworthie, enemie, threaten, abase, superstitious, prophane
F. false, vitious, seeke, receive, poore, curse
B. coward, tell, sett at liberty, pacifie, follow, defend
T. let goe, instable, yeeld, light, disburden, hope
B. small, doe, prosperous, quicken, godlie, free
N. unconstant, buy, cheap, leave of, worke, answere
M. ____, unchast, bring forth, comfort, wake, cloathe.

3. Ille

Foole, learne, doubt, denie, ignorant, forget
F. reject, dumb, come to passe, offend, content, hate
B. deafe, blind, obscure, performe, dishonour, unthankfull
T. condemne, ____, excuse, dispraise, wither, guilty
B. soft, end, ill, corrupt, die, decrease
N. obey, absent, loose, drawe, drowne, smoake
M. spare, full, drinke, silent, fast, soure.

4. Nos

Appeare, young, sottish, pricke, belch, weep
F. unpleasant, sad, sore, rubbe, black, haile
B. blunt, licke, cure, digge, ____, covet
T. poyson, fat, fertile, rotten, unsavory, suppe
B. cleane, odoriferous, boyle, rest, stand, spit
N. ____, dare, lighten, quench, happy, sparkle
M. improve, marry, play, conjure, graunt, unkind.

5. Vos

Pretious, strangle, speake true, rash, godly, unaccustome
F. lift up, ebbe, sigh, abuse, ____, valedico
B. consent, ____, unhonest, esteeme, unskilfull, fault
T. reap, imperfect, containe, nickname, ____, disinherit
B. weigh, annihilate, describe, shew, share, discover
N. respect, shine, brush, reject, faint, embrace
M. unwilling, deliver, attest, bend, plaine, harrow.

6. Illi

Prodigall, print, cast downe, browne, yellow, green
F. unequal, disorder, adde, disjoyne, blowe, poure out
B. unpowrfull, melt, wearie, bashfull, cut, brew
T. ____, win, mild, calme, slide, ____
B. impure, unfit, circumcise, discreet, meek, accompanie
N. lose, just, disarme, ____, dissemble, faile
M. ____, flie, astonish, leave, deformed, rowe.

7. Hoc

6. This *common writing* is very *satisfactory*, to *helpe sober preachers*
12. F. it *makes* them *prepare* their *thoughts*, by *judgement springing* from *numeration*
18. B. this *exercise belongs* not to *rebells*, who *endeavour treacherous councels*
24. T. this *excellent limitation* shall be *ordained*, that no *vaine boaster imitate* it
30. B. this *businesse* is a *glorious ornament*, *devised* for the *desert* of *ingenuous* men
36. N. this *ambitious purpose* is but a *dreame*, *crept* in and *dwelling* in *jealous* men
42. M. this *complaint* is *violently pleaded*, that it *hinders sinners* from *turning*.

8. Illud

6. That *theife* who *swears* he is not a *debtor*, should be *apprehended beaten* and *gelded*
12. F. that *Sacrifice offered* to a *redeemer* for him, is *blamed* as *crowning* him with a *slander*
18. B. that *stranger* who *besieges* & *cut's* him off, should be *recompensed* with *feasting entertainment*
24. T. that *hunter* who *vowed* to *attend* him, should be *chyded* and *banished* for his *payment*
30. B. he *sealed* a *pardon* to him in his *lodging*, and *acquainted* not the *barber* and the *miller*
36. N. that *exception* was *signifyed variously*, and *contrary wedgers* by *divers* men
42. M. the *strife* was so *charitably tempered*, that it was *committed* to the *watches* for *prevention*.

9. Aliud

6. Another *error* of *proud singers*, is to *defloure* maids with *wrestling temptations*
12. F. they *forbid* them to *spin* and *twist*, but *trie touching* and *smelling*
18. B. *another hindrance* is *put*, which *drives* them to *forsake* this *advantage*
24. T. another *disputation* is *diligentlie brought*, how a *drop stickes* in a *steep* place
30. B. the *hollownes* being *washed perishes*, and *sends* out *environing sinkings*
36. N. a *bald* man may *dip* a *bleired*, and *cast* him *revengfully* among the *planting*
42. M. another *carrier* may *stretch* him out and *plucke* him, and *separate* his *sound* from his *colour*.

The Table of Radicall Substantives.

[1. Ego]

6. I saw the *sun* rising in the *south east*, and a *hairie cat barking* at her
12. F. shee made the *sea* and *hils* like *blood*, and the *hornes* of the *sheep* like *trees*
18. B. the *wings* of the best *kind* of *foules*, covered the *fountaines* with the *feathers* of their *taile*
24. T. I put the *wheat barley* and *pease*, through my *kinsmens cheeks* to his *stomack*
30. B. the *bridegroome* my *schismaticall master*, stood in the *doore* & threw *stones* over the *wall* at me
36. N. I *needled* a *hole* in his *paps*, and *fingered* his *bastard beard*
42. M. I *sworded* his *arme* from the *elbow* downe, and *sad[l]ed* the *kings goose* for him.

7. Hoc

Proper, read, frustrate, _____, drunke, _____
F. undoe, _____, _____, _____, _____, _____
B. _____, _____, _____, _____, _____, _____
T. _____, _____, _____, _____, _____, _____
B. _____, _____, _____, _____, _____, _____
N. _____, _____, _____, _____, _____, _____
M. _____, _____, _____, _____, _____, _____

8. Illud

_____, perjure, _____, _____, _____, _____
F. _____, _____, _____, _____, _____, _____
B. _____, _____, breake, _____, _____, _____
T. _____, _____, _____, _____, _____, _____
B. _____, _____, _____, _____, _____, _____
N. _____, _____, _____, _____, _____, _____
M. _____, _____, _____, _____, _____, _____

9. Aliud

_____, humble, mourne, _____, yeeld, _____
F. bid, sowe, _____, _____, feele, tast
B. further, _____, _____, _____, prejudice
T. _____, slothfull, _____, _____, _____, _____
B. convexe, winnowe, _____, _____, _____, planting
N. _____, _____, _____, _____, _____, _____
M. _____, fold, _____, gather, _____, _____

Contraries

[1. Ego]

Moone, north, west, silke, mouse, hare,
F. river, valley, marrowe, hoofes, goate, herb,
B. fin, sort, fish, calcke, scale, maine
T. rye, oats, beanes, alliance, hips, guts
B. husband, heresy, servant, _____, _____, _____
N. pin, rift, navil, toe, _____, chin,
M. knife, legge, knee, bridle, subject, ducke,

2. Tu

6. Thou *eternally fabulous papist*, all thy *images* are gone to *hell* in a *morter*
12. F. thy *ship* was so *pumped* with *water*m, that the *waves* brake al the *plankes* of her side
18. B. thy *miraculous gifts* of *gold*, brought her *peaceably* to the *bottom* of the *rocke*
24. T. the *price* of they *glassen bells*, is *sensibly* worse then the *dirt* of the *street*
30. B. they could not *locke* the *deluge* of the *rainbowe*, & keep the *wind* from the *arche* of the *bridge*
36. N. the *sheets* of thy *bed* are not *lousie*, nor thy *cups* and *dishes sootie*
42. M. the *vessels* on the *table* of thy *church*, were *realy* the *almes* of thy *auncestours*.

3. Ille

6. It is a *qualifying attribute* of *faith* to love the *apostolicall ministers* of the *gospell*
12. F. the *halfe* of the *traditons* of the *old testament*, have no *materiall substance* of *grace* in them
18. B. every *word* and *letter* of the *proverbs*, is worth a *verse* of the *booke* of the *chronicles*
24. T. a *spirituall hearted man*, should give the *eucharist* every *yeare* to his *children*
30. B. *god* the *cause* of the *world*, dwell's not in *earthly houses* made with *hands*
36. N. every *day* in the *morning* in the *harvest*, he may fill their *bellies* with *butter* and *bread*
42. M. *hourly* all the *weeke* in the *summer*, he may make them *drinke wine* in the *kitchin*.

4. Nos

6. Wee are a *fortunate kind* of *people*, say the *honey bees* to the *flies*
12. F. a *heap* of *iron pens*, could not write all our *fellowes* in a *brazen table*
18. B. yet the *face* of a *wooden lion*, makes all the *parts* of our *members* as heavy as *lead*
24. T. we'll make a *woollen instrument* for *fruit*, and put *apples* and *cherreys* in his *waye*
30. B. the *axeltree* of our *cart wheels*, is as slow as a *snaile* after a *hart* or *salmon*
36. N. we'l take the *roses* and *lillies* from the *nettles*, & eat our *oynons* & *turnips* with *wormwood*
42. M. we'l pluck the *berries* from the *branch* of this *oake*, and *oyle* and *nuts* from the *shrubs*.

2. Tu

Tyme, history, protestant, idol, heaven, pistol
F. boate, bellowes, aire, cloud, board, midst
B. ____, reward, silver, warre, top, ____
T. ____, christal, ____, reason, ____, lane
B. key, ____, ____, ____, ____, ____
N. blankets, cradle, flea, jugge, spoone, chimney
M. ____, chaire, ____, person, ____, off spring.

3. Ille

Quantity, subject, misbelief, prophet, priest, law
F. whole, scripture, new-testament, forme, accident, nature
B. sentence, sillable, misterie, chapter, paper, revelation
T. body, head, beast, passeover, quarter, parent,
B. divel, effect, country, fire, towne, foot
N. night, evening, spring, back, cheese, drinck
M. minute, month, winter, ____, vinegar, hall.

4. Nos

Misfortune, sort, flock, wax, wasp, spider
F. ____, steele, inke, ____, copper, ____
B. ____, ____, ____, ____, ____, tin,
T. flaxe, ____, flowre, peere, plums, ____
B. pole, coatch, spoke, frogge, deere, trout
N. ____, ____, thistle, leekes, carrets, ____
M. ____, roote, ____, ____, ____, ____.

Broadsheet 3

News to the Whole World,
of the Discovery of an Universal Character,
and a New Rational Language (1658)

News to the whole World, of the discovery of an UNIVERSAL CHARACTER, and a new RATIONAL LANGUAGE.

This Design has been numbered as one of the chief *Desiderata* of Learning, and much longed for by the Learned, both of the present and former Ages, witness hereunto the renowned Lord *Verulam*,[1] the learned Doctor *Ward*,[2] D. *Pettie*,[3] Mr. *Comænius*,[4] Mr. *Lodovicke*,[5] with many others. High thoughts of advantage towards the advancement of all the parts of Humane Literature, and a more universal encrease of Knowledge, have been conceived from the discovery hereof; several attempts have been to this effect, but as yet without success of issue. I hope it shall appear from the following general Assertions, the truth whereof shall hereafter be demonstrated in particulars, that this present Undertaking shall be able to reach the production of all those desireable Fruits and Advantages to the World, which ever by any have been apprehended of it: Provided that, it being now ripe, and come to the birth, the cherishing care of the Supreme Authorities, and Universities of this Commonwealth (whom chiefly it doth concern) do tender its safe delivery, with suitable Encouragements to the exigency of the Affair; For if it be preserved from Injuries in its Birth, it will immediately thereafter be able both to nurse and arme it self against all prejudices, and will, as its nature requires, not onely spread it self, but carry along with it the fame and names of its first Patrons, over the whole World, to remain in an honourable remembrance to Posterity.

1. This Character shall immediately represent things, and not the sounds of Words, and therefore universal, and equally applicable to all Languages. 2. The Art hereof, shall not rest onely in a dumb Character, but by the same Rules it shall be made effable, in distinct and dearticulate sounds. 3. Which does chiefly commend the Art (though I know it will exceed the beleif of many) both the Character and Language shall be perfectly attainable by any of ordinary capacity and diligence, in less then a moneths time, so that two of quite different Languages may be made to understand one another, either in Writing or Speaking, within the said space. 4. This Character shall go far beyond all received Brachigraphy, for contraction and speed in Writing. 5. Whereas it is scarce known that Brachygraphy hath been improved in any Language but the English, this shall be equally practicable and useful in all Languages.

A copy of this broadsheet is preserved in the British Library, Add. MS 4377, fo. 143[r].

[1] Francis Bacon (1561–1626).   [2] Seth Ward (1617–89).   [3] Sir William Petty (1623–87).
[4] Comenius (Jan Amos Komensky 1592–1671).   [5] Francis Lodwick (1619–94).

6. This Character shall be more accommodated for an emphatick delivery of real Truths, and the grounds and precepts of Arts and Sciences, then any other Language; this will be easily apprehended by those, who are versed in late Mathematical Writers, who have begun to follow this way, by expressing words of frequent use with real Characters; and that partly because it works a more real and lively apprehension of the things treated of, and partly for compendiousness of delivery. 7. The Grammatical Rules of this Art, shall be few, plain, and easie, obvious to every capacity, because they shall be altogether grounded upon Nature and Reason, without any irregularities or exceptions (which Nature and Reason abhors) without any superfluity of univocations, or ambiguity of equivocations. 8. The construction and Phrasiology of this Character and Language, shall be such as Nature and Reason requires, and not to follow the impertinency, and non-sense of phrase of Languages; but to deliver Truth in plain and downright terms. 9. The true pronounciation and accent of this Language shall be easily attainable by the people of all Nations. 10. There shall be no occasion of error, or mistake in the Orthography of this Language; for the Writing shall be perfectly conformable to the speaking, and *è contra*. 11. This Character shall be a ready way, and singular mean, to convey Knowledge to deaf and dumb people (which is a secret of Learning heretofore not discovered) and it is conceived upon good ground that a deaf man might be taught to communicate in this Character, in the sixth part of the time that any other man could learn a foreign Language. 12. From the method and contrivance of this Design can be discovered, a more easie way of the Art of Memory then any commonly known. 13. From it may be drawn an exceeding useful *Janua*, whereby to enter the study of any Language. 14. It shall be a singular help to Discourse, affording variety of apposite words and epithets, and shall make a man understand his own Language, or any other he is Master of, more fully then he did, and shall teach him to distinguish betwixt Phrase and Sence. 15. All these things being made out, it cannot be denied, but that it will prove the most comprehensive, and advantagious peece of Knowledge that ever was received in Schools, for the education of Youth; for they shall be so far from losing of precious time in acquiring this Art, that by following the method and practice thereof, they shall redeem the half of that time, which others lose either in the study of Languages, or Philosophy, and besides have the practice of this Art, *gratis*, and by way of *over-plus*. If those whom it concerns, will mind the education of Youth, and Publick good so far as to make it practical this way; undoubtedly, the world will in a short time reap more plentiful fruits of it, then now can be apprehended. For 16. It may by Gods blessing be a great help for propagating the Gospel; and if neglected by reformed States and Churches, will certainly be improved by the Jesuits to that end. 17. It may be of singular use to civilize barbarous Nations, destitute even of the first elements of Literature. 18. It may unite the Nations of the World, by a more familiar and frequent intercourse and commerce, the cheif hinderance whereof is the diversity and difficulty of Languages. 19. Arts and Sciences may

flourish more every where, not onely because of the easiness of this Key of Language, whereby to enter them, but also because the method of this invention, discovers a way of abreviating and facilitating all other parts of Learning. From these brief Assertions, I leave it to every intelligent Reader to answer that great question to himself proposed to new Designs, *viz. Cui bono?*[6] Here I do profess that my main intent in publishing this Paper was to try if any would appear to own publick good, and the advancement of Learning so far, as to bring this design upon the Stage of a publick trial: For besides the testimony of several of the most eminent Doctors of both the Universities ready to be produced; I hope to rational men the thing shall be a sufficient testimony to it self. Any who desire the knowledge of this Art, or further satisfaction in those Proposals, may learn where to finde the Author, at the center of all useful and solid Learning, Mr. *Samuel Hartlibs* house, near Charing-Cross over against Angel Court.

By Geo. Dalgarno.

[6] 'For whose advantage?'

Broadsheet 4

Testimony by Richard Love (1658)

The possibilitie and great usefulnesse of an Universall character, whereby people of all the sundry nations of the World, how different soever in their proper languages, might with facilitie be inabled to hold a mutuall commerce, so far as not onely to understand each other by entercourse of writing, but also by way of a new-framed speech; is a businesse which in this latter age hath imployed the inquiry of many, and the endeavours of some ingenious and learned men. And doubtlesse were this attempt brought to its full perfection, it would evidence itself to be the rarest and most beneficiall invention which our times have given birth unto. I know no man whose industry hath carryed it on so far, or with so great dexterity, as the Bearer hereof Mr *George Dalgarno*: Conversing with whom about this subject, I found so much modestie in the Gentleman, so much rationality in his discourse, and probabilitie in the way of his designe; that for experiment I commended two young men, Bacchelours in Arts, to his directions in this way, for the space onely of one fortnight, allotting them no more for this business then one hour in the morning, and one other in the afternoon of the said dayes. In which small time they attain'd to that skill, that they both fully got the use of the character, and were able therein to expresse as well their own conceptions, as the conceptions of any other (for any matter of ordinary concernment) which were imparted to them, and what the one writ, the other (though absent and no wayes acquainted formerly with the least hint) was able both to read in this artificial new language, & to render the interpretation thereof in the *English* tongue. Which truth, as it was much beyond my expectation, so I think my self obliged to bear witnesse to; and withall (so far as is in me) to recommend this worthy and candid Person and his designe to all such men of a publick spirit, whose abilities or places afford them means to give encouragement to so hopefull an attempt, tending so much to an Universal good, in a way not onely of *Traffick* and generall learning; but also of *Religion*.

It seemeth to me a thousand pitties, that what in all likelihood will prove a means to bring much truth to light throughout the world, should prove it self abortive for want of help at home.

CORP. CHRISTI Coll. Cantabr.   RICHARD LOVE, *the Lady Margarets*
Calend. Maii, 1658   *Professour of Divinity in the Universitie*
                              of Cambridge.

A copy of this broadsheet is preserved in the British Library, Add. MS 4377, fo. 157^r.

*H*aving procured the Testimony of so Reverend and Learned a person, I thought it expedient (for inciting of others to put their helping hands to the production of this (as yet) Infant-designe, which now sticks at the birth) to publish therewith the Names of those worthie, and singularly ingenuous gentlemen, by whose Nursing care, (in their liberall contributions, according to their severall places) it hath heretofore been preserved from proving abortive: to whom with all other publick-hearted persons, who do with them joyn herein, the sole both praise and patronage of this work of so Universal concernment (what ever be the fruits of it reaped by posterity) shall be diservedly due.[1]

The University of *Oxford*
Attourney general *Predeaux*
Robert Boyle Esquire
Dᴿ *Theophilus Dillingham*
Dᴿ *William Dillingham*
Mᴿ *Thomas Woodward*
Mᴿ *Jacob Stock*
Colonel *Antony Morgan*
Captain *John Sparrow*
Captain *David Hembman*
Mᴿ *William Croon*
Mᴿ *William Bates*
Mᴿ *Francis Lodwick*
Mᴿ *Abraham Hill*
Mᴿ *White*
John Sadler Esquire
Sᴿ *Cheney Culpeper*
Dᴿ *John Bathurst*
Dᴿ *William Petie*
Mᴿ *Cooper*
Mᴿ *Staughton*
Mᴿ *Withers*
Mᴿ *Thomas Branker*
Mᴿ *Berrie*
Mᴿ *Gold*
Mᴿ *Floyd*
Mᴿ *Baccour*
Mᴿ *Cumberland*
Mᴿ *John Tillotson*
Mᴿ *Charls Bale*
Mᴿ *Thomas Slater*

[*Following names added in manuscript*]
Dᴿ *Joⁿ Wilkins*
Dᴿ *Joⁿ Connant*
Dᴿ *Joⁿ Owen*
Dᴿ *Edmund Staunton*
Dᴿ *Hen: Wilkinson*
Dᴿ *Wilkinson*
Dᴿ *Hen: Langley*
Dᴿ *J. Goddard*
Dᴿ *Jo: Wald*
Dᴿ *Jo: Palmer*
Dᴿ *Greenwich*
Mᴿ *Rob. Say*
Mᴿ *Tho: Barlow*
Mᴿ *Byfield*
Dᴿ *Ben: Whichcott*
Dᴿ *Ant. Tuckney*
Dᴿ *Fr: Walsell*
Mᴿ *Duport*
Mᴿ *L. Fogge*
Mᴿ *Tho: Pockley*
Geo: Crooke, Esquire

[1] This list of patrons includes a number of heads of Oxford colleges and others who would have been members of the body of University Delegates to which Dalgarno's scheme had been presented in April 1657. A modified list of sponsors, including only those who had contributed one English pound or more, was later printed in the prefatory matter of *AS*.

Broadsheet 5

Omnibus Omnino Hominibus (1660)

OMNIBUS OMNINI HOMINIBUS

Orbis Terrarum præcipue Dominis,
IMPERATORIBUS, REGIBUS, PRINCIPIBUS, DUCIBUS;
Qibuscunq; deniq; Dominationis, aut Dynastiæ Titulis,
Colendis, & Compellandis.

PRÆ OMNIBUS

Celsissimo & Augustissimo CAROLO

Magnæ *Britanniæ, Franciæ,* & *Hiberniæ*
Regi, Fideiq; Defensori, &c.
Bono Omine, & spe Magna, Regum Terrarum Maximo.

POST TANTUM REGEM

Subditis ipso dignissimis; Viris multis variisq; Honorum
Titulis compellandis, Generosissimis, Amplissimis, Rever-
rendissimis, Spectatissimis, Præestantissimis, &c.

Chen. Culpepper Baronet.	*Rob. Boile* Com. *à Corke, Frat. Germ.*
Edmun. Prideaux Armig.	*Jonath. Keat* Baronet.
Theoph. Dillingham T.D.	*Joha. Bathurst* M.D.
Guliel. Dillingham T.D.	*Gul. Pettie* M.D.
Jac. Stock Civ. Lond.	*Geo. Crook* Armiger.
Anton. Morgan Chiliarch.	*Cooper* A.M.
Johan. Sparrow Centur.	*Staughton* A.M.
David Henchman Centur.	*Withers* A.M.
Frans. Lodwick Civ. Lond.	*Tho. Branker* A.M.
Abrah. Hill Civ. Lond.	*Gold* Armiger
Whitle Civ. Lond.	*Baccous* Armiger
Johan. Sadler Armiger.	*Floyd* A.M.
Sam. Bifield A.M.	*Car. Bale* Civ. Lond.
Johan. Tillotson A.M.	*Tho. Slater* Civ. Lond.
Johan. Owen T.D.	*Fran. Walsel* T.D.
Johan. Wilkins T.D.	*L. Fogge* T.B.
Hen. Wilkinson T.D.	*Cumberland* A.M.

*Horum plurimis Ingeniossimis, Omnibus ingeniosorum fautoribus summis,
Patronis meis Munificentissimis, ideoq; Colendissimus.*

A copy of this broadsheet is preserved in the British Library, Add. MS 4377, fos. 139ʳ–142ᵛ.

TO ALL MEN OF THE WHOLE WORLD

<fo. 139ʳ>

and to rulers in particular,
EMPERORS, KINGS, GOVERNORS, DUKES;
by whatever titles to dominion and power
they are honoured and addressed.

ABOVE ALL OTHERS,

to the most Venerable and August CHARLES

King of Great Britain, France and Ireland,
Defender of the Faith, etc.,
by good fortune and grace, the greatest king in the world.

AFTER SO GREAT A KING

To his worthy Subjects; to those addressed by many and varied
Titles of Honour; the most Noble, Mighty,
Venerable, Revered, Distinguished, etc.

Chen. Culpeper Baronet	*Rob. Boile* Brother of the Earl of Cork
Edmun. Prideaux Esquire	*Jonath. Keat* Baronet
Theoph. Dillingham D.D.	*Joha. Bathurst* M.D.
Guliel. Dillingham D.D.	*Gul. Pettie* M.D.
Jac. Stock Citizen of London	*Geo. Crook* Esquire
Anton. Morgan Colonel	*Cooper* M.A.
Johan. Sparrow Captain	*Staughton* M.A.
David Henchman Captain	*Withers* M.A.
Frans. Lodwick Citizen of London	*Tho. Branker* M.A.
Abrah. Hill Citizen of London	*Gold* Esquire
Whitle Citizen of London	*Baccous* Esquire
Johan. Sadler Esquire	*Floyd* M.A.
Sam. Bifield M.A.	*Car. Bale* Citizen of London
Johan. Tillotson M.A.	*Tho. Slater* Citizen of London
Johan. Owen D.D.	*Fran. Walsel* D.D.
Johan. Wilkins D.D.	*L. Fogge* B.D.
Hen. Wilkinson D.D.	*Cumberland* M.A.

To the many most ingenious of men among these, to all of the greatest promoters of ingenious things, to my most munificent and thus most supportive patrons.

VOS omnes Adami posteri, vos (inqam) omnes omnino Orbis terrarum Homines, longe lateq; dissiti, variisq; Regionum terminis <fo. 139ᵛ> invicem dissociati. Primam vestram originem retrospicite. Hominum societatem non tam locorum longinqitate, qam linguarum diversitate, discontinuatam agnoscite. Scientiam omnem veram, fortuitorum signorum tricis involutam, aciemq; mentis ad altiora, Artiumq; ipsum fastigium, enixius aspirantem, verborum onere gravidam, depressam suspicite, Viros doctiores, hoc malum qerentes, frustra tamen remediam qærentes, tristes audite. Artem primam, maximeq; necessariam, hucusq; neglectam; alias vero (qantum fine hac poterant) laboriose, & ingeniose excultas, inertiæne genus humanum accusabo? Anne, Numinis decreto, majora & meliora Artis secreta, in ultima mundi tempora reservante, potius excusabo? En itaq; Mortales, Babelem corruentem, societatis humanæ vinculum, pontem animorum, Philosophiam vere primam, Scientiarum omnium januam, Artem deniq; Artium, ARTEM scilicet SIGNORUM: Eamq;, non tam industria humana inventam, qam casu divino repertam. En communia illa Rationis Principia, vobis omnibus pariter connata, oratione congruenti delineata. Ne igitur homo homini amplius brutum, sed vere homo esto.

Vos Orbis antiqi Incolæ, qotqot estis a Gadibus & ultima Thulæ, Auroram & Gangemusq; & ultra; Operosum, Barbarum; istum, docendi discendiq; medium, jam tandem, sero deponite. Mentes vestras, infinita, & confusa verborum farragine, nolite diutius excruciari; atq; in Scientiarum cortice, semper hærere.

Vos Judæi, Dei popule Antiqissime, qi nobis Terræ filiis, non solum Artium, sed ipsius Mundi, primam Originem patefecistis; Lingua vestra, aliarum onmium Antiqitate Sanctissima, huic tamen (Arte) Sanctiori, facilis cedat. Vos Sinæ oculatissimi, nolite qæsumus, nos monoculos, vestras res intentius intueri cupientes, fascinata spectra, pro Literis ostentando, excæcare. Ne Gentes cultas, barbarasq; (nullo habito discrimine) consuetudinem vestram ambientes, Monstrosorum Characterum, muris & turribus, societate vestra abarcete. Hoc certe, ultimum est Artis Remedium, ad vos in commune humanæ societatis consortium pelliciendos; qod si minus efficax fuerit, non amplius Artibus, sed Armis, ab ista pertinacia, pertrahendi eritis. Vos Indorum Brachmanes, Ægyptiorumq; Magi, Qid aliud est, homines vobiscum, Divinarum Humanarumq; rerum omnium scientiam, per brutorum simulachra haurire, qam homines brutescere. Vos Græci Romaniq; Artium Liberalium patres venerandi, vos tamen (valde mirum! sed magis verum!) vere barbaros esse, hinc certo discite.

Vos novi Orbis inculti Incolæ, fœlices vos præ nobis, qod animos qam agros, prius excolere liceat. Discite ex alienis malis sapere, rectamq; methodum Artium, prius qæ intra, qam qæ extra sunt erudire, cognoscite. Homines vos esse, non minus qam nos, ex facillimo omnium, qæ hic traduntur <fo. 140ʳ> traduntur intellectu, certo scitote. Qam autem Divina res sit Ars; hinc etiam, (non sine admiratione) erudimini.

All you descendants of Adam, all you people (I say) of the whole world, scattered far and wide, separated from each other by so many national boundaries. <fo. 139ᵛ> Look back to your first origin. Acknowledge that human society is fragmented not so much by spatial remoteness, but rather by the diversity of languages. See how all true knowledge is obscured by the trifles of arbitrary signs and how the sharpness of the mind, as it strives strenuously after the heights and very summit of those arts, is blunted by being weighed down by the burden of words. Heed those more learned men, who bewail this evil, and yet sorrowfully and in vain seek a remedy for it. Shall I accuse the human race of slothfulness for having until now neglected this first and most necessary art, while cultivating the other arts (as far as possible) with labour and ingenuity? Or shall I excuse it, since the divine will is reserving the greatest and best secrets of the arts for the last ages of the world? See then, mortals, the discovery (not so much by human endeavour as by divine chance) of the reversal of Babel—the fetter of human society—the bridge between souls, in fact the first true philosophy, the gateway to all of the sciences, namely the ART OF SIGNS. See here depicted in coherent language those public principles of reason that are known to all of you alike. Therefore let man be brutish to man no longer, but truly human.

You inhabitants of the Old World, however many you may be, from Cadiz or from Ultima Thula all the way to the Orient and the Ganges and beyond; now at last, put down, too late, that difficult and foreign medium of teaching and learning. Do not torture your minds any longer with that endless and confused mess of words; but stay always within the shell of the sciences.

You Jews, God's most ancient people, who revealed to us sons of earth the first origin not only of the arts but of the world itself; let your language, holiest of all others in its antiquity, yield place without difficulty to this more sacred art. You far-seeing Chinese, do not, we beseech you, render blind us one-eyed ones, anxious as we are to look more intently at your affairs, by displaying enchanting images in place of letters. Do not keep those civilized and barbarous peoples (there being no difference between the two), who seek your companionship, apart from your society by means of the towers and walls of monstrous characters. This is certainly art's ultimate cure, to allure you into full participation in human society. If this were less efficacious, it would take not arts but arms to drag you away from this obstinacy.

You Brahmans of the Indies, and Magi of the Egyptians, and those with you, what else is it, to derive the science of all things human and divine by means of images of brutes, than to brutalize men. You Greeks and Romans, venerable fathers of the liberal arts, learn clearly however from this (astonishing indeed! but nevertheless trueᵢ) that you too are indeed barbarians.

You savage inhabitants of the New World, happy in comparison with us, because you are permitted to cultivate your minds before your fields. Learn to become wise from observing other people's misfortunes; and understand that the true Method of the arts teaches you that which is inside your sphere of life

Vos deniq; (qidni dicam nos) fœlicissimæ Britanniæ, Incolæ cultissimi; non tam Orbe toto discreti, qam ex abstracta utriusq; orbis medulla, in centrum totius, firmissime concreti. Eja. Agite ocyus. Surgamus. Viros, vera virtute præditos, nosmet præstemus: Dedit nobis siqidem Deus O.M. hoc otium; non ut in eo, inutiles, turpiter consenescamus; sed, ut vires nostras omnes, in Artibus ornandis & augendis, intendamus. Pereat inter nos, omnis contentionis memoria. Homines de lana caprina certantes, consensu unanimi opprimamus. Sit nostra Britannia, Sanctum Sanctorum, Artium Officina, Mundi Schola, Domus Solis: non quidem vespertina, & occidentis, sed Meridiana clarissima, omnibusq; populis, hinc perpetuo orientis: Qo posito? Qis hodie Philosophorum, sic demonstrantem improbabit? Britannia est Solis Scientiarum Domus; ergo, Orbis Literati Centrum. Detur per nos, Scientiarum omnium continua circulatio: Sicq; nostra Britannia, si non primum vivens, saltem ultimum moriens, Mundi jam Literis animati, dicetur & erit.

Vos Mundi hujus Domini, & Moderatores, Monarchæ, Optimates, Populive; vobis in primis, Artibus opus est. Qis non novit, bellum ipsum, licet omnia fædans; qodq; vos solos penes est, Artibus gerendum esse. Novimus qidem, Furorem, aliquando unicum Armorum Artem extitisse: hic ministrabat, hic fabricabat, hic uti docebat. Nunc vero (Deus bone) [*illegible wordstem*]-tas vires furori, Ars furiosior addidit. Hiccine Artis Divinæ, mentisq; medicinæ usus, animatum hunc pulvisculum, qasi ex se non satis fragilem, Tormentis excogitatis conterere: Animamq; ipsam, nondum ad meliorem vitam maturam, crudelissime perdere? Permittite mihi obsecro, vos excelsi Judices Terræ, humani Generis causam (adeoqe revera vestram) liberius, coram Tribunali vestro, paucis agere. Qis Majestatis splendidior radius? Horridus Armorum strepitus, an dulces Musarum cantus? flamma ferrumq; an venusta Fana, Aurumq;? Eremus sqalida, an Paradisus amœna? Torridi cineres, an Turritæ Civitates? Mobilia Tabernacula, an splendida Palatia? Immatura Mors, an matura Senectus? Sed tœdet infinita recensere. Qid igitur Magnus Alexander? Qid Cæsar? Qid Pompeius? Qid Hannibal? Certe, me judice; Magni Latrones, sævi Laniones, vel, ut honestiori dicam nomine; Nobiles Carnifices. Qid autem Plato? Qid Aristoteles? Seneca? Cicero? Illis qidem multum contrarii: Peritissimi qoniam, morbidæ mentis humanæ Medici: Immortalitatis strenui assertores: adversus momentaneas hujus vitæ ærumnas, suavissimi Consolatores (qousq; nimirum naturæ lumen penetrare potuit.) Dicite igitur, vos pacis belliq; arbitri; Qid bello quæritis? Pacem? Nihil absurdius. An vivos <fo. 140ᵛ> inter mortuos? Horret animus. An vitam beatam, ex morte miserrima? Hoc sane, Divinum est qid. An Civitates ex Cineribus nascuntur? Reclamat experientia. Sed forte, iniquior sum in vos, & durus censor: vos mortalia spernitis, Mortem malorum omnium terminum, resq; mundanas, animæ inqinamenta, cernitis. Miseret vos hominum, fugaces & fallaces umbras, spe vana amplectentium; vitam vero æternam, propter has illecebras negligentium: Vobis itaq; pietas est, homines miseriarum hujus vitæ

before that which is outside. Know for certain, from your ability to understand with the greatest ease all those things that are being dealt with here, that you are human beings, no less than we are. <fo. 140ʳ> From this, you learn too (not without admiration) an art that is a thing divine.

Finally, you (and why not let me say *we*) most fortunate, most civilized inhabitants of Britain, not so much scattered through the whole world, as brought together most powerfully from the innermost parts of each half of the world, into the centre of the whole. Ah! Come, let us act more swiftly! Let us arise! Let us outstrip those men who have been endowed with true virtue! Since indeed God Almighty has given us this time of peace, not so that in it we might grow old, uselessly and shamefully, but so that we might direct all our energies to the embellishing and augmenting of the arts. Let all memory of contention amongst us perish. Let us with one accord crush those men who quarrel over goat's wool. Let our Britain be the Holy of Holies, the workshop of the arts, the school of the world, the house of the sun, not only at dawn and at dusk, but at the brightness of noon and for all peoples from this day, forever. Since this has been ordained, who today of the philosophers will condemn a man who is pointing it out in this way? Britain is the home of the sun of the sciences, and therefore the centre of the literate world. Through us, therefore, let the continuing evolution of all sciences be granted. And of the world now animated by letters, our Britain will be called, and will be, if not the first to have life, at least the last to die.

You Lords of this world, and governors, monarchs, aristocrats, or peoples, to you first of all the arts are necessary. Who does not know that war itself, although defiling everything, and although in your power alone, must be fought by means of the arts. Indeed we know that martial fury once was the only art of weapons: this used to supply, to build, and to teach men how. Now however (O gracious God!), a more furious art has added [*illegible word*] strength to the fury. Is this the use of this divine art, and of the mind and of medicine, to obliterate by contrived tortures this little piece of animate dust, as though it were not fragile enough by itself; and to destroy most cruelly the soul itself, not yet ready for a better life? Allow me, I implore you, lofty judges of the world, to plead in few words the case of the human race (and therefore truly your own) without hindrance before your court. What is a more splendid ray of majesty? The frightful clattering of arms, or the sweet songs of the Muses? The fire and the sword, or graceful temples, and gold? A barren wilderness or a delightful paradise? Burnt ashes, or turreted cities? Movable tents, or splendid palaces? Untimely death, or ripe old age? But it is a cause of boredom to recount an infinite number of things. What then of Alexander the Great? And Caesar? And Pompey? And Hannibal? Certainly, in my judgement, they were great brigands, savage butchers, or to call them by a more respectable name, noble executioners. But what of Plato? And Aristotle? And Seneca? And Cicero? These men are very much contrary to the former, since they were very skilful doctors of the sickly human mind, vigorously asserting immortality, the sweetest of

fluctibus jactatos, in portum salutis, qam brevissime, & recta deducere. Optime qidem dictum, si Dii essetis. Sed qis Deus aliqando docuit, omnibus ex æqo, & indiscriminatim, improbis probisq; vitam æternam esse paratam? Nonne potius certo constat, Deum unicum & verum, vobis nobisq; pariter Hominibus, hoc rapidum, vitæq; hujus instabile momentum, eo fine largitum, ut sordidas animarum maculas, in filii sui sanguine, unico salutis fonte, abluamus; nosq; (ut decet Regni Cœlorum Cives) Spiritus Sancti gratiis; omnibusq; qibus possumus, bonis Artibus, ornemus? His enim solis ducibus, ad portum salutis sempiternæ, tuto appellare licet. Vultis Nomina vestra, posteritati commendare? Vultis Regna perpetuare? Ditiones ampliare? Id tutius, certiusq; multo, Artibus, qam vi faciendam erit: Violenta enim omnia, suum accelerant interitum. Natura postulat Regem, sed Ars docet regnare. Qibus autem Artibus, ad regnandum opus est? Qamplurimis: Imo omnibus. Omnibus? Qid hoc est aliud; qam regnare, esse impossibile. Profecto, sine Consiliariis & Subregibus, ita se res habet. Qid autem causæ est, qod Ars regnandi, ita præ aliis, periculis plena sit? Dixi Artem hanc multiplicem esse, adeoq; difficilem. Triplicem vero cautelam, in Consiliariorum delectu, adhibitu necessariam (vel a Scriptoribus politicis, non satis explicatam, vel saltem, a Regibus non satis applicatam) sæpe mecum cogitare soleo. Primum expedit Regibus, in rebus sacris, & qæ ad Dei cultum pertinent, tales Consiliarios adhibere; qi ante omnia, pietatis sint singularis & eximiæ; summæ etiam eruditionis: qiq; inter contentionis flammas, notissimæ sint moderationis: Atq; qod præcipuum est, hic delectus fiat, non ex paucorum opinione, qi sæpissime partium studio abripiuntur; sed illi præferantur, qorum Nomina, popularis fama, superata invidia, propter dictas virtutes celebravit. In rebus vero, ad Rempublicam spectantibus, eorum consilia audire prodest, qi sint virtute Nobiles, sapientiæ exploratæ, experientiæ multæ, prudentiæ pluris, fortes pro Patria, a sordida avaritia in primis immunes; deq; suo sumptus impendentes, ut populi onera levent. Deniq; ut vigeant, crescantq; Artes, cum Liberales, tum Mechannicæ (in qibus omnis populi honos, opesq; posita sunt) ex singulis facultatibus & Artibus, viri ingeniosissimi ad consilium accersendi sunt: Præmiis simul propositis, Artium promotoribus. Hoc triplici, <fo. 141ʳ> Consiliariorum ordine stipatus, singulis intra suarum functionum Limites; se continentibus; tutius multo, qam in civitate; triplice munita muro, Rex qilibet regnabit. Sed qid facio? Qove dilabor? Qis, aut qantus ego? ut ad Regum consilia,[1] tam audacter accedam? Bona verba. Major forte hominum de me opinione. Qid si sine ullius Terræ Regum, læsæ Majestatis crimine, Rex ipse sim. Monstrum horrendum! Verissimum sane, & valde etiam dolendum; mentem humanam per omnia errori pronam, tot vanis conceptibus, monstrosisq; partibus sæpissime laborare. Sic ego nimirum, in dulcibus phantasiis, Utopiæ alicujus pacificæ, Rex sum: vel majori cum Gloria, Rebellium Oceanæ, debellator strenuus: aut etiam, qod ambitionis acmen terminet, Mundi Lunaris, universalis Monarcha? Hi Consiliarii mei, Hi Regni Proceres, hæ Artes Regnandi. Ast missis jocis, in re tam seria, esto. Deposita hac mea imaginaria Majestate:

comforters in the face of the momentary hardships of this life (as far, of course, as the light of nature could penetrate). Tell us therefore, you judges of peace and war, what do you seek in war? Peace? Nothing is more absurd. Or the living <fo. 140ᵛ> among the dead? The soul shudders. Or a blessed life, out of a most wretched death? This truly, is something divine. Or are civilizations born out of ashes? Experience loudly contradicts that. But perhaps I am being rather unfair to you, and a severe judge; you spurn mortal things and regard death as the end of all evils, and worldly things as pollutions of the soul. You pity men, as with vain hope they embrace fleeting and false phantoms, but neglect eternal life on account of these enticements: it is up to you, therefore, to have piety, and to guide men who are tossed on the waves of the miseries of this life, as quickly as possible and directly into the harbour of salvation. This would indeed be very well spoken, if you were Gods. But which God has ever professed that eternal life is ready for everybody equally and indiscriminately, for the wicked and the virtuous? Is it not certain on the contrary that the one true God has bestowed on you and us who are men alike, the rapidly passing and ever-changing brief time of this life for this purpose, so that we might wash away the filthy stains of our souls, in the blood of his son, the only source of salvation; and that we (as befits the citizens of the Kingdom of the Heavens) by the favour of the Holy Spirit and in every way possible, might adorn ourselves with the good arts? Only these guides to the harbour of everlasting salvation may be addressed safely. Do you wish to recommend your names to posterity? Do you wish to perpetuate your powers? To amplify your authority? This will be done far more safely and more certainly by means of the arts than by force; for all violence hastens its own destruction. Nature summons the ruler, but art teaches him how to rule. But which arts does one need for ruling? Very many. In fact all of them. All of them? What else is this than to say that it is impossible to rule. Truly, without advisers and subordinate rulers this would be the case. But what causes the art of ruling to be so full of dangers in comparison with the other arts? I have said that this art is manifold, and therefore difficult. I often think to myself that it is necessary to take a threefold precaution in the choosing of advisers (which either has not been sufficiently explained by political writers, or has at least not been sufficiently applied by rulers). First, it is useful for rulers, in holy matters, and those that pertain to the worship of God, to use such advisers as are, above all, extraordinary and distinguished in piety, and also of the highest learning; and who are, in the midst of the heat of the debate, most notable for their moderation; and, which is most important, this choice should be made not on the basis of the opinion of few, who are very often carried away by partisan zeal; but those are to be preferred, whose names are praised by public opinion, after envy has been overcome, because of the virtues mentioned. In matters concerning the public cause, however, it is useful to listen to the advice of those who are noble in their virtue, of tested wisdom,

<hr>

¹ The broadsheet has 'conlisia'.

Sim is, qi vere sum; Regis celsissimi, Subditus infimus, Consilione ideo abstinebo? Anne jam dicta retractabo? Minime faciam: Novi enim Regum esse, infimorum consilia non spernere; nec propter dicentis tenuitatem, Monita salubria rejicere. Verum ut eo insistam, qo primarius orationis scopus dirigitur: Vultis, vos Dii Mortales, ad Gloriam veram, vobisq; dignam, aspirare: Mittite hominum strages; Subditis vestris fovete, & in officio continete: Pacem cum proximis colite: qæq; in omne ævum, permanentia sint Monumenta, vos non inutiles vixisse in Terris: Edite præclara Artis facinora. Neve, sub NIL ULTRA, desidiæ Asylo, & Herculea Ignorantiæ Columna, vobis latitare permittatur. Ecce detectam, vastissimam Artis Americam: Qantam Gloriam reportabit, q[i pri]us[2] ex Regibus Terræ, ipsam occuperaverit? Via compendiosa est valde, & tuta satis, magno non est opus apparatu; ne igitur cunctemini. Sistite tamen paululum: Hæc enim omnia, ita sint licet; opus est nihilominus, itineris duce. Cui vero, ex tot magnis Mundi hujus Luminibus, operam meam hac in re offeram? Vah! Confundor! Nimius Majestatis splendor, me propemodum excæcavit! Sed, O me stupidum! Qid hic hæreo? Itane difficile est, Solem a Stellis discernere. Quis Gloria hac dignior, Rege meo, cui omnia mea, ipsumq; me (Mortalem scilicet), in solidum debeo. Rege (inquam) meo, Divinis patientiæ & pacis Artibus vincentissimo: Cujus Auspiciis, pax domi forisq; Orbi Christiano reddita est. Plaudite qapropter Huic, facilesq; cedite, vos Domini Sceptrigeri; neq; gravemini, Sceprtum Britannicum, recentis hujus Plantæ, (qandoqidem originis domesticæ) frondis; florisq; honores gerere; ubera enim fructuum Messis, erit vobis nobiscum communis.

very prudent, strongly for the fatherland, first and foremost free from base avarice, and making use of their own resources so that they might relieve the burdens of the people. Finally, so that the arts might flourish, and grow, the liberal ones as well as the mechanical ones (on which all the honour and wealth of the people depends), the most ingenious men of the particular faculties and arts must be summoned for their advice, while, at the same time, rewards are offered to these promoters of the arts. Attended by this threefold company of advisers, each keeping themselves within the limits of their functions, any king you please will rule far more safely than in a state fortified by a threefold <fo. 141ʳ> wall. But what am I doing? To where do I digress? Who am I, or how great am I, that I so boldly enter upon advising a king? Well spoken. Greater, perhaps, than people's opinion of me. What if I, without offending the majesty of rulers of any country, were king myself? A frightful disaster! It is indeed very true, and also very much to be resented, that the human mind, prone to error in everything, toils very often under so many vain misconceptions, and in monstrous tasks. Thus I myself am certainly, in sweet fantasies, the ruler of some peaceful Utopia; or with more glory, the vigorous subduer of the rebels of the Ocean; or even, which sets the limit of the height of my ambition, universal monarch of the lunar world. These are my advisers, these the princes of my kingdom, these the arts of ruling. But let jokes be dismissed, in such a serious matter. After I have put aside my imaginary majesty, let me be who I really am, the lowest subject of the loftiest king, shall I therefore refrain from giving advice? Or shall I withdraw what I have already said? I shall not do this at all, for I know that it is a mark of kings, not to despise the advice of the lowest, nor, on account of the insignificance of the speaker, to reject sound admonitions. But to emphasize that to which the scope of my speech is primarily directed: you mortal Gods, you wish to aspire towards a true glory that is worthy of you: give up the slaughter of men, cherish your subjects, and keep within the bounds of your office. Cultivate peace with your neighbours, and let those things be permanent monuments for all time, to show that you have not lived uselessly on earth; bring about beautiful products of art. And not so that you are permitted to lie concealed, under NIL ULTRA[3] (Nothing Beyond) the refuge of idleness & the Herculean Column of Ignorance. Behold the discovered vast America of Art: how much glory will he bring back, he who, first of the kings of the world[4] has taken possession of that very land? The road is very short, & safe enough, and there is no need of great preparation; therefore let us not delay. Yet stay a while. For, although all these things are thus, a guide for the journey is nevertheless needed. But to whom, among so many great lights of this world, shall I offer my work in this matter? Ah! I am confused! The excessive brilliance of majesty has almost blinded me! But, o stupid me! Why do I hesitate at this point? Is it so

[2] Lacuna in the broadsheet.
[3] This tag is used repeatedly by Dalgarno. See the dedicatory letter to Broadsheet 2 above.
[4] Reading *qui prius* for the two illegible words.

<fo. 141ᵛ> Serenissime Rex,

Rex Regum, frustra reclamante Terra, Cœlitus, tibi Sceptra, reddendo tradidit. Qam te decet, Christo Auspice, & Artibus Divinis, hæc tenendo regnare. Sit igitur, Celsissima Majestas, Ars prima Regnandi: Erga Deum, sincera, simplex, & non simulata Pietas. Homines tibi Subditos, Cœlestia spirantes, bene sperare jube. Legibus Divinis solutos, inq; omnia vitia humana solutos; fœlicissimo, qo cœpisti conatu, perge cohibere. Parasitarum impiorum adulationibus, *Vox Dei, non Hominis*, tibi acclamantium, Regio morbo perniciosissimo, summopere cave. Sit Ars secunda: Bonas Artes, animiq; culturam, omni studio promovere: Dumq; aliorum Terræ Regum, Sceptra sanguine madent; Tuum, ea, qa Rex tuus, tibi reddidit, Religione & Literis, hominum Mentes sanando, perpetua pace floreat: Pura enim Religione, Deum colendo; bonisq; Artibus, animum excolendo, ad summum hominis bonum, Tuumq; Thronum stabiliendum, unica est via. *HOMUNCIONEM ME*, ex obscuro prorepentem; humanoq; generi, novum hoc Scientiæ lumen, accendentem; Tibiq; insuper hoc splendidum Majestatis Jubar, offerre audentem, sereno qo soles vultu, propitius despice. Tu nostræ (vel potius tuæ) Britanniæ, Splendissime Sol; ex stupendo, & tristissimo abortu, nobis nuper (heu sero nimis) fœlicissime ortus: Sine, imo fac, ut scintillula hæc, scientiæ sublimioris, sub tuis carduis bis nata; tecumq; aliqamdiu obnebulata, tecum etiam, Mortalibus oboriatur: Atq; te Auspice, in omnem Orbis literati partem clarissimo splendore, effulgeat? Sicq; non solum nos, præsentis seculi homines; sed posteri nostri, per omnia futura secula, Te tantum rei literariæ Patronum, retrospicientes suspicient: & omni, sommoq; qo par est, huumano, Regioq; culta, venerabuntur, adorabunt.

Vos tandem, Patroni mei Munificentissimi, (salvo altorum honore) Angliæ flores & deliciæ; quod labores mei, serius opinione vestra, in lucem prodeant; non hic Morabor, causas docere. Spero tamen vestrum nonnullos percepturos, moram vires inventioni addidisse; Meq; tandem Policita & Debita mea, cum fœnere reddidisse. Ingratitudini forte a multis imputabitur, qod sicut vos, necessitates meas, Larga & Munifica Manu sublevastis; sic ego vicissim, Nomina vestra, lingua longiori, & vocifera non ebuccinem. Nihil sane est, qod Ingratitudine magis odi; nisi forte, a turpissima adulatione, adhc magis

difficult to distinguish the sun from the stars? Who is more worthy of this glory than my King, to whom I owe all that is mine, and me myself (although Mortal) in my entirety. My King (I say) who excels above all in the divine arts of patience and peace, under whose leadership the peace at home and abroad has been given back to the Christian world. Therefore applaud this man, and yield easily, you sceptre-bearing Lords, and do not regard it as a burden to carry the sceptre of Britain, the honours of the leaf and of the flower of this fresh plant (since it is of domestic origin). For the rich harvest of fruits will be shared by you and us.

Most Serene King,

<fo. 141ᵛ>

The Lord of Lords, while the earth cried out in vain against it, has from on high given back dominion to you. And taking possession of this dominion it befits you that you should rule under the auspices of Christ and the divine arts. Let therefore, most venerable majesty, the first art of ruling be this: a sincere, simple and unfeigned piety towards God. Order those who are subject to you, and who are bent on heavenly things, to be of good hope. Continue, with the same most happy effort with which you have begun, to hold together those who were released from divine laws and loosed into every human short-coming. Beware above all of the adulation of godless parasites acclaiming you *the voice of God, and not of man,* a most deadly affliction for a king. May the second art be this: to promote the noble arts, and the cultivation of the soul, with all zeal. And, while the dominions of the other kings of the earth are steeped in blood, may yours, which the Lord has returned to you, flourish in eternal peace through the healing of men's minds by means of religion and learning: for the only path to the highest good for men and towards securing your throne is by pure religion, the worship of God, and the cultivation of the soul by beneficial arts. Look down kindly upon me with your usual unruffled countenance, little man though I am, creeping out from obscurity, kindling this new light of science for the human race, and having the boldness to offer you this splendid light of majesty. O most brilliant sun of this Britain of ours (or rather, of yours) having risen most happily to us recently (alas, too late!) from an overwhelming and most tragic miscarriage. Allow it to be—nay, bring it about—that this little spark of a more lofty science should be twice born under your thistles. And with you, having for some time been surrounded by mist, and also with you, let it appear to mortals; and let it shine out, under your auspices, to every part of the learned world, with the clearest brilliance. And thus shall not only we, people of the present century, but also our posterity throughout all future centuries, look up to you in retrospect as such a great patron of the cause of letters. And they will venerate and adore you with all manner of the greatest reverence that is fitting for human and royal worship.

You finally, my most generous patrons (without offending the honour of others), beloved flowers of England; I shall not delay in telling you why my

abhorreat animus. Novi satis, hoc unicum a me vobis gratum fore, operam susceptam, in usum publicum, summa cum cura & diligentia perficere. Cumq; amplissima vestra Munera, <fo. 142ʳ> non tam mihi qam Reipublicæ Literariæ, sint donata; præcipuum (ni fallor) gratitudinis officium, in eo erit positum; ut omnes Musarum amicos, & alios qoscunq; generi humano bene optantes, ad gratias dignas vobis referendum, mecum provocem. Pergite, virtuosorum Antistites, vobis non nati, generi vestro (licet ignaro, ideoq; invito & ingrato) benefacere: Virtus enim sibi Sufficiens est præmium. Valete.

> *Humano Generi omnibus studiis deditissimus; ejusq; causa, Regibus Terræ omnia fausta, animitus comprecans; Regis veromei, Subditus Subditissimus; Patronorumq; meorum, Cliens & Alumnus Gratissimus.*

Geo. Dalgarno.

Epistolam hanc Dedicatoriam, ideo placuit sine ipso opere ad qorundam manus præmittere, ut certiores fiant ii, qibus vel officio, vel cordi est, Artes propagare; Conceptus meus de *Arte Signorum* (vulgo *charact. univers.*) jam maturatos in partu hærere. Characterem hujus Characteris, qantum patitur angustia hujus pagella dabo. Non suscipio (ut imaginantur plurimi) hominibus scientiam omnium Linguarum inspirare; nec talem Charact. describere, cujus significatio ex simplici intuitu, sine doctrina, omnibus innotescat. Sed Artem doceo, imponendi Nomina Rebus: Cujus praxis ad Communicandum tantæ sit facilitatis (qod fidem multorum super-abit) ut ea, homines diversissimorum Idiomatum (si mediocris ingenii & diligentiæ fuerint, spatio 14 dierum, majoris, minori tempore, minoris, majore) omnia animi sensa mutuo communicare possunt, qæ in lingua materna vel qalibet alia. Ingeniosos & capaces erudiet in Rerum natura: non enim casu sed ratione imponuntur signa. Signa Radicalia & Primitiva ad numerum 500 non pervenient; hæcq; non ex mero Arbitrio imposita, sed methodicæ Rerum dispositioni respondebunt. Soni Euphonici erunt, & omnibus populis pronunciatu faciles: nulla homonymia in vocum significatione: nulla anomalia in flexione; Ut paucis, & clare dicam; vocum *significatio, flexio, derivatio,*

labours should, rather late in your opinion, come forth into the light. Yet I hope that some of you will perceive that the delay has added to the strength of the invention; and that I have finally paid back what I have promised and owed, with interest. It will perhaps be considered ingratitude by many that, whereas you have alleviated my needs amply and with generous hand, I in my turn do not articulate your names at length and loudly. Truly there is nothing I hate more than ingratitude, unless perhaps my heart abhors the most disgraceful flattery still more. I know well enough, that this alone from me will be pleasing to you—namely, to complete with the greatest care and diligence the work that has been undertaken for public use. And since your very ample support has much been given <fo. 142ʳ> not so much to me, as to the Republic of Letters, the principal (if I am not mistaken) duty of gratitude will lie in this, that I call forth all friends of the Muses, and whoever else wishes good for human kind, to join me in giving you due thanks. Continue, O high priests of the virtuosi, to benefit your unborn offspring (although they be ignorant, and therefore unwilling and ungrateful), for virtue is its own reward. Farewell.

> *Most dedicated to all studies for the human race; and for its sake, praying with all my heart for all that is favourable to the kings of the world, the most humble subject of my true king, and my patrons' most grateful client and pupil.*

> Geo. Dalgarno.

I t seemed good to send this dedicatory epistle ahead, without the work itself, to certain people, so as to inform those whose task or pleasure it is to propagate the arts. My ideas concerning the art of signs (or a universal character) are now matured, but stick at birth. I will indicate the character of this character insofar as the narrow compass of this little page permits. I do not undertake (as many would imagine) to breathe into people a knowledge of all languages; nor to describe a character so structured that its meaning would become known to all men simply by intuition and without instruction. But I present an art for assigning names to things that is so easy to apply in communication (as will exceed the belief of many) that thereby people who speak completely different languages (in the space of fourteen days with average intelligence and industry, and more or less as the case may be) can communicate to one another all the thoughts that they can in their native tongue or any other language. It will instruct the talented and receptive in the nature of things, for the signs are established not at random but according to reason. The radical and primitive signs will not amount in total to 500; and these will not be established on the basis of pure arbitrariness, but will correspond to a methodical arrangement of things. The sounds will be euphonic, and easy to pronounce by all nations.

compositio, Constructio, phrasis, omnia, præceptis logicis regulabuntur. Hæc enim est regula principalis in hac Arte. *Ea tantum sunt derivativa vel composita, quæ talia sunt & in Re & in Signo, per regulam certam semper sibi similem.* Hæ igitur voces *mei, mihi, nos, fui esse, mors, vita, justitia, bonitas, fortitudo, ira, amor, gaudium*, &c. Secundum hanc regulam sunt vere primitiva; & non minus memoriam onerant (qod valde attendendum est) qam ipsa themata. Atq; hoc pacto, mihi constat, voces primitivas Linguæ Latinæ, numerum 60000 excedere: præter loquendi formulas rationi non consentaneas, ut Anglice, *Put out the Candle, bear with him,* <fo. 142ᵛ> *fie upon it,* &c. Qorum intellectio, ex ipsis vocibus separatim acceptis, non sequitur sine nova institutione, & memoriæ labore. Ars hæc, erit præ aliis, Poesi longe aptissima; Dicendi copiæ & ornatui, mire inserviens, Aptissimum medium ad gignendem Scientiam in surdis, & cum iis communicandum. Ad docendas Artes, sola hæc est idonei; & propter hujus defectum, Artes, vel potius Ars, Log. Metap. Gram. verborum caligine obscurata, imperfecta & inculta jacet. Cryptog. etiam longe aptissima. Præeter hos & multos alios usus practicos; in Theoria, veritates Philosophicæ variæ aperientur, *v.g.* Nullas dare notiones transcendentales, vel extravagantes; ut de *uno, vero, bono*, fabulantur, potius qam philosophantur, Metaphysici. *Substare* & *Accidere*, non esse primas, nec adæqatas *Entis* differentias: Multo tamen aliter Philosophando de conceptu *Substantiæ*, qam Tho. Hobbes: ad cujus Atheisticas ratiocinationes evertendas, prohibitur: impossibile esse, dari propositionem sine verbo Substantivo: & *Notiones* (non dico *Voces*) *Entis* & *Essentiæ*, non magis derivari ab (*est*) verbo, qam *Thomas a Lapide*. Secundum præsentem Philosophiæ constitutionem, nullam dari Definitionem proprie dictam; adeoq; nec Demonstrationem: Unica illa igitur definitio, in ore omnium jactata, *Homo est Animal rationale*, non est essentialis & propria. Hujusmodi Propositiones negativas, *Homo non est Lapis*, licat veras, secundum usum vulgarem, Stricte tamen loqendo, esse implicatorias. Has, *Non Homo est Lapis, Homo est non Lapis*, esse absurdas, ridiculas, & nihil significantes; nisi reductive. Haec & similia plura, solidis rationibus sine ullo Sophismate (Deo volente) probabo. Non dico omnes; (spero tamen plurimos eosq; viros doctiores) mecum consensuros. Qis aut qantus futurus sit fructus hujus Artis, parce hic dicam. Hoc tamen velim perpendant viri docti. Qid si Plato vel Aristot. hanc Artem detexissent, cum tanta facilitate practica qantam ego hic polliceor, eaq; in Artibus tradendis, usi fuissent? Profecto, mihi nullum est dubium, qin ante hæc mundi tempora, omnes homines mutua societate cum aliis fruentes, hac lingua usi fuissent: non qidem dico, usum vernacularum Linguarum, omnino fuisse aboletum, nec omnes hebetes & Idiotas, hujus usum calluisse. Nec minus est probabile, si Reges (nisi forte dici possit, utilitatem longe plus commendaturam, qam Regum authoritatem) Artem hanc omnium aliarum, ut facillimam, sic utilissimam, in Scholas introducerent, qin temporis progressu (modo tempus brevi non desinat) cum posteris nostris eundem successum haberet; & conseqenter mundi statum, ab eo qi

There will be no homonymy in the meaning of words, and no anomaly in the inflections. To put the matter clearly and in a nutshell: the *meaning, inflection, derivation, composition, construction,* and *phrasing* of words, *everything* will be regulated by logical rules. This is the principal rule of this art: *All that is derivative or composite is so both in the Thing and in the Sign, by a certain and invariable rule.* Thus the following words: *mine, to me, we, I was, to be, death, life, justice, goodness, bravery, anger, love, joy,* etc. are truly primitive according to this rule, and they will no less burden the memory (as should be carefully noted) than the topics themselves. And I am sure that in this fashion the primitive words of the Latin tongue exceed the number of 60,000, not counting idiomatic expressions that do not conform to reason, such as in English *put out the candle, bear with him, fie upon it,* etc., which cannot be understood on the basis of the meaning of the words taken individually, without a new convention and labour of the memory. This art will be most suitable to poetry, much more so than others, and will serve excellently for copious and embellished speech. It will be a most convenient means for instilling knowledge in deaf-mutes, and for communication with them. It will be uniquely helpful for the teaching of the arts; indeed the lack of it is the reason why the arts, or rather the single art, of Logic, Metaphysics, and Grammar remain imperfect and unimproved, obscured as they are by a mist of words. It will be likewise of great use in cryptography, and will have many other practical uses besides these. On the theoretical side, various philosophical truths will be uncovered, for example, that there are no transcendental or 'extravagant' notions, such as *one, true, good,* about which the metaphysicians ratiocinate rather than philosophize. It will be shown that *Substance* and *Accident* are not the first nor adequate differences of *Being,* and a quite different way of thinking about the concept of *Substance* than that of Thomas Hobbes will be defended, so as to overthrow his atheistic ratiocinations. Furthermore, that it is impossible to form a proposition without the substantive verb, and that the *notions* (I do not say the *words*) of *Ens* [Being] and *Essentia* [Essence] are no more derived from the verb *esse* [to be] than *Thomas* [*a Lapide*] derives from *Stone.* According to the present state of philosophy, there is no such thing as a definition properly speaking, nor indeed a proof either; therefore the definition that trips from everybody's lips, *Man is a rational animal,* is neither essential nor proper. Negative propositions such as *A man is not a stone,* even if true according to common usage, are strictly speaking incoherent. Those such as *Not-man is a stone* and *A man is a not-stone,* are absurd, ridiculous, and without meaning, unless reductively. These things and several others of this sort I shall demonstrate, on solid grounds and without any fallacies (God willing).[5] I hope that most even if not all men, and especially the more learned, will agree with me. What or how great will be the future benefit of this art, I will not venture to say. However, I would wish that the learned might bear the

---

[5] See *AS,* ch. 8, esp. pp. 62–5.

nunc est, valde transformaret. *Ne ingratus videar viris multis, de humano genere, & me bene merentibus: Sciatur, me propter hujus Schedulæ angustiam eorum Nomina tantummodo hic adscripsisse, qorum munera, Libram Anglicanam super-abant; vel ad minimum hanc summam complebant; qapropter aliis alibi gratiam debitam persolvam.*

following in mind. What if it had been Plato or Aristotle that had uncovered this art, one having as much practical convenience as I here promise, and had made use of it in transmitting the arts? I have no doubt that, before the present age of the world, all men who enjoy communication with each other would indeed have been making use of this language. This is not to claim that the use of the vernacular languages would have been completely done away with, nor that all feeble-minded and idiots would have grasped the use of it. Nor is it less probable that monarchs (unless it could perchance be said that utility is much more commendation than royal authority) would have introduced this art—more easy and more useful than all others—into schools; and that, with the passage of time (provided that time will not soon end), it will have the same success with our progeny, and consequently will fundamentally transform the state of the world from what it now is. *Lest I seem ungrateful to many men, to the human race, and to those deserving well of me, I wish it to be made clear that, because of the restricted space available in the present booklet, I have listed above only the names of those whose support was in excess of one English pound, or at least reached that amount. For this reason, I will pay due thanks to others elsewhere.*

PART II

THE ART OF SIGNS (1661)

Ars Signorum,

VULGO

CHARACTER UNIVERSALIS

ET

LINGUA PHILOSOPHICA.

Qa poterunt, homines diverſiſſimorum Idiomatum, ſpatio duarum ſeptimanarum, omnia Animi ſua ſenſa (in Rebus Familiaribus) non minus intelligibiliter, ſive ſcribendo, ſive loquendo, mutuo communicare, qam Linguis proprius Vernaculis. Præterea, hinc etiam poterunt Juvenes, Philoſophiæ Principia, & veram Logicæ Praxin,citius & facilius multo imbibere, qam ex vulgaribus Philoſophorum Scriptis.

Authore Geo. Dalgarno, ——— *hoc ultra.*

LONDINI,

Excudebat *J. Hayes*, Sumptibus Authoris, Anno reparatæ ſalutis, 1661.

Title-page to 'The Art of Signs'

The Art of Signs

OR

A UNIVERSAL CHARACTER

AND

PHILOSOPHICAL LANGUAGE.

By means of which speakers of the most diverse languages will in the space of two weeks be able to communicate to each other all the notions of the mind (in everyday matters), whether in writing or in speech, no less intelligibly than in their own mother tongues. Furthermore, by this means also the young will be able to imbibe the principles of philosophy and the true practice of logic far more quickly and easily than from the common writings of philosophers.

By Geo. Dalgarno, —— *hoc ultra.*

LONDON

Printed by *J. Hayes*, at the Author's Expense;
In the year of restoration, 1661.

<sig. A2ʳ>

Shod CAROLOI

KANEL Sʋfa, tηn Sefap,
sηf Britannoi sʋma, Hibernoi,
Francoi; tηn Krumel sηf
Tʋpu Siba Christoisa

Kanel Sʋfa

KANELLI suna sηf Nom, sʋmpomesi avvi sʋma, lul, Sava Kanel sηf Kanelli samesa bred Nam sas Lηl; Tηn lol-sas, lelilli punefi, Lηl <sig. A2ᵛ> samesu avvi sʋma ben Nom sas lelil; trim avvi sηf kusu shom krusu. Avvi sʋfa sηf krusu, tim, spηnu tηn sʋn-samu sηf Temmu, lul, samesi Stenu tipo, stηfo, tηn pomo. Tηn slun, tim stηfu sηf Stenu, lul-dan, Temmu tηn Tennu tim popo, slʋn, tim stηfu sηf Kanel, lul-dan tim Kanel sηf Kranelli tibo. Temmu samesi Stenu sefa, sʋn, shumu sηf uvvi tηn stηbbu, shʋn; sas, avvi lola tim sof-sefa shηg Temu. Kanel Sʋfa, lal Kranel Lηla shʋfa spηfesi shod Lηl Temu sʋfa, lul, spηnosa dan sηpdannu shuma sʋba: Lηl sʋb-dan tisesa sprηfu Lηla, stʋme tηn pemre trʋnu Lηla safesʋ tʋtu lola: Tηn Lηl tubesa, slam Trinnu Lηla, kranelli lηla tibo, pʋnesʋ Sagu Lηla Kana. Stηpu shʋma sisresu Temu lola <sig. A3ʳ> sʋma; tηn lolir samesu Tonu tηn Stηfu Lηla, tηn Tonu sηf Stenu, tηn (lul tim sʋn) Tonu sηf Sava, pemo bred daddu brepa sηf Nom. Lol-sas Kanel Sʋm-sefa, tupeso Kafelli, Tibelli, tηn Temelli Lηla, tηbesʋ pipai sibu tηn sigu sηf Temu lola; tηn lul-dan Lηl pemesa taggu sηf lelilli shop lela, sim-sodeso shod Sasel tηn Spηnel, sos satu sηf spηppu sηf lelil. Lal trim tunesi Stηffu tηn Stηbbu; shom, sηs-sηpu lela, lul, sefresu lal slemesʋ tηn sisresʋ Temu lola semo, sham skradu sηf Sava, Sηfu sηf Lηl Kanel lala,

To CHARLES

<sig. A2ʳ>

Greatest and Most Mighty KING,
of Great Britain, Ireland,
France; and Defender of
the True[1] Christian Faith

Greatest King,

ALL the kings of the earth greatly admire the great things that God the King of Kings has done in heaven for you; and for this reason they expect you <sig. A2ᵛ> to bring about great things on earth for him; not things of war but of peace. The greatest things of peace are invention and advancement of the arts, which make a nation famous, honoured, and admired. And as it is the honour of a nation when the arts and sciences are valued, so it is the honour of a king when [he is] the king of educated subjects. Arts make a nation the more powerful, a great number of people and riches make it the less; for these things are without power in the absence of art. Greatest King, I, your lowliest subject, offer to you the noblest art that has been invented[2] for many generations past. You have previously expressed your acceptance, promising and declaring your decision to help this enterprise. And you have encouraged, by your writings, your educated subjects to follow your royal example. A small outlay will perfect[3] this great art; <sig. A3ʳ> and this thing will make your name

---

[1] The word *sib* is not in the tables of the 'Lexicon Grammatico-Philosophicum' (see the fold-out table at the end of this volume), but in handwritten annotations made by Dalgarno in a printed copy of *AS* (Bodleian Library, 8° A 130 Linc), this form is added, and defined as 'truth'.

[2] The ending *-osa* does not occur in the list of grammatical inflections in the Lexicon Grammatico-Philosophicum, but is similarly used in an example on *AS* 76.

[3] The form *sisresu* is evidently composed of *sis-re-esu*: perfectio + make + future. The ending *-esu* is not listed in the 'Lexicon Grammatico-Philosophicum', but is defined in Dalgarno's annotations as indicating future tense. See Introduction, Sect. 3.3.2.

sim-tipu sηf Stenu lala, sigu sηf uvvi suna, tηn sηbu sηf Eiv lala. Lolirri tim shammu sυma, sham lul, lal <sig. A3ᵛ> pebesi sηpesυ; tηn lul-dan Sava sabesa lal sham lelirri, trim prebesυ shηpesυ. Tηn slem lel-dan, lal tim,

Kanel Sυf-sefa

Kranel Lηla krυba

Georgoi Dalgarnoi

and honour, and the name of the nation, and (which is more) the name of God, to be known in the farthest[4] places of the earth. Therefore, most mighty King, command your clerics, teachers, and artists, to test diligently the truth and utility of this art; and when you have learned their judgements of it, do well to the author and inventor, according to the merit of the labours of this person. I do not ask for honours and riches, but for such livelihood as will enable me to continue and perfect this now-initiated art, for the praise of God, the interest[5] of you my King, the glory of my nation, the benefit of all men, and the salvation of my soul. These things are great ends for which I am willing <sig. A3ᵛ> to live; and when God has employed me for these things, I am not unwilling[6] to die. And until then, I am,

Mightiest King,

Your obedient[7] subject,

George Dalgarno.

---

[4] Reading *bepa*: extreme + adjective, for *brepa*: middle + adjective.

[5] *Sηfu*: to pertain + substantive. We follow here the word-for-word gloss of Dalgarno's letter to Charles II made by John Wallis in a copy of *AS* in the Bodleian library (Savile Cc 18).

[6] *Preb* is not in the 'Lexicon Grammatico-Philosophicum', but clearly signifies the opposite of *peb*: appetitus.

[7] *Krυb* is not in the 'Lexicon Grammatico-Philosophicum', but must be the opposite of *kυb*: rebellio.

Charles R.

Whereas We have been informd, by the Testimonies of divers Learned Men [*in margin:* R. Love, D.D., J. Wilkins, D.D., J. Wallis, D.D., S. Ward, D.D. W. Dillingham, D.D.] from both the Universities of Our Kingdom of *England*, concerning the great pains taken by *George Dalgarno*, in a Schola <sig. A4ᵛ>stick and Literary Design, of a *Universal Character* and *Philosophical Language*; All of them approving and commending his Discovery, judging it to be of singular use, for facilitating the matter of Communication and Intercourse between People of different Languages, and consequently a proper and effectual Means, for advancing all the parts of Real and Useful Knowledge, Civilizing barbarous Nations, Propagating the Gospel, and encreasing Traffique and Commerce. We understanding moreover, by Certificates from several credible Persons, that through the various Vicissitudes of Providence, he hath suffered the loss of a considerable Estate, by reason whereof, he is wholly disinabled from affording that Charge and Expence, for the Effectual prosecuting of this Work, as the Nature of it requires.

We therefore out of a tender consideration of the Premises, and for manifesting Our Good Will and Affection towards the promoting of Art, and the encouraging all such ingenious persons of our Subjects who <sig. A5ʳ> shall attempt and Effect any thing tending to Publicke Good; As We do Declare, that, We will Our Selves express some Token of Our Royal Favour, for the helping forward this so Laudable and Hopeful Enterprize; So also, Reflecting upon its Common and Universal usefulness, We do by these Our Letters of Recommendation incite as many of Our Subjects (especially the Reverend and Learned Clergy) as are truly apprehensive and sensible of the defectiveness of Art, chiefly in this particular of Language; what great Loss mankind is at there through, how acceptable it will be before God, and praise worthy among Men, to Encourage and Advance those waies of Learning, wherein the general

Good of Mankind is intended; That such would, as their Affections shall encline them, and their places enable them, out their helping hands to the bringing forth this (as yet) Infant design, now sticking at Birth.

This will give just Cause to Our Posterity through succeeding Generations, while <sig. A5^v> they are reaping the Fruit of Our Ingeny and Industry, to look back upon Us with Reverence; And from Our Example they will be provoked, not to rest upon what they shall have received from Us; but still to be Endeavouring to proceed in a further repairing the Decayes of nature, untill Art have done its last, or, which is more probable, Nature cease to be, or be Renewed.

Given at Our Court at *Whitehal* this 26th of *November*, in the 12th Year of Our Reign.

Will. Morice.

Lectori Philosopho.

Judicio tuo (Lector Philosophe) Inventa hæc mea de Confusionis Linguarum remedio (qantum scil. malum hoc Arte reparabile est) visum est prius subjicere, qam inertis Vulgi manibus terantur. Lege, perlege, & relege. Cave autem ne inter judicandum, non separanda separes, id est, partem Logicam & Grammaticam; sed ut sententiam æqius feras, finem ultimum (Communicationis facilitatem) primo respice. Experire qid veri contineat sententia cujusdam Viri Docti de hac Arte. Tria Momenta ei assignabat. 1. Dixit Artem hanc videri plane impossibilem. 2. Possibilem qidem sed valde difficilem. 3. Vero, mire & supra fidem facilem. Forte erudite Lector, anteqam Libellum hunc in manus sumpseras, tibi videbatur hæc Ars omnino fabulosa & impossibilis; Sed ex iis qæ hic dicta sunt, jam vides possibilem, sed adhuc valde difficilem: Qare progredere adhuc ultra ad Praxin, eiqe paululum dili<sig. A6ᵛ>genter intende, & nihil dubito qin veritatem tertii maxima cum voluptate & emolumento percipies. Hominibus Sciolis qi hoc unicum possunt aliorum Scripta carpere, Artiumqe Prima Principia qantum in ipsis est funditus evertere (dum tamen ipsi nihil ponunt) mecum subride. Aut Artium omnium qædam Principia sunt stabilienda, aut omnis Ars ruitura est; maxime vero in Arte Signorum, præ aliis omnibus, Arbitrium est necessario admittendum. Pragmaticis vero, qi falcem in alienam messem injicere sunt parati, ut festinent lente, & caveant ne simul cum laboribus, honorem etiam qem ambiunt periclitentur, mecum consule. Absit autem hæc a me jactanter dicta sint, qasi existimarem me solum huic Suscepto parem: Tantum enim abest, meis viribus confidam, ut, per hæc ad omnes Doctos provocem qi Tractatulum hunc in manus sument; qorum Ingenia, studia, otiumqe & secessus Censores idoneos fecerint; ut, si qæ laus, si qis honor, si qis Generis Humani amor, si qod studium Artes & Rem Literariam promovendi, si qæ deniqe Posterorum cura: Per omnia hæc Menti Generosæ charissima, obtestor, rogo, flagito, obsecro; Doctrinam hanc novam, jam qinqe fere Annorum studio ad hanc maturitatem perductam, severe (simul tamen candide & sincere) examinent probent; mihiqe sua sensa de ea qam citissime renuncient. Si enim in aliqo ad melius consulant, <sig. A7ʳ> & Errorum meum non solum detexerint, sed sine majore Errore emendaverint, promitto me Animo facili & grato eorum monitis obtemperaturum. Cumqe expectandum non sit, unicum qemvis hominem, omnibus Notionibus Naturæ & Artis Nomina apta, Philosophice & secundum Rerum Naturas instituere posse; nisi prius earum accuratas Definitiones a variarum Artium peritis habeat: Vos igitur Viros Virtuosos & singularium Artium vere Magistros compello. Qisqe de suo penu ad hanc Babelam restaurandam materiam ministret. En jactum Fundamentum satis amplum & firmum: Non enim vel minimum dubito, qin omnes Notiones Naturæ & Artis ex Radicalibus hic positis satis perspicue definiri possint: Hoc tamen unum

To the Philosophical Reader   <sig. A6ʳ>

I t seems proper to submit these inventions of mine concerning a remedy for the confusion of tongues (in as far, that is, as this misfortune can be repaired by human art) first of all to your judgement, philosophical reader, before they are touched by the unskilful hands of the public. Read them, read them thoroughly, and read them more than once. Take care, however, that in forming your judgement you do not separate things that are not to be separated— namely, the logical and the grammatical parts; but so as to come to a fairer verdict keep foremost in mind the ultimate aim, namely ease of communication. See for yourself what truth there is in the opinion of one learned man about this art. He assigned it three different evaluations. 1. He asserted that this art seemed clearly impossible. 2. That it was indeed possible, but extremely difficult. 3. That it is in fact surprisingly and unbelievably easy. Perhaps, learned reader, before you picked up this little book it seemed to you that this art was quite incredible and impossible. But from what is here said you will already see that it is possible, although still very difficult. For this reason, I have no doubt that, if you now proceed still further to the practical material, and study this with just a little <sig. A6ᵛ> diligence, you will, to your great pleasure and profit, perceive the truth of the third evaluation. Share my derision for those men of little knowledge who are capable only of carping at writings of others, and of demolishing utterly, in as far as they can, the first principles of the arts (while they themselves establish nothing at all). For either certain principles must be agreed upon for every art, or else all art will be brought to nothing; and in the art of signs, above all others, it is necessary to allow the decision of an arbitrator. Take action with me against those advisers who are ready to put their sickles to the crops of others, so that they hurry slowly, and take care lest together with their labour they also endanger the honour after which they are striving. I am far from suggesting, however, that these things are said boastfully by me, as if I considered myself alone equal to this undertaking; for I am so far from having confidence in my own capabilities, that I hereby call on all learned men who pick up this little tract, whose talents and endeavours and whose leisure and solitude make them appropriate critics, so that, if there is any praise, if there is any honour, if there is any love for the human race, if there is any zeal for the advancement of the arts and letters, if, finally, there is any concern for posterity, in the name of all these gifts of a noble mind, I entreat, ask, summon, and implore them to examine and investigate closely (but at the same time honestly and sincerely) this new doctrine, brought to this stage of completion by nearly five years of endeavour; and that they should convey their opinions of it to me as soon as possible. For if they advise anything for the <sig. A7ʳ> better, not just pointing out my error but amending it without a greater error, I promise that I shall be guided by their counsels with goodwill

intendite, ut Rerum Descriptiones, Differentias maxime Communes & notas exhibeant, & ab aliis rebus maxime distinguentes; idqe qam paucissimis vocibus, ne voces hujus Linguæ ex iis componendæ in nimiam longitudinem excrescant. Homines Superstitiose nimis, susceptum hoc, Facinus Audax a Deo vetitum opinantes, ne audite. An Deus O. Homininbus libertatem indulsit, Carduos & Sentes ex agris eradicandi? Errores autem ex Cœlesti Animorum Solo exstirpare prohibuit? Absit! Ne credite. Deus ipse ejusqe Principaliores Ministri (hic in Terris) Natura scil. & Ars, eadem Methodo in operando utuntur, id est progrediendo <sig. A7�v> ab imperfectioribus ad Perfectiora. Qid hinc de hac Arte concludam facile est colligere. Qantus autem sit futurus ejus fructus (præcipue si in Scholas introducatur ejus usus) in Posteris Seculis, vos Viros Doctos variis vestris conjecturis relinqo. Valete.

Geo. Dalgarno

and gratitude. And since it cannot be expected that any one person alone can assign appropriate names to all the notions of nature and art, in a philosophical manner and according to the nature of things, unless he first has accurate definitions of them from others skilled in the various arts, for this reason I address you, men of learning and truly masters in the several arts. Let each one contribute material from his own stock for the reparation of Babel. Indeed, a foundation large and reliable enough has been laid. And there is not the least doubt that all the notions of nature and art can be defined clearly enough from the radicals here established. But take heed of this one thing: that the description of things should exhibit the differences that are the most general and well known, and that maximally distinguish things from other ones; and this is to be done using as few words as possible, so that the words of this language that are to be composed of these do not grow excessively long. Do not listen to those who superstitiously believe that this undertaking is too bold an endeavour, prohibited by God. Did God Almighty not grant to all men the liberty to rid fields of thorns and thistles? Did he then forbid errors to be eradicated from the divine ground of the mind? Far from it! Do not believe it! God himself, and his principal servants (here on earth), namely nature and art, use the same method in their operations, that is to say, by progressing <sig. A7ᵛ> from the imperfect towards the perfect. It is easy to gather what I conclude from the foregoing with regard to the present art. What or how great its success in future generations will be (in particular if its use is introduced into schools), that I leave, learned men, to your own several conjectures. Farewell.

Geo. Dalgarno

<sig. A8ʳ> # Alphabetum hujus Lingæ Philosophicæ.

Singulæ Literæ in principio dictionis sunt Characteristicæ Notionum Genericarum in Tabulis, ut infra indicatur.

A	Ens, res
H	Substantia
E	Accidens
I	Ens Concretum ex Subst. & Accid.
O	Corpus
Y	Spiritus
U	Concretum ex Corpore & Spiritu. 1. Homo
M	Concretum Mathematicum
N	Concretum Physicum
F	Concretum Artefactum
B	Accidens Mathematicum
D	Accid. Physicum Generale
G	Qalitas Sensibilis
P	Accidens Sensitivum
T	Accidens Rationale
K	Accidens Politicum
S	Accidens Commune, alias, servilis
R	Servilis, significat oppositionem
L	Servilis, significat medium inter extrema
V	Characterist. vocis numericæ.

Notæ Numericæ

A	1	M	1	Vado 154	
H	2	N	2	Ventum 32861	
E	3	F	3	Vapulo 17604	
O	4	B	4	Vel 30	
Y	5	D	5	Vendo 3254	
U	6	G	6	Vetuit 38608	
AI	7	P	7	Valili 10000	
EI	8	T	8	Void 95	
OI	9	K	9	Vestis 380	
I	0	L	0	Verrere 333	

The Alphabet of this Philosophical Language.   <sig. A8ʳ>

The single letters at the beginning of a word are characteristic of the generic notions in the tables, as indicated below

A	Being, thing
H	Substance
E	Accident
I	Concrete Entity from Substance and Accidents
O	Body
Y	Spirit
U	Concrete from Body & Spirit: Man
M	Mathematical Concrete
N	Physical Concrete
F	Artificial Concrete
B	Mathematical Accident
D	General Physical Accident
G	Sensible Quality
P	Sensitive Accident
T	Rational Accident
K	Political Accident
S	Common Accident, *or*, servile letter
R	Servile letter, signifies opposition
L	Servile letter, signifies medium between extremes
V	Characteristic of numerical words.

Numerical Marks

A	1	M	1	Vado 154
H	2	N	2	Ventum 32861
E	3	F	3	Vapulo 17604
O	4	B	4	Vel 30
Y	5	D	5	Vendo 3254
U	6	G	6	Vetuit 38608
AI	7	P	7	Valili 10000
EI	8	T	8	Void 95
OI	9	K	9	Vestis 380
I	0	L	0	Verrere 333

Lexicon Grammatico-Philosophicum

Tabulæ Rerum, & Notionum omnium Simpliciorum, & Generaliorum, tam Artefactarum quam Naturalium, Rationes & Respectus communiores, Methodo Prædicamentali ordinatas, complectentes: Quibus significandis, Nomina, non Casu, sed Arte, & Consilio, servata inter Res & Signa convenientia Analogica, instituuntur. Ex quibus, Rerum & Notionum aliarum omnium magis Complexarum & specialorum Nomina, vel Derivatione, vel Compositione, in una vel pluribus vocibus, per Regulas quasdam Generales & certas secundum Analogiam Logico-Grammaticam, formantur; Ita ut Nomina sic formata, Rerum Descriptiones ipsarum Naturæ consentaneas, contineant.

[A fold-out table with the above heading was positioned here in the 1661 edition. A facsimile reproduction can be found at the end of this volume.]

Grammatico-Philosophical Lexicon

Tables of things, and of all more simple and general notions, both artificial and natural, encompassing the more common grounds and aspects, arranged by the predicamental method; for signifying which, names are established not at random, but by art and design, observing an analogical conformity between things and signs. From these the names of all other things and notions that are more complex and more particular are formed, either by derivation or by composition in one or more words, by certain general and fixed rules, according to logico-grammatical analogy; so that the names thus formed contain descriptions of these things that correspond to their nature.

<sig. A8ᵛ> Placuit Gratitudinis ergo, & ut alii incitentur ad Artem hanc Novam ulterius propagandam, eorum Nomina adscribere, Qorum munificentia (cum meis laboribus) Ars hæc a primo Inventionis semine as hanc maturitatem crevit, jamqe Lucem Publicum videt. Horum nemo infra summam unius Libræ Anglicanæ, nemo supra decem, largitus est.

R. Boile Com. a Corke.	*J. Stock* Armig.
F[r]at. German.	*Whitle* Armig.
G. Morice Baronet Secret.	*Baccous* Armig.
Regius.	*Gold* Armig
C. Culpepper Baronet.	*J. Sparrow* Armig.
J. Keate Baronet.	*L. Fogge* T.B.
G. Crook Baronet.	*S. Byfield* A.M.
T. Dillingham T.D.	*J. Tillotson* A.M.
J. Wilkins T.D.	*Staughton* A.M.
S. Ward T.D.	*Floyd* A.M.
H. Wilkinson T.D.	*R. Cumberland* A.M.
F. Walsel T.D.	*T. Branker* A.M.
B. Whichcoat T.D.	*F. Lodwick* Civ. Lond.
J. Bathurst M.D.	*E. Bale* Civ. Lond.
G. Pettie M.D.	*T. Slater* Civ. Lond.
A. Morgam M.D.	*D. Henchman*

It was decided, by way of acknowledgement and also that others be encouraged <sig. A8ᵛ> to further this new art, to list the names of those by means of whose generosity (together with my own labours) this art has grown from the first seed of its invention to its present maturity, and is now presented to public view. Of those listed, none contributed less than one English pound, nor more than ten.[8]

R. Boile Brother of the
    Earl of Cork
G. Morice Privy
    Counsellor
C. Culpepper Baronet
J. Keate Baronet
G. Crook Baronet
T. Dillingham D.D.
J. Wilkins D.D.
S. Ward D.D.
H. Wilkinson D.D.
F. Walsel D.D.
B. Whichcoat D.D.
J. Bathurst D.M.
G. Pettie D.M.
A. Morgam D.M.

J. Stock Esquire
Whitle Esquire
    Baccous Esquire
    Gold Esquire
J. Sparrow Esquire
L. Fogge B.D.
S. Byfield M.A.
J. Tillotson M.A.
    Staughton M.A.
    Floyd M.A.
R. Cumberland M.A.
T. Branker M.A.
F. Lodwick Citizen of London
E. Bale Citizen of London
T. Slater Citizen of London
D. Henchman

[8] The list of names here may be compared with those printed on the broadsheet pamphlet 'Omnibus Omnino Hominibus' (see above, Part I, Broadsheet 5).

CAP. I.

DE PRIMIS SIGNORUM ELEMENTIS, SPECIATIM VERO DE SONIS SIMPLICIBUS.

Artem primam maximeque necessariam, *Artem* scil. *Signorum*, hucusque neglectam, alias vero (quantum sine hac poterant) ingeniose et laboriose excultas, inertiæne genus humanum accusabo? Anne potius Numinis speciali Decreto, Artem hanc tantas in rebus humanis mutationes portendentem, in ultima Mundi tempora reservante, excusabo? Artem igitur hanc ab aliis non inventam, mihi vero vere repertam patefacturus, a primis ejus Elementis *Literis* sc. exordium ducam; earumque Philosophiam paucis et perspicue tradam.

Optime meruit de genere humano, qui primus docuit voces humanas in quosdam simplicissimos primos et irresolubiles sonos resolvere; quam Inventionem certissimum est præcessisse Inventionem <p. 2> Literarum Alphabeticarum, quam nos vulgo miramur; hæ enim nihil sunt aliud quam Signa Signorum, id est sonorum, adeoque illis necessario posteriora. Non quidem dico hanc Inventionem omnem Literarum usum præcessisse; nam non minus certum videtur usum Characterum, quatenus Rerum ipsarum et mentis Conceptuum immediate significativi sunt, ante hanc prius longe cognitum fuisse: Imo judico usum Literarum hoc sensu fuisse ab initio, licet homines in materia solida et ad figuras conservandas apta nondum scribebant: qui enim caput nutat, oculo connivet, digitum movet in aëre, &c. (ad mentis cogitata exprimendum) is non minus vere scribit, quam qui Literas pingit in Charta, Marmore, vel ære. Ratio cur judicem Characteres extitisse ab initio, est quod non minus naturale sit homini communicare in *Figuris* quam *Sonis*: quorum utrumque dico homini *naturale*; licet scribere has vel illas figuras, vel loqui has vel illas voces, sit omnino ad *placitum*. Præterea Characteres *Reales* fuisse in usu ante Characteres *Vocales*, Synenses et Ægyptios, populos antiquissimos testes compello.

Sonorum simplicium numerus et differentiæ, a diverso modo aperiendi et claudendi Organa pronunciationis petenda sunt; quare primo dividi possunt Literæ, in *apertas* et *clausas*.

CHAPTER I

<p. 1>

ON THE PRIMARY ELEMENTS OF SIGNS AND
IN PARTICULAR ON SIMPLE SOUNDS

S hall I blame it on the inertia of human kind that the primary and most necessary art, that is the *Art of Signs*, has been until now neglected, whereas the other arts have been cultivated (in as far as this is possible without the former) with such ingenuity and labour? Or am I to plead as an excuse a special decree of the Almighty holding back this art, which portends such great changes in human affairs, until the last ages of the world? In order then to unveil this art, which I have succeeded in discovering where others have failed, I shall take my start from its primary elements—namely, the *letters*; and I shall touch upon the philosophy of them briefly and plainly.

The man who first discovered the method of analysing human words into the simplest, primary and irreducible sounds rendered the greatest of services to the human race. <p. 2> This discovery quite certainly preceded the invention of alphabetic letters, which we are generally wont to marvel at; for the latter are nothing other than signs of signs,[9] i.e. of sounds, and thus necessarily secondary to the former. That is not to say, however, that this discovery preceded all uses of letters, for it seems no less certain that the use of characters, such as immediately represent both things themselves and the notions of the mind, was known long before this. It is indeed my opinion that the use of letters, in this sense, existed from the beginning, even though men did not yet write on solid material capable of preserving figures; for someone who nods his head, winks his eye, moves his finger in the air, etc. (in order to express the thoughts of his mind) can no less truly be said to be writing than someone who forms letters on paper, marble, or bronze.[10] The reason I believe that characters existed from the beginning is that it is no less natural for man to communicate by *figures* than by *sounds*, both of which I claim to be *natural* to man; although whether one writes with these figures or others, and whether one speaks with these words or others, is entirely *arbitrary*. Furthermore, as evidence that *real* characters were in use before *vocal* characters, I may cite the most ancient Chinese and Egyptian peoples.

The number and distinctions of the simple sounds are to be discovered from the various ways of opening and closing the organs of speech; for this reason the letters can be divided first into *open* and *closed*.

---

[9] Cf. Aristotle, *De Interpretatione* 16ª4–6.
[10] Cf. the discussion in Dalgarno's subsequent work *The Deaf and Dumb Man's Tutor* (1680) (see below, Part III). On the background to Dalgarno's phonetic analysis, see Kemp (1972: 39–66).

Apertæ principaliores (non enim est animus <p. 3> differentias minutiores persequi) sunt septem; quarum valor, ordo, et soni differentia videantur supra. Hæ iterum sunt *Gutturales* vel *Labiales*. Gutturales sunt quatuor, quarum pronunciatio gradatim procedit, a fono maxime aperto *a*; per sonum paulo contractiorem *η*; et tertio *e* adhuc contractiorem, et gutture strictiore prolatum; ad quartum *i* sonum contractissimum, et strictissimo gutture formatum, ideoque acutissimum. Labiales sunt tres; quas sic voco quod sine labiorum ope et motu formari nequeunt. Harum *o* est maxime aperta, hoc est contractionem labiorum minime poscit; *v* contractiora labia in ipsius formatione requirit; *u* maximam labiorum contractionem et conatum postulat.

Quot modis hi soni simplices coalescere possunt in dipthongos, non morabor curiose inquirere: Hoc tantum teneatur, sex esse dipthongos sonatu et distinctu faciles, ni. ai ei oi au eu ou, qui efferri possunt continuato spiritu, ad modum unius simplicis soni: et ratio hujus est, quia componuntur ex sonis maxime apertis præcedentibus, et maxime contractis sequentibus; ideoque facilis est cadentia organorum eodem spiritu in his formandis.

Literæ clausis organis formatæ principaliores et omni populo pronunciatu faciles, et quibus solis idcirco hic usurus sum, sunt duodecim: Hæ dividuntur in *semiclausas* et perfecte *clausas*.

Literæ *semiclausæ* quæ et *semivocales* appellari <p. 4> possunt, sunt tres; *s r l* in quibus formandis organa oris non clauduntur perfecte, fed continuatur spiritus transpiratio per os; et ex varia percussione palati per linguæ extremitatem (quæ organum pronunciationis præcipuum est) formantur.

S formatur per contactum palati et laterum linguæ, media parte linguæ a contactu abstinente; per quam tanquam per fistulam, spiritus sono sibilo emittitur. De sono hujus Literæ audivi virum doctum hoc peculiare observantem, quod nequeat efferri sono *claro*, sed ad modum *susurri*: quod quidem verum est, sed non de hac litera sola; nulla enim est litera aspirata ex tribus mutis, quæ sono claro proferri potest. Ut hoc distinctius percipiatur, consulo ut inter pronunciandum diu hæreatur in harum literarum formatione: et sic observabit ingeniosus quilibet, licet altissima voce exclamet, proferendo vocem ex his literis et vocalibus conflatam, dum sonat vocales sonus erit clarus; sed cum ad has literas sonandas pervenitur, statim sonus clarus vanescit in susurrum, *e.g. as with life*.

Sonus *r* est fortis vibratio extremitatis linguæ contra palatum; hinc est quod qui nervos linguæ habent debiles, non facile formant hunc sonum.

The principal open sounds (for it is not my present purpose <p. 3> to pursue the more minute distinctions) are seven in number, and their value, order, and difference in sound may be seen above.[11] These divide again into *gutturals* and *labials.* There are four gutturals, whose pronunciation ranges by steps from the most open sound *a*; through the slightly more contracted sound *η*; the third sound *e*, more contracted still and produced with a narrowed throat; to the fourth sound *i*, the most contracted sound made with the throat most narrowed, and hence the most acute of these. There are three labials, which I call thus because they cannot be produced without the help and movement of the lips. Of these *o* is the most open—that is, requiring the least contraction of the lips; *v* requires more contracted lips in the same position; *u* demands the greatest contraction and exertion of the lips.

How many ways these simple sounds may be combined into diphthongs I shall not pause to investigate here, except only to note that there are six diphthongs that are easy to produce and to distinguish—namely, *ai, ei, oi, au, eu, ou*—which can be made with one uninterrupted breath in the same manner as one single simple sound. The reason for this is that they are compounded of one of the most open sounds followed by one of the most contracted ones; hence it is easy for the organs to make their movements in a single breath while forming these sounds.

There are twelve principal sounds made with the closed organs which are easy to pronounce by any nation, and to these alone I shall restrict myself here for that very reason. These are divided into the *semi-closed* and the fully *closed*.

There are three *semi-closed* letters, which may also be called *semi-vowels*: <p. 4> *s, r, l*. In pronouncing these the vocal organs do not make a complete closure but allow air to pass through the mouth; and they are formed by the different ways that the extremity of the tongue (which is the principal organ of speech) strikes the palate.

S is formed by the contact of the sides of the tongue and the palate, the middle part of the tongue not touching, so that air is expelled with a hissing sound as through a whistle. I have heard a learned man say of this letter that it cannot be pronounced as a *clear* sound but only *whispered*, but, while this is true, it does not hold for this letter alone, for none of the aspirate letters derived from the three mutes can be made as a clear sound. To perceive this more distinctly, I advise the reader to slow down the pronunciation of these letters; and anyone of any intelligence will observe that, when pronouncing a word composed of these letters plus vowels, even if speaking in a very loud voice, the vowels are produced with a clear sound, but when the letters in question are reached the clear sound diminishes into a whisper, e.g. *as with life*.

The sound *r* is a strong vibration of the tip of the tongue against the palate; which is why those having weak tongue muscles have some difficulty in making this sound.

---

[11] Cf. the list of letters on the page in the prefatory matter entitled 'The Alphabet of this Philo-sophical Language'.

L, formatur modo contrario quo *S*, extremitate scil. linguæ palatum tangente, lateribus vero a contactu abstinentibus, ut transmittatur spiritus. Hic notetur: nihil me unquam magis vexavit, quam <p. 5> invenire veram differentiam inter literas *n* et *l*; auribus enim percipiebam sonos distinctissimos, at vero in organorum contactu, unde omnem sonorum differentiam exoriri satis sciebam, vix quidem ac ne vix, per multos dies differentiam ullam observare potui; saltem quam describere poteram. Verum ex jam dictis et statim dicendis satis clare describi potest harum literarum differentia; in formatione enim *l* spiritus per os transmittitur, in *n* per nasum.

Soni perfecte clausi sunt novem, qui dupliciter subdividi possunt; vel primo, ratione diversitatis organorum quibus formantur; et sic in tres ternarios numeros dividuntur, *labiales m b p, linguales n d t*, et *gutturales f g k*. Vel secundo, distingui possunt secundum diversitatem soni editi in iis formandis; secundum quam differentiam ego eas hic disposui, utpote instituto meo accommodatiorem; et sic sunt vel *Nasales* seu *Transpirantes m n f*, vel *Suffocatæ b d g*, vel *Mutæ p t k*: Nam ratione organorum pronunciationis præcise, tres tantum sunt literæ perfecte clausæ; sed hæ tres clausuræ multiplicatæ per trinam differentiam soni faciunt novem.

Nasales ideo sic voco, quod dum organa oris clauduntur, continuatur sonus per emissionem spiritus per nares; clausis enim naribus, hæ literæ formari nequeunt. De his tria hic monenda sunt. Primo ex hac naturali et genuina sonorum analysi <p. 6> detegi (vel saltem confirmari) literam seu sonum vere simplicem dari, quæ vulgo per duas literas diversorum organorum, ideoque in eadem syllaba minime unibilium, absurde scribitur: Hic enim sonus ex natura rei ipsius, non minus facilis est vel in principio vel fine vocis sine alia consonante, quam aliæ duæ literæ nasales *m* et *n*; licet refpectu nostri non ita sit; nam nos nihil facile facimus nisi quod sæpe facimus. Secundo, cum in vulgaribus nostris linguis nullum habeamus Characterem simplicem ad exprimendum hujus soni valorem, ideo mutuatus sum Characterem *f* ad hunc sonum significandum. Tertio, propter hanc causam Characterem *f* pro dicto sono substitui, quia hic mihi propositum est omnibus modis facilitati consulere, (quæ etiam causa fuit, quod omnes alios sonos simplices rejecerim; quia pauci vel nulli eorum sunt, qui facile pronunciantur ab omnibus populis, sed apud varios populos admodum varius est eorum usus) ideoque hunc sonum, licet perfectissimum et distinctissimum ab aliis; cum tamen a nullo populo cujus literæ ad nos pervenerunt sit usitatus, nisi ante suffocatum vel mutum sui organi

L is formed in the opposite manner to *s*—that is to say, with the tip of the tongue touching the palate, but with the sides not touching and thus allowing the passage of air. I note here in passing that nothing has vexed me more than <p. 5> trying to identify the true difference between the letters *n* and *l*, for although I could hear two quite distinct sounds with my ears, for a long time I was scarcely able to perceive, and far less able to describe, any distinction at all in the contact of the organs, for which I knew full well that all differences between sounds arise. But from what has now been said and will be said here the difference between these two letters can be described clearly enough: in the pronunciation of *l* the air passes through the mouth, while in *n* it passes through the nose.

There are nine fully closed sounds, which can be subdivided in two ways. First, according to the various organs by which they are formed, whereby they are divided into three groups of three: the *labials*, *m*, *b*, *p*; the *linguals*, *n*, *d*, *t*; and the *gutturals*, *f*, *g*, *k*. Alternatively, they may be subdivided according to the different type of sound made in producing them, and I have set them out here in accordance with this distinction as being more suited to my undertaking: thus, *nasals*, or *transpirants*, *m*, *n*, *f*; *suffocates*, *b*, *d*, *g*; and *mutes*, *p*, *t*, *k*; for, following the method of distinguishing according to the organ of pronunciation, there are strictly speaking only three letters with full closure, but these multiplied by the threefold difference of sound make nine.

The *nasals* I call thus because, while the organs of the mouth are closed, the sound continues as the air passes through the nose; for, if the nostrils are held closed, these letters cannot be pronounced. Three comments are called for here. First, from this natural and proper analysis of sounds <p. 6> it can be discovered (or rather confirmed) that there is one truly simple letter or sound that is popularly and erroneously written with two separate letters representing different organs that cannot be combined in one and the same syllable.[12] This sound is in the nature of things no less easy to pronounce either at the start or end of a word without any accompanying consonants than the other two nasals *m* and *n*, even though for us[13] it may not be so, for we can only do easily what we do frequently. Secondly, since in our vulgar languages we have no simple character to express the value of this sound, I have borrowed the character *f* to represent it. Thirdly, for this reason I substituted the character *f* for the sound in question, since I am determined to make facility my main consideration in all respects (which is also the reason why I rejected all the other simple sounds, for few if any of them are easy to pronounce by all peoples, and their use is very varied with different peoples); for this sound, although quite discrete and distinct from the others, is not used by any nation whose letters have been passed down to us except before a suffocate or mute pronounced with the same organ (and even then it is not written with a character of its own, for Greek uses *γ*,

---

[12] i.e. the velar nasal, represented in English orthography by the digraph 'ng'.
[13] i.e. speakers of English.

(et tunc quidem Charactere proprio non scribitur; Græci enim per γ αγγελος; aliæ gentes per *n* ut *languor, anger*) ideo inquam, hunc sonum ex hac lingua ejeci, cujus loco substitui literam *f*, facilis et distincti soni. Si tamen aliter visum fuerit viris doctis, poterit retineri sonus proprius <p. 7> literæ gutturalis *Transpirantis*, seu *Nasalis* sub Charactere soni *f*.

Suffocatæ b d g formantur eadem clausura organorum qua *Nasales*; sed spiritu magno nisu retento et suppresso in gutture. Hic notetur literam *g*, ut vulgo in *Georgius* sonatur, non esse literam simplicem, fed compositam ex *d* et *sh*, quasi *dshordshius*.

Literæ *Mutæ* formantur eadem clausura organorum qua supra dictæ; sed omni interno spiritus motu et sono cessante post organorum clausuram factam.

Præter has duodecim consonantes principales jam enumeratas, omnibus hominibus organa illæsa habentibus pronunciatu faciles, quibusque solis (ut dixi) ideo hic usurus sum, alii sunt soni simplices ex his orti, ni. ex aspiratione dictarum *suffocatarum* et *mutarum* oriuntur sex; *v f* ex *b p*; *th* ut sonatur in *the* et *tithe*, ex *d*; *th* ut sonatur in *thrice*, ex *t*; *gh* (qui sonus est germanicus) ex *g*; et χ ex *k*. De his notandum primo, quasdam harum aspiratarum, licet duabus characteribus descriptas, esse tamen revera simplices sonos non minus quam *f* et *v* quæ unico charactere scribuntur. Secundo, Nationes exteræ male accusant nos Britannos *blæsitatis* dum literas *d* et *t* aspirate pronunciamus; qui soni illis durissimi sunt. Sic populo Anglicano vicissim peculiare est, abhorrere a gutturalibus aspiratis. Corrumpit etiam, ut plurimum, sonos *a* et *i*, <p. 8> quasi *e* et *ai*: non tamen omnino respuunt Angli sonos *a* et *i*, familiares enim satis illis sunt hi soni, licet diversis characteribus notati; *a* enim per *aw* scribunt, et *i* per *ee*, ut *law, saw, peel, feel*.

Contigit aliquando verba habere cum curioso quodam rerum naturalium causas scrutatore, qui causam varietatis hujus sonorum apud diversos populos, cœli solique temperiem assignabat. Non quidem diffiteor causas naturales esse operativas in sonorum diversitate; verum causæ proximiores reddi possunt, quam regionum temperies, ni. corporis temperamentum, quod sæpissime plus diversitatis producit in hominibus in eodem loco natis, quam videmus inter alios in diversis mundi climatibus. Quare hoc certum est, causas naturales variare sonos quoad eorum modulationem; hoc est, quod sint graviores, clariores, asperiores, &c. at vero adscribere causam differentiæ sonorum, qui ex distinctis organorum clausuis et contactibus oriuntur, vel regionis, vel corporis ipsius temperamento, est revera ignorantiam veræ causæ differentiarum sonorum prodere: mihi enim experientia comprobatum est, posse Anglos gutturales aspiratas satis distincte pronunciare, ut etiam alios

e.g. αγγελος, and other nations use *n*, e.g. *languor, anger*). For this reason, then, I rejected this sound from my language and substituted the letter *f* in its place, which is an easy and distinct sound. If however learned men are of a different opinion, the strict sound <p. 7> of the *transpirant* guttural letter, or *nasal*, can be retained for the character whose sound is *f*.[14]

The *suffocates*, *b*, *d*, *g*, are made with the same closure of the organs as the *nasals*, but with the breath forcibly held back and suppressed in the throat. Here it should be noted that the letter *g* as usually sounded in *Georgius* is not a simple letter but is compounded from *d* and *sh*, as it were *dshordshius*.

The *mute* letters are formed with the same closure of the organs as just described, but with all internal movement of air and all sound ceasing after the closure of the organs has been made.

In addition to the twelve principal consonants just enumerated, which are easy for anyone with intact speech organs to pronounce, and which are the only ones I shall use here (as previously noted), there are other simple sounds derived from them. Thus six sounds arise by aspiration from the just-mentioned *suffocates* and *mutes*: *v* and *f* from *b* and *p*; *th* (as pronounced in *the* and *tithe*) from *d*, and *th* (as pronounced in *thrice*) from *t*; *gh* (which is a Germanic sound) from *g*, and χ from *k*. Concerning these it should be noted, firstly, that those of the aspirates that are written with two characters are no less truly simple sounds than *f* and *v*, which are written with a single character. Secondly, foreigners wrongly accuse us British of *lisping* when we pronounce the aspirates corresponding to *d* and *t*, which for them are very difficult sounds. The English in turn have the peculiarity of shunning the aspirate gutturals. They also corrupt the sounds *a* and *i*, pronouncing them <p. 8> as η and *ai*. However the English do not avoid *a* and *i* altogether, for these sounds are indeed familiar enough to them but are written with other characters: thus *a* is written as *aw*, and *i* as *ee*, as in *law, saw, peel, feel*.

I have sometimes had occasion to debate with a certain careful investigator of the causes of natural things who ascribed the reason for the differences in the sounds used by different peoples to the climate and the condition of the soil. I do not wish to deny that natural causes are operative in the diversity of sounds; indeed more immediate causes can be adduced than the natural conditions of regions—namely, the effect of physique, which very often produces greater diversity in men born in the same locality than that to be observed in men from different regions of the world. But even though it is clear that natural causes produce variation in the sounds as regards their modulation—that is to say, whether they are deeper, clearer, sharper, etc.—nevertheless to ascribe the differences in sounds that arise from various distinct closures of and contacts between the vocal organs to the effects of the region or even of physique betrays a simple ignorance of the true reasons for the differentiation of sounds.

---

[14] i.e. the velar nasal 'ng'.

Populos gutturales linguales. Nulla igitur ratio reddi potest, cur Angli aversantur sonum χ, exteræ nationes vero *th*, quam cur Angli vocant *urbem town*, aliæ Nationes aliis vocibus.

Z est *S* suffocatum; hoc est, differt ab *s* ut *d* a *t* vel *b* a *p*, &c.

<p. 9> Est et alius sonus simplex, qui paululum differt ab *s*, qui vulgo scribitur *sh*: Hebræi proprio Charactere notant ש qui etiam dupliciter sonatur, ni. *muto* et *suffocato* sono; unde oritur duplex litera, cujus sonus *suffocatus* nobis Britannis non est usitatus, sed ni fallor Polonis familiaris.

Tota essentia literæ *h* consistit in forti spiritus impulsu in vocalium prolatione, sive id fiat spirando, sive respirando; et hæc de sonorum simplicium numero et principalioribus differentiis.

Quemadmodum soni simplices aperti coalescunt in unum sonum continuatum, qui dicitur dipthongus, sic clausi sæpissime in unum continuatum sonum in eadem syllaba coalescunt: quare explicatis sonis simplicibus clausis, quasdam regulas de earum compositione tradam; ni. de principalioribus sonis Compositis, ut monui de dipthongis.

Primo, Hæc est Regula certa et universalis: Nulla litera unius organi naturaliter præcedere potest literam alterius organi, in principio syllabæ. Hinc excipiatur *s* quæ ante quamvis aliam in principio syllabæ, vel post quamvis aliam in fine fyllabæ satis euphonice sonat, licet in nulla (quod sciam) lingua, suffocatis *b d g* præponatur, quod propterea nec ego hic feci. Raro etiam invenitur ante *r*; Analogia tamen hujus Linguæ coegit me in <p. 10> quibusdam vocibus componere *sr*: videbam enim sonum in se satis esse euphonicum et facilem. Lingua etiam Anglica admittit *r* post *sh*, sonum *s* maxime affinem, et quidem multo duriorem, ut *shrewd*, *shrine*. Videbitur fortassis *sf* (ubi per *f* jam intelligo gutturalem *nasalem*) sonus non naturalis: verum ut supra demonstravi *f* solitarie sonari posse in principio syllabæ, non minus quam *m n*; sic etiam compositio *sf* non minus est naturalis, quam *sm sn*.

I myself have established by experiment that the English are quite capable of producing aspirate gutturals distinctly enough, and likewise that other peoples are capable of producing the aspirate[15] linguals. There is, therefore, no reason that can be given to explain why the English should avoid the sound χ and foreign nations should avoid the sound *th*, any more than one can give a reason why the English should use the word *town* to signify a town while other nations use a different word.

Z is the suffocate equivalent of *s*; that is to say, it differs from *s* in the same <p. 9> way that *d* differs from *t*, *b* from *p*, etc. There is also another simple sound that differs slightly from *s* and that is popularly written *sh*. For this the Hebrews use a letter of their own ש, which can be pronounced in two ways—namely, with either a *mute* or a *suffocate* sound—whence arises a twofold letter, whose *suffocate* sound is unknown to us British, but is quite familiar, if I am not mistaken, to the Poles.

The essence of the letter *h* consists in a strong puff of air in the pronunciation of the vowels, made either by inhaling or exhaling.[16] So much for the number of and principal differences between the simple sounds.

Just as the simple open sounds may combine to form a single continuous sound that is called a diphthong, so also closed sounds combine very often to form a single continuous sound in one and the same syllable. Having therefore explained the simple closed sounds, I shall now give some rules concerning their combination—that is to say, concerning the principal compound sounds, as I did previously for the diphthongs.

First, there is the following fixed and universal rule: No letter pronounced with a given organ of speech may naturally precede a letter pronounced with a different organ at the beginning of the syllable. The exception to this is *s*, which can be pronounced euphonically enough before any other letter at the beginning of a syllable or following any other letter at the end of a syllable, although in no language (to my knowledge) does it precede the suffocates *b*, *d*, *g*, for which reason I have not done this here either. It is also found only rarely before *r*, but analogy in this language forced me <p. 10> to allow the combination *sr* in certain words, for I perceived that the sound was in itself euphonic and easy enough. Furthermore, the English language allows *r* after *sh*, a sound of close affinity to *s* and indeed rather harsher, e.g. *shrewd*, *shrine*. It might perhaps seem that *sf* (where *f* is intended to represent the guttural *nasal*) is not a natural sound. However, as I showed above that *f* could be sounded on its own at the beginning of a syllable no less easily than *m* and *n*, in like manner *sf* is no less natural than *sm* and *sn*.

---

[15] Reading *aspirates* for *gutturales*, which appears to be a simple slip.

[16] Cf. the discussion of 'h' and the aspirates in 'The Autobiographical Treatise', CC, fo. 74ᵛ (see below, Part IV).

Secundo, In fine syllabæ *Nasales* euphonice valde sonant ante *suffocatas* vel *mutas* ejusdem organi; ut *lamb, lamp, and, ant, long, ink*. Ubi notandum in *long* et *ink* non *n* sonatur, nec quidem sonari potest, sed gutturalis *Nasalis*. Durus tamen est Germanorum sonus componentium *Nasalem suffocatam* et *mutam* in eadem syllaba; ut *handt, landt*.

Tertio, *Semiclausæ r l* bene componuntur in principio syllabæ cum *suffocatis* et *mutis*, quæ compositio mihi in sequentibus magni est usus: durius tamen paululum sonat *l* post *d* et *t*, quia eadem fere (ut dictum) clausura organorum formantur. Et licet analogia hujus linguæ postulat sonum *l* componi cum *d* et *t*, tamen evenit in ista parte Lexici quæ sub *d* et *t* est, paucas notiones habere proprie dictum *medium* cujus *l* est characteristicum.

Quarto, *r* et *l* in fine syllabæ ante quamvis aliam consonantem bene sonantur, sed post nullam. <p. 11> Jamque doctrinam de sonis simplicibus cum his observationibus absolvam.

Primo, Omnium Linguarum Grammaticæ in Literarum numero vel defectivæ sunt, vel redundantes; quosdam enim sonos complexos unico charactere, alios vero sonos vere simplices duobus characteribus notant.

Secundo, Nulla ante-hac ratio *ordinis* literarum reddita est; sed non minus fortuitus est *ordo* literarum quam institutio vocum.

Tertio, Ex convenientia quam videmus respectu methodi in omnibus Alphabetis, manifestum est literarum Inventionem unicum Autorem habuisse; Literæ enim *A B* primum locum obtinent in Alphabetis omnium Linguarum. Quod ordo sequentium Literarum variet, ratio est, partim quod quædam literæ postea additæ sunt post primam inventionem; quædam etiam a quibusdam Gentibus eliminatæ sunt cum quilibet populus literas recipiens Linguæ suæ adaptavit: aliæ sunt variationes in numero et serie literarum apud varias nationes ex aliis accidentibus, quarum causas reddere est difficile.

Quarto, Ex sonorum Analysi hic tradita satis intellecta, statim sequitur eorum recordatio.

Quinto, Priusquam caput hoc de sonis absolvero, docebo ex supra dicta analysi Artem (quod quibusdam forte non ingratum erit) transmutandi voces cujusvis Linguæ in alias diversissimas, et <p. 12> tamen sermo sic transmutatus eandem gratiam et euphoniam retinebit; adeo ut facillime discerni posset, qua lingua quis utatur, licet sensus verborum maneat omnino occultus, etiam ab istarum linguarum peritis. Ars breviter hæc est. Fiat commutatio labialium *m b p* cum dentalibus *n d t*; quod etiam fiat in earum aspiratis; et commutatio *g* cum *k*, et *r* cum *l*; exemplum,

Secondly, at the end of a syllable the *nasals* can be pronounced quite euphonic-ally before a *suffocate* or *mute* formed by the same organ, e.g. *lamb*, *lamp*, *and*, *ant*, *long*, *ink*. It is to be noted here that in *long* and *ink* it is not *n* that is sounded, nor indeed could be sounded, but rather the *guttural nasal*. However, the combina-tion of a *nasal*, *suffocate*, and *mute* in the same syllable, as found in German, is harsh—e.g. *handt*, *landt*.

Thirdly, the *semi-closed r* and *l* combine freely with *suffocates* and *mutes* at the beginning of a syllable, and this combination is of great use to me in what follows, although to pronounce *l* following *d* or *t* is a little more difficult, since (as I have said) they are made with almost the same closure of the organs. And, although analogy[17] in this language demands that the sound *l* combine with *d* and *t*, it turns out that in that part of the lexicon that is under *d* and *t* there are but few notions that strictly have a middle degree, for which the letter *l* is the characteristic.

Fourthly, at the end of a syllable *r* and *l* can freely occur preceding any other consonant, but not following. <p. 11> I shall now conclude what I have to say about the simple sounds with the following observations.

First, the grammars of all languages are either defective or redundant as regards the number of the letters, for they represent some complex sounds with a single character, while representing some truly simple sounds with two characters.

Secondly, no reason has previously been given for the *order* of the letters, although the order of the letters is no less accidental than the institution of words.

Thirdly, from the agreement we can see in the method of all alphabets, it is apparent that the invention of letters must have had a single author. For the let-ters *A* and *B* have the first place in the alphabets of all languages. The reason why the order of the following letters varies is partly because certain letters were added after the first invention, while others were omitted by some nations when a people who inherited the letters adapted them to their own language. There are other variations in the number and order of the letters among various nations due to other circumstances whose causes are difficult to account for.

Fourthly, once the analysis of sounds that has been given here has been sufficiently grasped, they will be immediately recalled.

Fifthly, before closing this chapter concerning the sounds I shall propose, on the basis of the above analysis, an art (which some might find not unuseful) for transforming the words of any given language into quite different ones, <p. 12> whereby the text that is thus transformed will retain its beauty and euphony, so that it can easily be determined which language is being used, even though the sense of the words remains quite obscure even to one well versed in it. The method briefly is as follows. The labials *m*, *b*, *p* are to be interchanged with the dentals *n*, *d*, *t*; the same is done with their respective aspirates; and similarly *g* is to be interchanged with *k*, and *r* with *l*; for example:

---

[17] i.e. 'analogy' in the technical sense of 'regularity'.

Pipile pu tapuræ legudams sud peknime thaki.
Syrthesplen pemue Nusam nebipalis athema, i.e.
Tityre tu patulæ, &c.

Nemo linguæ Latinæ gnarus, dum audit has voces recte prolatas, qui non satis percipiet eas esse Latinas, licet ita inversas ut nihil intelligat ex iis.

Pipile pu tapurae legudams sud peknime thaki
Syrthesplen pemue Nusam nebipalis athema, i.e.
Tityre tu patulae, etc.[18]

No one who knows the Latin language, when hearing these lines correctly spoken, will be unable to recognize that they are indeed Latin, even though they are transformed in such a way that they are unintelligible.

---

[18] The lines from Virgil's *Eclogues* (1. 1) that are alluded to here read in full: 'Tityre tu patulae recubans sub tegmine fagi | Silvestrem tenui Musam meditaris avena' (Tityrus, you lie canopied beneath your spreading beech | and wooing the silvan Muse on your slender oat).

CAP. II.

DE CHARACTERIBUS.

Quemadmodum scientia transfertur a homine ad hominem per organum auris, mediantibus sonis, sic etiam per oculi organum mediantibus figuris. Potest fieri communicatio per reliquos sensus; sed tardius, ideoque ad nostrum institutum nihil pertinet, qui medium communicationis brevissimum et rationi maxime consentaneum quærimus. <p. 13> Si comparatio instituatur inter signa *vocalia* et *scripta*, communicatio in *sonis* multo est expeditior inter præsentes; sed hanc vincit communicatio per *figuras*, quod, cum *vox perit litera scripta manet*. Per figures enim communicari potest inter absentes, et ad quamvis distantiam; et quod præcipuum est, rerum memoriam præservant.

Hic diligenter est advertendum quod eadem sit Ars signorum *audibilium* et *visibilium*: quot modis enim componi possunt (secundum regulas Artis) figuræ simplices, et rebus significandis imponi, tot modis et eadem prorsus Arte, componi possunt et variari soni simplices. Veritatem hanc ulterius sic demonstro. Ubi Ars ibi Methodus, ubi methodus ibi numerus, ubi numerus ibi aptitudo, ut res numeratæ secundum ordinem numericum vel figuris vel vocibus significentur: quod satis est evidens ex signis numericis, a me in hoc opere traditis. Hoc noto propter imperitiam eorum (pro quo errore etiam homines docti sunt increpandi) qui Artem Signorum in *mutis figuris*, hoc est *Characterem Universalem* (ut vulgo appellari solet) mirantur, sed de lingua nova audire non ferunt: cum tamen nemo Artem communicandi per *figuras* tradere potest, quin eadem *Characteris* præcepta sint eadem ratione sonis applicabilia. Hoc quidem meipsum diu latuit, postquam detexerim hanc Artem in figuris: et sicut incredibile videbatur susceptum meum primum de Charactere muto, <p. 14> non solum vulgo sed plurimis viris doctis; hoc vero secundum adhuc magis fidem superabat, etiam multorum quibus abunde satisfactum erat de Arte figurarum.

Quamobrem hoc non me adeo movet, quod pauci apprehendant Artem *Sonorum* et *Figurarum* esse omnino eandem; est enim hoc Artis Mysterium satis arduum. Sed admodum moleste fero, quod videam omnes fere homines una voce *Characterem Realem* et *Mutum* expetentes, dum vero de *Lingua* audiunt, ab hac ut a vano et superfluo Commento abhorrent; quasi Linguarum confusio nullo alio pacto esset reparabilis, nisi exscindendo omnium hominum *Linguas*, ut solis *mutis Characteribus* fieret communicatio. An non qui legit hunc librum, habet me ipsi communicantem animi mei sensa in Charactere *Muto*; non enim audit meas *voces*? Sed dicet, hic Character est *effabilis*. Verum quidem est. An propterea pejor et minus desiderabilis? An voces aures offendunt? Si in signis inartificialibus (qualia sunt voces omnium Linguarum) detur resolutio *sonorum* in *figuras*, et *figurarum* rursus in *sonos*, quæ Ars est

CHAPTER II

ON CHARACTERS

As knowledge is transferred from one person to another by the instrument of the ear by means of sounds, so it is also by the instrument of the eye by means of figures. Communication can also be achieved by the other senses, but less immediately, and this therefore has no bearing on our present design, which is to find the means of communication that is the most concise and most in accord with reason. <p. 13> When a comparison is made between *vocal* and *written* signs, communication by *sounds* is by far the more expedient between people face to face; but communication by *figures* has this one advantage that, while *the spoken word vanishes, the written letter remains.*[19] By using figures it is possible to communicate with an absent person and at any distance, and, most important of all, figures preserve the memory of things.

It should be carefully noted that the art of *audible* signs and *visible* signs is one and the same; for, in as many ways as the simple figures can be combined (following the rules of art) and imposed to signify things, in so many ways also can these simple sounds be combined and varied according to the selfsame art. I shall demonstrate the truth of this further as follows. Where there is an art there is a method, where there is a method there is an enumeration, and where there is an enumeration there is a suitable way whereby the things enumerated are to be represented either by figures or by sounds following the numerical order, as will be clear enough from the numerical signs I have given in this work.[20] I emphasize this because of the ignorance of those (and even learned men must be reproached with this error) who have a high estimation of the art of signs in *mute figures*, that is to say a *Universal Character* (as it is usually called), but who wish to hear nothing of a new language. Whereas, of course, no one can produce an art of communicating by *figures* where the principles underlying the *characters* are not equally applicable to *sounds*. Indeed I myself did not perceive this for a considerable time after I had completed this art in figures. And just as my first undertaking towards a mute character seemed incredible <p. 14> not just to the uneducated but also to many learned men, this extension of it still appears beyond belief even among those who were fully satisfied with the art using figures.

It does not perturb me overmuch that few perceive that the art of *sounds* and *figures* is one and the same, since it is difficult indeed to penetrate this mystery of the art. Nevertheless I am irked to hear people very nearly unanimously

---

[19] A variant of this Latin motto is invoked by Bacon (1887–1901: i. 652) in the course of his discussion of real characters in 'De augmentis scientiarum'.

[20] Cf. the lower section of the page in the prefatory matter entitled 'The alphabet of this Philosophical Language'.

egregia et utilissima, quanto magis debet hæc perfectio reperiri in Signis Artificialibus? Rogarem cui fini vel bono expetitur Character Realis *Mutus*? Si dicatur ad communicandum cum hominibus diversæ *Linguæ*, consentio. Et ego hanc Artem hic doceo, longe compendiosius et facilius <p. 15> quam unquam cogitatum erat ab iis qui eam inter Literaturæ desiderata numerarunt, et quam est possibile ut fiat in tali *Charactere* qui in *sonos* non sit resolubilis. At dices, hic Linguam doceo. Resp. Si alicui non placuerit communicare per hanc artem in *vocibus*, compescat *Linguam*, et obturet *Aures*, et sic communicare poterit in solis *mutis figuris*: ego enim nullam aliam differentiam agnosco inter quemvis *Characterem* (Arte) excogitabilem ad communicandum, et *Linguam*.

Ratio autem quod homines adeo præjudiciis laborant contra *Linguam* novam, et *Characterem mutum* mirantur, est primo partim propter famam *Characteris Universalis* seu *Realis*, quo nomine indigitata fuit hæc Ars ab iis qui de Literaturæ desideratis tractarunt. Secunda hujus rei ratio (quæ etiam reddi potest ratio cur viri docti nihil vel parum dixerunt de Lingua Philosophica, desiderata Artis enumerantes) est propter ignorationem hujus egregiæ veritatis; quod quicquid præstari potest in *figuris*, idem eadem Arte præstari potest in *sonis*, ut supra ostensum est. Tertio, vulgus plus *novitatem* et *Raritatem* Artium admirari solet, quam *veritatem*: communicare autem per signa mere *muta*, est quid novum et rarum; per *figuras* in *sonos* resolubiles est ordinarium.

Suadebant mihi Rei Literariæ amici et etiam mei, Artem hanc primo in *Mutis Characteribus* exhibere, *Linguam* reticendo; quo hominum curiositati, <p. 16> ex rei omnimoda novitate magis placerem, atque sic ipsos ad ejus studium facilius allicerem. Verum hic non videbatur mihi bonus dolus, propter hanc rationem. Certum quidem est tantum esse hominis *curiositatem*, ut ad res *novas* et *raras*, quodam quasi curiositatis ardore et flamma omnes advolent: verum non minus certum est, *fastidium* quoddam occupare mentes humanas post visas res *novas* et *extraordinarias*, nisi *usus* aliquis in illis percipiatur. At vero in iis rebus, quarum *usus* ipsas plus commendat quam *novitas*, licet homines tanto impetu in illas non ferantur, attamen cum *usus* sit bonum *permanens* et *perpetuum*, *novitas* vero cito *transiens*, si non tam avide eas amplectantur, amplexas tamen majori cum voluptate retinent. In duobus autem demonstro usum *Linguæ*, id est facilitatem communicationis, majorem esse quam si in solo *muto Charactere* hanc Artem patefecissem. Primo, Nulla subsidia mnemonica haberi poterant ad Characteres Radicales memoriæ imprimendos, quæ hic valde memoriam adjuvant. Secundo, In *Charactere* solo patefaciendo oportebat novas *figuras* formare, quæ licet paucæ admodum fuerant, et eadem Arte unibiles ad unicum perfectum Characterem constituendum, qua hic literæ ad unam vocem faciendam, tamen aliquid oneris memoriæ necessario secum attulissent: hic vero, retinentur *Characteres* prius noti omnibus Europæ populis.

expressing their desire for a *real* and *mute character*, while recoiling from the idea of a *language*, when they hear it spoken of, as if it were some futile and superfluous fabrication; as if the confusion of tongues could be remedied by no other means than by doing away with all human *languages* so that the only form of communication would be by means of *mute characters*. Would not the reader of this book consider that I am communicating my thoughts to him in a *mute character*, since he is not hearing my *words*? Yet it must be admitted that this character is *effable*. Which, of course, it is. But is it for this reason of less worth or less desirable? Do words offend the ears? If signs that are not rationally instituted (and the words of all languages are such) allow the transformation of *sounds* into *figures* and of *figures* back into *sounds*, which is a noble and useful art, how much more is this feature of excellence to be desired in rationally instituted signs? The question I would ask is: for what end or benefit is a *mute* real character to be invented? If it is replied that its purpose is communication between people of different *languages*, I would fully agree. Indeed it is an art of this sort that I am proposing here, which is far more compendious and easy <p. 15> than any devised by those who reckon it among the desiderata of learning, indeed than any that could possibly be devised using *characters* that cannot be resolved into *sounds*. And, if it be objected that what I am proposing is rather a language, I would reply that, if anyone does not wish to communicate by means of this art using *words*, let him hold his *tongue*, block up his *ears*, and it will be possible thus to communicate purely in *mute figures*, for I recognize no other difference at all between any *character* whatsoever that can be devised (by art) for the purposes of communication, and a *language*.

One reason why people labour under so many prejudices against a new *language* whilst holding a *mute character* in high esteem is because of the long-standing repute of a *Universal* or *Real Character*, which is the name by which this art has been designated by those who have discussed the desiderata of learning. A second reason (which may also explain why learned men have said little or nothing about a Philosophical Language when enumerating the desiderata of art) is because of ignorance of the important truth that whatever can be expressed in *figures* can by the same method equally well be expressed in *sounds*, as has been shown above. The third reason is that people are wont to have a higher esteem for the *novelty* and *singularity* of an art than for its *truth*, and communicating solely by means of *mute* figures is something novel and singular while communicating by *figures* reducible to *sounds* is quite common or garden.

Some friends of mine who are also friends of learning urged me to put forward this art first of all in *mute characters* and to say nothing meanwhile about a *language*, by which means I would make greater appeal to people's curiosity <p. 16> by virtue of the complete novelty of the thing, and more easily inveigle them into studying it. But this did not seem to me a worthy deceit, for the following reason. It is certain that human *curiosity* is so strong that all flock avidly to things that are *new* and *singular*, as if driven by a certain heat and fire of inquisitiveness; but it is equally certain that after seeing *new* and *extraordinary*

<p. 17>   Cum igitur (ut dictum) Ars *Characteris* et *Sonorum* eadem sit, omnino par erat et rationi consentaneum, ut quod facilius erat primo proponeretur: qui enim *Linguæ* usum prius calluerit, possum illum *Characteris* Artem spatio unius horæ docere. Quare cum ex hac Arte *usum* vere intendam, hac Methodo Docendi usus sum, utpote fini meo maxime accommodato; ideoque impresentiarum de *Characteris* Arte nihil plus addam, nisi quod, sicut delectum feci *sonorum simplicissimorum* et maxime euphonicorum, sic etiam *Characteres* erunt *simplicissimi* et figuræ pulchræ et uniformes: nullæ erunt caudæ dependentes, nulli apices eminentes.

things the human mind fills with a certain feeling of *aversion,* unless some *use* can be seen in them. But in those things whose *utility* commends them more strongly than their *novelty,* even though people are not attracted to them with such passion, nevertheless, when their *utility* proves to be a *permanent* and *lasting* good and their *novelty* proves to be *transient,* if they do not embrace them so eagerly, yet having once embraced them they hold on to them with greater pleasure. There are two counts on which I maintain that the utility of the *language*—that is, facility of communication—is greater than if this art were presented solely in a *mute character.* First, no mnemonic aids would have been possible for imprinting the radical characters on the memory, such as here are indeed a great help to the memory. Secondly, if it were presented solely as a *character,* it would have been necessary to create new *figures,* which, even if they were quite a few in number and could be combined to form one complete character in the same way as letters are here combined to form words, would still necessarily involve some additional burden on the memory. The present design, however, employs *characters* that are already known to all the peoples of Europe.

Since then (as I have said) the art of *characters* and *sounds* is one and the <p. 17> same, it was entirely fitting and in accord with reason that the easier of the two should be presented first; for to anyone who has fully grasped the use of the *language* I can teach the use of the *character* within a single hour. Since my main concern in this art is its *use,* I have adopted this method of presentation as most appropriate to my aims. For the present therefore I shall say nothing further concerning the art of *characters,* except to note that, just as I chose *sounds* that will be the *simplest* and most euphonical, the *characters* likewise were of the utmost *simplicity* and the figures as elegant and uniform as possible; there will be no trailing tails or protruding apexes.

CAP. III.

DE RERUM SERIE PRÆDICAMENTALI.

A bsoluta Doctrina de primis Signorum Elementis, quantum præsentis Inftituti ratio postulabat, et brevitas sinebat, priusquam accedam ad *signa integra*, ex his componendum, *rebusque* ipsis imponendum, necessarium erit *Rerum* ipsarum naturas paululum introspicere: hoc enim est malum, cui remedium quærimus in aliis Linguis, quod prima nomina Rerum omnino fortuito, et sine <p. 18> ullo consilio vel respectu habito ad res ipsas pro quibus supponuntur, sint imposita. Cum enim *Signa* a nobis pro *Rebus* ipsis supponantur, omnino rationi consentaneum est, ut Ars *Signorum* Artem *Rerum* sequatur. Et sicut judico *Metaphysicam* et *Logicam* unicam tantum constituere Artem, sic *Grammatica* non aliter vel plus differt ab his, quam *Signum* a *Signato*; cumque hæc correlata sint, omnino eorum eadem debet esse scientia. Quare, qui cum Ratione *Nomina Rebus* imponere velit, primo oportet in Chaos istud Mundi Idealis in animo exiftentis, per quasi creationem Logicam, formam, pulchritudinem, et ordinem introducere; quo facto facile erit ejus partes Nominibus aptis appellare. Sicut enim manus pictoris in sculpendis Imaginibus, per internam Mentis Ideam ex objecto extrinsecus viso genitam, regitur, sic Grammaticus, secundum Ideas et Regulas Logicas a Rerum ipsarum natura extrinsecus existentium petitas, Nomina illis imponere debet. Hæc autem ordinata Series Rerum vulgo dici solet *Prædicamentum*: De quo in genere pauca hic dicenda sunt.

Opinio est quorundam hujus Sæculi Scriptorum, qui in quibusdam Philofophiæ partibus Inventores, in omnibus vero Reformatores se jactant, nullum esse usum *Doctrinæ prædicamentalis*; hoc est revera, strictam Methodum in Artibus docendis non esse necessariam: quo nihil absurdius et <p. 19> Philosopho indignius doceri potest. Quo enim tendunt omnium Philosophorum conatus in variis Philosophiæ partibus, nisi eo, ut Rerum naturas aperiant, differentias et convenientias scrutando, sicque, Methodo et ordine inter se collocando et disponendo? Quod postquam præstitum fuerit in particularibus Scientiis et Artibus, tunc officium est Logici, has sparsas Philosophiæ partes in inferioribus facultatibus ab aliis tractatas colligere, easque legitima subordinatione in unum Systema componere; quod recte appellari potest *Prædicamentum*, seu *Rerum* omnium *series* ordinata. Non mirum est igitur hos Autores in tam fædos errores fuisse lapsos, dum seriem prædicamentalem revera inutilem, nobis obtrudere velint. Quis Philosophus a risu continebit, cum audiverit duo esse Summa genera Rerum, *Corpus* scil. et *Non Corpus*. Dicerem hos homines *Manichæos*, nisi se *Saducæos* aperte profiterentur. Solent hi Terminis Artis, et vocibus ad res significandas a sensu et corporeo contactu remotas impositis, ut absurdis et insignificantibus irridere; cum tamen nulla detur vox magis absurda et

CHAPTER III

ON THE PREDICAMENTAL SERIES OF THINGS

Having outlined the doctrine of the primary elements of signs, within the limits that the purposes of the present design require and that the needs of brevity allow, before proceeding to the manner of combining them to form *integral signs* and assigning these to *things*, it will be necessary to examine briefly the nature of *things* themselves. For the imperfection whose remedy we seek in other languages is that the first names of things have been assigned quite haphazardly <p. 18> and without any regard for or consideration of the *things* themselves for which they stand. Since however *signs* are made by us to stand for *things*, it is wholly in accord with reason that the art of *signs* should follow the art of *things*. Just as I believe that *metaphysics* and *logic* constitute one single art, so *grammar* differs from these only in as much as the *sign* differs from the thing *signified*; and since these are thus interrelated, the same body of knowledge should underlie all of them. Hence whoever wishes to assign *names* to *things* according to reason must first, by an act of logical creation as it were, introduce form, beauty and order into that chaos of the world of ideas existing in the mind. When this has been done it will be an easy matter to assign appropriate names to its component parts. Just as the hand of the painter, in forming images, is guided by an internal mental idea which was produced externally by the object observed, so the grammarian must assign names to things according to the ideas and logical rules derived from the external nature of things themselves. This regular series of things is commonly called the *Predicament*, and there are a few things which need to be said here on this topic in general.

It is the opinion of some writers of this century, who boast of being innovators in certain parts of philosophy and of being reformers throughout, that the *predicamental doctrine* is of no use; which is as much as to say that a strict method is not necessary in teaching the arts, and nothing more absurd <p. 19> and more unworthy of a philosopher can be advanced than that. For where are the efforts of all philosophers in the various parts of philosophy directed other than towards laying bare the nature of things by examining their differences and similarities, and thereby distributing and arranging them in a methodical and orderly way? After this has been achieved in particular sciences and arts, it is then the duty of the logician to bring together the scattered parts of philosophy treated of by others in the subordinate disciplines and to organize them by a regular hierarchy into a single system, which can properly be called a *Predicament* or *orderly series* of all *things*. It is not surprising, therefore, that these authors have fallen into such vile errors when they wish to persuade us that the predicamental series is quite useless. What philosopher can keep himself from laughing when he hears

insignificans, quam *non-corpus* quæ illis summum Genus constituit. Rogarem hos, quid illis significat hæc vox *Deus*? Certe, nisi sibi aperte contradicant, est vox *absurda* et *insignificans*; nullo enim corporeo contactu, ipsis fatentibus, ad naturam Divinam perveniri potest.

<p. 20>   Quandoquidem probabile admodum sit, Libellum hunc ad multorum hominum doctorum manus perventurum, ideo placuit hic paucis inserere Rationes, propter quas seclusa fide ex Dei Revelatione, his duabus Maximis (et quidem mihi aliarum omnium primis) veritatibus ipse assentiam. 1. Esse *Deum*. 2. *Animam* Humanam esse *Immortalem*. Hocque eo libentius facio, quod videam maximam audaciam Mortalitatis assertorum hoc fermento plurimos corrupisse; et quosdam Autores Magni Nominis, hoc Argumentum leviter admodum tractasse.

Primo, præter naturæ vocem in omnibus hominibus Numen suspicientem et invocantem, ulterius sic colligo esse Deum. Esse Causam primam est prima veritas; ergo est prima veritas esse Deum: *Causa* enim *prima* et *Deus* mihi idem significant.   Verum

Secundo, *Animam* Humanam esse *Immortalem*, quod magis dubitatur et apertius contradicitur a multis (licet revera qui hoc negant per necessariam consequentiam *Dei* existentiam etiam negant) sic licet colligere. Nulla potentia *Materialis* et *Mortalis* elevari potest ad Deum *Immaterialem* et *Immortalem* apprehendendum et contemplandum; sed anima humana elevatur ad *Deum* apprehendendum et contemplandum, ideoque etiam appetendum et ut suo summo bono fruendum; ergo non est *Materialis* et *Mortalis*, sed germen et pro-pago Divinæ Naturæ: cui optime consentiunt <p. 21> *S.* Script. phrases, *Animam* appellando *Dei Imaginem, Candelam Domini,* et *Deum* Patrem *Spirituum.* Minor hujus Argumenti patet, nec ab adversariis negatur; Ratio Majoris est, quod inter omnem Actum et Objectum intercedere debet naturæ proportio: quod etiam principiis *immortalitatis* adversariorum est consentaneum, dum docent Mentem corpoream res incorporeas apprehendere non posse.

Renatus Des Cartes, vir in multis ingeniosissimus, videtur mihi hoc Argumentum tractans, fundamentum jecisse in arenis; magno enim apparatu verborum, et singularem Methodum affectans, ad hanc veritatem demon-strandum procedit; cujus tamen Argumenta mihi potius dulces phantasiæ vel Meditationes (ut ipse loquitur) quam rigidæ Demonstrationes videntur. Primum et maximum ejus Argumentum ad hanc veritatem evincendam, tale est. Possum ego supponere, nihil existere extra me, vel Deum, vel Cœlum, vel Terram; vel me habere manus, pedes, oculos, &c. et tamen omnibus his remotis, manet verum *ego Cogito*, ergo etiam hoc, *ego Sum.*

it said that there are two highest genera[21] of things—namely, *body* and *not-body*? I would call these people Manichees if they did not openly declare themselves to be Sadducees.[22] They are wont to scoff at[23] terms of art and at words assigned to signify things remote from the senses and from physical contact as being absurd and meaningless; and yet there is no word more absurd and meaningless as *not-body*, which for them constitutes a highest genus. I would ask them what they understand by the word *God*? It is clear that, unless they are flatly to contradict themselves, this word must be *absurd* and *meaningless*, for by their own confession it is not possible to reach the divine nature by means of physical contact.

Since it is probable that this little book will reach the hands of many learned <p. 20> men, it seems proper to outline briefly the reasons why, setting aside faith from divine revelation, I subscribe to the truth of the following two maxims (which for me indeed are prior to all others): (1) that *God* exists; (2) that the *soul* of man is *immortal*. I do this the more eagerly because I see the effrontery of those who assert its mortality, thereby corrupting so many with this contagion, and because certain authors of repute treat this topic so lightly.

First, besides the voice of nature calling forth and invoking the divinity in all men, over and above this I infer that God exists as follows. That there is a first cause is a primary truth, therefore it is a primary truth that God exists; for to me *first cause* and *God* mean one and the same thing. QED.

Secondly, that the human *soul* is *immortal*, which is more often doubted and more openly denied by many (even though those who deny this must by a necessary consequence also deny the existence of *God*) can be inferred as follows. No *material* and *mortal* power can be elevated so as to apprehend and contemplate the *immaterial* and *immortal* divinity; but the human soul is indeed elevated to apprehend and contemplate *God*, and so also to seek and enjoy the highest good as its own: it is, therefore, not *material* and *mortal* but an embryo and offshoot of the Divine Nature, which is wholly in accord with <p. 21> the sayings of the Holy Scriptures, which call the *soul* the *image of God*, *the candle of the Lord*, and call *God* the father of *spirits*. The minor premiss of this argument is clear and is not denied by my opponents. The justification of the major premiss is that there must be a natural proportion between any act and its object, which is in accord even with the principles of those who deny *immortality*, since they teach that the corporeal mind cannot apprehend incorporeal things.

René Descartes, a most ingenious man in many respects, seems to me to have built his foundations on sand when he deals with this argument, for he proceeds to demonstrate this truth with an immense verbal paraphernalia and aiming at a unique method. However, his arguments seem to me to be pleasant flights of fancy, or meditations (to use his own words), rather than solid proofs.

---

[21] Reading *genera* for *genere*.

[22] The Manichees were dualists, while the Sadducees denied the existence of spirits; both would thus deny the doctrine that man is a unity of body and spirit. Further on Sadducees, see Dalgarno's remarks in the tract 'On Interpretation', fo. 117ʳ (see below, Part IV, Unpublished Paper 2).

[23] Reading *irridere* for *irirdere*.

Miror neminem hujus suppositionis fallaciam detexisse: est enim non minus implicatoria quam hæc. Suppono nihil corporeum existere extra me, tamen verum manet, ego video, ego audio: omnis enim *Actus* tam *Spiritualis* quam *corporeus* necessario supponit *objectum*. Et qui per suppositionem <p. 22> tollit *objectum*, necessario tollit et ipsum *actum*; qui enim cogitat, de aliquo cogitet necesse eft, non minus quam qui videt, audit, necesse est *objectum* aliquod his facultatibus proportionatum habeat.

Si quis ad hanc suppositionem fulciendam diceret, posse *Animam* habere pro cogitationis *objecto seipsam*: Ad hoc Resp. 1. verissimum est, *animam* posse super suos actus directos reflectere, hoc est scire se scire: et hoc secundum est meum principale Argumentum pro *Animæ Immortalitate*, sic enim arguo.

Sicut primo, illa *Natura*, quæ ad Deum contemplandum, appetendum et fruendum elevatur, necesse est *Immaterialis* et *Immortalis* sit; Sic secundo, illa *Natura* quæ super suos Actus reflectere potest, et se contemplare, necesse est hanc Naturæ Divinæ participem esse: sed *Anima*, &c. Ratio Majoris est, quod sit perfectio soli Naturæ Divinæ competens, se contemplare, appetere et frui: Illa enim Natura quæ potest super se reflectere, se appetere et frui, nulla alia re existente, est *Deus*. Quare cum *Anima* possit super se reflectere, (licet non in supra dicta suppositione, sic enim esset revera Deus) certum est hanc potentiam esse partem *Imaginis Divinæ*.

Sed secundo, quid hoc ad dictam suppositionem fulciendam, quod *Anima* possit de se cogitare? Omnis enim *Actus Reflexus* (in Creatura) supponit <p. 23> *actum directum* super quem reflectit: omnis *actus directus* dicit essentialem respectum ad *objectum extrinsecus* existens. Qui igitur per suppositionem tollit omnia *objecta extrinseca*, is etiam *actum directum* omnem tollit; qui *actum directum* tollit, is etiam *actum reflexum*, cum *actus directus* sit *actus reflexi objectum. Actus* autem *Reflexus purus*, sine omni suppositione prioris *Actus directi*, est solius Dei. Quare supponere *Animam*, nulla alia re existente, de se cogitare posse, est supponere impossibile; vel *Animam* effe *Deum*, quod est adhuc magis impossibile.

Tertio, Neque verba ipsa Autoris patiuntur hunc sensum; explicans enim se quid intelligat per vocem *cogitare*, dicit esse, hoc velle, illud nolle, de alio dubitare, &c. qui actus aperte referuntur ad *objecta externa*, quæ modo per fuppositionem sustulerat.

His first and most important argument for demonstrating this truth runs as follows. It is possible for me to suppose that nothing beyond myself exists, neither
God, nor heaven, nor earth, or to suppose that I do not have hands, feet, eyes,
etc., and though these have all been taken away, it yet remains true that *I think*
and consequently also that *I am.*

I am surprised that no one has pointed out the fallacy in this supposition,
for it is no less contradictory than the following. Suppose that no corporeal
body exists beyond myself, yet it remains true that I see and I hear: for every *act*,
either *spiritual* or *corporeal*, necessarily presupposes an *object*. And whoever by
supposition <p. 22> removes the *object* necessarily removes the *act* itself; for if
one thinks, one must be thinking about something, no less than if one sees or
hears there must be some *object* corresponding to these senses.

If anyone should attempt to bolster this supposition by saying that the *soul*
may have its very *self* as the *object* of its thought, I would reply: (1) It is quite true
that the *soul* can reflect upon its own direct acts—that is, it knows that it knows;
but this is in accord with my main argument for the *immortality* of the *soul*,
which I argue as follows.

Just as a *nature* that is elevated to contemplate, desire, and delight in God is
necessarily *immaterial* and *immortal*, so also a *nature* that can reflect upon its own
acts and contemplate itself must necessarily partake of the divine nature; but
the *soul*, etc.[24] The reason for the major premiss[25] is that it is a perfection apper-
taining to the divine nature alone to contemplate, strive after, and enjoy itself.
The nature that can reflect upon, strive after, and delight in itself, nothing else
being in existence, is *God*. Hence, since the *soul* is able to reflect upon itself
(though not in the sense just mentioned, or else it would itself be truly God), it
is certain that this power is part of the *divine image*.

Secondly, how does the fact that the *soul* can think about itself in fact support
the supposition in question? For every *act of reflection* (in a created being) supposes <p. 23> a *direct act* upon which it reflects; every *direct act* implies some
essential connection with an *externally* existing *object*. If, therefore, by supposition, one removes all *externally* existing *objects*, one also removes the *direct act*;
if one removes the *direct act*, one must also remove the *act of reflection*, since the
direct act is the object of the *act of reflection*. The *pure act of reflection*, without any
presupposition of a *direct act*, pertains to God alone. Hence, to suppose that the
soul can think about itself, with nothing else in existence, is to suppose the
impossible; or else that the *soul* is *God*, which is even more clearly impossible.

Thirdly, do not the very words of the writer allow this interpretation; for, in
explaining what he means by the word 'think', he says that this is to want one
thing, not to want another, to doubt about a third, etc., acts that clearly relate
to *external objects*, which he had by supposition removed.

---

[24] The syllogistic argument is left for the reader to complete. The soul can reflect upon its own acts
and contemplate itself. Therefore, the soul partakes of the divine nature.
[25] i.e. the proposition expressed by the previous sentence.

Si dicat quis, quomodo dici possunt illa principia prima notissima et verissima, de existentia Dei et Animæ Immortalitate, cum ea homines docti habeant pro falsissimis? Resp. Hos homines loqui vel ex pravo affectu vel esse Mente captos. Sed quis ita mente captus, ut notissima et prima principa neget? Imo, vidi aliquando homines morbo corporeo laborantes, dum alios loquentes audiebant, et intuebantur, tamen negasse se vel videre, vel audire, et quanto clarius proponebatur iis objectum, tanto magis negabant se sentire. Sic contigit <p. 24> insanientem Atheum, dum conceptus clarissimos de Deo format, tunc strenuissime hoc idem negare. Sed hi homines multum sapientiæ in aliis rebus manifestant. Sic contigit aliquando quosdam homines absurde et ridicule de una aliqua re sentire, in aliis tamen satis sapere.

Sed ne diutius a proposito digrediar, summam dictorum in hanc brevem circularem ratiocinunculam colligo, quæ mihi principia prima et notissima continet (cum scil. non sensum, sed rectæ rationis ductum sequor) quæque ad omnia Atheorum Sophismata diluenda sufficiunt; *Aut ego sum Immortalis, aut Deus non est,—Aut Deus est, aut ego nihil sum*: jamque ad *prædicamentum* redeo.

Et interrogo illos qui *prædicamenti* nullum usum vident, quid significent hæ voces *genus, species, differentia, definitio,* &c.? Certe, sine prædicamenti suppositione funt omnino absurdæ et nihil significantes: omnis enim *demonstratio* supponit *definitionem, definitio genus* et *speciem, genus* et *species* ordinatam *seriem Prædicamentalem*. Et quidem si proprie loqui velimus, nulla est *definitio* vel *demonstratio* (licet Autorum scripta his vocibus abundent) quia nulla est constituta *series prædicamentalis*: hinc est, quod quæ habetur *definitio* ab uno, non merebitur *descriptionis* nomen (ut vulgo distinguunt) ab alio; sic quod huic est *demonstratio*, illi est *Sophisma*.

Jecit Aristoteles quædam rudia fundamenta <p. 25> *prædicamenti*, et nos nihil vel parum superftruximus. Posuit ille pro suo arbitrio decem Summa Genera Rerum, quasdam notiones quæ sub his comprehendi nequibant, *Transcendentes* et *Extravagantes* appellando; ex quibus duo alia *prædicamenta* eadem ratione et Autoritate constituere potuisset. Ratio quod hæc rerum ordinatio displiceat, eft primo, quod non satis accurate distinguat *Rerum notiones*; cum eadem *notio* sæpissime diversis respectibus, ad diversa *prædicamenta* referri potest, *Qualitatis, Actionis, Relationis,* &c. Secundo, quod in recta ordinata *serie Rerum*, nullæ sunt notiones *Transcendentes* admittendæ, nisi *genera* respectu *specierum* et *individuorum, Transcendentia* quis dicere velit. Qui enim notiones *Transcendentes* ullo alio sensu admittunt, contradicunt *prædicamenti definitioni* ab ipsis traditæ, ni. quod sit *Series Rerum sub uno summo genere contentarum*. Est igitur secundum hanc definitionem, sola notio *Entis* Transcendens.

How, it may be asked, can these be said to be the first acknowledged and true principles concerning the existence of God and the immortality of the soul, when certain learned men hold them to be false? I reply that such men are either talking from a warped disposition, or they are mad. But who can be so mad as to deny the first and most well-known truths? Indeed I have sometimes seen men suffering from a bodily malady, who, when they heard others talking about something and themselves looked, nevertheless denied that they could see or hear it; and the more clearly the object was displayed to them, the more firmly they denied perceiving it. Thus it is also <p. 24> with the insane atheist; when he forms the clearest concepts concerning God, he then most strenuously denies them. But these people show great understanding in other things. Thus it sometimes happens that some people have absurd and ridiculous opinions on one matter but have sound judgement on others.

But I shall not digress from my subject any longer, but sum up what I have said in a concise, circular statement of the argument, which contains what are to me the first and widely acknowledged principles (namely, when I follow not the guidance of the senses but of right reason) and which are enough to resolve all the sophisms of the atheists. *Either I am immortal, or God does not exist: Either God exists or I am nothing.* I now return to the topic of the *Predicament*.

I ask those who see no use in the predicament what these words signify: *genus, species, difference, definition*, etc.? Without supposing the predicament, these are clearly quite absurd and meaningless; for all *demonstration* presupposes *definition, definition* supposes *genus & species*, and *genus & species* suppose an orderly *predicamental series*. Indeed strictly speaking there is no definition or demonstration (even though the words occur frequently in the writings of these authors) where there is no *predicamental series* established. For this reason, what is held to be a *definition* by one person will not merit the name of *description* (as these two are commonly distinguished) for another person; thus what is a *proof* for one is a mere *sophism* for another.

Aristotle laid some basic foundations <p. 25> for the *predicament*, and we have built little or nothing upon them. He arbitrarily posited ten *highest genera* of things, calling some notions that could not be included under these *transcendental* and *extravagant*, from which he could have established two other predicaments by the same reasoning and authority. The reason why this ordering of things is unsatisfactory, is, first, that it does not distinguish the *notions* of *things* accurately enough, since often the same *notion* can, in its diverse respects, be assigned to several different predicaments: *Quality, Action, Relation*, etc. Secondly, because in a properly ordered *series of things* no *transcendental* notions are to be allowed, unless it is argued that *genera* are to be termed *transcendental* with respect to *species* and *individuals*. For those who allow *transcendental* notions in any other sense are contradicting *the definition of the predicament* which they themselves subscribe to—namely, that it is *a series of things contained under a single highest genus*. Following this definition there is only one transcendental notion—namely, *Being*.

Quid igitur fiet de his *unum, verum, bonum*? Omnino *Enti* subjugandæ sunt, sunt enim revera *Accidentia*. *Unitas* est Denominatio extrinseca, Rebus adveniens per Intellectus operationem, non minus quam *dualitas, trinitas,* &c. nihil enim est quod constituat Petrum *unum* hominem ante operationem intellectus, quod non eadem ratione, constituat Petrum et Paulum *duos* homines. Formalis etiam ratio *Veritatis* consistit in *relatione* inter *actum* Mentis et *objectum*. Sic denominatio <p. 26> *Bonitatis* dicit essentialem respectum ad *appetitum,* seu *voluntatem* aliquam. Imo Deus ipse *O. M.* ideo denominatur *optimus,* quod sit summe *appetibilis*: licet enim omnis *voluntas* creata cessaret esse, vel *appetere* Deum, nihilominus maneret semper summe *appetibilis,* et actu *appetitus* ab *appetitu perfectissimo,* hoc est suo; ideoque summe *bonus*. Voces autem *Res* et *aliquid* sunt omnino Synonymæ cum voce *Entis*.

Verum ad has notiones uberius explicandas, et in summa, ad terminos Metaphysicos, Logicos, et Grammaticos, (quæ ut dixi eandem constituunt Artem) multa verborum caligine obscuratos et intricatos, discutiendos, Tractatum specialem postularet: Nam propter defectum accuratæ Doctrinæ Logicæ, plurimæ reperiuntur absurdæ locutiones passim in scriptis Philosophorum et Theologorum; sæpius necessitate imposita, etiam viris doctis, loquendi cum vulgo, ut a vulgo intelligantur. Et quidem hæc Magna Philosophiæ *Reformatio* consistit in *Seriei prædicamentalis* legitima ordinatione, quæ fons est omnium *definitionum, divisionum, demonstrationum,* aliorumque Logicorum *Argumentorum,* et *terminorum*: ad quod *Nobile Susceptum* ut alios provocem, et ut quibusdam objectionibus contra sequentem Rerum Seriem in Lexico hujus Artis exhibitam, occurratur, mentem meam de *Prædicamenti Natura* quibusdam generalibus conclusionibus aperiam.

<p. 27>   Primo, Male representatur a Philosophis prædicamenti natura, *Arboris* similitudine; cum nihil sit quod clarius illustret hanc Rerum et Notionum Seriem, quam *Genealogia* Generis Humani. Sicut enim *fide* credimus, omnes homines ab uno primo Parente descendisse, sic *ratione* probamus, omnes particulares Notiones ab una prima *notione Entis* derivari. Hinc est quod recte vocari soleant Mentis humanæ apprehensiones, seu perceptiones, *Rerum Conceptus*: Res enim ipsæ sunt quasi *Pater,* gignens in mentibus nostris suam *Imaginem*; *Intellectus* vero est *Mater,* has imagines concipiens; et *Memoria* est *uterus,* in quo Rerum Imagines sic genitæ gestantur. Et quemadmodum videmus numerum *hominum,* ex successiva et continuata generatione multiplicari; sic etiam *notionum* numerus ex *Mente* humana, *corpore* non minus fœcunda, indies augetur. Et sicut is solus dicendus esset perfectus *Historicus,* qui omnia Adami gesta, et continuatam Seriem totius ejus posteritatis, omnesque eorum Actiones recitare poterit; sic ille solus dicendus esset perfectus *Philosophus,* qui totum numerum Rerum et Notionum, non minus numerosum quam est Adami Posteritas, descendendo et vicissim ascendendo recitare poterit, omnesque mutuos respectus horum inter se computare. Hinc apparet, quantillum sit quod nos Homines scimus; *Quam-quantum* vero quod nescimus.

What then is to be done with the notions *One, True, Good*? They are certainly to be subsumed under *Being*, for they are truly *accidents*. *Unity* is an extrinsic denomination that is put onto things by the operation of the intellect, no less than *Duality, Trinity,* etc., for there is nothing that makes Peter *one* man before the operation of the intellect, that does not, by the same reasoning, make Peter and Paul *two* men. The formal aspect of *truth* consists in a *relation* between an *act* of the mind and an *object*. Thus the designation <p. 26> *goodness* bears an essential relation to some *desire* or *wish*. Indeed God O[ptimus] M[aximus] himself is termed *best* because he is the most highly to be *desired*. Even if every created *will* should cease to exist or cease to *desire* God, nevertheless He would remain for ever the most highly to be *desired*, and by an act of *desire* that derives from the most *perfect desire*, which is his own. He is therefore the *highest good*. For the words *thing* and *something* are fully synonymous with the word *Being*.

But to explain these notions more fully, and to clarify the terms of metaphysics, logic, and grammar (which I have said all constitute the same art), which are obscured and confused in a great fog of words, would require a separate treatise. For, because of the lack of an accurate logical doctrine, various absurd locutions are found frequently throughout the writings of philosophers and theologians, not seldom because even learned men are forced to speak to the vulgar as they are to be understood by the vulgar. And, indeed, a great *reformation* in philosophy would consist in a proper ordering of the *predicamental series*, which is the source of all *definitions, divisions, proofs*, and of other logical *arguments* and *terms*. In order to call others forth to this *noble undertaking*, and to meet any objections against the following series of things as set out in the lexicon of this art, I will state my opinion concerning the *nature* of the *predicament* by way of some general conclusions.

First, the nature of the predicament is wrongly represented by philosophers <p. 27> by means of an analogy with a *tree*, for there is nothing that more clearly illustrates this series of things and notions than the *genealogy* of the human race. Just as we believe by *faith* that all men are descended from one first parent, likewise we can show by *reason* that all particular notions are derived from one primary *notion Being*. This is why the apprehensions or perceptions of the human mind are rightly called *conceptions of things*. For *things* themselves are like a *father*, begetting his image in our minds; the *intellect* is like a *mother* conceiving these images; and the *memory* is the *uterus* in which the images of things thus begotten gestate. And, just as we see the number of *people* increase by successive and continuing generation, so the number of *notions* of the human *mind*, which is no less fertile than the *body*, increases from day to day. And, just as he alone is said to be a perfect *historian* who can recite all the exploits of Adam, and the continued series of all his descendants and their actions, so he alone can be said to be a perfect *philosopher* who is able to recite the whole number of things or notions, which are no less numerous than Adam's offspring, both in descending and ascending order, and compute all the various mutual connections between them. From this it appears how little we humans know, and how much we do *not* know.

<p. 28> Secundo, si ex una parte, Rerum numerum pene infinitum, multiplicesque et varios ipsarum respectus mutuos, ex altera parte imbecillitatem Intellectus humani respiciamus; expectandum non est, talem *seriem Rerum* Arte humana construi posse, quæ omnibus numeris, et ita absolute sit perfecta, et quoad *numerum*, et quoad *methodum*, ut nihil vel *addi*, vel *demi*, vel *transmutari* possit: respectus enim Rerum ita multipliciter varii sunt, ut earum Methodus secundum varias suppositiones et varios respectus, multipliciter variabilis sit. Nominetur enim quælibet Philosophiæ pars, et ad hanc tractandam adhibeantur separatim mille viri doctissimi; inveniretur duos horum in omnibus inter se non consentire: quod non est soli *humanæ imbecillitati* imputandum (quod bene advertendum est) sed partim etiam, *Rerum* ipsarum *naturæ varietati*, et *respectui multiplici*. Nihilominus, licet talis perfectio expectanda non sit, maximi tamen esset usus in Philosophia, habere unam aliquam plenam *Seriem Rerum*, suffragiis multorum hominum doctorum comprobatam, omnes principales et notas notiones *Naturæ* et *Artis* legitima subordinatione prædicamentali per modum *Generis* et *Speciei* complectentem.

Tertio, Duplex est suppositio secundum quam hæc *series Rerum* constitui potest, et exinde Rerum *Definitiones* deduci: Vel primo, investigando per Analysin Logicam, certum numerum *primarum* et <p. 29> *simplicissimarum Notionum*, ex quibus omnes aliæ complexæ componuntur; et quidem hic Analyticus modus in penitiorem Rerum cognitionem ducit. Novi sententiam esse ingeniosissimorum hominum, numerum *Notionum simplicium* per strictam Analysin Logicam, pauciorem esse numero sonorum articulatorum simplicium per strictam Analysin Grammaticam. Vel secundo, constitui potest hæc *series* reducendo omnes Notiones *Naturæ* et *Artis*, tam *Complexas* quam *Simplices*, ad lineam rectam prædicamentalem. Utriusque hujus Notionum texturæ magnus esset usus in Philosophia.

Quarto, In serie secundum hanc secundam suppositionem stabilita, maxime naturale esset, eandem methodum observare in *substantiis*, et accidentibus ordinandis; cujus Methodi adumbrationem videre licet in *Tabulis* meis.

Quinto, *Divisio* Generum in hac Serie, procul omni dubio, optima et maxime naturalis esset *Dichotomica*, quæ omnium Distributionum est *optima*, quia *prima*; est enim primus discessus ab *unitate*. Nec verum est illud quod vulgo objicitur contra Dichotomiam, quod magis confundat *memoriam*; modo enim oppositio quæ est fundamentum hujus divisionis exhibeatur clara, nihil est quod magis adjuvet *memoriam*. Quotiescunque igitur *Memoria* confunditur ex *Doctrina Dichotomica*, revera non tam *Memoria* quam *Intellectus* confunditur, qui <p. 30> nondum satis clare percepit divisionis Rationem et Fundamentum.

Secondly, if we consider the near infinite number of things and the multiple <p. 28> and multifarious mutual relations between them, on the one hand, and, on the other hand, the feebleness of the human intellect, it is not to be expected that a *series of things* could be constructed by human art such as would be absolutely perfect as regards both *number* and *method*, so that nothing could be *added*, *taken away*, or *rearranged*. For the aspects of things are so multiply varied that their method, following various suppositions and perspectives, is accordingly variable. Name any part of philosophy and let a thousand of the most learned men be separately invited to treat of it: it will be found that no two of them will agree in all points, which is not to be ascribed solely to *human feeblemindedness* (which must be carefully noted) but partly also to the *varied nature* of *things* themselves and their *multiple interconnections*. Nevertheless, although such perfection cannot be hoped for, it would be of the greatest use in philosophy to have a *series of things* that was complete to some degree, acknowledged by the judgement of many learned men, and comprising all the principal and known notions of *nature* and *art* in a regular predicamental ordering by the method of *genus* and *species*.

Thirdly, the supposition following which this *series of things* might be constructed, and the *definitions* of things derived, is twofold. Either (1) by investigation through logical analysis of a certain number of *primary* and <p. 29> *most simple notions*, from which all other complex notions are composed, and indeed this analytic method leads to a deeper knowledge[26] of things. I know it to be the opinion of the most sagacious men that the number of *simple notions*, arrived at by strict logical analysis, is less than the number of simple articulate sounds arrived at by strict grammatical analysis. Or else, secondly, the series could be constructed by reducing all the notions of *nature* and *art*, *complex* and *simple* ones alike, to a uniform predicamental line. Either of these ways of disposing notions would be of great use in philosophy.

Fourthly, in the series established according to this second supposition it would be most natural to observe the same method in the ordering of *substances* as in the ordering of accidents, of which method an outline may be seen in my *Tables*.

Fifthly, the best and most natural *division* of the genera in this series, without any doubt, is by *dichotomy*, which is the *best* of all divisions because it is the *first*, for it is removed from *unity* by one step alone. Nor is there any truth in the common objection to dichotomy—namely, that it is more confusing to the *memory*; provided that the opposition that is the foundation of this division is clearly displayed, there is nothing that aids the *memory* more. If the *memory* is sometimes confused when taught by *dichotomies*, it is in fact not so much the *memory* that is confused as the *intellect*, which <p. 30> has not yet clearly enough perceived the reason and underpinning of the division.

---

[26] Reading *cognitionem* for *cogintionem*.

Sexto, Distributio omnis Prædicamentalis perfecta, est facienda per differentias et Species *positivas*; secus enim nulla est legitima Divisio facta: nullæ enim sunt species rerum *non existentium*, et Differentiæ *negativæ* nequeunt species *positivas* constituere. Philosophi et viri docti verborum fallacia hac in re valde decipiuntur; cum enim voces Linguarum vulgarium non sint Philosophice institutæ, et propterea cum nobis desint voces ad exprimendas multarum Rerum Differentias Categoricas, hinc est quod cogamur fingere voces *Negativas*, ex vocibus *positivis* diversæ vel oppositæ significationis, ad Notiones non minus *positivas* significandas, quam sunt istæ quæ vocibus *positivis* notantur: et sic propter defectum vocabulorum, Differentias *positive* contrarias, vocibus *negativis* exprimimus. Res hæc, licet a paucis observata, est tamen apertissima; ut patet in his exemplis, *æquale, inæquale, par, impar*: notio enim *inæqualitatis* non minus est positiva quam *æqualitatis*; dicit enim unam quantitatem esse alia *majorem*; et quid magis positivum? Idem dicendum de *par* et *impar*; quæ Anglice, vocibus *positivis* redduntur, *even, odd*.

Septimo, male omnino, et sine ulla ratione, arcent Philosophi *Artefacta* a Serie prædicamentali: *Artefacta* enim non minus sunt objectum <p. 31> nostræ cognitionis quam *Naturalia*; et non minus capacia sunt *ordinis*, et *methodi*, quam illa.

Octavo, Notandum in tali *Serie*, quamplurimæ darentur voces *genericæ*; quales sunt hæ, *Accidens, Qualitas, Quantitas, Relatio, planta, brutum, avis,* &c. quæ communiores Rerum respectus et convenientias notant. Supposito enim quod numerus *specierum infimarum* esset 4,000 vel 10,000, totidem esset numerus notionum *Genericarum*: quia scil. jam supposuimus omnem Generum divisionem esse dichotomice factam: et notiones Genericæ et communiores, unica voce expressæ, essent valde Emphaticæ, et ad docendum aptæ. Sic, daretur una notio communis *Generica*, ad omnes *Species* differentiis contrariis et prositivis distinctas: Sicut enim *sexus* est notio communis ad *marem* et *fœminam*, fic *calidum* et *frigidum, humidum* et *siccum, durum* et *molle,* &c. unicam notionem communem *genericam*, in qua convenirent, haberent. Specimen hujus Methodi videre licet apud Petrum Ramum, qui solus (quantum vidi) distributionem *Dichotomicam*, secundum strictas leges *prædicamentales*, in suis scriptis Philosophicis accurate observavit; licet illi defuerint *voces simplices* ad notiones *Genericas* distincte et compendiose sine periphrasi exprimendas.

Sixthly, for a predicamental distribution to be perfect, it is to be made by *positive* differences and species, for otherwise no legitimate division is made, there being no species of things *that do not exist*, and *negative* differences cannot constitute *positive* species. Philosophers and learned men are often led into error in this regard by the deception of words, since the words of vulgar languages were not instituted by philosophical method, and since therefore we lack words to express the categorical differences of many things, we are forced to invent *negative* words, derived from *positive* words with different or opposite meaning, to express notions that are in fact no less *positive* than those that are expressed as *positive* words; and thus, because of this defect in the vocabulary, we express differences that are *positively* opposed by means of *negative* words. Although this point has been observed by only few people, it is patently obvious, as emerges from the examples: *aequale, inaequale, par, impar*. For the notion of *inequality* is no less positive than that of *equality*; for it means that one quantity is *greater* than another, and what can be more positive? The same holds for *par* and *impar*, which in English are both expressed by positive words: *even, odd*.

Seventhly, quite wrongly and without any reason whatsoever, philosophers exclude *artefacts* from the predicamental series. *Artefacts*, however, are no less the objects <p. 31> of our knowledge than *natural things*, and are no less capable of being subjected to *order* and *method*.

Eighthly, it should be noted that in such a series there occur very many generic words, such as *accident, quality, quantity, relation, plant, beast, bird*, etc., which denote the more general aspects and similarities of things. If we suppose that the number of *lowest species* is 4,000 or 10,000, the number of the generic notions would be the same, because we have just posited that all divisions of the *genera* are by dichotomy, and that the generic and more common notions, expressed in a single word, are good for rhetorical emphasis and are most useful in teaching. Thus one common *generic* notion would be given to all *species* that are distinguished by contrary and positive differences. For example, *sex* is a notion common to *male* and *female*; and similarly *hot* and *cold*, *wet* and *dry*, *hard* and *soft*, etc., have one common *generic* notion uniting each pair. An illustration of this method can be seen in Peter Ramus,[27] who is the only person (as far as I have seen) who has consistently observed the distribution by dichotomy following strict predicamental rules in his philosophical writings, though he lacked *simple words* to express the *generic* notions distinctly and concisely without periphrasis.

---

[27] Pierre de la Ramée (1515–72).

CAP. IV.

COROLLARIA QUÆDAM GRAMMATICALIA EX DICTIS DE PRÆDICAMENTO.

E x iis quæ jam dixi de *prædicamento* in Genere, quod fundamentum est, et Materia *in qua* Grammatica, Corollaria quædam Grammaticalia deducam.

Primo, Constitutio illa Prædicamenti, quæ Notiones *primas* et *simplicissimas* (quarum numerum non superare decem opinio est quorundam) primo loco disponit; deinde compositas ex his paucis simplicibus, pro ratione varia qua ex his componuntur, et multiplici respectu quem ad se invicem dicunt, Fundamentum non est idoneum Artis Grammaticæ; idque propter duplicem rationem, unam a *Rebus* ipsis, alteram a *Signis petitam.*

Primo, qui Analysin accuratam omnium Notionum *Naturæ* et *Artis*, maxime *complexarum*, in prima sua Elementa, omnesque respectus mutuos *simplicium* in hoc Composito, curiose persequeretur; toties necessario ab illo assumerentur, et reassumerentur hæc *simplicia*, ad varios respectus *Compositi* significandos, illudque ab omnibus aliis <p. 33> rebus perfecte discriminandum; ut perfecta jam Analysi, Notio hæc *una* præ oculis poneretur, sæpissime, in tot *Partes* distributa a Philosopho curioso, quot corpus humanum, post dissectionem, a perito Anatomico. Et quidem non minus difficile esset, ex tot partibus per hanc Analysin jam separatim positis, colligere unam completam et integram formam hujus Compositi, ita clare ut ab omnibus aliis Compositis ex iisdem simplicibus distinguatur; quam ex dissecto cadavere in minutissimas partes, discernere cujus sit, an Petri, Jacobi, vel Thomæ, &c. Non nego (ut supra docui) hujusmodi Analyses in penitiorem et interiorem rerum cognitionem ducere; Imo dico hanc esse summam Philosophiæ perfectionem, posse quamlibet propositam Notionem in sua prima principia resolvere: qui modus philosophandi utilissimus nimis negligitur. Apparet tamen ex dictis, hanc Analysin parum conducere ad hanc Notionem, sub forma unius Compositi, statim unico Mentis actu, sine longo discursu, apprehendendum.

Secundo, Si signa respiciamus, idem manifestum erit; hoc principium omnino ineptum esse, ut secundum illud Nomina Rebus imponantur. Supponamus enim Notionum aliquam, per dictam Analysin distribui in centum, forte mille particulas, ad omnes minutas Differentias hujus Rei, quibus ab omnibus aliis distinguitur, notandas: oporteret, ut ad minimum, singulæ particulæ seu Differentiæ unam <p. 34> literam, ad illas distincte significandum haberent; his igitur literis in unam vocem collectis, Rerum Nomina in eam longitudinem excrescerent, ut vox una integram paginam impleret. Summe quidem cum illis consentio, qui majore acumine Philosophiæ partem Analyticam contemplant, quam Philosophorum vulgus; quanto pauciora fuerint Signa Primitiva,

CHAPTER IV   <p. 32>

SOME GRAMMATICAL COROLLARIES FROM
WHAT HAS BEEN SAID ABOUT THE PREDICAMENT

From what I have already said about the *Predicament* in general, which is the foundation of grammar, and the matter on which grammar operates, I draw the following grammatical corollaries.

First, the constitution of the predicament that in first place puts the *first* and *most simple* notions (the number of which, in the opinion of some, does not exceed ten), and next thereafter those that are composed out of these few simple ones, is not an adequate foundation for the art of grammar, by virtue of the various grounds on which the latter are compounded of the former, and the multiple respects that they bear to each other. This is for a twofold reason, the one drawn from the *things* themselves, the other from the *signs*.

First, whosoever carefully pursues to the end an accurate analysis of all notions of *nature* and *art*, which are extremely *complex*, resolving them into their first elements, and all the mutual relations of these *simple* elements within this composite, it will be necessary for such a person to assume and reassume these *simple* elements, in order to represent the various relations within the *composite*, and to distinguish it perfectly from all other things, <p. 33> so that, when the analysis has been completed, and this *one* notion is laid out before one's eyes, it very often happens that it has been distributed by the skilful philosopher into as many *parts* as a human body after dissection by a skilled anatomist. And indeed it would be no less difficult to put together, from so many parts separated out by this analysis, the single complete and whole form of this composite, so clearly that it could be distinguished from all other composite notions composed out of the same set of simple notions, than it would be to discern, from a dead body dissected into the minutest parts, whether it was Peter's, or James's, or Thomas's, etc. I do not deny (as I have said above) that analyses of this sort lead to a deeper and more interior knowledge of things. Indeed I affirm that it is the highest achievement of philosophy to be able to resolve any notion into its first principles. This most useful method of philosophizing is too much neglected. Nevertheless it is clear from what has been said that this type of analysis is of little use for the immediate apprehension of a notion as a single unified whole, by a single act of the mind, without requiring much mental ado.

Secondly, if we turn to the signs, it will be likewise apparent that this principle is quite unsuitable for the purposes of assigning names to things. Let us suppose some notion that by the aforesaid method of analysis has been distributed into a hundred, or even into a thousand, component particles, so as to indicate all of the minute differences of the thing, by which it is distinguished

ex quibus Rerum Complexarum Nomina, non ex mero Arbitrio, sed Logice et secundum Rei Naturam componentur, tanto perfectior erit Ars: Frustra enim fit per plura, quod æque, vel magis commode fieri potest per pauciora. Verum in tanta paucitate Primitivarum, ex nimia brevitate, nimia obscuritas oriretur: experientia etiam comprobaret, plus Arbitrii necessario fore in hujusmodi Compositis quam ipsis simplicibus.

Secundo, Nec illa constitutio Seriei Prædicamentalis, in qua omnes distinctæ Notiones Naturæ et Artis, tam complexæ quam simplices, per ordinatam seriem Generum et Specierum in linea Prædicamentali collocarentur, adeoque distinctis Nominibus Primitivis notandæ, esset structuræ hujus Linguæ principium accommodatum. Ratio est, quod numerus vocum Primitivarum esset pene infinitus; Bauhinus numerat 6,000 species plantarum; Brutorum ingens est numerus; vocabulorum Artis et Rerum Artefactarum, a nemine adhuc ad methodum Artis reductarum, multo <p. 35> major esset. Imo, ut docent Philosophi, continuum quodlibet minimum dividi posse in infinitum, sic non minus vere, quodlibet Genus vel species dividi potest per infinitas differentias: sic *numeri, colores, soni, passiones animi*, &c. Natura autem ipsa in omni homine docet Rerum Naturas sub communi et universali respectu confiderare, et ex paucis quibusdam Communibus Rerum rationibus, particulares Rerum naturas describere: quamobrem, omnino æquum est, ut Ars (quæ nihil est aliud nisi Natura Exculta) rationes Rerum maxime communes doceat, ex quibus particularium Rerum Naturæ describi possunt.

Quare Tertio, neutrum horum extremorum sequendum judicavi; sed viam mediam ineundam (quæ in Rebus multis maxime probatur) hoc est, selectum numerum principaliorum Notionum, ex primis et præcipuis Scientiis esse delegendum, earum scil. quæ respectus Rerum Communiores dicunt; et has pro primis supponere, iisque significandis voces Radicales imponere, ex quibus aliarum Rerum complexarum Nomina conficerentur.

from all others. It would be appropriate that, at very least, each of the individual particles or differences should have a single letter <p. 34> to signify it distinctly. Consequently, when all such letters are brought together to form words, the names of things would grow to such a length that a single word would fill a whole page. I wholeheartedly agree with those who consider the analytical part of philosophy with greater attention than the usual run of philosophers: the fewer the primitive signs are from which the names of complex things are composed, not from a merely arbitrary institution but in a logical fashion and according to the nature of the thing, the more perfect will be the art. For it is futile to do by means of more things, what can be done equally well, or even more easily, by means of fewer.[28] Yet, with such a very small number of primitives, excessive brevity will result in excessive obscurity. Experience also confirms that there is necessarily more arbitrariness in composites of this kind than in the simple notions themselves.

Secondly, nor would a disposition of the predicamental series in which all the distinct notions of nature and art, both complex and simple, were set out in a predicamental line by an orderly series of genera and species, such that they could be denoted by distinct primitive names, be an appropriate principle for the structure of this language. The reason for this is that the number of primitive words would be almost infinite. Bauhin[29] enumerates 6,000 species of plants; the number of beasts is vast; and the size of the vocabulary required for the arts and man-made things, which has not hitherto been reduced to the method of art by anyone, would be greater still. <p. 35> Indeed, as the philosophers teach us that even the smallest continuum can be subdivided an infinite number of times, so it is no less true that any genus or species whatsoever can be subdivided by an infinite number of differences—namely, *numbers, colours, sounds, passions of the soul*, etc. However, nature herself teaches every man to consider the natures of things from a common and universal respect, and to describe the particular natures of things on the basis of a small number of common grounds. For which reason it is entirely appropriate that art (which is nothing other than cultivated nature) should teach the most common grounds of things, on the basis of which the natures of particular things can be described.

Therefore, thirdly, I have decided that neither of these two extremes should be followed, but that the middle course (which proves best in many things) should be chosen: this is, a select number of principal notions, drawn from the first and foremost sciences should be assigned—namely, those that refer to the most common respects of things—and to take these as primitive and to impose radical words to signify them, from which the names of other complex things can be derived.

---

[28] An adaptation of the Latin motto 'Frustra fit per plura, quod fieri potest per pauciora', cited elsewhere by Dalgarno (see the treatise 'On Terms of Art', fo. 120ᵛ (see below, Part IV, Unpublished Paper 3)).

[29] Bauhin (1623).

Quot autem præcise numero sint hæ Notiones, et secundo, quænam nominatim tales sint habendæ, et tertio quo ordine inter se collocandæ; in his quæstionibus resolvendis, verissime dici potest, quot capita tot sententiæ. Censeo tamen omnes viros vere doctos mecum in hoc consensuros, nullam <p. 36> harum quæstionum determinari posse sine multo Arbitrii. Ingenii vero mei Mensura circa eas haberi potest ex Tabulis seu Lexico hujus operis: quas non offero ut Seriem Rerum summe perfectam, vel quoad Numerum, vel Methodum Notionum inibi contentarum; sed multum Arbitrii habere admixtum agnosco: hactenus enim docui, hanc Artem Signorum strictas Leges Philosophiæ non pati.

Exactly how many of these notions there are, and, secondly, which exactly are to be selected as such, and, thirdly, in which order they are to be brought together; in resolving these questions, it can truly be said, that there are as many opinions as there are heads.[30] Nevertheless I am sure that all truly learned men will agree with me in this, <p. 36> that none of these questions can be determined without a great deal of arbitrariness. The measure of my ability in this regard is to be judged from the Tables or Lexicon of the present work, which I do not submit as a perfect series of things, either as to the number or as to the arrangement of the notions contained therein, for I acknowledge that there is a large admixture of arbitrariness. My lesson so far is that this art of signs does not admit of strict philosophical rules.

---

[30] Latin motto: 'quot capita, tot sententiae'.

CAP. V.

EXPLICATIO TABULARUM.

Quandoquidem jam ad solos doctos scribo, quibus pauca verba sufficient, non morabor longam disputationem instituere de singularum Notionum natura et Methodo; sed paucis tantummodo seriem hanc Rerum adumbrabo, rationem dissensus mei a vulgari opinione in quibusdam breviter inuendo, quæ obvia sunt prætereundo.

Cum Philosophis omnibus sanioribus Consentio, dari unum Summum Genus, et primum et communissimum conceptum, quem solemus appellare *Ens*, seu *Res*. Verum in primis Differentiis *Ens* dividentibus, sententia mea ab illorum differt: <p. 37> Tam cito scil. oriuntur opinionum differentiæ inter nos homines, quam in ipsis rebus inveniuntur. Docent illi *substare* et *accidere* primo dividere *Ens*: Mihi vero videtur, Seriem perfecte prædicamentalem constitui non posse, secundum quam legitimæ prædicationes fieri possunt, nisi Differentias concipiamus magis latepatentes, quæ adæquate dividant *Ens*, sub conceptu et respectu communissimo: has ego vocavi, *abstractum* esse et *concretum* esse; vel *simplex* et *compositum*; vel statum rei *incompletum* et *completum*; Ens vero incompletum secunda divisione, in *Substantiam* et *Accidens* dividendo: nisi quis mallet uti divisione *trichotomica*, sic; *Ens* est *substantia*, *accidens*, et *Compositum*; quæ forte in hoc casu, et quibusdam aliis, non minus est perfecta quam dichotomia. Ratio dissensus est, quod omnis prædicatio Generis, sive immediati sive mediati de inferiore specie, sicut excludit a suo conceptu differentiam Generis oppositi, sic etiam a conceptu speciei de qua prædicatur eandem excludit: quare bene arguitur *lapis est corpus*, ergo omnem conceptum *spiritus* excludit: *Lapis est inanimatus*, ergo omnem conceptum *animati* excludit: at vero, hoc falsum erit; *Lapis est substantia*, ergo omnem conceptum *Accidentis* excludit; est enim conceptus *accidentis* non minus essentialis lapidi, quam *substantiæ*; saltem secundum opinionem hodie communiorem negantem Formas Substantiales Materiales. <p. 38> Cum igitur lapis nequeat dici proprie, vel *substantia*, vel *accidens*; consentaneum videtur, ut alia ratio Generica stabiliatur in serie prædicamentali, quæ de his Notionibus proprie prædicari possit. Eodem redit eorum sententia, qui substantiam dividunt in *incompletam* et *completam*; sed minus proprie meo judicio loquuntur, secundum strictas leges prædicamentales.

De divisione notionis *Concreti* (qua voce ego utar in sequentibus pro *substantia*) videtur eodem modo philosophandum quo de *Ente*; vel dichotomice, sic; in *imperfectius* et *perfectius*. Imperfectius continet Concreta vulgo Substantias *Corporeas*, et *Spiritus* a corpore separatos: perfectius, Hominem, id est, concretum compositum ex his incompletis; propter quam rationem et alias hic non nominandas, videtur mihi revera Hominem esse omnium creaturarum

CHAPTER V

EXPLANATION OF THE TABLES

Since I am at present writing only for the learned, for whom few words suffice, I shall not delay by entering into a lengthy discussion of the nature and method of the individual notions, but set out this series of things in a few words, giving the reasons why I disagree with the received opinion, which has to be opposed on certain issues.

I agree with all of the more sound philosophers that there is one highest genus, or first and most general concept, which we customarily call *Being* or *Thing*. But I differ from them in the division of *Being* into its first differences. <p. 37> For differences of opinion arise as quickly among us men as they are found in things themselves. They say that *Being* should subdivide first into *substare* and *accidere*. But it seems to me that we cannot construct a perfect predicamental series according to which appropriate predications can be made, unless we start from broader differences that divide *Being* adequately in its most general conception and aspects; I have called these *abstract* and *concrete*, or *simple* and *composite*, or the *incomplete* and *complete* states of the thing; incomplete *Being* subsequently dividing into *substance* and *accident*: unless anyone prefers to use a division by *trichotomy*, whereby *Being* divides into *substance*, *accident*, and *composite*, which perhaps in this case, and in certain others, is no less perfect than the dichotomy. The reason for this difference of opinion is that, whenever a genus is predicated of a subordinate species, either directly or indirectly, just as it excludes from its concept the difference of any opposed genus, so it also excludes the same from the concept of the species of which it is predicated. It is thus proper to argue: *a stone is a body*, therefore, it excludes any concept of *spirit; a stone is inanimate*, therefore it excludes any concept of *animate*; but it is false to argue: *a stone is a substance*, therefore it excludes any concept of *accident*, for the concept *accident* is no less essential to stone than *substance*, at any rate following the view nowadays most widely adopted that denies substantial material forms. <p. 38> Since, therefore, a stone cannot properly be said to be either *substance* or *accident*, it seems reasonable that another generical scheme should be established in the predicamental series that can properly be predicated of these notions. The opinion of those who would divide substance into *incomplete* and *complete* amounts to the same thing; but in my opinion they speak less correctly in terms of strict predicamental rules.

With regard to the division of the notion *concrete* (which is the term I shall use, in what follows, in place of *substance*), the same philosophical approach seems appropriate as with *Being*, either by dichotomy into more *imperfect* and more *perfect*: the category of more imperfect contains concretes commonly known as *corporeal substances* and *spirits* that are separated from the body; the category of more perfect is man—that is, a concrete composed out of both these types of

perfectissimum. Vel secundo, trichotomice sic, in *corporeum, spirituale,* et *compositum.* Hic Notandum ulterius de Notione *Hominis,* quod male collocetur in linea prædicamentali sub Genere mediato *animal,* et consequenter sub Genere Subſtantiæ *corporeæ*; si enim hæc sit vera prædicatio, *homo est substantia corporea*; sequetur a conceptu *hominis* removendum omnem conceptum *spiritus.*

Concreta Materialia divido in *Mathematica, Physica,* et *Artefacta.* Miratus sum semper has notiones Mathematicas, quas ego hic pro *Concretis* <p. 39> posui, a philosophis haberi *accidentia*: Quis enim non clare percipit has voces, *punctum, linea, superficies,* &c. esse *Concreta,* cum significent *subjectum* et *formam?* Quare hæc propositio *linea est longitudo,* est vel identica, vel falsa.

Notandum de his Notionibus, quod Nomina Rerum corporearum *Quantitatem* vel *figuram* essentialiter dicentium, hinc desumenda esse: sic, *scintilla, arena, pulvis, gutta*; mamnηm, mamnηf, mamnom mamnim, &c. id est, punctum ignis, lapidis, &c. Sic linea ignis, ligni, vel cujusvis materiæ, ubi longitudo præcipue innuitur: sic folium Chartæ, lamina, bractea, ad superficiem referuntur.

In concretis *Physicis* Methodum receptam sequutus sum, Corpora omnia simplicia sub uno genere comprehendi; nec judicabam necessarium addere istam vocem Genericam *Elementi,* cum satis exprimi possit hæc Notio *neim grʊpomp.* Partes Cœli posui solummodo tres; nec judicabam necessarium pro constellationibus omnibus (quæ Artis vocabula sunt) ponere voces Radicales; notio enim Constellationis satis commode exprimitur, *asind, stellarum aggregatum.* Nomina vero particularium Constellationum, imponi debent ex his, per descriptionem a forma, numero, situatione, aut alio accidente maxime distinguente: e.g. *asind vai, pleiades,* &c. quod faciendum Astronomis commendo; sicut et in aliis Artibus, terminorum <p. 40> Artis Nomina, ab Artium peritis imponenda relinquo. Vix enim expectandum est ab uno aliquo homine, ut sit par huic suscepto imponendi apta Nomina terminis Artium omnium, quod faciendum est per descriptiones ex primitivis desumptas; idque quantum cum claritate fieri potest, in una voce, per derivationem, vel compositionem: ubi vero natura rerum hoc non patitur, per periphrasin plurium vocum.

An detur elementum ignis non disputo, sed vulgarem opinionem hac in re sequor; ut etiam, sintne istæ partes quas ego posui, stricte loquendo sic dicendæ, et inter se distinctæ. Novi satis si detur elementum ignis, ibi nec *fumum,* nec *fuliginem,* nec *cineres* esse: Attamen nemo est qui non videt, has notiones dicere essentialem respectum ad ignem hic apud nos. Sic nolo asserere has partes esse stricte loquendo distinctas; novi enim *fumum* et *fuliginem* differre tantum ut eadem res *rarefacta* et *densifacta*: vel, si quis non ferat me sic loqui, *fumus* nihil est aliud nisi *punctula* (sic enim magis Philosophice dicuntur quam *Atoma*) materiæ combustibilis, per intensum calorem resoluta et dissipata; *fuligo* vero, est collectio horum sparsorum punctulorum in locum minrem. Sed rationem reddidi superius, cur omnes Notiones vere *compositas* non hic pro talibus habeam; et si de methodo et loco prædicamentali cujusque particularis Notionis curiose disputaremus, disputaremus <p. 41> in æternum; quare iterum dico hic

incomplete things; and for this reason, as well as others not to be discussed here, man seems to me to be indeed the most perfect of all creatures. Or secondly by trichotomy into *corporeal*, *spiritual*, and *composite*. It is further to be noted concerning the notion *man* that it is erroneous to place it in the predicamental series under the intermediate genus *animal*, and consequently under the genus *corporeal substance*; for if *man is a corporeal substance* were a valid predication, it would follow that any concept relating to *spirit* would be excluded from the concept *man*.

The category of material concrete I divide into *mathematical*, *physical*, and *artificial*. It has always surprised me that these mathematical notions, which I have placed here as *concretes*, <p. 39> have been held by philosophers to be *accidents*. Who would not clearly acknowledge the terms *point*, *line*, *surface*, etc. to be *concrete*, since they signify a *subject* and a *form*. Hence the proposition *a line is length* is either identical[31] or false.

In connection with these notions, it is to be noted that the names essentially signifying the *quantity* or *figure* of corporeal things are to be taken from here, thus: spark, sand, dust, drop; **mamnηm, mamnηf, mamnom, mamnim**, etc., i.e. a point of fire, a point of stone, etc.[32] Likewise a line of fire, a line of wood, or of any other material, whenever length is mainly implied; and likewise a leaf of paper, metal, gold leaf, etc. are all to be reduced to surface.

In the *physical* concretes I have followed the received method, including all simple bodies under one single *genus*; I did not think it necessary to include the generic notion *element*, since it can be adequately enough expressed by the notion **neim grυpomp**.[33] I have distinguished only three parts of the sky, and did not think it necessary to give radical words to all of the constellations (which belong to the vocabulary of science), for the notion of a constellation can be expressed conveniently enough by **asind**, *an aggregate of stars*. The names of individual constellations are to be assigned on this basis by a description derived from their form, number, location, or some other clearly distinguishing accident, e.g. **asind vai**,[34] *pleiades*, etc.; a task that I commend to the astronomer; and likewise in other arts <p. 40> I leave it to those skilled in them to assign names for the terms of art. It is scarcely to be expected that a single man should be equal to this task of assigning appropriate names to the terms of all arts, which is to be done by descriptions constructed from the primitive terms, in one word by means of derivation and compounding, if this can be done with clarity, or, where the nature of the thing does not allow this, by means of a periphrasis of several words.

Whether or not there is an element of fire I shall not here debate, but I follow the common opinion in this matter, and likewise as to whether those parts that I have established are strictly speaking to be thus identified and distinguished. I acknowledge that, if there is an element of fire, then there cannot be *smoke*, nor *soot*, nor *ashes*, etc. But yet anyone can see that these notions have an essential

---

[31] i.e. tautologous.

[32] **mamnom**—*punctum terra*—a point of earth; **mamnim**—*punctum aqua*—a point of water.

[33] **neim grυp-omp**: Simple inanimate physical concrete + corruption + '-able' (i.e. corruptible).

[34] **as-ind vai**: star + aggregate + seven.

multum Arbitrii necessario est admittendum. Omnibus igitur consideratis, non vereor asserere, recte et accommodate satis ad propofitum meum, has notiones positas esse ut *partes* ignis; quod etiam intelligendum volo in aliis partibus harum Tabularum, ad quarum particularem explicationem, memor polliciti, jam non descendam; sed explicationem *Concretorum Physicorum* his paucis Notandis absolvam.

Primo, In re *Herbaria* secutus sum Senertum, in *Arboribus* Spigelium, in *brutis* Jonstonum. Secundo, Non omnes differentias et Convenientias concretorum phyficorum quæ apud hos Autores inveniuntur, sed præcipuas tantum selegi: Quam inconveniens fuisset hos Autores in omnibus sequi, nemo doctus non videbit, cui scripta horum Autorum nota sunt, et qui naturam suscepti mei satis apprehendit. Tertio, Una et eadem res per variam compositionem potest multis appellari Nominibus; sic *Elephas*, *Nηkbeisap*, vel *Nηksofprηk*. Quarto, Quædam species vix possunt unica voce satis significanter exprimi, quo casu addendæ sunt plures voces; quod etiam videri licet in omnibus linguis, præcipue in numerosa *plantarum* familia. Quinto, Licet aliquando contingat, quasdam Rerum Species infimas non posse satis significanter Nomina habere a notione Generica, et superaddita Differentia, una, vel pluribus <p. 42> ex aliis radicibus, sine longa periphrasi; tamen magis eft philosophicum, et meo instituto congruum (cum hi casus omnino rari sint, rarissimi vero [quod præcipue attendendum est] in Notionibus communioribus et vulgaris usus) vel longa periphrasi uti, vel etiam differentiam mere fictam superaddere Notioni Genericæ, quod plus memoriæ opitulabitur, quam si omnes infimæ species fierent primitivæ, et ordine numerico disponerentur; nihil enim magis onerat memoriam, quam ordo numericus. Quinto, Si cui forte magis placeret definitiones Specierum *Naturæ* et *Artis* conficere ex Genere, et Loco numerico pro differentia posito, quam per differentiam petitam ex aliis radicalibus, et Generi superadditam; potest hoc fieri sine minima variatione harum Tabularum, ni. addendo literas terminales voci genericæ ordinis numerici significativas, *e.g.*

connection with fire as we know it. Thus I do not wish to assert categorically that these parts are strictly distinct, for I recognize that *smoke* and *soot* differ only in that they are *rarefied* and *densified* forms of the same thing; or, if this manner of speaking is objected to, that *smoke* is nothing other than small *particles* (better so termed than *atoms*, from a philosophical point of view) of combustible matter, loosened and dispersed by great heat, and that *soot* is a collection of these dispersed particles gathered into a more confined space. But I have put forward my reasons earlier why all notions that are truly *composite* should not be taken as such here; and if we were to debate in detail the method and predicamental location of each of these individual notions, we should be debating <p. 41> for ever more, which is why I repeat that in this matter there is much arbitrariness that necessarily has to be accepted. All things considered, I am not afraid to claim that these notions should quite properly and in accordance with my design be posited as *parts* of fire, and I should like things to be similarly interpreted in other parts of these tables, though I shall not, as promised, go into a detailed explanation of them, but simply make the following remarks to explain the category of *physical concretes*.

First, I have followed Senertes as regards the treatment of *plants*; Spigelius as regards *trees*, and Johnston as regards *animals*.[35] Secondly, I have not taken over all the differences and common characteristics of the physical concretes that are to be found in these authors, but have selected only the principal ones. Any learned man who knows the writings of these authors and who has a clear enough understanding of the nature of my design will see how inconvenient it would have been to follow them in every detail. Thirdly, one and the same thing may be called by several names, by means of different combinations of radicals, thus *elephant* can be **Nηkbeisap** or **Nηksofprηk**.[36] Fourthly, certain species can scarcely be expressed perspicuously enough in a single word, in which case several words are to be combined, which of course can be observed in all languages, especially in the numerous family of *plants*. Fifthly, although it may sometimes happen that for certain of the lowest species of things names cannot be adequately derived from the generic notion by the addition of one or more differences <p. 42> derived from other radicals, except by a lengthy periphrasis; yet it is more logical and in accordance with my design (since these cases are quite rare, and rarest of all (as should be especially noted) in the more common notions and those of everyday usage) either to use the lengthy periphrasis or else to add some *ad hoc* difference to the generic notion, which will assist the memory better than making all of the lowest species primitives and arranging them in numerical order, for nothing is a greater burden on the memory than a numerical ordering. Fifthly [*sic*] if by chance anyone should prefer to construct definitions for the species of *nature* and *art* from the genus

---

[35] Daniel Sennert (1655), Adrian Spieghel (1606), and John Johnson (1657).

[36] **nηk-beis-ap**: whole-footed beast + mathematical accident + superlative; **nηk-sof-prηk**: whole-footed beast + without + to rise.

Nηka		1. Elephas.
Nηkη	pro	2. Equus.
Nηke		3. Asinus.
Nηko		4. Mulus.

Sexto, Nil refert, quod quædam Genera aliquando coincidant in quibusdam eorum speciebus; necessarium enim duxi convenientias Rerum maxime communes seligere, licet aliquando coinciderent in aliquibus.

<p. 43> Concreta Artefacta quod attinet, nemo Philosophus (quod sciam) ante me tentavit reducere ad prædicamentum; multo minus ferunt Philosophi ea *Substantias* (hoc est entia concreta) vocari. Cum Notiones *Artis* non minus numerosæ sint quam Notiones *Naturæ*, ideo decrevi, non prosequi minutiores Differentias, sed quasdam Notiones Genericas disponere, ex quibus Nomina Inferiorum Specierum, vel per derivationem, compositionem, vel periphrasin exprimi possint. Via admodum intrita fuit in ordinandis Genericis Notionibus Artefactorum: Nihil tamen dubito, quin Notiones Genericæ quas hic posui, satis sint claræ, et obviæ, et inter se distinctæ, ut etiam comprehensivæ sub se omnium Notionum Artefactarum. In his explicandis non morabor, sed duabus factis observationibus ad alia transibo.

Sicut in Concretis Phyficis Nomina infimarum Specierum fiunt per compositionem ex Notionibus Radicalibus; sic etiam, hoc idem fit in Artefactis cum eadem prorsus sit ratio utrobique. Quare sicut Nomina *elephantis, equi, muli, asini,* fiunt ex hoc genere Radicali *nηk*, et differentiis ex aliis Radicalibus ascitis, fic *nηkbeisap, nηkpot, nηksofpad, nηkpim*; sic eodem modo, *poculum, cochlear, matula,* &c. fiunt ex Generica notione *fren*, et differentiis superadditis: *frenpraf, frenneis, frenirem,* &c. Sic, *palatium, carcer, templum, officina, tugurium, cubiculum*; *fankan, fancog, fanskas,* vel <p. 44> *fansava*, vel *fanskaf, fanspηd, fanstref, fanfrim*; sic, *pileus, chirotheca, thorax, calceus, braccæ, caligæ*; *freimmeis, freimsmvs, freimfeis, freimsmvr, freimsmηr, freimsmer,* &c. uno verbo. Nulla est Notio Radicalis in Tabulis Primitivorum Concretorum, sive Mathem. sive Physic. sive Artef. ex qua, tanquam Genere, et aliis aliunde ascitis differentiis, non fiant quamplurimæ inferiores Species. Et quidem modi hujus imponendi Nomina Rebus, vestigia quædam inveniuntur in omnibus Linguis; necessitate et Natura ipsa hoc dictante, ne fiat progressus in infinitum. Sed *Natura* hac in Re, hic *Arte* magis excolenda est.

and posit a numerical position for the difference, rather than by attaching to the genus some additional difference derived from other radicals, this can be done without any change in the tables—namely, by adding to the generic word a final letter indicating the numerical order, e.g.

Nηka	1.	Elephant.
Nηkη	2.	Horse.
Nηke for	3.	Ass.
Nηko	4.	Mule.

Sixthly, it makes no difference that certain genera sometimes overlap in certain of their species, for I considered it necessary to pick the most general of the common characteristics of things, even though some overlapped with others.

As regards the artificial concretes, no philosopher before me (to my knowledge) <p. 43> has attempted to reduce these to the predicament; nor indeed are philosophers wont to call these *substances* (i.e. concrete entities). Since the notions of *art* are no less numerous than those of *nature*, I decreased their number and did not go into the finer differences, but set up certain generic notions by means of which the names of the lowest species can be expressed by derivation, composition, or periphrasis. The road was virtually untrodden as regards the ordering of the generic notions of artefacts, but there is no doubt that the generic notions I have posited here are sufficiently clear, transparent, and mutually distinct to allow all the notions of artefacts to be subsumed under them. I shall delay no longer in explaining this but proceed to other matters, having first made two further comments.

Just as in physical concretes the names of the lowest species were made by composition from the radical notions, the same is also done in the artefacts, since the method is exactly the same in both. Thus, just as the names for *elephant*, *horse*, *mule*, *ass* were constructed from the generic radical *nηk*, together with a difference derived from other radicals, i.e. *nηkbeisap*, *nηkpot*, *nηksofpad*, *nηkpim*;[37] in the same way *cup*, *spoon*, *pot*, etc. are made from the generic notion *fren* with differences added, *frenpraf*, *frenneis*, *frenirem*,[38] etc. Likewise *palace*, *prison*, *temple*, *workshop*, *cottage*, *bedroom* are expressed as *fankan*, *fancog*, *fanskas*, or <p. 44> *fansava*, or *fanskaf*, *fanspηd*, *fanstref*, *fanfrim*;[39] And similarly *cap*, *glove*, *breastplate*, *shoe*, *trousers*, *boot* are expressed in one word as *freimmeis*, *freimsmυs*, *freimfeis*, *freimsmυr*, *freimsmηr*, *freimsmer*,[40] etc. There is no

---

[37] *nηk-beis-ap*: whole-footed beast + mathematical accident + superlative; *nηk-pot*: whole-footed beast + vehemence; *nηk-sof-pad*: whole-footed beast + without + sex; *nηk-pim*: whole-footed beast + simplicity.

[38] *fren-praf*: utensil + drink; *fren-neis*: utensil + mouth; *fren-i-rem*: utensil + urine, i.e. chamber-pot (n.b. use of euphonic -i-).

[39] *fan-kan*: house + king; *fan-kog* [reading *kog* for *cog*]: house + imprison; *fan-skas*: house + religion; *fan-sava*: house + god; *fan-skaf*: house + worship; *fan-spηp* [reading *spηp* for *spηd*]: house + work; *fan-strηf* [reading *strηf* for *stref*]: house + commonness; *fan-frim*: house + couch.

[40] *freim-meis*: garment + head; *freim-smυ-s* [hyphen added]: garment + hand; *freim-feis*: garment + trunk; *freim-smυr*: garment + foot; *freim-smηr*: garment + thigh; *freim-smer*: garment + shin-bone.

Secundo, Tenendum in Rerum Nominibus componendis, non esse necessarium ut differentia Generi superaddita sit tota rei Forma, quam docent philosophi esse unum aliquid simplex, occultum (ipsi nesciunt quid) latitans invisibiliter (et etiam inintelligibiliter) in Rebus; ad quam inveniendam nullum acumen penetrare potest. Verum hoc est commentum absurdum; omnium enim Rerum quarumcunque *formæ* sunt inadæquate cognitæ; nam quicquid cognoscimus de Re aliqua est pars ejus *formæ*: dico est *pars* Formæ; *Forma* enim nihil est aliud quam aggregatum omnium accidentium alicujus Rei. Sunt etiam formæ omnes inadæquate nobis cognitæ, nam multa sunt accidentia, qualitates, potentiæ, respectus, &c. in Rebus (etiam iis quarum Naturæ sunt nobis <p. 45> maxime notæ) quæ a nobis non intelliguntur. Satis igitur est, si differentia superaddita Generi, sit tale Accidens, quod diftinguat Speciem ab omnibus aliis. Atque hæc dicta sint de *Concretis*; sequuntur *accidentia*.

Tenendum in Genere de Notionibus Accidentalibus, quod methodus harum maxime naturalis sit eadem omnino quæ concretorum: ni. Primo, Accidentia Concretorum in genere; Secundo, Mathemat. Tertio, Physic. &c. ut patet ex comparatione Tabularum Concretorum, et Accidentium.

Primum igitur obtinent locum Notiones *Logicæ*, seu *Metaphysicæ*, quarum litera *S* est Characteristica: has qui probe intellexerit, et uti poterit, Logici Nomine vere dignus erit. Solent hæ Notiones a Philosophis *Transcendentes* vocari: modo intelligant, quod hæ Notiones sint Accidentia, quorum significatio communis est *spiritibus*, et *corporibus* absque ulla Metaphora, ego hunc loquendi modum admittam, secus non.

Inter has primum locum do *causis Rerum*; ad quem licet plures reduxerim Notiones quam vulgo solent alii, non tamen quam rerum Natura postulabat. Secundum locum dedi *modis existendi*; quæ Notio valde communis et frequens est, significat enim *statum*, seu *conditionem* rei. Tertium dedi *Modis agendi*; quæ Notio diversissima est a priori, quamvis Logici has confundant; nec quidem ullam <p. 46> accuratam distinctionem faciunt inter *Accidens, qualitas*, et *Modus*. Sed cum singula prosequi non vacet, de gradibus comparationis quos posui sexto loco, pauca notabo.

radical notion in the tables of primitive concretes, whether mathematical, physical, or artefact, which cannot be used as a genus from which, together with differences borrowed from elsewhere, any number of lower species can be constructed. Indeed there are vestiges of this way of assigning names to things to be found in all languages; necessity and nature itself require this, for otherwise naming would go on to infinity. But in this matter *nature* must be improved and refined by *art*.

Secondly, it is to be noted that in constructing compound names for things it is not necessary that the difference added to the genus should be the whole form of the thing, which philosophers teach us is something simple, occult (they themselves know not what), concealed invisibly (and even unknowably) in things, and which no ingenuity can ever penetrate far enough to find. This is truly an absurd fiction, for the *forms* of all things whatsoever are known inadequately, for whatever we know about a thing is part of its *form*: I say it is *part* of its form, for a *form* is nothing other than the sum total of all the accidents of a given thing. All forms are inadequately known to us, also because there are many accidents, qualities, powers, aspects, etc. in things (even in those whose natures are most <p. 45> well known to us) that we do not understand. It is enough, therefore, if the difference added to the genus is an accident such as will serve to distinguish the one species from all the others. So much, then, for the *concretes*; I now pass on to the *accidents*.

Note in general concerning the notions of accidents that the most natural method here is exactly the same as in the concretes, namely: first of all, accidents of the concretes in general; second, mathematical; third, physical, etc., as will be clear from comparing the table of concretes with the table of accidents.

First place is given to the *logical* or *metaphysical* notions, whose characteristic letter is *S*, and whoever understands these fully and is able to put them into practice is truly worthy of being called a logician. These are usually called *transcendental* notions by philosophers. Provided that by this they mean that these notions are accidents, whose signification is common to both *spirits* and *bodies* without any metaphorical extension, then I will go along with this way of speaking, but not otherwise.

Among these I put in first place the *causes of things*, to which I may have reduced more notions than others usually do, but yet not more than the nature of things required. In second place I put the *modes of existence*, which is a very general and frequent notion since it signifies the *state* or *condition* of a thing. In third place I put *modes of action*, which is a quite different notion from the preceding one, though logicians confuse them, <p. 46> for they do not draw any sharp distinction between *accident*, *quality*, and *mode*. However, since there is not room to discuss each of these in detail, I shall simply say a little about the degrees of comparison,[41] which I place in sixth position.

---

[41] On comparatives, see the discussion in Dalgarno's 'Autobiographical Treatise', fos. 66ʳ–70ʳ (see below, Part IV, Unpublished Paper 1), which includes a critique of the treatment in Wilkins (1668).

Notiones hæ sunt maximi et frequentissimi usus; est enim Actus Mentis *comparativus* longe excellentissimus in Rerum Scientia acquirenda: vix proferri potest sententia in qua Argumenta *Comparata* vel Causæ locum non habeant. Et tamen in nulla parte Logicæ magis cæcutiunt Logici, quam in Doctrina *Comparatorum.* Etiam ipse Petrus Ramus, me Judice, Logicorum Scriptorum acutissimus, hic in tenebris versatus est; nam inter Argumenta Comparata explicasse debuit *magnum* et *parvum,* et *maximum* et *minimum,* non minus quam *majora* et *minora:* licet enim hi gradus distinctionis causa, a Grammaticis dicantur *positivi* et *superlativi,* non, tamen minus proprie sunt Comparativi, quam *majora* et *minora.* Deinde, non fiunt hæ Comparationes in sola *quantitate,* ut ille opinatur; sed hæ notæ comparationis transcendunt et *quantitatem* et *qualitatem,* et utrique sunt æque applicabiles. Verum cum voces *majora* et *minora,* in usu vulgari appropriatæ sint solummodo Rebus *quantis,* ut veram naturam *comparatorum* intelligamus, necesse est abstrahamus a vulgaribus vocibus, ne vocum ambiguitate decipiamur: quare argumenta Comparata explico per voces Adverbiales, quibus secundum usum vulgarem, <p. 47> et recte, utimur indifferenter pro comparatis, tam in *qualitate,* quam *quantitate.* Notæ comparationis principaliores sunt hæ; *magis, æque, minus*; ex quibus oriuntur, *valde, mediocriter, parum,* et *maxime, minime*: sic dicimus, *magis* longum, et *magis* album; *æque* longa, et *æque* alba. Verum cum has Notiones Nominaliter et adjective exprimimus, utimur diversis vocibus, pro comparatione in *quantitate* et *qualitate*; et dicimus, *magnus* ignis, *intensus* calor; *major* ignis, et *intensior* calor.

Dico, licet stricte loquendo, omnes gradus comparationis possunt reduci ad *magis, minus,* et *æque*; tamen cæteri gradus, cum innuant diversitatem graduum, et modi comparandi res, ratio postulat ea in distincta Argumenta Logica Comparata distingui. *E* contra vero, male docetur *æqualia, inæqualia; similia, dissimilia; paria, imparia,* esse distincta Argumenta Logica, cum in gradibus Comparationis, et Actu Comparativo, ne minima sit diversitas, sed in solis subjectis; ut patet ex resolutione harum propositionum; parietes sunt *similes*; id eft, *æque* albi; hæ duæ lineæ sunt *æquales*; id est, *æque* longæ; hi numeri sunt *pares*; id est, *æque* multi, seu quanti: in quibus apparet idem omnino esse Logicum Argumentum.

De Accidentibus Mathematicis, quorum *B* est Characteristicum: Notetur 1. Præpositiones quæ cum verbis motus junguntur, hinc petendæ sunt; <p. 48> quæ voculæ (sicut omnes aliæ particulæ) admodum sunt ambiguæ, et incertæ significationis in linguis. Hujusmodi sunt, *per, præter, trans, supra, infra, ad, ab, ex, in,* &c. quarum significatio hinc determinanda est. 2. Posui sex principales differentias *situs,* sub terminis relativis, quæ ad *Mundum* applicatæ, significant *Oriens, Occidens, Septentrio, Auster, Zenith, nadir*: ad *hominem* relatæ, vel *brutum,* vel *Artefactum,* significant *ante, post, dextra, sinistra, supra, infra.*

These notions are of greatest and most frequent use, for the mental act of *comparison* is by far the most important one in acquiring knowledge of things. It is scarcely possible to find a sentence that does not involve arguments of *comparison* or of causes. Yet in no part of logic are logicians more blind than in the doctrine of the comparatives. Even Peter Ramus himself, in my judgement the most acute of logical writers, is lost in the shadows here. For among the comparative arguments he should have discussed *great* and *small*, *greatest* and *smallest*, no less than *greater* and *smaller*. Although these grades, in order to distinguish them, are called *positive* and *superlative* by grammarians, they are no less properly comparative than *greater* and *smaller*. Furthermore, these comparisons are not made solely with respect to *quantity*, as he asserts, but these signs of comparison transcend both *quantity* and *quality*, and are equally applicable to both. Since the words *larger* and *smaller* are, in common usage, applied only to the *quantity* of things, in order to understand the true nature of the *comparatives* we must detach ourselves from everyday language so that we are not led astray by the ambiguity of words. For this reason I analyse comparative arguments by means of adverbial words, which following common usage, <p. 47> and quite properly, are used indifferently for comparison with respect both to *quality* and *quantity*. The principal marks of comparison are: *more, same, less*, from which are derived *much, average, little*, and *most* and *least*; thus we say *more lengthy* and *more white*; *equally long* and *equally white*. But when we express these notions using a noun substantive and an adjective, we use different words for comparison in *quantity* and *quality*; thus we say *a large fire, intense heat, larger fire, more intense heat*.

Although strictly speaking all the degrees of comparison can be reduced to *more, less*, and *equal*, nevertheless there are other degrees that signify a diversity of degrees and ways of comparing things that reason dictates should be distinguished as distinct logical arguments of comparison. On the other hand, however, it is false to argue that *equal & unequal; similar & dissimilar; like & unlike* are distinct logical arguments, since in the degrees of comparison and in the act of comparison there is not the smallest difference, except in the subjects, as is apparent from the analysis of the following propositions. The walls are *similar*, that is, *equally* white. These two lines are *equal*, that is, *equally* long. These numbers are the *same*, that is, *equally* many, or great. From these it is clear that the logical argument is in each case the same.

Regarding the mathematical accidents, whose characteristic letter is *B*, it should be noted: (1) prepositions that occur with verbs of motion are to be found here; <p. 48> these words (as all other particles) being extremely ambiguous and of an uncertain signification in languages. Of this sort are *through, beyond, over, above, below, to, from, out of, into*, etc., whose signification is to be determined in this place. (2) I posited six principal differences of *position* under the relative terms, which when applied to the *earth* signify *East, West, North, South, Zenith, Nadir*; when applied to *humans, beasts*, or *artefacts*, these signify *in front, behind, right, left, above, below*.

Sub Genere *D* posui illas Notiones quæ solent a Physicis, in parte Physicæ generali tractari; de quibus hic nihil singulare notabo, nisi quod numerum harum multum auxerim (propter majorem facilitatem Communicationis) supra quem invenerim in Philosophorum scriptis.

Sub *G* complexus fum Notiones Physicas magis speciales, id est, *qualitates sensibiles*; quas distribui secundum ordinem sensuum, progrediendo ab imperfectioribus ad perfectiora. Deque his notetur. 1. Desiderari in Linguis vernaculis vocem Genericam ad significandum objectum *tactus*; cum tamen ratio postulet ut objectum *Tactus* una voce significetur, non minus quam *color, sonus, odor, sapor*. 2. Tanta est affinitas sensuum *gustus* et *olfactus*, ut vix censeam illos dicendos distinctos sensus: nec minori cum ratione, (meo judicio) secundum opinionem Scaligeri, appetitus venereus distingui potest a sensu tactus. 3. Cum <p. 49> duplex sit objectum generale *visus*, ego posui *colorem* ut principale *objectum*, et *lucem* ut speciem sub eo; non ignoro tamen multos Philosophos afferere, *Colorem* esse potius speciem *lucis*.

De Genere *P* Not. 1. Quod hic non expresserim potentias sensitivas *externas* [hic] quia satis commode formantur ab organis sensus, quæ Radicalia sunt inter membra corporis. 2. Differentiæ Genericæ in Tabulis positæ, stricte et proprie loquendo tales non sunt; nec tales (ausim afferere) possibile est invenire instituto meo applicabiles; quare docendi causa solum, passiones ita distinguuntur, in *principales, minus principales*, et *affines*, &c. 3. Me pleniorem Passionum enumerationem fecisse, quam inveniri potest apud quemvis Philosophum qui materiam hanc tractavit; et tamen præcipuas tantum enumeravi: numerus enim passionum in variis hominibus est infinitus; nemo est qui non habeat in se quasdam passiones, quæ in nullo alio inveniuntur. 4. Omnes *virtutes* hinc præcipue petendæ sunt; cum virtus nihil sit aliud, quam debita moderatio animi motuum, *vitium* vero, defectus vel excessus eorundem.

Atque hic filum Explicationis rumpam; multa consulto tacens, partim quod sciam Homines doctos, et hujus operis dignos censores, ex paucis quæ hactenus dicta sunt, rationem Methodi in sequentibus satis apprehensuros, partim etiam propter alias causas.

Under the genus *D* I have placed those notions that are generally used by physicists in the general part of physics; about these I will not note anything in particular, except that I have much increased their number (for greater ease of communication) beyond the number I have found in the writings of philosophers.

Under *G* I have included more special physical notions—that is, *sensible qualities*, which I distribute according to the order of the senses, proceeding from the less perfect to the more perfect. Concerning this it is to be noted: (1) The vernacular languages lack a generic word to signify the object of *touch*, although reason demands that the object of *touch* be expressible in a single word no less than *colour*, *sound*, *smell*, and *taste*. (2) Such is the affinity between the senses of *taste* and *smell* that I find it hard to call them distinct senses; and with no less reason (in my judgement) does Scaliger[42] find it impossible to distinguish the sexual appetite from the sense of touch. <p. 49> (3) Since the object of *sight* is generically twofold, I posited *colour* as the principal object and *light* as its subordinate species. I am not unaware, however, that many philosophers would claim rather that *colour* is a species of *light*.

Concerning the genus *P*, it is to be noted: (1) That I have not expressed the *external* sensitive powers here, because these can be conveniently enough formed from the organs of sense, which are radicals to be found among the parts of the body. (2) The generic differences set forth in the tables are strictly and properly speaking not such; nor (I am bold enough to declare) is it possible to discover any such as would be applicable to my design. For the purposes of teaching alone, therefore, the passions are to be distinguished as: *principal, less principal, associated*, etc. (3) I have made a more copious enumeration of the passions than I could find in any philosopher who has dealt with this topic, and yet I have listed only the principal ones, for the number of passions in different persons is infinite; there is no one who does not have certain passions within them that are to be found in no one else. (4) All of the *virtues* are principally to be sought here, since a virtue is nothing other than a due moderation of the motions of the soul, and a *vice* simply a defect or excess of them.

At this point, however, I shall break off the thread of my explanation. There are many things I have deliberately left unmentioned; partly because I know that learned men who are worthy judges of this work, will, from the few things that have been said so far, be fully able to grasp the rationale for the method in the rest; and partly for other reasons.

[42] Julius Scaliger (1484–1558). His best-known work is *De causis linguae latinae* (1540).

CAP. VI.

DE INSTITUTIONE VERBORUM,
SEU SIGNORUM APPLICATIONE AD TABULAS.

Qui in praxi hujus Artis versari velit, diligenter attendat Regulas hoc capite traditas.

1. Ordo literarum, ut capite primo docetur, perfecte tenendus et præ oculis ponendus est.

2. Conatus eram omni studio, tot Summa Genera Rerum constituere quot soni simplices sunt, idque methodo correspondenti inter *Signum* et *Signatum*; verum multa erant quæ huic conatui obstabant. Quantum tamen potui, convenientiam Symbolicam inter *Signum* et *Signatum*, etiam in prima signorum impositione observavi; ut consideranti patebit.

3. Summa Genera Rerum Septem primis literis notantur, id est, *vocalibus*; quibus subjungitur litera *v*, distinctionis causa, et ut voces flexionis sint capaces: *v* enim præcedens, semper est nota dictionis *numericæ*; ipsum tamen *v* nullum *numerum* significat, sed tantummodo distinguit voces *numericas* ab aliis vocibus; nam *ab* est *basis*, sed *vab* significat 14.

<p. 51> 4. Literæ *ei* et *s*, in vocibus *Genericis*, sunt tantummodo *serviles* et *Expletivæ*, ad faciendam integram vocem; nam in summis Generibus Concretorum et Accidentium, Litera Characteristica est unica: sic, *M* est concretum Mathematicum; *N* Concretum physicum; *S* Accidens Commune: quare his addendæ sunt Literæ in hoc casu serviles *eis*, sic *Meis, Neis, Seis.* In Generibus vero Intermediis Accidentium, quorum duæ sunt literæ Characteristicæ, sola *S* asciscitur in fine; ut *gos*, color, *gis*, sonus, &c. Sic etiam in Notionibus Genericis *partium corporis*; ubi Nomina *Specierum* formantur additione vocalium ante literam Genericam, *ei* additur ad vocem Genericam faciendam; ut *eim, ein,* &c. Cum vero species formantur subsecutione vocalium, Species distinguentium, tunc Nomen Genericum formatur additione terminationis *eis*; ut *meis, neis, feis*, &c.

5. Summa Genera Concretorum tribus consonantibus nasalibus notantur; quibus addenda est terminatio *eis*, ut voces integræ fiant, ut jam dictum.

6. Intermedia Genera Concretorum sæpius Polysyllabica sunt, propterea quod adsciscant literas Characteristicas Generum inferiorum. Sic cum Concretum Physicum dividitur in hæc tria intermedia Genera, *Inanimatum, Planta, Brutum*, tres literæ *m, n, f,* funt Characteristicæ *Inanimati*, et copulantur cum litera Generica *N*, per servilem <p. 52> dipthongum *ei*; sic, *Neimneif.* Sic *b d g* sunt Characteristicæ *Plantæ*, et fit *neibdeig: p t k, Bruti*, et fit *Neipteik.*

CHAPTER VI   <p. 50>

ON THE INSTITUTION OF WORDS,
OR THE APPLICATION OF SIGNS TO THE TABLES

A nyone who wishes to gain a practical knowledge of this art should pay careful attention to the rules given in this chapter.

1. The order of the letters, as explained in the first chapter, is to be firmly mastered and kept in sight.

2. I made great efforts to establish the same number of highest genera of things as there are simple sounds, in establishing a correspondence between *signs* and *signified*, but there were many things that stood in the way of this. As far as I could, however, I have paid attention to the symbolic relation between *sign* and *signified* in the initial assigning of signs, as will be evident from the perusal of them.

3. The highest genera of things are represented by the seven primary letters, that is by the *vowels*, to which is added the letter *v* for the sake of distinction, and so that words are capable of bearing inflections. When initial, the letter *v* always indicates a *numerical* expression; the *v*, however, does not itself signify a *number*, but serves only to distinguish *numerical* words from others: thus **ab** is *basis*, but **vab** signifies 14.

4. The letters *ei* and *s* in the *generic* words are only *servile* and *expletive* ones <p. 51> used to make up a complete word, for in the highest genera of concretes and accidents there is only one characteristic letter. Thus *M* is the category of mathematical concrete; *N* physical concrete; and *S* common accident; to which are added the letters *eis*, which are in this case purely servile, i.e. **Meis, Neis, Seis**. In the intermediate genera of accidents, each of which have two characteristic letters, only *S* is added at the end of the word, as in **gos**, *colour*, **gis**, *sound*, etc. Likewise in the generic notions for *parts of the body*; where the names of the *species* are formed by the addition of vowels preceding the generic letter, *ei-* is added to make the generic word, as in **eim, ein**, etc. When the species are formed by adding vowels following the generic letter, the generic name is formed by adding the ending *-eis*, as in **meis, neis, feis**, etc.

5. The highest genera of concretes are represented by the three nasal consonants, to which the ending *-eis* is added to make complete words, as just explained.

6. The intermediate genera of concretes are more often polysyllabic, because they take characteristic letters for the lowest genera. Thus when the category of physical concretes is divided into the three intermediate genera *inanimate*, *plant*, and *beast*, the three letters *m*, *n*, *f*, are the characteristics of the *inanimates*, and are joined to the generic letter *N* by a servile <p. 52> diphthong *ei*, i.e. **Neimneif**. Likewise *b*, *d*, and *g* are the characteristics of *plant*, i.e. **neibdeig**; and *p*, *t*, *k*, are the characteristics of *beast*, i.e. **Neipteik**.

7. In Nominibus Specierum infimarum componendis, quæ Characteribus minusculis in Tabulis distinguuntur, Literæ duæ posteriores, quarum prior significativa est Generis intermedii, posterior vero ipsius Speciei, solæ septem vocales, et novem principaliores Consonantes, locum habent.

8. In Tabulis Concretorum, Litera secunda (hoc est vocalis) est Characteristica Speciei; tertia vero, scil. Consonans, est Characterist. Generis intermedii. In Tabulis vero Accidentium, contrario modo se habet, ut patet comparando Tabulas.

9. Nomina Notionum incompletarum in Tabulis Concretorum, id est, Partium Rerum, funt etiam voces incompletæ et mutilæ: id est, biliterales (duplices enim literæ *fr, fl, sm, sn*, &c. habendæ sunt pro simplicibus, quæ loco simplicium literarum supponuntur, propter penuriam literarum simplicium) quæ quantum literarum distributio sinebat, habent præcipuam Characteristicam Literam sui Integri seu Totius, cujus sunt partes: Sic partes *Figuræ* habent *b*, quæ est Charact. Figuræ; idem videtur in partibus *Cœli, Ignis*, &c. ad quarum species distinguendas *s r l* sunt Characteristicæ, quæ nullo alio casu sunt Characteristicæ specierum. Sic Nomina partium *Animalis* (quod omnium <p. 53> corporum Naturalium est perfectissimum, ideoque pluriams habet partes) componuntur ex *m, n, f*, quæ Characteristicæ sunt *Animalis*, septem vocalibus distinguentibus species, nunc vocalibus præcedentibus, nunc subsequentibus. Verum tamen Notandum, quod Literarum distributio non sinebat, absque confusione cum aliis vocibus, omnes *partes* sic notare, per Characteristicon Nominis sui *Integri* seu *Totius*, ut patet ex partibus *Domus* et *Navis*.

10. Literæ *r* et *l* sunt Serviles in Tabulis Accidentium: *r* est signum oppositæ Notionis, *l* mediæ inter duas extremas. Eundem habent usum in Nominibus *Partium*, in Tabulis Concretorum; Verum in Nominibus Concretorum integrorum seu Completorum, hæ Literæ post *f* ponuntur, propter defectum Literarum simplicium, et copiam differentiarum Rerum; ut etiam aliquando *s* additur in initio, propter eandem causam, tam in Tabulis Concretorum, quam Accidentium.

11. Regula oppositionis et Medii locum habet in solis Accidentibus, et Notionibus incompletis inter Concreta; De quibus tenendum, Rationem Oppositionis non semper esse manifestam, sed ad modum oppositorum quædam disponuntur, quæ stricte loquendo talia non sunt: partim ad sublevandam Memoriam; sed præcipue, ut facilius comprehendi possint sub Generibus, et <p. 54> vocibus aptis insigniri, secundum Analogiam et Regulas Generales hujus Artis.

7. In compounding the names of the lowest species, which in the tables are set in lower-case letters,[43] for the last two letters, of which the first indicates the intermediate genus and the second the species itself, only the seven vowels and the nine principal consonants are used.

8. In the Tables of Concretes, the second letter (which is a vowel) is characteristic of the species; the third letter—namely, a consonant—is characteristic of the intermediate genus. In the Tables of Accidents, however, this is reversed, as will appear from a comparison of the tables.

9. The names of the incomplete notions in the Tables of Concretes—i.e. parts of things—are themselves incomplete and mutilate words. That is, they consist of two letters (where the double letters *fr*, *fl*, *sm*, *sn*, etc., are treated as single letters, filling the place of simple letters because of the paucity of the latter), which, as far as the distribution of letters allowed, borrow their principal characteristic letter from the integral or whole of which they are parts. Thus the parts of the *figures* have the letter *b*, which is the characteristic of figure; and the same will be seen in the parts of *sky*, *fire*, etc., where the species are distinguished by the characteristic letters *s*, *r*, *l*, even though these are not used elsewhere as characteristic of species. Thus the names of the parts of *an animal* (which of all <p. 53> natural bodies is the most perfect and which hence has the most parts) are composed of *m*, *n*, and *f*, which are the characteristic letters of *animal*, with the seven vowels, which sometimes precede and sometimes follow, distinguishing the species. It must be noted, however, that the distribution of the letters would not, without giving rise to confusion with other words,[44] allow all of the *parts* to be thus represented by borrowing the characteristic from the name of the respective integral or whole, as will appear from the parts of *house* and *ship*.

10. The letters *r* and *l* are servile ones in the Tables of Accidents, *r* indicating the opposite of a given notion, and *l* indicating the middle term between two extremes. They have the same function in the names of *parts*, in the Tables of Concretes; but in the names of integral or complete concretes these letters are used after an *f* because of the paucity of simple letters, and because of the great number of differences of things, just as elsewhere the letter *s* is added initially for the same reason, both in the Tables of Concretes and the Tables of Accidents.

11. The rule concerning opposites and middle terms applies only in the accidents and incomplete notions among the concretes. It should be noted that the grounds for the opposition is not always obvious, and that some notions are treated as opposites that strictly speaking are not such.[45] This is partly as an aid to memory, but mainly so that they can be the more readily subsumed under the genera and <p. 54> represented by appropriate words following analogy and the general rules of this art.

---

[43] i.e. in Dalgarno's Tables of Accidents (see the fold-out table at the end of this volume).

[44] Reading *vocibus* for *vocibns*.

[45] Wilkins also notes that some things that in his scheme are placed as opposites 'do not always fall out to be under the same Predicament or Genus with those things to which they are adjoyned' (1668: 290).

12. Litera *I* potest, ubicunque Euphonia postulat, addi fini vocis desinentis in consonantem; cujus usus sic erit mere Euphonicus, nisi quod necessario adsumenda sit in plurali numero, quia eadem consonans nequit duplicari sine vocali sequenti. Sic etiam, *i* servilis præcedit consonantem finalem, voci Radicali advenientem per flexionem Grammaticam, cum natura vocis non postulat aliam vocalem significativam præcedere.

13. Nullam reddo rationem Institutionis Nominum Animæ, Angeli, quæ concreta sunt Spiritualia, nisi simplex Arbitrium; sunt tamen eorum Nomina satis distincta ab omnibus aliis vocibus. Deum *O. M.* intra Prædicamenti limites non concludo, sed ejus Nomen est vel sic efferendum, *sasva*, Causa Prima; vel *Avav*, Ens Entium.

14. *S* est Litera servilis in vocibus numericis, quæ intervenit et distinguit inter literas numeri significativas, et literas Grammaticales Flexiones significantes.

15. Cum quælibet vox, ut ingreditur orationem, sit sub aliqua Grammaticali Flexione, hinc vox pure Radicalis est aliquid abstractum ab omni respectu Grammaticali: verum brevitatis causa, appropriavi vocem ex solis Radicalibus Literis constantem Notionibus Particularum significandis; quas omnes a Radicalibus Notionibus Tabularum <p. 55> derivari, Logicæ est Mysterium in hac Arte Revelatum.

16. Cum voces mutilæ, (id est, Nomina Partium) incipientes a vocali, ingrediuntur Compositionem, ad modum differentiæ (non Generis) adsciscunt *i* servilem, distinctionis causa, ne fiat confusio cum aliis vocibus.

17. Accentum quod attinet in hac Lingua, tenendum breviter. In vocibus dissyllabis penultima est longa; in plurisyllabis est brevis, nisi longa fuerit positione duarum consonantium.

18. Ad distincte et Euphonice efferendum voces seu sonos hujus Linguæ, hoc unicum requiritur: Accurate distinguere sonos septem vocalium, et Regulam de Accentu jam traditam bene attendere.

19. Vox primitiva pure Radicalis ex Tabulis Concretorum, significat ipsam notionem Concretam, Nominaliter, in casu recto; eadem ex Tabulis Accidentium, significat Notionem Particulæ, ut dictum.

20. In Compositione vox Generica præcedere debet, differentialis sequi; ut, *Nηkbeisam* elephas, non *Beisamnηk*, *Snηfgab* adamas, non *Gabsnηf*.

12. The letter *I* can be added at the end of words with a final consonant wherever it is required for euphony; and the use of this letter is purely euphonic, except that it is necessary to use it in the plural because a consonant cannot be doubled without a following vowel. Thus also a servile *i* precedes the final consonant that is added to a radical word as a grammatical inflection when the nature of the word does not require any other significant vowel to precede.

13. There is no reason to be given for the way the names of soul and angel are instituted, which are the spiritual concretes, other than arbitrary judgement. However, the names for these are sufficiently distinct from all other names. I have not included God Almighty within the boundaries of the predicament, but his name is to be expressed as **sasva**, *first cause*, or as **Avav**, *being of beings*.

14. The letter *s* is a servile one in numerical words, which separates and distinguishes between those letters indicating number and those signifying grammatical inflections.

15. Since any word when used in the context of speech occurs with some grammatical inflection, the purely radical word is something abstracted from all grammatical aspects. However, for the sake of brevity, I have allowed words consisting solely of the radical letters to signify the notions of particles, the method for deriving all of which from the Tables of Radical Notions <p. 55> is the inner secret of logic, as revealed in this art.

16. When mutilate words (that is, the names of parts) that begin with a vowel enter into a compound, a servile *i* is added, as with the difference (but not the generic), which is for the sake of clarity so that there is no confusion with other words.

17. The question of accent in this language can be dealt with briefly. In words of two syllables the penultimate is long; in words of more than two syllables it is short, unless it is long because of the position of two consonants.[46]

18. In order to pronounce the words or sounds of this language clearly and euphonically there is only one requirement: to distinguish accurately between the sounds of the seven vowels, and to pay strict attention to the rule of accent just given.

19. A primitive, purely radical word from the Tables of Concretes signifies the concrete notion itself in the manner of a noun in the nominative case; a similar word from the Tables of Accidents signifies the notion of a particle, as has been explained.

20. In compounds, the generic word must precede and the word for the difference must follow, as in **Nηkbeisam**,[47] *elephant*, not **Beisamnηk**; and **Snηfgab**,[48] *diamond*, not **Gabsnηf**.

---

[46] i.e. when two consonants follow the vowel of that syllable.

[47] Cf Ch. V, where the word for *elephant* is given as **Nηk-beis-ap**, using the ending '-ap'—superlative, rather than '-am'—'very'.

[48] **Snηf-gab**: precious stone + hardness.

21. Ultimo, consulo ne diu hæreatur in Præceptis et Regulis contemplandis, sed statim ad Praxin progrediatur; ex modica enim praxi, facilia admodum invenientur, quæ primo intuitu et non exercitato difficilia videntur. Et quod est bene <p. 56> observandum, licet hic signa non ex mero Arbitrio, sed cum ratione Instituantur; adeoque Memoriæ semel impressa, Intellectum erudiant de Rerum naturis; tamen in Committendo voces Radicales Memoriæ (quod est primum faciendum in ordine ad praxin) parum, vel nihil attendenda est Rerum et Signorum Methodus in Tabulis: via enim datur multo compendiosior imprimendi Signa Memoriæ, de qua pauca dicentur capite sequenti.

21. Finally, I urge the reader not to delay too long in studying these precepts and rules, but to proceed immediately to practice. For with only a small amount of practice things that appear difficult when first met with, before they are put into use, will prove to be quite simple. And it is to be carefully <p. 56> noted that, although these signs are not instituted by arbitrary judgement but according to reason, and once committed to memory will educate the mind about the nature of things, nevertheless, in memorizing the radical words (which is to be done first before going on to practical use), little or no attention should be paid to the arrangement of things and signs in the tables; for there is a much more direct way of impressing the signs on the memory, which will be dealt with briefly in the following chapter.

CAP. VII.

DE SUBSIDIIS MNEMONICIS.

Rerum et Conceptuum nostrorum Signa dupliciter in Memoria reponimus et conservamus. Primo frequenti repetitione inculcando; ita ut Signum auditum vel visum, frequenti usu, videatur Res ipsa, licet ab ea diverfissimum: Tantum scil. valet usus. Et quidem sola hæc actuum repetitorum frequentia efficere potest ut memoria extempore suo officio fungatur, sine Intellectus ductu, sive res memorandæ Methodice disponantur, sive omni Methodo sint solutæ. Nec facilius acquiritur facilitas et habitus memorandi certum <p. 57> aliquem numerum Rerum maxime methodice dispositarum (hoc est, ita ut earum quælibet separatim statim designari possit, sine mentis discursu) quam par numerus Rerum non cohærentium reponi potest in Memoria; Et Ratio hujus est, quod Memoria (si liceat Animi Facultates distinguere) sit Facultas omnino Passiva et receptiva Idearum, ab aliis animi Potentiis sibi concreditarum, et ad eam nihil spectat, (cum omnino cæca sit, et omnis cognitionis et judicii expers) quo pacto res ad ipsam deferantur, Arte, an Sorte, quocunque casu, vel Consilio; illa agit conservando et retinendo secundum suas vires naturales. Et quidem si proprie loqui velimus, in Memoria Artificiali, sive id fiat in Rerum Serie Legitima et naturali, sive per fictam mentis connexionem, Memoria hic nihil præstat Artificiale supra suas vires naturales. Sed totum hoc est Rationis opus, educentis ex Memoria Signa vel Res, in ipsa olim receptas et depositas.

2. Ratio humana, quæ Scientiæ Compendio quantum potest naturaliter studet, Memoriæ imbecilitati opitulatur, operando connexionem Rei Ignotæ cum Re Nota, vel Rei Memorandæ cum re Memorata: in hoc enim solo, tota Ars Memoriæ sita est. Et quidem hic est naturalis effectus Rationis in homine; videmus enim sæpissime in puero vel servo, si ipsis mandetur Nomen aliquod incognitum recordari, statim Ratio, quasi naturali <p. 58> instinctu, confugit ad compositionem hujus Rei Incognitæ cum alia Cognita affinis soni. Hæc autem compositio dupliciter sit; vel 1. Ubi est necessaria, et naturalis Rerum ipsarum connexio; vel 2. Fit per solam Mentis Fictionem. Cum compositio sit fecundum Rerum ipsarum Naturas, vel Generalem aliquam Regulam, eo firmior est et permanentior: Exempla harum sunt omnes Compositiones et Derivationes in Lingua Rationali, et etiam quæ in aliis Linguis regulariter fiunt. Sic, cum quis didicit primam conjugationem, ex verbo *amo*; postea si audiat hanc vocem *vigilabunt*, ejus significationem statim intelliget (modo quid significet *vigilo* prius intelligat) quamvis hanc vocem, *vigilabunt*, nunquam antea audiverit. Ratio est, quia intelligit per partes, 1. quid fignificet *vigilo*: 2. Quid terminatio *bunt*; quare etiam partes regulariter compositas, intelligit. Exempla compositionis Fictæ sunt voces Radicales sequentis Lexici, quæ longe facilius in

CHAPTER VII

ON MNEMONIC AIDS

There are two ways in which we store and preserve the signs of things and of our concepts in our memory. First, by impressing them by frequent repetition, so that, when the sign is seen or heard, it appears by dint of frequent use to be the thing itself, even though it is quite different from it. Such is the power of usage. And indeed only the frequency of such acts of repetition can cause the memory to fulfil its function spontaneously and without the guidance of the intellect, regardless of whether the things to be remembered are set out in a methodical fashion or in one devoid of any order. Nor is it any easier to acquire the facility and disposition to memorize a given <p. 57> number of things set out with the utmost order (that is, so that any one of them can be immediately recalled separately without a mental search), than it is to store in the memory the same number of things without any such order. And the reason for this is that the memory (if one may distinguish the faculties of the soul in this manner) is a completely passive faculty, receptive of ideas entrusted to it by the other powers of the soul. It is quite irrelevant (since it is quite blind and devoid of all thought or judgement) in what way the thing was presented to it, whether by art, or by chance, or by some coincidence, or by deliberation: it conserves and stores things according to its own natural powers. Indeed strictly speaking in Artificial Memory, whether it be by a proper and natural ordering of things or by contrived mental connections, the memory can achieve nothing in an artificial manner that is beyond its own natural powers. But the whole of this is the work of reason, retrieving from memory the signs, or things, that have previously been received and deposited there.

Secondly, human reason, which naturally strives towards compendiousness of knowledge as much as is possible, compensates for the *weakness* of the memory by making connections between things unknown and things known, and between things to be remembered with things already stored in the memory, for it is in this alone that the Art of Memory resides. Indeed this is the natural effect of reason in man, for we often see in a boy or servant, if they are told to remember some unfamiliar name, as if by natural <p. 58> instinct the reason instantly resorts to connecting this unknown thing with known ones of similar sound. This connection however is of two sorts: either (1) where there is a necessary and natural relation between the things themselves, or, (2) where the connection is made solely by a mental contrivance. When the connection is according to the nature of things themselves, or some general rule, it is correspondingly more stable and permanent. Examples of this sort are all the compounds and derivations in a rational language, as also those that in other languages are made by general rules. Thus, when a person has learned the first

Memoria reponuntur, per fictam hanc connexionem, quam per discursum Logicum; etiamsi supponeretur Methodum hanc Notionum ita Logicam et Naturalem esse, ut Ratio non minus facile posset eas percurrere, quam Literas Alphabeticas recitare. Hoc scio videbitur multis valde absurdum; est tamen experientia certissimum, et Ratio etiam evidens est hæc; Discursus Logicus, est via multo longior ad inveniendum Signum, quam connexio <p. 59> hæc ficta; dum enim ego ex discursu logico, quæsiturus sum vocem hujus Linguæ pro *animositate*, necesse est Ratio formet omnes hos distinctos Actus; est Accidens; est accidens physicum, sensitivum, cujus *P* est Characterist. 2. Est sub genere intermedio *quinto*, et est species *septima* sub hoc Genere. Quare licet Methodus esset ita perspicua, ut ratio sine errore posset omnia hæc percurrere, tamen hæc esset maxima tortura Mentis, tam longum discursum formare pro singulis vocibus. At vero, in ficta compositione, unicus tantum est actus Mentis ad inveniendum signum: sic, *v*, *g*, *pop æstimatio*; ego finxi connexionem inter *papam* et *æstimationem*: Cum igitur audio hanc vocem *æstimatio*, statim, etiam sine ullo discursu, recordor *pope*: Vel si audivero *pope*, vicissim statim recordor *æstimationis*. Et quidem, sicut parvo labore possunt voces Radicales memoriæ mandari per hanc Artem, fic parvo admodum exercitio, possunt homines satis expedite communicare, ex vocibus hac ratione in Memoria repositis. Fateor, ad recordandum voces extempore, sine ullo Rationis et judicii exercitio, habitum requirit; ad quem gignendum in Memoria, nec Ratio vera, nec ficta multum conducunt, sed sola repetitio frequens, ut supra.

Qui igitur recordatur per hanc fictam connexionem (quæ duarum Rerum tantummodo est) sine ullo respectu ad res alias, comparari potest ei qui <p. 60> quærens duos amicos, reperit eos solos in Domo aliqua Ampla: Qui vero recordatur per discursum Logicum, pertransiendo longam Seriem et Catenam Notionum, illi, qui quærit duos amicos in Templo inter mille alios homines. Vel possunt hi comparari duobus hominibus a Palatio Regio Londini, vicum Lambeth ex adverso petituris; alter Fluvium Tamefin cymba recta trajicit, alter circuitum facit per pontem. Quare consulo ei qui voces Radicales Memoriæ committere velit, ut prorsus negligat Methodum Philosophicam Tabularum, et hac sola Ficta Connexione, utpote multo compendiosiore utatur. Hic ponam exemplum 60 Vocum Radicalium, ex quibus judicari potest de cæteris.

conjugation from the verb *amo*, if he later hears the word *vigilabunt* he will immediately understand its meaning (provided he already knows what *vigilo* means), even though he has never heard the word *vigilabunt* ever before. The reason is that he interprets it by parts: (1) what *vigilo* means, and (2) what the ending *bunt* means; which explains why he also understands the parts when they are regularly combined. Examples of contrived connections are the radical words in the lexicon below, which are far easier to store in the memory by this contrived connection than by logical steps, even though it might be supposed that the ordering of notions is so logical and natural that the reason can run through them with no less ease than reciting the letters of the alphabet. This I know will seem quite absurd to many, but it is nevertheless clearly confirmed by experience, and the reason is also obvious, being as follows. Finding a sign by logical steps is a much lengthier method than by this <p. 59> contrived connection. For, if I wish to find the word in this language for *animosity* by logical steps, the reason needs to perform all of the following distinct acts: (1) it is an accident, and more specifically a physical, sensitive accident, for which the characteristic letter is *P*; (2) it occurs under the fifth intermediate genus, and under this genus it is the *seventh*[49] species. Although this method may be perspicuous enough that the reason may run through all these steps without error, nevertheless it would be an excessive torture for the mind to run through such a long process for every individual word. With the contrived connection, by contrast, a single mental act is all that is required to find a sign: thus, for example, for **pop**, *esteem*, I contrived a connection between *pope* and *esteem*, so that whenever I hear the word *esteem* I immediately and without further thought recall the word *pope*, and conversely if I hear *pope* I immediately recall *esteem*. And as only little effort is required to commit the radical words to the memory by this method, little training is likewise all that is required to be able to communicate readily enough using words stored in the memory in this way. It must be admitted, of course, that to recall words spontaneously and without any act of thought or judgement requires habit, and to engrain this on the memory neither reason nor contrivances are of any great help, but only frequent repetition, as has been previously said.

The person who memorizes by this contrived connection (which can only be made between two things) without any consideration of other things, can be compared to someone <p. 60> looking for two friends and finding them alone in some fairly spacious building. The person who memorizes by logical steps, on the other hand, running through a long chain or series of notions, is like someone looking for two friends in a cathedral among a thousand other people. Or they may be compared with two men, who are coming from the Royal Palace in London and are heading for the village of Lambeth opposite: the one crosses the river Thames directly by boat; the other makes a detour by

---

[49] For *seventh* read *eighth* (see the 'Lexicon Grammatico-Philosophicum' (on the fold-out table at the end of this volume)).

France, table   *Barbara*, rectus   *Podex*, ira
Flanders, aratrum   *Gomorrha*, lux   *Sand*, materia
Pomum, admiratio   *Dod*, solvere   *Bag*, concavitas
Adam, succuss   *Dog*, aperire   *Poket*, liberalis
Edmundus, cortex   *God*, ruber   *Ass*, stella
Ugly, arista   *Puf*, observare   *Ise*, mare
Pot, animositas   *Pudden*, attendere   *Flamma*, panis
Fanum, domus   *Pater*, concipere   *Toperie*, hasta
Actæon, ostium   *Grumble*, nutrire   *Dok*, spargere
Fens, pons   *Framea*, filum   *Sno*, vesica
Pope, aestimatio   *Fabula*, organum   *Foe*, venter
Marble, circulus   *Sibylla*, verum   *Ant*, humor
Samuel, efficiens   *Cobler*, proscribere   *Dik*, pungere
Sin, pulchrum   *Cogan*, incarcerare   *Globus*, flavus
Bed, extra   *Pipe*, diligens   *Tatle*, meditatio
<p. 61> *Before*, ante   *Pride*, affabilitas   *Tom*, litera
Smal, manus   *Purgatorium*, simulare   *Fringe*, Cathedra
Suggar, commune   *Prin*, ferus   *Faemina*, theca
Dig, percutere   *Beg*, extremum   *Sidney*, honestus
Sem, incipere   *Game*, dulce   *Gabulum*, durum

Poterit quilibet ingeniosus, bis vel ter relegendo has voces, eas ita Memoriæ committere, ut cogitatione facta de una, statim altera memoriæ succurrat. Sic cum ego audio vocem *sin*, statim recordor *pulchritudinis*; et vice versa.

Quamobrem ex hac instantia evidens satis videtur, facili negotio posse omnes voces Radicales hujus Linguæ, unius Septimanæ spatio, in Memoria reponi; et si altera ad Praxin accidat, poterit structura orationis ex his fieri, et mutua Communicatio inter Homines, non minus quam in aliis Linguis: Et hoc est quod ab hominibus habetur fabulosum, et impossibile, ideoque incredibile.

the bridge. For these reasons, I advise whoever wishes to commit the radical words to memory to disregard the philosophical method of the tables and to use only the contrived connection as being by far the quicker. I give here 60 radical words as an example, from which the method for the rest of them can be inferred.

France, table	*Barbara*, right	*Podex*, anger
Flanders, plow	*Gomorrha*, light	*Sand*, matter
Pomum, admiration	*Dod*, to untie	*Bag*, concavity
Adam, juice	*Dog*, to open	*Poket*, liberal
Edmundus, shell	*God*, red	*Ass*, star
Ugly, ear of corn	*Puf*, to observe	*Ise*, sea
Pot, courage	*Pudden*, to attend to	*Flamma*, bread
Fanum, house	*Pater*, to conceive	*Toperie*, spear
Actæon,[50] door	*Grumble*, to nourish	*Dok*, to scatter
Fens, bridge	*Framea*, thread	*Sno*, bladder
Pope, estimation	*Fabula*, organ	*Foe*, stomach
Marble, circle	*Sibylla*, true	*Ant*, moisture
Samuel, efficient	*Cobler*, to prescribe	*Dik*, to sting
Sin, beautiful	*Cogan*, to imprison	*Globus*, yellow
Bed, outside	*Pipe*, careful	*Tatle*, reflection
Before, before	*Pride*, courtesy	*Tom*, letter
Smal, hand	*Purgatorium*, to simulate	*Fringe*, arm-chair
Suggar, common	*Prin*, wil	*Faemina*, casa
Dig, to hit	*Beg*, extreme	*Sidney*, honoured
Sem, to begin	*Game*, sweet	*Gabulum*, hard

<p. 61>

Any ingenious person who reads these words two or three times will be able to commit them to memory in such a way that when one is thought of the other will immediately spring to mind. Thus if I hear the word *sin* I immediately recall *beauty*, and vice versa.

From the above it will be evident enough that with little effort all the radical words of this language can be committed to memory in the space of one week, and, if a second week is devoted to practice, these can be used to form the structure of speech and allow mutual communication between people no less than in other languages. And this is what is generally held to be fabulous, impossible, and indeed unbelievable.

---

[50] The 'Lexicon Grammatico-Philosophicum' has *ak* for 'ostium'.

CAP. VIII.

DE FLEXIONIBUS GRAMMATICALIBUS.

Hactenus explicatio Lexici et vocum Radicalium; sequitur quædam dicamus de Flexionibus Grammaticis, in derivatione, Compositione, et Structura orationis.

Docent Grammatici *octo* esse partes orationis: Logici melius, *duas* tantum statuunt. Ego vero, secundum libertatem Philosophandi quam hic mihi arrogavi, *unicam* tantum Orationis partem, Primariam, et proprie sic dictam agnosco; *Nomen* scil. Cæteras vero vulgo sic habitas, esse inter Flexiones, et Casus hujus, numerandas. Ratio assertionis hæc est; omne *Ens* quodcunque necessario primo locum habet in linea prædicamentali; omnis autem Notio prædicamentalis est Nomen. Quare sequetur, Verbum esse tantum Casum, feu Flexionem Nominis, non minus quam aliæ partes a Grammaticis enumeratæ.

Res hæc extra contraversiam erit, si evincam a Logicis unicum istud verbum Substantivum (Sum) derivari a Nomine prædicamentali: Quod conabor facere, 1. Negative, ostendendo *sum* non <p. 63> derivari ab *Ente*. 2. Positive, ostendendo veram verbi Substantivi originem.

Dico primo, Verbum Substantivum, quod copula est in omni Propositione, non derivatur ab *Ente* (non nego posse derivari verbum ab *Ente*, non minus quam a Notionibus *Substantiæ*, et *Accidentis*; verum hoc verbum longe aliud est a verbo Substantivo) quod ex resolutione harum duarum Propositionum demonstro. 1. *Homo est ens*. 2. *Homo est*. Si quis admittat primam propositionem esse legitimam, et constantem tribus terminis distinctis, Subjecto, Copula, et prædicato (quæ partes sunt essentiales omnis propofitionis) habeo intentum. Si dicatur hanc prop. esse Tautolog. et vocem *Ens* redundare, et quod hæc *Homo est*, significet totum quod *Homo est Ens*; Insto, vel hæc nulla est Propofitio, vel necessario est resolvenda in *Tres* Terminos Mentales, licet hic *duabus* vocibus expressos. Quare, hæ duæ voces vel non significant ad modum Propositionis, vel resolvenda est *est* in *duos* terminos, *copulam* scil. et *prædicatum*. Et sic habeo quod volo; *copulam* propositionis esse aliquid distinctum a Notione *Entis*.

2. Positive ostendo veram Verbi substantivi originem. Verbum, fatentibus omnibus, nihil est aliud, quam pars *Formalis* propositionis, id est, Signum Actus Mentis *Judicativi*. Cum vero Judicium dupliciter feratur de Objecto, vel per assensum vel dissensum, (qui actus vocibus <p. 64> expressi dicuntur *affirmatio* et *negatio*) hinc sequitur duplex esse Verbum Substantivum, respondens duplici Actui Mentis Judicativo; quæ duo verba sunt casus Notionum *affirmare*, et *negare*, quæ secundum leges prædicamentales primo concipienda sunt Nominaliter. Et bene hic tenendum est, Verbum (qua tale) esse meram copulam, et Signum Actus Judicativi; et Tempus esse quid extrinsecum ejus

CHAPTER VIII   <p. 62>

ON GRAMMATICAL INFLECTIONS

So far I have been concerned with explaining the lexicon and the radical words. I shall now say something about grammatical inflections, in derivation, composition, and the structure of speech.

Grammarians teach that there are *eight* parts of speech; Logicians say rather that there are only *two*. I myself, following the freedom to philosophize I have claimed for myself here, acknowledge only *one* primary part of speech properly so called-namely, the *Noun*.[51] For the others that are traditionally so termed should be counted as inflections and cases of the noun. The reason for this assertion is as follows: every *Being* of whatever kind must of necessity have a place in the predicamental series; but every predicamental notion is a noun. From this it follows that the Verb, no less than the other parts of speech enumerated by Grammarians, is only a case or inflection of the noun.

This point will be settled beyond controversy if I can prove on logical grounds that the singular substantive verb *to be* is to be derived from a predicamental noun. This I shall endeavour to do: (1) negatively, by showing that *to be* is not <p. 63> derived from *being*; (2) positively, by showing the true origin of the substantive verb.

I claim first of all that the substantive verb, which is the copula in every proposition, is not derived from *being* (which is not to deny that it is possible to derive a verb from *being*, as it is likewise from the notions *substance* and *accident*, but this verb is quite different from the substantive verb); I shall demonstrate this from the analysis of two propositions: (1) *Man is a being*; (2) *Man is.* If it is admitted that the first is a legitimate proposition consisting of three distinct terms, subject, copula, and predicate (which are the essential parts of every proposition), then my point is already established. If it is said that this proposition is a tautology where the word *being* is redundant, and that *man is* signifies exactly the same as *man is a being*; to this I reply either that the latter is not a proposition at all, or that it must necessarily be resolved into *three* mental terms, even though these are expressed here as *two* words. From which it follows that these two words either do not signify in the manner of a proposition, or that *is* must be resolved into *two* terms—namely, a *copula* and a *predicate*. I have thus established my point: that the *copula* in a proposition is distinct from the notion *being*.

2. The positive argument is to show the true origin of the substantive verb. The verb, as all would agree, is nothing other than the *formal* part of the

---

[51] Theories of the parts of speech varied widely in the seventeenth century; among grammarians, Dalgarno is unique in positing only one (Michael 1970: 241).

significationi. Non male igitur supponi possunt hæ voces (*ita*) et (*non*) pro propriis Verbis Logicis, et Signis actuum Judicativorum; quæ voces, etiam secundum usum vulgarem loquendi, ponuntur verbaliter. Ut, an Petrus est in domo? R. *ita, non.* id est, Petrus est in domo, Petrus non est in domo: vel magis Logice, sic. Petrus *ita* in domo; Petrus *non* in domo. Nam observetur has voces non significare adverbialiter, eo modo quo *docte, male, bene.* Sic enim voces *affirmative, negative,* sunt adverbia notionum *affirmare* et *negare.* Sed significant Judicium copulative: Et Ubicunque inveniuntur in oratione, significant ad modum copulæ inter subjectum et prædicatum, licet absurde ex vulgari usu, hæc vox *est* cum iis jungatur in propositione. Imo in propositionibus negativis est implicatio in ipsis terminis, dum nota *affirmandi* cum nota *negandi* jungitur. Homo *non est* lapis; quasi homo *non ita* lapis: Saltem nota *affirmationis* est redundans. Duo igitur sunt verba, *ita* et *non.* Cumque Verbum <p. 65> Negativum non ingrediatur propositionem Affirmativam, est non minus absurdum ut Verbum Affirmativum ingrediatur propositionem Negativam.

Ex dictis etiam patet, quam absurda sit eorum opinio, qui docent verbum Substantivum non esse necessarium ad faciendum propositionem: Pari enim ratione docere possunt, Subjectum vel Prædicatum non esse necessaria; est enim pars Essentialis et maxime Principalis propositionis. Hoc quidem verum est, posse Copulam, compendii gratia includi in eadem voce cum Prædicato, vel et Prædicato et Subjecto: *v, g,* hæc vox *amamus,* continet in se 4 distinctas Notiones; id est, *nos, præsenti tempori, sumus,* (vel potius *ita*) *amantes.*

Insuper ex dictis infero, nullam esse Negationem in terminis simplicibus; omnis enim Negatio est Actus Mentis, separans aliquid ab aliquo. Quare, maxima pars Doctrinæ Logicæ, quæ tractat de æquipollentia et conversione propositionum, est vana, inutilis, et absurda. Quis Bubulcus non docebit Logicum sic enuntiantem. *Homo est non lapis,* significantius dicere *homo non est lapis?* Nulla igitur est propositio terminis negativis constans, cujus Negatio, per resolutionem Logicam, non reducatur ad Copulam.

Hoc igitur stabilito, quod unica tantum sit Pars orationis principalis; tot dici possunt minus <p. 66> principales, quot Grammaticæ Flexiones, et variationes; quarum numerus potest esse vel major, vel minor, prout quis statuat pluribus vel paucioribus Particulis Auxiliaribus, in structura Orationis uti. Hinc quædam Linguæ, pro circumstantiis temporis, modorum, personarum, gradibus comparationis, utuntur vocibus distinctis et separatis; aliæ, has circumstantias terminationum varietate distinguunt. Quos autem diversos respectus et circumstantias ego hic admiserim terminationum varietate significari, ex Tabula Grammaticalium Flexionum patet; in quibus explicandis non insistam cum satis notæ sint ex exemplis.

proposition—that is, the sign of the mental act of judging. Since judgement of an object is made in one of two ways, either by assent or by dissent (which expressed in words <p. 64> are called *affirmation* and *negation*), it follows that the substantive verb must be twofold, corresponding to the twofold mental act of judging; and the two verbs are cases of the notions *affirm* and *negate*, which following the predicamental rules are to be conceived as essentially nominal. It must then be emphasized that the verb (as such) is merely a copula and a sign of the act of judging, and that tense is quite separate from its signification. The words *yes* and *no* may thus quite properly be substituted for the logical verbs themselves, which are signs of the judicative acts, and these words, even following ordinary usage, may be realized verbally. Thus *Is Peter in the house?* Reply: *Yes, no,* i.e. *Peter is in the house, Peter is not in the house*; or more logically: *Peter* **yes** *in the house, Peter* **no** *in the house.* Now it is to be observed that these words do not signify adverbially, in the same manner as *ably, badly, well*; for the words *affirmatively* and *negatively* are the adverbs corresponding to the notions *affirm* and *negate*. They signify judgement as a copula. And whenever they occur in speech they signify in the manner of the copula, between subject and predicate, even though vulgar usage is illogical in that the word *is* is joined with them in a proposition. Indeed in negative propositions there is a contradiction in these terms, when an *affirmative* sign is joined with a *negative* one. *A man* **is not** *a stone*, i.e. *A man* **yes no** *a stone.* At any event the sign of *affirmation* is redundant. There are thus two verbs, *yes* and *no.* And as <p. 65> the negative verb does not enter into an affirmative proposition, it is no less absurd for the affirmative verb to enter into a negative proposition.

From what has been said it will also be apparent how absurd is the opinion held by some that the substantive verb is not a necessary part of every proposition. By similar reasoning they might equally well claim that the subject or the predicate are not necessary either, for it is the essential and most important part of the proposition. It is, of course, true that the copula can, for the sake of conciseness, be realized in one word together with the predicate, or together with both subject and predicate, e.g. the word *amamus* contains within itself four distinct notions; i.e. *we, present tense, are* (or rather *yes*), and *loving.*

I conclude furthermore from the preceding that there is no such thing as a negation in simple terms; for every negation is an act of the mind, separating one thing from another. It follows that a very large part of logical theory, which treats of equipollence and the conversion of propositions, is vain, useless, and absurd. What country bumpkin would not tell the logician who says *A man is a not stone* that this is more clearly expressed as *A man is not a stone.* For there is no proposition consisting of negative terms, where the negation, if logically analysed, does not reduce to copula.

Having established that there is only one principal part of speech, it can be said that there are as many <p. 66> minor parts of speech as there are grammatical inflections and variations, whose number can be greater or less depending on whether one decides to use a larger or smaller number of auxiliary particles

Quod de numero Notionum Radicalium notavi, ni. quod viam mediam
inter duo extrema elegerim, hoc idem facio in Grammaticis Flexionibus;
non enim toties vario vocem Terminationibus distinctis, ad diversos modos
et circumstantias exprimendum, quoties compendii causa per Regulas certas
potuissem; cum non sit necessarium sic facere, et memoriam valde oneraret,
confusionem præterea pariens in Signis. Mirum est quot varias Terminationes
non necessarias quædam Linguæ admittant.

Nec. 2. Ita stricte Logicas Regulas sequor, ut eadem rigiditas observetur
in compositione et structura Orationis, quæ in Analysi; hoc est, ut omnes
distinctæ partes distinctis vocibus exprimantur: Certum enim mihi videtur,
omnem Grammaticam <p. 67> Flexionem distinctum aliquid superaddere
Radicali Notioni; qui respectus distinctis et separatis vocibus exprimi possunt,
nisi aliter fieret compendii causa. Quare ut dixi, media via incedo, præcipuas
modales Variationes Terminationum varietate distinguens, alias vero vocibus
separatis. Sicut igitur nulla vox Primitiva admittenda est in hac Lingua nisi
quæ in Tabulis habetur, sic nulla Derivativa, nisi quæ secundum has Gram-
maticas Flexiones fit. Non necessarium est moneam, non omnem Notionem
Primitivam capacem esse omnium harum Flexionum. Hoc tamen observatu
dignum est; hanc Linguam esse longe copiosiorem in Derivationibus et
Compositionibus quam quælibet alia Lingua; variabilitas enim in Notione est
Regula variandi vocem; Cum Derivationes Linguarum vulgarium coarctentur
inter breves gyros Regularum Grammaticalium. Quarum nulla alia ratio
reddi potest, nisi placitum et Arbitrium Majorum nostrorum; idque mero Casu
factum: Contra quem receptum usum loquendi, si quis loquatur secundum
Regulas Logicas, Barbarus habebitur; Quales essent hujufmodi phrases,
ignifica, luminifica candelam; *inignifica, inluminifica,* pro *extingue.* Sic non
licet dicere, *tenebile, dabile, scribibile, ridax, legax, ocululus, manulus, pedulus*;
Cum tamen hæ notiones, et hujusmodi feræ infinitæ, postulent eandem
Flexionem cum aliis, quam Linguarum Analogia iis contra omnem Rationem
denegat.

in the structure of speech. Hence certain languages will use distinct and separate words for the circumstances of tense, modes, persons, and grades of comparison; other languages distinguish these circumstances by varying the terminations of words. Which of the various respects and circumstances I have allowed to be represented by variations in terminations will appear from the Table of Grammatical Inflections,[52] which I shall not delay to explain since they will be self-explanatory from the examples.

What I have noted about the number of the radical notions—namely, that I have chosen the middle road between the two extremes—is again what I do with regard to grammatical inflections. For I do not vary a word with distinct terminations to express various modes and circumstances as many times as I would have been able to by means of certain rules for the sake of compendiousness: it is not necessary to do so; it would both overburden the memory; and it would also cause confusion in the signs. It is surprising how many unnecessary terminations some languages allow.

Nor, secondly, do I follow logical rules so strictly that the same rigidity appears in composition and the structure of speech as it does in analysis—namely, that all distinct parts are expressed by distinct words. It appears certain to me that every grammatical <p. 67> inflection adds something distinct over and above the radical notions, and these respects can equally be expressed by distinct and separate words, unless otherwise is done for the sake of compendiousness. For which reason, as I have said, I choose the middle road, distinguishing the principal variations of modes by a variety of terminations, and the others by separate words. Therefore, just as no primitive word is to be admitted into this language other than those contained in the tables, so no derivative is to be allowed that is not made according to these grammatical inflections. I need scarcely point out, that not every primitive notion is capable of taking all of these inflections. But it is worth mentioning that this language is far more copious in derivation and composition than any other language; for variability in the notion is the basis for variation in the word, while in vulgar languages derivations are confined within the narrow bounds of grammatical rules, for which no other reason can be given than the whim and convention of our ancestors, or indeed the operation of mere chance. Anyone speaking in contradiction to received usage, even if he speaks in accord with logical rules, will be held guilty of a barbarism. Expressions of this sort are: *ignifica* and *luminifica*, i.e. 'light', the candle; and *in-igni-fica* or *in-lumini-fica* for 'extinguish'.[53] Likewise it is not permitted to say *tenebile*, *dabile*, *scribile*; *ridax*, *legax*; *ocululus*, *manulus*, *pedulus*,[54] although these notions, and an almost unlimited number of

---

[52] See the list given under 'Etymologia præcipuarum particularum' in the rightmost column of the 'Lexicon Grammatico-Philosophicum' (see the fold-out table at the end of this volume).

[53] There are comparable lexical gaps in English, such as 'un-light' (to extinguish), 'un-find' (to lose).

[54] Parallel examples in English might be *hand-let* and *foot-let*, which are interpretable as 'a small hand' and 'a small foot' by analogy with *townlet*, *ringlet*, etc., but which happen not to have been sanctioned by usage.

<p. 68>   Notabilis est hæc differentia (inter plurimas alias) inter hanc Linguam et vulgares: In vulgaribus, habent Regulas quas vocant *Elegantiæ*, et *ornatus*, quæ sæpissime potius dicendæ sunt *Absurditatis*. Ita in malum omne sumus nos depravati homines proni, et in vetita ruimus; ut non solum pro maximis corporis nostri ornamentis habeamus, quæ corporis sanitati, et naturæ ipsi sæpissime adversantur, sed etiam Animas nostras, absurdis Figmentis, pro veris Scientiæ Dotibus corrumpimus. In hac lingua omnis Elegantia in hoc sita est, ut λογος externus sit interno perfecte conformis, ita, ut sermo sit Analysis Logica Conceptuum nostrorum: Et nemo hic potest ornate et eleganter loqui, et orationem construere, nisi bonus Logicus, qui eandem in suas partes noverit resolvere. Nec tamen hinc sequitur, neminem posse sensa sua hac Lingua exprimere, nisi Logicæ Artis peritus: potest enim quis Logicæ (Artis) rudis sensa sua hac lingua modo intelligibili patefacere; quod satis manifestum est ex aliis Linguis Potest enim Rusticus, sensa sua exprimere de Robus ipsi notis, ita ut ab aliis intelligatur: at vero Logicus plurimas absurditates in ejus sermone inveniet. Sed e contra, hoc bene sequitur; Ea quæ Logicus profert, facilia intellectu omnibus futura, ni. si materia sermonis sit ipsis nota: Et hoc satis etiam manifestum est ex Linguis vulgaribus, in quibus multo facilius est intelligere quam loqui; <p. 69> quod multo magis hic locum habet.

Hic insuper notari velim, quod Artis Logicæ ignarus, dum hac Lingua utitur, aptus erit Phrasiologiam suæ linguæ sequi, quæ sæpius absurda et insignificans est. Homines enim, priusquam præceptis Logicis imbuantur, loquuntur in multis more pfittacorum: Formulas quasdam traditione acceperunt, quibus utendi libertate sublata, obmutescent. Si enim inhiberetur Rusticus Anglus uti his phrasibus, *he must be born with*; *put out the candle*; mutis stabit. Ratio est, quod has phrases ex consuetudine quadam addidicit ad tales conceptus exprimendos, Logicam vero Analysin horum complexorum conceptuum perficere in mente nequit: Et quidem nonnulli sunt respectus Rerum, et concursus Notionum, quos Logice exprimere est perdifficile: Imo fastigium est acuminis Logici, posse bene Animi sensa hac Lingua exprimere. Quamobrem ad manuducendum Logicæ Artis ignaros in hanc linguam (id est, in veram praxin Logicæ) facienda est collectio quarundam Formularum ex Linguis vulgaribus, quæ Logice resolvendæ sunt per voces hujus Linguæ.

Hic etiam notatu dignum est, bene admitti posse variandi Formulas ad eandem Rem exprimendam in hac Lingua, non minus quam in aliis; sicut enim 4. et 4. vel 5. et 3. vel 2. et 6. faciunt octo, sic ex diversis simplicibus Notionibus potest idem sensus fieri.

the same sort, require exactly the same inflection as other expressions, which is denied them, contrary to all reason, by the rules of the language.

The following difference (among many others) between this language and <p. 68> the vulgar languages is worth noting. In vulgar languages there are what are called rules of *elegance* and *adornment*, which in many respects should rather be called rules of *absurdity*. Thus we fallen men are inclined towards every evil and rush towards what is forbidden. So that not only do we consider as being for the greatest adornments of our body things that are in conflict with the body's health and often with its very nature, but we also corrupt our minds by absurd fictions rather than the true gifts of knowledge. In this language all elegance resides in the fact that the external λογος is fully in accord with the internal one, so that speaking is in itself a logical analysis of our concepts. And no one can speak ornately and elegantly in this language, and fashion discourse in it, unless he is a good logician who knows how to resolve it into its parts. But it does not follow that no one can express their thoughts in this language unless they are skilled in the art of logic; for anyone ignorant of logic can make their thoughts known in this language in an intelligible fashion, as is clear enough in other languages. For a rustic can express his thoughts about things that are known to him so that others will understand him, even though a logician may detect various absurdities in his speech. But it does follow, on the other hand, that what the logician says will be the more easily understood by everyone, granted that they are acquainted with the topic he is talking about. And this too is evident enough from the vulgar languages, where it is much easier to understand than to speak, <p. 69> which applies all the more here.

I wish to add moreover that anyone who is ignorant of the art of logic, when he uses this language, will be inclined to follow the phraseology of his own language, which is often absurd and meaningless. For before people have been taught the principles of logic they speak mostly in the manner of parrots. They have inherited certain formulae by tradition and fall dumb if the freedom to use them is taken away. If an English countryman is not allowed to use phrases such as *He must be born with*, *put out the candle*, he will be struck dumb. The reason for this is that he has learned these phrases by custom to express their respective concepts, but he is not able to make a logical analysis of these complex concepts in his mind. And indeed there are several aspects of things and combinations of ideas that are extremely difficult to express logically. It is in fact the height of logical acumen to be able to express one's thoughts accurately in this language. For the purposes of initiating those ignorant of logic into the use of this language (that is, into the true practice of logic), it will be useful to make a collection of certain formulae from the vulgar languages, which are to be logically resolved by using words of this language.

It is further worth noting that in this language as in others it is quite allowable to vary formulae that express the same thing. Thus just as 4 plus 4 or 5 plus 3 or 2 plus 6 all make eight, so the same meaning can be expressed by combinations of different simple notions.

<p. 70>   Compositio in hac Lingua est duarum vel plurium dictionum in unam coalitio, majoris compendii causa in conceptibus nostris patefaciendis et communicandis. Atque hoc fieri potest pro re nata, quodlibet cum quolibet componendo; modo termini simplices eodem modo significent in Compositione quo extra compositionem. Cum enim rerum habitudines et Respectus mutui et Differentiæ ita infinite varient, nec ad hæc singula significanda dari potest vox simplex primitiva; et omnes Animi conceptus ex paucis primis vocibus sine ulla variatione exprimere impossibile esset sine longiffimis periphrasibus; ideo compendii causa necessario admittendæ sunt Derivationes et Compositiones. Et hic tenendum est, illas Notiones quas Derivativas appellamus, si stricte loqui velimus, esse revera compositas; distinctionem tamen facimus, quod illæ per additionem mutilæ Terminationis, vel etiam Præpositionis, fiant; hæ vero ex integris vocibus separatim significantibus. *Filiolus* enim est vox composita, ex *filio* et *parvo*; *durior* ex *duro* et *magis*, logice loquendo: appellantur tamen hæ voces Derivativæ, quia alter terminus compositionis mutila terminatione exprimitur.

Hinc est quod eo perfectior habeatur Lingua aliqua, quanto capaciores sint ejus voces Derivationis et Compositionis; ideoque Lingua Græca præ omnibus nobis notis præfertur, propter verborum <p. 71> copiam ex Derivatione et Compositione, eaque est sola Lingua quam adhuc habuerunt Philosophi idoneam ad Artes docendas: quod unicum Argumentum (seposita fide Historica) Græcos Gentem doctam et Philosophiæ primos cultores arguit. Et hodie observare licet, Gentes cultiores Compositionis et Derivationis Artem indies augere in suis Linguis vernaculis; sic Angli *self-denial, fellow-feeling*, et infinita fere similia quotidie excogitantur. Concludo igitur, licere in hac Lingua quodlibet cum quolibet componere, modo significanter et ad rem fiat; secus absurditas committitur.

Not. denique, Compositionem quod attinet; quasdam esse Notiones communes, quæ sæpissime Compositionem ingredientes in multis Linguis, per modum mutilarum Particularum, vocibus cum quibus componuntur, præponuntur, et ideo verius dicendæ funt derivativæ quam Compositæ: hujusmodi funt Latine, *re, con, am, se, in, ad, ab*, &c. quæ in hac Lingua Leges Compositionis servant; hoc est, tota vox simplex Compositionem ingreditur.

Composition in this language is the joining of two or more expressions <p. 70>
into one for the purpose of greater compendiousness in expressing and communicating our thoughts. And this can be done as the circumstances require, by
combining any one sign with any other, so long as the simple terms have the
same signification when part of a compound as they have when standing alone.
Since, however, the states, interconnections, and differences of things are
infinitely varied, and no simple and primitive word on its own can signify all of
these, and since it is impossible to express all the thoughts of the mind in terms
of a few primary words without variation except by very long periphrases, it is,
therefore, necessary for the sake of compendiousness to allow derivation and
composition. But it should be stressed that those notions that are called derived
ones are, strictly speaking, in fact composites; we draw the distinction because
the former are made by the addition of mutilate endings or prepositions,
which are themselves formed from integral words with their own independent
meaning. Thus *filiolus* [little son] is a composite word formed from *filius* [son]
and *parvus* [little]; *durior* [harder] is logically speaking composed of *durus* [hard]
and *magis* [more] but these are termed derived words because the second of the
two terms of the compound is expressed by a mutilate ending.

Hence it is that a language is deemed to be the more excellent, the greater is
the capacity of its words for derivation and composition. The Greek language is
thus thought better than all others known to us because of the <p. 71> richness
of its vocabulary resulting from derivation and composition, and it is the only
language previously considered suitable by philosophers for teaching the arts;
and this argument alone (aside from historical authority) reveals the Greeks to
have been a learned people and the first cultivators of philosophy. Nowadays
it may be observed that the more refined nations are constantly increasing
the capacity for derivation and composition in their own vernaculars. Thus the
English say *self-denial, fellow-feeling*, etc. and an almost infinite number of similar
words are invented daily. I have therefore concluded that in this language it is
permitted to combine any given term with any other, so long as this is meaningful and to the point, as otherwise an absurdity would result.

Note finally, regarding composition, that there are certain general notions
which enter very frequently into compounds in many languages and are placed
in front of the words with which they are combined in the form of mutilate
particles, and these are more correctly called derived rather than compounded:
of this sort are the Latin *re, con, am, se, in, ad, ab*, etc., which in this language
follow the rules of composition—that is, the whole simple word enters into the
compound.

CAP. IX.

DE SYNTAXI.

Structura orationis illi qui suos conceptus resolvere potest, facilis admodum est; pro qua hæc Regula generalis teneatur. *Idem sit ordo Signorum et Orationis, qui Mentis Conceptuum seu Actuum Rationis.* Mirum est, quanta sit transpositio vocum de suis locis propriis et naturalibus per hysteronproteron in quibusdam Linguis, præcipue Latina; adeo ut sæpissime eveniat, hominem omnia verba singulatim sumpta satis intelligentem, sensum tamen integræ orationis, sine longo discursu capere non posse. Cui rei procul dubio occasionem præcipue dedit Numerus, qui ab Oratoribus in oratione Soluta observatur, non minus quam in Ligata, quique ad Regulas Artis forte reduci poterit, non minus quam Poeticus. Verum in hac Lingua non est ferendum, ut aures demulceantur cum animi jactura, quod raro admodum aliter fit, præcipue a Poetis et Fictionum Amatoriarum Scriptoribus, cui generi hominum, qui nihil aliud quam spumam turbidæ Mentis ebullire solent, fateor me parum favere: Censeo enim hos Pestes <p. 73> Reipublicæ perniciosissimas; nam Mentes teneras Juvenum, honestis Artium præceptis et Virtutis praxi jam imbuendas, vitiant et polluunt. Utcunque, aliud remedium hic inventum est ad numerorum concentum harmonicum supplendum, absque orationis structuræ Logicæ perturbatione; ni. interpositio servilis literæ *i* quoties Euphonia postulat.

Regulæ particulares sunt. Primo, *Substantivum præcedat Adjectivum*; sic, *fη f goma, charta alba, fef groma, atramentum nigrum.*

2. *Agens præcedat verbum activum, patiens sequatur*; ut *sunilli ponesi Sava, omnes amant Deum; Sava ponesi lalli sunilli, Deus amat nos omnes.*

3. *Adverbium sequitur verbum*; ut, *lal trim sef trinesv simai, ego non possum scribere bene; lelil spηdesi pipai, ille laborat diligenter.*

4. Modus ille loquendi qui Latinis, *Ablativi absolute positi* dicitur, qui Græcis in Genitivo casu ponuntur, Angli vero Constructionem hanc per voces, *having, being,* exprimunt, est loquendi compendium quod in integram propositionem resolvi potest; verum propter frequentem usum admittendum est hoc compendium: Cumque hæc Constructio semper fere resolvatur in Tempus, per voces *cum, dum, post,* &c. ideo particula temporis erit hujus phrasis significativa; ut, *dan lollir tino, lel softinesa shvmdan; shvbdan lel slemesa tinesv,* his dictis, *siluit aliquandiu; postea vero progressus est loqui, seu continuavit sermonem: dan lolir samo* <p. 74> *lelil, sofslemesa spηdesv, hoc facto cessavit ab opere, vel operando: dan lal trineso, lelil bredprηdesa, me scribente ille ingressus est.* Notiones Temporis, ut Philosophis difficiles intellectu, sic Grammaticis expressu. Hæc constructio Anglice sæpe dicit respectum ad *causam,* et tunc per particulam causæ reddenda est; ut, *My hand being weary I cannot write longer*; id est, *sas smv lala spηgo, lal*

CHAPTER IX

ON SYNTAX

The structure of speech is quite straightforward for those who know how to analyse their concepts, and for these purposes the following general rule should be kept in mind. *The order of signs and of speech is the same as that of concepts of the mind or acts of reason.* It is surprising how often words are transposed from their natural and proper places by hysteron-proteron[55] in some languages, especially Latin, so that it often happens that someone can understand well enough each of the words taken individually and yet not be able to grasp the sense of the whole passage without running through a lengthy process. This is without any doubt for the most part occasioned by the rhythmic measures that are observed by orators, both in informal and formal discourse, which incidentally can be reduced to rules of art no less than can poetic metre.[56] But in this language one cannot express oneself in such a way that the ears are caressed while the mind is left vacant, which is usually the case with poets and writers of romantic fiction. I confess that I have little sympathy for such men, who are wont to do nothing more than spew forth the froth of a disordered mind. Indeed I consider them to be most pernicious enemies <p. 73> of the state, for they corrupt and pollute the tender minds of youth, whom we should be instructing in the rules of respectable arts and the practice of virtue. However, there is an alternative means provided in this language to furnish a harmonious concord of rhythm without disturbing the logical structure of speech—namely, the interpolation of the servile letter *i* whenever euphony requires.

The more particular rules are as follows: Firstly, *The substantive precedes the adjective*, e.g., *fnf goma, white paper*; *fef groma, black ink.*[57]

2. *The agent precedes the active verb, and the object follows*, e.g., **Sunilli ponesi Sava**, *All men love God*; **Sava ponesi lalli sunilli**, *God loves us all.*

3. *The adverb follows the verb*; **Lal trim sef trinesʋ simai**, *I cannot write well*; **Lelil spηdesi**[58] **pipai**, *He is working diligently.*

4. The construction that is known as the *ablative absolute* in Latin, which is expressed by the genitive case in Greek, and by a construction using the words *having* and *being* in English, is an abbreviation of speech that can be resolved into a complete proposition. Because of its frequency of occurrence, however, this abbreviation is to be allowed here. Since, however, this construction can

---

[55] Hysteron-proteron: the figure of speech in which what should come last is put first.

[56] See Dalgarno's unpublished tract on the reduction of poetic metres, 'On Terms of Art' (see below, Part IV, Unpublished Paper 3).

[57] Following Dalgarno's tables, *fηf goma, white paper*, should read *fηf gofa*; *fef groma, black ink*, should read *faf grofa*.

[58] **spηdesi** should read spηpesi.

trim sef trineso danibai, vel *svndan.* Multis modis possunt hujusmodi phrases variari, et omnes significare et Logice et Emphatice.

5. *Nomen Adjectivum et Genitivus casus, per strictam Analysin Logicam, eandem constituunt Notionem, seu Nominis Radicalis Flexionem, et ei superaddunt respectum pertinentiæ.* Hoc clarius apparebit comparando phrases diversarum Linguarum; Lingua Hebræa exprimit Flexionem, seu casum Adjectivum (jam enim bene advertendum, quod omnes variationes Notionis Radicalis, sive verbaliter, adverbialiter, adjective, &c. sunt vere Casus, seu Flexiones Nominis Radicalis) maxime proprie sic dictum, per Genitivum Casum, vel saltem per constructionem huic æquivalentem; ut, *homo albedinis, homo fortitudinis*; qua phrasi etiam aliquando Angli utuntur; *a man of might, a place of much Light.* Sic vicissim quædam Linguæ Genitivum casum propriissime sic dictum a Grammaticis, adjective exprimunt; ut, Anglice, *God's house,* John's *Father,* William's *Son, my hand,* <p. 75> *his foot*; sic Latini; *manus mea, pes tuus*: Ubi pronomina quæ pro Nominibus Substantivis supponuntur, redduntur Adjective. In omnibus quibus, Flexio Adjectiva, seu Genitivus Casus, significat Relationem pertinentiæ, possessionis, seu habitionis; Verum ego has Grammaticationes ut distinctas admisi, majoris compendii et claritatis causa. Perdifficile quidem est Regulas certas præscribere, quando Flexio Adjectiva, quando vero genitiva sit utenda; nam ut dixi, in stricta Logica Analysi, sunt eadem omnino flexio seu respectus: Hoc tamen hic offero. Utimur Flexione Genitiva (quæ exprimitur per particulam *sη f* a Radice *pertinere*) cum loquimur de duobus notionibus, ita, ut de una earum conceptus fiat in statu abstracto, vel quasi abftracto, separato, et distincto ab alia; ut, *albedo hujus parietis, Lux hujus diei,* manus Petri; Adjectiva vero, cum duas res concipimus in statu Concerto, composito, et unito; ut *paries albus, lux diurna, membra humana.*

6. Admitto Compendii causa distinctionem *personæ,* et *rei,* fieri per terminationes in eadem voce cum Nomine Adjectivo, sicut etiam fit in multis aliis Linguis; ut, *Sunirri tim samo sam,* vel, *sod Sava, omnia facta sunt a Deo. Simalli sodesi simai, boni homines bene faciunt.*

almost always be resolved into tense, by means of the words *when, while, after*, etc., a tense particle will be the indicator of such a clause, e.g., **Dan lollir tino, lel softinesa shʋmdan**; **shʋbdan lel slemesa tinesʋ**, i.e., *Having said these things, he was silent for a little time; afterwards he went on speaking, or continued to talk*; <p. 74> **Dan lolir samo lelil, sofslemesa spŋdesʋ**, *When he had done this, he left off his work, or stopped working*; **Dan lal trineso, lelil bredprŋdesa**, *While I was writing, he came in*. The notions of time, difficult as they are to understand philosophically, are to be expressed grammatically in this way. In English this construction often implies a *cause*, and in this case it is to be expressed by a causal particle, e.g., *My hand being weary I cannot write longer* is expressed as **Sas smʋ lala spŋgo, lal trim sef trineso danibai**[59] or **sʋndan**. Phrases of this sort can be varied in many ways, so that everything can be expressed both logically and with emphatic force.

5. *The adjectival noun and the genitive case, by strict logical analysis, constitute one and the same notion, or inflection of the radical noun, and they add to it the aspect of pertaining.* This appears more clearly by comparing constructions in different languages. Hebrew expresses the adjectival inflection, or what is more properly called the adjectival case (for it should be noted that all of the variants of the radical notion, verbal, adverbial, adjectival, etc., are really cases or inflections of the radical noun) by the genitive case, or at least by another equivalent construction, e.g., *a man of whiteness, a man of strength*, a construction that is sometimes also used in English, e.g., *a man of might, a place of much light*. Other languages again express by an adjective what is most properly called the genitive case by the grammarians, as in English: *God's house, John's father, William's son, my hand*, <p. 75> *his foot*, and in Latin: *manus mea, pes tuus*, where the pronouns that stand in place of the substantive noun are expressed adjectivally. In all of these the adjectival inflection or the genitive case expresses the relation of pertaining, possession, or state. I have allowed these to be distinct grammatications, for the sake of greater compendiousness and clarity. However, it is extremely difficult to lay down exact rules when to use the adjectival inflection and when the genitive, for as I have said, according to strict logical analysis they are one and the same inflection or aspect. However, I suggest the following. We use the genitive inflection (which is expressed by the particle **sŋf**, from the radical *to pertain*) when we are speaking of two notions such that one of them is conceived of as being abstracted, or quasi-abstracted, separate and distinct from the other, e.g., *the whiteness of this wall, the light of this day, the hand of Peter*. But the adjective is used when we conceive of two things as being concrete, composite, and unified, e.g., *a white wall, day-light, human limbs*.

6. For the sake of compendiousness I allow the distinctions of *person* and *thing* to be expressed by terminations included in the adjectival noun, as is done in many other languages, e.g., **Sunirri tim samo sam** or **sod Sava**, *all things were made by God*; **Simalli sodesi simai**, *good men act well*.

---

[59] Should probably read: **dan-i-bam**: time + long.

7. Constructio Ablativi et Dativi casus, seu quod idem est, particulæ *ab* et *ad* sunt significativæ relationis motus, ni. a termino, et ad terminum; <p. 76> id est, *actionis* et *passionis*; ideo optimo jure derivandæ sunt hæ particulæ a suis propriis Radicibus; ut, *Fef lola trinosa* sod *lal, hic liber scriptus erat* a *me. Lelil prηdesa* sod *fansava, stofdadu, ille venit* a *templo, foro. Sava spηbesi simarri suna* shod *lalli, Deus dat* nobis *omnia bona.*

8. Verborum impersonalium quædam redduntur per adjectivum *Rei*; qualia sunt hæc: *oportet, convenit,* &c. Sic, *Tim sedar sunilli shηpesv, oportet omnes homines mori.* Hujusmodi vero, *pluit, coruscat, &c.* sic reddenda sunt; *nan nanesi, ignis coruscat*; *nηn nηnesi, ventus spirat*; *nen nenesi, pluvia pluit.*

In propositionibus constantibus duobus Nominibus, ubi nullus habetur explicitus respectus ad differentiam temporis (quod licet non observatum sæpissime evenit, ut in propositionibus vulgo dictis æternæ veritatis, magis proprie, necessariæ connexionis) tunc Subjectum et prædicatum copulantur per duo verba substantiva *tim* et *trim,* pro ratione qualitatis propositionis affirmativa vel negativa; ut, *Sava tim sima, Deus est bonus*; *Tvsu tim tvma, voluntas est libera*; *sabtrin lola trim nη f, hæc penna non est lapis*; *Nam trim nom, Cœlum non est terra*; *lelil trim pono sod sava, ille non est amatus a Deo.* Cum vero temporis differentia innuitur, reddenda est per flexionem verbi temporis *dan,* sic; *Petrus danesa bred fan, Petrus fuit in domo.* Verum, si addatur particula temporis <p. 77> differentiæ significativa separatim, redundaret verbum temporis; ut, Petrus *tim bred fan lola svbdangom,* non, *Petrus danesa bred fan lola svbdangom, Petrus fuit in hac domo heri*: Sic, *Petrus tim bred fan lola loldan* vel *dlandan,* non, *Petrus danesi bred fan lola dlandan.*

9. Tenendum, in omnibus propositionibus affirmativis, ubi est verbum adjectivum (id est, conjugatum per flexiones temporis fignisicativas) omitti verbum substantivum, *tim,* compendii causa; in negativis vero semper exprimitur verbum *trim.*

Hic non addam plures Regulas de structura orationis; Logicæ enim peritus satis sciet ex paucis hic dictis, et capite sequente dicendis de particulis, quomodo connectere Notiones suas in aliis casibus: alii vero facile acquirent Logicæ praxin, ex praxi hujus Artis.

7. A construction with the ablative or dative case, or with the particles *from* and *to*, which is the same thing, expresses the relation of motion either away from or towards a particular point, <p. 76> that is of *action* and *passion*. These particles are therefore most properly to be derived from their respective radical notions, e.g., **Fef lola tinosa sod lal**, *This book has been written* **by** *me*; **Lelil prηdesa sod fansava, stofdadu**, *He came* **from** *the temple, or market*, **Sava spηbesi simarri suna shod lalli**, *God gives all good things* **to** *us*.

8. Certain impersonal verbs are expressed by the adjective of *thing*,[60] examples of which are *it is proper* [*oportet*], *it is agreed* [*convenit*], etc.; e.g. **Tim sedar sunilli shηpesv**, *All men must die*. Others, however, of the sort *it is raining, it is lightning*, etc., are to be expressed thus: **Nan nanesi**, *The lightning is flashing*; **Nηn nηnesi**, *The wind is blowing*; **Nen nenesi**, *The rain is raining*.

In propositions consisting of two nouns where there is no explicit reference to a distinction of time (and it very often happens that time is disregarded, as in the case of propositions that are commonly termed eternal truths, but that should rather be called propositions of necessary connection), the subject and predicate are linked by one of the two substantive verbs **tim** and **trim**, according to whether the quality of the proposition is affirmative or negative, e.g., **Sava tim sima**, *God is good*; **Tvsu tim tvma**, *The will is free*; **Sabtrin lola trim nηf**, *This pen is not a stone*; **Nam trim nom**, *The heaven is not the earth*; **Lelil trim pono sod sava**, *He is not loved by God*. When a distinction of time is implied, then it is to be expressed by an inflection of the temporal verb **dan**, e.g., **Petrus danesa bred fan**, *Peter was in the house*. However, if a particle is added that independently indicates a distinction <p. 77> of time, then the temporal verb is redundant, e.g., **Petrus tim bred fan lola svbdangom**, and not **Petrus danesa bred fan lola svbdangom**, *Peter was in this house yesterday*; and **Petrus tim bred fan lola loldan** or **dlandan** and not **Petrus danesi bred fan lola dlandan**.[61]

9. It should be kept in mind that in all affirmative propositions where there is an adjectival verb (i.e. one conjugated with inflections indicating time) the substantive verb **tim** is to be omitted for the sake of brevity; in negative propositions, however, the verb **trim** is always to be expressed.

I shall not list here any further rules concerning the structure of speech. From the few remarks that have been made, and from what will be said in the following chapter concerning the particles, anyone skilled in logic will know how to connect together his thoughts in other cases; and others will easily master the practice of logic from the practice of this art.

---

[60] i.e. **-a-** (adjective) plus **-r** (thing).

[61] The last two examples are the correct and an incorrect way of expressing the proposition *Peter is in this house now*. **dlandan** should read **dlaf-dan**: present + time.

CAP. X.

DE PARTICULIS.

Divina sorte magis quam Humana Arte ductus, felicissimo Auspicio, clavem hujus Inventionis primo reperi, propter cujus defectum, viri Docti, qui ante me hujus Artis Fores sedulo pulsabant, nequibant intrare. Per hanc Clavem intelligo <p. 78> Notiones vulgo *Particulas* vocatas, quæ ita se habent ad Orationem ut anima ad hominem, vel Tendines Nervi et ligamenta ad Corpus, vel Cæmentum ad Ædificium. Subductis enim Particulis ex Oratione, quid remanet? Nisi mortuum Cadaver sine forma hominis? Vel soluta membra sine forma corporis; vel cumulus lapidum sine forma domus? Et sicut Particulæ Formalem et Principaliorem partem Orationis constituunt, adeoque difficillimam (tota enim praxis Artis Logicæ et Grammaticæ in iis recte utendis sita est) sic etiam partem orationis maximam faciunt. Quare, dico harum resolutionem et reductionem sub regulis Artis, Inventionis Clavem.

Memini selectum numerum virorum Doctissimorum in Academia Oxoniensi, quibus primo Inventionem hanc communicavi, dum viderent Schema totius Artis in unica pagella exhibitum, Characteribus additis, brevitatem hanc incredibilem omnes mirabantur; præcipue illam partem quæ Particulas complectebatur. Ex his vir clariss. Sethus Ward *T. D.* et Aftronomiæ Professor in eadem Academia, postea mihi communicavit Tabulas Notionum Philosophicas, quas Artem hanc intendens ipse composuerat: et licet ad Particulas explicandas, et structuram orationis ex iis nondum descenderat, probabile tamen admodum est, quod labores ejus temporis progressu, serius aut citius in publicam lucem Artem hanc produxiffent. <p. 79> Postea vero mihi nunciatum est de aliorum propositis hac in re; circa enim idem tempus, prodiit Liber Anglice, sub Nomine Characteris Univerfalis, qui revera nihil aliud novi docebat, quam scribere vel loqui Anglice modo multo difficiliore quam vulgo fieri solet. Ingeniosius multo cogitata sua de hac Arte proposuerat Fransiscus Lodwick, Civis Londinensis; verum huic Suscepto impar, propterea quod Artis expers, et extra Scholas natus.

Primus igitur meus conatus in hac Arte longe alius erat a Methodo hic exhibita, præcipue in Particularum materia. Primo enim omnes Notiones Primitivas in duas Classes dividebam, Materiales scil. et Formales: Nomina et Verba et eorum casus partes materiales appellabam, easque Characteribus Majusculis notabam: Formales seu Particulas, punctulis minusculis circum Characterem Majusculum nominis vel verbi, designabam; eodem modo quo solent in Arte Brachygraphiæ, vocales per puncta notare circa Characterem consonantis. Et quidem hic modus maximum compendium scribendi docebat; sicut enim in vulgaribus Literis, quilibet Character significat partem vocis unius,

CHAPTER X

ON THE PARTICLES

L ed by divine guidance rather than human skill, by a most happy omen, I was the first to discover the key to this invention, for want of which the learned men who before me have industriously beaten at the doors of this art were not able to gain entry. By the key, <p. 78> I mean the notions usually known as *particles*, which are to speech what the soul is to man, what the nerves and ligaments are to the body, or what cement is to the building. For, if particles are taken away from speech, what remains? What else but a dead body without the form of a man? Or unconnected limbs without the form of a body? Or a pile of stones without the form of a house? And, just as the particles constitute the formal and most primary part of speech, and indeed likewise the most difficult one (the whole practice of logic and grammar residing in their correct use), so they also constitute the most important part of speech. It is for this reason that I call the analysis of the particles, and their reduction to rules of art, the key to the invention.

I recall that when a select number of the most learned men in the University of Oxford, to whom I first showed this invention, first saw the outline of the whole art displayed on a single small sheet, with characters added, they were all astonished by the incredible conciseness of it, and in particular the part that comprised the particles. One of these men, the illustrious Seth Ward T.D., professor of astronomy at the said university, later showed me some philosophical tables of notions that he himself had constructed for the purposes of this art. And, although he had not yet reached the stage of explaining the particles and the structure of speech from them, it is most probable that with time his labours would sooner or later have brought forth this art to public view. <p. 79> Afterwards indeed I was told about the proposals of other people in this area, for about that time there appeared a book in English under the title *Universal Character*,[62] which in fact offered nothing new, other than a way of writing or speaking English that was much more difficult than the customary one. In a more ingenious vein by far, Francis Lodwick, citizen of London, had set out his ideas on the subject,[63] but he was unequal to the undertaking, being deficient in art, and educated outside the schools.

My first efforts in this art were quite different from the method that is presented here, especially with regard to the particles. For at first I divided all the primitive notions into two classes—namely, material and formal. I classed as material elements the nouns and verbs and their cases, representing them by

---

[62] Cave Beck's *Universal Character* was published in 1657; see Dalgarno's negative judgement of the work in his letter to Hartlib dated 20 Apr. 1657 (see below, Part V).

[63] Francis Lodwick (1647, 1652), both in Salmon (1972).

forte *quartam, quintam, sextam, &c.* hic, minimum punctulum significabat integram Notionem; *v g,* hæc sentencia *ego amo illum valde bene,* scribebatur unico Charactere Majusculo pro verbo *amo;* cæteræ particulæ per puncta <p. 80> circum hunc Characterem affixa significabantur. Sic hæc sentencia: *Sed quoniam nos sæpe molestamur ab illis, ideo nos quoque illos aliquando molestabimus.* Tota hæc sentencia duobus Characteribus Majusculis scribebatur, cæteris vocibus per punctula circa Characterem affixa, expressis.

Verum postea, cum percipiebam multas notiones quibus pro particulis et primitive utebar (jam enim collectionem feceram circiter fere 300 particularum) esse vel revera compositas; quales sunt adverbia temporis, loci, conjunctiones causales; ut, *hic, illic, ubique, aliquando, quando, sæpe, quare, ideo, &c.* Alias vero nihil esse aliud quam adverbia modi, quales erant *bene, male, facile, &c.* Ideo Particularum numerum (quarum tot primo utebar, propter majus scribendi compendium) ex Analysi Logica indies minuebam.

Tandem vero mihi affulsit clarior lux; accuratius enim examinando omnium Notionum Analysin Logicam, percepi nullam esse Particulam quæ non derivetur a Nomine aliquo Prædicamentali, et omnes Particulas esse vere Casus, seu Modos Notionum Nominalium. Jamque inter hæc duo hærebam, an scriptionis compendium negligerem; an vero admitterem pro primitivis, quæ revera et Logice talia non erant; quod contra principalem hujus Artis scopum omnino erat. Quamobrem cum hæc duo conciliare nequibam, conclusi Logicam institutionem Nominum <p. 81> Rerum, utilitati Brachygraphicæ longe anteponendam; sicque omnes Particulas ex ordine Radicalium missas feci. Cumque jam respicio quot et quam varias Methodos et modos in hac Arte pertransiverim, quorum omnia longum esset recensere, experientia propria testatur, verum esse quod vulgo dicitur, Nihil simul natum et perfectum, et prima Artium lineamenta esse admodum rudia.

Tenendum me *sex* particulas Pronominales retinuisse, non necessitatis sed compendii causa, quia aliter sine longa periphrasi communicare non possumus; ponuntur enim hæ loco Nominum, ideoque Pronomina recte appellantur. Quod non sint absolute necessaria et primitiva, patet, quod quævis propositio illis constans resolvi potest per Nomina ipsa pro quibus hæc supponuntur. Sic *ego* scribo; id est, *Georgius Dalgarno* scribit: dum Petrum alloquor; *tu* scripsisti; id est, *Petrus* scripsit; dum Petrum alloquor de tertio aliquo, Johanne; *ille* scripsit; id est, *Johannes* scripsit.

capital letters. The formal elements, or particles, I designated by minuscular points arranged around the capital character of the noun or verb, in the same way as in the art of shorthand the vowels are marked by points around the character of the consonant. And indeed this produced a greatly abbreviated method of writing; for as in everyday writing any given character signifies a part of one word, say the *fourth, fifth, sixth*, etc., in my plan the smallest point signified a complete notion; for example, the sentence *I love him very greatly* was written with a single capital character for the verb *love*, and the other particles represented by points <p. 80> positioned around this character. Thus with the sentence: *But because we are often annoyed by them, we too will sometimes annoy them*. This whole sentence was written with two capital characters,[64] the other words being expressed by points positioned around the character.

Subsequently, however, I perceived that many notions that I was using as particles and treating as primitive (for I had now made a collection of around 300 particles) were in fact composite. Of this sort were adverbs of time and place, and causal conjunctions, e.g., *here, there, everywhere, once, when, often, wherefore, therefore*, etc. And I perceived that others were nothing but adverbs of manner, e.g., *well, badly, easily*, etc. For this reason, I started, by logical analysis, to reduce the number of particles (of which I was at first using so many for the purpose of greater brevity in writing).

But finally clearer light dawned on me. By examining more closely the logical analysis of all the notions, I perceived that there is no particle that does not derive from some predicamental noun, and that all particles are really cases or modes of nominal notions. At this point I hesitated between two alternatives: whether to disregard brevity of writing, or to admit as primitive what really and logically are not such, which would run quite counter to the principal aim of this art. When I was not able to reconcile these alternatives, I concluded that the logical establishment of names for <p. 81> things should clearly be given priority over the utility of shorthand, and I consequently dismissed all the particles from the rank of radicals. When I now look back on the many and diverse methods and approaches I worked through in this art, to recount all of which would take too long, my own experience bears witness to the truth of the popular saying that nothing is born perfect, and indeed the first outline of any art is rough and ready in the extreme.

It should be noted that I retained *six* pronominal particles, not out of necessity, but for the sake of brevity, since otherwise we could not communicate without lengthy periphrasis. These are used in place of nouns, for which reason they are quite properly called pro-nouns. That they are not absolutely necessary nor primitive is shown by the fact that any proposition containing them can be resolved by means of the nouns themselves which they are replacing. Thus **I** *am writing* is equivalent to **George Dalgarno** *is writing*; if I am addressing Peter, then **you** *have written* is equivalent to **Peter** *has written*; and if I am talking to

---

[64] Representing the two main verbs.

Hic bene observandum est, præcipuum quod reddit Linguas vulgares difficiles, est maxima ambiguitas particularum, ut videre licet apud Autores qui hoc subjectum tractarunt in variis Linguis: non enim sufficit ut aliquis Linguas vulgares intelligat, ut significationem omnium vocabulorum principalium separatim intelligat; Particulæ enim tam multiplices et incertæ sunt significationis, ut nequeant Regulæ certæ dari ad earum <p. 82> significationem determinandam, sed hoc ex solo usu et longa experientia est colligendum.

Judicia virorum doctorum varie expertus sum de modo instituendi voces ad *particularum* Notiones significandas: Quibusdam magis placebat modus ille prior, quo certum numerum Particularum pro Primitivis constituebam, a Notionibus Nominum in Tabulis positis distinctas. Ratio eorum erat; Primo, quod cum Particulæ sint notiones frequentis usus, voces iis significandis impositæ debent esse quantum fieri potest compendiosæ. Secundo videbatur illis in quibusdam Particulis quæ complexæ sunt significationis, ut vox longior, sic etiam obscurior: ut in vocibus, *sunsum* vel *sunshun*, unusquisque; *sυfshun*, vel *shυmsuf*, fere. Hæ enim voces sunt dissyllabæ, nec tamen totum sensum harum Notionum perfecte et plene exprimunt. Alii contra mecum hic sentiebant, quod cum notiones omnes Particularum fint ex natura Rei ipsius derivativæ a notionibus radicalibus Nominum (quod contra opinantes negare nequibant) ideo consentaneum esse, ut ab iis formentur, et omnino absurdum esse in Lingua Philosophica, admittere aliquam Notionem quæ non originaliter sit Nomen (vel saltem pro Nomine positum) et capax omnium flexionum Grammaticalium; quarum hæc est una, vocis scil. Radicalis mutilatio, qua denotatur vocem talem non significare partem aliquam materialem propositionis, fed <p. 83> formalem; id est, varios modos quibus intellectus notiones jungit in textura orationis, et varias rerum circumstantias situs, positionis, temporis, loci, &c. Quare hæ præcipue derivantur a notionibus transcendentibus et communioribus, et accidentibus sub Genere Accidentis Mathematici contentis. Præterea difficile est admodum determinare significationem harum vocum sine ambiguitate aliter: Imo omnino determinari nequeunt nisi ex notionibus Nominalibus ad quas dicunt essentialem respectum; quare æquissimum est sicut quoad *Rem* derivantur ab illis, sic etiam quoad *Signum*. Nec minori cum ratione derivantur, *et, ab, ad, per, sine,* &c. a radicalibus notionibus a quibus earum significatio determinatur, quam *bene, male, docte, &c.* a suis Primitivis.

Peter about some third person, John, then **he** *has written* is equivalent to ***John**
has written.*

It should be carefully noted at this point that the main feature that makes
the vernacular languages difficult is the great ambiguity of the particles, as
may be gathered from the writers who have dealt with this subject in various
languages.[65] For to understand the vernacular languages it is not sufficient
to understand the meaning of all the principal words in the vocabulary taking
each in isolation. For the particles are so varied and uncertain in their meaning
<p. 82> that no fixed rules can be given by which their meaning can be deter-
mined, but this can only be learned by usage and long experience.

I have profited in many ways from the opinions of learned men concerning
the method for setting up the words to signify the notions of the *particles*. The
method that some seemed to like best was the former one, whereby I set up a
certain number of particles as primitive, and distinct from the nominal notions
set out in the tables. Their reasoning was as follows. First, that since the particles are notions of frequent use, the words set up to signify them should be
made as concise as possible. Secondly, it seemed to them that in certain particles whose meaning is complex, the longer the word the more obscure it is,
e.g., in the words **sunsum** or **sunshun**,[66] *every single one*, and **sufshun** or **shumsuf**,[67]
almost. For these words are dissyllabic, and yet still do not accurately and fully
express the whole sense of these notions. Others, on the other hand, agreed
with me that, since the notions of all the particles are by the nature of the thing
itself derived from radical notions of nouns (which those of a contrary opinion
were not able to deny), it is appropriate that they should be formed from them,
and that in a philosophical language it is altogether absurd to admit any notion
that is not originally a noun (or at least put in place of a noun) and capable of
all the grammatical inflections. One of these is an inflection of the radical word,
by which is denoted that such a word does not signify any material part of
the proposition but <p. 83> a formal part, i.e., the various modes by which the
intellect joins notions together in the fabric of speech, and the various aspects
of things as regards location, position, time, place, etc. For this reason these are
chiefly derived from the transcendental and more general notions, and from the
accidents contained under the genus of mathematical accident. Moreover, it is
difficult to determine fully the meaning of these words in another way without
ambiguity, for they cannot be wholly determined except from the notions
of nouns to which they have an essential connection; for this reason it is quite
appropriate that, just as they are derived from them as regards the *thing*, so they

---

[65] Dalgarno might have in mind such works as Viger (1647) on the Greek particles, and Walker
(1655) on the English. Cf. Dalgarno's remark elsewhere: 'Thoe there have bin several accurat treatises
published upon the Particles both of the learned and vulgare Languages yet has there bin no Logical
analysis or Rationale attempted by any (for what I know) upon this Subject further than is to be seen
in the commone Systems of Grammare' ('The Autobiographical Treatise', fo. 60ʳ see below, Part IV).
[66] **Sun-sum**: whole + unity; **sun-shun**: whole + part.
[67] **Suf-shun**: maximum + part; **shum-suf**: little + rest.

Ad illud autem quod objicitur, voces esse longas nimis; Resp. Satis sunt breves quæ pro particulis primitivis supponuntur; secundum Regulam hujus Artis, *Vox Tabulæ Accidentis in oratione posita sine aliqua terminali litera addita est Particula.* Quod autem quædam particulæ sint propter compositionem longiores; quid hoc refert, quod aliquando sint dissyllabæ, trisyllabæ, quadrisyllabæ, modo satis distinguantur ab aliis vocibus? Sunt enim quædam Particulæ valde complexæ significationis, et cum capacitas Compositionis sit maxima excellentia in hac Lingua, absurdum omnino esset denegare Compositionem vocibus significantibus Notiones <p. 84> maxime complexæ naturæ; quales sunt quædam Particulæ. Videmus enim in omnibus Linguis, Logicam Naturalem hoc dictasse hominibus, Complexis Notionibus Particularum significandis, voces complexas imposuisse: ut quandoquidem, nihilominus, unusquisque; Anglice, *nevertheless, whensoever, &c.* Quare hæc abbreviatura vocum ad Brachygraphiam pertinet, nec est ejus confideratio admittenda in Lingua Philosophica, nisi secundario. Ad illud iterum, quod hæ voces aliquando non satis explicite dicant totam Notionem et conceptum Mentis; Resp. Fateor, aliquando sic est; non est enim expediens ad compendium et facilitatem communicationis, ut Notiones omnes nostras Simplices per rigorosam Analysin Logicam longa periphrasi semper explicemus. Sic vox *unusquisque*, significat distincte omnes distributive cum respectu ad singulas partes unatim; nimis autem esset laboriosum omnia hæc exprimere, in omni oratione ubi vox *unusquisque* occurrit: Quare vocem ex radicalibus *totius* et *partis*, vel *totius* et *unius* componimus, et supponimus pro hac complexa Notione, quod multo magis est rationabile quam vocem ex simplici instituto supponere. Concludo igitur, sicut Notiones Particularum derivantur a Notionibus Prædicamentalibus, sic etiam debent earum voces: Quod autem sic deriventur, abunde patet ex ulteriore earum resolutione. Unico exemplo instabo, de Particulis *tam* et *quam*. Hæc penna est *tam* longa *quam* illa; id est, hæ duæ pennæ comparatæ sunt *æqualis* longitudinis, vel *æque* longæ. Hæc <p. 85> penna est longior, vel magis longa quam illa; id est, Hæ pennæ comparatæ, hæc est longior, seu *magis* longa.

Ex his censeo abunde satisfactum esse iis qui resolutionem Logicam orationis perficere possunt, omnem Particulam derivandam esse a Notione Prædicamentali, et propterea facile erit illis, intelligere et recordari voces in sequentibus Tabulis, Particularum significativas: Rudiores vero quod attinet, voces Particularum ex Tabulis addiscant, tanquam essent ex mero instituto; idem enim signum potest esse respectu unius Rationale, respectu alterius qui rationem institutionis non apprehendit, simpliciter, arbitrarium.

should be derived as regards the *sign*. Thus it is just as rational to derive *and*, *from*, *to*, *by*, *without*, etc., from the radical notions that determine their meaning as it is to derive *well*, *badly*, *ably*, etc., from their respective primitives.

If it should be objected here that the words thus formed are too long, I would answer that those that are established as primitive particles are short enough, following the rule of this art: *A word from the Tables of Accidents used in speech without any suffix is a particle.* Certain particles are, of course, longer because they are compounded; but what does it matter if they are sometimes of two, three, or four syllables, so long as they can be clearly enough distinguished from other words? For certain particles have a very complex meaning, and, since the capacity for composition is the greatest excellence of this language, it would be quite absurd to disallow composition in words signifying notions <p. 84> of the most complex nature, and certain of the particles are of this kind. For we see in all languages that natural logic has dictated to men that they institute complex words for the complex notions of particles, e.g., *quandoquidem* [in as much as], *nihilominus* [nonetheless], *unusquisque* [every single one], and in English *nevertheless*, *whensoever*, etc. For this reason the abbreviation of words belongs in shorthand, but its consideration is not to be admitted in a philosophical language, except secondarily. If it be objected further that these words sometimes do not express explicitly enough the whole notion and concept of the mind, I answer, that I admit this sometimes to be the case, for it is not expedient for brevity and ease of communication that we should always express all of our simple notions by long periphrasis following strict logical analysis. Thus the word *unusquisque* [*every single one*] clearly signifies all distributively with respect to the individual parts one by one. However, it would be too laborious to express all of this whenever the word *unusquisque* occurred in speech. So we compound a word from the radicals *whole* and *part* or *whole* and *one*, and substitute this for the complex notion, which is much more rational than to substitute a word of a simple institution. I conclude, therefore, that, as the notions of the particles are derived from the predicamental notions, so their words should be also. That they are thus derived appears clearly from the further resolution of them. I shall give just one example, concerning the particles *tam* and *quam*. <p. 85> Haec penna est *tam* longa *quam* illa [*This pen is as long as that one*]; that is, These two pens when compared are of *equal* length, or are *equally* long; Haec penna est longior (*or* magis longa) quam illa [*This pen is longer (or more long) than that one*]; that is, If these two pens are compared, this one is longer or *more* long.

From what has been said I think it amply proved that, for those who are able to make a logical resolution of speech, every particle is to be derived from a predicamental notion, and for this reason it will be easy for them to understand and recall the words in the following tables that signify the particles. As far as the less learned are concerned, however, they should learn the words for the particles from the tables, as if they were instituted without reason; for one and the same sign may be rational from the viewpoint of one person, while for another who does not understand the reason of the institution it may be simply arbitrary.

Particularum Doctrinam absolvam, resolvendo quasdam Particulas et Constructiones difficiliores.

Totum Corpus, caput, terra, &c. absurde, pro, *totum* seu *totietas, corporis, capitis, terræ,* &c. Non enim dicimus, *partiale corpus, caput,* &c. sed, *pars corporis, capitis, terræ;* et eadem est constructionis ratio utrobique; vel si alterum horum verborum reddendum esset *Adjective* (nam supra docui Genitivam et Adjectivam Flexionem esse eandem) non *totum* et *pars,* sed *corpus, caput, terra,* adjective flectenda essent. Male sonarent hujusmodi phrases Latine, melius Anglice; *The bodies whole, the heads* <p. 86> *parts,* &c. Quare in hoc sensu collectivo, notio *(totum)* Substantive et abstracte est accipienda; in sensu vero distributivo, hæ notiones sunt reddendæ adjective, *uvvi suna, omnes homines;* vel per adjectivum *personæ;* sic, *sunalli, omnes homines; sunirri,* omnes res. De particula *unusquisque* hactenus. *Aliquis, nonnullus, particularis,* sunt adjectiva *partis* vel *unius. Ullus,* est adjectivum *entis.* Voces hæ, *quicunque, ubicunque, quandocunque,* &c. significant rem, personam, tempus, vel locum, &c. cum quadam Emphasi, quæ Latine exprimitur per terminationem *cunque;* quæ bene significari potest, per geminationem Particulæ relativæ *lul* his præfixæ; *lulluldan, lulluldad, lullulil, lullulir,* &c. Quo pacto etiam sit nonunquam Latine; *quotquot, quisquis, quoquoversum,* &c. Particula *in* est admodum ambiguæ significationis; numerant Logici octo modos inessendi (ut loquuntur) quibus nonum bene annumerare potuissent; ni. res *in tempore.* Verum unicus tantummodo est horum modorum, qui proprie dici potest modus inessendi: id est, res *in loco;* ut Petrus *in domo,* vinum *in poculo.* Proprie igitur dici potest lutum subjectum *inhæsionis,* cum quis *in* eo immergitur: improprie vero Anima respectu gratiæ, vel paries respectu albedinis, subjecta *inhæsionis* dicuntur: proprie tamen satis dicitur sanguis *in veste.* Cæteræ phrases ut plurimum resolvuntur per Genitivum casum; sic, *totum* et *pars* inter se comparata, *partes* sunt *totius partes;* non *in* <p. 87> toto. Nos sumus *in tempore;* id est, nos *temporamus* (si quis poterit notionem apprehendere ex hac barbara voce). Rex est *in* Regno; id est, habet, possidet Regnum, regnat. Longam orationem postularet omnem particularum ambiguitatem discutere; sed cum hoc noverint docti ad quos jam scribo sine me præunte præstare, cumque etiam satis determinatæ sint ex Tabulis, ideo hic amplius non expatiar.

Tenendum sub Nomine particularum contineri, Notiones vulgo a Grammaticis, Conjunctiones, Præpositiones, et Interjectiones appellatas, quæ posteriores formantur ab Animi passionibus, ut, *pom,* nota Admirationis, *puf,* ecce, *prob,* hei, vah, &c. Adverbiorum vero Flexio, est casus ab his distinctus, modum actionis significans; ut *pomesai,* admiranter, *ponesai,* amanter, &c.

I shall conclude this discussion of the particles by resolving certain more difficult particles and constructions.

The whole body, head, earth, etc., is an absurd construction and should rather be *the whole of* or *the totality of the body, the head, the earth*, etc. For we do not say *a partial body, head*, etc., but rather *part of a body, of a head, of the earth*, etc., and the logic of the construction is the same in both cases. Or, if one of the two words is to be expressed as an *adjective* (for I argued above that the adjectival and genitival inflections are one and the same), then the one to be inflected as an adjective is not *whole* or *part* but *body, head, earth*, etc. Phrases thus constructed sound bad in Latin, but better in English, e.g., *the body's whole, the head's parts*, etc. <p. 86> In this collective sense the notion *whole* is to be understood substantively and abstractly; but in the distributive sense the following notions are to be rendered adjectivally, **uvvi suna**, *all men*, or else by an adjective of *person*: **sunalli**, *all men*; **sunirri**, *all things*. The particle *unusquisque* has already been discussed. *Aliquis* [*somebody*], *nonnullus* [*some*], and *particularis* [*particular*] are adjectives of *part* or *one*. *Ullus* [*any*] is an adjective from *ens* [*entity*]. Words such as *quicunque* [*whoever*], *ubicunque* [*wherever*], *quandocunque* [*whenever*], etc. signify a thing, person, time or place, etc., with a certain added emphasis that in Latin is expressed by the ending *cunque*; this is well rendered by the geminated relative particle **lul** prefixed to them: **lulluldan, lulluldad, lullulil, lullulir**,[68] etc. This method is sometimes also used in Latin, e.g., *quotquot* [*however many*], *quisquis* [*whosoever*], *quoquoversum* [*every way*], etc. The particle *in* is extremely ambiguous in its signification: logicians enumerate eight modes of in-ness [modi inessendi] (as they say), to which they might well add a ninth: a thing *in time* [res in tempore]. Nevertheless there is only one of these modes that can properly be called the mode of *in-ness*, that is a thing *in a place* [res in loco], e.g., Peter is *in the house*; the wine is *in the goblet*. For mud can be properly said to be the subject of *inhesion* [inhaesio] when someone is immersed *in* it; but it is not correct to speak of the soul with respect to grace, or of a wall with respect to whiteness as subject of *inhesion*. It is, however, correct to speak of blood being *in clothing*. Many other phrases are resolved into the genitive case; thus when the *whole* and the *part* are compared, the parts are *parts of the whole*, not *in the whole*. <p. 87> We exist *in time* should be resolved into *nos temporamus* [we are timing] (if indeed one can grasp the notion from this barbarous expression). A king is *in reign*; that is, he has or possesses monarchy, or he reigns. It would require a very lengthy discussion to deal with all the ambiguities of the particles, but I shall not enlarge upon these here, since learned men for whom I am now writing will understand without my leading the way to show them, and since the particles are determined clearly enough from the tables.

It should be noted that included under the heading of particles are the notions commonly called conjunctions, prepositions, and interjections by grammarians,

---

[68] **lulluldan**: whenever; **lulluldad**: wherever; **lullulil**: whoever; **lullulir**: whatever.

Notandum etiam in Tabulis Accidentium, licet posuerim Notiones primitivas, vocibus Latinis expressas, aliquando Verbaliter, aliquando Nominaliter, idque nonunquam in sensu Adjectivo, nonunquam Substantivo concreto, nonunquam abstracto; tamen notio Radicalis et prima, concipienda est in sensu Abstracto, quod Lingua Latina (in hoc vere Barbara) sine Barbarismo exprimere non sinebat. Sic, hæ Notiones, *Dominus, Servus, Rex,* non sunt exprimendæ per solas voces Radicales, sed voci Radicali addenda est terminatio *el: e* enim est significativa Adjectivi <p. 88> agentis; *l* vero personæ; sic, *Kamel, Kramel, Kanel.*

Notandum ultra, *v* in principio dictionis est Characteristicon vocis numeri significativæ: Hoc sit ne fiat confusio inter voces Numericas, et voces aliarum notionum significativas hujus Linguæ. Præterea voces Numerorum Ordinalium formantur a vocibus Cardinalibus, adsciscendo literam servilem *s,* et *a* Flexionis Adjectivæ significativam; sic, *vasa, vηsa, vesa,* &c. primus, secundus, tertius.

Ultimum quod hoc loco addam erit de Mensuris. Mensuræ, cum non minus sint et arbitrariæ, et variæ apud varios Populos, quam sunt voces Linguarum, ideo æquum judico in hac Lingua Philosophica, ut rejectis omnibus vulgaribus Mensuris, non minus quam Vocibus, novæ Mensuræ prius formentur quam iis significandis Nomina instituantur. Verum quidem est, cum nulla detur determinata quantitas a Natura quæ sit primum Principium et Regula mensurandi, arbitrium necessario est admittendum in mensuris constituendis, non minus quam in primitivis vocibus instituendis: Verum si unum primum principium ex Arbitrio admittatur in unoquoque genere Mensuræ, hoc erit Regula Mensurandi quamlibet quantitatem; nec necessarium erit, dato semel hoc primo principio Mensuræ, instituere diversas et distinctas voces ad significandos distinctos gradus <p. 89> Mensuræ in eodem Genere; sed omnes aliæ Mensuræ exprimendæ essent per divisionem vel multiplicationem primæ Mensuræ. Sic, suppofito quod in genere Ponderis, *ounce* esset primum principium Mensuræ; Mensura vulgo *pound,* esset exprimenda 16 *ounces.* Nolo hic in me suscipere, quod sit istud principium mensurandi in singulis generibus Mensurarum determinare; sed rem hanc (cum aliis) virorum doctorum judicio, in hac Materia me magis versatorum subjicio; opinionem tamen meam hic sic offero: Minima Mensura quæ a viris doctis usum obtinuit in mensurando debet primum principium mensurandi constitui.

Aliam præterea rationem determinandi Mensuras, et sic Nomina illis imponendi in hac Lingua cogitavi, *viz.* Cum (ut dictum) omnis determinatio

the last category being formed from the passions of the soul, e.g., *pom* a sign of wonder; *puf*, *behold*; *prob*, *aha*, *oh*, etc. The adverbial inflection, however, is a case distinct from these, signifying a mode of action, e.g., *pomesai*, *surprisedly*; *ponesai*, *lovingly*, etc.

It is likewise to be noted in the Tables of Accidents that, although I have given the primitive notions expressed in Latin sometimes as verbs and sometimes as nouns, and this sometimes in an adjectival sense, and sometimes as a concrete substantive or as an abstract one, yet the primary radical notion is to be taken in an abstract sense, which in Latin (here truly barbarous) cannot be expressed without a barbarism. Thus the notions *dominus* [lord], *servus* [servant], *rex* [king] are not to be expressed by single radical words, but by the radical with the additional ending *el*: *e* indicating adjective <p. 88> of agency and *l* indicating person, i.e., *kamel*, *kramel*, *kanel*.

It should be further noted that the letter *v* at the start of an expression is the characteristic of a word indicating number. This is done so that there can be no confusion between numerical words and words in this language indicating other notions. Furthermore, the words for the ordinal numbers are formed from the cardinal words, with the addition of the servile letter *s* and the letter *a* indicating the adjectival inflection, i.e., *vasa*, *vηsa*, *vesa*, etc., *first*, *second*, *third*.

The last point I shall add here concerns measures. Since measures are no less arbitrary and variable from people to people than the words of different languages, I thought it proper in this philosophical language that, having rejected the vulgar measures as I rejected vernacular words, new measures should be invented before words be assigned to signify them. However, since no determined quantity is given by nature that would constitute the first principle and rule for measurement, it is necessary to allow arbitrary judgement in establishing measures no less than in instituting primitive words. But if one first principle is established arbitrarily in any one system of measures, this should be the rule for measurement of any given quantity whatsoever. It will not be necessary, once this first principle of measurement is established, to set up diverse and distinct words to signify distinct degrees <p. 89> of measure in the same system, but all other measures will be expressed by division or multiplication of the primary one. Thus, supposing that in the system of weights the *ounce* were the primary principle of measure, the unit commonly called the *pound* would be expressed as 16 *ounces*. I do not wish to take it upon myself here to determine what this principle of measure should be for particular systems of measure; in this matter (as in others) I submit to the judgement of learned men who are more knowledgeable than I. But the view that I am putting forward is this: the smallest unit that is accepted for measuring by the learned should constitute the primary principle.

I also considered another basis for establishing measures and for giving names to them in this language—namely, this: since (as I have said) every determination of measures is completely arbitrary, and measures vary from people to people, I should use as the method of measurement the measures used by us

Mensuræ sit res omnino arbitraria, et Mensuræ apud varias Gentes variæ sint, ideo Regulam mensurandi constituere Mensuras apud nos Britannos in usu: Si enim Arbitrium necessario sit admittendum, consentaneum videtur, ut nostrum Arbitrium hic præferatur; ut sciant aliæ Nationes unde hæc Ars primam originem duxerit. Verum cum nostræ Mensuræ, non minus quam aliorum populorum sint sine ratione institutæ; id est, variæ denominationes Mensurarum in eodem Genere Mensuræ, non distinguantur et excedant se invicem, secundum regularem et eandem <p. 90> quantitatis proportionem, *e.g.* 4 *farthings* (quæ est minima Mensura in Genere Pecuniæ) faciunt unum *pennie*, 12 *pennies* faciunt unum *shilling*; 6 *shillings*, unum *crown*, 4 *crowns*, unum *pound* (eadem est irregularitas proportionis in aliis Mensuris) omnino contra scopum Linguæ Philosophicæ fuisset, his Mensuris sic determinatis Nomina imposuisse. Deinde non est supponendum, licet hæc Lingua ita invaleret, ut usum omnium aliarum Linguarum exterminaret, quod valde est improbabile (licet enim mihi admodum probabile videatur eam ita invalituram in posteris sæculis, ut omnes Gentes cultæ et Literatæ ea usuri fuerint, quomodo nos Europæi utimur Lingua Latina; non est tamen probabile, eam usum omnium vulgarium Linguarum penitus aboleturam) quod propterea omnes Nationes, Antiquas et usitatas Mensuras simul cum Linguis rejicerent.

Quare tertio, omnibus his consideratis, concludo; nisi hunc arbitrarium morem mensurandi mutare possemus in Philosophicum, frustra esset Nomina Philosophica his Notionibus non Philosophicis instituere: Quapropter dum Gentes omnes consenserint mutare hunc mensurandi modum, retineant cum Arbitrariis Mensuris etiam earum Arbitraria Nomina: Cum igitur sermo habetur in hac lingua de Mensuris alicujus Nationis, exprimantur per Nomina ab ipsis usitata, tanquam essent propria Nomina virorum vel Locorum.

<p. 91>   Tenendum tamen est; bene institui posse Mensuras Temporis (adeoque etiam in hac Lingua, Nomina iis significandis) ad distinguendos diversos gradus vitæ in rebus Animatis: Ratio est, quia hic datur fundamentum in re ipsa; et ideo in omnibus fere Linguis vulgaribus, certi quidam gradus temporis vitæ, distinctis Nominibus insigniti inveniuntur: ut in homine, infantia, pueritia, adolescentia, juventus, status adultus, senectus. Quidam etiam distincti gradus notantur in plantis et brutis.

Quamobrem in homine Creaturarum viventium perfectissima, admitto quinque distinctos gradus temporis vitæ; quos distinguo per voces numericas voci speciei significativæ additis. Sic, 1. Infantia. 2. Pueritia. 3. Adolescentia. 4. Status adultus. 5. Senectus; *uvva, uvvη*, uvve, uvvo, uvvυ. Sic, proportione servata, distingui possunt 5 ætates plantarum: Prima, dum ex semine surgit (in Arboribus vocant Angli *kitkey*). Secunda Ætas est surculus tener. Tertia, Surculus procerior factus. Quarta, Planta adulta. Quinta, Vanescens et marcescens. Idem dicendum de Brutis, in quorum Nominibus (præcipue Brutorum nobis maxime familiarium) etiam quædam vestigia hujus distinctionis in Linguis vulgaribus inveniuntur; fic Angli dicunt, *foal, colt, calf, heifer*, &c.

Britons. For, if it is necessary to admit arbitrary judgement, it seems proper that our judgement is here preferred, so that other nations would know where this art had its origin. Our measures, however, no less than those of other peoples, are instituted without any regard for reason. That is, the various denominations of measure within the same system are not set up to follow on one from another, according to a regular and evenly <p. 90> proportioned progression. Thus 4 *farthings* (which is the smallest unit in monetary measures) make one *penny*; 12 *pennies* make one *shilling*; 5 *shillings* make one *crown*; 4 *crowns* make one *pound* (and other measures show a similarly irregular proportion); and it would, therefore, be quite in conflict with the aims of a philosophical language to assign names according to measures thus established. It is not, however, to be imagined, even if this language were to become so strong as to abolish the use of all other languages, which is extremely improbable (for, although it appears quite probable to me that this language will gain increasing strength in coming centuries, so that all the civilized and literate nations will use it in the same way as we Europeans now use the Latin language, yet it is not probable that it will do away with the use of all vernacular languages), that therefore all nations would reject their ancient and traditional measures along with their languages.

Thirdly, I draw the following conclusion from these considerations. Unless we can exchange this arbitrary system of measurement for a philosophical one, it is pointless to assign philosophical names to such non-philosophical notions. Hence, until all nations agree to change this method of measurement, they should retain along with their arbitrary measures, their arbitrary names as well. Therefore when in this language we speak of the measures of a particular nation, these are to be expressed by the names they themselves use, as though they were proper names for people and places.

However, it should be noted that it is very well possible to establish measures <p. 91> of time (and hence also to establish names in this language to express them) for distinguishing different stages of life in animate things. The reason is that a basis for this can be found in the thing itself, and therefore it will be found that in nearly all vulgar languages certain discrete stages of life are marked by distinct names, e.g., in man: infancy, boyhood, adolescence, youth, adulthood, old age. Certain distinct stages are likewise demarcated in plants and animals.

For this reason in man, the most perfect of living creatures, I allow five distinct stages of life, which I distinguish by numerical words added to the word indicating the species. Thus (1) infancy, (2) boyhood, (3) adolescence, (4) adulthood, (5) old age: *uvva*, *uvvη*, *uvve*, *uvvo*, *uvvv*. Keeping the same proportion, five ages may be distinguished in plants. First, when it emerges from the seed (which in trees is called *kitkey* in English). The second age is the young shoot. The third is when the shoot is taller. The fourth is the adult plant. The fifth is when it droops and withers. Similarly in animals, in the names of which (especially in the beasts best known to us) some traces of this distinction can be found in the vulgar languages: thus the English say *foal*, *colt*, *calf*, *heifer*, etc., which words distinguish the first two stages of life in these animals. The reason

quæ voces distinguunt duos primos gradus vitæ in his animalibus. Ratio autem quod hic <p. 92> admittam Numeros, ad harum Notionum differentias distinguendas, est quod hæ differentiæ essentialiter pendeant a numero; in hoc enim solo casu admittendi sunt numeri ad rerum Differentias significandas. Ratio iterum quod Numeri ita sint inepti ad Rerum differentias distinguendas, est hæc, quia aliarum omnium Notionum quæ sub cognitione humana cadunt, Numeri sunt a sensibus maxime abstracti; ideoque anima humana (quæ dum corpori alligata Sensuum ministerio utitur) dum notionum pure Numericarum recordatur, cogitur Numeros applicare ad res sensibiles: Ita ut vere dici possit, omnem Intellectus operationem ultimo resolvi in numeros, et hos si non necessario semper (quod non audeo positive afferere) saltem sæpissime, primo rebus sensibilibus applicari.

Admitto etiam sex gradus mensuræ temporis in genere, vocibus numericis distingui, ni. *minutum, hora, dies, septimana, mensis, annus;* sic, *danva, danvη, danve,* &c. dici etiam potest, *danvai* septimana, *daniar* mensis, *danial* annus.

Hic ultimo teneatur de gradibus consanguinitatis et affinitatis; modus maxime proprius et Philosophicus exprimendi has relationes (quia scil. maxime secundum ipsius Rei naturam) est per voces desumptas a notionibus Primis et Radicalibus, in quibus hæ Relationes fundantur. Sic, pater *pagel,* id est, persona gignens; mater *patel* vel <p. 93> *pratel,* id est, persona concipiens, vel pariens; avus, *pater secundus;* proavus, *tertius pater;* atavus, *quartus pater,* &c. Adeoque hoc sensu, Adam erit noster ultimus seu postremus pater. Sic filius *pagol,* id est, persona genita; nepos, *secundus filius;* pronepos, *tertius filius,* &c. Sic fratres, sunt *cognati primi* (nam teneatur, *steb* significare consanguinitatis relationem collateralem, non eam quæ est in linea recta) *cognati secundi,* qui habent eundem avum; *cognati tertii,* qui habent eundem proavum, *&c.* Avunculus, id est, *frater patris;* matertera, id est, *soror matris,* &c. idem intelligatur de gradibus affinitatis, id est, periphrastice exprimendi sunt *mariti pater, mariti frater,* &c.

Sequitur reductio præcipuarum vocum Linguæ Latinæ, ad Notiones Radicales hujus Linguæ Philosophicæ.

Et hic tenendum: Cum hic mihi tantummodo propositum sit principia et fundamenta hujus Artis ita proponere, ut a viris doctis apprehendantur; ideo 1. Voces in Tabulis positis brevitatis causa hic non repetivi. 2. Nec omnes voces Latinas hic posui; maxima enim pars vocum quæ reperiuntur in Lexicis, vel sunt Derivativæ et Compositæ, ut, *bonus, bene, bonitas, benefacio,* &c., vel tales sunt voces, quibus in aliis Linguis nullæ voces simplices respondent, sed periphrastice exprimuntur; quales sunt quamplurima Nomina *vestium, vasium, ciborum,* &c. quarum explicationem, <p. 94> per voces hujus Linguæ hic intendisse prolixum nimis fuisset, præterea etiam superfluum, cum viri docti satis sciant has voces resolvere per ea quæ hic tradita sunt: Auctius autem Lexicon in gratiam vulgi postea parabitur, 3. Nemo doctus expectabit me per voces hujus Linguæ redditurum eundem plane valorem omnium vocum

why I allow <p. 92> numbers here to distinguish between these differences is that the differences depend essentially on number; in this case alone, therefore, are numbers permitted to distinguish the differences of things. The reason why numbers are generally unsuitable to signify the differences of things is that, of all other notions that human thought can encompass, numbers are the most remote from the senses. And for this reason the human soul (which so long as it is tied to the body uses the services of the senses), when it recalls purely numerical notions, is compelled to apply numbers to sensible things. Thus it can truly be said that every operation of the mind can ultimately be resolved into numbers, and that numbers, if not necessarily in all cases (which I do not dare to assert categorically) at least in most cases, are related in the first place to sensible things.

I also allow six numerical words to distinguish six degrees in the measure of time in general; i.e., *minute, hour, day, week, month, year*: viz., **danva, danvη, danve**, etc. It is also possible to say **danvai** for *week*, **daniar** for *month*, and **danial** for *year*.[69]

A final point should be made concerning the degrees of consanguinity and affinity. The most correct and philosophical way of expressing these relationships (as being most in accord with the nature of the thing itself) is by words borrowed from the primary and radical notions upon which the relations are based. Thus father is **pagel**, the person who begets; mother is **patel** or **pratel**,[70] <p. 93> i.e. the person who conceives or gives birth; grandfather is expressed as *second father*; great grandfather as *third father*; great-great grandfather as *fourth father*, and so on. In just this sense, Adam will be our ultimate or final father. Likewise son is **pagol**, i.e. person begotten; grandson is *second son*; great-grandson is *third son*; and so on. Brothers are *first relatives* (note that **steb** indicates a collateral relation of consanguinity and not a relation of descent); *second relatives* are those who have the same grandfather; *third* relatives are those who have the same great-grandfather, etc. *Avunculus* [paternal uncle] is *father's brother*; *matertera* [maternal aunt] is *mother's sister*, etc.; and the same is to be understood with the degrees of affinity—that is, that they are to be expressed periphrastically, e.g., *husband's father, husband's brother*, etc.

There follows a list that reduces the principal words of Latin to the radical notions of this philosophical language.

This must be kept firmly in mind. Since my only aim here is to set forth the principles and foundations of this art in such a way as to be understood by learned men, therefore: (1) I have not, for reasons of brevity, repeated here all the words that are listed in the tables; (2) I have not included all Latin words here; for the majority of words found in dictionaries are either derived or compounded, e.g., *bonus* [good], *bene* [well], *bonitas* [goodness], *benefacio* [to do good]; or else they are words which have no corresponding simple items in other

---

[69] **Dan-vai**: time + seven; **dan-iar**: time + moon; **dan-ial**: time + sun.
[70] **Pag-el**: beget + person; **pat-el**: conceive + person; **prat-el**: give birth + person.

aliarum Linguarum sine periphrasi; hoc enim est impossibile, quia esset labor infinitus. 4. In explicandis vocibus Latinis hic positis non usus sum longa periphrasi verborum, nec omnes earum varias acceptiones enumeravi, sed breviter tantum expressi præcipuas Radicales voces hujus Linguæ per quas explicandæ sunt: possunt etiam quædam Notiones quas ego per voces compositas expressi, aliquando pro re nata, aptius periphrastice et divisim exprimi, et e contra; vocum tamen Compositioni, compendii et Emphasis causa, omnibus modis studendum est; et ad hoc faciendum cuique sua libertas linquitur, modo ratio Compositionis sit clara et evidens; in hoc enim summum Philosophiæ acumen apparebit, multiplicare per Compositionem et Derivationem signorum compendia Emphatica ex paucis Primitivis sine obscuritate.

languages, but are elsewhere expressed periphrastically. Such are, for example, the many nouns for *clothing*, *vessels*, *foods*, etc., to give definitions for which <p. 94> in terms of the words of this language here would have been too lengthy a matter; and besides, it would also have been superfluous, since learned men will know well enough how to resolve these words by means of those that I have given. An enlarged lexicon for the use of the man in the street will be provided later. (3) No learned man will expect me to be able to express by means of words of this language the exact meaning of all the words of other languages without periphrasis; this is impossible because the task would be infinite. (4) In explaining the Latin words listed here I have not used lengthy verbal periphrasis, nor enumerated all of their different subsenses, but only given briefly the chief radical words of this language by means of which they are to be expressed. Further, certain notions that I have expressed by composite words can in certain circumstances be better expressed periphrastically or in separate words, and vice versa. However, for the sake of conciseness and emphasis, the composition of words is to be striven for in every way, and freedom is to be allowed to any person to do this, so long as the reason for the composition is clear and plain to see. For the greatest skill in philosophy will be manifest in multiplying emphatic compendiums of signs by composition and derivation from a few primitives, and without obscurity.

LEXICON LATINO-PHILOSOPHICUM.

Abacus, *fran.*
Abbas, *kaf.*
Abdicare, *sofkafesv, trvd sofslem.*
Abdere, *dit.*
Abire, *bempηd.*
Abhinc, *shvb lol dan, bem lol dad.*
Abhorrere, *prebesv svmpron, trof.*
Abjurare, *scabe trimesv.*
Ablactatio, *soffηs, sofiηn.*
Abolere, *sofshanesv, grvpesv, sofiavresv.*
Abominari, *svmpronesv.*
Aboriri, *pratesv svb danu.*
Abripere, *dos don bemdep shekai.*
Abrogare, *sofiavresv, sofkebesv.*
Abrumpere, *domesv donesv.*
Absolvere, *kon shon sis.*
Abstemius, *sofprafemp.*
Abstinere, *trvs preb tim sodesv.*
Absurditas, *shib prem softos.*
Abundantia, *svmu slvdu.*
Abusus, *shig.*
Abyssus, *dadbaf.*
Academia, *dadtem fantem dadtis.*
Accendere, *nηmesv, semesv, nηm.*
Accidere, *sakesv pηk ded.*
Accingere, *drod sitresv.*
Accipere, *sprηb.*
Acclivitas, *blηmu.*
Accolere, *stid shvmbem.*
Accommodare, *stop sitresv.*
Acervus, *drotor,—ind* ut *nη find.*
Acetum, *flηm* vel *flem grηbe.*
Acies, *bηbu.*
Acquiescere, *dram tvp.*
Acquirere, *stis spηm.*
Aculeus, *sabdik.*
Acumen, *bηbu primu.*
Additamentum, *shunu drose, tηno.*
Adeo, *svm lolsηs ses.*
<p. 96> Adjuro, *skab.*
Adipisci, *spηn sprηb sηg stis.*
Administratio, *kas, kram.*
Admittere, *slaf prηdesv tvf*

Admodum, *svm.*
Adnihilare, *sofiavresv.*
Adolere, *nηmesv skagu gub.*
Adolescens, *vv daba vvve.*
Adoptare *tvdesv sηt pagol.*
Adoriri, *kum.*
Adorare, *skaf tud stη f.*
Adesse, *dap.*
Advena, *stred.*
Adversus, *shom.*
Adulterium, *kvf.*
Ædes, *fan.*
Æger, *grug.*
Æmulari, *pvt.*
Ænigma, *tidu trifo, shepa.*
Æqualitas, *slvn, stlηm.*
Æquanimitas, *pib pod.*
Æquilibrium, *slvn, dηm.*
Æquitas, *kef sid grat.*
Æquinoctium, *slvn dangom dangrom.*
Æquipollentia, *sefu slvna.*
Æquivocus, *tose shumir*
Ærugo, *grvpu sη f nef gob.*
Ærumna, *prob pred.*
Ærarium, *fanfum.*
Æstas, *dangam.*
Æstus, *gamu shvna, damu shvna sη f is.*
Ætas, *dansηp.*
Æther, *nam, nηm.*
Ævum, *danial vali.*
Affectus, *peb, pis, pos.*
Afferre, *bremdep.*
Affinitas, *streb sted.*
Affligere, *kofship prob kvm.*
Ager, *nom nvba, flan.*
Agger, *rvp nomind.*
Aggredi, *sem kum.*
Agrestis, *stran.*
Agilitas, *sprηt, dam, sod.*
Agmen, *shum——ind.*
Agricola, *nomspηpel.*
Agnatio, *steb.*
Agnomen, *ton svba.*

Agnus, *nekpimva.*
Ah, *prob.*
Ahenum, *fren nefgoba.*
Alabrum, *sabframdef.*
Alacer, *pob prim.*
Alapa, *digu sηf smvs.*
Albugo, *shunu gofa sηt mηs sηf snur.*
Alchymia, *temu sηf gakreu sηf nef.*
Alea, *mib spafa.*
Alias, *danslom.*
Alibi, *dadslom.*
Alienare, *gvg shηd strof.*
Alimentum *sangum.*
Aliquando, *shundan.*
Aliter, *slomses.*
Alius, *slom.*
Allevare, *drηmresv pobresv.*
Allicere, *tum spak.*
Allidere, *shomdenesv.*
Allucinari, *tren.*
Alludere *son spam pvp.*
<p. 97> Almus, *gum pok.*
Alere, *gum.*
Alphabetum, *tommu sηna.*
Altare, *fran skaga.*
Alter, *slomvη.*
Altercari, *spap.*
Alternare, *sηt shηd.*
Altitudo, *bafu.*
Alvearium, *dadu sηf snap nengηm.*
Alveus, *ab sηf ris.*
Alvus, *fos.*
Amanuensis, *trin.*
Ambages, *trommi spake sliba.*
Ambiguitas, *slib tose shumir.*
Ambitio, *trvbpebstηf.*
Ambitus, *eb beg.*
Ambo, *vη, lol tηn lel.*
Ambulare, *pηb.*
Ambulacrum, *dadpηb.*
Amentia, *grugrin.*
Amita, *stebpragva sηf pagel.*
Amnis, *ris.*
Amœnitas, *ped pob.*
Amphitheatrum, *fran spafa, fada, feda.*
Amplecti, *beg smv.*
Amplus, *svm beisam ban.*
Amussis, *sabbηf.*

Anathema, *truf.*
Anatome, *temdoniov.*
Anfractus, *brηf.*
Angere, *pred prob.*
Angina, *grugnir.*
Anhelare, *grugsheppam.*
Animadvertere, *puf, pem.*
Animal, *ov sηpe.*
Animus, *eiv tam.*
Annulus, *frvmsmus mab.*
Annus, *danial danvu.*
Ansa, *sunu dvn dvf.*
Annales, *sefdan.*
Anteferre, *svbpop befdad.*
Anticipatio, *svb bef sodesv samesv*
Antipathia, *shom.*
Antipodes, *shomsmvr.*
Antiquitas, *drab.*
Antistes, *stηf.*
Anus, *dobu sηf fvs.*
Anxietas, *pred, prob pum.*
Apex, *rab*
Apoplexia, *grugsofpies grugdod.*
Apostata, *sofslem.*
Apostema, *grugbrap.*
Apostolus, *kad.*
Apparere, *mηfosv, pem pef.*
Appellare, *ton.*
Appendix, *shunu tηno droso.*
Applicare, *dit dad.*
Approbare, *tad tvf.*
Aptitudo, *sit sos.*
Arbiter, *kηmel tvdo.*
Arcanum, *dit sofpem.*
Arcere, *krum shaf drηg.*
Arduus, *shep baf shηb.*
Arena, *nηfmamind.*
Argentum, *nef vηsa.*
Argilla, *nafgap.*
Argumentum, *sas, sog.*
Arguere, *tap trub kib.*
<p. 98> Arista, *vg.*
Arithmetica, *temtηg.*
Armentum,—*ind neikflanind.*
Arare, *flan.*
Armilla, *frvmsmη.*
Aroma, *neibdeig gema.*
Arra, *shunu sηf stηdu.*

Arrestare, *kod.*
Arridere, *spam ped.*
Arrogantia, *trvbsodpop prig.*
Articulus, *smeis drod.*
Arx, *fan kusa.*
Ascendere, *dam pηb pηd bηs ben.*
Aspicere, *mηs.*
Aspirare, *pam, dηf spηm.*
Assiduitas, *pip slem.*
Assuescere, *set.*
Astrologia, *temias.*
Asylum, *dad sηb.*
Atomus, *mam.*
Atrium, *rebak.*
Atrox, *pit pin.*
Avaritia, *trvd pvk.*
Author, *sas sam sem.*
Audacia, *put pot.*
Audire, *mηr.*
Auferre, *bemdep.*
Augere, *svn.*
Aurichalcum, *nefgod.*
Aurora, *semu sηf dangom.*
Aurum, *nefsimap.*
Austeritas, *grηn prid pin.*
Aut, *trηf.*
Automatus, *sabdan dame lvl.*
Autumnus, *danrag.*
Avunculus, *stebel vasη sηf patel.*

BACCA, *ragnog.*
Balbus, *grugshaftin.*
Balneum, *dadnimsif.*
Baptismus, *nimsif skapnim.*
Barba, *amnir.*
Barbarus, *pit softos.*
Barritus, *panu sηf nηksvf.*
Basium, *neis.*
Batillum, *frennηm.*
Beatitudo, *skan saku sima.*
Benignitas, *pokpon.*
Biblia, *sefsasva.*
Bilis, *ηm.*
Bilanx, *sabtηgdηm.*
Bitumen, *nafgap.*
Blæsitas, *grugshaftin.*
Blanditiæ, *pvp.*
Blasphemia, *truf sasva.*

Botrus, *ragsnug.*
Braccæ, *smηrfreim.*
Bractea, *mem.*
Braxare, *gvdesv flηm.*
Bucca, *nos.*
Bulbus, *mηb.*
Bulla, *mηb sηf nim.*

CACARE, *em dragresv fos.*
Cadaver, *ov shηpa.*
Cæcitas, *sofmηs.*
Cædere, *shηpresv.*
Cælare, *temdom trin.*
Cælebs, *trim stef.*
Cæremonia, *stam.*
Cæsius, *gop.*
Cæspes, *shunu fηf mem sηf nom.*
Cæspitare, *shaf smvs grugpηs.*
<p. 99> Calamitas, *skran prob.*
Calamus, *fam lηd.*
Calcar, *sabdik.*
Calceus, *freimsmvr.*
Calculus, *grugnηf sabtηgshum.*
Caliga, *freimsmer.*
Callere, *gab prim.*
Calva, *mas.*
Calvities, *grugsofiam.*
Calumnia, *kibu shiba.*
Campus, *lor.*
Canistrum, *fron.*
Canities, *am gof.*
Captivitas, *kug.*
Canon, *keb tok.*
Capere, *dvf.*
Capistrum, *sabmeisdrod.*
Capsa, *fem fron frvn.*
Carbo, *san sofnηm nafnηm.*
Carcer, *dadkog.*
Cardo, *ib.*
Caries, *grvp.*
Carina, *ab sηf fηn.*
Carminare, *drop sud.*
Carpentum, *flin.*
Carnefex, *kasshηprel.*
Carpere, *drid drot.*
Cartilago, *raf.*
Carus, *stηd svm.*
Casa, *fan strηb.*

Caseus, *flom.*
Castellum, *fankus.*
Castigare, *kof.*
Castrare, *sofsner.*
Castus, *tvbpap.*
Casus, *sak sηs tron.*
Catalogus, *fefton.*
Catena, *sabdrod frvm.*
Catulus, *nik potva nik primva,* &c.
Caudex, *lηd.*
Cautus, *tef prim pud.*
Caulis, *lηd.*
Caverna, *ol.*
Celebritas, *stηf stηn tip.*
Celeritas, *dηn.*
Cella, *fan.*
Celare, *dit.*
Centrum, *mam brepa.*
Cera, *nennηm.*
Certare, *spap kub spηg.*
Certitudo, *sib.*
Cervisia, *flηm nvpa.*
Cessare, *sofsod sofslem.*
Chaos, *ov sofshana shud.*
Character, *tom dip.*
Chirotheca, *freimsmvs.*
Chronica, *fefdan.*
Cicatrix, *dipu sηf domu fηf ef.*
Cicur, *prin.*
Cingere, *beg drod.*
Circa, *beg.*
Circumferentia, *eb.*
Circa, *loliηb.*
Cisterna, *frennim.*
Civitas, *fanind.*
Cithara, *fηb.*
Clam, *sofpem.*
Clamare, *svmpan.*
Claritas, *gon gid.*
Classis, *fηnind sud.*
<p. 100> Claudus, *sofsmvr grugpηb.*
Clavus, *ηt fim.*
Clavis, *sabdog.*
Clementia, *prit.*
Clivus, *blηn.*
Cloaca, *fam sηf avvi shiffa.*
Clunis, *fvs.*
Cochleare, *frenneis.*

Cæna, *steim, paf shemdangom.*
Cogitare, *tat.*
Cogere, *shek sed.*
Collegium, *stes fanstes.*
Colare, *freimmeir.*
Colon, *top.*
Colus, *sabfram.*
Comis, *prinstan.*
Comma, *top.*
Commercium, *stes stos.*
Communicare, *pemrefv tosresv.*
Compendium, *bram.*
Compositio, *shηn.*
Computatio, *tηgesv shum tηn.*
Conatus, *dηf.*
Concedere, *tad.*
Conscio, *trodu stηna, skasa.*
Conculcare, *brensmvresv.*
Conclusio, *trηm shηm tηt.*
Condire, *gηsresv.*
Conditio, *sηs tηm.*
Condonare, *stvp.*
Conducere, *strob sig.*
Condylus, *smeis.*
Consideratio, *tat.*
Consumere, *grvp sofshan.*
Contra, *shom.*
Convenire, *dim sprap sos.*
Conversatio, *stes sod.*
Convivium, *fleim shek slvbpafu.*
Copia, *svm.*
Coquere, *gvd.*
Corium, *ηf.*
Corona, *frvmmeis.*
Corrigere, *sensis sensham.*
Corrugare, *dek.*
Corrigia, *shundvf sηf freimsmvr, sabdig.*
Corrumpere, *grvp, sofsham.*
Coruscare, *gom.*
Cras, *danve dangom shvb.*
Creare, *samesv san sofavar.*
Crepusculum, *glom.*
Creta, *nafgof.*
Cribrum, *sabsinrer dobo.*
Crimen, *kvs.*
Cruditas, *grvd.*
Crumena, *fromsum.*
Crus, *smer.*

Crusta, *memgab.*
Crux, *sabshηpren brηna ship prob.*
Cubare, *pηk brηm.*
Cubile, *frun.*
Cubiculum, *fanfrun.*
Cudere, *dib dig.*
Culina, *fanfleimgʋd.*
Culmen, *rab.*
Culpa, *prem kʋs.*
Culter, *sabdom.*
Cumulus——*ind rʋp.*
Cunæ, *frunuvva.*
Cuneus, *sabdrob.*
Cupio, *peb tʋg.*
Currere, *sʋmpηb.*
<p. 101> Cuspis, *shundik bep.*
Custodire, *shad.*

DEBILIS, *sofsef.*
Decretum, *kom.*
Decere, *sit seb shanu sima sin.*
Decipere, *spak.*
Decorum, *shanu sima sin sudu sima sit.*
Decus, *stηf sin prog.*
Dedecus, *sofstηs shin pog.*
Dedicare, *spηf trʋn.*
Dedignari, *prop tagesʋ sofsat.*
Defetisci, *spηt.*
Deficere, *shʋd shηg.*
Degener, *sosslʋn pagel.*
Deinde, *shʋbsud shʋbdan.*
Dejicere, *dedresʋ denesʋ bηs bren.*
Deinceps, *shʋbdan.*
Delere, *sofshan.*
Demere, *dos trηn.*
Democratia, *kanstrηfu.*
Demonstrare, *pemresʋ sibresʋ.*
Denique, *shʋbapai.*
Deorsum, *bηs bren.*
Depsere, *gʋmesʋ flam sofgʋdo.*
Descendere, *pηb dam bηs bren.*
Designare, *tonesʋ shug trʋn.*
Desinere, *sofslem.*
Desistere, *sofslem dram.*
Desperatio, *sofpof.*
Detrimentum, *strηg shʋd.*
Dextera, *smʋ beba.*
Diabolus, *oiʋ shima.*

Diadema, *frʋm meis sηf kanel.*
Dialogus, *sηttinu slʋbtinu.*
Diæta, *sespaf danpaf dantut.*
Diameter, *ib.*
Diarium, *fef danve.*
Dico, *tin tim.*
Dies *danve dangom.*
Differre, *slom.*
Dignitas, *stηf stηd sat.*
Diluculum, *semgom glom.*
Diluvium, *nimdit.*
Dimidium, *shunu vηsa.*
Dirigere, *damresʋ babai sud.*
Disputare, *tap shom tap.*
Diu, *sʋmdan.*
Divortium, *strʋsu sηf stefu.*
Dolare, *gratresʋ.*
Dolus, *spak shib.*
Domare, *kut prinresʋ.*
Dos, *fum stηb stefa.*
Dubitare, *slib plem.*
Durare, *danesʋ slem.*

EBRIETAS, *trʋbpraf.*
Ebur, *nas sηf nηksʋf.*
Ecce, *puf pom.*
Ecclesia, *steskam.*
Ecstasis, *grug shηg sηp.*
Esurire, *pebpaf.*
Egere, *shηg.*
Egregius, *sin simap.*
Electrum, *ad sηf sneiggigema.*
Eleemosyna, *stifprit.*
Elementum, *shan vasa neim grʋpomp.*
Ellychnium, *fηm mηm bepa sηs frηn.*
<p. 102> Eloquentia, *temtin simtin.*
Embryo, *snus.*
Emungere, *sif.*
Ephippia, *frim nηkpota.*
Episcopus, *kaf.*
Epistola, *trin.*
Equitare, *nηkpotdeposʋ.*
Eremus, *nom gruna sofstido.*
Erigere, *bηmresu.*
Esca, *fleim gumer.*
Evangelium, *tibsηb.*
Eucharistia, *skappik skappaf.*
Evenire, *shed.*

Examinare, *tηb tid.*
Exsanguis, *sofien.*
Exanimare, *shηpresυ sofeiυresυ.*
Excellentia, *sis sim.*
Excommunicare, *sofstes.*
Excussio, *dos beddenesυ.*
Excudere, *trin dip dibtrin.*
Exercere, *set spηp.*
Exercitus, *kragind.*
Exhalatio, *nein.*
Exilis, *shυm grad.*
Existere, *aυ.*
Exlex, *kυb shηg keb.*
Exorcismus, *kυk.*
Exoriri, *sem guf ben.*
Explicatio, *tif.*
Expugnatio, *kut.*
Exter, *bed stred.*
Extinguere, *shemesυ nηm sofsham shηpresυ.*
Exilium, *kob.*
Exuere, *soffreim sofdit.*

FABER *temel.*
Fabula *tigshib.*
Facetiæ *pid.*
Facere *sam.*
Facultas *sef tem.*
Fæx *grυp.*
Falx, *sabdom braba.*
Fames, *grugshυg fleim.*
Farrago, *gυm shud.*
Farina, *mamind difo sηf nυb.*
Fas, *kef keb.*
Fascia, *srηmdrod*
Fascinare, *kυk.*
Fastidire, *preb prop.*
Fateri, *tυf kig.*
Fatigare, *spηt.*
Fatum, *sak komor trυnor sηf sasυa.*
Favere, *pon.*
Favus, *nengηmind*
Faux, *neir.*
Fax, *frηn.*
Febris, *gruggam.*
Ferax, *gun.*
Ferre, *dep.*
Ferrum, *nefgab.*

Festinare, *dηn.*
Festus, *skas.*
Fibula, *sabdrod.*
Fictio, *pug tηm shib.*
Fidelis, *sib sid sofpug.*
Fides, *tυp.*
Fiducia, *tυp sib.*
Figere, *dυmresu dramresυ.*
Figulus, *samel sηf frenni noma.*
Filius, *pagol.*
<p. 103> Fimbria, *bep.*
Firmus, *dram sfdam.*
Fistula, *fam fab.*
Flabellum, *sabdamnem.*
Flagellum, *sabdig.*
Fligere, *dig pronresυ ship.*
Flare, *nemesυ pam nηn.*
Fluere, *gak.*
Fluctus, *gaku sηf nim.*
Flumen, *ris.*
Fodere, *bagresυ nom.*
Fossa, *dadbog ol.*
Fædus, *stos.*
Fænus, *stηgfum.*
Fænum, *nab.*
Follis, *sabdamnem.*
Forceps, *fυm.*
Formosus, *sin.*
Fornix, *rep.*
Forte, *sak shed.*
Fortis, *sef dηb.*
Forum, *dadstof.*
Foveo, *shad gum pum.*
Fomes, *shan sηf nηm.*
Frænum, *sabdυnmeis.*
Frater, *steb υasa.*
Fremere, *sυmgis.*
Frendere, *nasdim.*
Frequens, *sηt shum*
Frigere, *gυd.*
Frivolus, *sofshem sofsig.*
Frustra *sofshem.*
Fuga, *pηp.*
Fulcire, *dηd.*
Fulgere, *gom sengom.*
Fulmen, *gisies.*
Funda, *sabden.*
Fundamentum, *ab.*

Fundere, *gakresv bedgakresv.*
Fundum, *ab.*
Fungi, *kas.*
Funus, *stam nomdit shηpalli.*
Furca, *sabdikvη*
Furfur, *shunsir sηf mamind.*
Furor, *svmpod.*
Fustis, *sabdig neiga.*
Fusus, *sabframdef.*

GALERUS, *freimmeis.*
Garrire, *pan neip tin svmtin.*
Gangræna, *gruggrup.*
Gelu, *gramgvb.*
Gemitus, *grugbredgis.*
Genealogia, *fefpag fefsteb.*
Genus, *tob sug pad.*
Generositas, *pot stηf.*
Generalis, *sug sun.*
Gens, *sten.*
Germinare, *guf.*
Germanus, *sib.*
Gigas, *uvim.*
Genius, *tam.*
Glaber, *sofiam.*
Glacies, *nimgvb.*
Glans, *rag snηg mηb.*
Glaucus, *gop.*
Gleba, *shunnom.*
Globus, *mηb.*
Glomus, *mηbfram.*
Gloria, *stef prog sin.*
<p. 104> Glubere, *dos ηf.*
Gluma, *ig.*
Gluten, *shangap rηp.*
Glutio, *paf.*
Grammatica, *temtos.*
Grando, *nenmam gvba.*
Granum, *gvpar suma rug.*
Gratia, *pon skam pik.*
Gratis, *stifai.*
Gratulari, *stat.*
Gremium, *shunu bem smηrri.*
Grex, *shum,——ind.*
Grundia, *ek.*
Gubernare, *kan sud.*
Gula, *snas.*
Gutta, *mam sηf nim.*

HABENA, *shundvf sηf sabdunmeis.*
Habitudo, *son sηf.*
Habitus, *set.*
Hamus, *rηbshηp sabrηb sabbrab.*
Harmonia, *sosgis.*
Harpago, *sabdrid sabdvs.*
Haurire, *deb.*
Hebdomas, *danvo danvai.*
Hebetudo, *pim tamu svm a.*
Herus, *kam.*
Hilaritas, *pob pid.*
Historia, *tig.*
Hodie, *loldanve.*
Horizon, *mab bepe mηsu.*
Horreum, *fanneib.*
Hortus, *dadneid.*
Hospitium, *steg.*
Humerus, *fes.*
Humilis, *prot bren.*
Hyems, *dangram.*
Hypocaustum, *fangam.*
Hypocrita, *pug.*

JACTARE, *prog.*
Jaculum, *fip.*
Janua, *ak.*
Idea, *sag.*
Idioma, *tin.*
Idolum, *sasva shiba.*
Jecus, *snes.*
Jejunus, *pebpaf drag grun.*
Ignominia, *trud pog.*
Ignorantia, *sofpem.*
Ignoscere, *krof kon stvp.*
Illidere, *dam den shom.*
Imago, *slvn sag.*
Imber, *non.*
Imminere, *lud tim ben meis dedemp*
Imo, *tim sib.*
Impensa, *stηp.*
Importunitas, *dan shit ship svd.*
Imputare, *kib.*
Incendere, *semesv nηm.*
Incestus, *kvf steb.*
Incitare, *spad tub.*
Incommodum, *sofseg strηg shηb.*
Incus, *sabbrendig.*
Indoles, *tam.*

Indulgere, *pon sʋmpum.*
Induere, *freimesʋ dit.*
Indusium, *bredfreim.*
Industria, *pip pum spηp.*
Infans, *uvva.*
Ingenuus, *pis sima, tʋb sid.*
Inguen, *snʋ snʋr.*
<p. 105> Initium, *sem.*
Innocentia, *sofkʋs keb.*
Inopinans, *sofpun.*
Insigne, *tos stηf toskus.*
Instituo, *tib trʋn sud.*
Integer, *sis sun sofdon.*
Intercapedo, *bem.*
Intercedere, *pηbesʋ bem lol brem lel sηtkif.*
Interdum, *shundanni.*
Interea, *trimshaf luldan leldan.*
Interest, *seg sig stηg.*
Intermitto, *sofslem.*
Interstitium, *bem.*
Intricare, *dop shep.*
Inventarium, *feffrein.*
Invicem, *sηt.*
Iris, *mabgosies.*
Irritare, *spad sofsham.*
Iter, *pηd.*

Jubere, *tup.*
Jubar, *mηm sηf gomu.*
Jugulum, *meir.*
Jugum, *sabdrosmeir.*
Jumentum, *neik spηp.*
Jungere, *dros.*
Jurgium, *spap.*
Juvenis, *uvve.*

Labare, *ded.*
Labarinthus, *shep.*
Lacertus, *smη.*
Lacus, *lir.*
Lædere, *predesʋ kʋm.*
Lætari, *pob.*
Lævigare, *gratresʋ.*
Lagena, *fren nηfa.*
Lambere, *naresʋ.*
Lamentari, *spab spram.*
Lamina, *mem.*
Lampas, *frηn.*

Lana, *am sηf nekpim.*
Lancea, *fip.*
Languere, *grugdrηb.*
Laniare, *dom dof kasneikshηprel.*
Laqueus, *sabspat.*
Largitas, *pok.*
Lascivia, *trʋbpap.*
Latere, *dit sofpem.*
Laterna, *femfrηn gona.*
Latrina, *faniem.*
Latro, *kʋn.*
Latrare, *panu sηt nikprim.*
Lavare, *nimsifesʋ.*
Legere, *tin tif.*
Legumen, *nʋb.*
Lentigo, *grugslomgos.*
Lentus, *drηn gap.*
Lepidus, *pid pobre.*
Lepra, *gruggofηf.*
Lethargia, *grugprab.*
Librare, *tηg dηm.*
Lienteria, *gruggratsnar.*
Lignum, *neig sneig.*
Limare, *gratresʋ.*
Limen, *abiak.*
Limes, *bep tos.*
Limus, *nomshif.*
Linire, *din.*
Lingere, *naresʋ.*
<p. 106> Linteum, *fremsnʋd.*
Lippus, *grugpredmηs.*
Liquor, *gan.*
Littus, *ηb sηf is.*
Livor, *pʋb pron.*
Locare, *dad stob.*
Lodix, *freimfrun.*
Lorum, *frηmfηm.*
Lues, *grugsʋmshηp.*
Lumen, *gom.*
Luscus, *grugbrηfmηs.*
Lutum, *nomshif.*
Luxuria, *trʋbped.*

Macer, *grad shʋmief.*
Machina, *sabkus.*
Macula, *slomgos.*
Madere, *gan.*
Magnus, *sʋm.*

Majestas, *svmu kana.*
Mala, *no nη.*
Malleus, *sabdig sabdib.*
Malle, *tvd svn.*
Mandibula, *nη.*
Mane, *semdangom.*
Manere, *dram slem danesv.*
Manica, *freimsmes.*
Manifestus, *pemo.*
Manipulus,——*ind drot.*
Mantile, *freimfran freimsmvssif.*
Mantica, *from.*
Manubrium, *shundvf.*
Margo, *bep.*
Marsupium, *from.*
Massa, *mim.*
Mater, *pragel.*
Matrimonium, *stefu.*
Maxilla, *nηs.*
Mederi, *gugresv.*
Meio, *remesv.*
Mel, *nengηm.*
Membrum, *shun sηf ov.*
Membrana, *ηf grada ed grada.*
Menda, *sir trenshvd.*
Mendacium, *tinshib.*
Mendicare, *tun fleimtun.*
Mens, *eiv tam, tat.*
Mentio, *tin.*
Mensis, *danvv daniar.*
Mereri, *sat.*
Meretrix, *kvb.*
Meridies, *brepdangom.*
Meta, *tos bep.*
Methodus, *sud.*
Metere, *dom drotesv raggi.*
Metrum, *trog.*
Messis, *dandrotrag danrag.*
Mica, *shunif.*
Migrare, *shηdesv stidu bemdam.*
Mimus, *pvn.*
Minuere, *shvmresv.*
Mittere, *pηdresvstin.*
Modus, *ev sηs ses.*
Modestia, *tvbpog.*
Molare, *dif.*
Momentum, *danva.*
Monachus, *kaf stes.*

Monere, *penresv tub.*
Moneta, *fum.*
Monstrum, *gvp shηk.*
Monumentum, *femshηp av penre.*
<p. 107> Mora, *dan shaf.*
Morbus, *grug.*
Mordere, *nasesv.*
Mortarium, *frendif.*
Mucere, *grvp.*
Mucro, *bep.*
Mulcere, *din prinresv.*
Mulgere, *baddib drid en.*
Mulier, *uv prag.*
Mulcta, *fumkof.*
Mundus, *avind.*
Mungere, *dib sif.*
Munire, *vpesv rvpesv feipesv.*
Munus, *stif.*
Murmur, *grid.*
Murus, *ip rvp vp.*
Musculus, *ef.*
Musica, *temgis.*
Mussare, *tinesv gridai gibai.*
Mutilus, *sir shηge shunu.*
Mutus, *softin.*
Mutuare, *stop.*

Nævus *shin shif.*
Nanus, *uvif.*
Nares, *doggu fηf mv.*
Nasci, *prat.*
Natura, *sasvη shan sek.*
Navigare, *fηndeposv.*
Nausea, *grug pebdag snal.*
Nebula, *nengrafes.*
Nebulo, *uv shima shiba, kvsel.*
Nec, *tηn trim.*
Necesse, *sed.*
Necare, *shηpresv.*
Nectere, *drop dop.*
Nefas, *sofkef sofkeb.*
Negligere, *prip.*
Negotium, *sar sod san.*
Nemus, *sneigdad.*
Nere, *framresv.*
Nequam, *shim kvs.*
Neuter, *sofiav fηf vη.*
Nictare, *dam mη.*

Nidus, *dadneipprat.*
Niger, *grof.*
Nimis, *svd.*
Ningere, *nen gofa gvba.*
Nitere, *gom bŋggom.*
Nocere, *shig kvm.*
Nodus, *drod dop.*
Norma, *sabbab tok.*
Noscere, *pem.*
Notio, *tab pemshan.*
Notorius, *svmpemo.*
Notare, *tos puf.*
Nothus, *pagol sofstefa.*
Novacula, *sabdom.*
Nox, *dangrom.*
Nubere, *stef.*
Nudus, *sofdit soffreim.*
Nugæ, *tinu pifa sofshama.*
Nullus, *sofiav.*
Numero, *tŋg shumu sus.*
Nuncius, *stinel tigel.*
Nutare, *damesv meis.*
Nux, *ragsnig.*

OBDUCERE, *dit.*
Objicere, *shomtin shomden.*
Obruo, *dit dedresv dib.*
Obscænitas, *pog tinu papa.*
<p. 108> Obscuritas, *grom shep.*
Obses, *stvf.*
Obsoleo, *sofset.*
Obstetrix, *safpratel.*
Obstinatus, *trvbpib.*
Occidens, *shunu breba sŋf nam.*
Occupare, *dvf stib.*
Ocrea, *freimsmer.*
Œconomia, *steis.*
Officium, *steis.*
Officium, *kas.*
Officina, *fanspŋp.*
Oleum, *ad.*
Olere, *ges.*
Olla, *fren.*
Omen, *tos.*
Omittere, *trim samesv sodesv.*
Omnis, *sun.*
Onerare, *dŋm.*
Opera, *stŋp.*

Opus, *spŋp sar.*
Opportunitas, *dansit.*
Oraculum, *tridu sŋf sasva keb.*
Orbis, *mab.*
Orificium, *dog.*
Oriens, *shun beba sŋf nam.*
Oscitare, *grugdogmeis.*
Ostendere, *samesv mŋsesv pemesv.*
Ostentum, *av shŋka.*

PASCISCI, *stos.*
Pagina, *ŋb.*
Palatium, *fan sŋf kanel.*
Pallium, *freimbed.*
Pallere, *gog.*
Palma, *shunu baga sŋf smv.*
Par, *slvnshum.*
Parabola, *slvntrod sagtrod.*
Parare, *sad sitre.*
Parvus, *shvm.*
Pascere, *gum.*
Passus, *pŋbu suma.*
Pater, *pagel.*
Patrimonium, *stŋbu stima.*
Patina, *frenfleim.*
Patria, *pratnom.*
Paucitas, *shvmshum.*
Pavire, *gratresv rukresv.*
Pacare, *sprad krus.*
Peccare, *kvs tren.*
Pecten, *sabdrop.*
Pecus, *neik.*
Pedere, *svsgis.*
Pendere, *bŋm dŋd.*
Pensum, *spŋpu tŋgo.*
Penetrare, *dob blŋn.*
Pera, *from.*
Perire, *sofiav sofshan.*
Perficere, *sisresv shem.*
Peripheria, *eb.*
Peritia, *tem ten prim.*
Pernio, *grugsmor.*
Perperus, *shim tren.*
Pessulus, *up.*
Petra, *nŋ find.*
Petulans, *prig put.*
Philosophia, *tem, temtef.*
Phlegma, *ran.*

Pius, *skas skam.*
Piger, *prip.*
Pila, *mηb spaf.*
<p. 109> Pileus, *freimmeis.*
Pingo, *trin fηd.*
Pinguis, *gad ef gηn.*
Pinaculum, *mub.*
Pistillum, *sabdib dif.*
Placeo, *spag ped.*
Planus, *grat.*
Platea, *dadpηb.*
Plaustrum, *flin.*
Plecto, *dop.*
Pleuritis, *grug fal.*
Pluvia, *nen.*
Poculum, *frrenpraf.*
Podagra, *grugsmυr.*
Pæna, *kof.*
Politia, *keis.*
Pollex, *smus suma vasa.*
Polliceor, *stυm.*
Pompa, *feid stam.*
Pono, *dam dad bηs.*
Populus, *uvind.*
Porrigo, *drek.*
Porta, *ak.*
Portentum, *tos shηk.*
Postis, *ep.*
Præceps, *blηm ded.*
Præcipuus, *suf.*
Præda, *kup.*
Prædico, *tin stηn subtin.*
Prædium, *stib.*
Præjudicium, *subtag.*
Prælum, *sabdib.*
Præmium, *stηt.*
Præposterus, *shυbsυb.*
Præsepe, *dadpaf.*
Præstigiæ, *shib spak.*
Præstolor, *pun dap*
Prætendere, *pug*
Prævaricari, *tren shib.*
Prandium, *pafu brepdangom.*
Pratum, *lornab.*
Primitivus, *sηm.*
Princeps, *kan suf.*
Privilegium, *kebstrηn.*
Procella, *dam shek.*

Proclivis, *blηm ded.*
Procus, *pon tun stef.*
Procul, *shυmbem.*
Prodigium, *pom.*
Prophanus, *skram skar.*
Proficio, *sig sim.*
Profiteor, *tim kig pem.*
Prodigus, *trυbpok.*
Progenies, *pagolli.*
Prohibeo, *tup shomtup.*
Promineo, *brap blηm.*
Promiscuus, *shud.*
Promptus, *sit.*
Promontorium, *rub sηf nom.*
Prosper, *sak sima.*
Proverbium, *tinu suga.*
Prudentia, *tef teg.*
Pruna, *ov nηma.*
Prurio, *grugdin.*
Puer, *uvvη.*
Pulvis, *mamind.*
Pupilla *mηb suf mηs.*
Purgo, *sif.*
Pus, *grυp.*
Pustula, *grυgmηbinf.*
<p. 110> Puto, *tag tat.*
Putris, *grυp.*

QUADRA, *vorηb.*
Quatio, *damresυ.*
Quatenus, *son.*
Qualis, *ev sηs geis.*
Quisquiliæ, *shif.*

RACEMUS, *ragsnug.*
Radius, *mηm.*
Rado, *dom din.*
Ranceo, *grυp.*
Rapio, *dos dυf.*
Rastrum, *flηn.*
Ratio, *tap sas.*
Raucus, *gruggig.*
Reus, *kυs.*
Recens, *dab.*
Reciprocus, *sηt.*
Recordor, *pen.*
Recreo, *sprηt.*
Reddo, *senspηb.*

Reformo, *senshan sendab.*
Rego, *sub pηt kan.*
Regnum, *kan.*
Relinquo, *suf.*
Remedium, *saf gug.*
Repagulum, *up.*
Reparo, *senshan sendab.*
Repentinus, *pun dηn.*
Repo, *pηf.*
Respublica, *sten stηbu stηna.*
Restis, *fηm.*
Resurrectio, *sengup.*
Rete, *fremspat.*
Rheda, *flin.*
Rigo, *gan.*
Ripa, *ηb snf ris.*
Ringo, *drit nassi.*
Ritus, *stam.*
Rivus, *rir.*
Robur, *sef dηb.*
Rodo, *din nas.*
Rogo, *tun tid.*
Ros, *nen grafa.*
Rostrum, *meis snf neip.*
Rota, *mab.*
Rotundus, *mηb.*
Rubeo, *god.*
Rubigo, *grup.*
Ructo, *grugnemsnal.*
Rudis, *softem gat stran.*
Rudo, *panu snf nηkpim.*
Ruga, *dek.*
Rumor, *tip.*
Rumpo, *don.*
Ruo, *ded.*

SABBATUM, *danve vaisa.*
Sacer, *skam.*
Sacrilegium, *kunskas.*
Sacerdos, *skagel.*
Sal, *nafgrηf.*
Salarium, *frennafgrηf.*
Saltem, *shuf.*
Sanctus, *skam.*
Sapo, *sansif.*
Sarcio, *senshan saf sis.*
Satur, *dag.*
Saucius, *grug.*

Saxum, *nηfind.*
Scaber, *gat.*
<p. III> Scabies, *gruggrupiηf.*
Scamnum, *frin dadpηk.*
Scandalum, *sprag.*
Scando, *dred.*
Scateo, *dot gak rir.*
Scelus, *kus.*
Sceptrum, *sabdrηd snf kanel.*
Scheda, *mem snf fηf.*
Schisma, *dos kud.*
Schola, *fantrib.*
Scintilla, *mamnηm.*
Scopæ, *sabsif.*
Scopulus, *nηfind.*
Scoria, *grupu snf nef.*
Scortor, *kuf.*
Sculpo, *trin dom.*
Scutum, *fup.*
Sebum, *ref.*
Secretus, *fofpem dit strηn.*
Seculum, *danial vali dansηp.*
Securis, *sabdom.*
Securus, *sηb prip.*
Sedeo, *pηk.*
Sedo, *sprad.*
Sedulus, *pum pip.*
Semita, *dadpηb.*
Senex, *uv draba uvvu.*
Sentina, *sabdebnim.*
Sentio, *peis.*
Sententia, *trod tag.*
Sepelio, *brennom dit.*
Sepio, *ip beg.*
Septentrio, *bref.*
Sera, *sabdrog up.*
Serica, *san snf frem sneipa.*
Sermo, *tin trod.*
Sero, *gup.*
Serra, *sabdom gata.*
Setæ, *am.*
Severus, *prid pin.*
Sibilo, *grid panu snf nuk.*
Significo, *tos.*
Sileo, *softin.*
Similis, *slun.*
Simulacrum, *slun fηd.*
Simus, *musbrab.*

Sindon, *fremsnud.*
Singularis, *sum shηk.*
Singultio, *grugdeksnal.*
Sino, *slaf.*
Sinus, *rηb snf is.*
Siphon, *fam.*
Sisto, *dram dus.*
Sitio, *pebpraf.*
Situs, *bηs grup shif.*
Solea, *ab snf smur.*
Sollennitas, *stηn.*
Sollicitus, *pum pip.*
Solidus, *gad graf.*
Solor, *trug.*
Solum, *ab sum.*
Solus, *sum ster.*
Somnio, *prab pef.*
Sorbeo, *paf.*
Sordeo, *shif.*
Soror, *stebprag vasa.*
Sors, *sak.*
Spatium, *bem.*
Species, *tlob shan.*
Specimen, *tηb preg.*
<p. 112> Spectrum, *mηsor profre.*
Specus, *ol.*
Sperno, *prop.*
Spina, *af snf far.*
Spinter, *dop drod.*
Spisso, *gaf gad.*
Splendeo, *gom.*
Spondeo, *stum.*
Sponsus, *stef.*
Spongia, *sabsif.*
Spuma, *memmηbind.*
Spuo, *ran.*
Spurius, *shib pagol sofstef.*
Stagnum, *lir.*
Stamen, *fram.*
Statuo, *tag trun.*
Statura, *bam tηg.*
Sterquilinium, *shifind emind.*
Sterno, *dit dedresv.*
Sternuo, *grug sifmus.*
Sterto, *grugprabpan.*
Stillo, *mam ded.*
Stimulo, *dik.*

Stipo, *krum prηp.*
Stipula, *lηd rηd.*
Stiria, *mηm mob snf nimgub.*
Sto, *bηm.*
Stabilio, *dramresv, keb.*
Stomachus, *snal.*
Strabo, *grug brη fmηs.*
Stragulum, *freimfrun.*
Stramen, *lηd snf nob nub.*
Strangulo, *shafpam sofpam.*
Strepo, *gis gig.*
Strideo, *gis gig.*
Stringo, *dib.*
Strophialum, *fremsmus freimsifmus.*
Struma, *grugmηb meir.*
Struo, *feinesv drot.*
Studeo, *tat.*
Stupa, *snud sir.*
Stupeo, *pom grugsofpeis.*
Stuprum, *kuf.*
Stylus, *ex sabtrin sestrin.*
Suadeo, *tut tub.*
Suavis, *gem sip.*
Subitus, *sofpun dηn.*
Submergo, *brednimesv brennim.*
Subsido, *ded dam bηs ab.*
Subula, *sabdob.*
Succedo, *shub.*
Sudus, *gon sofies.*
Sufficientia, *slud.*
Suffulcio, *dηd.*
Sugo, *deb drid.*
Sulcus, *dripu snf flan.*
Summa, *sun.*
Suo, *dros.*
Superbus, *trubpop.*
Superfluus, *sud.*
Supero, *sun kut.*
Sura, *smer.*
Surdus, *grugsofmηr.*
Sursum, *dred bηs ben.*
Suscito, *pabresv.*
Suspiro, *grugsheppam.*
Susurro, *trin grid.*
Sylva, *dadsneig sneigind.*
<p. 113> Symbolum, *tos.*
Syncerus, *sib sofpug.*

Tabeo, *gruggrupsflŋs.*
Tabula, *fef.*
Taceo, *softin.*
Tædeo, *spŋt.*
Talis, *lelsŋs lolsŋs.*
Talus, *af sŋf smʊr brapa.*
Tango, *brem gas.*
Tela, *frem.*
Temerarius, *softʊn.*
Temno, *prop.*
Temo, *shundʊn sŋf flin.*
Templum, *fansava.*
Tempestas, *dan damu sŋf nem.*
Tendo, *drek damesʊ bŋs.*
Tenor, *sud shan sot.*
Tento, *preg tŋb.*
Tepidus, *glam.*
Terebro, *dob.*
Tergo, *sif din.*
Tergum, *ŋf far.*
Termino, *bep shem.*
Tessera, *tos mŋb spafa.*
Testa, *frŋn noma mem gaba.*
Texo, *dop fremresʊ.*
Theatrum, *dadfad.*
Thesaurus, *fum stŋb.*
Thorax, *freimfeis.*
Tibialia, *freimsmer.*
Tingo, *gos.*
Tinnio, *gis nef.*
Titillo, *dinped.*
Titubo, *pŋb brŋf shaf pŋb.*
Titulus, *mam ked.*
Toga, *freim bam.*
Tolero, *prod slaf.*
Tondeo, *dom.*
Tono, *gis.*
Torculare, *sabdib.*
Tormentum, *pred.*
Torno, *temdomesʊ mŋbai.*
Torpeo, *spŋt drŋn.*
Torqueo, *mabdamesʊr.*
Torques, *frʊm begmei.*
Torrens, *ris.*
Torreo, *nŋm gʊd.*
Torvus, *pit prid.*
Trabs, *ap.*

Tranquillus, *dram.*
Tremo, *profdam.*
Tribunal, *frinkŋm.*
Tributum, *fumkan.*
Tripudio, *tempŋg.*
Tristis, *prob.*
Triumpho, *fed.*
Trochus, *sabspaf moba.*
Trudo, *did.*
Tuber, *grugbrap.*
Tubus, *fam.*
Tueor, *krum.*
Tumeo, *brap drek.*
Tumultus, *grim dimu sŋf uvvi shuga.*
Tundo, *dig did.*
Tunica, *freimfeis.*
Turba,——*ind shum.*
Turbo, *er mabdan.*
Turris, *fankus fanfub.*
Tyrannus, *kanel pita.*

<p. 114> Vaco, *drag sofspŋp.*
Vadum, *dradpraf sŋf ris.*
Vagus, *sofstid trenpŋd.*
Vah, *prob.*
Valetudo, *gug.*
Vannio, *nemsif.*
Vanesco, *sofslem mŋsosʊ.*
Vapor, *nein.*
Vapulo, *dig kof.*
Varius, *slom.*
Vasto, *drag sofstid.*
Ubertas, *gun.*
Udus, *gan.*
Vectis, *sabdeg.*
Vegetus, *gugsprŋt.*
Vehemens, *sʊm pin.*
Vellus, *ditu ama sŋf nekpim.*
Vendico, *krib.*
Venenum, *shŋpre.*
Veneror, *skaf.*
Venia, *stʊp.*
Venor, *pŋt spŋm.*
Ventus, *er.*
Ver, *danguf.*
Verbero, *dig.*
Verbum, *trom.*

Verecundus, *tvbpog.*
Verro, *sif din.*
Verruca, *grugbrapiŋf.*
Vertebræ, *drosu sŋf smeis.*
Vertex, *rab.*
Vertigo, *grugdebrin.*
Veru, *ib fleimgvd.*
Vesper, *shemu sŋf dangom.*
Vestigium, *dipu sŋf smvr.*
Vexillum, *toskus.*
Vexo, *ship.*
Via, *dadpŋb.*
Vibex, *dipu sŋf domu sŋf ŋf.*
Vibratio, *dam den.*
Victima, *skag.*
Vicus, *dabpŋb brana.*
Vicinus, *sted shvm bem.*
Video, *mŋsosv peisgosesv.*
Vigeo, *gud sprŋt.*
Vilis, *prop stŋd shuma.*
Villa, *fanind shvma.*
Villus, *am.*
Vincio, *drod.*
Vinum, *adsnug.*
Violo, *shin kvm.*
Virga, *mŋmdig.*
Virgo, *pragal sofpragel.*
Viscus, *vd gapa.*
Vito, *pub sŋb shaf.*
Vitulus, *nokflanva.*

Ulciscor, *pvd.*
Ulcus, *grugbrapgrvp.*
Ullus, *av.*
Ultimus, *shvb.*
Umbra, *gron.*
Uncus, *sabrŋbdvf.*
Ungo, *din dit dot.*
Unctuosus,
Universalis, *sug.*
Unusquisque, *sunsum sunshun.*
Vola, *shun baga sŋf smvs.*
Volvo, *deb.*
Vomo, *dragesv snal.*
Voveo, *stvm.*
<p. 115> Urbs, *fanind.*
Urna, *fren noma.*
Uro, *nŋmesv.*
Uter, *lul sŋf vŋ av.*
Utrum, *tid.*
Utor, *sab slam sig.*
Usurpo, *stibesv shom keb kef.*
Vulgus, *uvvi strŋfa.*
Vulnero, *dom.*
Vultus, *mar.*
Uxor, *stefprag.*

ZELOTYPUS, *pup.*
Zona, *eb mab.*
Zythum, *flŋm nvba.*

Sequitur specimen Artis instituendi Nomina Speciebus Naturæ significandis, complectens præcipuas Notiones sub Genere *Concreti Physici* contentas, quæ in S. Sc. occurrunt: Et hæc Exempla instar Regulæ sint, secundum quam omnium aliarum hujusmodi Notionum Nomina instituenda sunt.[71]

Naf Medium Minerale.

CARBO, *nafgrofnŋm.*
Sulphur, *nafgobnŋm.*
Sal, *nafgrŋf.*
Argilla, *nafgap.*

Nŋf lapis Vulgaris.

Silex, *nŋfgab nŋ fnŋm.*
Pumex, *nŋ fgraf.*
Tophus, *nŋ fgrap.*
Magnes, *nŋ fdeb nefgab.*

---

[71] English translation: There follows a specimen of the art of instituting names for signifying species of nature, encompassing the principal notions under the genus of *Physical Concrete* that occur in the Sacred Scriptures. And these examples are like rules, according to which names of all other notions of this kind are to be instituted.

Cos, *nηfbηbre.*
Alabaster, *nηfgofgrat.*
Marmor, *nηfgrat.*
Gypsum, *nηfrηp.*
Coralium, *nηfgod.*
Vitrum, *nηfgvbnηm.*
Crystallum, *nηfgvbnηm gona.*
Gagates, *nηfgen.*

Gemma Snηf.

Adamas, *snηfgab.*
Sapphyrus, *snηfgrob.*
Achates, *snηfshumgos.*
Jaspis, *snηfgrod.*
Carbunculus, *snηfnηm.*
Amethystus, *snηfgrog.*
Chrysolithus, *snηfgob.*
Smaragdus, *snηfsvmgrod.*
Topazius, *snηfgromgom.*
Chalcedonius, *snηfgof.*

<p. 116> Metallum Nef.

Aurum, *nefsis.*
Argentum, *nefgofsis.*
Stannum, *nefgofsil.*
Plumbum, *nefgofsir.*
Cuprum, *nefgod.*
Æs, *nefgob.*
Ferrum, *nefgab.*

Herba Neib.

Gramen, *nab.*
Cæpe, *nebgηn agmvba.*
Allium, *nebgηn agbana.*
Cucumis, *nib mvba.*
Cucurbita, *nib moba.*
Melo, *nib svma.*
Malva, *nηbiagban.*
Triticum, *nvbsim.*
Hordeum, *nvbflηm.*
Taba, *nobsvfbab.*
Zizania, *nobshvf.*
Pisum, *nobslvf.*
Sinapi, *nubgrηm.*
Lilium, *nadsin.*
Viola, *nηdgem.*
Urtica, *snvd oda.*
Linum, *snvd ruggrata.*

Cannabum, *snvd svfa.*
Cicuta, *snηdgen.*
Mentho, *snaibges.*
Hyssopus, *snedgem.*
Cuminum, *snηdgem.*
Coriander, *snηd rugbag.*
Nardum, *snaib aggob.*
Balsamum, *snaibgem.*
Nad, *agsvbrag.*
Aloes, *snudgrem.*
Laurus, *neggem.*
Erica, *nag grunnom.*
Ruta, *naggen.*
Thymum, *naggem.*
Rosa, *nηg lagsin.*

Arbor Sneid.

Fraxinus, *snagsvm bamrug.*
Tremulus, *snag agdam.*
Salix, *snag ηglag.*
Quercus, *snηgsvm.*
Abies, *sneg bab.*
Ficus, *snvg agban.*
Cedrus, *snegbam.*
Castanea, *snig aggat.*
Pomum, *snvg.*
Pyrus, *snvg ragmob.*
Morus, *snvg ladiηg.*

Bruta Exfanguia.

Apis, *snapgηm.*
Culex, *snηpshvf.*
Cicada, *snηkspan.*
Pulex, *snηkpηg.*
Pediculus, *snηkuv.*
Formica, *snηkpeg.*
Aranea, *snηkfiam.*
Limax, *snakdrηn.*
<p. 117> Vermis, *snak.*

Avis Neip.

Aquila, *napsvf.*
Cignus, *nupsvf.*
Columba, *nipprin.*
Gallus, *nippot.*
Pavo, *nipsin.*
Hirundo, *neipdηn.*
Vespertilio, *nηpbηppηn.*

Alauda, *nepbenpηn.*
Phœnix, *neipυa.*
Cuculus, *nepsompan.*
Ardea, *nυpsυmspis.*
Corvus, *napgrof.*
Regulus, *neipshυf.*
Strutheocamelus, *neipsυf.*

Quadrupes Neik.

Equus, *nekpot.*
Elephas, *nηksυf.*
Asinus, *nηkpim.*
Mulus, *nηksofpad.*
Camelus, *nekbrapfar.*

Unicornis, *nekiυmυa.*
Bos, *nekflan.*
Cervus, *nekdηn sυna.*
Dama, *nekdηn shυna.*
Canis, *nikprim.*
Lepus, *nokdηn sυna.*
Cuniculus, *nokdηn shυna.*
Leo, *nikpot.*
Pardus, *nikshυmgos.*
Sus, *nekshif.*
Felis, *nokditiem.*
Crocodilus, *naksofnar.*
Chamæleon, *nakshηdgos.*

PRAXIS

Primum Caput Genesios

1. Dan semu, Sava samesa Nam tηn Nom.

2. Tηn nom avesa sof-shana tηn draga, tηn gromu avesa ben mem sηf bafu: tηn υv sηf Sava damesa ben mem sηf nimmi.

3. Tηn Sava tinesa, gomu aveso: tηn gomu avesa.

4. Tηn Sava mηsefa gomu sima: tηn Sava dosesa gomu dos gromu.

5. Tηn Sava tonesa gomu Dan-gomu, tηn tonesa gromu Dan-gromu: tηn shem-gomu tηn sem-gomu avesa dan-ve vasa.

6. Tηn Sava tinesa, dad-dreku aveso bred brepu sυf nimmi: tηn doseso nimmi dos nimmi.

7. Tηn Sava samesa dad-dreku, tηn dosesa nimmi bren dad-dreku dos nimmi ben dad-dreku: tηn lel-sηs avesa.

8. Tηn Sava tonesa dad-dreku, Nam: tηn shemgomu tηn sem-gomu avesa dan-ve vηsa.

9. Tηn Sava tinesa, nimmi bren nam dekoso bred dadu suma, tηn granar mηsoso: tηn lel-sηs avesa.

10. Tηn Sava tonesa granar Nom, tηn tonesa <p. 119> deku sηf nimmi, Issi; tηn Sava mηsesa lolar suna.

11. Tηn Sava tinesa, nom gυpeso nab, neibeid gune rug, tηn rag-sneig gune rag sos sugu lυla, rug sηf lul tim bred lυl ben nom: tηn lel-sηs avesa.

12. Tηn nom gunesa nab, neibeid gune rug sos sugu lυla: tηn sneig gune rag, rug sηf lul tim bred lυl, sos sugu lυla: tηn Sava mηsese lolar sima.

13. Tηn shem-gomu tηn sem-gomu avesa danve vesa.

14. Tηn Sava tinesa, gommu aveso bred daddreku sηf Nam sham dosesυ dan-gomu dos dangromu: tηn lelli aveso sas dannu, tηn dan-vessi, tηn dan-vussi.

15. Tηn lelli aveso sas gommu bred dad-dreku sηf nam, sham gomesυ ben nom: tηn lel-sηs avesa.

16. Tηn Sava semesa vη gommu sυma, goma sυna sham sudesυ dan-gomu, tηn gomu shυna sham sudesυ dan-gromu: tηn samesa assi.

PRACTICE

<p. 118>

The First Chapter of Genesis

1. In the beginning God created the heaven and the earth.

2. And the earth was without form, and void; and darkness was upon the face of the deep. And the Spirit of God moved upon the face of the waters.

3. And God said, Let there be light: and there was light.

4. And God saw the light, that it was good: and God divided the light from the darkness.

5. And God called the light Day, and the darkness he called Night. And the evening and the morning were the first day.

6. And God said, Let there be a firmament in the midst of the waters, and let it divide the waters from the waters.

7. And God made the firmament, and divided the waters which were under the firmament from the waters which were above the firmament: and it was so.

8. And God called the firmament Heaven. And the evening and the morning were the second day.

9. And God said, Let the waters under the heaven be gathered together unto one place, and let the dry land appear: and it was so.

10. And God called the dry land Earth; and the gathering together of the waters <p. 119> called he Seas: and God saw that it was good.

11. And God said, Let the earth bring forth grass, the herb yielding seed, and the fruit tree yielding fruit after his kind, whose seed is in itself, upon the earth: and it was so.

12. And the earth brought forth grass, and herb yielding seed after his kind, and the tree yielding fruit, whose seed was in itself, after his kind: and God saw that it was good.

13. And the evening and the morning were the third day.

14. And God said, Let there be lights in the firmament of the heaven to divide the day from the night; and let them be for signs, and for seasons, and for days, and years.

15. And let them be for lights in the firmament of the heaven to give light upon the earth: and it was so.

16. And God made two great lights; the greater light to rule the day, and the lesser light to rule the night: he made the stars also.

17. Tηn Sava dadesa lelli bred dad-dreku sηf nam sham gomesυ ben nom.

18. Tηn sham sudesυ dan-gomu, tηn dan-gromu, tηn dosesυ gomu dos gromu: tηn Sava mηsesa lolar sima.

19. Tηn shem-gomu, tηn sem-gomu avesa danve vosa.

20. Tηn Sava tinesa, nimmi sυm-guneso neit, tηn neip pηme bred dad-dreku sηf nam ben nom.

<p. 120> 21. Tηn Sava samesa nυtti sυma, tηn neipteik sun-suma pηne, lul nimmi sυn-gunesa sos sugu lυlla tηn neip sun-suma spiso sos sugu lυla: tηn Sava mηsesa lolar sima.

22. Tηn Sava tufesa lelli tine, guneso tηn sus-sυnoso, tηn dageso nimmi sηfissi tηn neippi sus-sυnoso ben nom.

23. Tηn shem-gomu tηn sem-gomu avesa danve vυsa.

24. Tηn Sava tinesa, nom guneso sneikki tηn neikki sos sugu lυlla: tηn lelsη; avesa.

25. Tηn Sava samesa neikki tηn sneikki sos sugu lυlla: tηn Sava mηsesa lolar sima.

26. Tηn Sava tinsea, lalli sameso Uv sos sagu lalla sos sυnu lalla: tηn lelli kameso neitti sυf is, tηn neippi sηf nem, tηn neikki, tηn nom suma, tηn sneik sunsuma pηfe drηd nom.

27. Tηn Sava samesa uv sos sagu lυla, lelil samesa lelil sos sagu sηf Sava, lelil samesa lelilli pagel tηn pragel.

28. Tηn Sava tufesa lelilli tηn tinesa shod lelilli, guneso, tηn sus-sυnoso, tηn dageso nom tηn kameso lela, tηn kameso neitti sηf is, tηn neippi sηf nem tηn neikki tηn sneikki sηf nom.

29. Tηn Sava tinesa, puf, lal spηbesa shod lηlli neibeid suma gune rug, lul tim ben mem sηf nom suma tηn sneig suma lul gunesi rag tηn rug, lηlli sηgesu lella sηt fleim.

30. Tηn lal spηbesa, shod neikki suma, tηn <p. 121> neippi suma tηn sneikki suma, neibeid groda suma sηt fleim: tηn lel-sηs avesa.

31. Tηn Sava mηsesa avvi suna lul samesη: tηn puf, avesa sυm-sima: tηn shem-gomu tηn semgomu avesa dan-ve vυsa.

17. And God set them in the firmament of the heaven to give light upon the earth.

18. And to rule over the day and over the night, and to divide the light from the darkness: and God saw that it was good.

19. And the evening and the morning were the fourth day.

20. And God said, Let the waters bring forth abundantly the moving creature that hath life, and fowl that may fly above the earth in the open firmament of heaven. <p. 120>

21. And God created great whales, and every living creature that moveth, which the waters brought forth abundantly, after their kind, and every winged fowl after his kind: and God saw that it was good.

22. And God blessed them, saying, Be fruitful, and multiply, and fill the waters in the seas, and let fowl multiply in the earth.

23. And the evening and the morning were the fifth day.

24. And God said, Let the earth bring forth the living creature after his kind, cattle, and creeping thing, and beast of the earth after his kind: and it was so.

25. And God made the beast of the earth after his kind, and cattle after their kind, and every thing that creepeth upon the earth after his kind: and God saw that it was good.

26. And God said, Let us make man in our image, after our likeness: and let them have dominion over the fish of the sea, and over the fowl of the air, and over the cattle, and over all the earth, and over every creeping thing that creepeth upon the earth.

27. So God created man in his own image, in the image of God created he him; male and female created he them.

28. And God blessed them, and God said unto them, Be fruitful, and multiply, and replenish the earth, and subdue it: and have dominion over the fish of the sea, and over the fowl of the air, and over every living thing that moveth upon the earth.

29. And God said, Behold, I have given you every herb bearing seed, which is upon the face of all the earth, and every tree, in the which is the fruit of a tree yielding seed; to you it shall be for meat.

30. And to every beast of the earth, and to every fowl of the air, <p. 121> and to every thing that creepeth upon the earth, wherein there is life, I have given every green herb for meat: and it was so.

31. And God saw every thing that he had made, and, behold, it was very good. And the evening and the morning were the sixth day.

Psalmus primus. *Tudu vasa.*

1. Uv tim tufo lul trim pηbesi sos tutu sηf simalli tηn trim bηmesi bred dadpηbu kuselli, tηn trim pηkesi bred dadpηku sηf uvvi strabemp.

2. Sor, lelil pobesi shop kebu sηf kamel, tηn tatesi shop kebu lela dangom tηn dangrom.

3. Sas, lelil avesu slυn sneig gube sηmbem rissi sηf nimmi lul ragresu dan danu sima: ag lula trim grudesu; tηn lullulir lelil sodesu, simesu.

4. Kυselli, trim lolsηs, sor tim slυn ig, lul nηn didesi.

5. Lelfas simalli trim bηmesu bred dadkηnu, tηn kυselli bred stesu sηf simalli.

6. Sas, kamel pemesi soddu sηf simalli, tηn soddu sηf shimalli sofavrosu.

<p. 122>

Tudu Vηsa

1. Lulsas stenni podesi, tηn uvvi takesi sofshamar.

2. Kanelli sηf nom slυbkυdesi, tηn kamelli slυbstesesi shom Sasva, tηn shom pagol lυla.

3. Lalli doneso sabdroddu lella, tηn denoso fηmmi lella bem lalli.

4. Lelil lul stidesi bred Nammi spamesu, Sasva strabesu lelli.

5. Leldan lelil tinesu shod lellil podai, tηn shipesu lelli sas podu lυla sυma.

6. Lal dadesu kanel lala ben Zionoi or lala skama.

7. Lal pemresu trυnor, Sasva tinesa shod lal, lηl tim pagol lala: lal pagesa lηl lol-dangom.

8. Tuneso lal, tηn lal spηbesu shod lηl, stenni stimu lηla, tηn beppu sηf nom stibu lηla.

9. Lηn difesu lellil sab sabdonu nefgaba, tηn donesu lellil shunnu, slυn fren noma.

10. Lelfas, lηlli Kanelli refeso loldan: lηlli Kηmelli sηf Nom tiboso.

11. Krameso Sasva profai, tηn pobeso damprofai.

12. Neiseso Pagol, sham, lelil trim podesυ, tηn lηllil shηprosυ bred dadpηbu; luldan podu lηla nηmesu, sunilli lul tυpesi lηl tim skana.

First Psalm

1. Blessed is the man that walketh not in the counsel of the ungodly, nor standeth in the way of sinners, nor sitteth in the seat of the scornful .

2. But his delight is in the law of the Lord; and in his law doth he meditate day and night.

3. And he shall be like a tree planted by the rivers of water, that bringeth forth his fruit in his season; his leaf also shall not wither; and whatsoever he doeth shall prosper.

4. The ungodly are not so: but are like the chaff which the wind driveth away.

5. Therefore the ungodly shall not stand in the judgement, nor sinners in the congregation of the righteous.

6. For the Lord knoweth the way of the righteous: but the way of the ungodly shall perish.

Second Psalm   <p. 122>

1. Why do the heathen rage, and the people imagine a vain thing?

2. The kings of the earth set themselves, and the rulers take counsel together, against the Lord, and against his anointed, saying,

3. Let us break their bands asunder, and cast away their cords from us.

4. He that sitteth in the heavens shall laugh: the Lord shall have them in derision.

5. Then shall he speak unto them in his wrath, and vex them in his sore displeasure.

6. Yet have I set my king upon my holy hill of Zion.

7. I will declare the decree: the Lord hath said unto me, Thou art my Son; this day have I begotten thee.

8. Ask of me, and I shall give thee the heathen for thine inheritance, and the uttermost parts of the earth for thy possession.

9. Thou shalt break them with a rod of iron; thou shalt dash them in pieces like a potter's vessel.

10. Be wise now therefore, O ye kings: be instructed, ye judges of the earth.

11. Serve the Lord with fear, and rejoice with trembling.

12. Kiss the Son, lest he be angry, and ye perish from the way, when his wrath is kindled but a little. Blessed are all they that put their trust in him.

Tudu vesa

1. Lηl Sasva, lulsηs stretelli lala shumrosi? Lulsηs shumalli prηkesi shom lal?

2. Sumalli tinesi shod Eiv lala, Sasva trim safesu lelil.

3. Trim shaf, lηl Sasva tim fυp lala, progu lala, tηn benrel sηf meis lala.

4. Panu lala panesa Sasva, tηn lelil mηresa lal, bred or lηla skama.

5. Lal pηkesa tηn prabesa, tηn senprηkesa: sas, Sasva shadesa lal.

6. Lal trim profesu uvvi valili lul begesu lal.

7. Kamel, prηkeso: Sasva lala safeso lal: sas, lηl digesa afnos sηf stretelli lala suna; lηl donesa nassi sηf shimalli.

8. Sυbu tim sηf Sasva tηn lηl tufesi uvvi lηla.

Tuda vosu

1. Lηl Sasva lul skamresi lal, mηreso lal luldan lal panesu: lηl sηbresa lal, luldan lal shiposυ: priteso lal, tηn mηreso skadu lala.

2. Lηlli pagolli sηf uvvi, lulslemdan lηlli shηdesu progu lala sηt pogu, pone sofsigu, tηn spηme shibbu.

<p. 124> 3. Sas, lηlli pemeso, Sasva tυdesa simal sham lυlil: Kamel mυresu luldan lal panesu lelil.

4. Pυgeso, tηn trim kυseso: tηbeso flessi lηlla ben frunni lηlla, tηn prodeso.

5. Spηfelo skaggu sηf kefu, tηn tυpeso Kamel.

6. Shumalli tinesi lulil sasesu lalli mηsesυ simar ava? Kamel, saseso gomu sηf mar lυla gomresυ lalli.

7. Lηl sasesa lηl sηgesu pobu sυna sηf fles, lulai lelilli sηgesa, luldan nυb tηn flηmsnug lella sυmrose.

8. Lal pηkesu, tηn prabesu krusai: sas, lηl Kamel suma sasesi lal flidesu sηbai.

Third Psalm

<p. 123>

1. Lord, how are they increased that trouble me! many are they that rise up against me.

2. Many there be which say of my soul, There is no help for him in God. Selah.

3. But thou, O Lord, art a shield for me; my glory, and the lifter up of mine head.

4. I cried unto the Lord with my voice, and he heard me out of his holy hill. Selah.

5. I laid me down and slept; I awaked; for the Lord sustained me.

6. I will not be afraid of ten thousands of people, that have set themselves against me round about.

7. Arise, O Lord; save me, O my God: for thou hast smitten all mine enemies upon the cheek bone; thou hast broken the teeth of the ungodly.

8. Salvation belongeth unto the Lord: thy blessing is upon thy people. Selah.

Fourth Psalm

1. Hear me when I call, O God of my righteousness: thou hast enlarged me when I was in distress; have mercy upon me, and hear my prayer.

2. O ye sons of men, how long will ye turn my glory into shame? how long will ye love vanity, and seek after leasing? Selah. <p. 124>

3. But know that the Lord hath set apart him that is godly for himself: the Lord will hear when I call unto him.

4. Stand in awe, and sin not: commune with your own heart upon your bed, and be still. Selah.

5. Offer the sacrifices of righteousness, and put your trust in the Lord.

6. There be many that say, Who will shew us any good? Lord, lift thou up the light of thy countenance upon us.

7. Thou hast put gladness in my heart, more than in the time that their corn and their wine increased.

8. I will both lay me down in peace, and sleep: for thou, Lord, only makest me dwell in safety.

Tudu vʊsa

1. Kamel, mηreso trommi lala, tedeso tatu lala.

2. Kanel lala, tηn Sasva lala, sʊm mηreso sʊmpanu lala: sas lal skadesu lηl.

3. Kamel, lηl mηresu panu lala dan semdangom; lal skadesu lηl dan semdangom, tηn pudesu.

4. Lulsas, lηl trim Sasva, lul ponesi shimu; tηn shimal trim stidesu dap lηl.

5. Trefalli trim sηddapesu bef mηssi lηla: lηl pronesi kʊfelli suna.

6. Lηl shηpresu lelilli lul tinesi shibu: Kamel sumpronesu uv ηnpebemp tηn spakemp.

7. Slom, lal prηdesu bred fan lηla sas prittu lηla <p. 125> sʊma tηn lal profe lηl, skafesu bηs Fanskaf lηla skasa.

8. Kamel, pηreso lal, sos sibu lηla sas stretelli lala; babreso dadpηbu lnla bef mar lala.

9. Sas sibu ava trim bred neis lηlla, shunnu breda lηlla tim shimu sunai; neir lηlla tim fanshηpu dogo, nar lηlla pʊpesi.

10. Sasva, shηpreso lelilli; lelilli dedeso skam tuttu lʊlla: beddeneso lelilli sas kʊssu lella sʊna, sas lelli kʊbesa shom lηl.

11. Shom, sunalli lul tʊpesi lηl pobeso: lelli sundan sʊmpaneso sas pobu: sas lηl krumesi lelli: tηn lelli lul ponesi tonu lηla, pobeso sas lηl.

12. Sas, lηl Kamel, tufesu simal; ponu lηla krumesu lelil slʊn fʊp.

Fabula Æsopi 17.
Shop Neiteikpηggi tηn Kanel lʊlla.

[1.] Stenu snf neiteikpηggi, luldan sofkrama, tunesa Jupiteroi samesu Kanel sham lelli.

[2.] Jupiteroi strabesa tunu sηf neiteikpηggi.

Fifth Psalm

1. Give ear to my words, O Lord, consider my meditation.

2. Hearken unto the voice of my cry, my King, and my God: for unto thee will I pray.

3. My voice shalt thou hear in the morning, O Lord; in the morning will I direct my prayer unto thee, and will look up.

4. For thou art not a God that hath pleasure in wickedness: neither shall evil dwell with thee.

5. The foolish shall not stand in thy sight: thou hatest all workers of iniquity.

6. Thou shalt destroy them that speak leasing: the Lord will abhor the bloody and deceitful man.

7. But as for me, I will come into thy house in the multitude of thy mercy: <p. 125> and in thy fear will I worship toward thy holy temple.

8. Lead me, O Lord, in thy righteousness because of mine enemies; make thy way straight before my face.

9. For there is no faithfulness in their mouth; their inward part is very wickedness; their throat is an open sepulchre; they flatter with their tongue.

10. Destroy thou them, O God; let them fall by their own counsels; cast them out in the multitude of their transgressions; for they have rebelled against thee.

11. But let all those that put their trust in thee rejoice: let them ever shout for joy, because thou defendest them: let them also that love thy name be joyful in thee.

12. For thou, Lord, wilt bless the righteous; with favour wilt thou compass him as with a shield.

Aesop's Fables, 17:
Of the Frogs and their King[72]

1. The nation of the Frogs, when it was free, besought Jupiter, that they might have a King given them.

2. Jupiter laught at the petitions of the Frogs.

---

[72] The texts of the two fables reproduced here are from Hoole (1668). Dalgarno's selected fables are both from book one, the numbering being a standard one. Aesop's fables were widely used as texts for language instruction; a variety of editions—monolingual, bilingual, and multilingual—were available at the time Dalgarno was writing.

[3.] Trimshaf, lelli tunesa senai tηn senai slemdan lelil tumose;

[4.] lelil dedresa ap:

[5.] ap dη na damresa nimmi tηn samesa grimu sυma.

[6.] Neiteikpηggi profro foftinesa; lelli skafesi Kanel lυlla.

[7.] Lelli prηdesi shυmbem lelil shυmai tηn shυmai: Shema, lelli sofprofe dredpηgefi drηd lelil tηn dedpηgesi senai.

[8.] Kanel pripa <p. 126> strabosi tηn proposi:

[9.] Lelli sentunesi Jupiteroi sameso Kanel pota sham lυlli.

[10.] Jupiteroi samesi nυpbammeir Kanel lυlla.

[11.] Lelil pηbe drηd nom gana sυmpotai pafesi neiteikpηggi suna lul spηnesi.

[12.] Leldan neiteikpηggi spabesa sofshamai shop pitu sηf Kanel lυlla.

[13.] Jupiteroi trim mηresi lelli; sas, lelli spabesi slem danve lola.

[14.] Sas, luldan nυpbammeir dramesi dan shemdangomu, lelli pηdesi bed olli lυlla tηn panesi: lelli spanesi shod sofmηrel.

[15.] Sas, lolar tim tυfu sηf Jupiteroi, lelli lul tunesi shom Kanel prina sηgesu Kanel pina.

Fab. 41.
Shop nυkpυn tηn nυkprim.

[1.] Nυkpυn tunesi nυkprim spηbesυ shod lel shunu fηf om lυla sham ditesυ fυssi: sas, lelar dηmese lel, lul sigesu tηn stηfesυ lυl.

[2.] Nυkpυn tridesa, lυl trim sυgesa av ava sυda, tηn lυl tυdesu sυb om lυla dinesυ nom, shυb fυssi sηf nυkprim ditosυ.

Qantumvis nil dubitem qin posset ingeniosus qilibet debita diligentia adhibita, ex Doctrina hic tradita (cum praxi) in interiora hujus Artis penetrare; si qid tamen alicubi videatur obscurius dictum, paratus ero (si a viris Doctis ad hoc rogatus) sensum meum plenius & dilucidius explicare; Præcipue in Particularum materia, Structura <p. 127> Orationis, & quarundam Formularum loqendi Analysi Logica. Nec vereor hic afferere: Si Juvenes Praxi hujus Artis diligenter

3. Yet they pressed often upon him, till they made him do it whether he would or no.

4. He threw down a great Clog.

5. The heavy thing makes a great plunge in the River.

6. The Frogs being affrighted, hold their peace: they do homage to the King.

7. They come nearer by little and little: at the last, having cast away fear, they leap upon it, and leap down from it.

8. The idle King <p. 126> is a sport and a scorn to them.

9. They petition Jupiter again, they intreat they may have a King given them, that may be valorous.

10. Jupiter gives them a Stork.

11. He, walking very stoutly up and down the Fen, devours whatever of the Frogs come in his way.

12. Therefore the Frogs complained of his cruelty, in vain.

13. Jupiter doth not hear them, for they complain even yet to this day.

14. For when the Stork goes to his rest at even, they come out from their holes, and make a hoarse croaking; but they talk to one that hears them not.

15. For Jupiter's mind is, that they that petitioned against a gracious King, should now endure one that had no mercy in him.

Aesop's Fables, 41:
Of the Ape and the Fox

1. An Ape intreateth a Fox, that he would bestow a piece of his tail on her, to cover her buttocks: for it was a burden to him, which would be of use and an honour to her.

2. The Fox answers, That he had nothing too much, and that he had rather have the ground swept with his tail, than the Apes buttocks to be covered with it.

Although I do not doubt that, with the application of the necessary diligence, any talented person can, on the basis of the theory that has been presented here (together with the practice), penetrate into the inner secrets of this art; if nonetheless there are any places where what I have said appears obscure, I shall be willing (if it be asked of me by learned men) to explain my ideas more fully and

intenderent, majorem indefructum perciperent quam ex lectione multorum Voluminum Metaphysicorum; illinc enim inanem & inutilem (sine praxi) Artis Theoriam, maximo cum studio & labore, hinc vero usum maximo cum compendio acqirent. Præterea, si illis cordi fuerit qibus est officio Rei Literariæ prospicere, sumptus operi pares facere; Character Philosophcus, Typis aptatus, qi Rerum ipsarum immediate sit significativus parabitur. Singuli autem horum Characterum singularum Notionum Radicalium in Tabulis positarum significativi, paucioribus ut plurimum lineis, & pennæ ductibus formabuntur, quam singulæ vulgares nostræ Literæ Alphabeticæ; & eadem erit Ars variandi hos Characteres, qa Soni hic exhibiti diversificantur. Qantum autem scribendi Compendium hinc existet, judicium penes doctos esto.

clearly, particularly as regards the particles, the structure of speech, <p. 127>
and the logical analysis of certain idiomatic expressions. And I dare to assert
here that if youth apply themselves diligently to the practice of this art, they
will benefit more from it than from reading many volumes on metaphysics: for
in the latter they will, with great studiousness and labour, learn the empty and
(without praxis) useless theory of the art, where here they will with the utmost
brevity learn the use of it. Furthermore, if those who have the task of taking care
of letters and learning are willing to meet the expenses of the project, there
will be prepared a philosophical character, adapted for print, which would
immediately represent things themselves. Each of these characters signifying
the individual radical notions set out in the tables will be formed for the most
part with fewer lines and strokes of the pen than the individual letters of our
common alphabet, and the art of varying these characters will be the same as that
by which the sounds here presented are varied. To what extent compendium of
writing emerges from this, I leave to the judgement of learned men.

PART III

THE DEAF AND DUMB MAN'S TUTOR (1680)

DIDASCALOCOPHUS
Or
The Deaf and Dumb mans Tutor,

To which is added

A Difcourfe of the Nature and number of
Double Confonants: Both which Tracts
being the firft (for what the Author
knows) that have been publifhed upon
either of the Subjects.

By *GEO. DALGARNO.*

Printed at the THEATER in OXFORD,
Anno Dom. 1680.

Title page to 'The Deaf and Dumb Man's Tutor'

Imprimatur

TIMO. HAMILTON

Vice-Canel *Oxon*

The   <p. 1>

INTRODUCTION

With a KEY

to the following discourse.

About 20 years agoe, I published, *Latiali* but *rudi Minerva,*[1] a Synopsis of a Philosophical Grammar and Lexicon; thereby shewing a way to remedy the difficulties and absurdities which all languages are clogg'd with ever since the confusion, or rather since the fall, by cutting off all Redundancy, rectifying all Anomoly, taking away all Ambiguity and Æquivocation, contracting the Primitives to a few number, and even those not to be of a meer arbitrary, but a rational Institution; enlarging the bounds of derivation and Composition, for the cause both of *Copia* and *Emphasis*. In a word, designing not only to remedie the confusion of Languages, by giving a much more easie medium of communication then any yet known; but also to cure even Philosophy it self of the disease of Sophisms, and <p. ii> Logomachies; as also to provide her with more wieldy and mannageable Instruments of operation, for defining, dividing, demonstrating, &c.

What entertainment this design may meet with in following ages, I am not solicitous to know; but that it has met with so little in this present age, I could give several good reasons, which at present I forbear; intending, if God bless me with life, health, and leisure to do this in a more proper place.[2] To me 'tis enough to have the Testimony of some of the learned men of this present age[3] who are best able to judge in things of this nature, that I have there discovered a secret of Art, which by the learned men of former ages, has been reckoned among the Desiderata of Learning: To which I may add, that this discovery is made from more rational, easy, and practicable principles, than ever they imagined to be possible.

The text printed here is reproduced from the first edition of 1680, the pagination of which is indicated in angled brackets. The small number of errata on the verso of the original title page have been incorporated, with an explanatory footnote where appropriate. Various other typographical errors have been tacitly corrected. As is not unusual in seventeenth-century works, the heading of the appendix differs between the main title page and that of the subsection.

[1] 'In Latin, but without skill': Dalgarno may be responding here to the attack on *AS* by Roger Daniel in the introduction to his edition of Comenius (1662) (see above Introduction, sect. 4).

[2] This must refer to 'The Autobiographical Treatise' (see below, Part IV), which doubtless formed the basis for Dalgarno's paper to the Oxford Philosophical Society on 28 Feb. 1685.

[3] Printed in a marginal note: 'Dr Seth Ward now Lord Bishop of Sarum, Dr John Wilkins late Lord Bishop of Chester, Dr John Wallis, Dr William Dillingham'.

To this treatise I gave the title of *Ars Signorum*, which in compliance with the Dialect of the present Scene, I may properly enough <p. iii> change to *Sematology*. This soon after became a fruitful Mother of two Sister-Germans,[4] *Didascalophus*, and a *Discourse of double Consonants*; which having lyen as twins in the womb for many years, at last two severe fits of sickness did midwive them into the world, the latter here in order being *Senior* to the other by the space of full 7 years.

That the argument I have in hand is worthy to be treated of, will readily be confessed by *all*, but how worthily I have handled it must be judged by a *few*, to whose candor (passing by all apologies) I freely submit. The former treatise of *Sematology* had the Universality of all mankind for its object, but had nothing to recommend it *but* conveniency; This of *Didascalocophus*, is restrained (at least in its most proper ends and principal effects) to a small number of mankind; but comes recommended with the strongest arguments of Charity and Necessity. But at present I will dismiss the Mother, and betake my self to put the Daughter in a proper dress for the following Scene of action.

The Soul of Man in this state of union depending <p. iv> in its operations upon the bodily Organs; when these are vitiated it must needs follow, that the Soul it self is so far affected, as at least to be hindred in her external functions. Being therefore to treat of a way to cure a weakness that follows humane nature, equally affecting both: I will leave it to the skillful Physician, to discourse of the causes and cure of the Disease, as it concerns the Body, and will apply my self to consider of the means, to cure the better part of the Man, which is the proper work of a Grammarian.

And because the subject I have in hand is περὶ ἑρμηνείας[5] and more particularly one branch of it, which for what I know, has been hitherto *ex professo* treated of by no Author: I will first mention all the several wayes of Interpretation, whereby the Soul either doth, or may exert her powers: In doing of which I will be obliged to take the liberty of coyning some new words of Art, which hereafter I will explain.

It is true that all the Senses are Intelligencer to the Soul less or more; for tho they have their distinct limits, and proper Objects assigned them by nature; yet she is able to use their service <p. v> even in the most abstracted Notions, and Arbitrary institution: But with this difference, that nature seems to have fitted two, *Hearing* and *Seeing*, more particularly for her service; And other two *Tasting* and *Smelling*, more gross and material, for her dull and heavy consort the Body: whereas the fifth of *Touching* is of a midle nature, and in a manner equally fitted for the service of both, as will appear in the progress of the following discourse. Wherefore being here to speak of the Intrepretation of arbitrary Signs, imprest by the Rational Soule (and by it alone) upon the

---

[4] i.e. a sister through both parents, a full sister.
[5] 'Concerning interpretation': an allusion to the Aristotelian tract to be mentioned immediately below.

Objects of the Senses, most fitted for that use: I will take notice of the most usual, or at least of the most easy and practicable wayes of Interpretation which either are, or may be.

Here reflecting upon *Aristotles* περὶ ἑρμηνείας and περὶ ψυχῆς I expected both his help and Authority in Analysing the several kinds of Interpretation:[6] But finding little or nothing to this purpose in him, neither indeed in any other Author of old or new Philosophy (as wee now distinguish) that I have happened to look in, I was forced to adventure upon the following <p. vi> Analysis, for clearing my way, and enabling me to discourse the more distinctly on the Subject Argument.

Interpretation then in its largest sense, is *an act of cognitive power, expressing the inward motions, by outward and sensible Signs*: Of this there are three kindes, I. Supernatural, 2. Natural, 3. Artificial or Institutional; to which I give the names of Chrematology, Physiology, and Sematology. Chrematology, is when Almighty God reveals his will by extraordinary means, as dreams, visions, apparitions &c. and this in the division of Arts falls under Divinity. Physiology is when the internal passions, are expressed by such external Signs, as have a natural connexion by way of cause and effect with the passion they discover; as laughing, weeping, frowing, &c. And this way of Interpretation being common to the Brute with Man, belongs to Natural Philosophy: And because this goes not far enough, to serve the Rational Soul, therefore Man has invented Sematology; that is, an Art of impressing the conceits of the mind upon sensible and material Objects, which have not the least shadow of affinity <p. vii> to the images of the things they carry imprest upon them: And this is Interpretation, in the strictest and most proper sense; and to reduce this wonderful effect of Reason to such Rules of Art as the nature of it requires, is the proper Subject of *Ars Signorum*; which according to the commonly recieved distribution of Arts, is nothing else *but a* Rational Grammar.

Sematology then being a General name for all Interpretation by arbitrary Signs, or (to follow the most usual terms of Art) *voces ex instituto*, to any of the Senses; It may from the three Senses of Hearing, Seeing, and Touching, whose service the Soul doth chiefly make use of in Interpretation, be divided into Pneumatology, Schematology, and Haptology.

Pneumatology, (or if any think Echology more proper) is Interpretation by Sounds conveied thro the Ear; Schematology by Figures to the Eye; and Haptology by a mutual contact, skin to skin. Pneumatology again is divided into Glossology and Aulology: Glossology is a term proper enough for Interpretation by the Tongue, which is the first, and most common Organ of Interpretation, at least in Society, and <p. viii> face to face; for Man in the

---

[6] The primary reference here is to the Aristotelian tract 'On Interpretation'; see also Dalgarno's unpublished treatise, which is devoted to a similar range of topics (see below, Part IV, Unpublished Paper 2).

circumstances—*effert animi motus interprete Lingua.*[7] Aulology so styled by an easy Trope, interprets by a Musical Instrument; which is fully capable of as much, and manifest distinction as the Tongue, *but* not so natural and ready an Organ.

*S*chematology is divided into Typology or Grammatology, and Cheirology or Dactylology. By Typology or Grammatology, I understand the impressing of permanent Figures upon solid and consisting matter, which may be done two wayes; either by the Pen and Hand, or by the impression of Stamps prepared for that use; which makes only an accidental difference between Grammatology and Typology. Cheirology or Dactylology, as the words import, is Interpretation by the transient motions of the Fingers; which of all other wayes of Interpretation comes nearest to that of the Tongue. Haptology admitting of no Medium, nor distinction of Act and Object, but being body to body, doth therefore admitt of no subdivision. Tho I will not warrant all these Terms from Acyrology;[8] yet I am sure that they will both save me the labour of Periphrasis, and also from using words less proper.

---

[7] 'and with the tongue for interpreter, she [Nature] proclaims the emotions of the soul' (Horace, *Ars Poetica* 111).

[8] i.e. incorrect use of language (the *OED* cites Blount's *Glossographia* (1656) as the earliest attestation of this term).

CHAP. I

<p. 1>

A Deaf man as capable of understanding the expressing a Language, as a Blind.

Tho the Soul of man come into the world, *Tabula Rasa*; yet is it withal, *Tabula Cerata*;[9] capable throu study and discipline, of having many fair, and goodly images, stampt upon it. This capacity is actuated, by the ministry of bodily Organs. The Organs of the Body, serving the Soul in exerting her powers, in this state of union are four: the Eye and the Ear; the Hand and the Tongue: the first pair fitted for taking in, the other for giving out; Both the one and the other, equally necessary for communication and society.

That the Ear and the Tongue alone, secluding the other two, can perfect a man in knowledge (excepting of some few things which are the proper Objects of seeing) and enable him to express what he knows in Vocal Signs, or a Language <p. 2> spoken, is known by daily experience in blind people. That an equal degree of knowledge is attainable by the Eye, and expressible by the Hand in Characters, or a Language written, is no less evident in the Theory, for the reasons following.

All signs, both vocal and written, are equally arbitrary and *ex instituto*. Neither is there any reason in Nature, why the mind should more easily apprehend, the images of things imprest upon Sounds, than upon Characters; when there is nothing either natural, or Symbolical, in the one or the other.

Therefore that blind people should come sooner to speak, and understand, than Dumb persons to write, and understand, is not, because there is any more discerning faculty in the Ear, than in the Eye; nor from the Nature of Sounds and Characters, that the one should have a greater fitness then the other to conveigh those Notions imprest upon them, thro the respective doors of the Senses into the Soul: neither that pronounciation of articulate words is sooner, or more easily learned, then written Characters, neither <p. 3> yet, that the Ear is quicker in perceiving its object then the Eye: But it is from other accidental causes, and circumstances, which give the Ear many considerable advantages, in the matter of Communication, above the Eye. And yet, even in this particular, the Eye wants not its own priviledges; which if rightly used, may perhaps outweigh the advantages on the other side. For illustrating this, I will compare a Deaf man with a Blind. 1. The blind man goes to School in his cradle; this so early care is not taken of the Deaf. 2. The blind man is still learning from all that are about him; For every body he converses with is a Tutor, and every word he hears, is a lecture to him; by which he either learns what he knew not, or confirms what he had. The Deaf man not being

---

[9] 'A blank tablet, and yet a wax tablet.'

capable of this way of discipline, has no teacher at all: and tho necessity may put him upon contriving, & using a few signs; yet those have no affinity to the Language by which they that are about him do converse amongst themselves, and therefore are of little use to him. 3. The Blind man goes thro the <p. 4> discipline of Language in the best of his time, Childhood, and under the best of Teachers, women and children: The Deaf man is deprived of both these opportunities. 4. The blind man learns his Language by the by, and *aliud agens*; the Deaf cannot attain a language without instruction, and the expence of much time and pains. 5. The deaf man is confined to the circumstances of light, distance, posture of body, both in himself, and him he communicates with: the blind man is free from these streightening circumstances.

Lastly, all the advantages the Ear has above the eye, may be summed up in these two. First, more opportunities of time; secondly, quicker dispatch, or doing more work in less time: Both which may be in a great measure remedied by skill and care; by which if there were a timely application made to Deaf persons, I conceive they might be more improved in knowledge; and so their condition be much more happy than that of the blind: which will appear by the following advantages that the Deaf man has above the Blind.

<p. 5> First, the Deaf man has greater advantages of acquiring Real knowledge, than the blind; because the Eye has greater variety of objects then the Ear. 2. The Deaf man has a greater certainty of that knowledge he attains by the Eye, than the Blind can have of that he receives by the Ear; for *Pluris est oculatus testis unus, quam auriti decem.*[10] 3. As he has the better of the other in the knowledge of Nature; so also he exceeds him much, in Speaking and Reading the Language of Nature. For besides reading the Glory, and wisdom of God, in the book of the Creation; he is able also to read much of the minds of men, in the book of their Countenance; which, seconded with the postures, gestures, actions of the whole body; more particularly, the indications of the hands, feet, fingers, and other circumstances; laies open much of their inside to him: And he, by the same Dumb eloquence is able to notifie his desires to others. Of which way of communication, the blind mans condition renders him wholly uncapable. So that the one is able to prove himself a man, in any society <p. 6> of Mankind, all the world over: The other, take him from the company of his country-men, has little else left him wherewith to difference himself from a brute, but the childish Rhetorick of *Democritus*, and *Heraclitus*. But fourthly, to come closer to our purpose with the comparison. The Deaf man learns a Language by Art, and exercising his rational faculties; the Blind man learns by Rote; so that he gets a language and he himself knows not how. There is therefore as great difference in the point of language between a Deaf and a Blind man (supposing both to have made an equal progress,) as between one bred in the University, and a Clown that knows not a letter. Fifthly, tho the Blind man

---

[10] 'One eye witness is worth ten who rely on the ear' (Plautus, *Truculentus* 2. 6. 8).

have the start of the Deaf, yet the deaf man will be too hard for him in the long run: For he, after he has once got a competency of language, will be able to help himself, and direct his own course in the further pursuit of all Real knowledge. On the contrary, the blind man who is learning a language needed no particular Guide, because every body was his Guild; <p. 7> now he is at a stand, and cannot so much as advance one stop, without one to lead him. Sixthly, the Deaf man has this great advantage above the Blind, which weighs heavier then all that can be laid in the Scales against it: That he is able to write down his notions, and reflect upon them as often as he will. And now the advantage of having much time for study, and doing much work in little time is as much the Deaf mans, as at first setting out it was the Blind mans. Seventhly, in the superfetation of language the Deaf man will sooner be impregnate with a 2^d, or 3^d, language then the Blind, insomuch as one language learned by study and Art, is a greater step to facilitate the learning of another, then the mother Tongue which comes by meer use and Rote.

CHAP. II.

A Deaf man capable of as Early Instruction in a language as a Blind.

Taking it for granted, That Deaf people are equal, in the faculties of apprehension, and memory, not only to the Blind; but even to those that have all their senses: and having formerly shewn; that these faculties can as easily receive, and retain, the Images of things, by the conveiance of Figures, thro the Eye, as of Sounds thro the Ear: It will follow, That the Deaf man is, not only, as capable; but also, as soon capable of Instruction in Letters, as the blind man. And if we compare them, as to their instrinsick powers, has the advantage of him too; insomuch as he has a more distinct and perfect perception, of external Objects, then the other. For the Blind man has no certain knowledge of things without him; but what he receives, from the information of the gross sense of Feeling; which, tho <p. 9> it be a sure intelligencer; yet is its intelligence very scanty: For what he receives by the Ear, is but a second-hand knowledge, depending upon testimony, and the credit of others. So that the advantages I gave the blind man, at first setting out, are not in his own faculties, but from extrinsick and adventitious helps.

Therefore I conceive, there might be succesful addresses made to a Dumb child, even in his cradle; when he begins—*risu cognoscere matrem*:[11] if the Mother, or, Nurse had but as nimble a hand, as commonly they have a Tongue. For instance, I doubt not by the words, *hand, foot, dog, cat, hat*, &c. written fair, and as often presented to the Deaf childs Eye, pointing from the words to the Things and *vice versa*; as the blind child hears them spoken, would be known, and remembred assoon by the one, as the other. And as I think the Eye to be as docile, as the Ear; so neither see I any reason, but the Hand might be made as tractable an Organ, as the Tongue; and assoon brought to form, if not fair, at least legible Characters, as <p. 10> the tongue to imitate, and Echo back, articulate Sounds.

Here it may be doubted; whether it were more advisable, to train up the deaf child in Typology, or Dactylology. For the first, it may be said, That tho the institution is equally artibrary in both, and therefore equally easy to the learner: yet, writing is permanent, and therefore gives the young Scholar time to contemplate, and so makes the deeper impression: whereas, pointing to the fingers is transient, and gone before it can be apprehended. This made me at first incline more to writing: But upon further consideration, I judge the other way much more expedient. For tho it cannot be denied, but the permanency of the Character is in it self an advantage, if well improved; yet, transient motions, if often repeated, make as great an impression upon the memory, as fixt and

---

[11] 'To recognize the mother with a smile.'

immovable objects. A clear proof of this we have from young ones learning to understand a Language, from the Transient motions of the tongue: and which is yet more difficult; to imitate the same transient <p. 11> motions; where neither can the distinctions be so manifest, nor the formation so easy, as in the Hand-language. Which, as it confirms me; That pointing to the Hand, would be the better way of teaching, so it makes me think: That if closely followed, it might be easier attained, by young ones, then speaking; insomuch as the motions of the Hand, are much more easy then those of the tongue.

If here it should be objected; That words written are more distinct, and easy to be apprehended; for tho consisting of several distinct letters; yet being joyned, they pass in this rude discipline, for one individual Sign, for our Scholar is supposed as yet, to understand nothing of the distinction of letters: whereas in pointing to the Fingers; The distinct motions to make up a word, will be more manifest; and so will be a hinderance to the Scholars weak intention, to apprehend that, which is represented by many touches so distinctly, under the Notion of one word.

To this I answer. If we compare the action of writing, with pointing to the Fingers, this is much more simple then <p. 12> that; and therefore less amusing. But secondly, if we compare words written with pointing; this is still not only more simple, and therefore more easily apprehended; But also it is as easy to represent a word as one *Compositum* with a continuëd action of the Hand, tho there be many distinct pointings, as to make One Word by an aggregate of many distinct letters. Add to this, that pointing to the Hand is capable of more Emphasis; for frequent repetition accompanied with significant gestures, will come near to the way of teaching *viva voce*, which inculcates more then the beholding of a standing object. But here there is need of caution; That we follow the conduct of Nature; That is, to begin with Words most simple and easy. For we see that young children when they begin to speak are not able to pronounce long words, nor yet all letters. But here the only care to be taken is, to chuse short words; for all letters are equally easy. Now before I proceed I think it will be very proper to add some thing of the easiness of the whole Task; both to remove prejudices in <p. 13> others, and more particularly to encourage the careful Mother the more cheerfully to undertake it.

There are many mothers who (to their great praise) do teach their children to Read, even almost before they can speak. And yet (I hope) it will appear from the following considerations; That to read and write upon the Fingers, is much easier to the learner, than to read and write in Books; there being many difficulties in the one, which are avoided in the other. For, 1. in reading, single letters must be learned; which are very remote, and abstracted from sense, as being but parts of a Signs Sign, e.d. H. is the 4th part of the word *Hand*, which word written is a sign of the vocal sound, the vocal sound is the immediate sign of the thing itself. 2. Next to this difficulty is the learning to name the same letters in the precise abstracted notion of them *a*, *b*, *c*, *d*, &c. without borrowing names to them from other things; contrary to what the first fathers of letters have taught us, as appears by their naming the simple elements *Aleph, Beth, Gimel, Daleth*, &c.[12] And here by the by I <p. 14> cannot but observe; That we *Europeans* have been so dull Sholars, as not to take out the lesson: Yea our wise Masters the Grecians in this particular, are the greatest Dunces of the rest; For others have been truants and taken out no lesson; and they have taken it out false. For they have named them by Barbarous and insignificant words corrupted from the Hebrew; which is worse then to name them by their own powers alone. Which hallucination of theirs has a remarkable providence in it; For thereby they have given a convincing proof, and openly confessed (tho they neither designed, nor owned any such thing) that the Doctors of *Athens* have learned their a b c at the feet of *Gamaliel*. And here amongst our selves and neighbouring Nations, it is observable, that in this point of discipline, our Dames are wiser than our Doctors: for they find a necessity of bringing home these abstracted notions to young ones senses, by borrowing names from known and familiar things. But if there were one way of naming the simple Elements agreed upon, and this put in all Primers <p. 15> and Horn-books, it would not only be of good use to children and unskilful Dames; but also the thing being celebrated would give occasion to ingenious allusions and Metaphors, an instance whereof we have in A and Ω in the Greek. But to return to our purpose. A third difficulty in reading is true pronounciation of the simple letters. And 4. joyning them in syllables is yet more difficult; the single letters often times either quite loosing, or, changing their powers. And 5. the dividing syllables aright, and joyning them to make words. All which are such difficulties that one may justly wonder how young ones come to get over them: And how late, and with how great pains they are overcome by some, I appeal to those that know what belongs to the breeding of youth. Now the Deaf child under his Mothers tuition, passes securely by all these Rocks and Quick-sands. The distinction of letters, their names, their powers, their order, the giving them true shape or figure (which answers to others pronouncing true,) the dividing words into Syllables, and of them again making <p. 16> words, to which may be added Tone, and Accent. None of these puzling niceties hinder his progress. All the teacher has to do, is, to go with one continued motion over all the points that make up the word, pointing withal to the things. And at first it will be convenient to initiate the young Scholar with words of few letters, and a near affinity; as *Hat, Cat, Hog, Dog, Hand, Sand*. It is true, after he has past the discipline of the Nursery, and comes to learn Grammatically, then he must begin to learn to know letters written, by their figure, number, and order. But the rest of the difficulties I have but now mentioned, are proper to the Ear, and therefore do not concern him.

---

[12] According to doctrine of the letters, deriving ultimately from Stoic grammar, the 'name' of a given letter should naturally express its 'power', or phonetic value; the fact that the Hebrew names for the letters do so in a regular way is thus taken as evidence of the antiquity of the language.

And because the advantages the Blind man hath over the Deaf, are more considerably such, in the time of childhood; It cannot be denied, but the blind child, is in a greater capacity of learning the Mother-Tongue then the Deaf: yet so, as skill and care might advance the Deaf child in a vocabulary of the names of visible Objects, much above what the other can be supposed to get from the common <p. 17> use of the Mother-Tongue. For the one is still running the same round, in a narrow circle, hearing the same words redundantly: the other might be in a constant progressive motion.

And tho I perswade my self, that some time or other, there may be a mother found, who by her own care, and such directions as I am treating of, will lay a good foundation of Language in her Deaf child, even in the first stage of his Minority; yet seeing this is like to be but *rara avis*, I will advance our blind and deaf Scholars to a higher Form, and place them under a severer discipline then that of the Nursery; which I suppose none will deny them now able to bear: for I will suppose them entred in the 7th year of their age. Together then with this equality of age, let us suppose them every other way equal, in their natural parts, both faculties and inclinations, under Tutors equally both skilful and careful: And to make their capacities every way equal; the Deaf boy to write as fair and quick a hand, as can be expected from that age. In these circumstances, they are <p. 18> both of them to begin to learn a Language: the blind boy Latin, the deaf boy his Mothers-Tongue.

The case being thus stated, It is my own opinion, that the Deaf boy would come to read & write the Mother-Tongue both much better and sooner then the blind boy to understand and speak the Latin. For reasons of my so thinking, beside what may be gathered from chap. 1. I will here carry on the comparison between the blind boy and the deaf in some particulars coming closer to our present case.

1. The Blind boy has the advantage of knowing a language already, which is a great help to the learning any second <p. 19> language. For tho there be no affinity between the words of some languages; yet there is something of a Natural and Universal Grammar runs thro all Languages, wherein all agree. This contradicts not what I have said to the deaf mans advantage Chap. 1. Num. 6. Because there the blind and deaf are supposed both to understand the Mother-Tongue when they begin to learn a second language. Here the deaf is supposed to have no language, and the blind to have the Mother-Tongue; which tho by him learned, not by Rule, but by Rote; yet is it an advantage over him that has none.

2. Beside this notion of Natural and Universal Grammar, which the blindboy hath got with the Mother-Tongue; he not being to learn Words for Things, but Words for Words; and it falling out so, that oftentimes there is a great affinity between the words to be learned, and the words for which they are to be learned; this makes that he learns with less pains then the deaf boy, who learning words for Things, it can never happen, that a combination of Alphabetical Characters making up a word, should have any affinity to, or resemblance of the thing for which it is substituted.

3. Onomatopœia is a great help to the blind Scholar, for Example, *grunnitus*, *hinnitus*, *rugitus*, *ululatus*, &c. are easier to be learned by the blind man, then the deaf; because as they pass in Sounds thro the Ear, they are of a mixt Institution, partly Natural, partly Arbitrary; But <p. 20> these same words written in Characters are of a meer arbitrary Institution, whether they be considered with relation to the immediate, or mediate *Signatum*. So that our dumb Scholar has nothing to trust to, but diligence and strength of memory: Reason can do him no service at all, at least so far as either Primitive words, or words of an irregular inflexion from them extend; which make up the body of all languages. Neither can fancy help him much, which oftentimes is of great use by working a connexion between a strange and a known word, because as yet we suppose most words to be strangers to him.

The reason of this difference between words spoken and written is. Because speaking being before writing, has more of Nature and less of Art in it. For all languages guided by the instinct of Nature, have more or less of Onomatopœia in them, and I think our *English* as much as any: For beside the naming the voices of Animals, and some other Musical Sounds, which for the most part is done by this Figure in other languages, we <p. 21> extend it often to more obscure, and indistinct sounds. Take for example, *wash, dash, plash, flash, clash, hash, lash, slash, trash, gash*, &c. So *grumble, tumble, crumble, jumble, fumble, stumble, bumble, mumble*, &c. of which kind of words, The Learned and my worthy friend Dr *Wallis* has given a good account in his *English* Grammar.[13] In all these and such like words there is something Symbolizing, and Analogous to the notions of the things; which makes them both more Emphatic, and easy to the memory. But in words literally written and of a meer arbitrary Institution, there can be nothing Symbolical. But to draw something out of this digression to our present stated case. Tho Onomatopœia gives our blind Scholar some advantage over his Deaf Schoolfellow; yet is it short of what it would be if he were learning *English*. This is all that at present comes into my thoughts to say for maintaining the Paradox of a *blind guide*. I will now offer my reasons for giving him the precedency, that has two Eyes open in his head, which seems to be the more plausible opinion.

<p. 22>   1. The Deaf mans mind is like clean paper, and therefore takes the impression the more easily, fair and distinct: whereas the scriblings and blottings upon the Table of the Blind mans memory, as they leave little room for new impressions, so they breed confusion, and makes him ready to mistake, when he comes to read them.

---

[13] See Wallis (1653: ch. XIV, 'De Etymologia; sive Vocum Derivatione, seu cognatione mutua'. In this chapter, progressively enlarged by Wallis in each subsequent edition, he argues (i) that indigenous English words are characteristically monosyllabic (and thus structurally 'simple'), and (ii) that such simple English words are systematically onomatopoeic, and thus exhibit a 'natural' relation with the things signified.

2. Words laid up in the deaf Boyes memory, are like Characters engraven in Steel or Marble: The blind boyes words are but chalked out, or, *nigro carbone Notata*,[14] and therefore easily defaced. For the deaf boy having one word for every thing he knows, is therefore obliged to reflect upon it, as often as he has occasion to think, or speak of the thing it self: And it is this frequency of recognizing words, and using them upon all occasions that makes a man master of a Language: Whereas the blind boy having two words for one thing, the one an intimate and old acquaintance, even *a teneris unguiculis*,[15] the other a stranger to him; upon all occasions he loves to converse with his old crony, and keeps at a distance from <p. 23> the stranger; unless it be at set times, when force or fear commands his attendance. So that this considerations alone (specially if it be seconded with the care and diligence of those that are about him, in forbearing all other Signs with him but letters) may seem to outweigh all that can be said for the blind Boy.

3. The deaf boy can conn a lesson by himself, for *litera scripta manet*; The Blind Boy can do nothing without one prompting him for *vox perit*.[16]

Lastly, I think none will deny but that it stands with reason, That a deaf Scholar must be exact in Orthography. But for the blind I know it by experience, that it will be a hard matter to make him spel true.

---

[14] 'Marked with a black coal.'   [15] 'From one's earliest youth.'
[16] 'The written word remains . . . the spoken word vanishes'; this motto is also invoked by Dalgarno in *AS*, ch. 2.

CHAP. III.

Of a Deaf mans Capacity to speak.

That a Deaf man may be taught to speak, is no more a doubt to me, then that a Blind man may be taught to write: Both which I think not only possible, but also not very difficult; I will carry on the comparison in several particulars. First, both have the respective Organs, the Tongue, and the Hand, equally entire, and in a capacity to act. 2. Both are equally destitute of their proper guids, the Ey, and the Ear, to direct them in acting: and therefore, 3. both must be equally obliged to the sense of Feeling for direction.

And yet so Magisterial are the Senses of Hearing, and Seeing; that tho the Sense of Feeling alone may guide the Tongue, and Hand, in speaking, and writing, after a habit is acquired; yet for introducing this habit, directions from the Eye, and Ear are necessary. And which is observable <p. 25> in this point of discipline: The eye and ear seem to act out of their own Sphere, and to exchange their stations, and powers; for the Blind man learns to write by the Ear, and the Deaf man to speak by the Eye: From which to infer that community of Senses, which some Philosophers, and Physicians speak of, I think it would be absurd; the external objects still remaining distinct: But the true inference from this will be. That the soul can exert her powers, by the ministry of any of the Senses. And therefore when she is deprived of her principal Secretaries, the eye, and the ear; then she must be contented with the service of her Lacqueys, and Scullions, the other Senses; which are not less true and faithful to their Mistress, then the eye, and the ear; but not so quick for dispatch.

But to go on with the comparison. 4. It will be hard to teach the deaf man to observe tone, accent, and Emphasis in speaking; so will it be as hard to bring the blind man to write a fair hand, or diverse hands, yet the one may speak so as to be understood, and the other write so as what he <p. 26> writes may be read. 5. As there may be more simple, and therefore more easy Characters to be written, contrived for the use of the blind man; So may there sounds of an easier pronounciation than any in common use, be invented for the use of the Deaf, 6. They are equally uncapable the one of singing, the other of flourishing and painting. 7. As the Deaf man has this advantage above the Blind, that speaking in common commerce, and business is of more frequent and greater use than writing: So the Blind man comes even again with him in this. That there is one way of writing, and that of great use too, to the Deaf man; which the blind can learn both assoon and to as great a degree of perfection, as the deaf; whereas the deaf man cannot learn to speak without much time, and pains; and yet can never come to perfection in speaking. This way of writing is, by an Alphabet upon the fingers. 8. As to any direct tendency of improving either of them with knowledg, or dispatch of business and converse *in vita communi*,[17] I judge them both equally useless, or at least of <p. 27> no very great use; because I think scarce attainable to that degree of perfection, as to be ready for use upon all occasions. That there may be cases wherein they may be of great use I do not deny.

And of several that offer themselves, I will single out that of a blind Master, and deaf Servant, for stating of which the more clearly; I will premise. 1. That to read and write is a commendation in a servant. 2. It recommends him the more if he be to serve a blind Master. And 3. if his blind Master be a man of much business or learning, this enhances his service yet the more. These things premised; let our case be this.

Blind *Homer* hearing of an ingenious, but Deaf slave, called *Æsop*, who was trained up in all the forementioned waies of Sematology, and he himself being expert in Dactylology, he resolved to purchase *Æsop* at any rate. The first service he puts upon him, was to write out his *Ilias* fair, from his own blotted Copy: And because *Æsop* could scarce read his hand, he was alwaies present himself, correcting the faults of his Pen, upon his fingers. And <p. 28> here I leave them for a while till I have resolved another material doubt:

That which is my main design in this Treatise (to teach how to come to understand a language by reading and writing) suggests to me here to resolve this question. How a blind person might communicate with a dumb? The cause of doubting being upon the dumb mans part. I answer. The defect of his Tongue must be supplied with a musical Instrument, having the letters equally distinguished upon the Keys, or Strings, both to the Eye of the Dumb, and in the sounds to the Ear of the Blind; which I take for granted might produce the same effects with Oral speech. And here it is observable that that same action would very properly be, both Writing and Speaking; writing from the hands of the dumb touching the Keys, or Strings; speaking to the Ears of the Blind man from the sound of the Instrument.

After this short enterlude, let us bring *Homer* and *Æsop* upon the stage again. The old man was mightily pleaed with *Æsop*, till unfortunately on a certain <p. 29> time, the stuttering of his Tongue gave *Homer* occasion to suspect him of a ly: for which, in a sudden passion, he cuts out his Tongue: But afterwards repenting what he had done, resolved not to put him away; for he considered that he was yet as capable of serving him as ever; and perhaps more, the other waies of interpretation that he was skilled in, being more distinct than Glossology could be in a Deaf man. It happened soon after that *Homer*, had invited some friends to dinner, commanding *Æsop* to provide the greatest rarities the Market did afford. *Æsop* made a show of great preparation; but set nothing upon the Table, beside the tip of his own Tongue, in a large dish; upbraiding his Master with his pipe, that he did not tear his blotted papers

---

[17] 'In everyday life.'

when he could not read them; but had patience till he himself corrected them upon his fingers. *Homer* not enduring this affront before strangers throws *Æsops* pipe in the fire. *Æsop* fearing worse to follow, throws himself at his Masters feet taking him by the hand, and by rules of Haptology begs his pardon, promising if he <p. 30> would have patience, to make amends for his fault. *Homer* startled at this, to find both a Tongue, and a Pype, in *Æsops* fingers; was transported from wrath to fear, and admiration, concluding for certain, That *Æsop* was a conjurer, and that he deserved to be thrown in the fire after his pype. Yet resolving once more to try his wit and honesty: and for making satisfaction to his friends who had lost their dinner, he invites them to return to morrow, charging *Æsop* to provide the oldest, and leanest carrion, he could find. The night following, *Æsop* serves his blind Master with *lex talionis*[18] tongue for tongue, and repeated the same dinner to his friends the next day; excusing the matter, that he had from first to last obeyed his Masters commands, to the best of his judgment. *Homer* taking it ill, to be so often outwitted by a slave, by Dactylology begs of his provoked friends, to revenge him upon *Æsop*, by plucking out his Eyes; that his condition might not be more comfortable than his own. After this old age and a fit of sickness deprived *Homer* of his Hearing. This reconciled him again to <p. 31> *Æsop*; for he judged him the fittest companion he could find, with whom to bemoan his folly, and misery. After this, they lived good friends, passing the time in telling old stories; some times upon their fingers ends, and sometimes with hand in hand, traversing the Alphabetical *Ilias*.

This *Drama* being acted according to the Rules of Art, if there by any certainty in Art, that the promised effects will follow, it is no less true than it seems to be strange. And from this we may learn two things. 1. That tho hearing and seeing be the Principal, yet are they not the only Senses of Knowledg. 2. That the Hand is, (or at least is capable of being made) a more serviceable organ of interpretation to the Soul than the tongue. For it has access to its Mistress's presence, by the door of 3 Senses. 1. Of hearing by Aulology. 2. Of seeing, by both Species of Schematology, to wit, Typology and Dactylology. 3. Of Feeling, by Haptology. Whereas the Tongue can only enter by the door of one Sense, and do its message only by one kind of interpretation, Glossology.

---

[18] 'The law of requital of injury by injury.'

CHAP. IV.   <p. 32>

Of a Deaf mans Capacity to understand the speech of others.

I come now to the Deaf mans capacity of understanding the speech of others. That words might be gathered, and read from the transient motions, and configurations, of the mouth (if all the several distinctions of letters, were no less manifest and apparent to the Eye, than to the Ear from the speakers face) as readily as from permanent Characters upon paper, is not to be doubted: But that all the distinctions that are perceived by the Ear in speaking, cannot equally be perceived by the Eye; I will prove by an argument, which tho it be *à Posteriori*; yet I hope it will be of evidence and force sufficient to effect what is thereby intended.

If the same distinctions of letters and words did appear to the Eye from the motion of the speakers mouth, which are discernable to the Ear from the articulation of his voice; <p. 33> *Then it would follow; That the capacity of a Deaf man, would be equal to that of a Dumb (but not Deaf) for learning a Language, so far at least as to understand it.*

But the capacity of a Deaf man is not equal to that of a Dumb, for learning a language from speaking.

Therefore all the distinctions of letters, are not manifest to the Deaf, man from the speakers mouth.

The sequel of the Major is, I think, clear from what has been said before; there being nothing in sounds to the Ear either Natural, or Symbolical, more than in motion and figures to the Eye. And if any should say: That it is not so easy to read transient motions of the lips, even supposing them sufficiently distinct (which must alwaies be supposed) as permanent Characters. To this first, I oppose reading from poynting to a finger Alphabet; which is nothing but motion. 2. All reading from whatsoever immovable object, is as properly motion as hearing; for if there be no motion in the object, then it must be in the Organ of the Eye: which alters not our case, more than the Earths motion, or rest, <p. 34> alters the Phænomena of Astronomy.

If here it should be urged; that granting Signs to the Eye to be as fit for teaching, as signs to the Ear; and therefore, that a Deaf person must be supposed to be in as great a capacity of learning to understand a language spoken, as a blind, when the distinctions to the Eye and Ear are the same; yet, that the blind man learns to understand a language from hearing others speak, when the Deaf man learns not to understand from seeing others speak; is from the advantages the Ear hath above the Eye.

To this I answer, that all the advantages the Ear hath over the Eye, will be consistent enough with the Deaf mans capacity of learning to understand a language from speaking. It is true here, that the Eye is still at the loss of equal opportunities of time with the ear; but the other advantage I gave the ear over the eye, of doing more work in less time, is here quite taken away: and yet the Deaf man will still have as much opportunity of time (if there were no other defect) if his Nurse and all that are about him be <p. 35> not *Dumb*, as sufficiently to inculcate the common Notions of Language; For tho young people learn a Language by hearing others speak; yet the greatest part of what they hear is redundant, and like rain falling into a full conduit, runs over. So that a deaf man tho he have not so much opportunity of learning as a blind; yet has he opportunities enough, and to spare, for learning the common notions of language.

Now for the *minor* so far as concerns the Deaf man, it is known by sad experience, that he learns no language from his Mother or Nurse. And for the Dumb person, tho I can bring no instance; yet the case seems to me so clear, that I think nobody doubts of it, and therefore I will not enlarge to prove it.

But tho the Deaf man be not able to perceive all the distinctions of letters, neither indeed is it possible for him, the various motions by which some of them are differenced not appearing outwardly; yet if he be ingenious, I judge that he perceives a great many; and therefore I doubt not but Deaf persons understand <p. 36> many things, even without teaching, further than what they have from their Nurse. Tho here I must add: That they could understand but very little from the motion of the lips, which when most distinct must be full of ambiguity, and æquivocalness to them, without other circumstances concurring. For when dumb people make it appear, that they understand many things that pass in discourse where they are present, Children and fools cannot be perswaded but they Hear: Superstitious and ignorant people think they have a familiar Spirit: others despising the folly of the one, and impiety of the other, do judge, that they are able by the Eye, as distinctly to receive words from the speakers mouth, as others by the Ear. But the truth is, what they understand, is from a concurrence of circumstances, many of which are often as material, as the motion of the speakers lips; such as, his eyes, countenance, time, place, persons, &c.

To determine what, or how many distinctions of letters, the eye is able to discover in the speakers face; There can be no man so fit to resolve this doubt, as the <p. 37> Deaf man. And if there be no mistake in that well known passage of Sir *Kenelm Digby*;[19] A *Spanish* Deaf Lord hath already resolved it so, as to refute and destroy all that I have said. What is there said of him, will amount to this. *That the Eye can perceive all the distinctions of letters, in the speakers face, which the Ear can do in his voice.* I let pass that which increaseth the wonder: That this *Spanish* Lord should be able not only to know strange letters, in strange languages, instantly; but also to be able to imitate them, tho he had never been taught.

To neglect the Testimony of a person both of Honour, and Learning, who was an ear and eye-witness of all he relates, and had nothing to byass him from

---

[19] Digby (1644: 320). Wallis (1972: 12) refers to this passage, in which Digby describes the teaching of language to the deaf during a visit to Spain; it is quoted *in extenso* by Bulwer (1648: 56–61).

what he judged to be exact truth; and which is more, calling to witness to that relation a person much greater than himself, and beyond all exception for veracity; This would not only be disingenuous, but also arrogant. Therefore I will say what seems most probable to me for reconciling that relation to the truth. I will then first suppose, That Sir *Kenelm Digby* had not <p. 38> much considered this weakness of human Nature, nor of the way to remedy it, and therefore might be the more credulous (for I find nothing of suspition or caution, that he might not be imposed upon) and ready (as we are all in strange things) to magnify this rare and wonderful Art, which, 'tis like, he had never seen nor heard of before; and perhaps had even judged such performances impossible. Secondly, I will suppose that the Priest the Lords Tutor was ambitious to set off his Art, with all the advantages possible, before so great a Personage as the Heir of the Crown of *England.*

These things being supposed, I take it for granted that the Priest has used artifices of *Leger-de-main*, in these passages that seem most strange. What these have been (supposing the matter of fact to be true) tho I was not there an eye-witness; yet, without conjuring, I can tell as certainly, as if I had been a spectator, or, an Actor in that Scene. 1. His keeping up discourse with others, has been done in set forms, to acting of which he has been trained up before hand. 2. For returning <p. 39> any words that came from the mouth of another; this he has been prompted to by his Tutor, or any other standing by, with a finger Alphabet. 3. As for his Echoing back *Irish* and *Welsh* words, two things may be said. First, that he might have been taught to sound these guttural letters; which occur often in these languages, and were as easy to him as any other letters whatsoever: Or secondly, Because it is there said that the Priest affirmed, that he performed some things which were beyond the Rules of his Art; I know nothing can be said, but that he might perhaps chance upon the true sound of these letters, or something near them; which the relator thought good to represent with all his other performances (because indeed wonderful to those people that never had seen, or heard of the like, or knew by what art they were performed) to the greatest advantage. As for his returning words whispered at the distance of the breadth of a large room, there is no new wonder in this; for whispering and speaking loud were all one to him: But I suspect that this as well as other things, has <p. 40> been a set lesson, or, the Priest did *micare digitis.*[20]

I am not ignorant than many of Sir *Kenelms* relations, are looked upon, as fabulous and Hyperbolical. Well, be it so, and let this be as fabulous as any of them. It is not the *esse*, but the *posse* of the story, that I concern my self to maintain. That several passages related there, are impossible, and other circumstances very hyperbolical; in that sense, in which he understands them, I think, I have sufficiently proved: And yet, that the whole relation might be true, in that sense I have put upon it, I hope I have made no less evident.

---

[20] A game involving guessing the number of fingers held up for a brief instant.

CHAP. V.

Of the most effectual way to fill a Deaf mans capacity.

Hitherto I have been taking measures of the Deaf mans capacity. I come now to consider of the way to fill it. And here my design is not to give a Methodical Systeme of Grammatical Rules; But only such general directions whereby an industrious Tutor may bring his deaf Pupil to the vulgar use and ὅτι[21] of a language; That so he may be the more capable of receiving instruction in the δἰ ὅτι[22] from the Rules of Grammar, when his judgment is ripe for that study. Or more plainly; I intend to bring the way of teaching a deaf man to Read and Write, as near as possible, to that of teaching young ones to speak and understand their Mother-tongue.

I will begin with a Secret, containing the whole Mystery of the Art of instructing deaf persons. That is, I will <p. 42> describe such a powerful Engine, as may be able to fill his head as full of the Imagery of the world of words of mans making, as it is of the things of this visible world created by Almighty God: which Engine shall have one property more, that it shall not fail of success, even supposing both Master and Scholar to be the next degree to Dunces.

Here methinks, I see the Reader smiling at this *Fortunam Priami*;[23] and hear him whispering to himself, *Parturiunt Montes*, &c.[24] But I hope before I have done with my Notion, to reconcile him so far to it, as to bring him to judge that there is something considerable in it: And tho at first he meet not with all that this *hiatus* may seem to have promised; yet at last he may meet with something more than he expected. This powerful and succesful Engine, is not the Tongue of the Learned, but the Hand of the DILIGENT. The Hand of a *diligent* Tutor will not fail to make a *Rich* Scholar, if *Copia verborum*[25] may deserve the name of *Riches*. *Diligence* will be that same virtue in our Deaf scholars Tutor, that <p. 43> *Demosthenes* makes *Action* to be in his Eloquent Orator. Let the deaf child then have for his Nurses, not the 9 Muses, but the 9 Magpyes:[26] Let him be sent to School, not to πολύμητις Ὀδυσσεὺς, but to ἀμετροεπὴς Θερσίτης.[27]

---

[21] The 'that'.   [22] The 'wherefore'.

[23] 'Fortunam Priami cantabo et nobile bellum' (Of Priam's fate and famous war I shall sing) (Horace, *Ars Poetica* 137).

[24] 'Parturiunt montes, nascetur ridiculus mus' (The mountains will go into labour, and what will be born is a laughable little mouse) (ibid. 139).

[25] 'Wealth of vocabulary.'

[26] 'To see nine magpies is a proverbial sign of ill luck' (Brewer 1995 [1870]: 665).

[27] 'Not to cunning Odysseus but to Thersites of unmeasured speech.'

Diligence you will say is powerful in all Arts. True it is; yet as a Handmaid: But here I think, that without a *Catachresis*,[28] I may call it the principal point of Art. This with very few directions from Art, will do the work effectually; all the fine Tricks of Art, which the wit of man can contrive, will be ineffectual without this. The only point of art here is, how to make an application to your deaf Scholar, by the same distinction of letters and words to his Eye, which appear to the Ears of others from words spoken; that is to know his letters, and to write them readily; Diligence will do the rest. For Example: Let the same words be seen, as written as often by the Deaf man, as they have been heard and spoken by the Blind; if their faculties of memory and understanding be equal, the measure of knowledge also will be equal. But here it will be necessary that I explain what I mean by Diligence.

By Diligence I understand two things. 1. That which is properly so called, <p. 44> both in the Master and Scholar. This Sir *Kenelm Digby* calls much patience, and constancy in the experiment upon the *Spanish* Lord. 2. Many other adventitious helps. I summed up the advantages the Ear hath above the Eye into these two. 1. Having more opportunities of time; 2. Doing more work in less time. Here I will shew how Diligence, with a few directions from Art, may in a good measure remedy this inequality.

It is a received Maxim amongst those who have employed their thoughts, in that succesless enquiry, about a perpetual motion. *Reconcile time and strength, and this will produce a perpetual motion.* The application is easy from what I have said before, comparing the Deaf man with the Blind. Let them have equal time, and force of acting, and their proficiency will be equal. That care and diligence both in the general, and the particulars following, may remedy this inequality, in a great measure, I think no body will doubt. Neither ought this to <p. 45> be any discouragement, that the reconciling time and strength, as to a Geometrical equality, is not possible: For it is not here, as in the perpetual motion. There, if you fail of a minute, or a Dram, all your labour is lost: Here nothing is lost, but just so much as you come short of him you compare with. How much this is, we will see by the particulars following.

1. If the deaf Scholar could be brought to speak readily, this would lessen the inequality of *Force*, by one half: and if it were possible, that he could read the Speakers words from his face, this would make a Geometrical equality of force, in the Eye and Ear; so that the only inequality would be then, in time; the eye being confined to light, bodily posture, and distance; and out of these circumstances, the deaf and dumb man were perfectly cured. But because I am distrustful of this cure for which I have given my reasons chap. 4. I will confine my self to reading, and writing, most properly so called, as both the more certain and perfect cure.

---

[28] 'Improper use of words.'

Here the first piece of diligence must <p. 46> be, *frequens excercitate Styli*,[29] that is, as I understand it in this place, *using the pen and fingers much*. If this be so necessary for forming an Orator, (as *Cicero* teaches us in his *de Oratore*,[30] inculcating it with *ut sæpe jam dixi*) who has the use of the two principle Organs of Eloquence entire; how much more must it here be necessary, where the Pen must be both pen, and tongue. Great care therefore must be taken, to keep your Scholar close to the practice of writing; for until he can not only write, but also have got a quick hand, you must not think to make any considerable progress with him. It is true, that it were possible to teach a deaf man to read, without teaching him to write; as one may learn to understand a language spoken and not to speak it: But this would be but a half cure, and leave your Scholar uncapable of Society.

And because the conveniency of writing cannot alwaies be in a readiness, another great help will be, to have *Tabulæ deletiles*,[31] of stone or black wood, hanging up for expedition, in several convenient places. A third help will be, to have some <p. 47> common forms written in those Tables, there to continue, and to be filled up as accasion requires, like Virgils *Sic vos non vobis*, &c.,[32] such as, *where is? I pray give me? who? when? what?* &c. These may serve not only for expedition, but by them also, your Scholar may be taught to vary. Pocket Table books may sometimes be more ready then these. 4ly when neither of these is in a readiness, then practice by an Alphabet upon the fingers; which by frequent practice, as it is the readiest, so it may become the quickest way of intercourse and communication with dumb persons. But I shall have occasion to enlarge more on this, chap. 8. 5ly. another piece of useful care will be, to keep him from any other way of Signing, than by Letters. 6ly, Add to this; that his familiars about him be officious in nothing, but by the intercourse of letters, that is, either by Grammatology, or Dactylology.

If now lastly, I can make it appear that Diligence out-weighs wit in our present case; I hope my former Flash will not be thought to have ended in smoke. And <p. 48> this, methinks, is easily understood from obvious and daily instances: Do not we see that young ones, tho of very weak parts for understanding Grammar, yet come assoon, and some of them sooner, to understand and speak a language by use, without art, than those of stronger parts. One Boy has gone to School 7 years, and yet understands not the common accidents of Grammar; another in the half of that time, is able to expound an Author, and resolve all the Grammatications that occur to a Title: take the same two at play, or in things where there is no occasion to shew their learning, you will often

---

[29] 'Frequent practice with the pen.'   [30] Cicero, *De Oratore* 3. 190–1.
[31] 'Writing-tablets that can be wiped.'
[32] Pseudo-Vergil, from the Life of Vergil by Donatus (Diehl 1911: 35): 'Sic vos non vobis nidificatis aves. | Sic vos non vobis vellera fertis oves. | Sic vos non vobis mellificatis apes. | Sic vos non vobis fertis aratra boves' (Thus you birds make nests not for yourselves; you sheep bear wool not for yourselves; you bees make honey not for yourselves; you oxen draw ploughs not for yourselves).

find, that the slow boy, for the nimbleness of his Tongue, and *Copia verborum*, may seem to exceed the other, as far as he doth him in art.

Hence it will seem to follow; That the principal point of Art in teaching a slow Scholar, is, to use no other art but that of Diligence: and if so, a second inference will be: That there is none so fit to teach a slow Scholar, as a slow Master; This is, one Dunce to teach another. This I know will seem ridiculous and absurd to <p. 49> many; yet I declare, that I am much of this mind in earnest, in our present case, where Grammar is excluded. For an acute man will be impatient, and not able to stoop so much as the other. And to clear this further; I think it will be easily assented to, that a pratling Nurse, is a better Tutrix to her foster-child, than the most profoundly learned Doctor in the University.

My last instance therefore shall be. Take Master and Scholar qualified as before, adding *Diligence*, as I have described it, and let a liberal reward be proposed to the Master; if the work be not effectually done, let me be the Dunce for them both.

If therefore this cure may so easily be performed; what a reproach is it to mankind, that so little compassion is shewn to this infirmity of human nature; these wretched impotents being not only neglected in the point of education, like brutes; but also, as if this were not unkindness enough, the laws of men do most unhumanly deprive them of many priviledges wherein the comfort of life <p. 50> consists. As for former ages, I confess they are to be excused: For tho (as I have been proving) *Diligence* be the principal point of Art, yet was this a secret to them: But in this knowing age, in which proofs have been given both at home and abroad, that this weakness is cureable in a good measure; and if the reasons contained in these papers have any weight, curable even to perfection; so far at least as concerns the better part of the man. That is, these impotents may not only be instructed in the common Notions of Language, which is the bond of human Society; but also from this foundation may be raised the superstructure of all other arts, which are either for use or ornament to human Nature. I say then; for us to neglect so worthy and noble an experiment, and so great an object of charity and compassion; were at once to degenerate from the charity of our Ancestors, and to make their ignorance preferable to our knowledge.

CHAP. VI.

Of a Deaf mans Dictionary.

Tho a Diligent inculcating of the common forms of a Language, following no other Rule or Method but that of the Nursery, would undoubtedly bring the Deaf man to understand, and write it, so as the Vulgar understand and speak it. Yet some directions from Art (specially if your Scholar be ingenious) will both facilitate the work, and do it much better. That is, it will make him understand the nature of words better, and so prepare him for the study of Grammar; as also the nature of things, for which he sees words substituted, and so prepare him for the pursuit of other Arts. I will therefore give a few such directions, whereby the Teacher abstaining from Rules and words of Art, may be enabled to produce the proper effects of Art in his Scholar. But first I will resolve two preliminary Queries. 1. What language <p. 52> is easiest to be learned? 2. And what language will be the most useful?

For the first, a language of a Philosophical Institution, or a real Character, would be by much the most easy; as being free from all anomoly, æquivocalness, redundancy and unnecessary Grammatications: and the whole institution being suited to the nature of things; this verbal knowledge, would not only come more easily; but also bring with it, much real knowledge.

2ndly, The language of greatest use to be learned, will be that of the place where he lives, and of the people with whom he is to converse. And here with us, the Deaf man has several advantages above other Nations. First, that our *English* is freer from anomoly, and æquivocalness (as least in writing, which is enough for him) than many other languages. 2. It is not so much clogged with inflexions, as other languages, and 3. our words are for the most part Monosyllables, and therefore more easy to be remembered. I come now to the promised directions.

<p. 53> I will make way for particulars, by observing first in General; that the way of teaching here, must be something mixt, and as it were middle between the Grammatical way of the School, and the more rude discipline of the Nursery. The first initiation must be purely grammatical; But when your Scholar is got over this difficulty of knowing and writing his letters readily; Then imitate the way of the Nursery. Let *utile* and *jucundum*,[33] variety and necessity, invite and spur him on; specially if he be young or of a lache temper.

You must not be too Grammatical in teaching, till you find his capacity will bear it: He must not be dealt with as School-boyes, who are often punished for not learning what is above their capacity. It is enough for him to understand the word, or sentence proposed, without parsing every word and syllable:

---

[33] 'The useful and the agreeable.'

For this is all the use of language that not only children, but even people of age that are illiterate have: They understand the meaning of what is spoken; but can neither tell how many words, syllables, or <p. 54> letters came from the speakers mouth. So that the having the vulgar use of a language and the understanding it Grammatically, are very different things. And this preposterous way of learning the learned languages, first Grammar, & then the language, is the cause of so slow progress in those that apply themselves to the study of them.

The first exercise you must put your Scholar upon, is to know his letters written, or printed, and upon his fingers, and to write them himself; and when he comes to joyn, let his copies be of such words as he may be taught to understand; so that at once, he may be learning both to write and understand the meaning of what he writes. When you have got him to write fair, keep him to constant practice, that you may bring him to write a quick hand; which his condition requires.

Let him begin to learn the Names of Things best known to him, how Heterogeneous soever; such as the Elements, Minerals, Plants, Animals, Parts, Utensils, Garments, Meats, &c, and generally the <p. 55> names of all such corporeal Substances, Natural or Artificial; not only absolute, but Relative, as *Father, Brother, Master, Servant*; as also names of offices, and professions, as *Cook, Butler, Page, Groom, Taylor, Barber*, &c. For all these will be as easily apprehended as the most distinct *Species* of natural Bodies. Let his *Nomenclature* be written down fair, and carefully preserved; not only in a book, but on one side of a sheet of Paper, that it may be affixt over against his eye in convenient places. And let this his Dictionary be sorted three waies. 1. Alphabetically, 2. following the order of double Consonants, both in the beginning and the end of a word. 3. Reducing it to several heads, or *Classes*, with respect not to the words, but the things, as in *Junius Nomenclator*, for every one of these Methods will be of good use to him.[34]

After he has got a good stock of these concrete Substantives, then proceed to Adjectives; namly, Sensible Qualities, Quantity, with some Metaphysical Notions; which all of them, almost admit of proper contraries; which illustrate one another, <p. 56> and therefore will be of great use to the learner. Let him be made to understand Adjectives by joyning them to their proper subjects, taken out of his vocabulary of Substantives already understood; as *Hard Iron, Stone, Bone*, &c. *Soft Silk, Wool, Cloth*, &c. And sometimes instance the two contraries, in that same Subject; as *Iron hot, cold*: And thus he will make a further advance to complex Notions.

Observe here. That by the help of an Almanack and Watch, it will be easy to make your Scholar understand all the differences and words of that difficult Notion of *Time*.

---

[34] Cf. the discussion of alternative ways of structuring the lexicon in a philosophical language in Dalgarno's 'Autobiographical Treatise', fo. 23ʳ (see below, Part IV).

After he has practised sufficiently upon complex notions of Substantives, and Adjectives; let him proceed to words of Action, whether bodily or Spiritual, which Grammarians call Verbs, as, *break, cut, hold, take, laugh, affirm, deny, desire, love, hate*, &c. And thus much shall be enough to have been said of his Dictionary, in this rude discipline under which we suppose him as yet to be.

Here I would have it well observed: That tho in applying my self to the deaf <p. 57> mans Tutor, I have followed something of Method, *docendi Causa*;[35] yet I do not advise him, to take this course with his Scholar: But as I said before, That the names of things best known to him, how heterogeneous soever, were to be first learned: So here I say, that there is no regard to be had to the cognation, or Grammatical affinity of words. In a word, occasion will be the best Mistress of Method, till he have made a considerable advance; And then when his Dictionary begins to be numerous, it will be necessary to draw it up in rank and file. Nay further, I am so far from advising to follow any method at first, but what is occasional (excepting only the stated, and fixt order of letters in the Alphabet) that if your Scholar be not very young, you may propose sentences as early to him as single words; especially interrogatives and imperatives, as, *where is your hat? whose hat is this? who gave you this apple? Rise up, sit down, give me the cap, shut the door*, &c. And these may be easily varyed Indicatively, infinitively, affirmatively, negatively, &c. <p. 58>

And yet for all this, I cannot deny but the Teacher may, and must contrive some method for himself, even of those things which he has taught, following occasion and his Pupils capacity; that he may know the better to take the measures of his progress, and to make the best use of occasions offered.

---

[35] 'For the purpose of instruction.'

CHAP. VII.

<p. 59>

Of a Grammar for Deaf Persons.

Having dispatcht the Deaf mans Dictionary, I come in the next place to speak of his Grammar. I should contradict the principles I have formerly laid down, if I should insist much upon Grammar; neither indeed doth our *English* Tongue require or afford much to be said by him, who would be ambitious to shew himself γραμματιχώτατος.[36] I shall therefore only make some few reflexions upon Etymology and Syntax, supposing Orthography to belong to Lexicography, of which already: And for Prosody, our Scholar is no more able to receive its precepts, than a blind man is to judge of colors.

I shall only take notice of 5 Etymological Grammatications, and do but name them; for I judge that these and all other points of Grammar are to be differred, at least as to an accurate explaining <p. 60> of them, until he be fitted for the study of Grammar, in manner as I have said before.

The first is the plural number, for which the Rule is but one and easy. *Add s to the singular, pen, pens,* and the exceptions are not many, which here I pass by. 2. The Comparative, and Superlative degree, almost as easy as the other. They are formed by adding the terminations *er* and *est,* or by the auxiliary words, *more, most,* as hard *harder, hardest,* or *more* hard, *most* hard. The exceptions are not many. 3. The Participle Active or Neuter in *ing,* from which I think there is no exception: And the Participle passive, which is oftentimes the same with the preterimperfect Tense, without an Auxiliary word, as, I *loved;* or the preterperfect Tense, with an auxiliary word; as I have *loved:* But from this rule are a multitude of exceptions; which is the greatest irregularity in the *English* Tongue. 4. The adverb of the manner ends in *ly.* This also hath its exceptions, but not many. 5. The abstract ending in *ness* generally.

These things you need not teach your <p. 61> Scholar by Rule, for a little practice will enable him to make a Rule for himself, and to bring the exceptions too under his Rule; as, we hear Outlandish men, and children saying often: *mans, womans, foots,* for *men, women, feet.*

As for that ambiguity, that almost every concrete Substantive in English is used verbaly, as *pen, hand, foot,* &c. This adds much to the Copiousness, Emphasis and Elegancy of the language; and yet gives very little cause of mistake; the construction of the words determining the signification. But the Verbal signification of these words being Metonymical, it will be best to leave them to their own place. So much for Etymology shall serve in this place, now for Syntax.

---

[36] 'The most proficient of grammarians.'

The Learned languages make two general parts of Syntax, agreement and government; whereas it seems to me that with them, Syntax requires a distribution antecedent to this. To wit, that the Syntax of words is either *per se* or *per aliud*, i.e. The Grammatical coherence and connexion of words, is made by the Terminations of the words themselves, or, <p. 62> by auxiliary words, called *Particles*. But neither the one nor the other of these distributions does our language require, or admit of, being freed from all incumbrances of inflexions, by genders, and cases (except a few pronouns) and consequently from the Rules of Agreement, and Government: All our Syntax consisting in the cement of auxiliary Particles.[37]

To treat of Syntax then in English, is to shew the use of the *Particles*, in forming words into Sentences. For, to explain these Notions separately, were to build Castles in the Air; and to form sentences without them, were to make ropes of sand.

Here I will not insist upon explaining every single particle, as if I were dealing with a Dumb Scholar; But remembring that the present address is more to the Master then the Scholar; I will instance only in some few, which may serve for a Clew to guide any ingenious adventurer thro the whole Labarynth.

As I would advise the dumb Scholar to be often put to practice upon verbs of bodily action, varying the circumstances <p. 63> by the Particles; so will I single out the verb *Cut*, to be the Principal verb in the following Examples, for explaining the Particles.

I begin with Pronouns, which according to the Notation of the word, are words put for other words. Let therefore these things be present, for whole names the pronouns are the *provocabula*: and then it will be easy to make your Scholar understand the use of these pronominal words. I will instance, first in the Demonstratives, *I, thou, he, we, ye, they*. Let there be six persons present, as many more as you will. Write down. *I cut, thou cut, he cut, we cut, ye cut, they cut*. Let the Master take his Scholar by him, and place a third person over against him, all of them prepared with a knife, and apple, or stick, &c. Let the Master Cut first, pointing to the words *I cut*, 2. let the Scholar cut, the Master pointing to the words *thou cut*; 3. let the third person cut, pointing to *he cut*. And for the Plural number: let the Master and his Scholar stand first together, placing two more near them, and two over against them. Then let the Master <p. 64> and Scholar cut, pointing to *we cut*; let the two by them cut, pointing to *ye cut*; 3. let the two over against them cut, pointing to *they cut*. The possessives, *mine, thine, his, ours, yours, theirs*, may be taught after the same manner; *my apple, thy apple, his apple, our apple, your apple, their apple, mutatis mutandis*. In short, all pronominal words after the same manner, *all cut, none*, or *no body cut, this boy cut, that boy cut, the same boy cut, another boy cut*, &c. Let him practice much upon this and other Verbs till you find that he is able to make these distinctions of himself.

---

[37] Cf. Dalgarno's discussion of particles (*AS*, ch. 10).

When he can distinguish persons, it will be easy from many examples, *cuttest*, *cutteth*, *breakest*, *breaketh*, *holdest*, *holdeth*, to make him understand, that the 2d and 3d person singular are distinguished by termination from the other persons.

For the Signs of Tenses, *do, dost, doth, have hast hath, was wast were, shall will*: write down, *I have cut the pen, I do cut the apple, I will cut the stick*: cut accordingly pointing to your Scholar; or, write, *I have stood, I do stand, I will stand*, do accordingly. <p. 65> *I have walked, I do stand, I will sit*, do accordingly. Do not trouble your Scholar with too nice distinctions of words, such as *shall* and *will, did* and *have*; it is enough for him, as yet, that he understand the use of words in the common forms of speech, as illiterate persons do.

Let him practice much upon the Pronouns, and Signs of Tenses, with Verbs of Action, adding other circumstances of time, place, manner, &c. and that with all the variety possible, of familiar, plain, easy, most common, and most frequently occurring circumstances.

The *copula* will be easily understood, because of its frequent use, both affirmatively and negatively; *fire is hot, water is not hot*; *water is cold, fire is not cold*; So in all its inflexions; as, *I am tall, thou art short, he is thick, I am sitting, thou art standing, he is walking.*

The Particles OR and, AND, with the adjectives *Same* and *diverse*, are to be diligently inculcated, as being words of frequent use, and useful for explication, and declaring the sense of other words. *Or* in the explicative sense of it coming <p. 66> between words signifying the same thing; *And* between words signifying diverse things. It may be good to write down many examples of Synonymous words, and phrases which your Scholar understands, joyning them with, *or*, as

The same	{ I stand or I do stand or I am standing	{ to go or to walk	the same	{ wide or broad	

So for the Copulative, AND, give such examples as these.

Diverse	{ Hand *and* Foot	diverse	{ Pen *and* Ink	diverse	{ Sun *and* Moon

But the frequent recurring of these and many such like in common, familiar, and necessary forms of speech, will soon make them to be understood.

As for Particles signifying Motion, as *to, from, thro, by, into, out of, hither, thither, hence, thence*, &c. whether prepositions or adverbs: so Distance, as, *far off, near, at, hard by, close by*, &c. Position, as, *before, behind, above, upon, beneath, about, up, down, beyond, on this side*, &c. Their use and meaning is so plain and obvious, <p. 67> that there needs no more but choice of fit examples to make them understood. The Table is *before* your face; The Chair is *behind* your back; The book is *upon* the Table; My hand is *above* the Table; the nose is *between* the Eyes; the Eyes are *above* the mouth; the mouth is *under* the eyes; the tongue is *in* the mouth; to put *out* the tongue; to rise *up*; to sit *down*; go *to* the door, *from* the door, come *hither*, go *thither*, &c. These and such like words signifying circumstances perceivable by sense, are as easily apprehended as words signifying bodily substance or sensible Quality.

Even the Particles of a Metaphysical extraction, and more remote from sense, may be easily understood, if the Teacher be not too Metaphysical in his application. I will mention here only two Topicks of this kind of Particles; The causes and the Comparates, which are the two principal sinews of discourse. The particles from the causes are diverse, *from, of, with, by, wherefore, therefore, because, why,* &c. Use examples such as these. This Pen was made *by* the Master, *of* a Goosequil, <p. 68> *for* to write *after* my Copy. Explain *why, wherefore, what is the cause,* by expostulations, and interrogations, with your Scholar himself or others, and *Because* in answer to these.

Observe here, that many of these Particles being very equivocal, it will not be prudence to represent this difficulty all at once, lest is amaze and discourage your Scholar. For example, you have made him understand the causal particle *with,* in such examples as these, to cut *with* a knife; to write *with* a Pen: do not immediately put him upon the Particle of Society *with,* as go *with* me; but explain the various use of such particles, as they offer themselves occasionally in practice, and as you find his capacity is able to receive: For, improving of occasions, and complying with the Scholars capacity, will be the Masters greatest commendation. Not but that he may be put upon learning many set forms for exercise of memory; tho he understand them not perfectly. But do not put his understanding to the rack, by an undiscreet pressing upon his apprehensive faculty, Notions <p. 69> either simple or complex, which you find he receives not readily. But make a collection of such words, and watch opportunities of explaining them: I can give no better Rule for explaining words hard to be understood; then that which *Horace* has given, in a case not much unlike ours.

> *Dixeris Egregie notum si callida verbum*
> *Reddiderit junctura novum.*—[38]

Where the principal Verb of a sentence is clearly apprehended, it brings great light to other circumstantiating words. So that the skilful chusing of verbs of Action, well understood by your Scholar; and the like dexterity in placing a hard word, which you would have him to understand, amongst other words of circumstance already well understood, in construction with the verb; every word of the sentence will reflect some light upon this dark word.

The second classis of Metaph [ysical] (or perhaps more properly Logical) particles, are those that owe their Origine to the Topick of the Comparates;

---

[38] 'You will express yourself best if skilful positioning makes a familiar word new' (Horace, *Ars Poetica* 47–8).

such as, *than, much, more, most, less, least, by so* <p. 70> *much*, &c. explain these also by many fit examples, in which the several degrees of comparrison may be demonstrated to the senses. This water is *as* hot *as* that; This cheese, apple, egg, is *greater* or *more* great *than* that; This apple is the *greatest*, or *most great* of all the apples; *by how much* this stick, paper is *longer than* that, *by so much* that is *broader than* this; let the proportion be fitted and measured.

It will be necessary to make a collection of such forms of sentences as he understands, one or two examples of every form, that upon occasion he may have recourse to them as to rules, and precedents in the like cases: and amongst other forms, forget not imperatives and interrogatives, for which he will have early and frequent use. Gather up all the forms of interrogation; *when? who? what? where? whose? whence? whether? how long? many? great?* &c. Form sentences upon every one of these interrogations, in things familiar; and sub-joyn proper answers; as, *whose book is this?* A. *mine, thine, his, thy brothers, the Masters*, &c. *When shall we go to bed?* A. *by and by, at ten a* <p. 71> *clock, an hour hence*, &c. Imperative forms. *I pray give me the book, take up the pen, lay down the paper, sit down, rise up, put on your hat, open the door, shut the door*, &c.

For exercise, you may find great variety for him; such as, to describe things from their causes, from their contraries, by comparing them with other things; To form a narration of things seen, to write Epistles. Let him be put much upon the exercise of memory; and that not only in loose words, and incoherent sentences; But let him bestow much time and pains, in learning by heart, in the first place for his *Lectiones sacræ* upon the Lords day, and Holy-dayes, the Lords Praier, the Creed, and ten Commandements, with the Church-Catechism.

The solemnity and frequency of Divine Service, would have good effects upon him, being placed conveniently opposite to the Minister, with a book before him, and one to direct him, till custome enable him to direct himself. This would not only xcite him to piety and devotion; but in progress of time, he would come <p. 72> both to understand, and have by heart, the greatest part of Divine Service. Some other select passages of Scripture might be recommended to him, as the first Chap. of *Genesis*, the History of our Saviours Nativity, and sufferings. The most proper books among profane Authors for him to practice on (I think) of many, were *Æsops* Fables, and some playes where there is much of Action.

In the application of all I have said, respect is to be had to the quality of the person to be taught; whether young or old, dull or docile: How to comply with these circumstances, must depend upon the prudence of the Teacher. When his progress is so considerable that it may be said of him; He understands the English tongue tolerably well: He may then be put upon the study of Grammar; which will be the more easy to him; because the course of study he was in before had a mixture of Grammar in it, as I have said. Afterwards (or before if you please) he may be taught Arithmetick and something of Geometry.

CHAP. VIII.

Of an Alphabet upon the Fingers.

Because the conveniency of writing cannot alwaies be in readiness; neither yet tho it could, is it so proper a *medium* of interpretation between persons present face to face, as a Hand-language: It will therefore be necessary to teach the Dumb Scholar a Finger-Alphabet; and this not only of single letters, but also for the greater expedition, of double and triple Consonants, with which our English doth abound.

After much search and many changes, I have at last fixt upon a Finger, or Hand-alphabet according to my mind: For I think it cannot be considerably mended, either by my self, or any other, (without making Tinkers work) for the purposes, for which I have intended it; that is, a distinct placing of, and easy pointing to the single letters; with the like distinct, and easy abbreviation of double and triple Consonants. <p. 74>

I deny not but there may be many more abbreviations than I have provided for, namely of initial Syllables, and Terminations; but these I have past by at present, for two reasons. First, I think there will be little need of them; For I doubt not but that with the provision I have made, an habit equal to that in those who write a quick hand, may very near make the Hand as ready an Interpreter, as the Tongue. 2ly. If they should be judged needful, I have taken care, that with a few Rules they may be added, without altering any thing of the institution of this present Scheme.

The Scheme (I think) is so distinct and plain in it self, that it needs not much explication, at least for the single letters, which are as distinct by their places, as the middle and two extremes of a right line can make them. The Rules of practice are two. 1. *Touch the places of the Vowels, with a cross touch with any finger of the right hand.* 2. *Poynt to the Consonants with the Thumb of the right Hand.* This is all that I think to be needful for explaining the Scheme so far as concerns <p. 75> the single letters: and for the double Consonants.

I have made provision for abbreviating a threefold combination of them: I shall here only give the Rules of abbreviation of the several combinations I have made choice of, referring the reader for the reasons of my choice, to the following Treatise of double Consonants.

The first combination of double Consonants I make provision for is, when *h, l, r, s,* come in one syllable with other Consonants; and that two waies, either before or after another Consonant, as in these Examples.

1. H	{ light the	2. L.	{ falt title	3. R.	{ heart trie	4. S.	{ hast hats

Dalgarno's finger alphabet

1. When these 4 letters are prefixt to other Consonants, as in *light, salt, heart, hast*; the Rule is; *point skin to skin with the four fingers of the other Hand respectively to the Capital letter* (which in the present example is T) *to which they are prefixt*; which by Institution designs the double <p. 76> Consonants *ht, lt, rt, st.*
2. When the same four letters follow another Consonant as in, *the, title, trie, hats*; then, *point* (as before) *to T with nail to skin*, which gives, *th, tl, tr, ts.*

A second combination of double Consonants worthy of this care of abbreviations, because of their frequent use in English, is when the Liquids *m, n,* come before the Mutes and Semimutes, *b, p, d, t, g, k,* or *c,* That is, *m* before *b, p* and *n* before *d, t, g, k, c.* The Rule is. *Touch the place of these Mutes and Semimutes with the first and second finger joyned*; and this by institution gives the Liquid and the respective Mute or Semimute following, as in *lamb, lamp, hand, hunt, anger, ink, France.*

The third abbreviation is of Trible Consonants in the beginning of a word or syllable, where *s* is alwaies the first; as in, *schism, skrew, shrine, spread, strong, scrag, sphinx, softhenes, splinter, justle,* &c. The Rule is, *Joyn the thumb to the finger pointing to the other two Consonants.* And so much for abbreviation of double and trible Consonants.

But observe here, that as School-boyes <p. 77> are to learn *amavisse*, before *amasse*, and ποίεω before ποιῶ,[39] and to write words at length, before they learn short-hand; so let your Dumb Scholar, and others that would practice Dactylology, first know, and practice upon the single letters, before they come to practice upon the Rules of abbreviation.

Now tho this way of short-hand, or abbreviation of words be distinct, easy, quick and comprehensive; yet is there another way of practising, which comes nothing short of this in other respects, and in one respect seems to be preferable: That it supposes nothing necessary to be known for practising, but the places of the single letters, without making new Rules for distinguishing double and trible Consonants, from the single. The Rule is; *Point to all the single letters of the double or trible Consonant, simul & semel:*[40] which will be found to be as easy as poynting by the former institution with one single touch, as will appear in these examples; *when, which, the, light, blunt, brand, grunt, plaster, spread, strong,* &c.

If here it should be objected, that this <p. 78> will breed confusion, leaving the Reader doubtful what letter to begin with. To this I answer. 1. For double Consonants in the beginning of a syllable, this objection can never be of any force; for there is no English word found wherein their order is inverted, as will appear from the following Treatise of double Consonants. 2. For double Consonants in the end of a word, so far as concerns the second combination formerly mentioned, there can never be any mistake; for scarce (I think) is there any example occurs wherein their order is inverted; or if there did then the rule will be in that case, *point to the single letters distinctly.* So that the objection is of no force, except only against the first combination of double Consonants, and that only in the end of a Syllable: For there are some, but not many examples, where the order is inverted as, *salt, title, hast hats.* But to this it may be answered: That in a continued sentence, the sense will easily determine the case, and take away all ambiguity: as here lies one *hat*, there lie two *hats*. But if you have occasion to distinguish <p. 79> the word *hats*, from *hast*, then you must point to all the letters distinctly.

And this compendious and expeditious way of Cheirology may be extended further, than this abbreviation of double and trible Consonants: For they that are Masters of a Language, and have got a considerable readiness of practising, by distinct touches of single letters, will find it as easy, as it is useful, to express whole syllables, and whole words that are Monosyllables (specially in words of common use) with one multiplyed touch, *simul* and *semel.* My meaning by this multiplied touch *simul* and *semel* is, not to touch distinctly all the letters of a syllable or word, by the *Index* or any one single finger of the other Hand successively, making so many distinct motions from place to place, as there are letters in the syllable: But so to order the matter, than an equal number of the

---

[39] i.e. they are to learn the uncontracted forms before the contracted ones.
[40] 'Together and simultaneously.'

fingers of the other Hand may be used for a simultaneous touch to make the word or syllable, according to the number of letters it shall happen to consist of. This way of expressing syllables and words Monosyllables, <p. 80> with one multiplied touch, after a little practice, will be as easy and quick, as pointing to one single letter with a single touch; it will be also as distinct as pointing to every letter successively, with one finger.

But let it be well observed here, that tho I would have a whole syllable expressed with one single action, and motion of the whole Hand; yet let not the distinct touches be so simultaneous, but that it may appear where the word begins, and where it ends.

Here I think will be proper place to give a Rule, how to know when a word is ended, and it is this. *Let there be a continued actual touch of more fingers, or one at least, till the word be ended*; or if this happen (as it may in some words) to be uneasy, then make a quick motion from the place of the last letter of the word: But this difficulty after a little practice will vanish away.

Now because this discourse may fall into the hands of some that have trifling Heads like my own, to whom it will be acceptable to know what other waies of <p. 81> Dactylology I have had under consideration: I will, for satisfying their curiosity, and perhaps saving them the expence of vain labour, mention some other waies which I have considered, and after examination rejected.

The first way is to make the figures of the letters upon the Hand, which differs only from writing in this; that the one is transient, and the other permanent. It is true, that this is more ready upon all occasions than writing; but neither distinct nor quick enough to be taken notice of here.

A second way is the forming of the letters Symbolically; as to make an X by crossing two fingers; a cross touch upon the end of the thumb for a T; three fingers joyned for M, two fingers joyned for N, &c. This Symbolical way I reject, as being defective in two respects: First, it is defective in the point of symbolizing; for it will not be easy with the fingers to represent the shapes of all letters. This way of expressing the letters Symbolically, is somewhat like the conceit of a symbolical Character, and a Language of Nature, <p. 82> which some have talked much of; but without any foundation in Nature, and therefore all attempts of Art must be in vain. But secondly, this way is too laborious, and so defective in answering one of the principal ends for which Cheirology is desirable, and deserves the name of an Art: That is, a quick and ready expression, and interpretation of the conceits of the mind, coming as near as possible to that of the Tongue.

The third way is to design every single letter by a single touch; which I judge much the better way, than either of the other two; as being more simple, distinct, easy, and of quick dispatch. Having therefore resolved upon this, that the most proper way to express the simple Elements of the Alphabet would be, by a single touch; it remained that they should be distinguished amongst themselves by their places. And here again, after consideration and tryal, I have rejected several waies of distinguishing the letters by places. First, I provided places on both Hands, back and fore; but finding this laborious and intricate, and perceiving <p. 83> that there might be distinction enough found in one hand, I placed the whole Alphabet upon one Hand; yet so as to make use of an equal number of places on both sides of the Hand: But at last finding that all the necessary distinctions could be provided for, on one side of the Hand, I fixt upon the institution of the present Scheme; which I think is done with that consideration and care, that as I said before, it cannot be much improved.

Here I thought to have kept one secret of Art to my self; at least till I should see how other things I had discovered should please: But I must confess my own weakness, that in things of this Nature, I am *plenus remarum*.[41] I know not how considerable this secret will seem to others; But I declare (that I may confess another weakness) that I was much affected with it: For after a long and tyresome chase, and having pursued my Notion, as I thought, to a *nil ultra*; when I was set down, and pleasing my self with my purchase; on a sudden I fancied my self to see an one-handed deaf man coming to me, <p. 84> and asmuch as I could read in his eyes and countenance, expostulating with me thus? What? Have you done? Is there no help for me? Shall one Eye serve in Schematology? & one Ear in Pneumatology? one tongue in Glossology? yea one hand in Typology? And shall not one Hand serve in Dactylology? With this fixing my Eyes stedfastly on his Hand stretched out, I thought with my self, that I could discern a Mouth and a Tongue in his Hand: the Thumb seemed to represent the Tongue, the Fingers and the hollow of the Hand the lips, teeth, and cavity of the Mouth. Upon this I made signs to him to try to follow me, as I pointed to the letters on my own Hand; which he did so exactly that the surprise put me in a maze for some time. But when I had overcome my passion, reflecting upon this wonder both of Nature and Art, I observed that of the 24 letters, he pointed to 16 with his Thumb. Thus I dismissed my Deaf and lame patient, bidding him to be of good courage, and live in hopes of an effectual and speedy cure.

But after he was gone, I began to consider <p. 85> with my self. What? shall I magnify this as a mystery and wonder of Nature and Art, to find a way, to Metamorphize a *Chymæra* into a Man, or, to make a black Swan white? This will be *magno conatu magnas nugas agere*.[42] As I was thus thinking, it happened that I was smoking a pype of Tobacco; and having a present occasion to dispatch a speedy message; I was unwilling to let my Pype go out, and so at that present was deprived both of the use of my Tongue and one Hand: wherefore reflecting upon the lesson which I had lately taught the one-handed Deaf man, or shall I rather say, which he taught me: I call a boy to me, whom I had trained up in Dactylology, and delivered my message to him with one Hand. He staring in my face with a smiling countenance (for I had never spoken to him before that time with one Hand) performed the message very readily, and

[41] 'Full of leaks; unable to keep a secret.'
[42] 'To achieve great trifles with great effort' (Terence, *Heautontimorumenos* 4. 1. 8).

returned me a speedy answer, using the same Organ of Interpretation (for I surprised him eating an Apple) to me, which I had done to him. This gave me occasion to think, that this point of <p. 86> Art had not only one-handed Deaf men for its Object; but that there might be many other cases wherein it might be useful to speak with one hand: as to speak to a Dumb man riding on Horse-back, holding the reins with one hand, and with the other asking him. *How do you do?* or sitting at Table; holding the Cup with one hand, and with the other saying, *Sir my service to you.* Or, with one hand holding the knife, and with the other asking; *what will you be pleased to have?* &c.

And if any man could be supposed to have that readiness and presence of mind which is said to have been in *J. Cæsar* he might at once keep up discourse with 3 several persons, upon several subjects, talking to two with his two hands, and to a third with his Tongue. And here by the by, it is observable, that without any distraction of mind one may speak both to a Deaf and Blind man at once, expressing the *same* words by the Tongue to the Blind man, and by the hand to the Deaf.

Nay further I declare, that as much as I have as yet been able to discover by practice, I judge the way of speaking with <p. 87> one hand preferable to the other of using both, and that in all respects, unless it be in this one; That it is not capable of distinction enough for all the necessary abbreviations of double Consonants, which perhaps (after a readiness and habit acquired) may not be needful; or if it were, yet I know that one hand is capable of many more distinctions that I have as yet made use of: but at present I think if not *tanti*[43] to make use of them, for I foresee, that the conveniency will scarce ballance the inconveniencies.

Now tho the practising of this Hand-language be so plain and easy from the following Scheme, and the preceding explication of it, that any one who can but read (without knowing to write) may become his own Teacher; yet seeing the nature of all skill and cunning deserving the name of an *Art* is such, that something of instruction *viva voce*, is, if not necessary, at least useful; So here something of direction from one well skilled in the practice of this Art, either *viva voce*, or (which is the same thing, and as Emphatick a way of teaching if it were <p. 88> practiced) *digito demonstrante*,[44] will be of good use to young practioners.

I will add one help more, for enabling young beginners to practice more easily and readily: Let a pair of Gloves be made, one for the Master, and another for the Scholar, with the letters written upon them in such order as appears in the following Scheme. To practice with these, will be easy for any that do but know their letters and can spell; and a short time will so fix the places of the letters in the Memory, that the Gloves may be thrown away as useless.

---

[43] 'Of so great value.'
[44] 'Either by word of month or . . . by demonstration on the fingers.'

Having laid open the whole progress of my thoughts in this discovery of Cheirology, it remains that I make good my promise in the Title-page of shewing, that it is useful both in cases of necessity and conveniency.

First then I think none will deny, but that it is necessary for persons *Deaf* or *Dumb*; and therefore I shall spare my self the labour of proving it any other way, than by referring the Reader to the Series and scope of this whole discourse. But here it will be very proper to add something <p. 89> how it may be made *most* useful to the Deaf man, and in order to this let it be considered. That the nature of Cheirology is such, that it is only useful in society and converse with others: So that if the Deaf man be trained up in this Art, and have no body about him skilled in it but himself, it is of no use to him at all: As on the contrary, if all people were as ready in this Hand-language, as he may rationally be supposed to be; then the Hand between him and others, would be of the same use that the Tongue is to other people amongst themselves. But seeing (according to the received way of training up youth hitherto, by which no care is taken of teaching them Cheirology) he can have none, or very few to converse with him in this way: It will be the concern of the Deaf persons friends (beside the influencing all his familiars to acquaint themselves with this Art for his cause) to chuse some fit person to be a constant companion to him, and to be his Interpreter upon all occasions amongst strangers. And which is yet a more weighty concern: It would be their <p. 90> wisdom to project a match for the Deaf person, *man* or *woman* betimes; that the person they are to match with, may be trained up in Cheirology, which would add very much to the comfort of their life; they being thereby able to express and communicate their sentiments intelligibly, not only by Dactylology in the *light*, but also by Haptology in the *dark*.

In the second place I am obliged to shew the general usefulness and conveniency of this Art to all mankind. The particular cases wherein it may be convenient, are many more than can be expected, that I should instance in: I shall therefore mention only three generals. 1. Silence. 2. Secrecy. 3. Pleasure. In cases of necessary Silence, it may be useful to inferiors in the presence of Great persons; to those that are about sick people, as near relations, Nurses, &c. So for Secrecy, if people be in company, but not so near as to whisper one another in the Ear, it performs the office of whispering; it delivers, and receives secret messages, &c. And lastly for pleasure; it may be an ingenious and useful divertisement <p. 91> and pass-time for young people.

Here it may be objected, That all the conveniency will not ballance the pains that must be taken in learning this Art. This objection puts me in mind of another, and that a very considerable Conveniency; and therefore I answer. The pains that is taken about learning a Hand-language, if it were learned in due time, that is, in Childhood, would be so far from hindring, that it would contribute much to the Childs progress in learning to read, if he were taught both to know his letters, and to spell upon his fingers. This would please the Childs fancy, and imprint the letters the sooner upon his memory, having his

Book alwaies open before his Eyes. So that I look upon this as the greatest conveniency of Cheirology, That it would be of so great use, and learned with so
little pains.

And this consideration put me upon thinking of a more advisable way of
training up young ones, than any yet practised, that is: To begin children to
know their letters upon an Hand-book instead of an Horn-book; or at least to
<p. 92> have a Hand-book upon the backside of their Horn-book: For I make
no doubt but before they could come to know the names and Figures of the
letters, they would know their places upon the Hand, and be able to point to
them with the other, or the same Hand, as readily as to pronounce them with
the Tongue.

And who will not acknowledge that it were a thing desirable, and deservedly
to be esteemed as a peice of liberal education; to be able to speak as readily with
the hand as with the Tongue? And therefore who would not think it worth the
while, to train up young children from the a b c in Glossology and Cheirology,
pari passu? specially seeing the one is no hinderance but a considerable help to
the other, for I may truly say in the Poets words,

—— *Alterius nam*
Altera poscit opem res, & conjurat amice.[45]

I thought for the use of children, to have given some directions for facilitating the Elementary Discipline of knowing the letters, spelling, and reading;
whereby not only the old way might be <p. 93> made much smoother, but
also by one and the same labour, a considerable accession of useful knowledge
might be attained by the young Scholar: That is, together with reading in
Books, reading on the Hand; and as a necessary appendage of this, writing
upon, or speaking with (call it which you will) the Hand: whereas writing with
the Hand according to the common use of the word is by it self a distinct and
laborious Art. But I fear lest some may think that I have already stuft this discourse too much with trifles, and pedantry.

---

[45] 'So truly does each claim the other's help and form a friendly league with it' (Horace, *Ars Poetica*
410–11, in the context of a discussion as to whether a good poem is due to nature or to art).

AN APPENDIX
TO
DIDASCALOCOPHUS[46]

Containing

Some critical observations upon the
Nature and number of Double
and Trible Consonants.

Much hath been said by many learned men to describe the nature and causes of Simple Sounds, which are the first elements of Speech; as also of Diphthongs and Triphthongs (if any such be) coalescing or 2 or 3 Vowels into one Syllable: But of the coalition of two or more Consonants into one Syllable, little or nothing (for what I know) hath been said by any. And yet this composition of consonants deserves as much to be explained, or rather more <p. 96> than the other of vowels, because of its greater variety and use; Especially by him who would treat of a Philosophical Language or a Grammar for Deaf persons: So that my first Treatise of *Ars Signorum* or Sematology with this second of Didascalocophus[47] which is a legitimate offspring of that, obliged me to this enquiry.

If the Question should be put: whether in framing of words it were a more rational institution, that a single Consonant, and a single Vowel should alwaies succeed one another alternatly; or that there should be a mixture of Syllables allowed, made partly of Diphthongs, partly of double consonants? My own judgment in the case is. That both Nature and Art would make their first choice of an alternate succession of single Vowels and Consonants, and that their next choice would be, of such compounded vocal sounds, as are commonly called Diphthongs, and described by Grammarians; and such compounded close sounds, as are most natural and of an easy pronounciation, for describing of which this discourse is intended.

<p. 97>   But that such a Language could derive its origine from blinded Nature, and not from Art, or a Divine institution, is no waies probable: For I conceive that there is now no Language upon the face of the Earth in common use, but

---

[46] 'Didascalocophus' has been substituted for 'Cheirology' here, following the printed list of 'Errata' in the 1680 edition. Dalgarno clearly first intended to give *The Deaf and Dumb Man's Tutor* the general title of 'Cheirology' but changed his mind during the production of the volume. See Introduction, Sect. 5.1.

[47] Reading 'Didascalocophus' for 'Cheirology', following the errata list.

admits of a mixt composition of Diphthongs, and Double Consonants. And the more rude and uncivilized the people are, the more frequent this composition is with them, and the sounds the more harsh and unpleasant. That roughness of speech wears out with roughness of Manners, and smoothness of the one is a natural consequence of the smoothness of the other, the English Language and Nation is a sufficient proof. And if this be granted it is argument enough to prove; that Nature without Art or some more powerful assistance, would never bring forth a language in which there should be no Diphthongs or, Double Consonants. Nature, I say, as it is now in its degenerate estate: How she would have decided this Question in her primitive integrity and perfection, or rather how she did actually decide it, as we are assured from Gods word <p. 98> she did, cannot be otherwaies known to us, than by some probably conjectures.

It is generally thought by the learned, that *Adam* was the Author both by Invention and Practice of the Hebrew Tongue; not as we have it now in any of its Dialects; yet if it be granted that the Hebrew had for its mother that Language which *Adam* did invent and speak; we may with good reason conclude, that corrupted as it is, it still retains the substance and *Genius* of its Mother; There being some indelible Characters upon all Languages which common accidents cannot deface. For tho the tract of time from *Adam* to *Moses*, was longer than that from *Augustus*, or *Alexander* the Great, to this present age; yet the common accidents which are known to change a language could not be so many and effectual, for changing the first language to that which is now called Hebrew, as they have been known to be for changing the pure Greek, into that which now is used by a remnant of the Grecians, and called Modern Greek; or for changing the pure Latin *extant* in Classick Authors, into <p. 99> that which is now called Italian; which languages notwithstanding keep still so manifest Signatures of their origine, that it is easy to discern what Stem they are branches of.

Now amongst several other defaced reliques of that first and Divine language remaining not only in the Hebrew, but also to be found in many other of the Eastern Languages, this seems to be very considerable. That the Hebrew admits of no composition either of Vowels or Consonants in that same Syllable; But all their Radical words consist generally of a single consonant, and a single vowel, succeeding one another alternatly; which cannot well be supposed to be the effect either of degenerate Reason or Chance.

There are two things more in that ancient language which seems to me unaccountable without referring them to a supernatural cause. One is, that their radical words consist generally of 3 consonants, and for the most part are Dissyllables; and these Radical words how different soever in their consonants, yet have still the same points, *Cametz* and <p. 100> *Pathach*; which in oral prolation make the same vocal sound with א, which, as it is the first letter of their Alphabet, and from them in all other Languages; so is it the first vocal sound in Nature. And that originally all their words were Dissyllables (as some conjecture) is not improbable: whereas in all other Languages their

Radicals are generally Monosyllables, and I think originally have all been so; yea so far so, that there are many Monosyllables found to be *Composita*, and *Decomposita*, as the Learned *Doctor Wallis* has ingeniously observed in his English Grammar.[48]

Another thing is, that the Hebrew does often contract a whole sentence into one word, incorporating not only pronouns both prefixt and suffixt, but also prepositions and conjunctions with the radical word. And this *compendium* did first excite me to do something for improving the Art of Short-hand; That drove me before I was aware upon a real Character; That again after a little consideration resolved it self into an Effable language.[49] This at last has carried on my thoughts to <p. 101> consider of a way how a language may be attained by Reading and Writing, when it cannot be attained by Speaking and Hearing. So that this Series and chaine of thoughts has for its first link an Hebrew Grammatication.

I take notice of three things more in the Hebrew, which are considerable upon the account of a rational Institution, which is not to be found in the common usage of other Languages; but not so mysterious as the other three which I have already mentioned. The first is their separating the Vowels from the Consonants, both by place and Character; which has something Natural, and Symbolical in it: For there is something in the structure and composition of the words, analogous to *Man* the Author of them; the Characters of the consonants being of large dimensions, and divisible into many parts, represent the gross and material part of Man, the *Body*: the Vowels being exprest by indivisible pricks or points, do answer to that which is more properly indivisible, the *Soul*. This, together with a more accurate distinction of Vowels into <p. 102> long and short; as also a more accurate division of Consonants from their Physical causes, that is, the Organs of formation, tho of late use (according to some later writers) in that most ancient language; yet it shows (at least) how the *Genius* of the Tongue is fitted not only to comply with such an Institution; but also that from all Antiquity there have been some *vestigia* of that Primitive and Divine, or purely rational Sematology; taught by Almighty God, or invented by *Adam* before the fall (unless any should have the confidence to affirm, that this among many other unhappy consequences of the fall, was one; that it did not only in part deface, but totally wipe out all former impressions, leaving our first Parent as the blind Heathens would have him, *Mutum & turpe pecus*.[50] That is, having his Soul as much *Tabula rasa* as ours is when we come into the world) which have given occasion to Grammarians of later times to bring that part of Grammar to the present establishment. But whatever be the decision of that grand controversy about the antiquity of the <p. 103> Hebrew points, the

---

[48] See the discussion in Wallis (1653: ch. XIV, 'De Etymologia').

[49] The story of the origin and development of Dalgarno's universal language scheme is recounted in detail in 'The Autobiographical Treatise', (see below, Part IV).

[50] 'Dumb, shapeless beasts' (Horace, *Satirae* 1. 3. 100, with reference to the first animals created).

observation I have made here will still be considerable.[51] Wherefore I pass to a second thing considerable, which without all controversy is more ancient and of longer standing than some would have the points to be. It is agreed upon all hands that there are three principal and cardinal Vowels א י ו of as ancient a date as the first invention of letters; which without giving offence to those that are for, or advantage to those that are against the Antiquity of Points, may *sano sensu*, be styled *Matre Lectionis*; Because all other Vowels are but intermediate sounds and as it were the *Proles* or ofspring of these three. Wherefore, without interposing as to the main state of that so momentous question; That which I take notice of here as considerable, is this: That it has been a thing done with great care and judgment, the establishing these three letters for the Cardinal vowels or *Matres Lectionis*;[52] For they are the three most distinct vocal Sounds that are in nature; even as distinct as the two extremes and the middle of any thing that has dimensions can be; all other <p. 104> Vowels being but intermediate Sounds to, and gradually differing from them. א is a Guttural Sound, and of all other Vowels the most apert; ו is Labial and of Vocal Sounds the most contracted; י is Palatine and equally distant from both. And as it is possible that there might be a Language copious enough, allowing only the use of three Vowels, and secluding double Consonants in that same syllable, provided that the Radical words were Dissyllables; which some think to have been the Institution of the pure and uncorrupted Hebrew: So would such an institution be much more easy and distinct than any language in being; the intermediate sounds to these three radical vowels being less distinct, and therefore oftentimes giving occasion of mistakes.

I have had occasion to mention the third thing considerable in the preceding Treatise of Didascalocophus;[53] to wit, Their naming the simple Elements of letters by significant words; *Aleph*, *Beth*, *Gimel*, &c. which without doubt is as ancient as the use of letters, or at least as *Moses*; The truth of this the Grecians have confirmed <p. 105> by a very convincing, but withal a very inartificial argument in naming the letters corruptedly after them, *Alpha*, *Beta*, *Gamma*, &c. as I have noted before.

Tho I have in *Ars Signorum* given such an Analysis of simple Sounds, both Vowels and Consonants, as seemed to me proper upon that occasion; yet I must here repeat what has been said there of the nature and number of simple Consonants; otherwise the Rules of compounding I am to give, cannot be understood.[54]

Consonants then are first to be divided into, close [and] semiclose: 1. Close, when the appulse of the Organs stops all passage of breath thro the mouth;

---

[51] On the contemporary controversy concerning the antiquity of the Hebrew points, see David (1965).

[52] 'The basis of pronunciation.'   [53] Reading 'Didascalocophus' for 'Cheirology'.

[54] Cf. the discussion of speech sounds in *AS*, ch. 1, and at various points in Dalgarno's unpublished papers.

and they are in number 9, *m, b, p, n, d, t, ng,* Γ, *K,* This closure is again three-fold. 1. A perfect shutting of the lips and this produces *m, b, p,* 2. the fore part of the Tongue with the Palate, hence *n, d, t,* 3. the hinder-part of the Tongue with the Palat hence *ng,* Γ, *K.* These nine Consonants are capable of another threefold division, upon the account of a threefold accident which <p. 106> equally happens to the foresaid closure of the Organs respectively. For 1. if the breath and voice be *simul* and *semel*[55] stopt with the closure of the Organs, like the throwing of a stone against a Rock; this produces the 3 mutes *aP, aT, aK,* 2. If after the closure of the organs, a *conatus* of breathing be continued, and the repercussion of the breath from the passage stopt, making an inward murmuring like the breaking of a wave against a Rock, which is quickly spent and husht into silence; the same closure of organs produces the 3 Semimutes, *aB, aD, a*Γ. 3. If upon the closure of the organs, there be a free passage of breath and voice thro the Nose, like the sounding of an Organ-pipe, when the key is touched; this produces a third distinction of Sonorous letters from the same closure, *aM, aN, a NG,* (by *ng* I mean that sound which is heard in *anger, hunger* not in *danger, hinge.*) And these 3 sounds may be continued after the closure of the Organs, as long as one will. I have placed a vowel before these consonants, because their *power* appears more distinctly, than when the vowel follows.

<p. 107>   Hence I infer, that the number of close consonants is 9, neither more nor less; not more I say, because I find that some add 3 more, *hm, hm, hng,* calling them Mutes, making only this difference between them and, *m, n, mg,* that the one is uttered vocally, the other whisperingly:[56] But if a whispering and a vocal breath makes distinct letters, there will be more distinctions of letters than the Authors of this opinion seem to approve: and if this be reason enough to multiply letter, I know not but soft speaking, and crying about the Streets, may have the same power.[57] That certain other distinctions in the forming of these, or any other letters, may be fancied by curious and Musical ears, from the modes and degrees of shutting the organs, the intention and remission of the voice, the Tone being more grave, acute, &c. I readily grant: But how to make more distinctions from these 3 closures, plain and easy to be discerned, and worthy to be so far taken notice of, as to be placed in the Alphabet, is a thing I could never reach.

Again, I said no less than 9, because <p. 108> common custome has made one of these a double Consonant, writing it with two letters *ng* the sound of neither of which is to be heard in pronounciation; but a perfectly distinct simple sound from the power of both, as in *sing, ring, long,* and from all letters whatever. And it is observable that our English is very unconstant in expressing the power of this letter: sometimes by *ng* in the end of a word,

[55] 'Together and once.'   [56] Wilkins (1668: 367).
[57] Dalgarno is here employing Occam's razor so as to establish a distinction similar to that between phonetics and phonology in modern linguistic theory. For a contemporary discussion with a similar agenda, see Ray (1691).

as *sing, hang, long*; where nothing of the sound either of *n*, or *g* is heard; Sometimes by *n* alone before its brother consonants, *k, g*, before *k* every where; as *ink, rank, drunk*, before *g* in the middle of a word, as *longer, hunger*, tho not alwaies so, for in *danger, stranger* &c. *n* keeps its own power.

If any be so far prejudiced with the use of the Latin (which alwaies expresses the power of this letter by *n*) and other modern Languages; let him look a little higher to the Greek, where he will find three things considerable of this letter. 1. That it is no double consonant, but exprest with one single Character, γ. 2. That it is exprest not by a letter of a distinct <p. 109> tribe (as in the Latin) but by one of its own fraternity, that is, by a letter formed with the same closure of the organs with it self. 3. That it never goes before any other consonant in that same Syllable, but those of its own tribe γ, κ, χ, ξ, which is according to the true reason and Rules of compounding consonants in the end of a syllable, as I shall make appear by and by. The *Romans* finding that it was a sonorous letter, reject γ as being a Semi-mute, and substitute for it *n* agreeing with it formally in that same analogy of sound, but differing from it materially, as being formed by a distinct closure of Organs.

Great *Vossius* may excuse my being so long upon this one letter: For he after spending a whole Chapter upon it, concludes with a profest uncertainty of judgment, whether to make it a single letter, a *Sesquilitera*,[58] or a double consonant.[59] I thought once I had been singular in my opinion about it; But afterwards meeting with *Doctor Wallis's* English Grammar, I perceived that he had given the same account of it long before me.[60]

The Semiclose sounds are of two sorts, some of them are formed from the <p. 110> whole-close sounds and are called Aspirats, because they are formed by a partial opening of the Organs, and sending forth the breath thro the mouth; hence the number of them are six, *f, th, χ*, from *p, t, k*, and *v, th* (as in *that*) *gh*, from the Semi-mutes *b, d, g*; for there can be no aspirats from *m, n, ng*. 2. That nimble instrument of articulate voice, the top of the Tongue brings forth three more semiclose sounds *l, r, s*, and so doubles the number of letters formed by the other organs. 1. L is formed by a close appulse of the top of the Tongue to the palat, the sides not touching, but leaving an open passage, which distinguishes it from, *n*, where the appulse makes a perfect closure. 2. The appulse is from the sides of the Tongue the top not touching, but leaving an open passage to force out the breath; hence is formed the letter S. 3. A repeated or multiplyed appulse of the tongue to the palat, by a quick motion of trepidation which produces R. S, has affinity to the close mutes *p, t, k*, and therefore admits <p. 111> of being raised to a semimute, Z, both of which are capable of

[58] i.e. a letter and a half—the notation that Vossius gives consists of a nasal symbol 'N' together with a diacritic that indicates velarity.

[59] See Vossius (1635: bk. 1, ch. 20).

[60] See the section 'De Loquela' in Wallis (1972 [1653]: 158–62) and Kemp (1972: 56). Cf. Wilkins (1668: 367).

aspiration, as the close mutes and semimutes *Sh*, *Zh*. These seem to me to be all the simple consonants in nature perfectly distinct, and to be made use of in a Philosophical Language for which this was first intended. And I think that this Analysis of them from their Physical causes is plain & easy, for to pursue all the minute differences of sounds, as it were endless, so were it useless.

I come now to speak of compounding two or more consonants into one syllable, and that two waies, either in the beginning or end of it; a thing well to be considered by him who undertakes to frame a language by Art from the principles of Nature, and of no small use in fitting a Grammar for Deaf persons.

That I may proceed the more distinctly in this enquiry, I will begin with the definition of a Syllable, and passing by several other descriptions, I will keep to that of *Priscian* and approved by *Vossius*; as being most full and apposite to my purpose. *Syllaba est vox literalis, quae sub* <p. 112> *uno accentu, & uno spiritu indistanter profertur.*[61] Where I suppose by *sub uno accentu*, and *uno spiritu*, there can be no more than one Vowel or Diphthong in a Syllable; which as a *terminus communis* unites the extreme consonants on each side; Even as the *copula* units the Subject and the Predicate making one Proposition.

My first Rule shall be: To speak properly and in a strict sense, There can be no composition of Consonants amongst themselves, either in the beginning or end of a Syllable, but what is preternatural and inconsistent with the definition of a Syllable. Who does not perceive, that even in the composition of Mutes and Liquids in the beginning of a syllable as *prat*, *plot*, which of all compositions of consonants is most common, and also judged most easy, as not making the preceding Vowel long by position; yet I say even in those it is easy to perceive a *distantia terminorum*, and that they are united by a rapid spirit, as a *terminus communis*; and cannot possibly be otherwise, seeing they are formed by distinct closures of the <p. 113> organs; and therefore there must be a *Transitus* from the one to the other, which appears yet much more evident in the end of a syllable; with which kind of composition our English abounds very much as, *Table, ridle, sadle, little,* &c.

It is true in some compositions of consonants the *transitus* not being from organ to organ, but from one degree of vocality to another, as in *lamp*, *hand*, *ink*, the *transitus* here is so quick, that it may be said to deceive the Ears; much like the colours of the Rainbow to the Eye, as it is that ingenious description of *Arachnes* Web. *Ovid. Lib. 6. Met.*

> *In quo diversi niteant cum mille colores,*
> Tansitus *ipse tamen spectantia lumina fallit:*
> *Usq; adeo quod tangit idem est; tamen ultima distant.*[62]

---

[61] 'A syllable is a verbal sound which is produced as a unit under a single accent and with a single breath' (Vossius, 1635: bk. 2, ch. 1).

[62] '. . . though a thousand different colours shine in it, the eye cannot detect the change from each one to the next; so like appear the adjacent colours, but the extremes are plainly different' (Ovid, *Metamorphoses*, bk. 6, ll. 65–7).

But passing by the dictates of right reason and Art, which certainly have not been followed in the primary Institution of any language unless it be of the Hebrew alone; let us look to Use which is the Sovereign Lawgiver to all languages. And more particularly to the usage of the Greek, which gives laws of Orthography to all the Occidental Languages: and <p. 114> first for the compounding of Consonants in the beginning of a syllable.

Had the Grecians been as careless of Euphony and polishing their words in the terminations, as they have been in the initial syllables, their language had been as much inferior to some others in Euphony, as now it is esteemed more pleasant and graceful. What more rude sounds, uneasy to be pronounced, and harsh in the ear, then ψάλλω, ζάω, ξαίνω, χθών, φθίσις, πτῶσις, δνόφος, βδήλυγμα, μνῆμα, γνῶσις, κτῆμα, κνάκων, πνεῦμα, θνήσκω, τλήμων, &c. What cause to ascribe this to I am uncertain, whether to the rudeness of their language, together with others, in its first origine; or to some modish affectation of times and humors, or more particularly to a Poetical humor of Syncopizing and contracting their words, which seems to me most probable. But this we see is certain, that they have taken to themselves such a liberty of compounding Consonants in the beginning of a syllable, that their greatest admirers the *Romans* have forsaken them in this; there scarce being any such double consonants, as any in the fore-mentioned <p. 115> examples in the beginning of a word, in all the Latin Tongue; unless it be in some few words, which are manifestly of a Greek origin. They have gone so far, that almost no Rule can be formed for their initial Syllables, but *Quidlibet cum Quolibet*.[63] Howbeit I will endeavor to reduce the usage of the Greek in this particular to some General Rules.

First, *There is no double consonant to be found in the beginning of a Greek word, but one of them is a Lingual*: these are, n, d, t, l, r, s, z, th, θ, sh, zh. Hence I observe that *Vossius* goes too far, when he bids in imitation of the Greek to divide *a-gmen*, *te-gmen*; unless he could have produced authority for a short vowel before this position, or a word beginning with *gm*, neither of which I think can be found.

2. The liquids (commonly so called) *l*, *m*, *n*, *r*, add, *ng*, never come before other consonants, or one another in the beginning of a word, except μνάομαι.

3. *None of the close Consonants*,

Labials	⎧	p, b, m,
Linguals	⎨	t, d, n,
Gutterals.	⎩	ng, Γ, k,

<p. 116>

Or their aspirats.

Labials	⎧	φ, ν,
Linguals	⎨	θ, th,
Gutterals.	⎩	χ, gh,

---

[63] 'Anything with anything'; cf. the invocation of this motto in connection with compounding in *AS*, ch. 8.

If they be of the same Organ, can be compounded with one another. Except δν as δνόφος, θν, as θνήσκω. In these negatives the Latin, and I think other modern languages do agree with them.

For affirmative Rules the first shall be: *The liquids L, R, come frequently after the Mutes and Semimutes, with their aspirats* as,

πλέω	δράω
πρὸ	γλάφω
τρήω	γραῦς
τλῆμα	φλέβω
κλείω	φρουρέω
κραυγή	θλίβω
βλάπτω	θρέω
βρέμω	χλαμὺς
δλ—	χράομαι

The Rule is universally true *de jure*, tho not *de facto*; or, it is true *de generibus* <p. 117> *singulorum*, tho not *de singulis generum*.[64] Hence tho there be no δλεπω, yet analogy would bear it as well as βλέπω, or γλάφω. So in Latin, tho there be no words beginning with *tl*, yet *tlarus* would be as Analogical, as *clarus* or *planus*. So in English *tlash* were as Euphonick as *plash*, *clash*.

2. *S, in the beginning of a word comes before all kinds of Consonants in that same Syllable*; i.e. it is compounded with *Genera singulorum*, tho not with *Singula Generum*.

1. For the Mutes *p*, *t*, *k*, and their aspirats φ, θ, χ, it is compounded with them all; as, σπάω, σύπτω, σκέπτω, σφεῖς, σθενοσ, σχῆμα. 2. The Semimutes β, δ, γ, it is only found with β, as σβέννυμαι; and by the Dorick Dialect with δ, as κωμάσδω for κωμάζω. 3. Of the Sonorous or Nasales μ, γ, γγ, it is found only with μ, as σμέρδω. *S.* is not to be found before any of these three consonants in Latin, unless it be in words taken from the Greek; and yet our English abounds with examples both of *sm*, and *sn*, as *small*, *smooth*, *smite*, *snatch*, *snow*.

Except from the former Rule, its two sister-semiclose linguals, *r*, *l*, before which <p. 118> it never comes in Greek or Latin; Tho *sl* frequently in English, as *sleep*, *slow*; and tho *s* it self comes not before *r* yet its aspirate *sh* is found with *r* as *shrine*, *shrewd*.

3. *S* in the beginning of a word comes after some both of the Mutes and Semimutes, *de facto* and therefore might come after them all *eodem jure*, ψ, ζ, ξ, i.e. *ps*, *ds*, *ks*. Here it comes after two Mutes, *k*, *p*, and one Semimute, *d*. The reason in Nature were the same for *bs*, *gs*, *ts*, in the beginning of a Syllable; but *s* after any other Consonant in the beginning of a Syllable sounds harsh, and

---

[64] 'The rule is true for general classes of individual cases, but not for every individual case within each class.'

layes a force upon nature. What could induce the Grecians to single out these three double Consonants ψ, ζ, ξ, contracting them into one single Character, and placing them in the Alphabet amongst the simple Elements of letters, is not easy to guess. Had they made a more soft and melting sound than other double consonants, this might have past for a tolerable Reason; But the case is quite contrary; for they make a stronger position after a short vowel than many other double consonants do: or if frequency of use had been the induce-
<p. 119>ment this also had been tolerable; but even in this they must give place to many other double consonants: unless perhaps it may be thought, that the frequency of ψ and ξ in the future tenses of Verbs might have occasioned this abbreviation. *Vossius* guesses at the Origin of ψ, that it has been an imitation of the Hebrew צ.[65] If he had made ζ and ξ to be of the same origine, his conjecture had been by much the more probable; for there is fully as great reason for these as for that. The affinity of ξ to צ is all one with ψ to צ; for both of them are compounded of S following a Mute. Again the affinity of ζ to צ is no less, for tho the one be mute, the other Semimute; yet they belong both to one organ of formation, which the Hebrews take notice of as the greater affinity: so that if an imitation of the Hebrew pass for a probable reason of this Grammatication, it is much more likely, that a threefold abbreviation would induce them to this imitation, sooner than a single one; specially considering that *s* never follows another consonant in composition in the beginning <p. 120> of a word, but in these three. I might add that the Hebrew Grammarians will scarce allow צ to be a double Consonant, tho I dare not undertake to defend them in this.

My next Rule shall be for trible Consonants in the beginning of a word. 1. *There can no word begin with three consonants but where* s *is one.* This is not only true in Greek and Latin, but I think also in our vulgar Europæan Languages. 2. *S, never makes a triple consonant in the beginning of a word, but with a mute and liquid following*; And this but rarely in Greek, as σπλην, στλεγγὶς, στρατὸς; so in Latin, as *scribo, spretus, stratus*; Tho the composition of *s* with any either single or double consonant in the beginning of a word, seems to be of no difficult pronounciation. And now I come to double and Triple consonants in the end of a Syllable.

I think our English Tongue with its Mother Saxon, abounds more with this kind of closure or ending of words, with double and triple Consonants, than any other common Language; which makes us censured by neighboring Nations, by comparing our pronounciation to the <p. 121> barking of Dogs: For our words being for the most part Monosyllables, and often ending with a harsh collision of double and trible consonants, and admitting no Apostrophe; this makes us take the more time, and use the more force to utter them.

---

[65] Vossius (1635: bk. 1, ch. 21).

1. *The most natural and easy composition of Consonants, either in the beginning or ending of a Syllable, is that of the Mutes and Semimutes, following the Sonorous letters of their own respective organs of formation*; as in these examples.

mb	*Lamb, dumb, comb,*
mp	*lamp, imp, lump,*
nd	*hand, blind, round,*
nt	*Ant, hint, hunt,*
ngg	*thing, long, dung,*
ngk	*think, rank, drunk.*

2. *The composition of two consonants next for facility to the former, is when the three semiclose linguals, l, r, s, come before other consonants in the end of the syllable.* Examples in English are obvious: It is true, not of these three coming before *all* other letters; yet the reason is the same for all, tho use be not. <p. 122>

3. *S in the end of a word, according to the use of our English, makes a double consonant after any other letter, unless it be after q, z.* Other double consonants there are in the end of a word; but being very irregular and of a harsh sound, I pass them by; such, as, *soft, length, right, apt,* &c.

4. *For trible Consonants in the end of a syllable there is none found in any language but where S makes one.* I know the *Dutch* write **Handt**, but I suppose they must pronounce either *hand* or *hant*; for a mute and semimute of that same organ are inconsistent sounds. And as for our *strength*, and *length*; 1. Tho they be written with four consonants; yet we sound but two neither of which can be written in English, but with two Characters; But 2ly, I think the most genuin pronounciation of these two words is, as if they were written *strenth* and *lenth* according to the Northern Dialect.

5. *And lastly, allowing two s s in two distinct places* (which often happens) *there may be, and are de facto, in English four consonants after a vowel in that same syllable,* as in *firsts, thirsts.*

<p. 123>   This doctrine of double and trible consonants so far as concerns the ending of words, has but little place in the learned languages; yet examples are found both in Greek and Latin, even of Trible consonants; as λάρυγξ, *stirps*. Where observe that there are no words in Greek ending either in double or trible consonants, but where *s* either virtually or expressly is the last; and but very few in Latin ending in other double Consonants; Some in *nt* as *amant sunt*, some few in *ne*, as *hinc hunc*, in *st*, as *est post*.

My last enquiry about double Consonants shall be. How many may come together in one syllable? To which I answer. First, if we follow reason & the Authority of the ancientest language, there can come no more than two, one before and another after the vowel. 2ly If we follow the usage of the other two learned languages Greek and Latin; secluding the letter *s*, there can be no syllable of above four consonants, two before, and two after the Vowel. 3ly Admitting *s*, which comes both before and after most letters, there may be a syllable of six consonants, three <p. 124> before and three after the vowel.

I grant there is no example found either in Latin or Greek of above five consonants; yet there are many examples in both of three consonants in the beginning, as στρατός, scribo; so of three in the end, as σαρξ, *stirps*, whatever is above this, is harsh and Barbarous.

I have heard learned men of the Polish Nation affirm, that there is a Monosyllable of nine letters in that Language, the Orthography of which I took from the hand of a person of Honor of that Nation,[66] thus *Chrzaszcz*. This word I have often heard pronounced by Natives, and have my self been commended by them for my imitation: But to strangers it seems a barbarous sound, and reaches not the expressing of the power of all the letters with which it is written. *Vossius* affirms as much of the *Dutch*. The word he instances in is, **t'strengst**. But I am sure if this be allowed for a Monosyllable, there may be a monosyllable of eleven letters, according to the Analogy both of the *Dutch* and *English*; or rather I may say, that there can be no bounds set to the Tongue in this particular. For, first <p. 125> if **t'strengst**, why not **st'strengst**; for it is clear even from the same instance, that *s* may come before *t* in that same syllable. If it be said that the letter *s* cannot be repeated thrice, in distinct places of that same syllable. First, I answer by retorting; much less can *t* be repeated thrice, as here; for laying this one word aside, I think it will be hard either to prove by reason, or to bring another instance out of any language whatever, where a word consisting of three *t t t* disjoyned from one another by the intervention of other letters is esteemed a monosyllable. 2ly The Analogy of the English allows of such a Monosyllable, as *Spasms, Schisms*.

Again if **ststrengst** why not **ststrengsts**, and so *in infinitum*. That *s* after *t* is consistent in the end of a syllable, our English abounds with Examples, as *Tasts, fasts*. But here it is observable that this composition we admit of, *s* coming both before and after another Consonant in the end of a syllable, is very harsh and uneasy, and scarce to be found in any other language. The *French* make many shifts to avoid <p. 126> the harshness of *s* either before or after another consonant, and chiefly in the end of a syllable: if *s* go before, they leave it out, as in *haste, viste*; if it comes after they leave out the consonant that goes before it; as in *loups, animaux*. Another thing observable of *s* with its affinis *l*; when they come alone without the implication of other consonants: they are of an easy and graceful pronounciation. *Homer* seems to have loved them, as in these,

Αλλα συ σησιν εχε φρεσι——
——Ενι φρεσι βαλλεο σησι.[67]

---

[66] This person may with some certainty be identified as Faustus Morstyn, the Polish nobleman who first introduced Dalgarno to Hartlib; see Introduction, Sect. 2.1.

[67] Two formulaic phrases: 'but keep (this) in your mind' (Homer, *Iliad* ii. 33); 'cast (this) in your mind' (ibid. 1, 297; cf. i. 607; xxi. 94).

That the Press should have stript these broken ends of Verses of the unnecessary and troublesome luggage of Spirits and Accents, is neither the Compositor nor the Correctors fault: I am obliged to excuse them and take the fault, if there be any, upon my self; or rather lay it over upon the Author; who were he alive, he would excuse both me and himself, by the Use of the times he lived in: and *use* we know is the supreme Law in all languages. But if all this do not satisfy the Critical Hellenist; Them I must add further, that *Use* in the present case, will even dare to <p. 127> appeal to right Reason: For whatever may be said for the cumbersome tackling of Spirits and Accents in Prose; yet in a Verse, Accents are down-right non-sense, unless it be *tollendæ ambiguitatis causa*[68] in æquivocal words.

That all other Appendages beside the letters are unnecessary and troublesome, I shall instance only in one word, which is so overgrown with the Rickets, that the Head is much greater than the whole Body; for whereas the letters of the word are but three, the other appurtenances of it are five: And had it all that swelling furniture about it in the Glossology, which it hath in the Typology, it would choke one to pronounce it. But he must have more critical Ears than mine, that can perceive five distinctions in ἔῤῥ which are not to be heard in our English ERR. that this is not a word either made or sought by me, appears by this passage of a common Epigram.

$$\epsilon\rho\rho\epsilon\ \pi o\theta'\ a\delta\eta\nu$$
$$\overset{\prime\prime}{\epsilon}\overset{\epsilon}{\rho}\overset{\prime\prime}{\rho}\ \epsilon\pi\epsilon\iota\ \epsilon\psi\epsilon\upsilon\sigma\omega\ \pi a\tau\rho\iota\delta a\ \kappa a\iota\ \gamma\epsilon\nu\epsilon\tau a\upsilon^{69}$$

And here I shall take the liberty to go one step further out of my road, by taking <p. 128> notice that the Grecians have lasht out a little too far, in that which is thought to be the greatest grace of their language: That is, *their words ending much in Vowels and Diphthongs; and these frequently making* pure *syllables, one, two, or more, without the intervention of a Consonant.* One, two, or at most[70] three, one would think were enough for Euphony; but four, five, or sometimes six in the end of a word, I think is too much; specially, if they make so many syllables, ἀργύρου τόξου sounds well; ἀργυρέου βιοὺ is yet more soft and melting; and ἀργυρέοιο βιοῖο sounds high and lofty from the mouth of a Poet, and Symbolizeth with the more Symbolical Hemistich preceding it.

$$\text{———}\varDelta\epsilon\iota\nu\eta\ \delta\epsilon\ \kappa\lambda a\gamma\gamma\eta\ \gamma\epsilon\nu\epsilon\tau'\ a\rho\gamma\upsilon\rho\epsilon o\iota o\ \beta\iota o\iota o.^{71}$$

But βιοῖο and by a Dialysis βιοῐο, is too soft and lushious. And for *ææa* and βοῶo, I know not what other censure to pass on them, but that they are childish and ridiculous Traulisms. It is true that βοῶo, in the Typology of the word, has its Syllables distinct enough; but the best can be said of it will leave

---

68 'For the purpose of removing ambiguity.'
69 'Go to hell! Off with you, since you have deceived your fatherland and your begetter' (anon.).
70 Reading 'most' for 'least', following the printed Errata of the 1680 edition.
71 'Terrible was the twang of the silver bow' (Homer, *Iliad* i. 49).

them too identical in the Glossology. Again for *ÆÆÆ*, which <p. 133[72]> is the word of the greatest number of vowels without a consonant, that I have happened to meet with; tho it be manifestly of a Greek origin, yet I know now where to father it upon any Greek Author, *totidem literis & syllabis*:[73] which makes me strange the more to see the grave and Manly *Roman*, who in his imitation of the effeminate *Greculus*, hath with a wonderful judgment, shall I say or happiness, equally avoided the extremes of too much harshness in the beginning of his words, and too much softness and delicacy in the end of them; yet in this one word to have outdone him in number of vowels, tho not of syllables. *Ovid*, is my Author for this. *Metamorph. lib.* 4.

Nec tenet ÆÆÆ genetrix pulcherrima Circes.[74]

But to return from this digression to another observation upon the letters, L, and S. These two letters seem to me to make a great impression upon the body of the French tongue (as the particles and chiefly the pronouns do in all languages) because of their so frequent use in the *pro-vocabula* of that language. I have often been pleasantly affected to hear two talking <p. 134> *French*, when the pronominal words recurred often; such as, *ce, cett, c'est cettui, cettuici, cettuila, lui, celui, icelui, elle, icelle, celleci, cellece*, &c. and many such like descending from the fruitful stock of *ca & la*: for these words comming from a French mouth, make a pretty soft whispering noise affecting the Ear pleasantly. Our own English pronominal words are none of the most graceful pronounciation, chiefly because of the so frequent use of *th* as *thou, thy, that, the, this, those, their*, &c. This makes Outlandish men call us *blæsi*, the sound of *th* never being heard amongst them, but by lispers; who pronounce *s* vitiously by the power of this letter. I will conclude with rectifying an Universal mistake of all that have written of Grammar, for want of considering the Nature of double consonants. It has past for currant amongst all Grammarians, that we are to divide words in all other Languages, following the use of double Consonants among the Grecians; as, *ma-gnus, do-ctus, le-ctus, a-ptus*, and not *mag-nus, doc-tus, lec-tus, ap-tus*, Vossius goes yet further (as I have had occasion to <p. 135> mention before) and bids us divide *se-gmen a-gmen*; tho their be no precedent for this in Greek. One Ancient Grammarian goes yet a step further, and bids follow this Rule even in compounded words; as *o-bruo, o-bligo*, which notwithstanding others do except. But *Priscian* does well refute this Authors opinion by this argument, That Poets never used these syllables short; So that for the very same reason, we must not divide *le-ctus, do-ctus*, because they are used still long by position.

---

[72] The pagination of the 1680 edition jumps at this point from 128 to 133 and following.
[73] 'In as many letters and syllables.'
[74] 'nec te Clymeneque Rhodosque | nec tenet Aeaeae genetrix pulcherrima Circes' (Neither Clymere seems fair to you, nor the maid of Rhodes, nor Aeaean Circes' mother, though most beautiful) (Ovid, *Metamorphoses* 4. 205).

Tho this reason be convincing enough; yet there is another reason worthy to be mentioned in this place, which also illustrates and confirms what I have said before: that the primitive words of other languages (excepting the Hebrew) are for the most part Monosyllables. In all primitive words I distinguish between radical and servile letters: the radical part of the word generally both in Greek and Latin is effable in one syllable, *amo, doceo; am* and *doc* are the radical letters, *o* in the one and *eo* in the other being serviles; and so changeable in the oblique <p. 136> inflexion of the words, therefore I think it were reasonable in dividing the word to distinguish between what is radical, and what is servile.

Post-Script

Tho I make no question, but I have said as much as may enable any person of ordinary capacity, with extraordinary diligence, to become if not a Didascalocophus, as least a Hypodidascalus to some more expert Master; yet my main design being not so much to make every Grammaticaster a Didascalocophus, as to satisfy learned men, that Cophology is none, either of the ἔργον ἀδυνάτων, or δυσνοήτων;[75] This has made me the shorter in the practical part. So that any practitioner in this Art, not more Master of it than my self, must be beholding to me for some more particular directions. Wherefore if any Philocophus should challenge my self, to make good the Title of my book: let him bring a Subject duely qualified, male or female, the younger the better; and he shall find me ready to answer his challenge, either personally or by proxy.

---

[75] 'Neither impossible nor unfamiliar works.'

PART IV

DALGARNO'S UNPUBLISHED PAPERS

Unpublished Paper 1

The Autobiographical Treatise

THE AUTOBIOGRAPHICAL TREATISE <fo. 20ʳ>

Tho most Arts owe their Invention more to chance than a deseigned search, yet the History of so lucky a chance [is] so acceptable to learned men, that where it is neglected, they complaine of it as an irrecoverable loss. This consideration has obliged to give a brief relation of the first occasion of *Ars Signorum*, together with my first rude thoughts upon that subject, and further progress of them to the stop I made in publishing that treatise, as also some reflexions I have made upon [it] since.

It happened that in the year 165[7][1] there came a man to Oxford who profest to teach the Art of short-hand and, as was pretended, much more compendiously than any that had bin Masters of that Art before him. I understood that way of Short-writing which was commonly practised, and from it had contrived a more compendious way (as I conceived) for my own use. This made me have the curiosity to make enquiry wherin this man had exeeded others. After therefore I had understood his way, I perceived the man to be ingenious, and that he had made a Collection of many commone phrases, for expressing of which he had contrived a more compendious way than any I had seen. This gave me occasion to compare the labours of several men for perfecting this Art and to apply myself if possible to advance it a step further, and to remedy some defects I perceived in all the ways of that Art I had seen. And in my first attempt to that purpose, the Hebrew Language, which at that tyme was my study, <fo. 21ʳ> afforded me great light, which not only encouraged me with assurance of good success in the prosecution of my present deseign, but also became an open doore to lead me in to discover a more Universal way of writting, which at that tyme I was so far from seeking, that I never had heard nor read any thing of it. And after I had found it by chance and by the by in the prosecution of another enquiry, I knew not how to name it.

I perceived then in the Hebrew, that the most part of the particles in the contexture of words were joyned to the primary Radical by way of affixes and suffixes, so that one word in that language many tymes could not be rendered into another language [in] under 4 or 5 words. This consideration suggested to me that the like might be done for the more compendious writting of English, viz, to make a collection of the particles, and so to order them that they might be exprest by points, some before and others after the principal word of the

---

From MS 162, Christ Church, Oxford. On the foliation of the MS, see the Textual Note. The heading has been added by the editors.

[1] The year of the decade is left blank in the MS, but can be supplied by a letter from Faustus Morstyn to Hartlib dated 11 Apr. 1657 (Hartlib MS 49/22/1) concerning the recent arrival of the brachygrapher and Dalgarno's attempts to improve his shorthand system. See Introduction, Sect. 2.1.

sentence as their nature required, even so as the vowels are to be exprest in Shorthand, partly by points and partly by distinct places about the principal letter of the word.

But here a great difficulty did occurre, how to distinguish these points, when they were put literally for vowels, and when they were put realy for the notions of Particles. I laboured much to overcome this difficulty, but all was in vain. At last having <fo. 22ʳ> run over all the Topicks of Invention, I perceived that there was no other way of remedying this evil, but to use these points realy for particles with such Characters as were Real and not literal, for some few such real Characters signifying things of most comone and frequent use are used in the commone way of Short-Hand. But these were so very few, and for the most part such as the particles had little dependence upon, that this new Rule for compendizing the particles seemed to be of little use, and scarce worth the while to be taken notice of or practised. Yet this compendium, upon the first discovery of it, seemed so pregnant and promising, and did so much affect me, that I could not lay it aside, till I had spent more thoughts about it, the final result of which was this. That the particles for the most part accompany Verbs, and verbs, of commone use in familiare and ordinary discourse, are not very numerous. Therefore to make a collection of such verbs, and to assign distinct Characters to each of them, not literal but Real, with those at least the [Particles]² might be exprest by points and places without confounding them with the points assigned to vowels by the commone Rules of Shorthand, which are alwise placed about Literal Characters, and this I thought would make a considerable improvement of the way of compendious writting.

Having therefore run over a Dictionary and excerpted such verbs as I thought proper for my deseign, when I looked back upon the Collection I had made, I was again discouraged to see a heap of words, for which I thought <fo. 23ʳ> it would be difficult to provide easy and distinct Characters; and thoe this were done, yet they would be a great burden to the memory. However, I resolved, being now so deeply plunged in this gulfe, not to give over till I had dived to the bottom if there were any. The first thing that offered itself to my thoughts, to guide me out of this Labyrinth, was the excellency and usefulness of the thred of order by which I perceived that at once the confusion of this Chaos might be remedied, and also the memory much eased. Here again I was at a stand what method of many that offered themselves to follow, whether: 1. The Alphabetical order of the words,³ or 2. if I should distribute them under certaine commone Heads as Junius in his *Nomenclature* and Comenius in his *Janua Ling[uarum]*,⁴ or 3. if I should order them in a predicamental series of

---

² The MS has 'Particulars': clearly a scribal slip for 'Particles'.

³ The alphabetical ordering was used in Beck (1657), on which Dalgarno commented unfavourably in a letter to Hartlib dated 20 Apr. 1657 (BL Add. MS 4377, fo. 148 (see below, Part V)).

⁴ Cf. Junius (1577) and Comenius (1631). Dalgarno understood Comenius to be working on a universal language scheme, as indicated in his letter to Hartlib of 3 Nov. 1659 (Hartlib MSS 42/7/1 (see below, Part V)).

Genus, Species and difference, or 4. and lastly, if neglecting all affinity either of words or things I should use an artificial Method as more subservient to the Memory in dealing with a multitude of loose and inconherent words. After some tryals made of other wayes, I concluded this [last way] would be the best for my present purpose. To mention all the rubs I met with, and how I was often forced to take my throw againe, would make me transgress the bounds of that brevity is here intended.

Having made this progress, I began to gather up my loose papers, as so many scattered limbs about me, and to piece them together on one side of a sheet of paper, ranging a numerous collection of particles above for a Frontispiece to be exprest by <fo. 24ʳ> points and places, and a considerable collection of Integrall words under them, for which I had provided the simplest and easiest Characters that I could think of.

{[*from* fo. 23ᵛ] After the whole piece was finished, at first lifting up of my eys upon it, I pleased myself at least with this: that what ever Monsterous shapes were in the lower part of it [yet] was it in my judgment then, and afterwards owned to be so by others, *Mulier formosa superne.*[5] But when I began with greater attention to contemplate it in all its aspects,}[6] on a sudden I was struck with such a complicated passion of admiration, fear, hope and joy, that it would need a more skilfull hand than my own to paint it upon paper; and therefore if any desire to see the Picture of this Passion drawn to the lyfe, in orient colors and by an excellent Artist, let him read the story of the passionate lover Cherea in Terence *Eunuchus*, where he'l finde that to be the Allegory of this. I seemed to myself to sie, thoe at a distance and darkly, and as it were throw a veil, a *nova figura oris*,[7] of so inviting a beauty, that after I had personated Cherea in the first Scene, I was lyke to act the unfortunate Narcissus in the last, for I had not one houres natural rest for the 3 following nights together.

But in one word to unriddle this Allegory more plainly, I perceived that that which I had deseigned only for English, was equally applicable to any Language whatsoever, {[*from* fo. 23ᵛ] lyke some pictures that looke to every body that look to it.} And thoe the scheme I had before me was not comprehensive of all the Notions of comone discourse, yet some few more additions might make it comprehensive of all that Artists understand by *corpus orationis*, so that I did clearly see by comparing what I had <fo. 25ʳ> done with what was as yet wanting, that the body of Language, by which I understand the comone notions of familiar and ordinary intercourse and dayly use in *vita communi*, secluding terms of Art and the numerous species of Natural bodies, might be exhibited both Dictionary and Grammar upon one face of a sheet of paper.

---

[5] Cf. Horace, *Ars Poetica* 4: '... ut turpiter atrum / Desinat in piscem mulier formosa superne' (Make what at the top was a beautiful woman have an ugly ending in a black fish's tail).

[6] This insert replaces: 'This done, I applyed myself with great attention of mynde to contemplate this Scheme which had bin the product of so great pains. In this fixedness of mynde . . .'.

[7] 'An utterly different face' (Terence, *Eunuchus* 317).

When I had recovered myself out of this Maze, finding that I had unawares killed two birds with one stone, or to use a more Illustrating Simile, that by courting the waiting maide I had won the faire Lady, who seemed now to put off her veil and with open face to afford me a smile, I resolved to continue my due respects to both. Therefore my next care was to cast my Scheme into a new mould. I enlarged the Tables or Dictionary, partly by adding more primitive and Radical words, and partly by enlarging their signification by the affixing of Transcendental particles. I made provision for Analogy and necessary Grammatications, yet so as to keep within the bounds of the Notions of commone discourse, and still to carry on my first deseign of Short-Hand.

The work being now this far matured, by the advyce of an old Skool-fellow who was then the only acquaintance I had in Oxford, I discovered my thoughts to Dr Owen at that tyme Vice-Chancellour,[8] with whom this man was in great favour. Dr Owen, assoon as he look't upon my Tables, told me that the deseign I had in hands was an Universal Character; but for his own part he would <fo. 26ʳ> not take upon him to judge of my labours, but would recommend me to one, to whose judgment he would trust, naming Dr Ward, then professor of Astronomy, now Lord Bishop of Sarum.

He upon my first address to him received me courteously and dealt very generously and openly with me. He told me he lyket well of what I had done, adding further that I had imparted a deseign that it were an easy matter for him to wrong me in, but assured me with repeated protestations that he would not wrong me in the least but would be my friend and encourag me so far as to become my Scholar and recommend me to others, and he was as good as his word. And as a further proof of his candour and ingenuity he imparted to me (which I conceived he did partly if not wholly to free me from all suspicion of looking upon him as a rival) a Collection he had made of the Species of Natural bodies, in order to the fitting of Real Characters for them, and was so free as to put his papers in my hands to peruse. To all this he added another favour in advysing me to become acquainted (which he offered to mediate if I thought good) with Reverend and Learned Author of the *Essay towards an Universal Character and Philosophical Language*,[9] giving me such a Character of his worth and learning which almost seemed to me incredible. But afterwards I knew by my own experience that it was nothing more than was deserved. But still he added this caution, that I should doe nothing rashly, or against <fo. 27ʳ> my own inclinations upon his persuasion, assuring me that he would keep my secret in his own brest from all men living, without my own consent to the contrary. I thanked him for his good counsel, and prayd him that he would be pleased to comunicate the papers I left in his hand to his Learned friend.

---

[8] John Owen (1616–83) was vice-chancellor of Oxford from 1652 to 1658.
[9] John Wilkins (1614–72), author of the *Essay*, is never referred to by name throughout the present treatise, for reasons that emerge below.

It happened that the first tyme I saw this great man was casualy walking the streets, where meeting him and Dr Ward he made a stop, for Dr Ward had told him who I was. All that past then beside Salutation was barely this: that he had seen my papers and was so well pleased with them that he would present my labours to the supreme powers of the nation,[10] and that he should be glad to see me at Wadham College.

I was overjoyed at so favourable a providence, that I was lyke to have the Authority of two so eminent persons to make myself and my deseign known, for both of us were as yet great strangers at Oxford.

When I came to Wadham College, Mr Wardan made [me] welcome and for conveniency of having me nearer him invited me to battle in the College, giving privileges not usual, and frequently invited me to his own table. He honoured me lykewise by listing himself amongst the number of my Scholars, and recommended me to many others [of] his friends and acquaintance, among whom I am obliged to place in the first <fo. 28ʳ> rank the Honourable and famous Mr Boyle as one of my most bountifull.[11]

But of all my Scholars Mr Wardan was the greatest proficient, for out of his singulare curiosity he took more paines than they all to understand me. Soon after, when I had resolved to make it publick by professing to teach it, he desired me to provide a copy of my Tables to be presented to a company of learned men that met frequently at his lodgings, for the same ends that the Royal Society at London, and the *conventus curiosorum* at Oxford propose to themselves. There were present at this meeting a company of learned [men], most of which yet alive, and all of them have either left or will leave behinde them such monuments of learning as will make their names famous to posterity. They all of them comended the whole contrivance, but chiefly insisted upon the ordering and reducing the particles,[12] acknowleging that this was the Key of the whole discovery, for want of which all that ever had bin or would be attempted upon this Subject must be unsuccessfull.

Here, I think it not impertinent to take notice that to secure me the more against the cavills and obloquies of incredulous and prejudiced persons, who for want of due consideration prest severe censures upon me that I was a Monster-Monger and obtruded them upon credulous persons; as also satisfy others that are not so rash as to disbelieve and condemn evry thing impossible, even thoe at <fo. 29ʳ> first appearance it may seem so to them, but rather to have their curiosity excited to enquire into and examine what is proposed; for these reasons I desired to have a Testimony from the hands of this loving

[10] Wilkins was one of those, along with Richard Love, Seth Ward, John Wallis, and William Dillingham, who were instrumental in obtaining for Dalgarno a letter of recommendation from Charles II, which was printed in *AS*.

[11] Robert Boyle's financial support is acknowledged in the printed lists of sponsors both in the early broadsheets (BL Add. MS 4377, fos. 139ʳ, 157ʳ (see above, Part I, Broadsheets 4 and 5)) and in *AS*.

[12] Cf. *AS*, ch. X.

and learned couple, which they readily granted. The Original was written by Mr Wardans own hand and both of them put their names to it, the Copy wherof followes:[13]

. . . .

<fo. 30ʳ> After I had conversed with this learned man for a considerable tyme, and fully opened up my whole minde to him, laying before him the whole series and progress of my thoughts by producing all the rude and unpolished papers that I had blotted upon that Subject, he began to suggest that my Tables were not full, more particularly defective in the predicament of Substance, having made no provision for the Species of Natural bodies. He was very urgent with me to apply myself to make up this defect and he was so zealous for hastening the work and so much concerned for this part of it that he offered his assistance in drawing up a Scheme of Natural bodies, which he did and put into my hands. But when I had perused it and perceived that it quite destroy the principles that I had laid down to myself to be guided by, specially it did thwart that which was my grand principle, to finde out the shortest, easiest and distinctest Medium of communication for the commone use of all mankinde, I returned it, excusing myselff that I reverenced his judgment but could not goe against the dictates of my own.

Wee argued the case often but without conviction on either side. My Lord of Sarum did hear our reasons on both sides but was not free to interpose. I was willing and offered so much, for preventing a breach which [I] forsaw would prejudice the deseign much and me more in the profite I promised myself from it, in things of arbitrary institution {[*from* fo. 30ᵛ] to submitt to his judgment, but this was not thought submission enough. Hence followed a perfect and declared breach of judgment, though not of friendship, for I conversed with him a long tyme after this, somtymes personally and sometymes by letters, as familiar as ever before.}[14]

<fo. 31ʳ> If any suspect the truth of this relation let him consult the Author of the *Essay*'s Epistle to the reader, where he will finde the same account for substance with this; neither (I hope) will any censure me of immodesty for affirming the person of one described anonymously there by an obscure circumlocution, for not vanity and ostentation but truth and necessity have forced me to doe soe.

After this Breach was noysed abroad I founde that all my former and great hopes and expectations for a reward of my labours were almost quite defeated. Both Scholars and benefactors fell off; some civilly excusing themselves that they would come in, some to learn, others to put to their encouraging hand,

[13] The remainder of the page is left blank in the MS. The testimony from Ward and Wilkins is mentioned by Dalgarno in a letter to Hartlib dated 20 Apr. 1657 (BL Add. MS 4377, fo. 148ᵛ (see Part V)), but no copy appears to be extant.

[14] This insert replaces: 'to submitt to his judgment: But this was not thought submission, neither was I free in this matter to submitt any further. And therefore from this followed a final and declared breach of judgment, but not of friendship for I conversed with him a long tyme after this somtymes personally and somtymes by letters as familiarly as ever before.'

when they should see the deseigne established by the approbation of learned men, especially of one great man who had taken more paines to understand it than others and was a more competent judge than others; others again that knew not the truth censuring me for a plagiary.

This disappointment discouraged me much, and caused me to make haste <fo. 32ʳ> to cast it lyke an abortive out of my hands.

Yet this comforted me again, that I should no [*sic*] lay it down.

The suspicion of my being a plagiary was much encreased by [a] book of Dr Owen's, who above all men living was obliged in honour and conscience to doe me right because he was the first man to whom I had disclosed my secret, and that not upon the account of his Learning, but his Authority by which he was obliged to doe me justice. In this book (and his books were much read in these tymes) he told the world, that an Universal Character so much talked of and desired was now ready to be published by a person of known abilitys, naming the Author of the *Essay* without mentioning any thing of my labours.[15] It happened about this tyme that I had an occasion to goe down into Scotland for about a quarter of a year. At my return I was told of Dr Owens Booke and how he had served me in it. I took an occasion to complain to him that he had not done me that justice which I had cause to expect from him above all other men. His answer was, that he had heard that I had given [up] the deseign and gone down to Scotland, but that he knew as well as he knew that 3 and 4 make seven, that if I had [not] crackt the shell, others had never come to the kernel.

Yet under all these unexpected disappointments and discouragments this <fo. 33ʳ> did at least comfort me that I should not lay it down dishonourably.

I have already given an account by what chance I fell upon a Dumb Character; now I come to that part of the Relation which concerns the second part of the discovery, that is, how I chanced (for I must confess all was chance) to make this Dumb Character vocal by turning it into a Language.

And here in the first place it is well to be observed that there is a near affinity and cognation between these two. They are not only *Germani* but *Gemelli*; both the sons of Jupiter, not Hercules and Iphicles, but Castor and Pollux, *eodem ovo prognati*, living and dying by turns, serving humane Society interchangeably, the one the ey the other the Ear.

Now for clearing my way to this narrative I must resume and enlarge upon some particulars I have formerly touched. I mentioned 4 ways of Method to which I reduced the Radical words of my Tables. The first two were scarce

---

[15] Cf. Owen (1659: 277): 'Speaking lately with a worthy learned friend, Dr Wilkins, Ward: of Wad. Col., about an *universall Character*, which hath been mentioned by many, attempted by divers, and by him brought to that perfection, as will doubtlesse yield much, if not universall satisfaction unto learned and prudent men, when he shall be pleased to communicate his thoughts upon it to the world . . .'.

capable to admitt the Institution of a Language, at least with any tolerable shew of Art. The last two were equally and excellently fitted for that purpose, thoe [for] no such matter deseigned. The method I was pursuing <fo. 34ʳ> then was not the predicamental way of genus, species and difference, which now appears in my Tables[16] as my last choyce, but the Technick way taken up in imitation of the other and in all respects the same with it as to the Instituting and applying a Character either Real and immediate or mediat and vocal, which distinction has not that *fundamentum in re* that many doe erroneously imagine.

This Technick way[17] was briefly this; 1. I had reduced the whole Collection of Radical words I had made to the number (as I remember) of 17 or 18 Strophes or Stanza's which answered to so many Genus's in the predicamental way. 2. Every Strophe consisted of seven lynes or verses. This answered againe to the Generical differences in the predicamental way. 3. Evry lyne contained 6 Radical words distinguished by a different letter from the expletive and arbitrary words which connected them into a sentence. For evry Strophe I had provided a Radical Character capable of 7 distinct marks for distinguishing the 7 lines, and these markes [were] to be diversified 6 wayes for the 6 Radical words of each line, all which is clearly exemplified *mutatis mutandis* in the Shorter Tables of the *Essay*[18] for I did not goe to the charge of founding a new Character. All the difference between the Character which I used and that to be seen there, [is that] myne is perpendicular, that is Horizontal.[19]

This done and having occasion to consult the Table often, for greater expedition and conveniency of naming them, which could not be done by the dumb Character which I had provided, <fo. 35ʳ> I resolved therefor to imitate the Mathematicians, who name all their lines and Angles in their operations by Alphabetical letters, by naming my Stanza's and lynes at first from letters appropriated to them. This I did at first by using letters according to the inartificial order they are placed in our Alphabet. I had gone but a little way in contriving this expedient when I perceived that by making an Artificial distribution and choyce of letters I could name evry Stanza by a consonant, evry lyne by a vowel or diphthong, and evry radical word againe by a consonant; so that by joyning the Characteristical letter of the Stanza, the vowel deseigning the lyne, and againe the consonant noting the Radical word of the lyne, there did result from this contrivance a Triliteral Monosyllable, guiding me as it were an Index to the Stanza, line and word of the line; e.g. supposing I had

---

[16] i.e. in the tables of *AS*, which are arranged in predicamental order (Method 3), in contrast to the tables of the earlier broadsheet (BL Add. MS 4377, fos. 145ʳ-146ᵛ (see above, Part I, Broadsheet 2)), which are arranged in mnenomic verses (Method 4).

[17] A fuller explanation of the earlier scheme is contained in the letter to Pell, Dec. 1657 (BL Add. MS 4377, fos. 150ʳ-152ʳ (see below, Part V)); Pell's notes and comments are preserved in BL Add. MS 4377, fos. 158ʳ-161ʳ.

[18] Cf. the 'Summary of Directions both for the Character and the Language' in the fold-out 'Shorter Tables' of Wilkins (1668), attached between pages 442 and 443.

[19] Cf. Dalgarno's characters entered by hand in his broadsheet tables (BL Add. MS 4377, fo. 145) and illustrated in his letter to Pell (BL Add. MS 4377, fo. 151ʳ) with those of Wilkins (1668: 387-8).

followed the Alphabetical order of letters (which I did not) then *Bad* was the first Stanza, first line, and third word; *dog* was [third] Stanza, fourth line, fifth word.[20] The same might have bin done by syllables, so that according to the Institution *Bad* will be *Babadi*, *dog* will be *didigu*.[21] Where single consonants failed to begin a word I made use of double, and encreased the number of vowels by adding diphthongs. This further advance and improvement of my first thoughts pleased myself as much as it displeased others, whose reasons I shal consider hereafter.[22] <fo. 36ʳ>

It was near a quarter of a year after my first acquaintance with the Author of the *Essay* that I started this new notion of a Language. And when I communicated it first to him (as I concealed nothing that came into my thoughts upon that Subject from him) he was so incredulous, that if I had not given him proofs of lucky hits in things of that nature he would have slighted it. But it is easy for any one to see from what had bin said, that the bare producing of my Tables as formerly described was sufficient to unriddle the matter to one of a meaner apprehension. I forbear to speak of his judgment in this particulare till its proper place when I have finished the Historical part of this discourse, which I now hasten to doe.

After the breach of judgment formerly mentioned between this great man and me, I saw a necessity of betaking myself to another province. Yet that I might not lay this down dishonourably, being to deliver it up to so brave a successor, I resolved to rally my forces, and having corried all the frontiers and outworks so succesfully, to *invadere ipsam Arcem causae*[23] and give my last assault. When I had sumoned in all my best thoughts, the summe of that consultation was this. That hitherto the hope of gaine had had a great influence upon {[*from* fo. 35ᵛ] and bin the confusion of } my thoughts. Now this hope

---

[20] Annotations along these lines, which appear to be in Dalgarno's hand, are preserved in the copy of the tables in the Bodleian Library (Wood 276 a 20). Phonetic values are there assigned as follows:

Stanza	1	2	3	4	5	6	7	8	9	10	11	12	13
	A	B	D	F	G	L	M	N	P	R	S	T	BR

Line	1	2	3	4	5	6	7
	A	E	I	O	U	Y	OI

Word	1	2	3	4	5	6
	B	C	D	F	G	L

Thus B-A-D = stanza 1, line 1, word 3; D-O-G = stanza 3 (not 1 as in the MS), line 4, word 5. (Following the printed tables, B-A-D would represent the radical meaning 'place', and D-O-G the radical meaning 'flourishing').

[21] Using syllables, phonetic values would be assigned as follows:

Stanza/Line/Word	1	2	3	4	5	6	7	etc.
	Ba	Ce	Di	Fo	Gu	Ly	Moi	etc.

The equivalent of B-A-D (stanza 1, line 1, word 3) by this method is thus Ba-Ba-Di. The equivalent of D-O-G (stanza 3, line 4, word 5) should correspondingly be Di-Fo-Gu, and not Di-Di-Gu as in the MS.

[22] Cf. the comment later in the treatise, fos. 70ʳ ff.

[23] Cf. Cicero, *Epistolae ad Familiares* 1. 9. 8: 'Num potui magis in arcem illius causae invadere' (Could I have more uncompromisingly invaded the very stronghold of the triumvirs' party).

being dasht, it highly concerned me to look into my selfe, that I might not at least suffer in my reputation, which I reckoned much the greater loss. Therefore beginning now as it were to take new measures of the whole deseign, <fo. 37ʳ> the first thing I suggested to myself here was to examin narrowly, not it the Goldsmiths but the Philosophers Scales, whether Shorthand, which I had carried alwise in my ey, did consist with the shortest medium of communication, which was the grand quaesitum. The decision of this question in the Negative brought with it a new light which convinced me that that part of the deseign which seemed both to myself and others to be most firmly established was quite to be pulled to pieces and put into a new frame. The *Mulier formosa superne*[24] was now to be metamorphosed into a *Barbatus Philosophus*. The reason of this great change was brought from two Rules I had laid down as fundamental principles: 1. That in a Philosophical Language no redundancy is to be admitted. 2. That evry Radical word must be a noun Substantive, or rather signifying the notion of the thing indefinitely. Both which rules are grounded in that well known maxime, *Entia non sunt multiplicanda* [*praeter necessitatem*], which challenges to itself a more peculiar right in our present case.[25]

Short-Hand required the particles, both separate and most properly so called as also the Transcendentall, to be provided for by distinct marks from the Integrals. Philosophy teach[es] that they ought not to be so, but that all the particles as the[y] derive their signification from the integrals so they ought their Signs. The logical part of speech lying chiefly in the particles, it adds much to the force and weight of periods and channels of reasoning to see plainly in the words themselves whence these nervous parts of <fo. 38ʳ> discourse proceeds: as for instance, *quando, nunquam, semper,* &c. are good compendiums of speech, but redundancys and illogical.[26]

I am obliged to discuss this nice point it being my last push, and *nodus vindice dignus*[27] with more accuracy. It is therefore to be observed that to speak strictly and logically there is no such thing in nature as a primitive and underived particle, but are all of them contrived for compendiums of speech, as the literal points in Shorthand and the Real points in an Universal Character, first thought of by me and now rejected, are in writing. To this purpose its worth the observation that Logicians styling the particles *Syncategoremata* teach us that they belong to the predicamental series of things only reductive. They might have said as well deductive, that is, as they are *ex parte rei* but modale variations of the predicamental Notion, so *ex parte Signi* they ought to be

---

[24] Horace, *Ars Poetica* 4 (cited above, n. 5).

[25] 'Entities are not to be multiplied beyond necessity.' Occam's razor, which Dalgarno invokes elsewhere as a fundamental principle in both grammatical and phonological analysis, is particularly appropriate in the present context, since *Ens* is the superordinate category in the predicamental series.

[26] Cf. *AS* 80.

[27] 'Nec deus intersit, nisi dignus vindice nodus inciderit' (Neither should a god intervene, unless a knot befalls that is worthy of his interference) (Horace, *Ars Poetica* 191).

inflexions of the Radical word. Hence the rule in *Ars Signorum* is for particles that can be exprest in one word, the Radical word, without any addition, is to signify as a particle, ex. gr. the Radical words for *Cause, Instrument, Matter, efficient, end,* &c., having no more but barely the Radical letters in them stand for, *because, with, out of, by, to the end that,* &c.[28] The reason of this Institution was partly to avoid an unnecessary redundancy of words, partly for emphatical-ness of signification, the words having express marks stampt upon them of their natural origine, <fo. 39ʳ> partly to Symbolize with the indefinite and as it were mutilate nature of these notions, for throughout the Table of Accidents, which are the proper fountains from which the particles are derived, the bare radical word[s] without inflexion signify the notion indefinitely, and the modale variations of Substantive, adjective, active, passive, &c. are made off by terminations.

All therefore that can be said for providing distinct Signs for the particles having no relation to nor dependance upon the Integrals is the conveniency of gaining tyme and saving labour in speaking and writting. But to this it is Answered: that somthing indeed is got in writting, but nothing in speaking; but to take so far notice of this petty conveniency, as to set it up for a principle to be guided by in the Institution of a Rational Language is below a Philosopher. Did it contribute any thing to shorten the work of the minde as well as of the hand, I should be by all means for following that way. But so far is it from easing the labour of the minde that it layes a double burden upon the memory by obliging it to learn two distinct words for one thing, so that in effect this compendium of the Hand is a dispendium of the minde.

This new modelling of the particles was the only considerable change which I made in my Tables upon this last review. The success I had here made me press forward hard but I found that I was come to a *nil ultra.* Here therefore I made <fo. 40ʳ> a stop, and after bemoaning myself and my unfortunate labors I made all haste possible to forme that model of them which appears in *Ars Signorum.* Others may wonder to see one so unskilfull in the present Universal Language of the world to venture upon setting up a new one in its place. But to me it is a wonder, when I reflect upon the way of my education, how I could adventure then to putt my thoughts upon this or any other Subject. Many objected to me that I was too young a man for so great an undertaking. The little acquired knowledge I had went little further than Hurtado, Arriago, Oviedo &c., and some other Schoolmen of the same stamp.[29] As for those books called Classical Authors, I had heard of them but had very small acquaint-ance with them. But to leave this Apologizing for the outside, that which is the greatest wonder to me, when I strip it naked and wander all over it with my most

---

[28] Cf. *AS* 83. Thus, for example, the radical in the Table of Accidents under 'causa', SAS, occurs also in the list of particles as equivalent to 'propter', etc.

[29] i.e. Petrus Hurtado de Mendoza (1578–1651), Rodericus de Arriaga (1592–1667), and Franciscus de Oviedo (1602–51) (cf. Risse 1964).

piercing thoughts, I cannot yet after the experience of near 30 years, and sieing the accurate thoughts of other learned men that have followed upon the same argument, I say for all this, I cannot discern any considerable blemish in *Ars Signorum*, but remaine still fixed in the same judgment, wherof I was then.

Some Alterations (I confess) may be made in the Table of Radicals; some more may be taken in, some left out, and others <fo. 41ʳ> transposed, and this is all the change that I can approve of.

There is one necessary accomplishment of this deseign, which, thoe extrinsic and accessary, yet requires great care and judgment and one well skilled in Philology to labour in it. That is the reducing of the words of other Languages to the Tables of this. And in this the Author of the *Essay* was so happy as to have the assistance of a person so excellently qualified for this Taske, that whoever hereafter engages in that deseign will find himself much obliged to the accurate and judicious labour of that learned man in the English Dictionary placed after the Tables of the *Essay*. This learned person was then Mr Floyd Commoner Master in Wadham College, now Lord Bishop of St Asaph, to whom for his favours I have bin often obliged, more particularly for honouring me in taking the name of my Scholar.[30]

I have now done with the Historical part of this discourse; I come in the next place to compare the Method of *Ars Signorum* with that of the *Essay*. The end I doe this for is to recommend this neglected, and (by many) contemned piece of knowledge to all cordial lovers of learning and well-willers to mankind; and to invite and encourage such as are qualified to put their helping hand to finish the superstructure, when so fair a foundation is laid. And let us for once suppose that the world will never be so wise in my opinion, or so great fools in <fo. 42ʳ> the opinion of others as to receive it, yet let me suppose withal that no considering man will deny, but the Theory of this Art, secluding practice, is as rational a speculation as many other parts of Philosophy which have bin and are daily cultivated by learned and grave men. Let me add further, that it is a worthy undertaking to convince the incredulous, that the *Literati* of Mankind in following ages may be happy if they will in having a medium of commun-ication by many degrees both more easy for commone, and more fitted for learning and learned converse than any Language since the confusion. So that this added to the most ancient invention of writting and the late improving of that Art by printing, I know not what more can be Instrumentally desired for the perfecting and propagating humane learning, and contracting an Universal acquaintance amongst mankinde.

Another reason of this undertaking is because the Author of the *Essay*, thoe he hath declared his different from *Ars Signorum* in the number of Radicals and actualy dissents from it in many other particulars, giving no reason for his

---

[30] William Lloyd, who prepared the dictionary printed as an appendix to Wilkins' *Essay* (1668), is listed as one of the sponsors of *AS*.

so doing further than is to be gathered from the thing done, I think it well usefull to enquire after the reasons of this dissent *hinc inde*, that others may be the better able to judge what comes nearest to the truth. And if both be found to miss the mark, yet it may give an occasion of a luckier hit to a third person. <fo. 43ʳ>

To make way for the first thing I intend to observe, I will premise, that I have often taken notice of a commone failing in the works of ingenious men: that for setting off some specious and pretty fancy of their own, they have laid a force upon nature to follow them in tricking up their beloved darling, and this is somtymes so far pursued that one may clearly see the poets lordship of *Delphinum Sylvis*, and *fluctibus aprum*.[31] I shal [goe] no further for instances than *Ars Signorum* as it was first revealed and the present establishment of the *Essay*. The joyning of Short-Hand to an Universal Character was preternatural, and consequently a Monster in Philosophy. So the stating of the number of Radical words in a Philosophical Language from a full enumeration of genus, difference and species in a predicamental series of things seems to me, with submission to better judgments, too large a foundation for building a Language upon. The specifically distinct roots planted in the great wood of Nature, even thoe all know by us, are too numerous to be followed by any Language of humane Institution. Humane frailty is scarce able to count them all distinctly and keep them clear, much less to imitate nature in the Institution and bearing in mind so great a multitude of Arbitrary Signs, were it possible to find words or Characters that signify φυσει and not θεσει, then our knowledge of Things and words should be of equal extent. <fo. 44ʳ> But nature itself and the commone dictates of right reason have taught men that the number of words must not answer the number of things that are in the world, but that this invincible difficulty is to be remidyd by Analogy, in composition and derivation, and circumlocution, by which a few Radicals may be infinitly multiplyd and reach all the Notions both of Nature and Art that wee have any knowledge of. {[*from* fo. 43ᵛ] And here 'tis to our purpose that all Languages when they come to call out the notions of any numerous Tribe either in Nature or Art, when they find the Tribe subdivided in families all the persons of each family, that is all the species under their several Genus's, are named by the father or the genus with the addition of some distinguishing accident.} I doe not think that any Language in the world has so many as 3000 Radicals, as Grammarians and Criticks define a Radical;[32] but if wee grant that all aequivocal words make as many Radicals as they have diverse Interpretations, and that all inflexions wanting analogy doe multiply the words into so many

---

[31] 'delphinium silvis appingit, fluctibus aprum' (he adds a dolphin to the woods, a boar to the waves) (Horace, *Ars Poetica* 30).

[32] Cf. the discussion in Wilkins (1668: 450–4), where Wilkins claims that his language, having 3,000 radicals, will be easier to learn than a language such as Latin, which he estimates as having 30,000.

Radicals, which sense, reason but chiefly memory assures us that it is so; then it is evident enough that some Languages have above a 100000 Radicals.

I expected, because this was a controverted point as he confesses himself, that he should have given some reasons of his judgment in differing from what I proposed. It is true that judicious persons may suggest somthing of reason to themselves from the bare comparing of our tables. Yet the thing being new, and but few that will take the paines to compare the Tables so accurately as to pass judgment in the case, I will therefor, as far as I can, call to minde what reasoning past between us upon this point.

First then he suggested, as bin said page [30^r],[33] to order all the Species of natural bodys predicamentaly <fo. 45^r> and then to sute Radical Characters and words for each of them so ordered. I told him that I had resolved at first setting out to keep within the bounds of that which I called the body of a Language and not to medle as yet these appurtenances which would swell my Tables to such a Bulk as to discourage any to learn it. He urged that if I did so I would fall under the censure of learned men for putting forth a lame deseign, and so have it taken out of my hands by others. To this I answered, it could not be called a lame deseign, for I intended to make it comprehensive of the notions of some select and choyce author {[*from* fo. 44^v] wherin there was variety of matter} , and as I was deliberating what author to chuse My Lord of Sarum did either advyse or approve (I remember not whether of the two) of pitching upon the Bible. Beside, I would take care that the foundation I laid should be fitted to bear all the superstructure that be advysed. All this did not satisfy, but still he prest further, that in a Philosophical Language that part was not to be omitted that was most capable of a Philosophical Institution. To this I replyed that it was not ignorance but prudence made me omitt only *in presens tempus*. When I saw that there was no satisfying of him but by that of the deseign in its full latitude and using that Tables which he with great paines [had] drawn up for me, I was forced at last to open up my [mind] to him and tell him that I was not free in judgment to follow that method he proposed in making all the Species of Natural bodies radical. He took no offence at this, but to bring me to be of his opinion he reasoned thus. That a Philosophical <fo. 46^r> Language should containe a regulare enumeration according to the received Theory of all the Notions of nature and Art, that so the Lexicon of Radicals might be a Synopsis or Index of the whole Encyclopedy or Arts digested in a Predicamental Series. To this I returned several things. Firstly, that I doubted much if the nature of things were capable of that predicamental exactness, or if they were, if any one single man, or society of men, could presume to be either so wise or so happy as to finde this out to that perfection as to have all mankinde to subscribe to their judgment. But secondly, suppose this possible from the Nature of things, yet 1. an exact and full predicament

[33] The MS has a blank for the cross-reference to be added; cf. fo. 30^r.

will still be impossible from their number: the distinct Species of Natural bodies; the same may be said of bodies factitious (I mean all natural bodies having the Characters of Art imprest upon them, which require method and distinct appellations no less then the other, and therfore I see no reason why Philosophers should exclude them from their Categories); add to this the minute differences of things from their modes and respects varying infinitly; all which render this undertaking in its full latitude impossible. But because it may be thought that such a nicety as this might have bin spared, therfore 2. supposing a stop be made and wee proceed no further but to those notions of things which [have] bin described and taken for single terms in theire appellations, even those will amount to so many thousands that it were ridiculous to attempt to build a Language <fo. 47ʳ> upon so large a foundation. This even to imitate the people of China, for other nations can use 24 letters to as good purpose as they doe 24 thousand or nearly double that number. As he therfore that first founde out the way to resolve all articulate sounds of humane voice into 24 letters according to the vulgar account deserved well of mankinde, so my judgment has alwise bin that he that shews himself so good a philosopher as to state the fewest Notions of things, which in my opinion should be the *Genera* and *communes rationes rerum*, and so skilfull a Grammarian to fitt radical words, which in my opinion again must be short, distinct and Euphonical, {[*from* fo. 46ᵛ] and then from this stated number of things and words, by the fewest and plainest Rules of Analogy and Grammare to deduce the appellations of the numerous proles of inferior notions by derivation, composition and often tymes circumlocution of more words than one, I say he that does this skillfully has laid the best foundation for a Philosophical Language. Neither is it to be thought strange that a Philosophical Language should allow of periphrasis, for necessity has obliged all Languages to doe so,}[34] neither can Art devise a Language free from this necessity. Thoe I must add that a Philosophical Language built upon such a foundation as I have described, thoe it admitt of periphrasis, and in many cases when other Languages serve their use with one word, yet will it not only come even with them, but have the odds by far in using the compendium of one word in other places, where they must use two or more.

His last and (I must confess) his strongest reasoning upon this debate <fo. 48ʳ> was this. If it were possible to give accurat definitions of the Species of Natural bodies and hence to take their names he would be fully of my judgment. But sieing the formes of things, if there were any such, were unknown to us, and therefore there could be no definitions by essential differences by this Hypothesis; or if these formes were nothing else, according to that which

---

[34] This insert replaces: 'which may be a firm foundation for the numerous inferior proles of things by deducing their appelations from these few Radicals following analogy in derivation, composition and often tymes circumlocation of more words than one, which necessity has obliged all languages to doe'.

is called new philosophy which he seemed to encline to, but a multitude of modes of matter Constituting the Species, their definitions would be [too] long for the purpose of Instituting Radical words, and therefore it seemed most rational to put them in predicamental rank and file, and give them their names by instituting such words and Characters as might denote their numerical place and order.

To this I returned for answer, in the first place, that a full collection of all the specifically distinct {[*from* fo. 47ᵛ] (I mean according to the commone theory)} notions of Nature and Art predicamentally methodized, {[*from* fo. 47ᵛ] many wherof have bin treated of in the commone Systems, and some as yet wanting that care,} was in my own opinion to be reckoned among the desiderata of learning. And let me add by the by, which may be to purpose thoe not much to the present purpose, that from the confused Idea I forme to myself of such Tables done with due skill and care, they might be made as usefull ornaments to a Skolars Study as Globes and universal maps.[35] But that this was not the proper foundation for the Radicals of a Language I offered these reasons.

<fo. 47ᵛ>   Secondly, I granted that essential definitions by formal differences expressable in one or few words seemed to be, if possible at all from the nature of things, yet to be above the reach of human skill, and so impracticable in our present case. But I would by no means grant that numerical order (let the order be never so clear) was to be admitted for the specifical differences in case where our grand business was to ease memory, but that the difference best known to us was to be made out by some distinguishing accident [rather] than with essential forms. Let examples clear the matter. That plant which from its figure is commonly called fox taile: *Ars Signorum* thinks that *Plant Fox taile* is better defined for the use of memory, than *Gramineouse plant not used by men for food, first of the second paire.*[36] The lyke may be said of Mouse taile, feather grass, hairy grass, quaking grass &c. under that same difference in the *Essay*, as also of many other Species of natural bodies, stones, metalls, animals, in which its agreed by the commone consent of mankinde not to give primitive words, but compounded, taken from such distinguishing accidents are as most obvious to our senses. [For this way] of giving names to things appears sufficiently warranted by the great Examples 1. of Almighty God giving Adam his name, 2. of that great and perfect Philosopher Adam in the state of innocency giving names to all living creatures, and 3. the practice of all mankind, all Languages known to us (neither do at the least doubt of others) following this Institution less or more imitating nature and yielding to necessity. Neither has the *Essay* bin able to <fo. 48ᵛ> overcome this necessity; for it cannot be denied but there

---

[35] Five botanical tables, based on Wilkins (1668) and 'fitted to hang up in the manner of maps', were made by Andrew Paschall in 1678. In a letter to Aubrey he suggests that such tables 'might become a fine ornament for summerhouses & very usefull for any that delight in that pleasant piece of knowledge [i.e. Wilkins's real character]' (see Turner 1978).
[36] Cf. Wilkins (1668: 73).

are many Species of Nature omitted, perhaps more than taken notice of, whose names must either follow the Institution of *Ars Signorum* or all pass under one of the ineffable Mysteries of nature. But these institutions shall [be] more fully exemplified page [77ʳ ff.],[37] from which it will be easy by comparing to pass judgment upon this grande controverted point.

Thirdly, I excepted that this provision made the Radicals too numerous, <fo. 49ʳ> there being no Language in the world that had so many. But to this objection, so far as it concerned a Philosophical Language compared with other Languages, there was a clear and full answer at hand. That there was a vast difference between the Radicals of this Language and those of other Languages, for 1. the Radicals of other Languages, according to the true notion of a Radical given page [44ʳ],[38] will far surmount the number of Radicals stated here; 2. and chiefly, there is no reason at all can be given for the Institution of the Radicals of other Languages, but here, after the Arbitrary Institution of a few Generical words and Characters all the rest are by rational inference deduced from them {[*from* fo. 48ᵛ] and so are not *signa ad placitum.*}

But al this did not satisfy, for I had this further to urge: that the keeping of the numerical order and places of things in minde was of all other things most uneasy for the memory, especialy where the things so to be remembered were many, which was the case here. To this it was answered that the reason of the order appearing in the Larger Tables did facilitate the work of the memory much. To this it was replyed: 1. that thoe where the reason of the order did appear clearly the memory was much eased in remembering a few things in their numerical order, yet this would not hold proportionally in greater numbers; 2. it is evident enough that the reason of the order that appears in the Tables of the *Essay*, thoe done with great Art and judgment, is not alwise so clear as to guide infallibly to the numerical place. And thoe such an uncontroverted clearness of method could be found, yet still it lays so uneasy a Taske upon the Learner <fo. 50ʳ> by obliging him to move from one set of Numbers to another and from that to a third, lyke Theseus with his thred seeking his way from post to post, that it quite tyres him out, and finds it easyer in the end to trust to the strength of Natural memory. This prevailed so far with the Author of the *Essay*, thoe not to retrench the number of Radicals, yet to give a caution to learners not to committ them to memory from their numerical order, but from their Signification, page 441.[39]

And I remember that My Lord of Sarum, when this point was a debating, thoe alwyse he forbore to interpose his judgment, yet he declared that if one

---

[37] The MS has a blank for a cross reference to be added; cf. fos. 77ʳ ff.

[38] The MS has a blank for a cross reference to be added; cf. fo. 44ʳ.

[39] Wilkins (1668: 441), in the chapter on 'Directions for the more easie learning of this character', says: 'the Differences belonging to each Genus . . . though they are in the Character expressed by that numerical institution of First, Second, and Third &c., yet are they to be committed to memory from their real signification.'

should name some one of the ten comandments, he could not readily tell its numerical order in the Decalogue. I know the reasons that have bin brought here against the Method of the *Essay* may be retorted upon *Ars Signorum*. But yet thoe it must be confest to, so they doe not pinche so much here as there, 1. because of the great disproportion in the number of Radicals, 2. because *Ars Signorum* is more capable of an artificial and subsidiary help for memory than the *Essay*, by linking its Radicals together in Sentences, which was done in the first Essay of it[40] as has bin said, and had come first with the double advantage of natural and artificial order had not the Edition bin precipitated for reasons formerly mentioned. There are some parts of the *Essay* at least, namely plants and insects [and] fishes, that these mnemonick sentences will make but poore sense.

<fo. 51ʳ>   There are two inconveniencies more that follow the method of the *Essay* yet are avoided by *Ars Signorum*. First, if one be to learn one or two words only out of differences that contain 10, 12 or more, as falls out often in plants and elsewhere, he quite loses the reason of the institution so far as concerns the Species, see page ____.[41] Secondly, if there be any single Species omitted, as cannot be denyed but many are omitted, these Species when known cannot be provided for in the Tables without disturbing the order of the other Species under that difference to which they are to be reduced.

My last and strongest argument (as I conceive) against the method of the *Essay* is because it burdens the memory much more then *Ars Signorum*. The best way I judge to prove this will be by appealing to experience. I will not here transcrib the whole Tables and compare them but only add some few examples from which it may be easy to judge of the case.[42]

. . . .

<fo. 52ʳ> Now having dispatcht the Grand difference between the Tables of the *Essay* and *Ars Signorum*, the lesser differences (if they may be so called, for some of them seem to me no less considerable then that which first caused the breach) come now in the next place to be discoursed of.

All the tyme I conversed with this learned man, he objected but little against either the number or method of my Tables of Accidents. But after a declared diversity of judgment about the Table of Substance, he engaged into the Table of Accidents. But of his labours in this part of the work I never saw nor heard any thing till I saw them in print, and then I perceived that the distance of our thoughts was near as wide in this as in the other. I have alwise thought and acknowledged that the number of Radicals might be augmented in my Table of accidents, and perhaps some placed there left out, yet am I far from thinking that they should amount to the number stated in the *Essay*.

[40] i.e. in Dalgarno's broadsheet tables.
[41] Dalgarno was presumably intending to add a page reference to Wilkins's section on plants (1668: 67–120).
[42] The remainder of the page is left blank, presumably for examples to be added later.

If it should be asked how I would have these supernumerary Radicals provided for, I answer that some of them are Synonymous and so no provision to be made for such. And for others that are not so they are to be made off from Notions truly Radical by Derivation, Composition and Periphrases. There is one whole Genus in the Tables of the *Essay*, to wit that of diseases, which by the Authors own concession may be spared, see page 351.[43] There are two Genus's more, Possessions and Provisions, which for the most part to be left out.[44] Wee ought to be sparing in making the works of Art Radical for the same reasons which have bin brought against <fo. 53ᶜ> the making the Species of Natural bodies Radical, and those that are for their being Radical must by a parity of reason allow a much fuller collection of the works of Art to be Radically provided for in the Tables. My own opinion [is] that from a few Generical Radicals the Species are to be made off from their figure, matter, use &c. There is a whole Difference under the Genus of Motion put redundantly, namely the 4th.[45] There it is evident that the Notion of Purging added to the parts or matter to be purged does fully and distinctly express the particular Motions there Radicaly provided for as distinct Species.

Beside this Redundancy, I find also many Synonymous Radicals in the Tables of Accidents, which is less Tolerable than the other in a Philosophical Language. For this, compare the Genus's of Natural power, Habit, and Spiritual action, more particularly in the Radicals, Strength, power, Sprightliness, Sagacity, Sobriety, Seriousness, gentleness, Moderation, Stoutness, Hardiness, faith, love, hope, Salvation.[46]

When I consider the Learned Authors maine Scope to be the accurate Stating the Number and order of all the Idea's and Notions wee [have] of things in this world, I doe not so much admire to finde the Task redundant in order to Grammatical deseign as to finde a deficiency in one place which above all others ought to have bin full, I mean the Topick of the causes. I can not finde by the Tables of the *Essay* to express a *Malefactor* or *sinner deserves punishment*. This I mention, not as if I thought to procede <fo. 54ᶜ> much less of judgment, but to Apologize for my own oversight of this notion.

Thoe there be many greater and sadder Instances of the weakness of humane understanding that ought to beat down all high thoughts of mens own abilities {[*from* fo. 53ᵛ] and to keep them humble} yet have I bin much affected to sie two proposing themselves that same end, and at first setting out agrieing about the means to compass it, and yet at last to be so much divided. This

---

[43] 'It may likewise deserve some farther inquiry, whether some of these particles here nominated may not be spared to make room for others; as . . . Flowers, Fruits, Disease, &c.' (Wilkins 1668: 351).
[44] Cf. Wilkins (1668: 254–63).   [45] Cf. ibid. 241.
[46] Cf. ibid. (pp. 195–232), where the radicals Dalgarno lists can each be found under more than one heading, e.g. 'gentleness' is listed: (a) under 'natural power/ tempers of the spirit/ 4' (p. 197); (b) under 'habit/ affections of intellectual vertue/ 4' (p. 202); and (c) under 'manners/ vertue/ 9' (p. 207).

I mention because in a late treatise of near affinity with this I promised to give some reasons why an Universal Character so much desired by the learned of former ages when discovered and brought to light and to greater perfection too than ever was thought possible, yet should meet with so cold entertainment by the learned of the present age.[47] Its first appearance upon the stage from diverse hands and in diverse dresses made learned men suspect it for a Proteus or some greater Monster.

But wheras I said two persons proposing to themselves the same end &c., this requires correction. I should rather have said proposing two subordinat ends but with this difference; that for my own part I deseigned as my chiefe and ultimate end the easiest medium of Interpretation, and subordinatly to that the most natural order of the *Summa genera rerum* which were to be the Radicals. On the other hand the Reverend and learned Author of the *Essay* seemed to me, and I have often told him so much, to invert this order, that is, to make the Grammatical part subordinate to the Philosophical, or at least to carry on both *pari passu*, as I myself did at first Shorthand and an Universal Character, as has <fo. 55ʳ> bin formerly observed.

I would not have any to think that this freedom of myne proceeds from a spirit of contradiction, for I knew that excellent man so well, and had so high an esteem of him for his worth, that I have known but few so ingenious and scarce any to be compared with him for a zealous promoter and encourager of what he conceived usefull knowledge. And if he had not bin (as I conceive) under a strong prejudice of joyning two inconsistent deseigns into one, he could have done either, or both of them apart, excellently well.

I have now done with the grande difference between the Tables of *Ars Signorum* and the *Essay* about stating the number of Integral Radicals,[48] I come now in the next place to that of the Particles, which though not so wide for number as the other about the Integral Radicals, yet is it if wee consider the reasons of the Institution on both sides much wider. And here the Scene seems to be inverted from what it was in the Integrals, *Ars Signorum* pretending at least to follow a rational Institution here, on the other side the *Essay* following that which is purely arbitrary and Redundant. Neither can I think of any other reason of his following this way, but that it was after our Correspondence ceased that I changed my thoughts, as has bin said, about the ordering of the particles, and never had an opportunity after that to discourse the reasons of this change with him. Only once it happened that I saw him with Mr Hooke[49] in Westminster Abbey, and of the few words that past between us then this

---

[47] Cf. the introduction to *D&D* (1680): 'what entertainment this design [i.e. a philosophical language] may meet with in following ages, I am not solicitous to know; but that it has met with so little in this present age, I could give several good reasons, which at present I forbear, intending, if God bless me with life, health, and leisure, to do this in a more proper place.'

[48] Dalgarno returns to the question of the radicals later in the treatise, fos. 77ʳ ff.

[49] Robert Hooke (1635–1703), a close friend of both Wilkins and Lodwick, was involved in plans to improve the *Essay* after Wilkins's death (see Salmon 1974).

all I remember: I told him that I had rejected all <fo. 56ʳ> Radical particles as redundant. To which he returned that he had lessened the number of my first Tables and intended yet to make them fewer.

As now for the suffixed particles termed Transcendental in the *Essay*, I rejected them as being yet more redundant then the Separates, the same notions being expresly provided for in the Table of Integrals; and secondly because this contrivance made the laws of composition too restrained. The *Essay* allows no composition of Integral with Integral; *Ars Signorum* allowes of composition in its fullest latitude *Quidlibet cum quolibet pro re nata*, but with this caution, that the Simple Terms change nothing of signification in composition. That this latitude of composition is one necessary qualification of a Philosophical Language wee have a famous Instance of the Greek, the most Philosophical Language that ever the world yet knew, this very thing being the greatest commendation of that most copious Language, and making all other Languages beholding to it. But the want of this necessary caution is one reason that makes it as difficult, if not more, than any other Language.

This Instance of the Greek brings into my thoughts one Topick of composition omitted in the *Essay* which seems to challenge a right in a Philosophical Language as much as any, for it makes it copious, Emphatick, elegant and withall perspicuous. This Rule of composition is to compound the passions with their objects, the word signifying the passion alwise preceding, as *philopater*, *philadelphus*, not *Theophilus*, *Theostygus*.

This inconveniency of superdeducing a redundancy of Transcendental <fo. 57ʳ> particles and restraining composition to them alone has bin occasioned (as I suppose) from another grammatication, which makes another considerable difference between *Ars Signorum* and the *Essay*. All the Radical words in the Tables of *Ars Signorum* are Monosyllables, except a few Generical words in the Table of Substance. All the Radicals in the Tables of the *Essay* are Dissyllables. Now that one inconveniency did beget another seems to me may be gathered thus. If composition be allowed in its fullest latitude, compounding and sometymes decompounding Radical with Radical, this will produce too long words. Therfor for avoiding of this it will be expedient to confine composition to a few select Notions for which when they enter into composition, thoe they be provided for in the Table of Radicals and keep still their primary and native signification, yet for conveniency of composition there may be new marks and words of one Syllable provided for them.

Having now dispatcht the most material points wherin these two discourses differ, there are some lesser matters remaining yet to be compared. First for the Integral Character, besides that difference already mentioned of the one being perpendicular [and] the other Horizontal, there is this further difference, that the Character of *Ars Signorum* was more simple, the body of evry generical Character being a perpendicular straight line, the mark of distinction still <fo. 58ʳ> in one of the extrems, never in the middle, {[*from* fo. 57ᵛ] every one of which could be easily formed with one ductus of the pen;} p, q, b, d, were the most complex and laborious characters. The marks of distinction to be afixed upon the body of the Generical Character, for the difference and Species were much the same with the *Essay*.

The Characters of the particles, partly for symbolizing with the things they were to represent, and partly that 3 of them might [be] placed distinctly upon each side of [a] square, which space was to be allowed to every Integral Character; for these reasons theire Character was to be little, and because of their littleness to be contrived very distinct. Therefore the Characters which I did chuse for this use as most [clear] and most distinct and lyable to least mistake were: 1. one single point {[*from* fo. 57ᵛ] and circle} capable only of one position, and twelve places about a square as all the rest were; 2. two points with their 4 positions, perpendicular, horizontal, sloping both wayes as accent grave and acute; 3. a straight line with the same 4 positions; 4. a straight line angle in 4 positions, prone, supine, right and left hand (here I did not admitt the distinction of right, acute and obtuse angles, for thoe in greater Characters these be distinct enough, yet [this] is not so in so minute figures); 5. a semicircle with the same 4 positions; 6. p, q, b, d, in small Characters with the same 4 positions of a straight line.[50] These I conceived to be the most simple and easie to be formed, and with them I could serve all my occasions. For at first when the collection of particles I made was numerous I allowed 12 places for them about each Character, but afterwards contracting the number of particles I provided only 6 places, 3 before and 3 after the Character, so that the same Character did serve my <fo. 59ʳ> turne still. At last turning off all the particles except a few pronounes[51] I needed no more marks but that which confest to be both the most simple and easy of all Characters, that is single and double points.

<fo. 60ʳ> Thoe there have bin several accurat treatises published upon the Particles both of the learned and vulgare Languages yet has there bin no Logical analysis or Rationale attempted by any (for what I know) upon this Subject further than is to be seen in the commone Systems of Grammare. I shal content myself here to examine the nature of some few of the most difficult of them.

I shal begin with that which is called copula[52] and makes the formal part of evry proposition.

The *Essay* and *Ars Signorum* agrie in this, that this Notion of the copula is no Integral but a Particle; but differ in this, that the former following the commone theory makes it one single terme, the latter makes it double, and my following thought enclines me to be of the opinion that it is rather 3 fold.

---

[50] Although Dalgarno did not go to the expense of founding type for his characters (see fo. 34ʳ), we have examples of those he inserted by hand on the printed tables that he sent to Pell (BL Add. MS 4377, fo. 145ᵛ (see below, Part V)). The characters for the particles differ from the list given here only in that p, q, b, d, are replaced by two characters O and T.

[51] An isolated note on the cover of the MS reading 'pronownes no particles but integrals' indicates that Dalgarno further envisaged doing away with the category of particle altogether, including the remaining pronouns.

[52] Cf. the discussion of the copula in *AS*, ch. VIII.

The reason of this being interwoven with a score of consequents and comitants differing from the common Theory both of Logick and Grammar, I will set them down briefly and as clearly as I can and leave the learned to judge.

First, that seing evry proposition is a judicative act of the minde following upon the comparing of two terms mentally apprehended, now these two extrem terms being compared, either they seem to agree, or to differ, or it is uncertaine whether they agree or agree not. Hence follows a 3 fold act of judgment, and consequently a 3 fold vocal enunciation must [be] formally distinct. For in the first case the judgment unites the terms, and this is called affirmative; in the second, it separates them and this is called negation; or thirdly <fo. 61ʳ> it enclines equally to both sides, but determines for neither, lyke a Traveller coming to two unknown paths not knowing which to chuse goes no further but leaves of walking and stands, and this is called doubting.

Hence it seems clear that there are three kinds of propositions:

(1) Affirmative
(2) Negative
(3) Dubitative

This will plainly appear by answering the following questions

An Petrus est homo? Affirmatur
An Petrus est lapis? Negatur
An Petrus est doctus? Dubitatur

Here observe, 1. that according to the commone use of words an affirmative proposition may indeed be enuntiated in 3 words. *Petrus est homo*, but then the copula is improper; neither does the tyranny of custome excuse Logicians for their not defining of the true Notion of the copula, and telling us what words should have bin used for *est*. But 2. there is yet a greater impropriety in Negative propositions, *Petrus non est lapis*. For firstly the copula is not one single terme but double; and secondly, which is most absurd, these two termes are implicatory, *est* affirming, *non* denying. And here it is worth <fo. 62ʳ> the while to observe that in some cases the vulgare speake more properly than Logicians. The vulgar say *praeceptor non docet*, and this proper Logicians say *praeceptor non est docens*, which is absurd and implicatory. 3. a dubitative proposition, thoe as simple as the other two, consisting only of two extreme terms and the copula, yet can it not be enuntiated according to the use of vulgare Languages without a Periphrasis of many words. Here it is to be observed also that all Interrogatives are dubitative propositions, *an Petrus doctus, legit, docuit*.

By the Institution of *Ars Signorum* these improprities of Speech and other inconveniencys that follow are avoided, the 3 former propositions being worded thus:

Petrus affirm. homo
Petrus neg. lapis
Petrus dubit. doctus

for there all particles being derived from Integralls, and the copula of propositions being properly a particle and not single but 3 fold, this 3 fold particle from
the 3 Integral Radicals of *affirmare, negare, dubitare*.

If here it should be objected, that doubting is no act of the judgment,
but rather a suspending of the judgment from acting, I answer: if wee consider
doubting abstractly and *in actu signato* it is as properly an act of the minde
as affirming or denying; but if <fo. 63ʳ> wee consider it *in actu excercito*, with
relation to two terms apprehended, it is no transient act, but suspending the
judgment from acting by the transient acts of affirming or denying.

Here againe, it is to be observed that *est* is not only improperly used for
the copula, but it gives occasion to a greater mistake. For Logicians doe teach
that *est* does not only signify the bare judicative act, but also that it formally
and explicitely predicats and attributes to the Subject entity. So that when I say
Petrus est homo I attribute as formally and explicitly entity as humanity to Peter.
To which I answer, that entity is predicated of Peter virtually, as being virtually
included in *homo*, but not as it is in *est*. For *est* signifies no more than this, that
the judgment attributes all that is in *homo* to Peter, otherwise it would be
complex term containing both the copula and predication, and this proposition *Petrus est ens* would be a tautology, *ens* being twice predicated of Peter.

Its worth the enquiry, how this absurdity of speech came first into use. My
own conjecture is that wee have learned it from the Grecians, the first Masters
of Logick, for it is manifest that most of our European Languages have
followed them in using the substantive verb *sum*, as they call it, for the copula
in propositions; and which is observable, this inflexion of *est*, which is either
actually or virtually the copula in all propositions, is less changed than other
inflexions of that same verb. This confirms my conjecture, that the orientall
Languages use not the verb *sum* for the copula, but the bare enuntiation of
the predicat and <fo. 64ʳ> Subject makes an affirmative proposition; and in
negatives, a bare note of negation is the copula, which is truly Logical.

Its to our present purpose to observe that there can be no proposition where
either Subject or predicat is negative, but only reductively by mak[ing] the
negation the copula; and the reason of this is because a negation, as the notation of the word imports, is nor can be nothing else but the act of the minde
separating two terms, and so becomes the formal part of a negative proposition; and that negation which the Schoolmen would make distinct from
this is a *purum putum nihil*. The last shift that I finde in some of the acutest
of them is, that *negationes existunt suo modo*; if you ask them what that *modus*
is, they cannot tell you, wheras a country clown that never saw Oxford or
Cambridge will tell you bluntly that nothing is nowhere, or, which comes all
to one, *negationes existunt suo modo*, that is, *nullo modo*.

From this same mistake in Logick of making the verb *sum* the copula in all
propositions has followed a gross mistake in Grammare. It has past as currently
among Grammarians that *sum* governs a Nominative case after it, as with
Logicians that it is the copula in all propositions. But this is manifestly false,

for still the Nominative after *sum* if it be adjective has nothing to do with *sum* but agries with its Substantive before it; if it be a substantive, it agries with the substantive before by that figure which Grammarians call apposition, which is another great error in grammare, for there is no figure in this construction, but it is one of the plainest constructions in Grammare, and to be made as it <fo. 65ʳ> is the first and most proper concord.

Having given the true nature of the copula, and discovered the several <fo. 85ʳ> mistakes both of Logicians and grammarians about it, I come in the next place to that most subtle and nice notion which in the learned Languages has no other Signe allotted it but the construction of the Integral words, but modern Languages I think generally provide a separate particle for it. The Hebrew allowes no marke of distinction for it, neither separately, nor joyntly either by prefix or suffix, but barely puts down the two integral Substantives, and this they call *status regiminis*. The Greek and Latine for the most part provides for it by turning the latter Substantive into the Genitive case. Our English uses the particle *of*, one of the most equivocal words wee have.

Now this notion of the Greek and Latine Genitive case, thoe much more restrained then our Particle *of*, yet is it full of ambiguity, as denoting *forme*, *matter, part, Subject, object, correlate, possessor*, &c. [ex. gr.]

{genera animalium, species herborum &c, *Sub*[*stantia*].   <from fo. 15ʳ>
crateras auri, *matter.*
Cornua bovum, *Tot.*
vir magni nasi, *part.*
facundia Ulyssis, *Sub*[*ject*].
puer boni ingenii, *Adjunct.*
Ilias Homeri, *Effic*[*ient*].
cogitatio belli, *Object.*
codex fratris, *poss*[*essor*].
Incola urbis, *locus.*
sinum lactis.}

And therefore if wee would speake Logically and accurately, that which is done confusedly by the genitive case must be done distinctly by making off particles from the several notions they refer to as the occasion requires. For example *Timor Domini*, The fear of the Lord, is ambiguous both in Latine and English. The Genitive Case and *of* may denote either Subject or Object, so that one sense of the same word is good and pious, the other is impious and blasphemous. And here I cannot but take notice that these words cannot be expressed by the Tables of the Essay in the good sense of them, thoe in the bad they may: sie the definition of the Particle *of*, Part 3, Chapter 3.[53] In a philosophical Language the words in the good sense must be translated *The fear Ob*[*ject*]

---

[53] See Wilkins (1668: 309).

God; in the bad, *The fear Sub[ject] God*. But thoe it cannot be denied that this confounding many distinct notions into one begets great mistakes, as appeares in the instance I have produced, yet must it withall be confest that the custome of the received Languages in this particulare has something of reason in it which is not lightly to be rejected even in a Philosophical Language.

<fo. 86^r>   The reason for this Institution seems to be this. That it is not only an usual thing with orators, but also reckoned amongst the ornaments of discourse, to use the genus for the species, and the species for the Individuum, or as the Masters of Rhetorick phrase it, *commune pro proprio*, when the series of the discourse doth sufficiently determine and restraine the generality of the word to its proper and intended sense. So in our present case it seems to be agreed upon by all nations by a tacite consent, that so many specifically distinct notions as are reckoned up by grammarians [are] to be exprest by one Generical Sign having the proper sense to be determined by the sentence and its circumstances. And if a sentence thus worded be found faulty either for ambiguity or obscurity, then the safest way of remedy is to declare the true and proper sense exegetically, e.g. *The fear of the Lord is the beginning of Wisdome*, i.e. That fear which hath the Lord for its object &c.

    Now it remains that wee enquire what that notion is for which 1. the Hebrews use their *status regiminis*, 2. the Greek and Latine the genitive case, and 3. the vulgare Languages a separate particle. My own opinion at present is that it comes from the Integral *Relation*, thoe in my Tables of *Ars Signorum* I brought it from *Pertinere*, a notion of near affinity to the other.[54] For thoe it signify more specialy and properly between correlates, as *genitor Petri* and *genitus Petri*, yet in all other places where this form of speech is used there is still a respect between the terms thoe not falling under the special denomination of correlats. But thoe it be allowed to received Languages that in this institution they have followed the dictates of right reason so far as they all agrie (for I have not to dispute against the unanimous sentiments of all mankinde, at least of all civilized nations which I think to be concerned in the present case, especialy when that wherin they doe agrie cannot be called the mear effect of imitation, which cannot be said here for they differ widely one from another in the point of arbitrary institution but in the general above recited they all agrie), yet doth it not follow but the precepts of a Philosophical Language may interpret some notions more distinctly, when they have rested upon a confused and general knowledge.

<fo. 66^r>   I expected to have found the Comparates[55] all under one difference in the *Essay* no less than the causes. I have taken notice of one deficiency in that of Causes, but I finde no greater Redundancy throughout all the Tables than in the Radicals belonging to Comparates. The 3 degrees of comparison in *Ars Signorum*, *magis*, *aequae*, *minus*, for to speak strictly there are no more, in

---

[54] See *AS* 75.   [55] Cf. the discussion of the comparates in ibid., ch. V, §15.

the *Essay* are multiplyed to near 27 Specifically distinct Radicals, and yet all comparates come not under this difference, for *even* and *odd*, *lyke* and *unlike*, many [and] *few*, come under other differences.[56] I confess that in order to the framing of a Language it is more tolerable to encrease the number of Radicals in Metaphysical notions than else where, because they contribute much to the describing the nature of things below them in the predicament and of a more limited nature. Yet me thinks the *Essay* has bin a little too lavish in the number of Radicals belonging to this Head, and that not only in the Table of Transcendentals, which is the proper place, but also throughout the whole body of the Tables, where are many Radicals differenced only by more or less, greater or lesser.

Excellency and *sorriness* belong to the superlative degrees *maximus, minimus*. AEquality is the midle notion between *majority* and *minority*, improperly termed superiority and inferiority; *inaequality* is opposite privatively and so no Radical. If *betterness* and *worsness* be allowed distinct Radicals, then so must all comparative degrees as well as their positives: *encrease* and *diminution* is properly *majurari* and *minurari*; intention and *remission* is the same, and as easily distinguished as great fire, great heat. *Similia* relating to quality is *aeque-qualia*. Aequalia relating to quantity is *aeque-quanta*. Even relating to number is *aequal-parts*; odd, *unequal-parts*: 4 is an aequal-part number, 5 is an unequal-part number.

That I should deny distinct Radicals to *lyke* and *unlyke*, *aequal* and *unequal*, <fo. 67ʳ> may seem strange, seing they are treated of by Logicians as distinct arguments of discourse. But let Logicians say what they will, *aequalia* and *similia* belong properly to the Topick *majora* and *minora*, as being most properly the midle notion between these extrems. And as Logicians doe not subdivide *majora* and *minora* into *magis tanta* and *magis talia*, making them distinct arguments, so neither ought they to make *aequalia*, which is logically *aeque-tanta*, and *similia*, which [is logically] *aeque-talia*, distinct arguments.[57]

These 3 words, *quantus, qualis, aequalis*, have bin as very improperly so very unhappily taken up in the Latin Tongue to express those common Notions in Philosophy for which they are used; for persons that are not wary and considerate enough to distinguish between words and things are led into many mistakes by these words. *Aequalis* is plainly from *aeque-qualis*, and ought most properly to signify that Notion that has *similis* for its signe, which aryseth from a comparison in quality and is not that midle notion between the extrems of *major* and *minus* as they relate to quantity, which by grammatical Analogy ought to have bin termed *aequantis*.

---

[56] The main section on comparates in Wilkins's *Essay* is under the category Transcendental Relations of Action, pt. II (1668: 39); but *many-few, even-odd*, and *like-unlike* are elsewhere under Transcendental Mixed, pts. III.1, III.5, and V.1 respectively.

[57] See also the isolated note on CC, fo. 19ʳ: 'great and small are commone and indefinite notions commone both to quantity, continued and discret, as also to quality.'

Again these words, *qualis* and *quantus*, *talis* and *tantus*, are very improper and occasion mistaks in their predicamental signification, which ought rather to have bin *antitas* and *alitas*, leaving to them as that most common, so their most proper signification: that is for *quantus* and *qualis*, Interrogative or relative; and *talis* and *tantus* their Redditives, the former pair being compounded of *quam*, the latter of its redditive *tam*. <fo. 68ʳ> For both which particles of comparison, whether in quantity or quality, our English is the only Language that I know that uses the one and the same particle *as*, which is truly Logical.

Here I think I may safely venture to give this for a rule in a Philosophical Language. In all sentences figured by comparison, if the comparison be in aequality, the protasis and apodosis is the same *aeque* as if in inaequality the protasis and apodosis is exprest by the particles *magis* [and] *minus*, more [and] *less*, respectively. ex. gr.

> Peter is as learned as John
> Petrus est aeque doctus aeque Joannes
> Peter is not as learned (so learned is improper) as John
> Petrus non aeque doctus aeque Joannes

This appears to be so the more clearly by varying thus:

> Petrus et [Joannes] sunt aeque docti
> Petrus et Joannes non sunt aeque docti

In inaequality againe thus:

> Peter is more learned than John
> Petrus est doctior (or magis doctus) quam Joannes

Log[ically]:

> Petrus est doctus magis, Joannes minus

So that these 3 particles, *magis*, *aeque*, *minus*, are to make both protasis and apodosis in all Comparative sentences.

When I compare the Table of Radicals with the [Table] of Particles in the *Essay*, I finde that beside that redundancy which is commone to all the particles there, there is also a more particulare redundancy in the Comparat particles compared amongst themselves. [In] chapter 4, part 3,[58] there are five combinations of adverbial particles, wherof only the second is allow[ed] <fo. 69ʳ> to be comparats, and yet the last paire in the first combination, and the first in the third, are as properly comparates as they; but all [of] them [may be] resolved into *magis*, *aeque*, *minus*, *maxime*, *minime*.

{[*from* fo. 68ᵛ] *Magis*, *aeque*, *minus*, are properly adverbs derived, and by them all the Comparats, both in the Tables of integrals and Radicals, are to be resolved, partly by composition, partly by periph[rasis].}

---

[58] See Wilkins (1668: 312–13).

When I first gave it out that I could make the Real Character which I had <fo. 70ʳ>
cont[r]ived Effable by turning [it] into a Language, I cannot but think strange
to consider with what prejudice this improvment of my first thoughts was
received. To obtrude a new Language upon the world was thought to add a
new curse to that of the confusion. Neither did the prejudice stop here, but
after this many began to have lower thoughts of a Real Character which before
they had so much admired.

I was so much affected with this unexpected Rub, that I had once resolved
to say no more of a Language. But when I considered again with myself that it
was more than probable that so easy an inference from the principles I pro-
ceded upon would be deduced and brought to light by some other hand; and
in the next place, that it would be a meer cheat to conceal one halfe, and in my
own judgment the better halfe by much, of that which rightly understood was
the true desideratum; and withall forseing that I was not lyke to have that
encouragement which might enable me to devote the labours of my whole life
to polish the new Theory with variety of practice as the nature of it required;
I say for all these reasons I resolved fully to disclose and set down a summary of
my best thoughts upon the subject, and so cast it out of my hands.

First then {[*from* fo. 69ᵛ] every Language written to every man is a real
Character, but when he vocaly pronounces it. And because here it may be said
that in this case words written cannot be properly called Real Characters, seing
they are the mediate Signs of sounds and so *Signa Signorum* and not *Signa
rerum*, therefore I add further,} to satisfy the prejudices of those that are for
a Character but against a Language: Let it be considered, that any Language
whatsoever may be learned by a person born deaf and dumb, which has bin
partly proved by experience, and has I think bin clearly demonstrated in a
treatise[59] written by me upon that <fo. 71ʳ> Subject, containing such plaine and
easy directions for effecting so charitable a work, that this weakness of humane
nature may be both better and more easily cured than ever it has bin heretofore.
Now it is undeniably evident that to such persons a Language is most properly
a Real Character.

And to confirm and clear this further, let us suppose a deaf and dumb man
cured of this bodily weakness after he is Master of a Language; yet books to him
are still Real Character till by a new course of discipline he be taught the vocal
power of letters and the Art of reading. And if wee suppose this care not to be
taken of him then the learning to speake and understand that same Language
wherof he is already Master in books will be as new a thing to him and cost him
as much pains and labour as the learning of any other Language whatsoever.
And when he has learned to speake the same Language, the case with him is
quite contrary to what it is with other men. The Characters of letters to others
are properly the immediate Signs of articulate voice; to him they are still the
immediate signs of things, and so most properly a Real Character.

[59] i.e. *D&D.*

From all this I gather, first, that all Languages to all men are in some sense Real Characters, and to those thay are deprived of the faculty of hearing, in the strictest and most proper sense of the word they are so. Secondly, that no Real Character can be invented, if it be done by Art, but will Naturally resolve itself into vocal sounds. I speak now of such a Character as may reach the whole designe of a Language and deserve the name of a perfect System of Interpretation, by which I exclude Hierog[lyphics], Emblems, [and] Sym[bolic] Ch[aracters], <fo. 72ʳ> which because of their obscurity, ambiguity, want of inflexion, ligaments, &c., which make the formal part of a Language, can never be made a full medium of Interpretation in *vita communi*.

Seing then Characters written and a Language spoken are so near a kin that they are indeed not two but two names for the same thing: two they are in dress and enter throw two doors to their Mistress; but by her order, without which they can doe nothing, they bring exactly the same intelligence.

If then it be clear from what has bin said that a Language and a Real Character are not really distinct, and so the one no Clog to the other, I see no reason why any should be prejudiced with a Language proceeding from or rather advantageously accompanying a Real Character.

But one may think that all this I have now said might have bin spared, seing now I am to declare that which I know will meet with stronger prejudices in persons that take not the paines to examine and scan the matter thorowly.

It has alwise bin my judgment, since I had a full comprehension of the deseign, that Signs of a Rational Institution for Interpretation, which is the true desideratum, if we consider it in its two aspects, a Character and a Language, and compare these two so far as they are distinguishable, the Language is to be preferred. Before I give the reasons of my judgment I will first take notice, that learned men that have reckoned an Universal Character amongst the desiderata of learning have had false notions of it, for I take it for granted that they understood such a Character as is already received <fo. 73ʳ> in some parts of learning, such as numbers, weights, &c., which have no relation to, nor can be resolved into sounds. I must also take it for granted from what has bin said that there can be no Character invented by Art which can be truly said the easiest medium of Interpretation and fitted to reach all the ends and uses of Language but must necessarily be resolvable into Alphabetical simple sounds. Hence I infer that such a Character considered as effable {[*from* fo. 72ᵛ] and conveighing knowledge by the ear} seing even as such it is fitted for preserving of the memory of things past no less than a Real Character, is much more useful than a Character that is only fitted for converse by the ey.

Neither can I stop here, but further declare that which I look upon as the most considerable improvement of my thoughts set down in *Ars Signorum*: that my present judgment is that a Real Character provided distinct from the Character of the Language is quite to be rejected. My reason for this is the same that obliged me to reject Radical particles and transcendental particles, to wit the old rule *entia non* [*sunt multiplicanda praeter necessitatem*]. For seing the Real Character and the Alphabetical, which still must be allowed with a Real Character for expressing proper names and exotick words, are virtually the same thoe differing in figure, it is a manifest redundancy to provide for the same thing twice. Neither can there any reason be imagined why a Real Character should be provided distinct from the Alphabetical but one of two: 1. For the conveniency of short writting; but this [should] not stand in competition with the great end of a Philosophical Language, which it does considerably obstruct, to wit the shortest and easiest medium of Interpretation. This conveniency, if worthy of that care, is not to overrule the whole deseigne but to be provided for apart by a second institution. <fo. 74ʳ> 2. I confess it even more convenient for the use of dumb people than an Alphabetical Character. But it will be of little use in this case unless wee should suppose all mankinde to be mutes, or for a fews sake that are so that the rest would [be] so kinde as to teach them and themselves learn this dumb Character. If any should yet think that the very fame and novelty of a real Character would recommend [it] this is childish and deserves no answer.

I have this one thing more to add relating to the Character. Thoe I allow that the simple elements of speech ought to be otherwise stated, both for their number, order, powers, and figure, than they are to be found in the common Alphabets of any Language, yet seing this is the most arbitrary part of the whole worke I think that at first setting out at least it might be convenient enough to use our European Character. And if it should happen to take amongst other Nations that use a different Character then it might be tyme to apply a Character of a more rational Institution; unless any should think that because all Characters in their first Institution are equally *Signa ad placitum*, the use of our European Character might still be continued as a badge of its origine.

What my own opinion is of the number, order and powers of the simple letters I have made appear in *Ars Signorum* as also in a latter treatise of the nature of double consonants,[60] a Subject which I know never treated of before. It has bin received as an uncontroverted principle amongst learned men that the accession of aspiration to a mute, or Semimute <fo. 75ʳ> some goe further, make so many formally distinct simple Elements, and not double letters. I will not be so arrogant as to reject that which is so firmly established by the commone either express or tacite consent of the whole learned world known to us. Neither is there any part of learning that deserves to be or has bin more accuratly discust by the men of greatest learning of all ages, especialy of this present age. Yet with due reverence to so great names, and submission to better judgments, I will offer some reasons which suffer me not give my full assent on this point.

First then taking it for granted that the aspiration H having a distinct power from all other letters (and if any doubt this let him consult the acute

---

[60] See *AS*, ch. 1, and appendix to *D&D*.

Dr Littleton upon the letter H[61]) therefore makes a distinct simple letter of itself, it must needs follow that this letter being joined to any other single consonant makes a double consonant, for it is granted by all that S which is of near affinity with H, sie Littleton *loco citato*, joyned to another single consonant makes a double consonant, witness ξ ψ ζ. But for my own part, as I think I have sufficiently proved that any two consonants cannot come together in the beginning or end of a syllable, so I think that the power of the letter H cannot easily be sounded either before or after any other single consonant in that same syllable. {[*from* fo. 74ᵛ] And if it be the use of any Language then that letter before or after which H is sounded keeping still its proper power and H its are still two single letters and not one.}

I know many will be startled at this and be ready to ask the question: what then shall become of φ χ θ, of which it was never yet doubted but that they were the true aspirats of π κ τ.[62] To this I answer that *sano sensu* they may be called the aspirats of π κ τ as being formed by the same organs, but not the same configuration of the organs which give the distinct and essential forme to letters. But that they are not compounded <fo. 76ʳ> of the genuine powers of ph, ch, th, as wee absurdly resolve them, I appeal to the judgment of sense. To say then that φ χ θ are simple letters, which all acknowledge, and yet to make them have the distinct powers of ph, ch, and th is a contradiction both to sense and reasone.

<fo. 77ʳ>   The right stating of the number and nature of the Radicals being the greatest difficulty, and the Institution of *Ars Signorum* in that particular being so deficient in the judgment of so great a man as to oblige him quite to reject the method there proposed and to substitute in its place a fuller of his own; the clearing of this point is of so great consequence I will dwel a little longer upon it, and beside what has bin said already[63] I will sume up what I have further to say to these three heads: [1.] reason, 2. example, 3. experience.

1. The reasons of this Institution I bring from nature and necessity.

It is the nature of principles, if wee consult all Arts, that they be few for number, for nature distinct and easy, that it may plainly appear that all other notions are compounded of and resolved into them. I shall not enlarge upon instances taken from other Arts but content myself with the great and universal Art of Interpretation and the several ways of it.

Firstly, for a Real Character it is evident from the people of China's Character and the Aegyptians Hieroglyphicks what ill consequences there are from want of principles and analogy. On the contrary wee sie how a few Alphabetical Characters rightly stated can make all the Languages of the world

---

[61] See the comments under 'H' in the Latin–English section of Littleton (1678). (Littleton says that in compiling the English–Latin section 'no small assistance hath been afforded us by the Reverend Dr. Lloyd, Dean of Bangor, in his Philosophical Dictionary at the end of Bishop Wilkins his Universal Character'.)

[62] Cf. the discussion of the aspirates in Wilkins (1668: 371–2).   [63] See fos. 41ʳ–51ʳ.

legible; ten numerical figures can perform the whole business of numeration. Againe wee sie how the multiplying of the figures of the simple Elements in some Languages, namely the Arabick, makes the Art of reading more difficult, as the misapplying of their powers does the same in other Languages, more particularly the English and the french.

But to come nearer to the present case. The nature of Signs are servile, and <fo. 78ʳ> their only use to be representative vicars of all things and persons, without which they are but so many nothings. Now the fewer of these servants wee entertain, provided they doe our worke as well as a greater number, they are the less charge and burden to the memory, which chiefly they serve. The servants employed in *Ars Signorum* are few but nimble and active: *tradunt mutuas operas inter se*[64] one servant with the help of his fellow servants does as much work as a great many by the institution of the *Essay*. That is, one Generical word in the Tables of substance, taking its difference one or more as the nature of the thing requires from the Table of accidents, calls out the Species under that Genus as distinctly as a great many new coyned words in the *Essay*.

If here it should be objected that the Institution of the *Essay* guids us to the Natural order and essentiall differences of the Species amongst themselves, to this I answer that this piece of knowledge strictly considered is quite a distinct discipline from the Art of Signs, neither can this knowledge in the least depend upon arbitrary Signs. For Suppose one should learn all the Characters and words in the *Essay* under some one Genus without consulting the declaration of the larger Tables, these new words are of as arbitrary an Institution to him as so many En[g]lish words. It's true the order of the letters may guide him to the numerical place and order of the Species under that Genus, but if he be not either so good a philosopher already or else take paines to learn what [he] is ignorant of, this new Character or word helps him not in the least to understand the reason of the order or any thing else said there to describe the Species, so that in effect and by the Authors own concession the name of evry Species there is as great a burden <fo. 79ʳ> to the learners memory as if it were taken from any other Language whatever. {[*from* fo. 78ʳ] And this barely too with relation to the substituting of a new mark for the old one wee had of the confused Idea of the notion for which it is substituted. But if this new name must be a marke also of a new and more distinct Idea of the thing than wee had before, then such a mark becomes a double charge to the memory. For besides representing to us all that the old name did, it must now represent somthing more: that same thing of specifical difference which is purely of arbitrary institution no less than the generical marke, ex. gr. *elephant, fox taile.*}[65] Now as *Ars Signorum* has the Grammatical advantage of the *Essay* of not coyning new words for the Species, so I think that in many of them it may compare with it

---

[64] 'They help each other out' (Terence, *Phormio* 267).
[65] Cf. the discussion of 'fox tail' on fo. 47ᵛ.

in the Philosophical part of the Institution, even thoe account given of them in the Tables were as explicitly provided for as the difference in *Ars Signorum*.

There are some considerable objections here to be answered. 1. Thoe it be allowed that the Institution of *Ars Signorum* may doe well enough for naming some species, yet will it not be able to reach them all by single words, no more many of them without long periphrasis. To this I answer first that this is unavoidable by any Institution whatsoever, the differences of things varying so infinitly. That it is so not only in vulgar Languages but even in Greek and Latine Natural History is sufficient proof, more particularly those parts of Natural History where the species of natural bodies are numerous, such as Insects and plants. Yea further the *Essay* itself is proof for this, for besides the leaving many species of Natural bodies to be exprest periphrastically, which in universal philosophy challenge a right of having an equal care taken of them with others, there are many other notions which thoe not allowed specifically distinct by philosophers, for I think it is not yet agried upon amongst philosophers what makes a specifical distinction, yet they require distinct appellations, and by the use of most Languages are distinctly provided for, no less than notions most specifically distinct, and yet the *Essay* leaves them, and I <fo. 80ʳ> think with good reason, to be exprest by periphrasis. I might bring many instances of the works of [Art],⁶⁶ such as vests, vessels &c., but I shal chuse rather to insist upon the natural bodies and for instance of such I shal take dogs and Hawks, the varieties of which thoe not reckoned specifically distinct yet not only the common use of Languages but even learned men in natural history have given them distinct name. And yet sie in the English dictionary of the *Essay* what long names are provided for Mastife, cur, spaniel &c. From which I infer, that if so considerable varieties of that same Species requiring and allowed distinct appellations be left to periphrasis, I sie no reason but the lyke varietys of notions called distinct species of that same genus, may be the same way provided for. But here I must add that in this way of institution *Ars Signorum* has a vast advantage above the *Essay*, for in the one the names of the greater part of the Species may be mad off in one word, by the other it is point blank against the Institution of the other to give a compounded name to any notion further than the Transcendental particles goe, which reach none of the Species of nature and therefore by that Institution they must either be provided for by radical words, or a periphrasis of more than one.

<from fo. 79ᵛ>   {And here I cannot forbear deploring the condition of those [terms] that are deseigned for learning and liberal education, and that not only upon the account of the difficulty of the Vulgare part of Languages, for remedying which never any thing yet has bin attempted, but even upon the account of that which may be called the Learned Part, under which Head I place all terms of Art. Now it is manifest that those vocables ought not to be of a primary and

---

⁶⁶ The MS has 'works of Nature', clearly a scribal error for 'works of Art'.

Arbitrary but a Rational Institution, because wee must suppose that they were upon due deliberation imposed by Artists. And yet wee finde by experience, thoe all this be pretended to be so, yet many of them doe neither inform our judgment, nor ease the memory, both which they ought to doe. The instance I give here shal be taken from poetry, that much cultivated part of learning. I appeal to the judgment of the greatest Masters of that Art how difficult a thing it must be for Novices to remember the vocables, and understanding the meaning of all the names of feet simple and compound. In most of them there is no shadow of reason appears in the word for its institution, and in others the reason is so far fetcht that its as good as none at all, wheras it were an easy matter to fitt such Names as at first appearance might be clearly apprehended and so easily remembered, which would be a great encouragment to young ones. ex. gr. for *pyrrichius, proceleusmaticus, spondeus, Molossus, Dactylus, anapestus, Iambus, Choreus* &c.

What has bin complained of here of the Irregularity of Poetical feet, <fo. 80ᵛ> which are the Rule of numbers, may be extended to the tropes and figures of Grammare and Rhetorick, and generally to all Arts and Sciences. I pitty all Scholars in General travelling through this mist of hard words, yet I cannot without indignation think of the condition of young ones, who are often struck blind with this thick Ægyptian, and Hieroglyphick darkness.}[67]

I have one thing more to add by way of reason which if it be not nervous and solid enough <fo. 81ʳ> let it pass for flourish and fancy, I hope it will not be found impertinent. All naturall bodies consisting of matter and forme (I take the word forme laxely) the naming them by a Generical word with the addition of a distinguishing difference taken from the Tables of accidents Symbolizeth with the nature of things, for the Generical word represents the substantial and material part, and the difference added the forme.

This much shal serve for the first argument drawn from reason, so far as concerns the first branch of it, the Nature of things; I mean not simply the nature of things but chiefly the Nature of interpretation by Signs and the nature of things considered under their hability and relation to Signs. The next thing to [be] spoken to is the necessity of following this way. And here againe I mean not an absolut but rather a rational necessity facilitating the labour of a great and difficult work. This necessity appears [1.] from the almost infinite number of things, for which to provide single and distinct marks were, if not absolutely impossible, yet to imagine this practicable were very wild and extravagant, 2. all the Languages that I have any knowledge of, neither doe I doubt but all Languages all the world over thoe some more some less, to keep within the bounds of this necessity, 3. even the *Essay* itself, which is the only Institution that I know that has adventured to encounter with necessity in this particulare,

---

[67] The content of this excursus, apparently written at the same time as the main text, is reworked by Dalgarno as a separate tract on metrical terms (see below, Unpublished Papers 3); see also fo. 14ʳ.

is sufficient proof that all the simple notions, I doe not say of art but of nature for which it is more concerned, cannot be provided for by single and simple words; and yet discounting for Synonymous words it is my opinion that there is no Language in the world that has <fo. 82ʳ> so many Species of Natural bodies provided for by I will not say primitive, but single words.

I have done with the first argument taken from reason, I come to the second from example.

And for examples, besides some vestiges of this way of institution to be traced in all Languages, which I look upon more as the effect of chance and necessity than of right reasoning, I have others to produce and those great above all comparison: Almighty God himself and Adam in the state of Innocency. God himself named Adam, thoe a single individuum and the most perfect of all corporeal beings, by a derivative not primitive word. Adam as a perfect Philosopher following nature and the example of his maker gave names to all living creatures, not primitive and independent words, being antecedently to this imposition meer insignificant sounds, but words of a secondary institution inflected from other words, the primary and proper sense of which contributed to the describing of the nature of that thing whereof it was to be the name or which it was to represent. For unless this be granted, the commone opinion of Adams giving names to all living creatures suited to their natures will be absurd.

<fo. 83ʳ>   I agrie with the commone Theory, that *Ens* or *Esse* is the Summum genus in the predicamental Series of things.[68] But I take the liberty to place immediately under it as its first difference, *Abstractum* and *Concretum* {[*from* fo. 82ᵛ] or (with the dichotomists leave, whose way of teaching I subscribe to as most exact, but not alwise so convenient and easy) by a trichotomy into *Substantia, accidens,* and *Compositum.*} From which I infer two things: 1. That the words *Entitas* and *Essentia* are very improper and illogical thoe coyned by Logicians, 2. That *Substantia* can only be properly predicated of *Spiritus* and *corpus* or *Materia,* and therefore all other predications where *Substantia* is the predicate, such as *homo* est Substantia, *lapis est Substantia* &c., by the Categorical test are absurd and false. And this must be equally acknowledged both by those that are for and those that are against substantial forms. And seing all Physical Concrets

---

[68] At the beginning of the treatise (fo. 2) there are diagrammatic jottings in Dalgarno's hand that relate to this section (see also the discussion of the predicamental series in *AS*, ch. V).

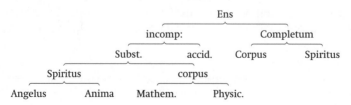

{[*from* fo. 82ᵛ] (by concrete here I doe not understand according to the vulgare use of the word matter vested with some commone accident, as *album, dulce* &c., but matter as it is subjected to a concurring multitude of modes according to the commone Laws of nature and Art)} consist of Matter, which is specifically the same in all, and formes, modes, or accidents, for here I take these words promiscuously, which vary infinitly, I will leave to Philosophers to consider what number and order of such notions are to be fixed for making up a full and complete Predicament. And sieing necessity of Nature obliges men to make use of sensible Signs to communicate their thoughts, the Grammarians business is to furnish the Philosopher with such a Systeme of Signs as may not only be a proper means to remedy the confusion of Signs that are in the world already, but also may be able to ease this invincible necessity of being obliged to the use of Signs, as much as human skill and Art can doe. And by the Philosophers leave, in such an undertaking I think the commone Notions of mankinde are principally to be taken care of and provided for, and the vocables of Art are to be provided for by a secondary Institution.   <fo. 83ᵛ>

This inference I bring from a fundamental principle. That no notion is to be expressed by a primitive Sign, which by its nature is capable of being exprest by a derivation or composition. And because my deseign in this discourse is not to state an uncontroverted Number and Method of primitives, for this I am so far from pretending to that I judge it above the reach of humane skill, neither will I take it upon me to put the stamp of my own Authority upon this scheme, which yet must be done either by some single person or society of men if eve[r] it be received. This I doe not decline lest I should undergoe the censure of Arrogance, for as I think the right will not be denied me, so all things considered I presume it will be owned by such as are competent judges, that all requisite extrinsic advantages be allowed me for so great a taske, I might be as qualified for digesting an established Systeme [of] Signs worthy to be received and practised without any material alteration as any other person. But thoe I resolve to decline this Taske myself yet I will contribute my best assistance in these papers to any that shall hereafter think it worthy of their care. I hope the reader will excuse my loose way of writting for I take things as they come into my thoughts by starts, having no deseign to form a new System but to explain my first rude modele which now I proceed to doe.

The primitives of a Philosophical ought to differ from those of other <fo. 84ʳ> Languages *ex parte Signati* 1. in number, they must be fewer, 2. and chiefly, in nature, they ought to be genericals. That is, the first and principal notions are to be with great care and judgment selected for this establishment out of the principal sciences of Metaph[ysicks], Math[ematicks], Phys[icks], Gram[mar], Log[ick], Ethicks, under which I comprehend OEconomi[cks], Pol[iticks] and Eccles[iasticks]. And of all these sciences it will be usefull to make the fullest collections out of Math[ematicks] and Metaph[ysicks], 1. because the notions taken from these two commone places are so large and comprehensive that they contribute much to the describing of notions of an inferior and more restrained nature, 2. from these fountains flow all the particles which make the formal part and are as it were *sublig[a]men orationis.*

Againe *ex parte Signi* [1.] the words ought to correspond with the notions of things they represent by an artificial symbolizing, 2. they should be distinct and Euphonical, free from harsh collisions of consonants which cannot be avoided by those that have not thorowly considered the nature of simple sounds and more particularly the nature of double consonants, 3. they should be short, *id est* monosyllables. The reason of this is not only to make way for regulare inflexions, but chiefly for composition in its fullest latitude, a necessary condition of a Philosophical Language. This condition seems to have something of nature in it, for I am enclined to believe that the truly radical words of all Languages are monosyllables, for it is manifest that our Europeans are so, excepting only the oriental languages descended of the primitive and first Language, the reasons wherof I have discoursed else where.[69]

---

[69] See *D&D* and the treatise 'On Interpretation' (see below, Unpublished Papers 2).

Unpublished Paper 2

On Interpretation

ON INTERPRETATION

It is a masterpiece of Art, and much to be studied by any that undertakes to <fo. 117ᵛ> discourse accurately on a Subject, to finde out proper and significant terms; especially this is to be observed in finding words adequate for the *Summum*, and *Subalterna genera* of the argument he is to handle. The nixt care is to define his *summum genus* aright, and to give a full and regulare enumeration of the species, or *subalterna genera*. This gives both the Author himself, and his readers a clearer propect of his whole design.

Among all the discourses that ever yet have bin published to explaine the Philosophy of Language I finde none that has given an adequat terme, and comprehensive of the subject in its full extent, but Aristotle in his treatise περι ἑρμενέιας, for Interpretation is comprehensive of all the wayes of communicating by instituted signes that either are, or can be. But as Cicero finds fault with Panaetius in his offices, that at first setting out he falls lame both in his definitions and divisions,[1] so may Aristotle in that Treatise be justly charged with *parturiunt montes* &c.[2] For after the specious Title of Interpretation, he neither gives a good account what he means by Interpretation, and not a word of the severall kindes of it. Had Aristotle pursued this subject so far as to say all that it could bear, and the nature of it required, shewing the defects of the received wayes of interpretation, and remedying them by a new and more rational institution, he might in all possibility have remedied the confusion of Languages, at least amongst the Literati of mankinde, and so got himself greater and more lasting glory by this one Treatise, then all that he ever wrote beside.

I will resume with some amendments and enlargements, what I have said on this subject in the preface of another Treatise.[3] There I defined Interpretation to be *an act of cognitive power expressing the inward motions of the minde by outward and sensible signs*. Here I chuse rather to put for the Genus *an act of rational power*; <fo. 116ᵛ> and for the better understanding of this definition it will be necessary also to give the definition of a *Sign*, signs being the proper object of Interpretation.

A Sign is a material or sensible subject representing an Image imprest upon it by a rational minde. There is the same union between matter and the Image

---

From MS 162, Christ Church, Oxford. On the foliation of the MS, see the Textual Note above. The heading has been added by the editors.

[1] Cicero, *De Officiis* 1. 7.

[2] 'Parturiunt montes, nascetur ridiculus mus' (the mountains will be in labour, and what will be born is just a ridiculous little mouse) (Horace, *Ars Poetica* 139).

[3] i.e. D&D.

imprest upon it, as between the body and soule of Man; with this difference, that in man the prototype, the Image, is imprest by Almighty God; in Signs, the Image is imprest by Man. So that books are the transcripts of the Images imprest by God on men; neither can the most skilfull painter draw the picture of a mans face so exacty, and to the lyfe, as a man skilled in the Art of Signs is able to draw the picture of his owne minde. I place for Genus in the difinition of a Sign, *Sensible Subject*, because thoe figures and sounds are fitter vehicles for these images then the objects of the other senses, there being a quicker passage through the organs of the ey and ear to the Soule than by the other senses; yet all other sensible qualities are equally capable to receive the same impressions, if the other Senses were equaly capable of transmitting and receiving. By the difference *representing an Image imprest upon it by a rational minde*, I remove all Natural Signs, such as the cause and effect, the antecedent and consequent, the concomitant, &c. Secondly I remove all significant words uttered by brutes, whether by articulate voice, as the parrot, Magpye &c., or in letters written, as is reported of the Elephant. For these animals doe only imitate the material part of the signs, but have not the least power, either of impressing, or perceiving the Image imprest upon them.

If here it should be objected, that brutes, thoe they have not a power of impressing, yet have they a perception of Images imprest by men, otherwise how could a dog know his own name, Lye down, rise up, and the lyke. I answer, that these Signs, coming from brutes, have only a material Image of figure and sound imprest upon them. Neither doe they conveigh any thing more to the eys and ears of other brutes lyke themselves; thoe coming to the eys and ears of men they carry two <fo. 115ᵛ> Images, one material formed by the brute, and the other Immaterial formed by man, the first Author of them. Againe when Signs come from the mouth or hand of a man, to the eys or Ears of a brute, they perceive only the material Image; for as they have no power to forme, so have they no capacity to receive the Immaterial Image; and therefore the effects produced have for the proper and natural cause either the modulation of the voice, with frowning of the countenance, as a natural sign of passion, and command, which excite the lyke passions of fear and submission in the brute. Or supposing the brute to have contracted such a habite, that upon the bare hearing of words, without any thing of threat, or terror in the voice, or countenance; yet the same natural Signs which were the concomitants, or rather the proper causes of the first force that brought the brute to submitt, excite the same passion by a reminiscentia, which was the first, and continues still to be the only cause of obedience. I say, by such a sensible passion as enclines to self preservation; not by a *funiculus* or hooke in the nose, issuing from the speakers mouth, and drawing the brute lyke a wheel-barrow where the man pleases, according to the opinion of some late Philosophers, who would have brutes, yea, and some of them man himself, to be nothing else, but mechanical machines, therby taking away all natural and voluntary motion, and action, as also confounding the grand differences, and degries of excellency, which almighty God has established amongst his creatures, wheras the true end of Philosophy is to explaine and illustrate the nature of things, by a diligent search of their true differences, and hence to forme accurate definitions.

Thoe it were too great boldness in mortals to determine by what medium of Interpretation Separat Spirits doe communicate, yet two things, I think, may safely be asserted. First negatively, that they need not our material and sensible Signs of sounds and Character; 2. affirmatively that their way of intercourse whatever it be is much more excellent than ours, particularly, more distinct and quick. (The necessity of using material signs is annexed to humane nature upon the account of the mysterious and near connexion of soule and body). Thirdly it seems consonant to [the] excellency of their nature, that they should be able to understand Images of the elicite acts of mens mynds when they are imprest upon matter. <fo. 114ᵛ> This is confirmed by all apparitions wee read of Spirits conversing with men.

Here I think it will be a proper place to speak somthing to that πολυθρυλητον[4] amongst the ancient Philosophers, whether words signify φυσει or θεσει. This has given occasion to some opiniastres of this age to talke much of the Language of Nature, and a Symbolical Character. I confess I have often laughed at so groundless a conceit both in ancient and moderns as to imagine there a Systeme of Signs whether words or Characters signifying naturally the things they represent of sufficient extent to Interpret all the notions of discourse and humane affairs. Something symbolical there might be in words instituted to represent the diversity of sounds that are in nature, and somthing Symbolical in Characters representing things differing by shape and figure, but even the few of those that can be pretended to be most so without a defined and restrained sense put upon them by arbitrary institution, in the contexture of a discourse would be found so obscure and mystical as the Ægyptians Hieroglyphics. But when I consider the antiquity of this opinion and that it was disputed by Plato and likely he had it from Socrates, I dare not think that so great men would have taken notice of so extra[va]gant an opinion unless they had received it from antient tradition before their tymes with some color of reason, especially seing their own Language was so little concerned in this dispute. For I think the observation is obvious that the more of Art be in Language there is the less of nature, and the ruder and more unpolished Languages are wee finde the more of onomatopoeia in them.

I will give my own conjectures about this matter in the following conclusions. 1. If the question be thus stated whether it be natural to men to speake, or if all Language were by imitation, to this I answer that thoe it be true that all Languages (excepting the first and miraculous gifts) comes by imitation <fo. 114ʳ> yet does this not hinder the faculty of Interpretation in general from being natural to man. To prove this *de facto* I confess is very hard, neither

---

[4] i.e. 'Controversy'. The MS has the spelling πολυθρυπλετον.

can I by any means approve of the way a late french Author goes about it to prove it by supposing a shower of men to fall from the clouds. This is wilde, for nothing is to be supposed here but what is naturally possible. The only way imaginable to trye this experiment is to suppose a company of young ones to be taken as soon as they come into the world and separated from all humane society so far as never to sie or hear any thing of arbitrary Signs till they come to be of perfect age. That this Society of mutes would invent and use Signs I doe not in the least doubt, but then I take it for granted that all their signs would not be vocal, for it must be supposed in them that the distinction of Signs to the ey would be easier than to finde out the articulations of voice. This exp[eriment] in all the due circumstances of I confess would be very difficult but not either naturally nor morally impossible.

If here it should be urged that all this granted yet it does not prove that its natural in man to invent and use Signs, for let one single person be kept apart with all the former caution and care he would not be supposed to invent as having no occasion to use Signs. To this I answer first by retorting thus. Its granted to be natural for a dog to gro[wl] yet he'l never doe so unless you vex him. The cat is thought naturally to hate the mouse, yet no signs of this before she sie her, so the use of signs being chiefly in society no marvel if he that never saw a mans face never spoke a word, nor write a letter. But supposing this Hermite to have but the bare book of nature open before him, his senses and natural faculties intire and vigorous, I doubt not but his contemplation would prompt him to marke and lay up good store of notions by arbitrary Signs which after he had learned a Language would be able to give an account of. 2. It is lykely that amongst the other rudiments of philosophy which the wise men of greece brought over from Ægypt this might be one, how to imitate their Hieroglyphics in a Language, they being of a mixed institution. 3. Lastly, which is most probable, they might fetch this notion from Phoenicia <fo. 115ʳ> whence its well known they had their first letters. If plato and others have read the History of the creation, as probably they did, it is no marvel, if when they find the first man at his first appearance amongst his fellow creatures to be so far Master of a Language as that his sovereigne Lord was pleased to leave it to him to give names to all living creatures, I say when they met with this passage it was no marvel if it should start many doubts to them about the matter of Language as whether the Language was natural to man, and if so whether their words did not signify naturally &c.

And now this brings me from a trifling and unlearned controversy (at least so far as I [have] seen it managed) to that which is more worthy to be considered in this place.

Seing it is clear from revelation that Adam in the state of innocency was Master of a Language, This may give just cause of doubting whether this hability was a supernaturaly inspired gift or a faculty proper to humane nature in its first perfection. If the first, then it will follow that man of all creatures is the most imperfect in his kinde for herby he is utterly incapable of society which notwithstanding is one of the great ends for which he was deseigned. Secondly it seems probable that seing Adams natural abilities were much weakened by the fall that supernatural assistances should quite cease, and so Adam left mute. On the other side if it be said that Language in Adam was a natural faculty, then it will follow that there is such a thing as a Language of Nature, and has bin *de facto* in the world, and consequently all Languages consist not [of] arbitrary signs as the commone opinion is. This dilemma presses hard with both horns. I will safe my self by getting between them as near as I can.

It is my own opinion then that Adam by the strength and excellency of his natural faculties did himself invent the Language which he and Eve did then speake without any supernatural assistance, which therefore to them was truly and properly a natural Language. But then it will not follow that any of Adams degenerated posterity can invent such a Language no nor understand that first and natural Language neither if it were extant, for even the words of it would be as arbitrary to him as any words whatever. I confess had wee a Dictionary and grammar of Adams Language wee might sie great singularities in it differing from other Languages but quite above our reach to comprehend the reasons of them.

Thoe this cannot be denied to be so, yet may it further be confirmed from <fo. 116ʳ> some vestigia and fragments of this first Language yet remaining in the Hebrew, which (as is highly probable) is a true dialect of the first mother Language. I have proved by undeniable arguments that there is something of Art in the primitive institution of that Language which nothing lyke can be found in all the Languages of the world beside. And here I must add further, that thoe I judge the first Language was rational yet in some sense it might be called arbitrary, that is he had more ways than one of expressing the same thing, as there are many to get over a river, by bridge, by boat, by horse, &c.

Before I proceed I will first guard my following reasoning with a twofold <fo. 117ʳ> precaution. 1. I doe not undertake to convince preadamites[5] and sadduccees.[6] 2. neither will I rashly intrude into the divines province by urging texts of scripture taken from the history of the creation against those that denie original sin; only the arguments I have in hand obliging me to do so I will suppose with the greatest part of divines. That our first parents before the fall were not only in a state of Innocency which all grant but also that this state did consist in such a degree of perfection both of soule and body as did become the image of God and his viceregent in the government of this inferior world. That is his natural faculties were clear and distinct, not subject to error, but naturally illuminated with such a degree of knowledge that never any of his posterity can arrive at or

---

[5] Those believing that preadamites, speaking a preadamitic language, existed before the creation of Adam; see the discussion in Stillingfleet (1662: III. iv, §2).
[6] Those denying the existence of angels and things supernatural; cf. *AS* 17.

so much as comprehend what the extent of his knowledge was. So in his will and affections was such a rectitude without any byas or obliquity that it alwise had a direct tendency to do the will of his lord and master and that in a higher degree not only of the Hethenish Stoicks but even of the Christian Enthusiasts proportionable to that of his understanding.

This position is warranted both by Scripture Authority, right reason and antient tradition of all civilized nations. From scripture, every thing that God made was good and perfect in its own kinde, wee have one of the greatest arguments of the perfection of his intellectuals that could be brought, for first it is clear he was Master of a Language and wee may suppose a perfect one too, and from thence we may infer the excellency of his knowledge in those notions which wee term Metaphysical, Logical and Grammatical, for without this he could never have bin able to have done that which is further recorded of him to wit the giving of names to all living creatures, which is another argument of his perfection, that without studying he understood the book of Nature.

Secondly this is consonant with the dictates of right reason. For what is more reasonable than that a creature made after the image of his creator, and sent from heaven to be governor of so considerable a province of the universe should understand the works of creation and providence which were the proper object of his contemplation.

Thirdly to prove the [position] by antient tradition I need say no more to those that are acquainted with mythology but name the Golden Age. But I will not insist <fo. 118ʳ> on this proofe partly because not only the poets but even the gravest of the antient Philosophers have debauched it into Romance and fable, but chiefly because that wherin they all agree to wit a primitive state of perfection, was no notion of their own but was brought with other things to Greece from Phoenicia.

Fourthly I must add that which seems to me a very considerable argument a posteriori. That now after nearly 6000 years there are some reliques of that Language which make it evidently appear to us that there was some superlative excellency, I must say of Art as it respects us, but of nature as it respects both this Language itself and its Author. My reasons for this I forbear to repeat here having discoursed them largely in another treatise. There were large scope here to expatiate upon the subordinate faculties of the will and affections, but my subject not being concerned in that, I come now to consider a difficult probleme wherin the divine and Grammarian seem equally concerned.

<fo. 116ʳ>   Taking it then for granted from right reason that Adam was capable to invent, and from Divine revelation that he did invent a perfect Language, and thirdly that there are as yet some relicks of that Language extant that argue its perfection above other Languages; from these permisses I gather the following inferences. 1. That Language was the first of all Arts. 2. That it was necessary it should be so even to man in his most perfect state, it being organically necessary for all the elicite acts of our natural faculties. And from the same premisses I think the opinion received by many that letters were

from the beginning is clearly deducible, for it seems not only rational that he should but also probable that he did set down a register of the names of all living creatures.

Beside that instance of the excellency of his reason in giving names to all things <by such an excell[ent] Inst[itution] that it deserves the name of a natural and Rational Language and> which can never be done by any of his degenerate posterity in this life, there are two points of Art more in this Great Art of interpretation which justly deserve our admiration. 1. the distinction and articulation of humane voice by which it is resolved into so many simple and indivisible sounds which wee commonly call Alphabetical, and first elements of Speech, and 2. the inventing and appropriating distinct Characters for representing these first vocal elements, so that adding only the charge of learning to know the figure and power of a few single letters the whole business of Interpretation becomes as easily performable by the hand as by the Tongue.

For clearing this difficult and nice point[7] I will first suppose that it is irrational <fo. 92ᵛ> and superfluous to resolve any difficult case in to supernatural when it can be clearly resolved into natural causes. Now that the present case is such I will endeavour to prove by divine authority, by reasons deducible thence, and lastly from matter of fact.

From divine Authority the case seems so clear that one may think it needs no further proof but barely producing Genesis 2.19 which is express and full beyond contradiction that Adam was Author of a language and a perfect one too, but it is far from giving the least intimation that this was a supernatural gift, that if the whole series and circumstances of the History be considered, the contary seems rather to follow; for what should be the meaning of these words, Genesis 2.19: *And brought them to Adam to SIE what he would call them, and whatsoever Adam called every living creature that was the name therof.* But the cause is not so weak as to wrest and force texts of Scripture to support it.

Yielding therefore that this opinion cannot be maintained by express Scripture proof, I will sie what can be done by inference, for effecting which I will sett down the following premisses. 1. That Interpretation by arbitrary and Sensible Signs is proper to man and not communicable to any creature of an inferior rank. 2. I will suppose that angels good or bad as they are a superior order of beings thoe they need not this gross medium of communication amongst themselves yet by the great excellency of reason in them they are able to communicate upon occasion with men in any Language. 3. I will suppose that the Soule of man with its primitive purity was equal to Angels in this faculty of using arbitrary signs, because he was so much concerned in the use of them. But 4. that which I lay the greatest stress upon is the perfection of mans faculties whereby he knew more naturally than any of his posterity can ever

---

[7] This excursus on the language of Adam, which recapitulates and expands on the arguments in the foregoing section, is inserted from elsewhere in the MS (fos. 92ᵛ–93ʳ).

attain to by study. Now this one thing granted it follows clearly that he must needs be well skilled in that which is the most necessary piece of knowledge belonging to humane nature without which he could not be fitted for the actions of humane life and therefore it seems most rational to believe that this faculty was breathed into mans nostrills with the first breath of life. Now this perfection is so fully confirmed by plaine texts of Scripture that no thing can be more. First in the General, Genesis 1.26,27: how emphatically there is man said to be made after the image of God. And that this was no imperfect image, sie v.31, where it is affirmed that every thing God made was good, very Good that is in its own kinde, and then I hope man was not excluded out of this summum of every thing. Again Eccl[esiasticus 39.16:] *God made man perfect*, what can be more plain and full.

<fo. 92ʳ>   There are particularly instances of his perfection, and some of them relating to that I am contending, for as first his being master of a Language and thereby being able to give names to all living creatures, which to me is an argument of the perfection of his nature till I sie better reasons than I have brought here to prove that this action was super natural. Then further the perfection of his knowledge of nature appears by his giving names to all living creatures. 3. There not being ashamed of their nakedness shews they were above all impure thoughts, but wee sie immediately upon the fall what a change was wrought in them, now they were ashamed of their nakedness. 4. The opening of their eyes to sie their nakeness shews a great change wrought in them from innocency to guilt and a sense of sin and shame.

<fo. 93ʳ>   I am not ignorant that I am now prying into an abstruse point and above the reach of degenerate reason to determine any thing certainly; yet if it appear that what is here offered proceeds from a desire to resolve a hard problem by the united force of divine revelation, right reason, and experience, I hope that thoe my endeavours may not deserve praise yet they may deserve a pardon. Let us then state the case thus by supposing that all mankind were at this day in that same state of perfection that Adam was before his fall. And then let the question be whether all mankind would understand one anothers Language. To this I answer 1. That it seems probable that even in the midst of so great a confusion yet they would understand one another, that is that all men would understand all Languages. My reason is because I think it becomes the dignity of rational Soul to be perfect in all its rational faculties, and not only so, but also by consequence to be able to sie and correct all the errors of those of their own kinde who are degenerated from that primitive perfection for *rectum est iudex sui et obliqui*.[8] 2. I think it credible that a pefect understanding should be able

---

[8] There is a sentence deleted in the MS that reads: '2. I think it consonant to rason yt the rational Soule should be endowed wt a natural power to impress such lively images of his notions upon matter as thereby to conveigh them to others.' Dalgarno has put parentheses round this sentence with the marginal note 'ob', indicating that the point is taken up and expanded on the obverse page (fo. 93ᵛ).

to know more, and more perfectly than can be acquired by any mortal man in his uttermost endeavour, but wee know that all Languages are attainable by study and that some men have actually understood a great many. But 3. I conclude that thoe men would understand all Languages now in use in the world yet would they use none of them but as a Master among a company of School-boyes when he hears them pratling barbarous and broken Latine he understands them but does not talke as they doe, but observes grammare rules and Authority. So an Adamite conversing with us mortals would understand us and so speake to us in our own Language. But with other Adamites would converse in a perfect Language, which Language would be as unintelligible to us as any Language in America, but much easier learned than any Language in the world because it would be frie from all irregularities that make Languages so difficult.

And here to prevent mistakes I will explain my meaning when I call Adams <fo. 93ᵛ> Language a Natural and Rational Language. By Natural here I doe not understand such sounds or Characters as have a natural Connexion with the things they represent, but that it was natural to this great Philosopher to impress such distinct images of his conceits upon any arbitrary signs that they were intelligible to others so that every notion had not [a] peculiar word and character whereby and by none else it could be represented, but it was easy for him to make this or that word or Character the vehicle of his notion as it is for us to impose what signification wee will upon words or Characters, but with this difference, that images of things that wee impress upon material objects of sounds or Characters by compact and so carry them in our memories and learn them by Art and industry, all this he did by the natural strength of his faculties without compact or study; all sounds and Characters then were indiffferent to him but he was better able then wee to chuse what was in all respects most convenient. The reason of all this because all the knowledge that wee can possibly acquire by labour and paines this and much more was in him naturally without any thing of Labour or paine.

Thoe many have pretended to treat of the Philosophy of Language <fo. 113ᵛ> abstractedly,[9] and have published discourses with the specious Titles of *a Rational Grammar*, *The Art of Speech*, &c., yet it is obvious enough, that the principal scope of these discourses, is either to modell a more Artificial Systeme of Rules for some instituted Language or to make some Philosophical reflexions and observations upon the nature of Language in general, by instances taken from several particulare Languages. But to discourse of the nature of Interpretation in its full extent with the *species* of it abstractedly from all instituted Languages or to give directions for instituting a Language by Rules of Art has bin a thing indeed talked of and desired by learned men, but never attempted by any (for what is known) before *Ars Signorum.*

---

[9] This final section (fos. 113ᵛ–106ᵛ), although a continuation of the ideas in the preceding discourse, might have been intended to stand as a treatise in its own right.

It is true that in some sense, there is no Language in the world but has much of Art in it. For as the inventing of a Language, which I suppose the Barbarous of mankinde capable to doe, would be a great piece of Art, let the Language be never so rude and unpolished, so imitation and receiving a Language by tradition which all mankinde actually doe, is not the more contemptible, because performed by children; but rather gives us occasion to admire the excellency of our rational faculties, that exert themselves so early, as to make a considerable progress even in childhood, in the most difficult of all Arts. Further there never was, is, nor indeed can be a Language but besides the being reduced to some general Rules of Art commone to all Languages it will also be reduceable to specificall and distinguishing Rules of Art within itself. For it is a great mistake in some learned men, that in some Languages there is no Analogy; it being impossible to contrive a Language without Analogy, for this would suppose an infinite number of words necessary to express the commone notions of mankinde. Numeration alone which is a smal part of Language but a very necessary piece of knowledge would require an infinite number of words.

But in another and more strict sense there is no Language in being of a rational institution, unless it be the <fo. 112ᵛ> Hebrew alone, in its primitive institution, the reason of which institution is wholly lost to us, as also the primitive words themselves, either lost, or, much corrupted; and for the primitive words of other Languages there is not so much as any shadow of reason pretended for their institution; and for other words of a second institution, how conjectural their origin is. Take for instance one of many out of Vossius, *Frequens*, from *fere cum ens*.[10] And in other words where the Etymology is manifest enough *ex parte Signi*, yet the reason *ex parte rei* is either forced, very far fetcht, or rather none at all. And how weak arguments are brought *a notatione nominis*, I leave to Philosophers to judge.

And as the origination of words is often both conjectural, and irrational, so is it never more so, then when we would force all words from the Hebrew; for it is not to be doubted but that there are many words which are not only lyke, but the same both for sense, and sound in diverse Languages.

This conceit of thinking that the words of all other Languages must ow their origin to the Hebrew (thoe it be manifest that many words of a second institution have with the river Nilus lost the fountaine whence they did first spring) proceeds from the confest antiquity of the Hebrew and a received maxime amongst Criticks that *all Languages come from one*. By which maxime if they meant no more than this; that there was one Language before there were many, I should willingly from Scriptural authority subscribe to their judgment. But if they mean (as I think they doe) that all other Languages are the legitimat offspring, and the natural issue of this first mother Language I think it is at no hand to be granted.

---

[10] See the discussion in Vossius (1662), under the entry 'fraxatores'.

That the first Language was lost by the fall of Adam, is nowise probable, more than that he lost his faculties and senses. But his understanding and memory being vitiated, his Language became changeable with himself, and lyable to the fate of all other Languages, that is gradually to change and degenerate. If wee consider the long lives of men before the flood, it is probable that the first Language was not much changed in that long tract of tyme at least in the eastern parts <fo. iii^v> of the world where the Seniors and princes of mankinde reigned.

But what ever changes Language was subject to before the flood, it is certaine both from reason, and from Scripture Authority, that from the flood to the building of Babel there was but one Language. Neither can it with any reason be denied, but that this Language was the principal dialect of the first Language spoken by Adam. And I think, that it is demonstrable both from Scripture and reason, that this Language was multiplied at the building of Babel by miracle; and that this change was not into Dialects but independent and mother Languages. I know that this is plainly denied both by some antient writters, as also by some learned men of our own age, who affirm that there was no sudden, or miraculous change, either into mother Tongues, or Dialects, but that the people falling out among themselves, were dispersed into diverse contreys and coloneys, and so the Language did degenerate gradually by the commone fate of all Languages in all ages into as many Dialects (mother Tongues they cannot call them) as there were Colonies. And as this is the profest opinion of some, so all that hold the forecited Maxime, that all Languages are sprung from one, that is, almost the whole tribe of Etymologists and Criticks, by necessary consequence run into the same opinion, wheras in the mean tyme they acknowledge the confusion of Languages and so become guilty of a palpable contradiction.

This being *nodus vindice dignus*,[11] I will endeavour to unty it both by Scripture Authority and reason. First the iith of Genesis seems to be so full and clear, that without manifest violence, there can be no other sense fastened upon it. And I think, there is none will have the confidence to denie, that the commone received literal sense of these texts, is the most obvious and natural. And for that evasion of recurrring to a trope, and Hebraism, of putting the lip for the heart, granting that sometymes in Scripture this trope occurrs, yet will it not follow but that this word may be used in a more proper <fo. 110^v> sense; and that it is so here the words immediatly following *that they may not understand one anothers speech* doe expressly declare.

I dare not charge the contempt of Scripture Authority upon the authors of this opinion; but they themselves must needs confess that the Phaenomena of Language in all ages are better salved by acknowledging a confusion; nay,

---

[11] 'Nec deus intersit, nisi dignus vindice nodus incident' (Neither should a god intervene, unless a knot befalls that is worthy of his interference) (Horace, *Ars Poetica* 191).

I add, that there are some Phaenomena which cannot be resolved into any other cause. And therefore I judge that the so express account of the confusion is a great argument for establishing the Authority of Scripture, shewing its exact consistency with itself, in relating the miraculous manifestations of Gods power and providence, in the grand effects of it, the Creation, the Deluge, and the Confusion of Languages. To wrest the plaine, natural and Grammatical sense of words, should be the last refuge in any case. But to lay a force upon words, where the natural and obvious sense of them can only be true, and that they should be so is a matter of so high concern as in the present case, must proceed from strong prejudice or something worse.

The only reason I can imagine of these learned mens incredulity is, that they are unwilling to resolve any Phaenomenon into a miracle, where it may be resolved into natural causes. And in this in general I doe fully agrie with them; for a superstitious credulity of prodigies, as it is one of the greatest weaknesses of humane nature, so has it abused the world much. But I wil take it for granted that these Authors doe agrie, that God Almighty doth manifest himself by miracles, that is extraordinary effects of his power; and that he did work miracles to confirme the doctrine both of the Old and New Testaments. And that the confusion of Languages was such an extraordinary and miraculous effect of his power and will, I will by clear evidence of reason make appear to all that own the Creation and Universal Deluge. I will first premise my reasons from which it will be easy to infer the conclusion. <fo. 109ᵛ>

First I take it for granted that there are somthings eternal in all Languages, some indelible Characters, which length of tyme can scarce deface and wear out. Every Language has a Genius, which thoe as modish as a French man as to its outward dress, and attire, yet his lineaments, countenance, features, symmetry, and proportion of parts continue still the same; so that a discerning ey may easily perceive after many ages that the person is not changed, but the outward dress. And this either corrects Horace own judgment, or gives light to that well known passage and often abused by Criticks

> Ut Sylvae foliis pronos mutantur in annos
> [prima cadunt: ita verborum vetus interit aetas][12]

If Horace by Leavs understood the whole body of a Language he was in a manifest mistake. But if he understood only vocables for customs, and things in their nature changable, and modish inflexions of them, he could not have found a more illustrating *simile* to help our understandings to conceive aright of the nature of Language if he had pursued it as far as it would goe. But his deseign obliging him only to place the *Somnia vana verborum* amongst the

---

[12] 'As the woods change their leaves with each year's decline, and the earliest fall off; so with words the old race dies' (ibid. 60 ff). Reference to this passage is a commonplace in seventeenth-century discussion of language change cf. Wilkins (1668: 8).

leaves of this *ulmus opaca*,[13] I hope I may be allowed with as good reason to lodge my *Genius Linguarum* in the same old stock; for I think the *Genius* of a Language may hold out under as many changes of the tribe of modish words, as the stock of an elme or oake can change its cover of leaves.

And because similes doe rather illustrate than prove, for confirming a standing Genius in Language I wil appeal to experience, by instancing in the most part of Languages known in these parts of the world. And first in the three Learned Languages who can deny that their Genius is yet alive, not only in books, for wee have them lyke an embalmed Mummy entire to a haire, but even in the Tongues of the vulgare, to this present age, at least in some of <fo. 108ᵛ> the principal Dialects of them, neither is it lykely, that as many ages more to what they have already lived will be able to destroy them. The same may be said of the Dutch and Slavonick with all their dialects. That there be cases supposed and perhaps such have bin, as to extinguish a Language quite, I doe not deny; but these cases are very rare, and must have somthing extraordinary in them, and therefore cannot with any shew of reason enervate my proofs.

My second postulation shall be, that the Language of the whole earth (as the Scripture affirms, and reason infers from the truth of the deluge) was one at the building of Babel. To which I will take leave to add, that there is no Language now on the face of the earth, so much one as that was then; which, together with the long lives of the men of these first ages, must be allowed for an intrinsick cause of keeping it from corruption; and that the external causes of working a change were neither so many, nor so powerful, as in following ages, is evident enough.

Hence I infer, that it was morally impossible, that many mother Tongues, distinct not only in dialect and dress but in a standing *Genius* should appear so early in the ages after the flood, without a miraculous change. For confirming this evidence, I will first instance in the oriental Languages. It is manifest enough that many of them, the Arabick, Syriack, &c., differ but dialectically from the Language spoken by the people of Israel at their coming out of Ægypt and written by Moses. Which of these Languages was the mother is not to the purpose now to enquire; but this is certaine that they are all dialects of one of the Mother Languages at the confusion; and it is highly probable that this mother Tongue was the principal at the confusion, being the same that was spoken by Noah, and continued at the confusion without change. Again for the Greek, If wee compare the vulgare Greek as it is spoken in many places to this day with what it was near 3000 years agoe, it is no less manifest that so long a tract of tyme and the many changes and <fo. 107ᵛ> revolutions that the people have bin exercised with, has not bin able to destroy the *Genius* of that

---

[13] 'In medio ramos annosaque bracchia pandit | ulmus opaca, ingens, quam sedem Somnia volgo | vana tenere ferunt' (In the middle an elm tree, vast and shadowy, spreads her boughs and aged arms, the home, so they say, which false dreams hold) (Virgil, *Aeneid* 6. 283).

Language. The same may be said of the antient Roman Language compared with the Italian, Spanish and French to this day; and no doubt, the Genius of many other mother Languages has proved as durable, but cannot be so evidently proved, because of their late use of letters.

My last instance shall be in our own Language which is the same in substance, with what it was a 1000 years agoe. For proof of this compare the Lords prayer, as wee have it now, with that translation in the 700 year after Christ in Cambden.[14] Now if the *Genius* of these Languages has remained uncorrupted through so many ages, how is it credible that one Language should produce so many distinct Languages in a very few ages after the flood, when yet the causes of corrupting it were neither so many nor so powerfull to worke a change, as they are now and have bin for so many latter ages.

There is one Hypothesis indeed which would give a satisfactory account of the diversity of Languages in the world without a miracle; and that Metaphysically possible enough, but withall so highly improbable that I think never any did, or will adventure to defend it. That is, to suppose that at the dispersion of Colonies after the flood, the several princes of families did employ trifling heads lyke my own to make new Languages for their new plantations. And yet (if a moral possibility of imposing these new Languages were granted, which were not very absurd, considering the authority of the imposers and the small number of which colonies did then consist) this opinion in all other respects might be better defended, than many other bold assertions of this nature, which have got their Authors immortal names, and drawn the world after them.

Such is in the first place the diurnal and annual motion of the earth,[15] with a multitude of other monstrous productions spawned from this great <fo. 106ᵛ> monster as 1. a world in the moone.[16] And why not in the other planets too? That so that beastly *Metempsychosis*[17] of Pythagoras being exploded, or at least left for Mr Hobbs kingdome of darkness,[18] way may be made for introducing a nobler opinion of a *metachoresis animarum*, taking their flight from stage to stage, that is from planet to planet, till at last after a long pilgrimage, and many lustrations, they arrive at the region of light and glory, the center of rest. 2. The discovery of this new world being so taking, that it give occasion to some aspiring Hero's to soare a little higher, and discover a multitude of worlds to us; and these such vast systems too, that wee may be ashamed to call our Epitome by the name of world.[19] 3. Lastly, upstarts an Herculean race defying

---

[14] See Camden (1605). Versions of the Lord's Prayer given by Camden are reprinted (with a marginal source reference) in Wilkins (1668: 7).

[15] There is a separate unpublished tract by Dalgarno on diurnal and annual motion in CC, fos. 105ᵛ–94ᵛ.

[16] In 1638 Francis Godwin published a tract entitled *The Man in the Moone* (Godwin 1638). In the same year, Wilkins argued that the moon might be inhabited in a treatise entitled *The Discovery of a World in the Moone* (Wilkins 1638).

[17] 'Transmigration of the soul.'   [18] See *Leviathan*, pt. IV ('Of the Kingdome of Darknesse').

[19] Cf. Wilkins (1640), in which it is argued that the earth is one of the planets.

all mankinde with a *Nil ultra*,[20] of infinite worlds. But Mr Hobbs, startled at this boldness, cryes out: Theeves, if *nil ultra* be yours, *nil supra*[21] is mine, for my one infinite world swallows up all your infinite finite worlds.[22] Hence I infer that for men to broach opinions (especially if they thwart the commone sense of mankinde) grounded upon bare possibility, is a great vanity. But seriously and dogmatically to defend them, turns fools into madmen, and that not of the lowest, but highest forme; for these are the only men of whom it may be truly said that *cum ratione insaniunt.*[23] I have drawn the parallel of these two specious, but false hypotheses, to shew how dangerous and unsure it is, to infer an *esse* from a bare *posse*. This liberty indeed, has alwise bin, if not given, yet liberally enough taken, by poets and Romancers. But there can be nothing more unworthy of a philosopher, than to build upon precarious principles; especially when such opinions have an ill influence upon Religion, as is but too manifest that the two opinions I am now shooting at, the one directly the other obliquely, have.

[20] 'Nothing beyond.' Cf. Part I, Broadsheet 2, fo. 146ᵛ, and Broadsheet 5, fo. 141ʳ; Part II, *AS* title page.

[21] 'Nothing above.'

[22] Hobbes maintained that the world or universe consists entirely of bodies of various sizes: 'that which is not Body, is no part of the Universe.' In particular, abstract essences and incorporeal spirits do not exist. See *De Corpore*, ch. 26, and *Leviathan*, ch. 46.

[23] 'There would be method in their madness' (Terence, *Eunuchus* 63).

Unpublished Paper 3

On Terms of Art

ON TERMS OF ART

Amongst many other causes from without, and therefore out of the reach of <fo. 123ᵛ> Art to remedy, there are two grand internal causes of perpetuating the confusion of Languages in the world:

1. The multiplying of words without necessity
2. The want of Art in their Institution.

That it is morally possible to remedy this evill, as to the vulgare use of Language, by all the engines either of Art, or power, were a fonde thing to conceive. Neither yet is it to be expected, thoe much to be desired (at least in many ages) that the *Literati* of mankinde will agree among themselves upon a common Language of a rational institution, for propagating and improving those parts of humane knowledge which are reduceable to Systems of Art.

But supposing this disease to be equally incurable, both in the *Literati*, and the vulgare; yet, me thinks that it should pass without any attempt of remedy in the terms of Art, many wherof are of a late institution, and not warranted by the authority of antient writters (and I fear that our new Philosophers who pretend to be reformers of antient errors, will be found as faulty here as others, and yet this was the first thing they ought to have begun with), I say, that this sore should rather spread than heal seems to be a reproch to Art and Artists.

That multiplying of terms without necessity, and want of Art in their Institution is a great difficulty and discouragement to young students in any Art, I will take for instance the Art of poetry, so much cultivated by the most polite wits of all civilised nations, and all ages of the world.

First for multiplying of words without necessity: the greatest Masters of the Art have invented a multitude of compounded feet which I doubt if they can justify by the Authority of the antient poets, whose scholars they profess themselves to be. And thus they lay a force both upon the poet and nature, that in spight not only of his teeth but even of nature itself, he must come not running but jumping along after them, when they hold up their finger, as if he were fast in the <fo. 122ᵛ> stocks or fetters.

But here it will be said that there are some kinds of verse that cannot be measured but by compounded feet. But this is a manifest mistake, and the reason why it is so is no less manifest; for there is no compounded foot but resolves itself naturally into two simple, so that measuring by simple and compounded feet is like going and jumping, and I think there is none but will confess that it is easier to goe by steps than to jump about the streets.

From MS 162, Christ Church, Oxford. On the foliation of the MS, see the Textual Note above. The heading has been added by the editors.

But I will descend to some particulare instances out of Horace Lyricks which are commonly measured by compounded feet: and first by Choriambus. Now let us first take notice, that Horace has 3 kinds of Choriambick verses: (1) consisting of one Choriambus, as:

> Sic te Diva potens Cypri.[1]
> Lydia dic per omnes.[2]

(2) of two Choriambus's, as:

> Maecenas atavis edite regibus.[3]

(3) of three Choriambus's, as:

> Tu ne quaesieris scire nefas, quem mihi quem tibi.[4]

Now it is undeniably manifest, that all these 3 kinds can be measured by dactyles, viz., the first without a caesura, the second with one caesura, and the third with two caesura's. And because I doubt if ever this way of measuring the third has bin taken notice of (which I hope to make appear to be the true measures that Horace tyed himself up to in this verse, and never thought of a Choriambus), nor yet dividedly by Trochaeus and Iambus, I will measure the verse thus:

> Tū nē quāesiĕ, rīs, scīrĕ nĕ, fās, quēm mĭhĭ, quēm tĭbĭ

And so all the Choriambicks of this kinde in Horace, which are 3 odes, doe exactly answer to this way of measuring by 2 caesura's.

Now that Horace deseigned this way of measuring and not by Choriambus's <fo. 121ᵛ> I prove it thus. If Horace had deseigned any of these 3 kinds of verse to be measured by Choriambus's, he would have taken the same liberty in all places where this foot was to be used, which is manifest he has not, but has tyed himself strictly to the laws of caesura: for in his verses of one Choriambus this foot ends indifferently either with the end of a word, or the beginning of another. In his verses measurable by two Choriambus's the last Choriambus ends likewise indifferently either with the last or first syllable of a word, but the first ends consistently with the last syllable of a word, and so make a Dactyle with a caesura. And in lyke manner the verses measurable by 3 Choriambus's: the last still ends indifferently as the former with the last or first syllable of a word, but the two first Choriambus's both of them doe constantly end with the last syllable of a word, and never ends with the first syllable of a word. For this reason it seems to be clear that Horace never thought of Choriambus's, but intended them all to be measured by dactyles and caesura's.

---

[1] 'May the goddess who rules over Cyprus . . .' (Horace, *Odes* 1. 3. 1).
[2] 'Lydia, tell me, by all [the gods] . . .' (ibid. 1. 8. 1).
[3] 'Maecenas, sprung from royal stock . . .' (ibid. 1. 1. 1).
[4] 'Don't ask (we cannot know) what [the gods plan] for you or for me' (ibid. 1. 11. 1).

That caesura's are not unusual to Horace, and even in his dactylick verses, appears by:

arboribusque comae.[5]

where I cannot but take notice that this verse is as properly Choriambick as any in Horace. And therefor I wonder much that those that are so great lovers of compounded feet, and expecially Choriambus, should measure this by dactylus.

Secondly, that Horace intended these verses to be measured by dactylus and caesura is evident for this reason. A caesura makes a pause in a verse next to that which is to be observed when a verse is ended, and this no doubt is the true reason why the poets allowed [a] short syllable long in any part of a verse, as they did the last syllable in evry verse.

Now whoever considers attentively the last two kindes of Choriambus will finde that the respective caesuras by which they are to be measured will easily discover themselves <fo. 120ᵛ> by a natural pause offering itself in reading, unless the reader come with a prejudice, and so offer force to nature.

Hence I infer that these verses have never bin rightly read, or if any have read them true, by so doing he has contradicted the received way of measuring. The single caesura in the first is so manifest that a child that can but read distinctly will observe a pause in reading. But the double caesura in the second not being so usual, thoe manifest enough, this verse could never be rightly pronounced by those that are under the prejudice of Choriambick measures, unless nature have overcome prejudice in the reader, even when he was not aware of it; which I think must be so, for it is a hard matter to read these verses without observing the pauses, they offer themselves so naturally; thoe it cannot be that they should be so accurately observed as they ought by those who have measured these verses by Chorimabus, and have not seen that Horace did industriously seek and fix these pauses as the great grace of this kind of verse.

There is only one jumping ode more in Horace, which I think may have its fetters knockt off as well as the rest:

Miserarum est.[6]

Why not by Pyrrichus and Spondaeus alternatly, as well as by Ionicus a minore?[7] Neither of them will be Hypermeter by this means: the first will be trimeter and the second tetrameter in Horace own sense of the words. I know nothing can be said against measuring here by single feet, as evry where else, but that it is the most natural, easy and usual way. But against compounded feet wee have the celebrated maximes: *Entia non sunt multiplicanda* [*praeter necessitatem*][8]

---

[5] And the foliage [is returning] to the trees (ibid. 4. 7. 2).

[6] 'Poor girls, it is [their fate]' (ibid. 3. 12. 1).

[7] An ionic foot consists of a pyrrhic plus a spondee; *ionicus a minore* is where the pyrrhic precedes.

[8] Dalgarno appeals to Occam's razor elsewhere as a principle for establishing the set of radicals in a Philosophical Language; his argument is that one should not invent a new term for a *complex* notion that can adequately be expressed by a combination of two or more *simple* notions (see 'The Autobiographical Treatise', fo. 37ʳ).

and *Frustra fit per plura* [*quod fieri potest per pauciora*], which are not to be <fo. 119ᵛ> departed from without weighty considerations. And if any should say measuring by compounded feet is more compendious, I answer this is a mistake. For there is no compendium in the names of feet; and for the compendium of pronouncing 4 syllables in one breath, which by the other way must make a double hiatus, what is got in tyme is lost in distinction of numbers, which is the greater loss of the two.

I come in the second place to instance in terms of Art that want of Art in their institution: and these shall be the received names of feet, whether single or compounded. For compounded feet, if ther were any use of them, it were easy to give to all of them vocables of a rational institution, even as some of them already have, such as Choriambus, Dichoraeus &c. And why not with as much ease and much greater reason: Dijambus, dipyrrichus,[9] &c. than such monstrous insignificant words, or at least of a far fetcht signification, commonly used, which burden the memory and confound the understanding.

---

[9] Dalgarno is here proposing compound terms such as *di-iambus, di-pyrrichus*, where the meaning of the whole is transparent from the meaning of the component morphemes, on the model of *chor-iambus, di-choraeus*, etc. One of Dalgarno's chief criticisms of Wilkins's Philosophical Language is that he coins new terms where transparent compounds would be readily possible.

PART V

DALGARNO'S CORRESPONDENCE

Dalgarno to Samuel Hartlib, 20 April 1657

Oxford 20 Apr[il] 1657

Much honoured Sir,

The tender respects you manifest to Ingenious Designes, tending to the advancement of Literature, does sufficient plead an Apologie for my boldnes & presumption in saluting you by these Lines, without any other acquaintance or interest unto you. Sir, The occasion of my present writing was the sight of a Letter of yours, to my Honourable & worthie Friend Mr Morstyn, wherein having seen my own name mentioned & perceiving that something of my tendencies to the discovery of an Scholasticall Mysterye, attempted by many of the more learned sort of all ages, though in vaine, hath been imparted unto you, I judged it therfore my dutie for your further satisfaction of the realitie of the affaire, to certifie something from my oune hand. Sir, you shall know therfore, that the whole designe is now pefected & a Testimony & Approbation of the same granted by those two Learned Doctors Dr Wilkins & Dr Ward, who were by the Vice-Chancellor appointed my examinators. It is also at the desyre of the Vice-Chancellor & the foresaid Doctors to bee propounded before the Delegates of the Universitie this weeke, & I am immediately to go upon the practise of it herafter at this place. I have likewise an testificat from the Vice-Chancellor & some of the most learned Doctors of Cambridge, having beene there occasionally of late. It is to bee taken notice off, that this Art conteineth an other Excellencie in it (:besides of being an Common Character applicable to all languages:) little inferior in use to the same, viz. An compendious and contracted way of writing for any language, farre exceeding all Inventions of Tachygraphy in this Nation for writing of the English language, & this my certificat does beare. This I conceive to bee a thing which doth very much commend the Invention, two Arts both of singular use, being attainable by the same Precepts & Rules, so that I may call it Grammatically one Art, but Logically two. Sir, I am informed by Severall Persons of Quality at this place (:besides that I learne from your owne Letter:) particularly Dr Ward, a Gentleman of great deserving for his eminent parts of Literature, that you are the most singular promotor of Scholastick designes, that this Nation doth affoard. Wherefore Sir I am very ambitious of the honour, & shall esteeme it me exceeding great happiness to have a fuller acquaintance confirmed with you upon that Account. I hoped Sir you are not insensible, that the best way of promoting of Literature, & Ingenious Inventions, tending to the publick good is the encouradging with some gratitude those spirits, whom it pleaseth the Lord to fitt to bee the Inventors. Wherfore Sir if you can contrive a way off

Letter preserved in the British Library, Add. MS 4377, fo. 148.

encouradgment to me for the further improvement of my Labours in publick
sevise, I will undertake by the blessings & assistance of God shortly to discover an Invention of higher worth & unspeakable utilitie, not only to this
Commonw[wealth] but all the civilized Nations of the World. As for that latlie
put forth Treatise entituled, The Universal Character by Cave Beck M. A.
wherof you desire my impartial Judgment, you shall know Sir that I did see
it long agoe from Dr Wilkins in an Manuscript by the Authors owne hand,
which was sent to him for his censure of it: who did shew me; that hee did
peremptorily dissuade the Author from publishing off it. As for my owne
Judgement Sir if it can be taken for impartiall, I find it nothing else, but an
Enigmaticall waye of writing the English Language. So that as I conceive the
title of it is false. And wheras the Author of it promises the knowledge of it
shall be attained in two hourse tyme, if hee can let me see the Man two yeares
hence, who can readily & extempore, either write, reade, speake, or understand
by his Grammatical Rules, without any other helpe, but his owne memory,
I shall say *peccavi* for my rash censure. I have another Treatise by me, which was
put forth the year of God 1647 to that same purpose, which doth farre exceed
the other, & yet comes very farre short of doeing the thing. Sir you should very
much oblige me by communicating the thoughts of any other Person upon this
subject. For if I knew, but in one line or two, the Method & way I could easily
from thence gather the rationalitie of their designe. Sir if your more serious
employments can dispense with so much spare time, you shall honour &
gratifie me much in bestowing one line upon

> Honoured Sir
> Your truly reall servant
> Gdalgarno

Dalgarno to John Pell, 26 December 1657

R[ight] Worshipfull

Leaving to use many apologies for these my abrupt addresses, the chieffe motive which has induced me to direct these papers to your hands was the fame not onlie of the singulare excellence of your literarie induments but also your zeale and forwardnes for the advanncment of learning and all usfull and ingenious designes tending therunto. Sir it having pleased the Lord to make me Instrumentall in discovering a clearer light of that long desyred designe of an Universal Char[acter] than ever has yet appeared by anie others labours or endeavours in that affaire, I have by his grace and assistance brought it alreadie to that perfection as that it is capable of accomplishing all those uses and ends (if the world will improve it) which I doe assert in my printed paper, and this I have testified and approven by the most learned of both the universities and several other eminent persons here at London, and having learned from my most singular friend and promoter Mr Samuel Hartlib that he had communicated a copie of my first printed papers to your Wor[ship] I presumed by his warrant and desyre to direct these few lynes with the enclosed papers for a farder explication and unfolding of the designe, hoping therby that if your Wor[ships] spare houres can suffer you to take a narrow and exact surveighe of the nature and particulars of the contrivance somthing advantagious for the farder perfecting of it may be suggested by the acutnes of your piercing judgment and certaine of your satisfaction you maye become an encouradger and a patron of the worke. Sir it would take a larger discourse than I can now enlarge to explaine evrie particulare fullie, therfor fore the present I shal contentment [*sic*] myselffe to referre you to the perusal of the print paper and onlie give some general observations for the understanding the grounds of the designe; and because *longum iter per praecepta, breve et efficax per exempla*[1] I shal sett doune some few examples in practice for a clearer Illustration and if this be acceptable I shal endeavour a farder explication and more particulare satisfaction at the nixt opportunity.

First I desyre to be considdered that I reduce the simple notions of language necessarie for communication and commone intercourse to a certaine number, taking away the superfluitie of synonymous words and the ambuguitie of aequivocal words. I take of all grammatical irregularities and unnecessarie rules

---

Letter preserved in the British Library, Add. MS 4377, fos. 150–2. This letter contains a detailed and illustrated account of Dalgarno's early scheme for a real character. Letters with similar contents must have been sent out to the other worthies from whom Hartlib solicited an evaluation at this time (see 'Chronology of Dalgarno's Life'). The contents were not self-explanatory to all the recipients; thus Mercator complains in a letter to Hartlib that the amanuensis must have made a mistake in copying Dalgarno's characters (Hartlib MS 56/1/115a).

[1] Long is the road to learning by precepts, but short and successful by examples.

and flexions &c. Then I divid the parts of speech into two, to witt, auxiliarie words commonlie called particles, and radical words expressing the notions of things. The particles I express not with anie radical character seing they do not properlie represent anie notion of the mynd but are simplie *veicula notionum* but writt them by poynts or affixes distinguished by the several places, as it will appeare from the table, so that manie tymes one radical character makes up a compleat sence and period with the particles affixed about it, as will appeare in the <fo. 150ᵛ> examples. The whole number of radical and primitive notions consisting of verbs and nouns I reduce first to two classes, the first containing verbs and adjectives, and the second such substantives as are not properlie derivative notions from verbs or adjectives, where I give a rule that as sub-statives are derived from verbs and adjectives, so verbs maye be derived from radical substatives. Neither think I it fitt to be too nyce or curious in deter-mining what nouns are to be placed radicallie as verbs and adjectives and what as substantives seing several languages varies in this, but for my designe it is eneoghe if I have evrie necessarie notion whether I express it radicallie as verb or noun, seing as the nature of the notion requires a verb can be turned to a noun, and a noun radical to a verb.

The whole number of radical notions I divyde, following a memorative method (memorie being the cheiffe thing here to be consulted and which is the cheiffe excellence of this designe above other languages, it being practicallie attainable in less than twentieth part of the tyme that anie language can be learned) and abstracting from philosophie, into several periods wherof evrie one contains fourtie two notions. Every one of these periods are subdivyded in seven lynes wherof evrie lyne contains six notions and three of those six going alwaies together by waye of one sense. Againe in evrie period the first lyne is the narration of a fictitious storie, the second an illation by the particle *for*, the third comes in by that same current of fictitious sense or non sense with an exception by the particle *but*, the fourth brings in an inference from that by the particle *therefore*, the fyfth renders a reasone of that by the particle *because*, and because varietie is operative on the memory, the two last lynes (*nevertheless* and *moreover*) give a contradiction to what has bene spoken before. This uniforme method is observed thurouout all the periods, which is exced-ing helpfull to memorie, for I now know it by experience that anie of ordinarie capacitie and memorie is able by this method to have al the common notions of discourse so readilie in less than a fortnights tyme as presentlie to writt anie notion as its oune proper character without booke, or to read what is written in it. For it is to be observed that the character is so artificialie contrived that ther needs no more for having the character of evrie notion but simplie to gett the tables by heart, which being done the character ipso facto is had by two or three general directions. It is therefore againe to be observed that evrie period has but one radical character to express the fourtie two notions contained [in] it, but is capable of fourtie 2 distinct poynts of numeration upon it so that what ever word occures to be expressed by this character we must first recurre to the period it is in, nixt to the lyne, thirdlie to the numerical word of the line, and so the character is had. The points of numeration stand thus answering to the numerical disposition of the notions in the table, to witt, six simple poynts upon the top of the character as is represented in the following <fo. 151ʳ> figure using express the six notion of the first lyne; six on the middle of the character for the 2 lyne (which for memories cause is to be called *for*); six at the bottome for the 3 lyne, *but*; six againe on the top hooked poynts for distinction for the lyne *therefore*; six in the middle for *because*; six at the bottom for *Nevertheles*; and six quite thorou the character for *Morover*.

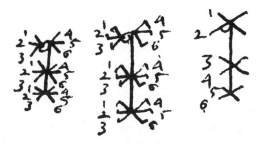

Dalgarno's diagram representing the various positions of strokes indicating radical words in his initial scheme.

All the characters being perpendiculare are equalie capable of these distinct poynts of numeration, and it is much to be noted that anie who getts by heart these periods has not to remember alwaies from one to fourtie two for finding his character but remembering the lyne of the period he has onlie the order of the six words of that lyne to remember, as ꝗ, I know,[2] is the fourth character of the lyne *because* of the table *ille*; ꝑ writt; ꝉ salute; ꝗ thanke; ꝗ light, &c. Manie things are altered in these print tables and there are four more added; the table of substantives I have quite altered for several reasons I can not here enlarge.

Two more great advantages of this designe commending both the rationalitie and facilitie of it I shal onlie name, to witt expressing of all contraries by one rule, to witt by the contrary position of the same character: as ꝺ true, ꝺ false; ꝅ proud, ꝉ humble. Secondlie to make all notions wherof a certaine number can be reduced to one head derivatives from the radical character of verbs and adjectives, making the ground of derivation some use or other qualitie most certain and known in the thing for by this meanes the memorie shal be much helped and we shal have a description of the thing to witt the genus of it in the title which represents what classes of things it belongs to and the propertie of the thing expressed in the radical from which it comes. This waye I derive all the members of the bodie, diseases, all the species of nature, the young of living creatures, diminutives, arts, aggregata, of every one of these I have great companies brought together where ever the nature of the thing will

---

[2] Following Dalgarno's rules, the character for 'to know' should be ꝗ.

beare to be reduced to one of those heads which in other languages are a
difficile to be learned as other notions, but here the radicals being had and the
title of derivation for evrie head presentlie the derivative notion is had. The
order of my periods is taken from the order of the particles, the first containing
storie all in the first persone, the second in the second person &c. Sir, manie
learned persons here advyse me to order the simple notions in a philosophical
method withal joyning the memorative helps, cheifflie Doctor Wilkins advyses
this and is taking paines himself to put them in praedicamental order. This
method I did choose at the beginning but therafter deserted it for two reasons,
first I found all the mnemonicke helps would not answere to the philosophical
method, 2dlie I feared if I did pretend a philosophical order ther <fo. 152ʳ>
wold be quot capita tot sententiae among philosophers which might occasion
alteration and so the cheiffe intended end of the designe to be lost. I should
be glad to have your Wor[ships] judgment both in this and other things.
Manie particulars remaine to be explained conducing to the full understanding
of the designe which were too taedious to enlarge here wherfor I shal content
my selffe at present to have sett doune these few general observations and
according as this shal find acceptance I shal be readie herafter to accomodat
my selffe to your Wor[ships] farder desyres of satisfaction. Mr Hartlib I hope
will testifie what satisfaction the most learned and ingenious persons both here
and at both the universities with whom I have conversed have received, but my
real encouradgments have beene yet so small that it hinders my progress much.
I feare your Wo[rship] maye be wearied in reading this rather undigested
comentarie than a missive, for my prolixitie wherin I begg pardon, remaining

Sir
Your very faithfull thoe unknown servant
Gdalgarno

praxis

Praxis

He who can read this will soon understand this writing but because no man knows that which he nere did see he ought therfore to considder well and then lett him judge for he who condemns anie thing before he trie verilie dothe but make knowne his own weaknes

Sample of Dalgarno's real character, with running English translation, in his letter to Pell dated 26 December 1657.

Dalgarno to William Brierton, 17 February 1658

Ry[gh]t honourable Sir,
having now after long deliberation fully matured my thoughts in the Designe
of an Universal Character and a rational language, I have presumed to acquant
you, that (God willing) my purposes are shortly for satisfying the expectations
of many worthie persons who have been verie liberal patrons to me in the
carrying on of the worke to give a public account of my Labours. Sir you wil
perceive by the enclosed testimony what the practical facilitie of the designe
is, which is one of the cheife things commending it, I know it wil exceed
the beliefe of manie but it being upon experiment I hope to rational men the
evidence is so clear that it can not be contradicted. Sir you wil also see a list
of my patrons names (some wherof I doubt not are well knowne to yourself)
to whom with all other public spirited persons who shal contribut with them
dutie oblidges me to dedicat my Labours. Sir, I am sufficiently perswaded of
your good wishes and affections to all undertakings of a publick nature and in
particular to this and if you can engadge anie of your more ingenious friends to
doe some thing by way of encouradgment heerin I hope you shal find heerafter
that you have therby done service to the Common-wealth of Learning besydes
the putting a singulare obligation upon

Honourable Sir
Your most humble and obledged servant
Gdalgarno

London 17 Febr[uar]y
1658

Letter preserved in the British Library, Add. MS 4377, fo. 155.

Dalgarno to Samuel Hartlib, 20 May 1658

Honoured Sir

Nothing worthie of your observation having occurred since I came from London I have purposelie forborne to trouble you with letters knowing what multitude of employments you lye under and indisposition through bodilie infirmities for overcoming them. You will perceive by the enclosed testimonie what satisfaction the University of Cambridge has received of my designe; this testimonie being upon Experiment of the practical part of the designe I conceive it is omni exceptione major, and may fullie take of the prejudices of such incredulous persons who can give credit to the truth of nothing but what comes within the Compas of their owne sense and Apprehension. To the more ingenious sort I am Confident it wil be aboundantlie satisfactorie and wil engadge them to appeare the more forward in giving their best assistance towards the propagation of it; the Vice Chauncler Dr Worthington hes been verie Civil to me [and] I have grounds to hope that the University wil be generous in their Contribution for my encouradgment. I do not doubt Sir, if it please the Lord (which shal be my prayers as I know it is of manie others) to restore you to healthe, but you wil be readie (having so good grounds as both the Ample testimonies of so manie learned men as also the example of so manie worthie persons who have been liberal benefactors hertofore) to draw in all publick hearted persones you have anie interest in to doe somthing for carrying on the worke. Sir, I earnestlie entreat you with the verie first Convenience to spare a lyne upon me and if anie letters from Scotland or elswhere have come to your hand directed to me that you would be pleased to send them. I long to heare what becomes of the business in Ireland. Sir, if in anie thing I can be servicable to you here or else where you may verie readilie Command

Sir
Your verie much Obleidged friend and servant
Gdalgarno

Cambridge May 20th 1658
from my Chamber at John Smiths a shoemaker neare Sidney Colledge.
[*Postscript in margin*:] Sir, I purpose (godwilling) within a fortnight or little more to be at London at which tyme you shal expect a more particular account of my affaires. If anie gentlmen of my acquaintance come to give you a visit I pray you communicat this testimony to them that they may know there is yet lyfe in the designe and that there is good hopes that it shal dayly increase to a greater strengthe.

Letter preserved in the Sheffield University Library, Hartlib MS 49/1/1.

Dalgarno to Samuel Hartlib, 3 November 1659

Bishopston in Wiltsshire
No[vembe]r 3 1659

Honored Sir

Since the Lord called me forth to that great worke of preaching the Gospel I have (Blessed be his name) enjoyed myself with a great deale of tranquillity & Contentednes, wanting no accomodation of use to a Contemplative lyfe but Converse with men and bookes, which I can so much the easier dispense with that the path I have traced by my late studies hath been for anie thing I know traced by none before me. Any spare houres I wholly employ in revising & endeavouring a farder perfection of my first thoughts and truly I have found by experience that solitarines does fitt and dispose an Inventive spirit to dive to the bottom of his invention. I pray you Sir therfore let all my friends & bene-factors & others of your ingenious acquaintance as you have occasion under-stand that what hath been undertaken & promised to the world by me in the designe of a Real Character & Rational Language shall G[od] willing shortly appear & what it hath lossed in tyme it hath gained in strength & perfection. I feare my too much friedome & openes while I Conversed with men may be by some not made good use of, but if the worke it selfe & the publick suffer not the privat injurie to me shal be easily pardoned. If you heare anie thing of this subject or what hath affinity with it be pleased to impart it as you have done formerly, particularly if you can learned anie thing to come forth from Comenius, Sir Tho. Urquhart my countrie man, or Dr Wilkins, who, if he publish anie thing he deales neither ingeniously nor justly with me & I feare if he attempt anie thing on this subject he shal have small credit of it for besides that all he wil doe wil be to discover another mans labors, this cheifly wil reflect that (as I am verie confident) he wil doe it with several material defects for albeit I did for almost a yeers tyme by dayly Converse with him open up the whole mysterie so farre as the veine of my invention had then gone yet since the tyme of my retirement I have discovered advantages which I perswade my [selfe] have not fallen under his Consideration. If anie thing come to your knowledge which may be usfull to me in my studies as they relate

Letter preserved in the Sheffield University Library, Hartlib MS 42/7/1.

to publisk usfulnes I hope you will be willing to Communicat it withall, leting me know how you enjoy your health which I pray the Lord Continowe or restore according as your Condition is

Remaining
Sir
Your and the Publicks heartily wel wishing servant
Gdalgarno

[Postscript]
Sir, when you write to me send your leter to Mr Keate his house in Clements Lane neare Lumbard Street.

Dalgarno to Lord Hatton, 9 June 1672

Oxford June 9th
1672

Right Honorable
My Lord

as the onely reason that moved me to come over into England was for the cause of my health; so that same reason enclines me to continue here at Oxford which I hope will give no offense either to your Lo[rdship] or any of my good friends in Guernsey, seing without health I can in nowise be usefull to them yet I dare not take a final resolution in this matter till I understand your Lo[rdship's] pleasure. In the mean tyme I recommend my wife and children to your Lo[rdship's] favour and with my prayers for your Lo[rdship] and all your Honorable family, I rest

My Lord
Your Lo[rdship's] most obliged and most humble servant
Geo. Dalgarno.

Letter preserved in the British Library, Add. MS 29553, fo. 445.

Dalgarno to Lord Hatton, 22 June 1672

Oxford June 22nd
1672

Right Honorable
My Lord

The concernment of the matter, and the danger of miscarriage have moved me to write again these same things which I signified to your Lo[rdship] by a former letter to wit That since my coming to Oxford by your Lo[rdship's] favour and permission for my healths cause; my friends here advyse me not to return again into that air which hath agried so ill with my constitution: To whose advyce I must confess I ecline to hearken, if it may be with your Lo[rdship's] favour, together with the favour and good-will of my good friends the people of Guernzey. I hope your Lo[rdship] will be pleased to take into your consideration my great sufferings not only in my body but also in my goods, occasioned by willingness to serve my friends in Guernzey. I recommend my wife and children to your Lo[rdship's] favour, and that it may please Almighty God to protect and bless your Lo[rdship] and your honourable family is the prayer of

My Lord
Your Lo[rdship's] most humble and most obedient servant
Geo. Dalgarno

Letter preserved in the British Library, Add. MS 29553, fo. 453.

Dalgarno to Lord Hatton, 30 September 1672

Oxon. Sept 30th
1672

Ryght Honorable
My Lord,

I received a letter from your own hand enclosed in another from your brother, the contents of both of which (being the same) I satisfyed by a Resignation of the Latine frie Schoole of Guernzey under my hands seal; which I returned by the first post according to his desire. My Lord, althoe, when I weigh your late favours in the balance of strict justice I find myself too light for them; yet did I not dare, when I reflected upon your equity and goodness, be distrustfull; but that I should have further cause to love and honour you, and to pray for your welfare and prosperity, together with all your Noble Relations, and to be ready not only here, but upon all occasions to give real testimonies that I am

My Lord
Your Lo[ordship's] most obliged and most humble servant
Geo Dalgarno

Letter preserved in the British Library, Add. MS 29554, fo. 39.

GLOSSARY OF RADICALS AND PARTICLES

I. RADICALS

A

ab	basis
acre	salsum
ad	succus
af	os
ag	folium
aiv	concretum spirituale
ak	ostium
al	sol
am	crinis
an	humar
ap	tignum
ar	luna
as	stella
at	malus
av	ens, res

B

bab	rectum
bad	continuum
baf	profundum
bag	concavum
bam	longum
ban	latum
bap	planum
bas	affectiones primae
beb	dextra
bed	extra
bef	ante
beg	circundans
beis	accidens mathematicum
bem	distantia
ben	supra
bep	extremum
bes	situs

blηm	inclinans
blηn	secans
brab	curvum
brad	discretum
braf	breve, depressum
brag	convexum
bram	breve
bran	augustum
brap	gibbosum
breb	sinistra
bred	intra
bref	post
brem	contiguitas
bren	infra
brep	medium
brηb	obtusus
brηd	refractus
brηf	obliquus
brηg	reflexus
brηm	jacens
brηn	transversum
brηp	pronus
bηb	acutus
bηd	incidens
bηf	rectus
bηg	directus
bηm	perpendiculum
bηn	parallelum
bηp	supinus
bηs	positio

D

dab	novum invenis
dad	locus
daf	praeteritum
dag	plenum

This list was compiled by the editors of the present edition so as to enable easy reference to the meaning of expressions of Dalgarno's language. The list consists of two sections, together including all words enumerated on the tables of the Lexicon Grammatico-Philosophicum. As Dalgarno indicated, the list of particles presented there is not exhaustive. For grammatical inflections, see the fold-out table, seventh and eighth columns, and Introduction, Sect. 3.3.2.

dam	motus
dan	tempus
dap	praesentia
das	maxime communia
deb	trahere
ded	cadere
def	vertere
deg	tollere
deis	physicum generale
dek	contrahere
dem	flectere
den	jacere
dep	portare
des	motus simplex
dib	premere
did	pulsio
dif	terere
dig	percutere
dik	pungere
dim	concursus
din	fricatio
dip	sigillare, imprimere
dis	motus cum contactu
dit	tegere
dlaf	praesens
dob	forare
dod	solvere
dof	lacerare
dog	aperire
dom	scindere
don	frangere
dop	plicare
dos	motus retentio
dos	motus separans
dot	spargere
drab	antiquum
draf	futurum
drag	vacuum
dram	quies
dran	aeternitas
drap	absentia
dred	surgere
dreg	deponere
drek	dilatare
drid	vulsio
drod	ligare
drog	claudere
drop	explicare
drot	colligere
drηd	inniti
drηg	resistere
drηm	levitas

drηn	tarditas
dηb	vis
dηd	sustinere
dηf	conatus
dηg	cedere
dηm	gravitas
dηn	celeritas
dηs	modi motus
dυf	prendere
dυm	haerere
dυn	tenere

E

eb	perimetrum
ed	cortex
ef	caro
eg	calix
eif	spermaticae
eik	partes aedificii specialiores
eim	excrementitiae
ein	partes fluidae utiles
eiv	anima
ek	grundia
em	stercus
en	lac
ep	columna
er	ventus
es	nubes
et	remus
ev	accidens

F

fa	pectus
fab	organum pneumaticum
fad	ludus
faf	atramentum
fam	canalis
fan	domus
fap	gladius
fe	scapula
feb	cumbalum
fed	spectaculum
fef	liber
feib	suppellex musicum
feibdeig	suppellex voluptuarium
feid	suppellex oculum delectantia
feif	suppellex ad communicandum
feim	victus et amictus

feimneif	concretum artefactum necessarium	frʋm	ornamentum
fein	aedificium	frʋn	arca
feip	arma	fub	campana
feipteik	suppellex perniciosa	fum	pecunia
feis	concretum artefactum	fη	mamma
feis	truncus	fηb	lura
fem	theca	fηd	pictura
fen	pons	fηf	charta
fep	arcus	fηm	funis
fi	costa	fηn	navis
fib	pandura	fηp	bombarda
fim	acicula	fʋ	nates
fip	sagitta telum	fʋb	tuba
fla	diaphragma	fʋm	forfex
flam	panis	fʋp	clupeus
flan	aratrum		
fle	cor	**G**	
fleim	victus	gab	durities
flein	suppellex rustica	gad	crastitias
fleis	partes mediae cavitatis	gaf	densitas
flem	jus Condimentum	gag	arriditas
flen	ligo	gak	fluiditas
flim	buturum	gam	calor
flin	currus	gan	humiditas
flom	caseus	gap	lentor
flum	artocreas	gas	tactus
flη	pulmo	gat	asperitas
flηm	potus	geis	qualitas sensibilis
flηn	occa	gem	fragrans
flʋm	fartum	gen	graveolentia
fo	venter	ges	odor
fob	tumpana	gib	fortis
fom	acus	gid	clarus
fop	hasta	gif	acutus
fram	filum	gig	asper
fran	mensa	gim	articulatus
fre	coxa	gin	echo
freim	amictus	gis	sonus
frein	suppellex domestica	gob	flavum
frem	pannus	god	rubrum
fren	vas	gof	album
fri	spina	gog	pallidum
frim	pulvinar	gom	lux
frin	cathedra	gon	diaphanum
fro	lumbus	gop	caesium
from	saccus	gos	color
fron	sporta	grab	mollities
frun	lectus	grad	subtilitas
frη	umbilicus	graf	raritas
frηm	vitta	grag	lubricitas
frηn	candela	grak	consistentia
		gram	frigus

gran	siccitas
grap	friabilitas
grat	laevitas
grem	faetidus
grib	debilis
grid	obscurus
grif	gravis
grig	aequabilis
grim	confusus
grob	caeruleum
grod	viride
grof	nigrum
grog	purpureum
grom	tenebrae
gron	opacum
grop	fuscum
grub	decrescere
grud	marcescere
grug	morbus
grum	fames
grun	sterilitas
grup	immaturitas
grηb	acidum
grηm	amarum
grηn	austerum
grυp	corruptio
gub	crescere
guf	pallulare
gug	sanitas
gum	nutritio
gun	fertilitas
gup	maturitas
gus	affectiones vegetabiles
gηf	insipidum
gηm	dulce
gηn	pingue
gηs	sapor
gυb	concretio
gυd	concoctio
gυd	florere
gυf	temperamentum
gυg	alteratio
gυm	mixtio
gυn	fermentatio
gυp	generatio
gυs	communes affectiones mixtorum

I

ib	axis
id	geniculum
if	vena
ig	palea
ik	vestibulum
im	mucus
in	modulla
ip	cancelli
ir	fons
is	mare
iv	ens completum, vel concretum

K

kab	tutor
kad	legatus
kaf	clericus
kag	dux
kam	dominus
kan	rex
kap	consiliarius
kas	relatio officii
keb	lex
ked	titulus
kef	jus
keis	(accidens) politicum
kem	res
ken	actio causa
kes	judiciorum materia
kib	accusare
kid	appellare
kif	causam agere
kig	confessio
kim	citare
kin	allegare
kis	partes litigantium
kob	proscribere
kod	arrestare
kof	punire
kog	incarcerare
kom	decernere
kon	absolvere
kop	confiscare
kos	partes judicis
krab	pupillus
kraf	laicus
krag	miles
kram	servus
kran	subditus
kref	factum
krem	persona
krib	excusare
krid	submittere
krim	apparere
krin	probare

krof	parcere		meis	concretum
kron	damnare			mathematicum
krum	defendere		mem	superficies
krut	dedere		mi	cilium
krηf	reus		mib	cubus
krηm	litigans		mim	solidum
krηn	cliens		mo	tempora
kub	praeliari		mob	conus
kud	induciae		mra	facies
kuf	obsidere		mre	occiput
kug	captivare		mreis	collum
kum	invadere		mrη	aurus
kun	excubare		mub	piramis
kup	spoliare		mη	oculus
kus	bellum		mηb	sphaera
kut	vincere		mηm	linea
kηb	testis		mυ	nasus
kηd	officialis		mυb	cilandis
kηf	actor			
kηm	judex		**N**	
kηn	patronus		na	dens
kηs	relatio officii in judiciis		nab	herba bestiae vesca
kυb	rebellio		nad	herba flore insignis bulbosa
kυd	factio		naf	minerale medium
kυf	fornicatio		nag	herba lignosa suffrutex
kυg	haeresis		nak	brutum sanguineum terrestre oviparum
kυk	incantatio			
kυm	injuria		nam	coelum
kυn	furtum		nan	meteoron ignitum
kυp	crimen falsi		nap	avis carnivora
kυs	delicta		nat	piscis squamosus
kυt	proditio		ne	palatum
			neb	herba vesca homini in radice
L				
lag	flos		nef	metallum
led	caro		neg	herba lignosa semper viridis
lir	palus		neib	herba vesca
lor	planities		neibeid	herba
luk	paries		neid	herba flore insignis
lηd	truneus		neidbeig	planta
lυk	teguli		neif	minerale
			neig	herba lignosa
M			neik	brutum sanguineum terrestre
ma	cranium			
mab	circulus		neim	inanimatum simplex
mam	punctum		neimneif	inanimatum
me	frons		nein	meteoron
meb	spira		neip	brutum sanguineum aerium id est, avis
meib	figura			
meim	species simplices		neipeit	brutum imperfectum
meis	caput			

neipteik	brutum	nʋ	gula
neipteik	brutum sanguineum	nʋb	frumentum
neis	concretum physicum	nʋk	brutum sanguineum
neis	os		terrestre sub terra degens
neit	brutum sanguineum	nʋp	avis aquatica
	aqueum id est piscis	nʋt	piscis caete
neiteik	amphibion		
nek	brutum sanguineum	**O**	
	terrestre bisulcum	ob	gumphus
nem	aer	od	spina
nen	meteoron aqueum	of	nervus
nep	avis canora	og	spica
net	piscis cartilagineus	oiv	angelus
ni	labium	ok	contignatio
nib	herba vesca homini in	om	cauda
	fructu	on	chylus
nig	herba lignosa non	ool	cavea
	spinos. seminif.	op	scala
nik	brutum sanguineum	or	mons
	terrestre multifidum	os	continens
	majus	ot	branchia
nim	aqua	ov	corpus
nin	meteoron terrenum		
nip	avis domestica	**P**	
nit	piscis planus	pab	vigilare
no	bucca	pad	sexus
nob	legumen	paf	edere
nog	herba lignosa bacciferus	pag	mas gignere
nok	brutum sanguineum	pak	educare
	terrestre multifidum minus	pam	spirare
nom	terra	pan	vocem edere
nop	avis pulveratricea	pap	libido
not	piscis fluviatilis	pas	generaliora
nri	mentum	pat	concipere
nu	gurgulio	peb	appetitus
nub	condimentum	ped	voluptus
nuk	brutum sanguineum	pef	phantasia
	terrestre serpens	peg	providentia
nup	avis palmipes	peis	accidentia sensitiva
nη	gingiva	pem	cognoscere
nηb	herba vesca homini in folio	pen	memoria
nηd	herba flore insignis non	pes	sensus interni
	bulbosa	pib	constans
nηf	lapis	pid	affabilis
nηg	herba lignosa frutex	pif	gravis
	spinosus	pig	sobrietas
nηk	brutum sanguineum	pik	gratitudo
	terrestre solidipes	pim	simplicitas
nηm	ignis	pin	ferus
nηn	meteoron aerium	pip	diligentia
nηp	avis nocturna	pis	inclinatio naturalis
nηt	piscis laevis	pit	crudelitas

pob	gaudium	pηs	motus animalis
pod	ira	pηt	ducere
pof	spes	pʋb	invidia
pog	pudor	pʋd	vindicta
pok	liberalitas	pʋf	zelus
pom	admiratio	pʋg	consternatio
pon	amor	pʋk	concupiscentia
pop	aestimatio	pʋm	paenitentia
pos	passiones principales	pʋn	imitatio
pot	animositas	pʋp	adulatio
prab	dormire	pʋs	passiones minus
praf	bibere		principales
prag	faemina (gignere)	pʋt	aemulatio
prat	parere		
preg	experientia	**R**	
prib	mutabilis	rab	cacumen
prid	morosus	raf	cartilago
prif	levis	rag	fructus
prig	affectatio	rak	fenestra
prim	sagacitas	ram	unguis
prin	mitis	ran	pituita
prip	ignavia	rap	asseres
prit	misericordia	rat	transenna
prob	laetitia	reb	area
prod	patientia	red	medulla
prof	metus	ref	adeps
prog	gloriatio	rem	urina
prok	parsimonia	ren	semen
pron	odium	rep	arcus
prop	contemptus	ret	velum
prηd	venire	rib	polus
prηk	surgere	rid	internodium
prηp	sequi	rif	arteria
prʋb	commiseratio	rig	siliqua
pub	cavere	rik	postica
pud	attendere	rin	cerebrum
puf	observare	rir	rivus
pug	simulare	ris	fluvius
pum	curare	rob	impages
pun	expectare	rod	lanugo
pup	suspicio	rof	fibra
pus	passionum affines	rol	rupes
put	audere	rom	juba
pηb	gradi	ror	vallis
pηd	comparare	ros	insula
pηd	ire	rug	nucleus
pηf	serpere	ruk	pavimentum
pηg	saltare	rηb	angulus
pηk	discumbere	rηd	ramus
pηm	volare	rηf	membrana
pηn	natare	rηk	fornax
pηp	fugere	rηm	melancholia

rηn	spiritus	shom	oppositum
rηp	caementum	shon	absolutum
rηr	fuligo	shop	objectum
rηs	flamma	shot	circumstantia
rηt	anchora	shug	proprium
rυk	capreoli	shum	multitudo
rυm	ungula	shun	pars
rυp	agger	shηb	periculum
rυt	pinna	shηd	mutabile
		shηg	carere
S		shηk	extraordinarium
sab	instrumentum	shηm	dependens
sad	preparans	shηn	compositum
saf	auxilium	shηp	mori
sag	exemplum	shυb	posterius
sak	fortuna	shυd	defectus
sam	causa efficiens	shυf	minime
san	materia	shυm	parum
sap	occasio	shυn	minυs
sas	causa	sif	purum
sat	meritum	sig	utile
sava	deus, id est, causa prima	sim	bonum
seb	debere	sin	pulchrum
sed	oportere	sip	jucundum
sef	potentia	sis	perfectio
seg	expedire	sit	aptum
seis	accidens commune	skab	jurare
sek	spontaneitas	skad	orare
sem	incipere	skaf	colere
sen	repetere	skag	sacrificium
sep	facile	skak	miraculum
ses	modi agendi	skam	gratia
set	solere habitus	skan	felicitas
shad	conservans	skap	sacramentum
shaf	impedimentum	skas	religio
shak	consilium	skat	mysterium
sham	finis	skrad	laudare
shan	forma	skraf	profanare
shek	violentia	skram	natura
shem	finire	skran	miseria
shep	difficile	skras	superstitio
shif	impurum	slaf	permissio
shig	noxium	slam	medium
shim	malum	slem	continuare
shin	deforme	slim	indifferens
ship	molestum	slom	diversum
shit	ineptum	slop	medium
shob	inconsistens seu	slυb	simul
	contradictorium	slυd	satis
shod	passio	slυm	mediocriter
shof	positivum	slυn	aeque
shog	adjunctum	sma	manus

smar	pes	snib	herba miscellanea convolvula
sme	cubitus		
smeis	artus	snid	herba miscellanea lactaria
smer	tibia		
smi	cubitus	snig	arbor nucifera
smir	genu	snir	fel
smo	carpus	snit	brutum exangue aqueum crustaceum rotundum
smor	calx		
smu	digitus	sno	vesica
smur	digitus pedis	snob	herba miscellanea spinosa
smη	brachium		
smηr	femur	snod	herba miscellanea nervosa
smυ	manus		
smυr	pes parvus	snog	arbor prunifera
sna	aesophagus	snor	ren
snab	herba miscellanea marina	snot	brutum exangue aqueum testaceum turbinatum in anfractum
snad	herba miscellanea tomentosa		
snag	arbor sterilis	snu	foetus
snak	brutum exangue terrestre apodum	snub	herba miscellanea scabiosa
snal	ventriculus	snud	herba miscellanea semper viva
snap	brutum exangue aerium volatile detectipennis	snug	arbor acinifera
snar	intestina	snur	ovum
snat	brutum exangue aqueum molle apodum	snut	brutum exangue aqueum conchae
sne	epar	snη	peritoneum
sneb	herba miscellanea junci et arundines	snηb	herba miscellanea lacustris
sned	herba miscellanea corimbifera	snηd	herba miscellanea umbellifera
sneg	arbor conifera	snηf	lapis pretiosus
sneib	planta imperfecta	snηg	arbor glandifera
sneibeid	herba miscellanea	snηk	brutum exangue terrestre paucipedatum
sneig	arbor		
sneik	brutum exangue terrestre	snηl	omentum
sneip	brutum exangue aerium volatile	snηp	brutum exangue aerium volatile bipennis
sneipteik	brutum exangue	snηr	mesenterium
sneis	partes organicae ventris infimi	snηt	brutum exangue aqueum molle pedatum
sneit	brutum exangue aqueum	snυ	uterus
snek	brutum exangue terrestre multipedatum	snυb	herba miscellanea filices
snep	brutum exangue aerium volatile vaginipennis	snυd	herba miscellanea linosa
		snυg	arbor pomifera
sner	testes	snυr	virga
snet	brutum exangue aqueum crustaceum caudatum	snυt	brutum exangue aqueum testaceum turbinatum in orbem
sni	lien		

sob	consistens	sted	proximus
sod	actio	stef	maritus
sof	privativum	steg	hospes
sog	subjectum	steis	(accidens)
som	idem		oeconomicum
son	respectivum	stek	creditor
sop	actus	stem	familia
sos	consentanea	sten	natio
sot	substantia	step	familiaris
spab	quaerela	stes	relatio societatis
spad	provocare	stet	amicus
spaf	ludere	stib	possessio
spag	placere	stid	habitatio
spak	fallere	stif	donatio
spam	ridere	stig	praescriptio
span	canere	stim	haereditatio
spap	lis	stin	legatio
spas	effectus passionum	stis	modi acquirendi dominium
spat	insidiari	stlηm	aequalis
spe	penna	stob	locare
spi	ala	stod	deponere
spo	crista	stof	emere
sprag	offendere	stog	sponsionem facere
spram	flere	stom	tractare
spran	plorare	ston	permutare
sprap	concordia	stop	accommodare
spre	pluma	stos	contractus
sprηb	recipere	strab	irridere
sprηd	dimittere	straf	valedicere
sprηf	acceptare	stran	rusticitas
sprηn	perdere	streb	affinis
sprηp	otiari	stred	peregrinus
spηb	tradere	strek	debitor
spηd	sumere	stret	hostis
spηf	offerre	stris	modi tenendi dominium
spηg	luctari	strob	conducere
spηm	quaerere	strof	vendere
spηn	invenire	strηb	paupertas
spηp	laborari	strηf	plebeitas
spηs	alii effectus	strηg	damnum
spηt	lassitudo	strηm	inferior
sros	dissentanea	strηn	privatus
stab	jocare	strυm	praestare
stad	comitari	strυs	modi dissolvendi
staf	salutare	stηb	divitiae
stag	visitare	stηd	valor pretium
stam	ceremonia	stηf	nobilitas honor
stan	civilitas	stηg	lucrum
stap	tractare	stηk	merx
stas	relatio morum	stηm	superior
stat	congratulari	stηn	publicus
steb	cognatus	stηp	sumptus

stηs	variae denominationes personarum et rerum	teis	accidens rationale
		tem	ars
stηt	merces	ten	scientia
stʋb	fidejubere	tes	habitus intellectuales
stʋd	solvere		
stʋf	pignerare	tib	docere
stʋg	acceptillare	tid	interrogare
stʋm	promittere	tif	interpretari
stʋn	stipulare	tig	narrare
stʋp	condonare	tik	restringere
stʋs	modi obligandi	tim	affirmare
stʋt	compensare	tin	loqui
sub	proportio	tip	fama
sud	ordo	tis	intellectus expressio
suf	reliquum	tit	definire
sug	commune	tlob	species
sum	unitas	tlom	sullaba
sun	totum	tob	genus
sus	relatio numeri	tod	propositio
sηb	salus	tof	figura
sηd	permanens	tog	prosa
sηf	pertinere	tok	regula
sηg	habere	tom	litera
sηk	ordinarium	ton	nomen
sηm	independens	top	periodus
sηn	simplex	tos	signum
sηp	vivere	tot	sectio caput
sηs	modi existendi	trad	distensus
sηt	vices	trib	discere
sʋb	prius	trid	respondere
sʋd	excessus	trik	ampliare
sʋf	maxime	trim	negare
sʋm	valde	trin	scribere
sʋn	magis	trit	distinguere
sʋs	gradus comparationis	trob	individuum
		trod	oratio
		trog	carmen
T		trok	exceptio
tab	apprehensio perceptio	trom	dictio
tad	astensus	tron	casus nominis
taf	curiositas	trop	accentus
tag	judicium	trub	reprehendere
tak	machinatio	trud	vituperare
tam	ingenium	truf	maledicere
tan	conscientia	trug	consolari
tap	discursus	trum	dissuadere
tas	actus intellectus primi	trun	deprecari
tat	meditatio	trup	obedire
teb	opinio	trηf	dividere
ted	intelligentia	trηm	inferre
tef	sapientia	trηn	subducere
teg	discretio	trηt	excludere

trʊb	vitium	**U**	
trʊd	rejectio	ud	surculus
trʊf	dissensus	ug	putamen
trʊm	coactio	uk	tectum
trʊn	determinatio	up	obex
trʊp	diffidere	uv	compositum, id est, homo
tub	hortari	uv	homo seu concretum
tud	laudare		compositum
tuf	benedicere		
tug	minari	**H**	
tum	suadere	ηb	latus
tun	petere	ηd	radix
tup	imperare	ηf	cutis
tus	voluntatis expressio	ηg	pappus
tut	consulere	ηk	caminus
tηb	probare	ηm	cholera
tηf	multiplicare	ηn	sanguis
tηg	mensurare	ηp	later
tηm	supponere	ηr	cinis
tηn	addere	ηs	fumus
tηp	conjicere	ηt	clavus
tηs	ex primis orti	ηv	substantia
tηt	includere		
tʊb	virtus	**Y**	
tʊd	electio	ʊd	gummi
tʊf	consensus	ʊf	ligamentum
tʊg	optare	ʊg	arista
tʊm	libertas	ʊk	transtra
tʊn	deliberatio	ʊm	cornu
tʊp	credere	ʊp	vallum
tʊs	voluntas	ʊt	squama
tʊt	suscipere	ʊv	spirit

II. PARTICLES

A

av   ullus

B

bed   1. e, ex
      2. extra

bef   1. ante
      2. coram
      3. prae
      4. pro

beg   circum

bem   1. ab
      2. apud
      3. inter

ben   supra

blηn   per

bred   1. in
      2. intra

bref   post

breg   inter

brem   1. ad
      2. iuxta
      3. tenus

bren   1. sub
      2. super

brηn   1. per
      2. praeter
      3. trans

bηs	1. tenus
	2. versus
bηsben	sursum
bηsbren	deorsum
D	
dan	in
dap	cum
dlaf	interim
drap	sine
drηd	super
dηd	sub
G	
gʋm	inter
L	
lal	ego
lel	ille
lelbes	tam
leldad	illic
lelsas	1. ergo
	2. ideo
lol	hic
lolbes	tam
loldad	hic
loldan	1. interim
	2. jam
	3. nunc
loliηb	citra
lul	1. qui
	2. quis
luldan	interim
lulsas	cur
lηl	tu
lʋl	ipse
M	
mηssi	coram
S	
sab	1. cum
	2. per
sag	per
sak	forte
sam	1. ab
	2. per
san	e, ex
sas	1. nam
	2. ob
	3. propter
sen	iterum

ses	quasi
sham	1. ob
	2. propter
	3. ut
shep	vix
shod	ad
shom	1. contra
	2. ob
	3. sed
shomieb	trans
shop	de
shumbem	iuxta
shun	aliquis
shundan	interdum
shηg	1. citra
	2. sine
shʋb	1. post
	2. praeterea
	3. sub
shʋbapdan	denique
shʋbdan	deinde
shʋbdanbam	tandem
shʋbsud	deinde
shʋmbem	1. apud
	2. prope
	3. propter
	4. secundum
shʋmsuf	prope
slam	1. cum
	2. per
slem	adhuc
slom	1. at
	2. aut
slʋb	1. cum
	2. simul
slʋd	satis
slʋn	1. iuxta
	2. quasi
	3. quoque
	4. tam
	5. ut
sod	1. ab
	2. per
sof	sine
sos	1 iuxta
	2. pro
	3. secundum
srʋd	nimis-parum
subdan	adhuc
sufshun	prope
sum	1. aliquis
	2. invicem

sun	omnis	trηb	1. aut
sηf	1. de		2. vel
	2. nam	trηf	1. at
sηt	1. invicem		2. sed
	2. pro	trηm	ergo
sʋb	pro	tηf	1. ac
sʋd	nimis		2. et
sʋfshun	fere		3. etiam
sʋmshʋf	fere		4. item
sʋs	quam		5. praeterea
			6. quoque
T		tηg	quam
tid	an	tηm	1. etsi
tim	ita		2. tamen
trim	1. ne		
	2. non	**V**	
trimshaf	1. at	vη	iterum
	2. tamen		

References

AARSLEFF, HANS (1976), 'John Wilkins', in C. C. Gillispie (ed.), *Dictionary of Scientific Biography* (New York: Scribner's), xiv. 361–81. (Reprinted in Subbiondo 1992: 3–41.)

ABERCROMBIE, DAVID (1993), 'William Holder and other Seventeenth-Century Phoneticians', *Historiographia Linguistica*, 20: 309–30.

ALSTON, R. C. (1967), *Bibliography of the English Language from the Invention of Printing to the Year 1800*, vii. *Logic, Philosophy, Epistemology, Universal Language* (Bradford: Printed for the author by Scolar Press).

ANDERSON, PETER JOHN (1889), *Fasti Academiae Mariscallanae Aberdonensis* (Aberdeen: New Spalding Club).

ANDRADE, E. N. DA C. (1936), 'The Real Character of Bishop Wilkins', *Annals of Science*, 1: 4–12. (Reprinted in Subbiondo 1992: 253–61.)

ARISTOTLE (1949), *Categoriae et Liber de Interpretatione*, ed. L. Minio-Paluello (Oxford: Oxford University Press). (Trans. *Aristotle's Categories and De Interpretatione*, trans. with notes by J. L. Ackrill. (Oxford: Clarendon Press, 1963).)

ARNAULD, ANTOINE, and NICOLE, PIERRE (1970 [1662]), *La Logique ou l'Art de Penser* (Paris: Flammarion).

ARRIAGA, RODRIGO DE (1653), *Cvrsvs philosophicvs* (Lugduni: Sumptibus Claudii Prost).

ASBACH-SCHNITKER, BRIGITTE (1984), 'Introductory Essay', in John Wilkins, *Mercury: or the Secret and Swift Messenger* [1641], reprinted from the third edition: *The Mathematical and Philosophical Works of the Right Reverend John Wilkins* (1708) (Amsterdam / Philadelphia: Benjamins).

AUBREY, JOHN (1950), *Brief Lives*, ed. from the original manuscripts by Oliver Lawson Dick (London: Secker & Warburg).

BACON, FRANCIS (1605), *The two bookes of Francis Bacon. Of the proficience and aduancement of learning, diuine and humane* (London: H. Tomes).

—— (1887–1901), *The Works of Francis Bacon. Philosophical Works*, ed. J. Spedding, R. L. Ellis, and D. D. Heath (London: John M. Robertson).

BAUHIN, CASPAR (1623), *Pinax Theatri Botanici Caspari Bauhini* (Basileae Helvet.: sumptibus et typis Ludovici Regis).

BECHER, JOHANN JOACHIM (1661), *Character, pro Notitia Linguarum Universali* (Frankfurt).

BECK, CAVE (1657), *The Universal Character* (London).

BENNETT, JIM, and MANDELBROTE, SCOTT (1998), *The Garden, the Ark, the Tower, the Temple: Biblical Metaphors of Knowledge in Early Modern Europe* (Oxford: Museum for the History of Science).

BIRCH, THOMAS (1756), *The History of the Royal Society*; 4 vols. (London: Printed for A. Millar).

BLUNDEVILLE, THOMAS (1599), *The Art of Logike* (London: John Windet. (Reprinted Amsterdam and New York: Da Capo Press, 1969)).

BONET, JUAN PABLO (1620), *Reduction de las letras, y arte para enseñar a ablar los mudos*. Madrid: F. Abarca de Angulo. (Trans. *Simplification of the Letters of the Alphabet and Method of Teaching Deaf-Mutes to Speak*, trans. H. N. Dixon (Harrogate: A. Farrar, 1890).)

BORST, ARNO (1960), *Der Turmbau von Babel: Geschichte der Meinungun über Ursprung und Vielfalt der Sprachen und Völker*; 6 vols. (Stuttgart: A. Hiersemann).

BOYLE, ROBERT (1772), The *Works of the Honourable Robert Boyle. Edited by Thomas Birch*; 6 vols. (London: J. and F. Rivington). (Repr. Hildesheim: Olms, 1965–6.)

BREWER, EBENEZER COBHAM (1995 [1870]), *Brewer's Dictionary of Phrase and Fable, fifteenth edition, revised by Adrian Room* (London: Cassell).

BUCKLER, BENJAMIN (1756), 'A Table of the Succession of the Delegates of the Press from the Year 1633 to 1756', printed as an appendix to *A Reply to Dr Huddesfield's Observations Relating to the Delegates of the Press* ([Oxford] n.p.).

BULWER, JOHN (1644), *Chirologia: or, the naturall Language of the Hand. Whereunto is added Chironomia: or, the art of manuall rhetoricke. By J.B. Gent. philochirosophus* (London: Richard Whitaker).

—— (1648), *Philocophus: or, The deafe and dumb mans friend. By I.B. sirnamed the Chirosopher* (London: Humphrey Moseley).

BURSILL-HALL, G. L. (1972), *Grammatica Speculativa of Thomas of Erfurt* (London: Longman).

CAMDEN, WILLIAM (1605), *Remaines of a greater work, concerning Britaine* (London: Simon Waterson).

CAMPANELLA, TOMMASO (1638), *Philosophiae Rationalis partes quinque, videlicet: Grammatica, Dialectica, Rhetorica, Poetica, Historiographia* (Paris: apud Ioannem du Bray).

CARTER, HARRY GRAHAM (1975), *A History of the Oxford University Press*, i. *To the Year 1780* (Oxford: Clarendon Press).

CHRISTENSEN, FRANCIS (1946), 'John Wilkins and the Royal Society's Reform of Prose Style', *Modern Language Quarterly*, 7: 179–89, 279–90. (Repr. in Subbiondo 1992: 133–52.)

CICERO, MARCUS TULLIUS (1961), *De Officiis* (Loeb Classical Library; London: Heineman).

—— (1972), *Epistolae Familiares: The Letters to his Brother Quintus*. (Loeb Classical Library; London: Heineman).

CLAUSS, SIDONIE (1982), 'John Wilkins's Essay toward a Real Character: Its Place in the Seventeenth-Century Episteme', *Journal of the History of Ideas*, 42: 531–53. (Repr. in Subbiondo 1992: 45–67.)

COHEN, JONATHAN (1954), 'On the Project of a Universal Character', *Mind*, 63: 49–63. (Repr. in Subbiondo 1992: 237–51.)

COHEN, MURRAY (1977), *Sensible Words: Linguistic Practice in England 1640–1785* (Baltimore: Johns Hopkins University Press).

COMENIUS, JAN AMOS (1631), *Janua linguarum reserata aurea sive seminarum linguarum et scientiarum omnium* ([Lezno] n.p.).

—— (1662), *Janua linguarum trilinguis* (London: Roger Daniel).

—— (1668), *Via Lucis* (Amsterdam: apud Christ. Cunradam).

—— (1966), *Panglottia*, in J. Ñervenka and V. T. Mikovská (eds.), *De Rerum Humanarum Emendatione Consultatio Catholica*; 2 vols. (Prague: Academia Scientianum Bohemoslovaca), ii. 147–204.

CORNELIUS, PAUL (1965), *Languages in Seventeenth- and Eighteenth-Century Imaginary Voyages* (Geneva: Droz).

COUTURAT, LOUIS, and LEAU, LÉOPOLD (1903), *Histoire de la langue universelle* (Paris: Hachette).

CRAM, DAVID (1980), 'George Dalgarno on "Ars Signorum" and Wilkins' "Essay"', in E. F. K. Koerner (ed.), *Progress in Linguistic Historiography* (Studies in the History of Linguistics, 20; Amsterdam: Benjamins), 113–21.

—— (1985), 'Language Universals and Seventeenth-Century Universal Language Schemes', in Klaus D. Dutz and Ludger Kaczmarek (ed.), *Rekonstruktion und Interpretation* (Tübingen: Gunter Narr.), 243–57. (Repr. in Subbiondo 1992: 191–203.)

—— (1989), 'J. A. Comenius and the Universal Language Scheme of George Dalgarno', in M. Kyralová and J. Prívratská (eds.), *Symposium Comenianum* (Prague: Academia Scientianum Bohemoslovaca), 181-7.

—— (1990), 'George Dalgarno and Guernsey'. *Reports and Transactions* (Guernsey: La Société Guernesaise), 22: 808-26.

—— (1994), 'Universal Language, Specious Arithmetic and the Alphabet of Simple Notions', *Beiträge zur Geschichte der Sprachwissenschaft*, 4: 1-21.

—— and MAAT, JAAP (1996), 'Comenius, Dalgarno and the English Translations of the Janua Linguarum', *Studia Comeniana et Historica*, 26: 55-6, 148-60.

DALGARNO, GEORGE (1661), *Ars Signorum, vulgo character universalis et lingua philosophica* (London: J. Hayes). (Repr. Menston: Scolar Press, 1968.)

—— (1680), *Didascalocophus or The Deaf and Dumb mans Tutor, to which is added A Discourse of the Nature and Number of Double Consonants* (Oxford: at the Theater). (Repr. Menston: Scolar Press, 1971.)

DAVID, MADELEINE (1965), *Le Débat sur les écritures et l'hiéroglyphe aux xviie et xviiie siècles* (Paris: SEVPEN).

DEBUS, ALLEN G. (1970), *Science and Education in the Seventeenth Century. The Webster–Ward Debate* (London and New York: MacDonald & American Elsevier).

DEMOTT, BENJAMIN (1955), 'Comenius and the Real Character in England', *Publications of the Modern Language Association*, 70: 1068-81. (Repr. in Subbiondo 1992: 155-81.)

—— (1957), 'Science versus Mnemonics, Notes on John Ray and on John Wilkins' Essay toward a Real Character, and a Philosophical Language', *Isis*, 48: 3-12.

—— (1958), 'The Sources and Development of John Wilkins' Philosophical Language', *Journal of English and Germanic Philology*, 57.1: 1-13.

DESCARTES, RENÉ (1902), *Œuvres de Descartes*, ed. Charles Adam and Paul Tannéry (Paris: Léopold Cerf).

DIEHL, ERNST (1911), *Die Vitae Vergilianae und ihre antiken Quellen* (Bonn: A. Marcus und E. Weber's Verlag).

DIGBY, SIR KENELM (1644), *Of Bodies*, in *Two treatises, in the one of which, the nature of bodies; in the other, the nature of mans soul; is looked into in way of discovery of the Immortality of reasonable soules* (Paris: Gilles Blaizot), 1-346.

DOLEZAL, FREDRIC (1985), *Forgotten but Important Lexicographers: John Wilkins and William Lloyd* (Tübingen: Niemeyer).

DUTZ, KLAUS D. (1989), '"Lingua Adamica nobis certe ignota est". Die Sprachursprungsdebatte und Gottfried Wilhelm Leibniz', in Joachim Gessinger and Wolfert von Rahden (eds.), *Theorien vom Ursprung der Sprache*; 2 vols. (Berlin and New York: Walter de Gruyter), i. 204-40.

ECO, UMBERTO (1995), *The Search for the Perfect Language* (Oxford: Blackwell).

ELLIOTT, RALPH W. V. (1957), 'Isaac Newton's "Of an Universal Language"', *Modern Language Review*, 52/1: 1-18.

EMERY, CLARK (1947), 'John Wilkins' Universal Language', *Isis*, 38: 174-85.

—— (1948), 'John Wilkins and Noah's Ark', *Modern Language Quarterly*, 9: 286-91. (Repr. in Subbiondo 1992: 279-84.)

EVERARDT, JOB (1658), *An Epitome of Stenographie; or An Abridgement and Contraction, of the Art of short, swift, and secret writing by Characters* (London: Lodowick Lloyd).

FIRTH, J. R. (1964 [1937, 1930]), *The Tongues of Men and Speech* (London: Oxford University Press).

FOSTER, JOSEPH (1891), *Alumni Oxonienses: The Members of The University of Oxford, 1500-1714; Their Parentage, Birthplace, and Year of Birth, with a Record of their Degrees; Being the Matriculation Register of the University* (Oxford and London: Parker and Co.).

FUNKE, OTTO (1929), *Zum Weltsprachenproblem in England im 17. Jahrhundert* (Heidelberg: Carl Winter).

—— (1959), 'On the Sources of John Wilkins's Philosophical Language', *English Studies*, 40: 208–14. (Repr. in Subbiondo 1992: 183–9.)

GODWIN, FRANCIS (1638), *The Man in the Moone: or a Discourse of a Voyage Thither by Domingo Gonsales, the Speedy Messenger* (London: J. Kirton and T. Warren). (Repr. in Grant McColley (ed.), *Smith College Studies in Modern Languages*, 19 (1937), 1–48.)

GOODWIN, G. (1908), 'George Dalgarno', in *Dictionary of National Biography*, v. 389–90.

GUNTHER, ROBERT T. (1925), *The Philosophical Society* (Early Science in Oxford, 4; Oxford: Oxford Historical Society).

HOBBES, THOMAS (1839–45), *Thomae Hobbes opera philosophica quae Latine scripsit omnia*, ed. William Molesworth, 5 vols. (London: apud Joannem Bohn).

—— (1991), *Leviathan*, ed. Richard Tuck (Cambridge: Cambridge University Press).

HOLDER, WILLIAM (1668), 'An Account of an Experiment, Concerning Deafness', *Philosophical Transactions*, no. 35, 18 May 1668, pp. 665–8.

—— (1669), *Elements of Speech: An Essay of Inquiry into the Natural Production of Letters: With an Appendix Concerning Persons Deaf ad Dumb* (London: John Martyn).

—— (1678), *A Supplement to the Philosophical Transactions of July, 1670, with some Reflexions on Dr John Wallis, his letter there inserted* (London: Henry Brome).

HOOLE, CHARLES (1668) (ed.), *Æsopi Fabulæ Anglo-Latine* (London: S. Griffin, pro Societate Stationariorum).

HORACE (1960), *The Odes and Epodes* (Loeb Classical Library; London: Heineman).

—— (1970), *Satires, Epistles and Ars Poetica* (Loeb Classical Library; London: Heineman).

HOWELL, WILBUR SAMUEL (1956), *Logic and Rhetoric in England, 1500–1700* (Princeton: Princeton University Press).

HÜLLEN, WERNER (1986), 'The Paradigm of John Wilkins's *Thesaurus*', in Reinhart R. K. Hartmann (1986) (ed.), *The History of Lexicography* (Amsterdam: John Benjamins), 115–25.

—— (1989), *'Their Manner of Discourse': Nachdenken über Sprache im Umkreis der Royal Society* (Tübingen: Gunter Narr).

JONES, RICHARD FOSTER (1951), *Science and Language in England of the Mid-Seventeenth Century* (Stanford, Calif.: Stanford University Press).

JUNIUS, ADRIANUS (1577), *Nomenclator, omnium rerum propria nomina variis linguis explicata indicans* (Antwerp: Ex officina Christophori Plantini).

KATZ, DAVID S. (1981), 'The Language of Adam in Seventeenth-Century England', in H. Lloyd Jones, V. Pearl, B. Worden (eds.), *History & Imagination, Essays in Honour of H. R. Trevor-Roper* (London: Duckworth), 132–45.

KEMP, JOHN ALAN (1972), 'Introduction', in *John Wallis: Grammar of the English Language: A New Edition with Translation and Commentary* (London: Longman).

KIRCHER, ATHANASIUS (1663), *Polygraphia Nova et Universalis* (Rome: Varesius).

KNEALE, WILLIAM, and KNEALE, MARTHA (1962), *The Development of Logic* (Oxford: Clarendon Press).

KNOWLSON, J. R. (1965), 'The Idea of Gesture as a Universal Language in the Seventeenth and Eighteenth Centuries', *Journal of the History of Ideas*, 26: 495–508.

—— (1975), *Universal Language Schemes in England and France, 1600–1800* (Toronto and Buffalo: University of Toronto Press).

LAIRD, JOHN (1935–6), 'George Dalgarno', *Aberdeen University Review*, 23: 15–31.

LANCELOT, CLAUDE, and ARNAULD, ANTOINE (1660), *Grammaire générale et raisonnée* (Paris: Chez Pierre le Petit).

LARGE, ANDREW (1985), *The Artifical Language Movement* (Oxford: Blackwell).

LEIBNIZ, GOTTFRIED WILHELM (1903), *Opuscules et fragments inédits, édités par Louis Couturat* (Paris: Félix Alcan).

—— (1923 ff.), *Sämtliche Schriften und Briefe* (Herausgegeben von der Preussischen Akademie der Wissenschaften; Darmstadt: Reichl). (1950 ff. Berlin: Akademie Verlag.) [Academy Edition, abbreviated as A. References are to series number, volume number, and pages.]

LITTLETON, ADAM (1678), *Linguæ latinæ liber dictionarius quadripartitus* (London: T. Basset, J. Wright & R. Chiswell).

LOCKE, JOHN (1975 [1689]), *An Essay concerning Human Understanding*, ed. Peter H. Nidditch (Oxford: Clarendon Press).

—— (1976), *The Correspondence of John Locke*, ed. E. S. De Beer (Oxford: Clarendon Press).

LODWICK, FRANCIS (1647), *A Common Writing* (London: for the author). (Facsimile in Salmon 1972.)

—— (1652), *The Groundwork, or Foundation laid (or so intended) for the Framing of a New Perfect Language* ([London] n.p.). (Facsimile in Salmon 1972.)

MAAT, JAAP (1995*a*), 'The Logic of Dalgarno's "Ars Signorum" ', in Kurt R. Jankowsky (ed.), *History of Linguistics 1993* (Amsterdam and Philadelphia: Benjamins), 157–66.

—— (1995*b*), 'Leibniz on Wilkins and Dalgarno', *Beiträge zur Geschichte der Sprachwissenschaft*, 5: 169–83.

—— (1999*a*), 'Leibniz on Rational Grammar', in David Cram, Andrew Linn, and Elke Nowak (eds.), *History of Linguistics 1996. Selected Papers from the Seventh International Conference on the History of the Language Sciences*, 2 vols. (Amsterdam and Philadelphia: Benjamins), ii. 113–22.

—— (1999*b*), *Philosophical Languages in the Seventeenth Century: Dalgarno, Wilkins, Leibniz* (Amsterdam: ILLC dissertation series).

—— and CRAM, DAVID (1998), 'Dalgarno in Paris', *Histoire, Épistémologie, Langage*, 20: 167–79.

—— (forthcoming), 'Universal Language Schemes in the Seventeenth Century', in Sylvain Auroux, Konrad Koerner, Hans-Josef Niederehe, and Kees Versteegh (eds.), *History of the Language Sciences, an International Handbook on the Evolution of the Study of Language from the Beginnings to the Present* (Berlin and New York: de Gruyter).

McCLURE, J. DERRICK (1979), 'The "Universal Languages" of Thomas Urquhart and George Dalgarno', in J.-J. Blanchot and C. Graf (eds.), *Actes du 2e. colloque de langue et de litterature écossaises* (Strasbourg: Institut d'études anglaises de Strasbourg), 133–47.

MERSENNE, MARIN (1636), *Harmonie universelle, contenant la theorie et la pratiqve de la mvsiqve* (Paris: Sebastien Cramoisy).

MICHAEL, IAN (1970), *English Grammatical Categories and the Tradition to 1800* (Cambridge: Cambridge University Press).

OVID (1977), *Metamorphoses* (Loeb Classical Library; London: Heineman).

OWEN, JOHN (1659), *Of the Divine Originall, Authority, self-evidencing Light, and Power of the Scriptures* (Oxford: Tho. Robinson).

PADLEY, G. ARTHUR (1976), *Grammatical Theory in Western Europe, 1500–1700: The Latin Tradition* (Cambridge: Cambridge University Press).

—— (1985), *Grammatical Theory in Western Europe, 1500–1700. Trends in Vernacular Grammar I* (Cambridge: Cambridge University Press).

PLOT, ROBERT (1676), *The Natural History of Oxford-shire, Being an Essay towards the Natural History of England* (Oxford: Leonard Lichfield).

POMBO, OLGA (1987), *Leibniz and the Problem of a Universal Language* (Münster: Nodus Publikationen).

PORPHYRY (1975 [*c*.270]), *Isagoge*, translation, introduction and notes by Edward W. Warren (Toronto, Ont.: Pontifical Institute of Medieval Studies).

PORTA, GIOVANNI BATTISTA DELLA (1602), *De furtiuis literarum notis vulgò de ziferis libri quinque. Altero libro superaucti, & locupletati* (Naples: apud Joannem Baptistam Subtilem).

PRÜMERS, RODGERO (1899–1900), *Tagebuch Adam Samuel Hartmanns über seine Kollektenreise 1657–1659*, in *Zeitschrift der historischen Gesellschaft für die Provinz Posen*, 14: 67–140; 15: 95–160, 202–46.

RAY, JOHN (1691), 'An Account of Some Errors and Defects of our English Alphabet Orthography and Manner of Spelling', printed as an appendix to the second edition of Ray's *Collection of English Words Not Generally Used* (London: Christopher Wilkinson).

RÉE, JONATHAN (1999), *I See a Voice: A Philosophical History of Language, Deafness and the Senses* (London: HarperCollins).

RICH, JEREMIAH (1659), *The Penns Dexterity: By theise incomparable Contractions by which a Sentence is Writt as soone as a Word. Allowed by Authority and past the two universitys with great aprobation and aplause* (London: Samuel Botley).

—— (1669), *The Pens Dexterity compleated: or, Mr. Riches Short-hand now perfectly Taught, Which in his Life-time was never done, by any thing made publique in Print, because it would have hindred his Practice* (London: H. Evesden & T. Jenner).

RISSE, WILHELM (1964), *Die Logik der Neuzeit* (Stuttgart-Bad Cannstatt).

ROBINS, ROBERT H. (1990 [1967]), *A Short History of Linguistics* (London: Longman).

ROBINSON, HENRY W., and ADAMS, WALTER (1935) (eds.), *The Diary of Robert Hooke 1672–1680* (London: Taylor & Francis).

ROSSI, PAOLO (1960), *Clavis Universalis. Arti Mnemoniche e Logica Combinatoria da Lullo a Leibniz* (Milan and Naples: Ricciardi).

SALMON, VIVIAN (1966a), 'The Evolution of Dalgarno's "Ars Signorum" ', in M. Brahmer *et al.* (eds.), *Studies in Honour of Margaret Schlauch* (Warsaw: Polish Scientific Publishers), 353–71. (Repr. in Salmon 1988: 157–75.)

—— (1966b), 'Language-Planning in Seventeenth Century England: Its Context and Aims', in C. E. Bazell *et al.* (eds.), *In Memory of J.R. Firth* (London: Longmans), 370–97. (Repr. in Salmon 1988: 129–56.)

—— (1972), *The Works of Francis Lodwick: A Study of his Writings in the Intellectual Context of the Seventeenth Century* (London: Longman).

—— (1974), 'John Wilkins' Essay (1668): Critics and Continuators', *Historiographia Linguistica*, 1: 147–63. (Repr. in Salmon 1988: 191–206, and in Subbiondo 1992: 349–64.)

—— (1975), ' "Philosophical" Grammar in John Wilkins' "Essay" ', *Canadian Journal of Linguistics*, 20: 131–59. (Repr. in Salmon 1988: 97–126, and in Subbiondo 1992: 207–36.)

—— (1988), *The Study of Language in Seventeenth-Century England* (Studies in the History of the Language Sciences, 17; Amsterdam: Benjamins).

—— (1992), 'Caratéristiques et langues universelles', in Auroux Sylvain (ed.), *Histoire des Idées Linguistiques*; 2 vols. (Liège: Maidaga), ii. 407–23.

—— (1996), 'The Universal Language Problem', in Marcelo Dascal, Dietfried Gerhardus, Kuno Lorenz, and Georg Meggle (eds.), *Philosophy of Language: An International Handbook of Contemporary Research* (Berlin and New York: Walter de Gruyter), 916–28.

SALTER, H. E. (1923), 'The Poll Tax of 1667', in *Surveys and Tokens* (Oxford Historical Society, 75; Oxford: Clarendon Press), 213–336.

SCHOTT, CASPAR (1664), *Technica Curiosa, sive Mirabilia Artis* (Nuremburg: sumptibus Johannis Andreae Endteri, & Wolfgangi juniori haeredum).

SHAPIRO, BARBARA J. (1969), *John Wilkins 1614-1672. An Intellectual Biography* (Berkeley and Los Angeles: University of California Press).

SHUMAKER, WAYNE (1982), 'The *lingua philosophica* of George Dalgarno', in *Renaissance Curiosa* (Binghamton, NY: Center for Medieval & Early Renaissance Studies), 132–72.

SIGER, L. (1968), 'Gestures, the Language of Signs and Human Communication', *American Annals of the Deaf*, 113: 11–28.

SLAUGHTER, MARY M. (1982), *Universal Languages and Scientific Taxonomy in the Seventeenth Century* (Cambridge: Cambridge University Press).

STILLINGFLEET, EDWARD (1662), *Origines sacræ. Or A rational account of grounds of Christian faith, as to the truth and divine authority of the Scriptures, and the matters therein contained* (London: Henry Mortlock).

STILLMAN, ROBERT E. (1995), *The New Philosophy and Universal Languages in Seventeenth-Century England: Bacon, Hobbes, and Wilkins* (Lewisburg: Bucknell University Press, and London: Associated University Presses).

STRASSER, GERHARD F. (1988), *Lingua Universalis. Kryptologie und Theorie der Universalsprachen im 16. und 17. Jahrhundert* (Wolfenbütteler Forschungen, 38; Wiesbaden: Harrassowitz).

SUBBIONDO, JOSEPH L. (1977), 'John Wilkins' Theory of Meaning and the Development of a Semantic Model', *Cahiers Linguistiques d'Ottawa*, 5: 41–61. (Repr. in Subbiondo 1992: 291–306.)

—— (1992) (ed.), *John Wilkins and Seventeenth-Century British Linguistics* (Amsterdam and Philadelphia: Benjamins).

SWIFT, JONATHAN (1985 [1726]), *Gulliver's Travels* (London: Penguin Books).

TERENCE (1912), *The Plays* (Loeb Classical Library; London: Heineman).

TURNBULL, G. H. (1947), *Hartlib, Dury and Comenius* (London: Hodder & Stoughton).

TURNER, ANTHONY JOHN (1978), 'Andrew Paschall's Tables of Plants for the Universal Language 1678', *Bodleian Library Record*, 9: 346–50.

URQUHART, THOMAS (1652), *Ekskubalauron, or the Discovery of a Most Exquisite Jewel* ([London] n.p.).

—— (1653), *Logopandecteison, or, an Introduction to the universal language* (London: G. Calvert & R. Tomlins).

VAUGHAN, ROBERT (1839), *The Protectorate of Oliver Cromwell, and the State of Europe during the Early Part of the Reign of Louis XIV*; 2 vols. (London: H. Colburn).

VIGER, FRANÇOIS (1647 [1627]), *De Praecipuis Graecae Dictionis Idiotismis* (Cambridge: Roger Daniel).

VOSSIUS, GERARDUS JOANNES (1635), *De Arte Grammatica libri septem* (Amsterdam: Apud Guilielmum Blaev).

—— (1662), *Etymologicon linguæ Latinæ* (London: Jo. Martin & Ja. Alestry).

WALKER, WILLIAM (1655), *A Treatise of English Particles* (London: T. Garthwait).

WALLIS, JOHN (1653), *Grammatica Linguae Anglicanae* (Oxford: Leonard Lichfield).

—— (1670), 'A letter of Dr. John Wallis to Robert Boyle Esq, concerning the said Doctor's Essay of Teaching a person Dumb and Deaf to speak, and to Understand a language', *Philosophical Transactions*, no. 61, 18 July 1670, pp. 1087–99.

—— (1678), *A Defence of the Royal Society and Philosophical Transactions, Particularly those of July, 1670. In Answer to the Cavils of Dr. William Holder* (London: Thomas Moore).

—— (1686), *Institutio Logicae, ad communesusus accommodata* (Oxford: Leonard Lichfield).

—— (1972 [1653]), *Grammar of the English Language: A New Edition with Translation and Commentary by J. A. Kemp* (London: Longman).

WARD, SETH (1654), *Vindiciae Academiarum, containing, some briefe animadversions upon Mr Websters Book, stiled, The Examination of the Academies* (Oxford: Leonard Lichfield). (Facsimile in Debus 1970.)

WILKINS, JOHN (1638), *The Discovery of a World in the Moone. Or, a Discourse Tending to Prove, that 'tis probable there may be another habitable World in that Planet* (London: Michael Sparke and Edward Forrest).

—— (1640), *A Discourse concerning A New Planet. Tending to prove, That 'tis probable our Earth is one of the Planets* (London: Iohn Maynard).

—— (1641), *Mercury, or the Secret and Swift Messenger* (London: John Maynard & Timothy Wilkins). (Facsimile edition of the third edition, 1708, with an introductory essay by B. Asbach-Schnitker, Amsterdam and Philadelphia: Benjamins, 1984.)

—— (1668), *An Essay towards a Real Character and a Philosophical Language* (London: Samuel Gellibrand & John Martyn).

WOOD, ANTHONY (1691), *Athenæ Oxonienses: An Exact History of all the Writers and Bishops who have had their Education in the University of Oxford to which are added, the Fasti, or Annals, of the said University*; 2 vols. (London: Tho. Bennet).

WORTHINGTON, JOHN (1847–86), *The Diary of John Worthington, edited by J. Crossley* (Remains, Historical and Literary Connected with the Palatine Counties of Lancaster and Chester, vols. 13, 36, 114; [Manchester]: Printed for the Chetham Society).

YATES, FRANCES A. (1966), *The Art of Memory* (London and Henley: Routledge & Kegan Paul).

YOUNG, ROBERT FITZGIBBON (1932a), *A Bohemian Philosopher at Oxford in the Seventeenth Century: George Ritschel of Deutschkahn (1616–1683)* London: School of Slavonic Studies in the University of London).

—— (1932b), *Comenius in England* (Oxford: Oxford University Press).

INDEX